Books by Frederick L. Schuman

RUSSIA SINCE 1917
Four Decades of Soviet Politics
(1957)

THE COMMONWEALTH OF MAN
An Inquiry into Power Politics and World Government
(1952)

SOVIET POLITICS
At Home and Abroad
(1946)

NIGHT OVER EUROPE
The Diplomacy of Nemesis, 1939–40
(1941)

EUROPE ON THE EVE
The Crises of Diplomacy, 1933–1939
(1939)

THE NAZI DICTATORSHIP
A Study in Social Pathology and the Politics of Fascism
(1939, 1936, 1935)

In Collaboration with Major George D. Brodsky
DESIGN FOR POWER
The Struggle for the World
(1942)

THESE ARE BORZOI BOOKS,
PUBLISHED IN NEW YORK BY ALFRED A. KNOPF

RUSSIA
SINCE
1917

Frederick L. Schuman

WOODROW WILSON PROFESSOR OF GOVERNMENT,
WILLIAMS COLLEGE

RUSSIA
SINCE
1917

Four Decades of Soviet Politics

MAPS BY GEORGE D. BRODSKY

NEW YORK

ALFRED A KNOPF

☼ 1962 ☼

L.C. catalog card number: 57–7553

© *Frederick L. Schuman, 1957*

THIS IS A BORZOI BOOK,
PUBLISHED BY ALFRED A. KNOPF, INC.

PUBLISHED JULY 22, 1957

SECOND PRINTING, AUGUST 1962

To the memory of my parents:

Preface

WHEN GEN. NATHAN F. TWINING, Chief of Staff of the
USAF, returned from the Soviet Union on July 4, 1956,
he was quoted as saying: "Nobody is an expert on
Russia. There are just varying degrees of ignorance." A similar comment was made by British journalist Paul Winterton during World
War II, when the course and outcome of the savage combat across
the steppes confounded most Western "experts."

If wisdom regarding Russia were proportionate to the staggering number of books, monographs, and articles on Soviet affairs published since 1917 in English, French, and German, all literate citizens
and statesmen throughout the Atlantic communities would be wise
indeed. All seekers after truth are deeply indebted to these many
laborers in the vineyards of Russian studies. Without their toil no
such task as is here attempted could be contemplated.

Yet darkness and fear have not been dispelled by these millions
of printed pages. Few are available to the peoples of the USSR.
Even the Lenin State Library in Moscow, claiming to house the
largest collection of books in the world, contains almost no works in
any language by writers who are hostile toward, or critical of, or
"objective" about, the Soviet way of life. The gigantic output of the
Soviet publishing business, catering to a domestic market which is
insatiable, is far more readily available to Western scholars, particularly to readers of Russian—with much accessible in translation for
those to whom the Cyrillic alphabet, the Slavic root-words, and the
two aspects of the verb are impenetrable mysteries. This literature,
however, answers only a few of the questions about Russia in which
Western peoples are most interested. When reality is projected
through the lenses of dogma, truth is seen only through a glass
darkly. Many Western efforts to "explain" Russia display similar

distortions, with more heat than light generated in the processes of refraction and reflection.

The sheer volume of publications about Russia obliges anyone who adds to the mass to try, as best he can, to justify his conduct. What new "truths" are here revealed? What claims, if any, to *expertise* can the perpetrator of these pages plausibly put forward? Such queries are better answered by readers and by critics than by authors. One man's view of the problem may yet be worth setting down.

From time to time, it seems to me, some semblance of insight into the Marxist Muscovy of the 20th Century can best be attained by trying to see beyond specialized studies of particular aspects of Soviet experience and to transcend the polemics of Marxism, Leninism, and Stalinism—and of anti-Marxism, anti-Leninism, and anti-Stalinism. The rarefied atmosphere at the summit of an intellectual Mount Kazbek may, to be sure, induce dizziness rather than clarity of vision. But if the searcher in Sovietland will keep his eyes on people as well as on programs, on the imposing spatial dimensions of his subject along with the color of localities, and on the equally imposing temporal dimensions of a society which has endured through many vicissitudes for more than a thousand years, he may be able to arrive at a synoptic view, at a new synthesis, and at an illuminating reinterpretation of this incomparably dramatic and dynamic chapter of the human adventure.

Such, at any rate, is the purpose of this book, as it was of my earlier book, *Soviet Politics at Home and Abroad,* published by Alfred A. Knopf in 1946 and by Iwanami Shoten of Tokyo in a Japanese translation in 1956. The close of World War II appeared to me, a decade ago, an appropriate time for such a venture. The fortieth anniversary of the Revolutions of 1917 strikes me as another suitable occasion for a fresh attempt at synthesis and revaluation in the light of recent documentation and the contemporary Soviet scene. Whether the purpose has been fulfilled is for others to say.

I have here sought to present, insofar as this can be done in a single volume, the whole story through forty years of what some Westerners once called the "Soviet experiment" and others the "horrors of Bolshevism." Lincoln Steffens, returning from Moscow in March of 1919, exclaimed ecstatically: "I have seen the future and it works!" Never was anyone so wrong in so few words about so much. Moscow in 1919 was not "the future," nor is Moscow in 1957

in any sense "the future" even for the third of mankind under Communist rule. The Soviet polity, economy, and society of 1919 did not "work" at all but spelled chaos. Today they "work" very well, though in ways never foreseen by the Marxist conspirators of a generation ago. Like most other acts on the stage of man's endless quest for salvation, the drama of Russia since 1917 is a tangled tale of tragedy and triumph, of frustration and success, of hopes realized and of dreams turned to dust. Here, more vividly than elsewhere in our time, sin and virtue, crime and retribution, inspiring achievements and ghastly disasters alternate in the course of human fortunes. The whole is a black paradox, a bright vision, and a baffling enigma which it behooves Americans, along with other peoples, to try to comprehend, lest they blindly repeat the mistakes of the past in a new time when the price of ignorance and error may be the thermonuclear coannihilation of most of the human race.

In these pages I have, I trust, made no pretense of supplying all the "right answers." The liberal-democratic formula for wisdom in public affairs presupposes that no one has the right answers but that all, if informed, may ask the right questions in a free market for talk—and that out of discussion, observation, decision-making, and the pragmatic testing of hypotheses truth may emerge in the form of operationally workable means toward social goals subscribed to by most men and women of good will. The Marxist formula, like that of other dogmatists, presupposes that truth and wisdom can be derived from sacred scriptures as interpreted, intolerantly, by high priests. Happily the Marxists of Muscovy are lately displaying an increasing disposition to test their "truths" by consequences and to accept the biblical injunction: "By their fruits ye shall know them!" My hope is that these pages pose some of the right questions; that they will contribute modestly to comprehension of Russia's travails and accomplishments; and that they will prove useful as a detailed and documented record of the words and deeds of the rulers of Russia since the October Revolution in their responses to the challenges posed both by internal problems and by the external environment of world politics in an age of world wars, "cold wars," and incessant rivalry among Powers and priesthoods for influence over the minds of men.

The narrative and analysis here presented include some scattered passages from my earlier book on *Soviet Politics*. The perceptive reader will see that many judgments on many matters offered

a decade ago have been much modified in view of new facts—
precisely as many of the evaluations here set forth may well be in
need of alteration a decade hence. These pages also include a few
passages from my annual articles on the USSR in Funk and Wagnall's *New International Year Book.* I am most grateful to Editor
Henry E. Vizetelly for permission to reprint these passages—and
for the opportunity he has granted me over the past dozen years to
attempt an annual survey of Soviet developments, without which
this book could not have been written.

The footnote references, all of which are indexed, comprise a
select but fairly complete bibliography of the most informative and
suggestive books in English on Soviet history and politics in recent
years. Earlier works are cited in the Notes to *Soviet Politics.* Publications in Russian, which are unlikely to be perused by many readers
of this volume, are cited only where translations are unavailable
and where some unique contribution has been made.

In expressing my gratitude to those who have aided me in the
enterprise, I am embarrassed by their numbers and by their gen-
erosity and by the difficulty of establishing priorities among them.
But my warmest thanks are due in the first instance to Alfred A.
Knopf, Inc., for granting me a royalty advance that enabled me to
revisit the USSR in May and June of 1956. (My earlier visits in
1928 and 1933 are briefly recounted in the Preface to *Soviet Politics.*
My "travelogue" of 1956 can be found in *The Berkshire Eagle* of
Pittsfield, Mass., edited by "Pete" Miller, in eight articles beginning
in the issue of May 29, and in *The Nation,* edited by Carey McWil-
liams, in four articles beginning in the issue of July 14, 1956.) I am
also most grateful to President James Phinney Baxter III and the
Trustees of Williams College for a sabbatical leave in the spring of
1956 and to my colleagues, Fred Greene, Robert Gaudino, E. Drexel
Godfrey, Jr., Dwight Simpson, Vincent M. Barnett, and Paul Clark
for "carrying on" during my absence and for lightening my burdens
upon my return by way of helping me to get on with writing. My
Williams students over the years in "Pol. Sci. 3–4," "Pol. Sci. 18,"
and "Pol. Econ. 20" and my graduate students in Berkeley (1955)
and in Chicago (1956) have brought much to the task in the way
of stimulation and a cooperative quest for truth.

I cannot begin to express adequate appreciation to Sally Carle-
ton Foote of Williamstown for the accurate typing of the entire
manuscript and for other work far beyond the call of duty, and to

my Chicago friend of many years, George D. Brodsky, for drawing
the maps which embellish the book. Of these, two are *de novo:*
"Russian War Fronts, 1918–21" and "Russia and the Far East." Two
others—"War in Russia, 1941–5" and "Soviet Imperialism, 1944–8"—
were originally drawn for the fourth and fifth editions (1948 and
1953) of my *International Politics*, published by the McGraw-Hill
Book Company, to which I am indebted for permission to include
them here.

On another level of obligation, I herewith tender thanks for
much aid in many matters to Gabriel Reiner of the Cosmos Travel
Bureau of New York; to the pilots and hostesses of Scandinavian
Air Lines and of Aeroflot for invariably courteous and efficient
service; to Alexander Rogov, head of Intourist in Moscow; to my
local guides and counsellors: Roman Tuchkanen in Leningrad,
Zoya Kurantcheva and Lily Karnit in Moscow, Olga Tcherkassova
in Kiev, Konstantin Mikhailovich Strelnikov and Saissaya Cher-
nenko in Rostov, and Olga Ivanovna Ivanova and Dr. Ivan Ershov
of Hospital No. 5 in Stalingrad; to Vladimir D. Kazakevich of the
Institute of Economics and Emily Grace Kazakevich of the Institute of History, both in Moscow, for hospitality and much information on current Soviet life; to Joseph Livingston, financial editor of
The Philadelphia Bulletin, Morris Rubin, editor of *The Progressive*
of Madison, Wisconsin, and Anita Nicholson of TWA, among
American transients in Muscovy during my sojourn, for sharing with
me many of their explorations into the mysteries of Sovietland; and,
among the then more permanent American residents in the Soviet
capital, to Irving R. Levine, Jack Raymond, John C. Guthrie (Williams Class of 1937 and now First Secretary of the U.S. Embassy),
and Ambassador Charles E. Bohlen, all of whom were most gracious
and helpful.

I also appreciate very much the kindness of various writers and
publishers for permission to quote from their works: Harvard University Press, for the concluding sentences of Merle Fainsod's *How
Russia Is Ruled*; *Harper's Magazine*, for a passage from George F.
Kennan's "Overdue Changes in Our Foreign Policy" in the August
issue, 1956; *Newsweek*, for a passage from "White Star vs. Red"
in the issue of May 17, 1948; *The Saturday Evening Post*, for an excerpt from "If War Comes," by Joseph and Stewart Alsop, in the
issue of September 11, 1948; Oxford University Press, for passages
from Vol. III of Edward Hallett Carr's *The Bolshevik Revolution*

and from Vol. IX of Arnold J. Toynbee's *A Study of History*; Henry Regnery Company, for a passage from William H. Standley's *Admiral Ambassador to Russia*; and John Scott, for the excerpt from his *Political Warfare*.

It is customary in all Prefaces to absolve all persons and organizations thus thanked for their help from any responsibility for errors of fact or judgment in all that the writer has written. The discharge of this duty is peculiarly important in the present instance. No one named above would subscribe to all of the interpretations here offered. Everyone named above, including all the Russians, would vehemently repudiate many of my judgments. The verdicts here rendered on four decades of Soviet politics may indeed prove to be wrong, in whole or in part. I believe them to be right on the basis of the record and of currently available evidence. But let it be emphasized that they are exclusively my own and that no one else in the USA or the USSR who has aided me in my quest is even remotely responsible for any mistakes of data or conclusions here committed.

Last, but far from least, I am grateful to Henry Robbins of Alfred A. Knopf, Inc., for many useful suggestions for improving the style and content of these pages. And I am warmly grateful to my wife, Lily Abell Schuman, for enduring stoically the agonies of authorship, for making many helpful criticisms in the course of composition, and for lending invaluable aid in the complex task of indexing. For help with the Index, my thanks are also due to Grace Perez.

The assumption behind this book is that peace is desirable, necessary, and possible between the halves (or thirds) of a divided world, lest more war bring us all to ruin. The soundness of the assumption can be tested only by the validity of the analysis of things past here essayed and by the shape of things to come. If the assumption proves wrong, nothing much matters. If it proves right, then promising vistas loom before us in the way of creative competition—not in the techniques of death, but in the arts of life. It is my hope that this book of record and evaluation may contribute to the constructive use of the opportunities of tomorrow.

FREDERICK L. SCHUMAN

Williamstown, Mass.
March 21, 1957

Contents

Contents

Maps

[BY GEORGE D. BRODSKY]

Contents

Maps

[BY GEORGE D. BRADLEY]

RUSSIA
SINCE
1917

To everything there is a season, and a time to every purpose under the heaven: A time to be born, and a time to die; a time to plant, and a time to pluck up that which is planted; a time to kill, and a time to heal; a time to break down, and a time to build up; a time to weep, and a time to laugh; a time to mourn, and a time to dance; a time to cast away stones, and a time to gather stones together; a time to embrace, and a time to refrain from embracing; . . . a time to keep silence, and a time to speak; a time to love, and a time to hate; a time of war, and a time of peace. . . . I know there is no good . . . but for a man to rejoice and to do good in his life. And also that every man should eat and drink and enjoy the good of all his labor, it is the gift of God.

—ECCLESIASTES, *Chapter* 3

Call unto me and I will answer thee, and shew thee great and mighty things which thou knowest not. . . . They came to fight . . . and for their wickedness I have hid my face from this city. (But) behold, I will bring it health and cure, and I will cure them, and will reveal unto them the abundance of peace and truth. . . . And I will cleanse them from all their iniquity, whereby they have sinned against me. . . . And it shall be to me a name of joy, a praise and an honor before all the nations of the earth, which shall hear all the good I do unto them. . . . Again there shall be heard in this place, which ye say shall be desolate without man and without beast . . . the voice of joy, and the voice of gladness, the voice of the bridegroom, and the voice of the bride, the voice of them that shall say: Praise the Lord of Hosts; for the Lord is good; for his mercy endureth forever.

—JEREMIAH, *Chapter* 33

CHAPTER ONE

Marxism and Muscovy

1. A TIME TO BE BORN

O N THE west bank of the Volga, midway between Samara and Kazan, the provincial town of Simbirsk, now called Ulianovsk, sprawls across low hills overlooking the broad waters of Europe's longest river. The settlement was founded in 1648 as a Muscovite bastion against the Mongols—who, although broken a century earlier by the armies of Ivan the Terrible, still sought to plunder the villages of the victors. Simbirsk achieved fame in 1670 as the scene of the decisive defeat of the rebel serfs and Cossacks who, under Stenka Razin, had swept over the steppes burning manor houses and killing landlords.

Here in a time of peace, in April of 1870, a pious and virtuous woman gave birth to a boy. Maria Alexandrovna Blank was the Lutheran daughter of a Volga-German army surgeon. Her husband was Ilya Nikolayevich Ulianov. Bald and bearded, he was a sober scholar, conservative and Orthodox. He taught mathematics and physics in high school, originally in Astrakhan and later in Penza and Nizhni Novgorod. His work was much respected and won national recognition. He became a school inspector in Simbirsk and was awarded the rank of "State Counsellor." He therewith became, despite his humble origins, a member of the honorary aristocracy, with his children inheriting "noble" status.

The baby, christened Vladimir Ilyich, was a third child after Anna (1864–1935) and Alexander (1866–87). These parents were to rear three more: Olga, Dmitri, and Maria. During Vladimir's first five years the family lived in a modest two-story, green-painted residence, and then moved to a larger brown "ranch house." The birth-

day of Vladimir was April 22 by our reckoning, or April 9 by the uncorrected Julian calendar, which Russians followed until 1918. Father and mother had no doubts regarding their way of life and no fears that any of their children might grow up to be devils or delinquents. Their first son was to die on the gallows. Their second was fated to shake the earth, whether for good or ill men will long debate.

Remote events, unforeseen by any of the participants, were to entangle curiously many lives and ultimately alter the destinies of most of mankind. In April of 1870, when Vladimir Ulianov came into the world, a grizzled, red-eyed man was living in London in a small house at 9 Grafton Terrace, Maitland Park, Haverstock Hill. On near-by Hampstead Heath he liked to walk on Sundays with his beloved wife, Jenny von Westphalen, and to play with his children. Of these, three died in infancy and three grew up: Jenny, Laura, and Eleanor. This man of 52 was long an exile from his native Rhineland. His father had been a Jewish lawyer of Treves, some of whose forebears had been rabbis. When the son was six, his father became a Christian convert. The youth was a prodigy. After study in Bonn and Berlin, he won his Ph.D. at the age of 23. He was already alienated from his class and his countrymen, from his God and his King. As an atheist and iconoclast who "hated all the gods," he was barred from an academic career and became a revolutionary journalist. In 1849 he was expelled from both Prussia and France as a subversive.

Karl Marx, despite piles, boils, liver complaints, and lung troubles, was still a dynamo of energy in April of 1870, often toiling all day in the library of the British Museum and working far into the night in his disorderly study, amid scattered papers and books, pawn tickets, cigar ashes, and unwashed dishes. The first volume of *Capital* had been published three years previously. But his research and pamphleteering brought in no money. He had, in fact, no regular income except between 1852 and 1861, when he was correspondent for Horace Greeley's *New York Tribune*. His patron was his gay fellow radical Friedrich Engels, who prospered from cotton mills in Manchester. In 1869 Engels gave up the business and relieved the chronic poverty of the Marx ménage with part of the proceeds.

In the autumn of 1870 Engels was to move permanently to London with his Irish mistress, Lizzy Burns (successor in this role to her later sister, Mary), whom he was to wed in 1878, at her tearful request on her deathbed. In April of 1870 Marx and Engels were

much preoccupied with the Irish question and with a pending Russian version of *Capital*, the first translation from the German. The Tsarist censors permitted it to be published on the ground that, although it was "completely socialist," it was unreadable and thus could do no harm. Marx was moved to study Russian and to interest himself increasingly in Russian events. Of the obscure Ulianov family in Simbirsk he knew nothing.

No more did another spinner of words, who also knew not Marx. In April of 1870 he was at work in a Dresden pension on a prophetic book. This man, too, in his youth was an alien among his people and long a wanderer among strangers. His father, a Moscow physician, was murdered by his own serfs on his country estate in 1839 when his son was 18. Ten years later the son, already a well-known writer, was arrested for participation in a subversive conspiracy and condemned to death. Following a mock "execution," after which the victim's epilepsy was much worsened, commutation of the sentence was announced: four years in the Siberian convict prison in Omsk, followed by five years of military service in Central Asia. His novel *The House of the Dead* was the product of these years of servitude. A later novel, *Memoirs from the Underground* (1864), was a rejoinder to *What Is to Be Done?* (*Shto Dyelat?*), by N. G. Chernyshevsky (1823–89). This disciple of John Stuart Mill was a convinced Utopian who had no doubt that heaven on earth was to be had if all men were free to follow the dictates of reason. Our writer was already beginning to perceive that man is more irrational than rational and may, if free, prefer evil to good. Such was the insight of Fyodor Mikhailovich Dostoevsky—at a time when Sigmund Freud was still a small boy.

The author of *Crime and Punishment* (1866), *The Idiot* (1869), and *The Brothers Karamazov* (1880) spent his middle years, after the death of his first wife, in debauchery, gambling, and anguish, driven by poverty to go on writing in order to secure advances from his publisher, Mikhail N. Katkov. At 45 he married his stenographer, a girl of 20, Anna Grigorievna Snitkina, who brought him happiness and managed his affairs. In 1867 they went abroad. The husband relapsed sporadically into roulette, lawful in Germany until 1872 when a federal ban drove the gambling-houses to Monte Carlo. After two years in Switzerland and Italy (during which their first child, Sonya, died in infancy in Geneva) they spent two years in Dresden before returning to Russia. Here it was, during the spring

of Vladimir Ulianov's nativity, that Dostoevsky began writing *The Devils*, rendered into English as *The Possessed*.

The inspiration of the work was threefold. The author had quarreled with his friend Ivan S. Turgenev, whose *Fathers and Sons* is a tragedy of devout parents whose children follow false gods. In Geneva, Dostoevsky had attended with distaste a gathering of exiled revolutionaries assembled in the name of a "League for Peace and Freedom." In 1869 he learned of a scandal in Moscow: one Sergei Nechaiev had formed a subversive "cell" with four students, one of whom, Ivanov, lost faith and was killed by his colleagues, who feared he might expose them. Dostoevsky, now an ex-radical turned conservative, was persuaded that nihilism leads to crime. *The Devils* is a mordant portrait of a sentimental liberal, Verhovensky, and a caricature of sundry reformers, rebels, and conspirators, some of whom commit murder, while one, Stavogrin, ends by hanging himself with a well-soaped rope. A minor character, Shigalov, has a formula for Paradise:

> I am perplexed by my own data and my conclusion is a direct contradiction of the original idea with which I start. Starting from unlimited freedom, I arrive at unlimited despotism. I will add, however, that there can be no solution of the social problem but mine. . . . Mankind must be divided into two unequal parts. One-tenth enjoys absolute liberty and unbounded power over the other nine-tenths. The others have to give up all individuality and become, so to speak, a herd. . . . Every member of the society spies on the others, and it's his duty to inform against them. Everyone belongs to all and all to everyone. All are slaves and equal in their slavery. . . . We'll reduce all to a common denominator. . . . [But] slaves must have directors. Absolute submission, absolute loss of individuality, but once in thirty years let them have a shock as a precaution against boredom.[1]

The Devils was serialized in *Rusky Vestnik* during 1871 and issued in full in 1872, the year in which the Russian translation of Volume I of Marx's *Capital* was published. Vladimir Ulianov was 2

[1] Condensed from pp. 376–8 and 391–2 of Constance Garnett's translation of *The Possessed* (Macmillan, 1931).

years old. Years later, like his dear brother Alexander, he attended the Simbirsk Classical High School, whose principal was one Fyodor Kerensky. The principal's son, another Alexander, was born in Simbirsk when Vladimir Ulianov was 11 years of age. When he was 16, Vladimir's father died of a stroke. When he was 17, a month before his graduation, news came from St. Petersburg that sister Anna and brother Alexander, then a student of zoology, had been arrested for participation in a plot against Alexander III. The Tsar's father, Alexander II, had been blown to pieces on March 13, 1881, by members of a terrorist organization calling itself *Narodnaya Volya* "People's Will" or "People's Freedom." The authorities were vigilant.

Maria Alexandrovna hurried to the capital to help her children. Anna was released as knowing nothing of the conspiracy. But Alexander Ulianov proudly acknowledged that as a member of *Narodnaya Volya* he had prepared explosives in his apartment and planned with his confederates to kill the Tsar on the 6th anniversary of the earlier assassination. The police brought 15 of the plotters to trial. Alexander sought to console his mother: "There is no other way." He told the court: "Terror is our answer to the violence of the State. It is the only way to force a despotic regime to grant political freedom to the people. We do not fear to die. There is no death more honorable than death for the common good."

At dawn of May 20, 1887, in the courtyard of Schlusselberg Fortress, Alexander and four of his friends were hanged by the neck until dead. His embittered family moved that summer to Kazan where Vladimir entered the university law school. He was arrested in December for attending an illegal student meeting. Expelled and exiled to a neighboring village, he returned to Kazan in midyear of 1888. There he played chess with brother Dmitri, as he had once done with brother Alexander, and began reading Karl Marx. After an interlude on his mother's small estate near Samara, he resumed his studies on his own and in 1891 was allowed to take the law examinations at the University of St. Petersburg. His grade was the highest of the 124 participants.

His joy was changed to grief by the death of his sister Olga (1871–91). He returned to Samara to practice law. But in 1893 he was back in St. Petersburg, writing revolutionary pamphlets; then abroad in Salzburg, Geneva, Paris, and Berlin; and, late in 1895, again in Peter's city, where he was arrested and exiled to Siberia.

His police pictures reveal a broad-faced, bulletheaded, mustached and bearded young man, already half bald.

From January 1897 to February 1900 Vladimir Ulianov lived in the village of Shushenskoye, near the upper Yenesei, most of the time in a peasant log cabin. Here, in July 1898, he married a Marxist comrade, Nadezhda Konstantinova Krupskaya. In later life a goitrous disease made her ugly, but in her youth she was fair, full-lipped, and wistful. Her husband's devotion to her, and hers to him, persisted throughout their life together. In Siberian exile he wrote articles and pamphlets and a book: *The Development of Capitalism in Russia*. Like other revolutionists, he used pen names: Elin, Tulin, and finally Lenin.

On February 10, 1881 (new style), when Lenin was a boy in Simbirsk, Dostoevsky, then at the height of his fame, died in his St. Petersburg apartment. The master had fittingly closed his public career the preceding June by a moving address in Moscow at the dedication of a memorial to Pushkin. Here he urged that the essence of "Russia's Shakespeare" was universality and that the "mission" of the Russians was to become "truly Russian" by becoming the brothers of all men and "to pronounce the final word of the great general harmony, of the final brotherly communion of all nations in accordance with the law of the gospel of Christ!" The audience sobbed and cheered and cried: "A prophet!" At his funeral 30,000 people followed the procession to the monastery of Alexander Nevsky and, on the morrow, to the cemetery. Many were the speeches and the wreaths.

Two years later, in March of 1883, when Lenin was a student at the Classical High School, death came to Karl Marx in the house at 41 Maitland Park Road, Haverstock Hill, to which the family had moved in 1875. Within the preceding year he had lost his wife and his daughter Jenny. "The Moor," as his children called him, never recovered from his sorrow. At the simple burial in Highgate Cemetery, attended by a mere handful of friends, Engels spoke: "On the afternoon of the 14th of March at quarter to three, the greatest living thinker ceased to think. Left alone for less than two minutes, when we entered we found him sleeping peacefully in his chair, but forever. . . . As Darwin discovered the law of evolution in organic nature, so Marx discovered the law of evolution in human history. . . . Marx was above all a revolutionary, and his great aim in life was to cooperate in the overthrow of capitalist society and the

State institutions which it had created, to cooperate in the emancipation of the modern proletariat. . . . His name will live through
the centuries and so also will his work." [2]

2. THE SOURCES OF HERESY

MACHIAVELLI'S dictum that it is better for a Prince to be feared than
to be loved, since "mankind in general are ungrateful, fickle, timid,
dissembling, and self-interested," was faithfully followed by most of
the rulers of Russia in the 19th Century: Tsars, bureaucrats, and
landlords, and later the new entrepreneurs who emerged with the
advent of the factory system. The difficulty with the formula is that
rulers who rule by fear are themselves fearful. Their anxiety inspires
contempt among the ruled, some of whom may prove defiant. These
dangerous spirits, even when striving to replace the rule of fear by a
rule of love, are readily moved to violence. What they will do in
pursuit of their goal in incalculable, but always hazardous to those
who rule.

The danger is small in static societies where each knows his
place. The peril is large in communities racked by storms of change.
Such a nation was the Russia of the 1800's—half Asiatic, dark and
backward, on the edge of Europe yet inexorably entangled in the
politics of the "Powers" and slowly being transfigured by European
technology and capitalism. Over the land blew winds from the West,
bearing to this dark soil wild seeds destined to grow into strange
flowers and exotic fruit.

[2] Among the numerous biographies of the lives here touched upon, the
most illuminating in English seem to me to be the following: David Shub:
Lenin: A Biography (Doubleday, 1948); Gustav Mayer: *Friedrich Engels:
A Biography,* translated from the German by Gilbert and Helen Highet (Knopf,
1936); Franz Mehring: *Karl Marx: The Story of His Life,* translated from the
German by Edward Fitzgerald (Covici Friede, 1935); Edward Hallett Carr:
Dostoevsky (1821–1881): A New Biography (Houghton Mifflin, 1931); and
Ernest J. Simmons: *Dostoevsky: The Making of a Novelist* (Little Brown,
1940). See also Leopold H. Haimson: *The Russian Marxists and the Origins of
Bolshevism* (Harvard University Press, 1955); Tomáš Garrigue Masaryk: *The
Spirit of Russia: Studies in History, Literature, and Philosophy,* translated from
the German original (1913) by Eden and Cedar Paul (Allen & Unwin, London,
and Macmillan, New York, 1919); Ernest J. Simmons (editor): *Continuity and
Change in Russian and Soviet Thought* (Harvard University Press, 1955); Mark
Slonim: *Three Loves of Dostoevsky* (Rinehart, 1956); and Bertram D. Wolfe:
Three Who Made a Revolution (Dial Press, 1948).

Weird doctrines of rationalism, liberalism, and radicalism found converts among the literate few or "intelligentsia." These were the sons and daughters of aristocrats or officials or of the new merchants and bankers. Few among them were peasants or workers, for whom the ancient ways were the only ways, despite resentments and groping hopes, and among whom the world of ideas was long a closed book that, even if opened, they could not read. Excited by ideas from abroad, the intellectuals achieved miracles of creativity in fiction, music, poetry, drama, and science. But the ideas they borrowed were, more often than not, subversive of the old order whereby the rulers of Russia lived and governed and preserved their privileges. Dangerous thinkers, isolated alike from the blind elite and the deaf masses, were moved to guilt and shame, to profound alienation from the faith of their forebears, and to clamant demands for reform or revolution.

Let others dispute as to whether the destructive elements of the new "nihilism," as Turgenev first named it, were products of the neuroses of the intellectuals or of the insensitivity of the holders of power. It is enough to note that the midcentury ferment was less productive of affirmations than of negations. That existing realities were intolerable many could agree. How matters were to be mended few could perceive. How this vacuum was to be filled none could foresee. Most of the reformers and preachers of revolt ultimately became "socialists" of one or another variety. The gospel of social revolution to achieve a cooperative commonwealth is doubtless most attractive to those most dependent upon Church and State for a sense of community and most alienated from the religious and political order of their ancestors.

Some among the literati, to be sure, rallied to the defense of the *status quo*. Against the "Westernizers" and revolutionists, the "Slavophiles" sprang to the aid of Orthodoxy, Autocracy, and Holy Mother Russia. These apostles of conservatism included Alexei S. Khomyakov (1804–60), the brothers Ivan (1823–86) and Konstantine (1817–60) Aksakov, the brothers Ivan (1806–56) and Peter (1808–56) Kiriyevskii, Yuri F. Samarin (1819–76), and, with qualifications, Vladimir Solovyov (1853–1900).[3] Their ranks included Dostoevsky

---

[3] I am much indebted to my former student Richard B. Holton for new light on these writers in his Williams College honors thesis, unfortunately unpublished, "The Slavophiles: Their Tradition and Legacy," 1955, which includes many hitherto untranslated excerpts from their works.

and the philosopher of history Nikolai Y. Danilevsky (1822–85), an anti-Darwinian Pan-Slavist and pre-Spenglerian prophet of the doom of the West. Their common themes, mingled ambivalently with xenophobic distrust and grudging admiration of "decadent" Europe, were Russia's "mission" to save the world, Slavic purity and superiority, and the sacred principle of *sobornost* or "collectivity" in contrast to Western individualism. Such ideas, forged by the defenders of the Romanov Tsardom as weapons against reformers and rebels, were sufficiently rooted in Russian experience to insure their survival, in semantic disguise, long after 1917.[4]

The same may be said for many of the concepts of the most articulate foe of heresy and apologist of Autocracy, the jurist, censor, and "Grand Inquisitor" of the Tsardom, Konstantine Petrovich Pobedonostsev (1827–1907), who was Procurator of the Holy Synod from 1880 to 1905. In his voluminous writings he contended that men are evil, false, and self-deluded, and that equality is a fantasy. Russia is "an icy desert and the abode of the Bad Man." Its people are at once lazy and filled with ferocious passions. Reason is a snare. Only strong rulers, able and willing to employ force, fraud, and favors with firmness, can govern such a society. Rulership is the task of an enlightened and disciplined minority. Democracy spells abasement and vulgarization. Parliamentarianism is "the great lie of our age." The unity of the community, moreover, requires one single Orthodoxy, intolerant of all dissent. The State must be arbitrary, authoritarian, absolute, monolithic, and all-embracing. Yet Europe should be told that freedom of speech and conscience prevails in Russia, and that all accusations against the regime are false.[5]

That some among the revolutionaries should ultimately adapt to their own purposes the ideas and practices of the reactionaries is evidence that people are more shaped by conditions than conditions

---

[4] For a fascinating account, with quotations, of other 19th-Century Russian writers whose messianism—whether Slavophile or "Western," Muscovite or Petrine—anticipated the Russia of the 20th Century, see Hans Kohn: "The Permanent Mission: An Essay on Russia," *The Review of Politics*, July 1948.

[5] Punsters had fun with Pobedonostsev's name, which means "bringer of victory." *Bedonostsev* means "bringer of evil." *Donostsev* means "informer." For his ideas, see *Moskovskii Sbornik* (Moscow Collection), containing in successive editions many of his essays, and, in translation, his *Reflections of a Russian Statesman* (R. C. Long, 1898). Cf. Ernest J. Simmons (editor): *Continuity and Change in Russian and Soviet Thought* (Harvard University Press, 1955), pp. 113–28, "Pobedonostsev on the Instruments of Russian Government," by Robert F. Byrnes, who has a book in preparation on the same subject.

by people; that timeless Russia conquers her conquerors; or that men are subtly transformed into the image of what they hate and fight against. The more famous Russian intellectuals of a century ago were iconoclasts and rebels. Spectacular among them was Mikhail Bakunin (1814–71), revolutionary anarchist who first worked, and then quarreled, with Marx and involved himself fantastically in most of the revolutions of his time. Long before, in December of 1825, a group of liberal army officers in St. Petersburg, led by Colonel Paul Pestel, had vainly attempted a *coup d'état,* halfway between a "palace revolution" and a popular rebellion. The "Decembrists" were hanged, beheaded, or exiled to Siberia. Pestel was an early "socialist." Most of his successors believed, however vaguely, that the Good Society could somehow be achieved through the community ownership of private property. Alexander Herzen (1812–70), bastard son of a nobleman, was, before his exile in 1835, a leader of heretics at the University of Moscow, where Bakunin, the Aksakovs, and Vissarion Belinsky were his contemporaries. He preached a mystical socialism to be attained through the peasantry and the village *mir* (this Russian word, significantly, means "community," "peace," and "world"), wherein land was owned and tilled in common.

Such agitation came to political fruition in the 1860's in the emergence of sundry groups committed to faith in the peasantry and to the uses of murder as a weapon of reform or revolution. Obscure conspirators, calling themselves *Zemlya i Volya* ("Land and Freedom"), plotted a peasant uprising in 1863 and the killing of the Tsar in 1866. Both enterprises failed and led the plotters to the gallows or Siberian exile. Peter Lavrov preached the need of propaganda among the peasant masses and inspired many intellectuals in the early 1870's to go to the villages—where the usual response of the *muzhiks* was incomprehension and hostility.

In 1879 *Narodnaya Volya* was organized, with Lavrov becoming editor of the journal of the same name, to preach a cult of peasant emancipation, a constituent assembly, and the assassination of officials. The converts became known as *Narodniki* or Populists. Their movement waned toward the century's end, but found new life in the establishment of the Social Revolutionary (SR) Party, formally created in 1902. The leader and chief theoretician of this group was Victor Mikhailovich Chernov (1876–1952). The SR's killed many agents of the Tsardom and by 1917 had won the support of a majority of the Russian peasantry. Their blueprint for the new order was cloudy. Chernov later fought the Soviet regime, fled to Germany and France as an *émigré*, and died in New York a year before Stalin's demise.

A grim caricature of the terrorists is furnished by Sergei G. Nechaiev, born the son of a serf in 1847 and dead in the dungeons of the Peter-Paul fortress in 1883. He it was who in November 1869, in Moscow, murdered his fellow student Ivanov as a "traitor" to the cause. Earlier in the year, while abroad, he had formed the secret "Society of the People's Assize" and collaborated with Bakunin in the writing of a *Revolutionary Catechism*. Here was expounded a harsh gospel. The Revolution must be the work of a devoted fellowship of conspirators. Each must abandon all human ties, even his name, and dedicate himself solely to the profession of revolutionist. All together must obey the Leader. The end is freedom for the workers. The means, justified by the end, are dissimulation; lies; liaisons with prostitutes, criminals, and policemen; assassination; enhancement of social evils to provoke the masses to revolt; and anything else, beyond good and evil, which will contribute to the total destruction of the existing order. "A true revolutionary excludes all romanticism, all sensibility, all enthusiasm, all spontaneity . . . even personal vengeance and hate. Revolutionary passion becomes for him an unceasing habit and allies itself with cold calculation."

After Ivanov's murder, Bakunin condemned Nechaiev as a scoundrel and denounced his Jesuitism and Machiavellianism. Yet Nechaiev's formula was, in the end, to prove irresistibly attractive to other rebels, including those who most loudly repudiated his methods as immoral or futile.[6]

With the wit of afterthought, it is easy to see that the handful of Russian intellectuals who were converted to Marxism were the most farsighted and potent among their confreres. Yet the perception is false, for there was nothing "inevitable" in the final triumph of the Russian Marxists. How this came to pass we shall examine in due course. Here let us recall how the business began.

In the year 1879 a split took place among the adherents of

[6] On the intellectual and political ferment of the waning Tsardom, the best book by far is still Tomáš G. Masaryk's superb survey and evaluation, *The Spirit of Russia* (1913). A vivid portrait of a typical terrorist is presented by David Footman: *Red Prelude* (Yale University Press, 1945), a biography of Andrei I. Zhelyabov, organizer of the assassination of Alexander II.

Zemlya i Volya. Marx was 61. Lenin was 9. Neither knew of the event. The dissidents opposed terrorism—i.e., murder as a political weapon. One among them was Georgii Valentinovich Plekhanov, born in 1856 and fated to die of tuberculosis in 1918. In 1881 he went abroad and was converted to Marxism. In September 1883, six months after Marx's death, he, along with Paul B. Axelrod, Leo G. Deutsch, and Vera I. Zasulich, established in Geneva a pretentiously named "Emancipation of Labor Group," designed to convert the Populists to Marxism. In 1884 and 1887 the Group prepared drafts of a program of a Russian Social Democratic Party, still toying tentatively with terrorism, which Marx had vigorously opposed. Under the pen names Volgin and Beltov, Plekhanov smuggled Marxist literature into Russia in the 1890's and thereby earned his title as the "Father of Russian Marxism." His subversive activities were not fruitless. Here and there, across Russia's vast expanse, alienated intellectuals came upon his work and experienced a great vision.

Two among them, apart from the young Lenin, are noteworthy by virtue of their later roles. Both were born in 1879, one on November 7 and the other on December 21 by our calendar. The elder of the two, by seven weeks, was the fifth child of Anna and David Bronstein. The parents were Jewish. She was a Ukrainian townswoman, literate and mildly religious. He was quite un-Jewish in being illiterate, irreligious, and a farmer—indeed, a *kulak* ("fist") or well-to-do peasant. He had just purchased a large farm, Yanovka, near the village of Bovrinetz in Kherson Province in the southern Ukraine. Here the son, named Lev or Leon, spent his first nine years in an atmosphere of hard work, thrift, and waxing prosperity.

Since Jews were forbidden to buy land by a ukase of 1881, the father, who flourished by shrewd dealing and driving his workers hard, rented new hectares from the debt-ridden Polish and Russian gentry near by. Little Lev lived his next seven years with liberal-minded relatives, the Spentzers, in cosmopolitan Odessa, where he did brilliantly at school. At 16 the youth destined for fame as Leon Trotsky was already handsome, eloquent, polished, self-centered, and proud.

How and why do young bourgeois gentlemen become Marxists? Lev Davidovich Bronstein soon saw that his hard-fisted parents were uncouth. He sometimes quarreled with his father on his return to the farm. It is arguable that sons who break with their fathers sometimes become alienated from their fatherlands. Yet the

man who became Trotsky was long indifferent to politics. In Niko-layev, where he went in 1896 to complete his high-school education, he resisted the efforts of the family with whom he lived to interest him in socialism. But soon he felt "pity for the oppressed" and found himself, nebulously, a "socialist." Then he came upon a Czech gar-dener, Franz Shvigovsky, who talked much in his orchard hut with radical students and workers. This "circle" consisted of *Narodniks*. Lev condemned Marxism and, half in love, quarreled with a girl in the group who was a Marxist, Alexandra Sokolovskaya. When his father, alarmed at loose talk, forbade him to see Shvigovsky, he spurned his family allowance, took up tutoring, and moved to the hut. 1897 found him studying mathematics at the University of Odessa and then plunging abruptly, more than half a Marxist, into a frenzy of conspiratorial activity leading to the emergence among the laborers of Nikolayev of the clandestine and illegal "Southern Russian Workers' Union." Lev was not yet an orator. But he was al-ready a skillful agitator and journalist, vastly excited by his new mission.

The sequel was not unique but common in the experience of thousands of young Russian radicals at the turn of the century. In January of 1898 the police swooped down on all, including Alex-andra and Shvigovsky, who were suspected of having a hand in the Nikolayev "Union." Bronstein pined in various jails, often in soli-tary confinement for defiance. Refusing to rot, he penned verses, wrote literary essays, learned languages, studied theology, and tried his hand as a Marxist historian by writing an account of Freema-sonry, of which the manuscript was later lost. Sentenced without a trial to four years of Siberian exile, he was sent first to a transfer prison in Moscow. There, in 1900, he married Alexandra and, before leaving for Siberia, spent his time reading Lenin and Bernstein and endlessly writing revolutionary articles.

The newlyweds finally reached the Lena River and the miser-able gold-rush ghost village of Ust-Kut, filled with mosquitoes, cockroaches, and drunken peasants. Lev studied *Capital*, begot a daughter, and became bookkeeper to an illiterate millionaire. Later he moved to Verkholensk, near Lake Baikal. He made friends in Irkutsk and achieved distinction as a literary critic and Marxist journalist. He was called Pero ("The Pen"). In the summer of 1902, with his wife's approval despite the birth of a second daughter, he escaped on a false passport on which he wrote the name of one of

his jailers in Odessa: Trotsky. After conferring and conspiring with other Marxists along the Volga and in the Ukraine, he went abroad to report to the editors of *Iskra*. In October 1902 he arrived in London and called at once on a "Mr. and Mrs. Richter," who were living in a one-room flat near King's Cross in a tiny three-story brick tenement. His hosts were Lenin and Krupskaya. Trotsky had arrived, in Isaac Deutscher's phrase, "at the door of history." [7]

Trotsky's contemporary, later comrade, and ultimate nemesis was born on December 21, 1879, in the Georgian town of Gori. His father, Vissarion I. Djugashvili—earlier a serf and the son of serfs—had moved some years previously from the village of Didi-Lilo near Tiflis. In Gori, 40 miles away, he set up a cobbler's shop and married a girl of 15, Ekaterina Gheladze, daughter of a serf. They lived in a shack with one window and a brick floor. Three babies were born. All died. The fourth lived and was baptized Joseph Vissarionovich Djugashvili. He survived smallpox in childhood and an infection that permanently stiffened his left elbow. His father failed in his little business and lived on Ekaterina's earnings as a washerwoman. He then took to vodka and to beating his wife and son, and tried in vain to recoup his fortunes by working in a shoe factory in Tiflis. He died in 1890.

His pious and illiterate widow took in more washing and dreamed of better things for her "Soso." In 1888 she sent him to a church school and imagined him becoming a priest. The boy from the slums learned easily and outshone his upper-class schoolmates. He acquired Russian, while doubtless resenting "Russification." (His mother spoke only Georgian.) He often dominated his boyhood friends. In the fair countryside of the land of the Golden Fleece, rich in legends of invasion, resistance, and feuds among clans, all

---

[7] See Isaac Deutscher's brilliant biography, *The Prophet Armed: Trotsky, 1879–1921* (Oxford University Press, 1954), for more details of Trotsky's subsequent career, and a useful bibliography of books in English, Russian, and other languages by and about Trotsky. See also Leon Trotsky: *My Life* (Scribner, 1930); Trotsky's indictment of his foe, *Stalin* (Harper, 1941), about two-thirds complete when Trotsky was murdered, and later translated and edited by Charles Malamuth; Isaac Deutscher: *Stalin: A Political Biography* (Oxford University Press, 1949); and Bertram D. Wolfe: *Three Who Made a Revolution* (Dial Press, 1948). The last-named work is an invaluable "biographical history" of Lenin, Trotsky, and Stalin up to 1914. See *The American Slavic and East European Review*, February 1956, for a belated and somewhat quibbling criticism by Marc Szeftel, along with Wolfe's masterly rejoinder.

boys played "bandit" and "warrior." In 1894–5 he was precociously writing Georgian poetry (and getting it published) and beginning his studies on a scholarship in the Theological Seminary in Tiflis.

How did a shoemaker's son, destined for the priesthood, become a Marxist? The Seminary combined the worst features of a monastery and a barracks. Many students were rebellious, some in the name of Georgian patriotism, others influenced by Russian subversives exiled to Georgia—Populists, terrorists, and finally Marxist proletarians, such as Mikhail Kalinin and Sergo Alliluyev. Before Joseph's arrival, one principal had been assassinated and a student strike had led to the expulsion of 87 pupils. Soso was a model student, but the spying monks discovered in 1896 that he was borrowing forbidden books from the town library and smuggling them into the Seminary. By summer of 1898 he had joined a students' secret debating club and, in the town, a Marxist society known as the "Third Group," founded in 1893 by G. Tseretelli, K. Chkheidze, and others. The first strikes of Tiflis workers contributed to Joseph's conversion, as did contacts with local revolutionists. They assigned him in his off hours to lecturing secretly on Marxism to small groups of factory hands. At the Seminary he deceived the monks, resented their searches for books, and was punished for disrespect and rudeness. On May 29, 1899, he was expelled.

At the dawn of the year 1900 he had a clerk's job and a room at the Tiflis Observatory. May Day found him giving his first public speech to several hundred workers who gathered in a suburb to evade the police. They sang socialist songs and carried red flags and crude drawings of Marx and Engels. A year later the police raided his room. Being away, he escaped arrest, but was obliged to give up his clerkship and go "underground" into the precarious life of a professional subversive. He was not to emerge until 1917. Joseph Djugashvili began writing for an illegal Marxist journal, *Brdzola* (*The Struggle*). In November 1901 he became a member of the Social Democratic Committee of Tiflis and was sent to Batum on the Turkish frontier as a Marxist agitator.

Here he called himself Koba ("The Indomitable"), from the name of a legendary Georgian brigand and champion of the poor. His efforts, including a secret press, were effective in promoting strikes and riots. He condemned his Marxist comrade Chkheidze for "faintheartedness." Chkheidze called him a "madman." On April 5,

1902, Koba was arrested. After confinement in Batum and other Caucasian jails, he began a long cycle of imprisonments, exiles, escapes, and revolutionary exploits.

For the future "Stalin," as for most of his comrades similarly dedicated to Marxism as a career, family life was irrelevant and almost impossible. He was to marry a simple soul, sister of one of his fellow conspirators and not unlike his mother: Ekaterina Svanidze. They had one child, Jacob. Little is known of this marriage. Even the date, 1903 or 1904, is uncertain. She died in 1907 and was given an Orthodox funeral. Whether, as Trotsky later wrote, Stalin was so heartbroken as to become henceforth heartless toward all mankind is doubtful. He was not to remarry until 1919. His second wife, Nadezhda, was the daughter of Sergo Alliluyev, a worker whom he first met in Georgia and who, much later, was to befriend the conspirator destined to become dictator over Russia. This marriage, too, is a mystery, including its tragic ending.

Meanwhile, other Marxist plotters had sought to unify their scattered efforts by founding a party. Several local "Leagues of Struggle" joined with the Bund, or Union of Jewish Marxists, in sending "delegates" to a secret "congress." Only nine arrived. The appointed place was Minsk, and the time March 1898. They proclaimed the establishment of the "Russian Social Democratic Labor Party" (RSDLP), named a "Central Committee," and issued a "Manifesto" written by Peter Struve which noted, vaguely, that the workers of Russia possessed none of the Western civil rights essential in the struggle "for final liberation, against private property, for socialism." The Russian bourgeoisie is "weak, mean, and cowardly." Therefore the proletariat must "conquer political liberty" as "the first step to the realization of the great historic mission of the proletariat, to the foundation of a social order in which there will be no place for the exploitation of man by man." There was no mention of Marx's formula of "the dictatorship of the proletariat" and no program of action. All the participants were soon arrested. None achieved later fame.[8]

The nine unknown who met in Minsk in March of 1898 appar-

---

[8] The names of the nine delegates were S. Radchenko (Moscow League of Struggle), A. Vannovsky (Ekaterinoslav League of Struggle), K. Petrusevich (Kiev League of Struggle), P. Tuchapsky, two delegates from a Kiev paper, Eidelman and Vigdorchik, and three delegates from the Bund: A. Kremer, A. Mutnik, and S. Katz.

ently accomplished nothing. But among the Russian disciples of Marx their meeting was to be named "Congress I" of the Party that has ruled Russia since 1917.

3. THE MESSAGE OF THE BOOK

THE NINE men of Minsk were converts to a cult. So also were count-less other Russians, along with millions elsewhere throughout the world. The content of the cult was found, to begin with, in the works of Marx and Engels. Both authors denied the sanctity of their scrip-tures. Disgusted by the dogmatism of some of his followers, Marx in his last years thanked the Lord that *he*, at least, was "not a Marxist." The revered writings of the founders nevertheless came to be re-garded by all disciples as a revelation. They included *Capital* (com-pleted by Engels); the original "Communist Manifesto"; *The Pov-erty of Philosophy*; *The Holy Family*; *Value, Price, and Profit*; *A Critique of Political Economy*; *Anti-Dühring*; and sundry other books, pamphlets, and letters. Revolutions are verbose. This light was not hid under a bushel.

Forty years after 1917 the visitor to the capital of Muscovy could find fabulous collections of the scriptures, coupled with all glosses by all writers in all tongues. The Marx-Engels Institute, behind the Museum of Fine Arts, contains a large library on Marxism up to 1914. The Marxist-Leninist Institute, off Gorky Street (formerly Tverskaya) on Soviet Square, houses additional archives. The Lenin State Library, southwest of the Kremlin at Mokhovaya and Frunze streets, comprises a vast enlargement of the original (1787) Rum-yantsev Museum and boasts 2,000 employees, 5,000 daily visitors, and 18,000,000 books, pamphlets, and periodicals. Yet this "largest library in the world" contains few anti-Soviet books in any lan-guage. Moreover, its collection of the writings of Trotsky, Bukharin, Zinoviev, and other victims of the Great Purge is available freely in 1956–7 only to professors and holders of doctors' degrees, with other readers barred unless they have special permits.

Such monumental compilations of sacred writings demonstrate that Marx and Engels, quite apart from other evidences of their in-fluence over the minds of men, were "prophets." They were also pol-iticians, although frustrated by hopes ever deferred. In their youth

they founded in Brussels a "German Workers' Society" and joined a conspiratorial "League of the Just," soon renamed the "League of Communists." Late in 1847 they wrote the "Manifesto." The League lapsed with Marx's flight to London after the upheavals of 1848. In 1863 he was one of the founders of the "International Working Men's Association," dissolved in Philadelphia in 1876 following the break between Marx and Bakunin, and later known as the "First International." Marx died without seeing the realization anywhere of the "Proletarian Revolution" that he confidently forecast, save for the transitory "Red Republic" in France in 1848 and the tragic "Paris Commune" of 1871. The latter enterprise in insurrection he envisaged in his *Civil War in France* as the prototype of the "Proletarian Dictatorship" of days to come.

The Marxist creed, born of German philosophy, English political economy, and French "Utopian" socialism, was at once a cosmology, a hypothesis of history, a theory of economics, a system of sociology, and a science of politics. Its essence comes to this: the basis of the cosmos is matter, not energy or ideas. Hence philosophical "idealism" is wrong and philosophical "materialism" is right. All things are in flux, with change proceeding in the fashion postulated by George Wilhelm Hegel, though Hegel's "idealism" was erroneous and must be "stood on its head" by the tenets of "materialism." Hegel saw all transitions in terms of a "dialectical" process whereby each entity (thesis) begets its opposite (antithesis), with interaction between them leading to a fusion (synthesis) which, in turn, reinitiates the process. Marx's revision of Hegel thus came to be called "dialectical materialism."

This conception of cosmic processes, when applied to human affairs, led Marx and Engels to their own version of economic determinism: "historical materialism"—i.e., the view that what is fundamental in all human societies is the system of producing goods and services. Economics, thus defined, is the "base" of all community life. All else—State, law, religion, art, philosophy, etc.—is "superstructure," having meaning only in relationship to the "base." Thus far all societies, thanks to their systems of production, have generated antagonistic social classes: slaves and masters, serfs and lords, workers and capitalists. Human history is significant, argued Marx and Engels, only as the record of class struggle.

Early and for long in our era of the Western world, lords exploited serfs in a predominantly rural economy. The rise of the urban

middle class or "bourgeoisie" marked the slow transition from "feudalism" to "capitalism." But the bourgeoisie, in turn, brought into being, willy-nilly, a new counterclass by virtue of its ownership of the means of production in the new factory system born of modern science and technology. The counterclass is the "proletariat" of wage slaves, owning no property and compelled to live by selling its labor to the capitalist entrepreneurs. The latter's sole motive is profit-seeking and the accumulation of wealth for luxurious living or for reinvestment in industry with a view toward greater profit.

At this point Marx borrowed from Ricardo and his precursors the "labor theory of value," according to which the worth of all commodities in the market is, ultimately, a function of the labor required for their production. If wage-earners received the full value of their contribution, no profit would be possible for the owners of the means of production. All profit therefore represents "surplus value," over and above what workers are paid for their labors.

From this it follows that "capitalism," while vastly more efficient than "feudalism," is an even more monstrous system of exploitation whereby capitalists enrich themselves by stealing from workers a large share of what the workers in fact produce. This scheme of production, while immensely profitable to the owners of capital, is nevertheless self-defeating and finally doomed to self-destruction. For its net result, so Marx and Engels contended, is the bipolarization of society into an ever smaller and more bloated class of plutocrats and an ever larger and more impoverished class of proletarians. All other social strata will be ground to pieces between the millstones. The capitalists, thanks to their competition with one another in exploiting the workers, will experience a declining rate of profit, marked by "crises," panics, and depressions of ever increasing severity. They will thus be obliged to resort to ever more rigorous means of exploiting their wage-earners, who, as consumers, will be less and less able to buy back what they produce at prices profitable to the owners of the means of production. The end can only be an economic and social débâcle.

The State, in the Marxist view, is never anything more than a tool of the ruling class, designed to insure the effective exploitation of the ruled by the rulers. Bourgeois democracy is thus a sham. When "capitalism" collapses, the starving proletariat must be prepared to take over the means of production through revolutionary action, thus establishing a "dictatorship of the proletariat" as a new

form of State which will "expropriate the expropriators"—i.e., dispossess and liquidate the bourgeoisie. The proletarian State will nationalize all industry and establish "socialism," whereby the exploitation of man by man will be ended in a cooperative commonwealth. In the words of the original Manifesto:

> Political power, properly so called, is merely the organized power of one class for oppressing another. If the proletariat during its contest with the bourgeoisie is compelled, by the force of circumstances, to organize itself as a class; if, by means of a revolution, it makes itself the ruling class, and, as such, sweeps away by force the old conditions of production, then it will, along with these conditions, have swept away the conditions for the existence of class antagonisms and of classes generally, and will thereby have abolished its own supremacy as a class. In place of the old bourgeois society, with its classes and class antagonisms, we shall have an association, in which the free development of each is the condition for the free development of all. . . . The Communists disdain to conceal their views and aims. They openly declare that their ends can be attained only by the forcible overthrow of all existing social conditions. Let the ruling classes tremble at a Communist revolution. The proletarians have nothing to lose but their chains. They have a world to win. Workingmen of all countries, unite!

After the Revolution comes the Millennium. By establishing "socialism" and ultimately "communism," the proletarian State will for the first time in history create a "classless society." Since the State, by definition, is nothing more than an executive committee of the ruling class, a society without classes will need no State. This venerable institution will therefore "wither away." In Lenin's words: "So long as the State exists, there is no freedom; when freedom exists, there will be no State." The end result of the expropriation of the bourgeoisie by the proletariat will thus be the inauguration of a wholly new epoch in human affairs, characterized by such freedom and justice as were hitherto inconceivable in all the class societies of the past.

The "truth" or "falsity" of the premises of Marxism have been disputed for over a century by thousands of writers pouring forth millions of words. Non-Marxists are entitled to test the validity of

Marxism by the facts of life and the record of the times. Those who do so fairly must concede that the new gospel offers valuable insights into many of the processes of economic, social, and political change in all human communities. Yet the verdict is inescapable that the major premises and predictions have been invalidated by experience, which is the only possible criterion for judging propositions alleged to be "scientific." [9]

This negative judgment need not here be elaborated. Such notations as these will suffice. If "matter" and "energy" are now seen to be, by the light of Einstein, merely two aspects of one entity, then the age-old quarrel of "materialists" and "idealists" is no longer meaningful. The trinity of the dialectic is equally dubious as a description of change in the universe. *Homo sapiens,* moreover, cannot be comprehended simply as "economic man," moved by rational self-interest, for he is a creature—admirably exemplified by the Marxists themselves—of loves and hates, fears and guilts, conscience and sin, as often moved by unconscious unreason as by calculation. As for "base" and "superstructure," the very history of the USSR refutes the relationship that Marx assumed. Class conflict, moreover, is not normal but abnormal in most societies, appearing only in times of rapid shifts in the fortunes of men, begetting tensions, frustrations, and aggressions.

The economics and sociology of Marxism are simply wrong as an analysis and prognosis of "capitalism." In advanced industrial communities the "proletariat" grows richer, not poorer, and becomes a waning rather than a waxing segment of the social hierarchy, while the new middle class comes to embrace most of the population. In such societies slumps and breakdowns may generate Fascist despotism but never the "workers' revolution"—which has come to pass, beginning in the Russia of 1917, only in backward rural economies. Marxism in practice serves purposes and fulfills functions that have

---

[9] Among the voluminous literature on Marxism, the following recent contributions seem to me to be informative and suggestive: G. D. H. Cole: *The Meaning of Marxism* (Gollancz, 1948); G. D. H. Cole: *A History of Socialist Thought* (4 vols., St. Martin's Press, 1954–7); Eugene O. Golob: *The Isms: A History and Evaluation* (Harper, 1954); Sidney Hook: *The Ambiguous Legacy: Marx and the Marxists* (Van Nostrand, 1955); R. N. Carew Hunt: *Marxism: Past and Present* (Macmillan, 1955); William N. Loucks and J. Welson Hoot: *Comparative Economic Systems* (Harper, 4th ed., 1952); H. B. Mayo: *Democracy and Marxism* (Oxford University Press, 1955); Alfred G. Meyer: *Marxism: The Unity of Theory and Practice* (Harvard University Press, 1955).

nothing in common with the postulated aims and goals of Marxist theory. And since the State has many roles in serving or disserving human needs, apart from the occasional role that Marxists assert is its sole role, its prospects of "withering away" are negligible, particularly under conditions of total socialism. How any complex society can become "classless" or how any concrete meaning can be given to an economic "communism" wherein each will be rewarded according to his "needs" has never been explained by any Marxist to the satisfaction of anyone save other Marxists.

So much said (and much more might be said), it behooves Marxists and non-Marxists alike to note that all these considerations are almost irrelevant to the question of the appeals and prospects of Marxism. Despite its pretense, Marxism is no "science" to be accepted or rejected on the basis of empirical evidence. Marxism is a cosmology, a creed, and a gospel, offering to its converts symbols of identification no less emotionally potent than those offered by other "higher religions." Here, as in every well-articulated theology and eschatology, are the bearded Prophet, promising salvation; the pantheon of saints and martyrs; and the books of Holy Writ, ponderous, ambiguous, read by few but revered by all the faithful as the source of all wisdom. Here are a key to the cosmos, a resolution of all mysteries, a revelation of all truth, an explanation of beginnings and endings, a vision of the ultimate triumph of Good over Evil at Armageddon, and a dream of the Millennium of days to come when men, at long last, will be saved from the miseries of this vale of tears and will find their way to peace through love and brotherhood.

The cult of Marxism may be deemed, depending upon taste, an adaptation to socialism of what Bertrand Russell has called "the Jewish pattern of history"; the fourth of the Judaic Higher Religions, after Judaism, Christianity, and Islam; or, in the formulation of Arnold J. Toynbee, the great Jewish-Christian Heresy of our time.[1] It first emerged as a Western faith, having its sources in the spiritual heritage of ancient Israel, Athens, and Rome and the modern middle-class credo of liberalism with its aspirations toward a fuller freedom and a more perfect democracy. That Marxists in action have often seemed to betray these aspirations and to negate that heritage does not distinguish them from many votaries of other

---

[1] See Bertrand Russell: *A History of Western Philosophy* (Simon and Schuster, 1945), pp. 363 f., and Arnold J. Toynbee: *A Study of History* (Oxford University Press, 1954), VIII, 469, 478; IX, 450, 461, 583–4, 620–1 etc.

creeds or lend credibility to the view that Marx was anti-Christ and that contemporary Communism is exclusively the work of the devil. Converts find in the Marxist dogma, as others have found in other doctrines, a satisfaction of their quest for certainty, a protest against social injustice, and a summons to action to save their souls —if not within the pearly gates beyond the grave, then here and now in heroic struggle to realize heaven on earth.

This creed had a peculiar fascination for many of the members of the groping and guilt-ridden intelligentsia of the Romanov Tsardom in the days of its decay. The initial appeal, in East and West alike, was to alienated intellectuals of noble or bourgeois origin rather than to the industrial wage-earners to whom the cult was addressed. The "proletariat" long remained indifferent or hostile, completely and permanently so in America and largely so in England. Where workers became converts in appreciable numbers, this result was the work of upper-class missionaries who dedicated themselves to propagating the faith and organizing the faithful for the tasks of parliamentary or revolutionary politics. How this labor proceeded in Muscovy is the next object of our inquiry.

4. THE FORGING OF THE SWORD

DURING the first 17 years of the 20th Century the Russian Marxists fashioned the weapon with which they were to conquer power in the October Revolution, undertake the "liberation" of the world, and, failing this, transform utterly the Muscovy of old in ways unforeseen by the Marxists themselves. The weapon was the "Party," a misnomer for a subversive conspiracy of plotters, fanatically consecrated to rebellion. Its fabrication was not a masterwork of craftsmanship executed according to prior design. It was rather a disorderly muddle of venomous wrangling among the conspirators —interspersed with plots, counterplots, police spies, arrests, exiles, escapes, murders, bank robberies, an abortive revolution, despair, hope, and endless frustrations reducing the whole enterprise to a futility at once tragic and absurd from which, incredibly, it was finally rescued and brought to victory by the blunders of its foes.

To reduce this jumble of struggle to a logical maturing of revolutionary strategy and tactics does violence to the facts. To narrate

the events of these turmoils in darkness would require many volumes.[2] A few episodes will suggest the noisome and turbulent climate of the "underground" out of which Russia's new rulers were to emerge.

In the spring of 1900 Lenin, released from Siberia, returned to St. Petersburg and conferred with Vera Zasulich, Peter Struve, Julius Ossipovich Martov (Tsederbaum, 1873–1923), and other Marxists. He was troubled by the rise of "revisionism" among the faithful, a doctrine reflecting the views of Eduard Bernstein, who doubted the débâcle of capitalism and urged a program of evolutionary reform. Lenin sought to establish a Russian Marxist periodical abroad. He was no man to be discouraged by difficulties or dismayed by opposition. In July he went to Germany and soon saw Plekhanov, Axelrod, and other exiles in Switzerland. Lenin, Zasulich, and A. N. Potresov became editors in Munich of the new journal of the "Russian Social Democratic Labor Party" (RSDLP), printed in Leipzig. They called it *Iskra* (*The Spark*), echoing the exiled Decembrists' reply to greetings from Pushkin: "From the spark will spring the flame!"

The first issue of *Iskra* was dated December 11, 1900. In its pages Lenin presently argued that the RSDLP should not seek to become a large, loose, democratic mass movement, since such qualities would doom it to failure under the conditions imposed by the Tsarist autocracy, but should rather seek its model, *à la* Nechaiev, in the Carbonari, the Jacobins, and the Jesuits. The Party must be a small, carefully selected, highly disciplined, and wholly consecrated fraternity of comrades, financed by Party funds so that every leader might devote himself wholly to the profession of revolutionist. Decisions should be arrived at through free discussions and votes among delegates at periodical "Congresses," where a "Central Committee" should be elected to direct the struggle. But all members must be bound in iron obedience to carry out decisions and orders regardless of personal views. This organizational ideal, to be known as "democratic centralism," was sketched by Lenin in "Where to Begin?" in the fourth issue of *Iskra*, May 1901, and developed in

[2] In addition to sources of Party history cited in subsequent chapters, see Nicolas Berdyaev: *The Origins of Russian Communism* (Scribner, 1937); William Z. Foster: *History of the Three Internationals* (International Publishers, 1955); Donald W. Treadgold: *Lenin and His Rivals* (Praeger, 1955); and Edmund Wilson: *To the Finland Station* (Harcourt, Brace, 1940) and *Red, Black, Blond and Olive* (Oxford University Press, 1956).

Shto Dyelat? (*What Is to Be Done?*), published in Russian in Stuttgart in March 1902. Here Lenin quoted Lassalle to Marx, June 24, 1852: "Party struggles give a party strength and life. The best proof of the weakness of the party is its diffuseness and its blurring of clear-cut differences. . . . A party becomes stronger by purging itself." And here Lenin pleaded for:

> A small, compact core, consisting of reliable, experienced and hardened workers, with responsible agents in the principal districts and connected by all the rules of strict secrecy with the organizations of revolutionists, can, with the wide support of the masses and without an elaborate set of rules, perform *all* the functions of a trade-union organization, and perform them, moreover, in the manner Social-Democrats desire. Only in this way can we secure the *consolidation* and development of a *Social-Democratic* trade-union movement, in spite of the gendarmes. . . . If we begin with the solid foundation of a strong organization of revolutionists, we can guarantee the stability of the movement as a whole, and carry out the aims of both Social-Democracy and of trade unionism. If, however, we begin with a wide workers' organization, supposed to be most "accessible" to the masses, when as a matter of fact it will be most accessible to the gendarmes, and will make the revolutionists most accessible to the police, we shall neither achieve the aims of Social-Democracy nor of trade unionism. . . .
>
> "Broad democracy" in party organization, amidst the gloom of autocracy and the domination of the gendarmes, is nothing more than a *useless and harmful toy*. . . . Only abroad, where very often people who have no opportunity of doing real live work gather together, can the "game of democracy" be played here and there, especially in small groups. . . .
>
> The only serious organizational principle the active workers of our movement can accept is: strict secrecy, strict selection of members, and the training of professional revolutionists. If we possessed these qualities, "democracy" and something even more would be guaranteed to us, namely: complete, comradely, mutual confidence among

revolutionists. And this something more is absolutely essential for us because, in Russia, it is useless to think that democratic control can serve as a substitute for it.[3]

This stern dogma of a militant elite to plot the seizure of power was at once denounced by other Marxists. On July 30, 1903, in a warehouse in Brussels some 50 "delegates" of Russian Marxism at home and abroad secretly assembled as "Congress II" of the RSDLP. Plekhanov gave the opening address, followed by the singing of the "International." Heated debate on credentials and a program ensued. "Secrecy" proved fictitious. When the police deported one delegate, warned others to leave, and spied on all, the Congress moved to London, where it met in a church August 11–23 through hot days and nights of disputation. These dedicated men and women were not workers but intellectuals. Their word-splitting would have seemed ludicrous to outsiders, if any had been interested. Yet these controversies among obscure agitators were, years later, to have world-shaking consequences. They revolved around the gospel that Lenin had expounded in *Iskra.*

The delegates approved a platform that was to remain the Party program until Congress VIII in 1919. The maximum demands were: social revolution and a "dictatorship of the proletariat"; the minimum: an end of the Tsardom, a democratic republic, and social reforms. When Lenin, at first supported by Plekhanov, urged his view of a monolithic brotherhood, Martov pleaded for a democratic mass organization. This able champion of "freedom" was later described by Sukhanov as "an exceptional intellect" and "an incomparable political analyst" who, however, was as irresolute as Hamlet. "An intellect that dominates everything is a source of softening of the will and indecisiveness in action." [4] The first vote, 28 to 22, was in favor of Martov's "soft" line and against Lenin's "hard" view. But when the Bundists left in protest at the refusal of the Congress to concede that they were exclusive spokesmen of Russia's Jewish workers, the "hards" secured a majority. They were dubbed *Bolsheviki* or members of the majority in contrast to the *Mensheviki* or minority. A Central Committee of Lenin's supporters was elected. But his triumph was brief. Soon after the Congress adjourned, Mensheviks

---

[3] *Collected Works of V. I. Lenin* (International Publishers), Vol. IV, *The Iskra Period,* Book II, pp. 159 f., 198, 213.

[4] Sukhanov, pp. 354–6. See footnote 2, p. 68, on the source.

Martov, Plekhanov, Axelrod, and Trotsky took over *Iskra* and began opposing Lenin's Bolshevik position.

This initial schism was never healed. In the summer of 1904, amid the Russo-Japanese War, the Menshevik faction took over the Central Committee. Lenin's followers called for a third Congress, which convened in London in April 1905. But the Mensheviks refused to attend and held their own Congress in Geneva. "Two Congresses, two parties!" Lenin commented bitterly. For him, compromise was inconceivable since it would involve a betrayal of Marxism as he understood it. His stubbornness evoked reproof from Marxists of a milder persuasion. Plekhanov in 1904 accused him of fostering "a sectarian spirit of exclusiveness," of "confusing the dictatorship of the proletariat with the dictatorship *over* the proletariat," and of espousing "Bonapartism if not absolute monarchy." Martov penned a pamphlet: *The Struggle Against Martial Law in the RSDLP.* Zasulich asserted that Lenin's idea of the Party was Louis XIV's idea of the State. Trotsky in *Our Political Tasks* assailed Lenin's view as "a dull caricature of the political intransigence of Jacobinism" and predicted that the time might come when "the Party is replaced by the organization of the Party, the organization by the Central Committee, and finally the Central Committee by the Dictator." Plekhanov later said that if the Bolshevik view should prevail, "everything will in the last resort revolve around one man who *ex providentia* will unite all powers in himself." [5]

The issue of "democracy" was posed in a broader form in the quarrels of 1905. Trotsky, in collaboration with Parvus (Alexander I. Helfand), denounced Lenin's conception of the Party, but urged a revolutionary State to be controlled only by Marxists. Lenin replied that the Marxists and the proletariat as a whole were a small minority of Russia's people and must cooperate with other groups to ensure the democratic character of the revolutionary regime. "Whoever wants to approach socialism by any other path than that of political democracy will inevitably arrive at absurd and reactionary conclusions, both economic and political." In 1917 Trotsky and Lenin were to join forces, with each tacitly accepting the position advanced by the other a dozen years earlier. This synthesis contributed to (even if, as we shall see, it was not the prime cause of)

[5] Cf. Edward Hallett Carr: *The Bolshevik Revolution, 1917–1923* (Macmillan, 1951–4), in four volumes, hereinafter cited by number, as here: Carr, I, 32–3.

the shape of the Soviet polity as a fusion of Party and State, with the State a one-party dictatorship and the Party commanded by a self-chosen oligarchy and finally by an autocrat. But the great constitutional questions of the 1930's and the 1950's were mere semantic disputations among the unknown conspirators of 1905.[6]

These quibbles, seemingly trivial but portentous of things to come, were overshadowed by the outbreak of revolt in Russia in the wake of the defeat of the Tsardom by Japan. According to the Marxist exegesis, the workers' revolution was possible only in mature, fully industrialized societies in a condition of disintegration because of the "contradictions of capitalism." Russia was agrarian and semi-feudal with a "capitalism" still so primitive as to be far away from the final débâcle forecast by Marx. How, then, should Marxists act and what should they expect or strive for?

According to the scriptures, nothing was possible under such circumstances save a bourgeois-democratic revolution against the Tsardom and the aristocracy, with the "proletarian revolution" inexorably deferred to the remote future pending the full development in later decades of a capitalist economy. Most Mensheviks envisaged a bourgeois-proletarian coalition to cast down the Autocracy, with the RSDLP holding aloof from the resultant democratic regime. Lenin conceived of a proletarian-peasant alliance that might support the business classes in completing the bourgeois revolution or, if one could entertain so un-Marxist a hope, might somehow achieve a swift transition to socialism. Late in 1905, in notes not published until 20 years later, he developed the thought that after the triumph of the bourgeoisie over the Tsardom and the landlords, the rich peasants or kulaks and much of the middle peasantry would support the bourgeoisie while the poor peasants and the proletarians might struggle for a "socialist revolution." This struggle would be hopeless, however, "unless the European socialist proletariat comes to the help of the Russian proletariat. . . . Then we together with them will make the socialist revolution." [7] Ultimately most Russian Marxists were agreed that no socialist revolution in Russia was possible without a European or world revolution.

Since nothing was less likely in 1905, the comrades were baffled by their own formulas. In October spontaneously organized

6 See Bertram D. Wolfe's astute analysis of this issue in *Three Who Made a Revolution*, pp. 289–94.

7 Carr, I, pp. 56–7, quoting Lenin: *Sochinenya* (*Works*), VIII, 424–7.

Councils or Soviets of Workers' Deputies arose, first in Ivano-Voznesensk and then in St. Petersburg, Moscow, and elsewhere, to lead a nationwide general strike and transmute popular grievances into revolt. Lenin, who returned in November, perceived, albeit ambivalently, that these bodies might become the units of a provisional revolutionary government. Trotsky was sure of this. He was soon a vice-chairman and the most energetic leader of the Petersburg Soviet, which was controlled by Mensheviks under a radical lawyer, Khrustalev-Nosar. The 550 delegates represented 250,000 workers. A paper was published: *Izvestia* (*News*). At the end Trotsky became President when Khrustalev-Nosar was arrested. The Moscow Soviet, under Bolshevik leadership, planned an armed insurrection.

All the returned exiles were incessantly scurrying about, exhorting, organizing, and inciting to rebellion, although many were unclear as to the nature of the new order to be striven for. In December, in a mood of exaltation, sundry leaders of the RSDLP met in a conference in Tammerfors, Finland. Koba (Stalin) emerged for the first time from the murky underground of the Caucasus, now all in ferment. And for the first time he met Lenin, "the mountain eagle of our Party." Years later the cobbler's son acknowledged unwittingly his Oriental provincialism and his own secret ambitions by saying he had "fancied Lenin as a giant, stately and imposing. How great was my disappointment to see a most ordinary-looking man, below average height, in no way distinguishable from ordinary mortals. [I found him] in a corner, unassumingly carrying on a conversation, a most ordinary conversation, with the most ordinary delegates." The mature Satlin as ruler over Russia was seldom to permit himself to be confused with ordinary mortals. But in December of 1905 only a madman could have forecast for him such a role.

The delegates at Tammerfors saw the downfall of the Tsardom as imminent. Their purpose was to reconcile Bolsheviks and Mensheviks and decide whether the Party should boycott, or participate in, elections for the new Duma. Lenin proposed participation. Most of the rest, including Stalin, opposed him, believing that the victory of the revolution through direct action would sweep away the promised parliament. Lenin yielded. The conference ended on the last day of the year.

But hope soon waned. The sword was blunted. The Party was inadequate for its mission and uncertain as to its course. As the dele-

gates departed, Admiral Dubassov's troops in Moscow were mopping up after smashing the barricades and shelling for three days the workers' tenements in the Presnaya district. A thousand died. The Soviet was ended. So, less violently, was its counterpart in St. Petersburg, with most of the leaders in jail. The great strikes were broken, the peasant uprisings crushed, the mutinies suppressed. The tide of mass revolt, never at the crest required to topple the Autocracy, was now swiftly ebbing. The revolution had failed.

What ensued among the Marxists through dreary years need only be sketched. In April 1906 the 111 delegates of Congress IV gathered in Stockholm, with Bolsheviks and Mensheviks ostensibly reunited. Congress V, with 336 delegates, met in a London church in May 1907. Trotsky sought in vain to organize a middle faction between the factions in the name of anti-factionalism. Stalin was present but obscure. Among new Bolshevik figures, destined later to be famous and then to be devoured by the Moloch of their own devising, were Lev Borisovich Kamenev (Rosenfeld, 1883–1936) and Gregory Evseyevich Zinoviev (Radomyslsky, 1883–1936).

Hot words could not alter cold reality. No new Congress was to meet for ten years. Lenin and Krupskaya lived incognito in Finland. He affected good cheer and wrote tender letters to his mother. He attended the Stuttgart Congress of the Second International, established in Paris in 1889, and was named a member of its Bureau in August 1907. Back in Finland, he sensed the police on his trail. In December he went to Switzerland, oppressed by poverty and despair. He was not to return to Russia for a decade. In what he called "this damned Geneva," he said: "I feel just as if I had come here to be buried." The next year, having moved to France, he wrote his mother: "Paris is a rotten hole. . . . I have not been able to adapt myself." When, in 1909, he learned of the suicide of Laura Marx and her husband, Paul Lafargue, he observed to his wife: "If one cannot work for the Party any longer, one must be able to look truth in the face and die the way the Lafargues did."

The Party, in truth, had disintegrated. Members at home fell away in hopelessness. Exiles abroad alternated between depression and angry feuding. Tsarist police spies and double agents infiltrated the organization. One such, Roman V. Malinovsky, became a member of the Central Committee and in 1912 won Lenin's complete confidence, thus effecting the arrest of many Party agents in Russia. Even Stalin was to be charged in later years with playing such a

role, although on the basis of dubious evidence.[8] At a fifth Conference of the Party, held in Paris in December 1908, Lenin condemned both the *Otzovists* or "Recallers," who were demanding that the Marxist deputies quit the Duma and go underground into illegal work, and the "Liquidators," who wanted an end of all illegal activities. He insisted that the Party must function simultaneously as a legal political group and as a revolutionary conspiracy. A sixth Conference in Prague in 1912 found Trotsky once more seeking to reconcile Mensheviks and Bolsheviks, now more sundered than ever. The Conference voted to expel the Mensheviks, to change the Party name to "RSDLP (Bolshevik)," and to choose an all-Bolshevik Central Committee, of which Stalin and Sergei Ordjonikidze became members. In December of 1912 Koba conferred with Lenin in Cracow and wrote an article (his first signed "Stalin") on "The National Question and Social Democracy," published in a review *Prosvyeshchenye (Enlightenment)*. Lenin wrote to Maxim Gorky: "We have a wonderful Georgian here who is writing a great article."

Despite a fanatical faith presumably capable of moving mountains, each of the leading Russian apostles of Marxism during this dismal epoch came to terms with circumstances as best he could and expressed his frustration more often by insulting comrades than by serving the common cause. Martov accused Trotsky of "the worst habits of literary individualism." Trotsky called Lenin a "petty squabbler" and a victim of "sectarian spirit, individualism of the intellectual, and ideological fetishism." He wrote to Chkeidze that Leninism "flourishes on the dung-heap of sectionalism" and is "founded on lies and falsifications." Lenin called Trotsky a "Judas," a "most despicable careerist and factionalist," a "poser," a "phrasemaker," a "plagiarizer," a "diplomat of the basest metal," and the "plague of our time."

Lenin took refuge in the writing of a philosophical work, *Materialism and Empirio-Criticism* (1909), assailing those Marxists who had become Neo-Kantians, "positivists," and followers of Ernst Mach and Richard Avenarius. A few of his comrades plunged into Marxist politics in their countries of exile and became leaders: the brilliant Parvus and the fiery Polish-born Rosa Luxemburg in Germany and the flaming Angelica Balabanov in Italy.

Trotsky, having abandoned Alexandria and their two daughters in his first escape from Siberia, met Natalia Ivanova Sedova in Paris

[8] Cf. Isaac Don Levine: *Stalin's Great Secret* (Coward-McCann, 1956).

in 1902 and made her his mate and helpmeet forever after. He spent 15 months in prison following the suppression of the Soviet. After orating eloquently at his trial, he was exiled to the northern Siberian village of Obdorsk, whence he escaped in a sleigh drawn by reindeer. After moving with his new family to Vienna, he began publishing in 1908, with Adolf A. Joffe, a journal called *Pravda* (*Truth*) dedicated to "permanent revolution," meaning that the Russian Revolution, once victorious, could have no terminal point short of the destruction of capitalism everywhere in the world. By 1912 Trotsky was a correspondent of *Kievskaya Mysl*, covering the Balkan wars.

Stalin's activities during the years of waiting are still obscure in some details because of his later penchant for suppressing or rewriting history. Yet the known facts of his crimes and punishments are more improbable than the most picaresque fiction, as is fitting and proper in the career of a Caucasian adventurer infused with a Western faith and destined to become an Oriental despot dedicated to Westernizing a semi-Asiatic land. On the morning of June 26, 1907, in Erivan Square in Tiblisi (Tiflis), while Cossacks escorted two carriages from the Post Office to the Central Bank, bombs were thrown, shots were fired, men were killed, and a bogus "officer" in hot pursuit of the thieves made off with the loot: 341,000 rubles, largely in 500-ruble notes. The "officer" was an Armenian, Semyon Arshakovich Ter-Petrossian, alias Kamo, a fellow townsman and co-conspirator of Koba (Stalin), who undoubtedly organized the enterprise. Arrested in Berlin in November with some of the notes on his person, Kamo feigned madness and was returned as a lunatic to Tiblisi, whence he escaped to Paris and was cordially greeted by Lenin as "the Caucasian brigand." His later daring exploits ended with his demise in a bicycle accident in 1921.

This episode was one among many. The Party was starving. Money was raised by counterfeiting and by theft from the Tsarist banks, dignified as "expropriation" of the bourgeoisie. A certain Meyer Wallach, alias Maxim Litvinov, was arrested in Paris, January 18, 1908, in the Gare du Nord as he was about to depart for London. He had many false names and a dozen of the missing banknotes on his person. When he proved that he was in Paris, not in Tiblisi, when the "ex" occurred and had got the notes from comrades for Party work, he was released and deported. The Minister of Jus-

tice, Aristide Briand, refused to extradite anyone accused of a "political" crime. Litvinov in London married Ivy Low and long tarried on the fringes of the Russian revolutionary exiles. Other "exes" were numerous, though not all were organized by Stalin. The Party piously condemned such outrages. Its Transcaucasian Committee secretly expelled Koba for planning Kamo's deed. Stalin later denied his expulsion and hounded to death all who had a hand in it. Lenin tacitly condoned the thievery. Revolutions require propaganda and weapons, which require money, which may as well be seized in advance from the class that the Revolution will expropriate *in toto*. Among all fanatics the distinction between acts of faith and acts of criminality is shadowy.

Stalin was arrested in March 1908 and spent eight months in jail, preaching Marxism to his fellow inmates and once winning their respect by walking unbowed, book in hand, between rows of soldiers beating prisoners with rifle butts. In July 1909 he escaped from exile in Soloychegodsk in Vologda Province. After eight months in hiding in St. Petersburg and Baku, he was again exiled, escaped, was rearrested and exiled anew to Soloychegodsk, once more escaped, and by the end of 1911 was secretly working for *Zvezda* (*Star*) and for the new *Pravda* of St. Petersburg. Again arrested in April 1912 and sentenced to exile in Tomsk, he escaped in September—only to be caught for the nth time in February 1913 and exiled for four years to Siberia, where his new attempts at flight were thwarted by the machinations of Roman Malinovsky. Such a sequence of experiences is incredible. That it is true may explain, in part, what is otherwise incredible in Stalin's later career.

With the crack of doom the dismal comrades of Muscovite Marxism took new heart. The year was 1914. On June 28 in Sarajevo, capital of Bosnia, the Hapsburg Crown Prince, Archduke Francis Ferdinand, and his wife were murdered by Pan-Siberian terrorists in connivance with politicians in Belgrade. On July 28, following rejection of an ultimatum so devised as to insure rejection, Austria-Hungary declared war on Serbia. On August 1, following rejection of an ultimatum against mobilization, Germany declared war on Russia. On August 3 Germany declared war on France. On August 4 Britain declared war on Germany. To all Bolsheviks it was clear that "capitalism" and "imperialism" were bent upon suicide.

Therefore, at long last, the Revolution was (again) around the corner.

Lenin, in Poronino at the fateful moment, was arrested by the Austro-Hungarian police as a Russian spy. Soon released, he went to Berne in September to speak, write, agitate, and judge the cosmic events of the day. All Marxists had long supposed that if the bourgeoisie unleashed war, the proletariat would rise as one man in all countries to impose peace via revolution. In the event, most Marxists discovered to their surprise that they were patriots. Only the Bolshevik deputies in the Imperial Duma opposed the war, and they were sent to Siberia for their pains. Lenin, although scarcely astonished, feigned shock at the disposition of other Marxists to support their warring governments.

On November 1, 1914, in No. 33 of the *Sotsial Demokrat* he opined, with renewed exuberance, in "The War and Social Democracy" that the "working masses," dedicated to peace and "a republican United States of Europe," will create "a new International" to replace the defunct Second International whose members supposed themselves internationalists and found themselves nationalists. "Turning the present imperialist war into civil war is the only correct proletarian slogan. . . . Long live the international brotherhood of the workers united against the chauvinism and patriotism of the bourgeoisie of all countries! Long live a proletarian International, free from opportunism!"

Very few non-Russian Marxists responded to such appeals. In February 1915 a conference of Socialists of the Entente countries gathered in London. The RSDLP was represented by Litvinov, who appeared to protest at the exclusion of the Bolsheviks and walked out when the chairman sought to silence him. Swiss and Italian Marxists called a conference of anti-war Socialists in the village of Zimmerwald near Berne, September 5–18, 1915. Among the delegates were Trotsky, Rakovsky, Balabanov, Chernov, Radek, Axelrod, Martov, Zinoviev, and Lenin. As usual, they soon split into feuding factions. Lenin, for the "Left," demanded a clean break with the Second International and an appeal for global proletarian revolution to end the war. A second "Zimmerwald Conference" gathered in Kienthal, April 24–30, 1916. Most of the delegates were still unwilling to proclaim a "Third International." The "Zimmerwald Left" demanded revolution, but to no immediate purpose. Lenin wrote in December 1916:

We should not permit ourselves to be blinded by the present imperialist war. . . . There can be wars against other bourgeois and reactionary countries waged by a socialism which had been victorious in one country only. Disarmament is the ideal of socialism. There will be no wars in a socialist society. Consequently disarmament will we realized. But he is not a socialist who waits for the realization of socialism *without* a social revolution and a dictatorship of the proletariat. Dictatorship is a government power which leans directly on *violence*. In the epoch of the 20th Century, as in any epoch of civilization generally, violence is not a fist and a club, but an *army*. . . . The oppressed class which would not strive to learn to handle arms or to possess arms would deserve to be treated as slaves. . . . Our slogan should be: the arming of the proletariat in order to defeat, expropriate and disarm the bourgeoisie. . . . Unless the struggle against imperialism is bound indissolubly with the struggle against opportunism, it is but an empty phrase or a deception. One of the chief defects of Zimmerwald and Kienthal, one of the basic reasons for a possible fiasco of these embryos of the Third International, consists precisely in that the question of struggle against opportunism has not even been posed openly. . . . The chief defect of the demand for disarmament is precisely that it evades all concrete questions of revolution. . . . We do not wish to ignore the sad possibility that, at the worst, mankind will live to see a second imperialist war if in spite of numerous outbursts of mass ferment and mass discontent and in spite of all our efforts, a revolution does not grow out of this war. . . .[9]

In September 1917 a third "Zimmerwald Conference" assembled in Stockholm, but was poorly attended and did no more than reiterate earlier resolves. By 1919 the Zimmerwald Right and Center had rejoined the restored Second International. Lenin in exile was thus unable to bring into being a revolutionary Third International. He consoled himself by writing another book: *Imperialism, the Highest Stage of Capitalism* (1916). Here he argued that mo-

[9] *Sbornik Sotsial-Demokrata*, No. 2 (December 1916), in Olga H. Gankin and H. H. Fisher: *The Bolsheviks and the World War: The Origin of the Third International* (Hoover Library, Stanford University Press, 1940), pp. 493–500.

nopoly capitalism postpones its breakdown by the exploitation of colonial peoples, thus temporarily "buying off" its own proletariat through Cecil Rhodes's formula of 1895 to Wickham Steed: "If you want to avoid civil war, you must become imperialists." But the cataclysm, of course, is still "inevitable." Where and when it would come, and how in a half-feudal, almost pre-capitalist land it would create the conditions needful for a Marxist seizure of power, even Lenin, for all his political vision, did not foresee. As late as January 1917, in his 46th year, he told a Swiss audience that it was doubtful whether "we, the old, will live to see the decisive battles of the coming revolution." [1] Six weeks later the last of the Romanovs was to lose his throne.

[1] Carr, I, 69.

CHAPTER TWO

Echoes of the Past

1. NOMADS OUT OF ASIA

FOUR DECADES beyond 1917 and a dozen years after the defeat of the German invaders, the wayfarer in Muscovy in search of monuments of medieval Russia would find little to sate his curiosity and nothing remotely comparable to the cathedrals, castles, and quaintly mellow towns of Western Europe. In Holy Kiev, "mother of Russian cities," with its handsomely reconstructed Kreshchatik Boulevard, he would find in a pleasant park on the terrace of Vladimir Hill a tall copper image, erected in 1853, of Prince and Saint Vladimir. The name means "Lord of the World." Holding cross and crown, he gazes eastward across the winding Dnieper toward the broad flatlands that once were his.

To the west, in old Kiev, is the golden-domed Byzantine Church of St. Sofia, containing 11th-Century mosaics and frescoes and the tomb of Yaroslav the Wise, who died in 1054, twelve years before the Norman conquest of England. To the south, overlooking the river, are the chapels, tombs, and workshops of the Kiev Pechersky Lavra or monastery of the caves, oldest in Russia and long the largest and richest. All its buildings have been restored, save the most ancient of all, the Uspensky Cathedral, reduced to rubble by the Nazis. In near-by Spass Church is the new sarcophagus of Yuri Dolgoruki (1090–1157), Grand Duke of Vladimir and Suzdal, surnamed the "Long-armed" and regarded as the founder of Moscow. In Soviet Square in the Muscovite capital a heroic equestrian statue of Yuri in armor was raised in 1947 as part of the celebration of the 800th anniversary of the city.

By going far afield our wayfarer could find a few other relics of long-lost yesterdays. In Novgorod (New City), on the banks of the

River Volkhov near Lake Ilmen, stands a 12th-Century Kremlin or stone citadel, another Cathedral of St. Sofia, first built in 1045, and the Millennial Memorial of Russia, erected in 1862 in honor of Russia's first thousand years. Northeast of Moscow, on the river Kliazma, the city of Vladimir was founded in 1108 by Vladimir Monomakh. This "capital" of Russia in the late 12th Century still has its Kremlin, its early churches, and its Monastery and Cathedral of the Assumption (Uspensky Sobor). To the north is ancient Suzdal with another Kremlin and sundry ecclesiastical structures. Little else can be found of the visible works of the men of old. Most of these few have been many times demolished and rebuilt.

This scarcity of medieval mementoes is not due to architectural or artistic backwardness on the part of the Russians of a millennium ago, for they were then as creative as the people of the West. It stems rather from innumerable and savagely destructive invasions, both before and after the long Mongol darkness. This pattern of recurrent violence from abroad, unparalleled in frequency and ferocity in any other modern State, was decisive in shaping the attitudes and lifeways of the steppe-dwellers. Russian character and institutions have been "explained" in terms of the swaddling of infants, the absence of any Renaissance or Reformation, the tyranny of a harsh climate, and the mystic influence of the great plains on the gray masses, ever driven to seek an escape from anarchy in despotism.[1] Without dismissing these phases of ancestral experience as factors influencing the outlook of today's children, it is nevertheless probable that the incessant march across the endless prairies of alien warriors bent upon Russia's destruction played a decisive role in molding the responses of successive generations of Russians to foreigners, to their own fears and hopes, and to all the problems of politics.

Our prime concern is with the years since 1917. What Russians have felt and said and done during these years, however, is not to be comprehended without awareness of what was done by, and done to, these people of the plains during the long centuries of their common life together. The great epochs, looking backward,

---

[1] Cf. John S. Reshetar, Jr.: *Problems of Analyzing and Predicting Soviet Behavior* (Doubleday Short Studies in Political Science, 1955); Edward Crankshaw: *Russia and the Russians* (Viking, 1948); Margaret Mead: *Soviet Attitudes toward Authority* (McGraw-Hill, 1951); Geoffrey Gorer and John Rickman: *The People of Great Russia: A Psychological Study* (Chanticleer Press, 1955).

were the 304 years of the Romanov Tsardom (1613–1917), the 133 years of the independent Muscovite principality (1480–1613), the 240 years of Mongol rule (1240–1480), and the 378 years of Kievan Russia (862–1240). The shape of each must be outlined if the present is to be understood and the prospects of the future assessed.

The gigantic stage on which Russia's stormy drama played itself out was from the beginning what it is today: the northern Eurasian "sixth of the world." These eight and a half million square miles are as immense as all of North America and almost as large as the USA, China, and India combined. Ten time zones span this vastness, on which the sun never sets during the summers of "white nights." When clocks in Leningrad strike midnight, the time is ten in the morning in Kamchatka.

Most of the vast and lonely land of Tsars and Commissars, bright green under blue skies in short summers and snow-clad in the long polar darkness of winter, is a flat and featureless saucer remotely circled by a rim of rocks. From west to east the major mountains, in order of their best-known names, march as follows: the Carpathians; the Caucasus, rising to the highest peaks in Europe— Mount Kazbek (16,346 feet) and Mount Elbruz (18,465 feet); the lofty Pamirs, here and there reaching skyward 20,000 feet or more; the Hindu Kush; then the Tien Shan, the Altai, and the Sayan ridges reaching in serried ranks toward Lake Baikal, loftiest and deepest lake of Eurasia; and, beyond the lake, the Yablonai, Stanovoi, Kolyma, and Anadyr ranges stretching toward the Bering Strait, with the Maritime Provinces, the coastal plain, and Kamchatka Peninsula lying southeast of the highlands. The low Urals, in the center of the platter, are no barrier between Asia and Europe. The twelve seas into which the slow rivers flow embrace five arms of the Arctic Ocean (the White, Barents, Kara, Laptevykh, and East Siberian Seas), three of the Pacific (Bering, Okhotsk, and Sea of Japan), the two landlocked salty shallows of mid-Asia (Caspian and Aral), and the Black and Baltic Seas giving access to the Atlantic by way, respectively, of the Mediterranean and the North Seas. Of the myriad lakes, the largest are Baikal, Balkash, and Ladoga. The most important, historically, are Onega, Peipus, and Ilmen.

The lazy streams, with west banks commonly higher than east, meander idly through the plains and often spread in spring over wide areas with the melting of winter snows. Of the half-million rivers, the longest, proceeding from east to west, are the Amur

(2,900 miles), the Lena (2,860), the Yeneisei (2,800), the Ob-and-Irtish (3,900), the Syr Daria (1,700), the Amur Daria or Oxus (1,500), the Ural (1,400), the Volga (2,300), the Don (1,100), the Dnieper (1,400), the Dniester, the Danube, the Western Dvina, and the Northern Dvina. In the Valdai Hills, west of the site of Moscow, the Dnieper, the Western Dvina, and the Volga all have their sources. The Don rises near by to the southwest.

Along these waterways early migrants wended their way and slowly knit together a community thinly scattered across an immensity of primeval forests and measureless meadowlands. All this Eurasian wilderness is clothed by wind and cloud, rain and sleet, and an endless overarching sky, with a mantle of infinity reducing all human effort to insignificance and yet challenging men to adventure and achievement. Even today, after a thousand years of human habitation, much of northern Russia looks from the air like empty forest land.

The major zones of vegetation are plainly distinguishable. In the far north, fringing the Arctic, is the treeless tundra, with its subsoil frozen all the year. South of it the woodlands, 5,000 miles long and 1,200 miles wide, stretch in majestic grandeur from the Baltic to the mountain chains of Eastern Asia. They contain a quarter of the world's timber reserves, solidly evergreen south of the tundra and mixed coniferous and deciduous at the opposite edge, where forest and meadow alternate. Next comes the steppe zone, 2,600 miles long and 600 miles wide, containing a broad belt of *chernozom* or rich black earth, ideal for cereal crops. The steppe was originally carpeted by feather grass or *stipa,* with few trees save in the river valleys. South of the steppe are the deserts of sand and salt, 1,800 miles long and 600 miles wide, extending from the Caspian to Lake Balkash. Only in the extreme south, along the Black Sea coast and in Transcaucasia, is there abundant rainfall, no frost, and semitropical vegetation. The Great Plain is dryer and colder than mid-America, making its agriculture less productive. Leningrad is in the same latitude as the tip of Greenland. Moscow parallels Labrador. Warm Turkmenistan and Tadjikistan are on a line with San Francisco, St. Louis, and Washington.

When and whence the first humans found their way across these far-flung horizons of prairie and forest is unclear. But it is likely that the barbarian ancestors of Greeks and Romans, and of Celts and Germans, all came into Europe from Asia along the steppes that ex-

tend from Mongolia to the Danube. The earliest Slavs, having doubtless traversed this same route, settled about 300 B.C. between the Carpathians and the Baltic, where they were known to the Romans as Venedi and to the Germans as Wends. From this center emerged the forebears of the South Slavs, the West Slavs, and the East Slavs. Some spread southwestward and became Slovenes, Croats, and Serbs. Some mingled with the Bulgarians, who were soon speaking a Slavic tongue. Others moved westward and evolved into Slovaks, Czechs, Poles, and the original Prussians. Still others, pushing toward the north and east by river boats and pack horses, became Great Russians, "White" or Byelorussians, and Ukrainians or "Little Russians." All these labels are names not for "racial" groups or "national" units (the sentiment of nationality, here as elsewhere, was a slow and late phenomenon), but simply for the modern variants of the Slavic language. The common name for all stemmed from *slava* ("glory"). These people were fond of such names as Boguslav ("glory of God"), Jaroslav ("glory of spring"), etc.

This *diaspora* and differentiation of the Slavs tells us little of the origins of the earliest Russian State. The clue to its genesis is to be found in the tedious migration of sundry nomads along two primitive highways. One was the "river road" from the Gulf of Finland by way of the Neva, Lake Ladoga, the Volkhov, Lake Ilmen, the Lovat, and a short portage over the site of modern Smolensk to the upper reaches of the Dnieper, whence early boatmen could reach the Black Sea and Byzantium. The other was the "steppe road" from Asia, whereby the riders of the grasslands, ferrying their families, goods, and steeds across the rivers intersecting the prairie, could reach Danubia and Balkania. Where the two highways cross, the first recognized "Russian" community came into being from the mingling of nomads-by-boat with nomads-by-horse.

Two thousand years before this marriage of migrants the steppes north of the Black Sea were traversed and sparsely peopled by tribes known as Cimmerians. Four centuries before Athens became the glory of the world, earlier Greeks were establishing colonies in and around the Crimea and calling the newer steppe people Scythians. These wanderers—pressed westward by Mongoloid nomads called Huns, whose efforts to penetrate China had been beaten back—allied themselves with mighty Assyria and drove out or absorbed the Cimmerians. When the Great Alexander died of

drink and fever in Babylon in 323 B.C., the Scythians were already being assailed by other Asian tribes crossing the grasslands. These newcomers were called, variously, Antes or Alans or Sarmatians. In the valley of the Dnieper they later met and mixed with Slavs drifting southeastward from their pristine homelands.

During the 2nd Century A.D. the Germanic Goths, initially settled in Gothland and then on the southern shore of the Baltic, began moving southward on the river road at the behest of their king, Filimir. "In search of suitable homes and pleasant places," wrote Jordanes, Gothic historian, "they came to the land of Scythia" —to the distress of the Slavs and Sarmatians, upon whom they imposed their rule, and ultimately of the Romans, whose Danubian frontiers were soon assailed by land and sea. Under pressure from the Huns, the Goths invaded Thrace, slew the Emperor Valens at Adrianople in 378, and pillaged the Eternal City in 410. The demise of the Western Roman Empire, insofar as it was encompassed by outer barbarians, was a consequence of happenings on the steppes before there was a "Russia." The Huns, now permanently thwarted in their designs on China by the Great Wall, rode the prairies ever westward, driving Germanic tribes into the realms of Rome. The frightful Hunnish host, under Attila ("Scourge of God"), swept through Central Europe and into Gaul, where, at Chalons-sur-Marne in 451, it was beaten and turned back to lose itself amid the confused incursions of many barbaric peoples.

Behind the Huns rode the Bulgars (A.D. 400–500), next the Avars (550–650), and then the Khazars (650–750), a seafaring folk of obscure origin. The Kakhans, or rulers of the Khazars, founded an "empire" north of the Black Sea in the 7th Century. After considering the Moslem creed of the Arabs as well as Christianity, which they knew from the Eastern Romans or Byzantines, the Khazars adopted Judaism as their faith. Their ability to protect, and thus command obedience from, their Alanic-Slavic-Iranian subject peoples was weakened by Arab invaders crossing the Caucasus and by the appearance on the steppe road of the Magyars (750–850). As early as the 5th Century the Rukhs-As or "light clan" of Alans were sometimes called Hros, Ros, or Rus, though the "Normanists" among Slavic historians would have it that *rus* was a corruption of the Finnish word *ruotsi* ("rowers") or of *rusij* ("fair-haired," a trait of many early Scandinavians and Slavs), echoed in the Latin *russus* ("red") and in the English adjective "russet."

2. THE VARIAGS

BETWEEN the years 700 and 1100 of the Christian era bands of daring seamen poured periodically out of the pagan wilderness of Scandinavia, sailing and rowing swift vessels girt with shields and gay with colored sails and painted dragon-headed prows. These Norsemen or Vikings, adept at battle, piracy, and plunder, made themselves masters of Sicily, Normandy, and England and even reached America. They likewise sailed through the rivers of Russia and were known to the Byzantines as Varangians and to the Slavs as Variags.

When and by whom they were first called (if indeed they were called) to help defend the subjects of the Khazar Kakhans is wholly obscure. Some of them seem to have portaged to the Volga and the Don in the middle decades of the 8th Century, taking the name Rus and establishing a State of sorts, later called the "Russian Kaganate," around Azov, north of the Black Sea. That they fought Khazars as well as Magyars for control of the western reaches of the steppe road is attested by the plea of the Kakhan to the Byzantine emperor in 833 to help him build on the Don a "white tower" or fortress (in Ugric *sarkel*) for defense against them. Their kinsmen were settled in the north around Novgorod and Staraya Rusa on Lake Ilmen and sought to trade, in the face of Khazar resistance, with the Russian Kaganate in the south. A "Russian" fleet tried without success to raid Byzantium in 860.

What is known of the foggy events to follow is derived from the *Chronicle* of Nestor (*c.* 1050–1114), a monk of the Kiev Pechersky Lavra who wove earlier records, tales, and legends into the first Russian attempt at writing history. Here is set forth how the people of Novgorod invited a renowned Norse freebooter, Roric or Rurik of Jutland, to become their ruler. This he did in 862 and promptly sent two barons or *boyars*, Dir and Askold, down the river road to "liberate" Kiev from the Khazars.

Some years earlier the Patriarch Photius, head of the Byzantine Church, had sent two missionaries, Cyril and Methodius (both later canonized), to convert the Khazars and the "Russians"—i.e., the Variags. In this they failed. But in 862 they went to Moravia to convert the West Slavs. A Prince Rostislav received them. Since the Slavs had no written language, the two saints devised variants of Greek letters in order that the Scriptures might be rendered into

Slavic. These symbols became the medium of "Church Slavonic" throughout Slavdom and, with alterations, evolved into the alphabet of modern Russian. In 869 St. Cyril died in Rome. His Moravian converts to Byzantine or Greek Orthodox Christianity were later persuaded or coerced by German princes into becoming Roman Catholics. Yet the invention of the "Cyrillic alphabet" was an enduring achievement.

Another lasting fact of life stemming from these remote times is the centuries-old rift between the Catholic and Orthodox churches, which became final in 1054. By this time the Poles (in 966), along with the Czechs, Slovaks, Slovenes, and Croats, had embraced Roman Catholicism, while the Serbs, Rumanians, Bulgars, Greeks, and Russians became Orthodox, thus dividing Slavdom forever into rival variants of the Christian creed.

Meanwhile, to return to the nascent Russia of the 9th Century, Rurik went west in 870 to consult with Charles the Bald, King of the West Franks and later Holy Roman Emperor, from whom he received a fiefdom over Friesland in 873—following which he promptly died. His kinsman from Norway, Helgi or Oleg, assumed rulership of Novgorod in the name of Rurik's infant son, Ingvar or Igor. (Norse names henceforth become Slavic.) Oleg, being bent upon all of the "Russia" he had inherited, sent warriors down the Dnieper. Askold and Dir were slain. Oleg became "Prince of Kiev." Igor succeeded him and was followed in turn by Igor's widow, Olga, who was baptized in Byzantium in 957. Her son was Svytoslav I (the name means "glory to sanctity"), who seized Sarkel and Itil on the Volga from the Khazars, defeated the Bulgars on the Danube, and ruled a wide realm along the river road and all the western reaches of the highway of the steppes.

This earliest Russia of the Kiev Principality was a feudal State wherein the slaves or serfs tilled the soil owned by the boyars. From being pirates, plunderers, and later merchants, the boyars became an aristocracy of *druzhina* (royal bodyguards) and *dvoryane* (courtiers). As in the West, only the nobles could bear arms and own land. In Novgorod and other northern trading towns, a kind of urban "democracy" evolved, centering in the *Veche* or popular assembly. Had Novgorod rather than Kiev or, much later, Novgorod rather than Moscow become the political heart of medieval Russia, it is conceivable, though not certain, that this far-flung polity of the Eastern Slavs might have grown into some semblance of a free and open

society instead of developing into an Autocracy, combining all the worst features of absolutism and feudalism. But this is speculative. The outcome, as we shall see, was less a product of intent than of circumstances that seemed to offer no alternative.

Kievan Russia acquired its written language, its standards of art, and its religion from golden Byzantium, bright capital of the Eastern Roman Empire—more Greek than Latin and fated to outlive the ancient Empire of the West by a thousand years. Nestor depicts Prince Vladimir, son of Svyatoslav, deciding to renounce paganism and accept a "higher religion." He debates with his counselors the respective merits of the available choices. The Judaism of the Khazars is rejected, for the Khazars are foes and the God of the Jews has too much punished his worshippers for their sins. Islam is unacceptable: the Arabs are enemies and (we may surmise) the Moslem ban on alcoholic drinks is deemed incompatible with warmth, or the illusion thereof, in the harsh Russian winter. Roman Catholicism, embraced by the Poles 23 years previously, seems an alien creed that subordinates State to Church. Emissaries back from Byzantium remind Vladimir of the conversion of his grandmother and dwell ecstatically on their feelings at services in the great Basilica of St. Sofia: "We do not know whether we were in heaven or on earth, for there is not on earth such sight or beauty. . . . There God lives among men." Vladimir decides. The year is 989. The base of his contemporary monument in Kiev depicts the baptism of his subjects in the Dnieper. Vladimir marries Anne, sister of the Byzantine Emperor.

Although its surviving artifacts are few, Kievan Russia left its indelible imprint on all the Russias to come after. Its politics, over much of its four centuries of life, was a chaos of anarchy made better by occasional despotism and made worse by recurrent dynastic rivalries. This luxury of feudal disorder was permissible in a Western Europe unthreatened by Asian conquerors. But medieval Russia was constantly exposed to assault by new barbarians coming westward over the steppes. By beating them back, century after century, the Russians of Kiev helped mightily, with no help from Europe, to save Europe from Asian conquest. Yet, while temporarily successful in defense, they were too fond of their own disorders to organize themselves for permanent survival.

The end, to be sure, was long in coming, despite repeated disasters. New nomads called Pechenegs or Patzinaks assailed Kiev

throughout the 9th Century and beyond. One chronicler called them "the carrion eaters, the godless, unclean folk, the wicked, blood-drinking beasts." They reached the Dnieper in 895, pushed the Magyars under Arpad into Hungary, and killed Svyatoslav I in 972, after crushing his armies. His skull was fashioned into a drinking-bowl for a nomad chieftain. Kiev endured. Prince Yaroslav in 1036 defeated the foe. The Pechenegs wandered into the Balkans and vanished.

But no peace was to be had on the crossroads of the highways of river and steppe. New invaders appeared on the Dnieper in 1095. They were called by the Russians Polovtsi, and by other victims of their fury Falven or Cumans or Kipchaks. They rode through Russia, despoiled Hungary and the border provinces of the Byzantine Empire, and finally disappeared through absorption, with the last living speaker of their strange tongue dying in the land of the Magyars in 1770. In the year 1185 a Prince of Kiev, defending his realm against these invaders, was vanquished and lost his life. The tragedy was celebrated by an unknown poet in the "Tale of the Host of Igor," which Alexander Borodin (1834–87) transmuted into the opera *Prince Igor*. Wrote the poet: "Igor leads his soldiers to the Don. . . . The eagles screech and call the beasts to a feast of bones. . . . The Russians bar the long fields with their crimson shields, seeking honor for themselves and glory for the Prince." All died. Yet this Russia of long ago somehow survived the Polovtsi and endured for another half-century.

In the spring of the year 1223 the Polovtsi chieftains, faced with a new foe out of Asia, appealed to Kiev for aid: "Today they have taken our land. Tomorrow they will take yours." The new enemies had conquered Georgia, crossed the Caucasus, and reached the steppes of the Don. They rode swift steeds and drank mares' milk and horses' blood. They carried round shields and wore lacquered black armor. They displayed uncanny skill in launching lances and arrows from the saddle. They made use of a primitive artillery. They were organized into light and heavy cavalry, grouped into troops of 10, squadrons of 100, regiments of 1,000, and divisions of 10,000, with each army comprising three divisions. Experts in communication, espionage, and psychological warfare accompanied all their hosts. Their commanders were master strategists. Here was no new horde of clumsy barbarians, but a conquering army come

from nowhere and weirdly following a battle standard of nine yak tails. The Russians of Kiev knew nothing of these matters.

Prince Mstislav the Daring gathered his men-at-arms. His subjects, though given to much feuding, were loosely united under the heirs to Vladimir Monomach (1113–25). Spokesmen from the invaders came to parley. The Prince ordered them put to death. A rejoinder came from the unknown foe: "As you wish for war, you shall have it. We have done you no harm. God is impartial. He will decide our quarrel." Mstislav led 80,000 warriors, Russians and Polovtsi, to meet the enemy. On a June day in 1223 the battle was joined near the River Kalka, north of the Sea of Azov. By day's end all was lost. The Prince and his vassals, unable to flee the dark horsemen, were seized and crushed to death under heavy planks. The invaders raided the Crimea and then vanished. Kiev again survived, but briefly. Wrote a chronicler: "Only God knows whence they came and whither they went."

The latest riders of the prairies were the Mongols, last and most formidable of the nomads out of Asia. They were destined to come closer to "conquering the world" than any of their precursors or successors. They were fated to subjugate and all but destroy medieval Russia and to subject the survivors to an enslavement centuries long. The encounter on the Kalka was a sign of calamity to come.

3. THE EMPEROR OF ALL MEN

IN Mandarin *Cheng-sze* means, or once meant, "perfect warrior." The Mongolian equivalent, linked with *Khan* or "Prince" and having the connotation of "Heavenly Ruler," is *Chingiz*. In the year 1206, on the banks of the River Onan, Mongol chieftains gathered to confer upon one of their number the name and title of Chingiz Khan, known to the West as Ghenghis Khan.

The leader thus honored was born in 1162 in a felt tent or yurt on the Mongolian plateau north of the Gobi Desert. His people were herdsmen and hunters. His father, son of Kabul Khan, was Yesukai the Valiant, Khan of the Yakka and master of 40,000 tents. His was the clan of Grey-Eyed Men, descended from the Blue Wolf. When the boy was born, the father was away on a raid in

which he vanquished a rival named Temujin—whose name, quaintly, he gave to his son. This Temujin was to be later named, not without reason, "Master of Thrones and Crowns" and "Emperor of All Men." His horsemen were the last of the nomads to invade Europe from Asia via the steppes.

Having united the Mongol tribes by beating in battle all his foes, Ghenghis made his capital at Karakorum, a city in a desert of black sand. In a campaign of eight years he breached the Great Wall and conquered the Kingdom of Cathay. From Pekin, which the Mongols took in 1215, he acquired the scholarly and civilizing services of an able statesman, Yeliu Chutsai. After subduing rebels in his western provinces, he proposed to make peace and enjoy himself in quiet. But the envoys he sent to the Shah of Khorezm, a mighty Moslem empire spread over Central Asia, were put to death, leaving him no honorable choice but war. In 1219 the Mongol cavalry, some 250,000 strong and led by Chepé and Subotai, descended upon the realm of the Shah, slaying all who stood in their way and sacking and burning Bokhara, Samarcand, and other fabled cities that once had been the light of the Orient.

In pursuit of the Shah the invincible horsemen ravaged northern India, traversed Iran, and then, as an afterthought, conquered the knights of Georgia, threaded their way through mountains higher than the Alps, and appeared like a nightmare in the valley of the Don. It was this host of Subotai and Chepé which outflanked, encircled, and destroyed the Russians on the Kalka in 1223. The invaders returned to Karakorum along the steppe. Ghenghis, off in China, saw five planets in conjunction and knew that his time had come. He sickened on his homeward journey and expired near the frontiers of his original realm. The year was 1227. He died as master of the most extensive empire ever brought under a single rule, although its expansion had barely begun. Mongol habits of deception, trickery, savage cruelty, fierce vengeance, and callous disrespect for human life were to be spread over Eurasia, leaving a permanent imprint upon their Russian victims. These habits were exemplified in the funeral journey back to Karakorum. That his death might be kept secret until his son, Ogdai Khan (1227–42), should safely ascend the throne, all wayfarers encountered along the road were killed.

Ogdai, hearing reports of the richness of Russia, charged his nephew, Batu the Splendid, with the conquest of all the lands be-

tween the Urals and the Dnieper. For these mounted fighters who lived in the saddle, expeditions across thousands of miles were routine. Like a hideous apparition, Batu appeared on the Volga in 1236 with 300,000 warriors. Proceeding northward along the river, his men fanned out, overran the petty town called Moscow, and besieged the city of Vladimir, which they destroyed in 1237. In the following March the devils out of Asia overtook and annihilated the army of Grand Prince Yuri. Novgorod yielded and was spared. The dark riders now raced southward along the water road. Despite heroic defense, Kiev was taken and razed in December of 1240. Most of its people were butchered. As an independent community the first Russia thus came to an end.

For the Mongols the end was not yet. Batu and Subotai, pushing westward, reached Galicia in the spring of 1241. Most of the princes and knights of Middle Europe gathered formidable armies to safeguard Christendom. But resistance was futile. Unlike the Huns and Arabs before them and the Turks of a later time, the Mongol invaders were ever victorious against Christian arms, thanks to superior mobility, firepower, and strategy. In April 1241 a portion of Batu's host, led by Baibars and Kaidu (grandsons of Ghenghis), crushed a mixed Polish-German-Bohemian-French army at Liegnitz in Silesia while Subotai and Batu entered Hungary and destroyed the forces of King Bela IV at Mohi. Budapest was stormed, Austria was invaded, and all the towns of the Dalmatian coast were ravaged, save only Dubrovnik behind its mountain-girt wall. All Europe was helpless. But in 1242 news came from Karakorum that Ogdai was dead. His captains went home, abandoning Hungary, Bohemia, Germany, and Poland, but not Russia.

Africa was spared invasion when, in 1260, Islamic armies from Egypt defeated the Mongols for the first time at Ain Jalut in Syria, following the Mongol conquest of Baghdad and Jerusalem. Genghis's grandson, Kubla Khan (1260–94), genial host to Marco Polo, conquered all of China and moved his capital to Pekin, where he founded the Mongol dynasty. He likewise subjugated Burma, Indochina, and part of India, though his designs on Japan and Indonesia were frustrated. This most gigantic of all empires was not the creation of men with a mission, bent upon "saving" or "liberating" the world. Its builders, like the Romans, had no creed of salvation and were devoid of racial, religious, or ideological fanaticism. They asked no more than tribute and obedience. Those who agreed were

spared. Those who resisted were killed. This simple precept of power, coupled with military invincibility, brought into being the most extensive and populous empire of all time. Its dissolution through internal disintegration was long delayed.

The western Mongols became converts to Islam, while their kinsmen in the east became Chinese. Vast satrapies ruled by Ilkhans slowly went their way with little central direction. In Turkestan one of the major Khanates fell under the sway of Timur the Lame, or Tamerlane (1369–1405), who beat the Seljuk Turks, wrecked the ancient irrigation works of Mesopotamia, and converted many prosperous provinces into deserts embellished with heaps of skulls. Other Mongols under Baber conquered all of India a century later and established the Mogul dynasty, whose brightest star, the Emperor Akbar (1556–1605), was not a destroyer but a beneficent statesman. The black riders were thus builders of realms that endured in sundry guises for half a thousand years.

In the darkness engulfing Russia, rulership rested with the Khanate of the Golden Horde (so-called from Batu's gilded pavilion), with its capital east of the lower Volga at Sarai near the site of modern Tsaritsin or Stalingrad. Under Uzbek Khan (1314–41) these Mongols embraced Islam, though displaying a most un-Moslem patience with all creeds and faiths and eschewing all intolerance as inconvenient for the administration of so mixed a realm. To Sarai, and initially to Karakorum in far Mongolia, came the envoys of the local princes and churchmen of vanquished Russia to pay tribute and to receive their *yarliki* or investitures, authorizing them by the will of the Khan to rule their subjects and ensure taxation, submission, and order.

Amid the gloom, at the very time of its descent, a feeble light gleamed forth. The Prince of Novgorod in the tragic year 1240 was one Alexander, surnamed Nevsky because of his victory over Swedish invaders on the Neva in 1236. Six years later, in a memorable battle on Lake Peipus in April of 1242, he defeated other invaders: the Teutonic Knights of the Baltic. Centuries later he became a sacred symbol of Slavic resistance to *Deutschtum*. The largest cathedral in the Balkans, donated by the "liberating" Tsar of all the Russias to his Bulgarian protégés, is the Cathedral of Alexander Nevsky in Sofia. In the 1930's and 1940's this Prince of Novgorod was heroized anew in the Soviet press, theater, and cinema as the original champion of Slavdom against the Germans.

Alexander's immortality was the reward not of romanticism but of practicality. He understood that the Mongols were invincible. Despite local opposition, he went to Batu in 1242 and agreed to pay tribute and acknowledge Mongol supremacy. Only in this way was he able to exercise some semblance of local independence. After his passing in 1253, his successors were able, with Mongol assent and with the support of Novgorod's *Veche* or Town Meeting and its *Soviet Gospod* or Council of Masters, to wield wide power over all the scattered communities northward to the White Sea and eastward to the Urals. All other surviving Russians lived in spiritless servility.

The curse of the "evil Tartars" seemed to its victims an irreparable calamity. And so it was, since it severed Russia from the West and inspired Russians to adopt Mongol methods to achieve ultimate emancipation. In medieval Russia, as in medieval Spain under Arab subjugation, the undying hope of freedom from the rule of alien infidels fostered imitation of the ways of the conquerors—royal absolutism, a union of Church and State in a Holy Crusade against Islam, and deep fear and suspicion of all foreign influence. Yet the Mongol impact upon Russia, like the Moorish impact upon Spain, was not wholly negative. The local agents of the Golden Horde, in their zeal for law, order, and tribute, taught their Russian subjects various arts of which they had known little hitherto: census-taking, tax-gathering, coinage, customs dues, military conscription, a postal system, and, finally, the uses of militarism and absolutism. The Russians of the darkness learned from their conquerors the only means of attaining emancipation, and in learning devised a system of power which subordinated all personal freedom to the supreme end of liberating the community from pagan domination.

4. THE THIRD ROME

IN the center of European Russia on the banks of the River Moskva —which flows into the Oka, which flows into the Volga—a tiny town of wooden houses and stockades came into being sometime in the 12th Century. It is first mentioned in the chronicles in 1147. Its alleged founder was Yuri the Long-Armed, Prince of Vladimir and Suzdal and later of Kiev. The site was fateful, for it was near the headwaters of the Don to the south and, to the west, of the Volga,

Western Dvina, and Dnieper. In these times the rivers were high-ways for those in search of adventure or trade or power. In the late 1200's Daniel, son of Alexander Nevsky of Novgorod, became Duke of Moscow. He was followed, in the years from 1328 to 1462, by Ivan Kalita (John Moneybags), Ivan II, Dmitri, Basil the Blind, and Ivan III. In exchange for payment of tribute and acceptance of their *yarliki* from the Khans at Sarai, they were charged by their Asian overlords with taxation and the maintenance of order throughout Central Russia. The Principality of Muscovy extended its authority at a remarkable rate, ultimately embracing a sixth of the world. In early Moscow settled the Metropolitans of the Church to administer to the needs of the faithful and to aid the rulers of the new State in their hopes through many generations of securing freedom from the Khans.

The hope was long deferred. But it was presently apparent that its realization could be accomplished only by the Muscovites. Kiev was dead. Novgorod was moribund. All other Russian communities were impotent. After 140 years of Mongol rule, in 1380 Prince Dmitri of Moscow, aided by St. Sergius of Radonezh, rebelled, and for the first time the Mongols were defeated in battle at Kulikova near the Don. He was henceforth called Dmitri Donskoi. The victory was in vain, for the Mongols under Mamai, even in defeat, had slain most of the Russian warriors. Two years later the dread horsemen, under Toktamish, sacked and burned Moscow once more. A century passed before Ivan III (1462–1505), surnamed "the Great," was able in 1480, in alliance with the Khan of the Crimea, to halt payment of tribute to the Golden Horde, thus achieving, after 240 years, the independence of a new Russia.

Ivan the Great annexed Tver and Novgorod, claimed suzerainty over "all Russia," hired Italian architects to help build the Moscow Kremlin, and founded the immense realm inherited by the Commissars four centuries later. In the year 1453, a decade before he ascended the Muscovite throne, the Ottoman Turks breached the long-invulnerable walls of Istanbul and extinguished the Eastern Roman or Byzantine Empire. With the fall of the city of Constantine, Ivan took the Byzantine title of "Autocrat," borrowed the Byzantine symbol of the double-headed eagle as his emblem, and, in 1472, married Sofia, niece of the last of the Cæsars, Constantine Paleologus, who had been slain by the Turks when they conquered the "Second Rome." The mission of the new Muscovy as heir to the lost

Byzantium was suggested by the greeting sent to Ivan in 1475 by the Abbot Philotheus of Pskov Monastery:

> The church of ancient Rome fell because of the Apollinarian heresy; as to the Second Rome—the church of Constantinople—it has been hewn by the axes of Ishmaelites, but this Third new Rome—the Holy Apostolic Church, under thy mighty rule, shines throughout the entire world more brightly than the sun. All the Orthodox Christian realms have converged in thine own. Thou art the sole Autocrat of the Universe, the only Caesar of the Christians. . . . Two Romes have fallen, but the Third stands, and no fourth can ever be. . . .

The story of this Third Rome prior to 1917 is no part of the present enterprise.[2] Yet the highlights of this venture in statecraft must be noted, since nothing makes sense in the vast realm of the Soviet Muscovites without some knowledge of the estate they inherited and of the attitudes, problems, and policies stemming from the pre-revolutionary past. Let the peaks therefore be sketched and some generalizations offered as to how the power-holders of this ever expanding empire, growing at the rate of 60 square miles a day for 300 years, met their tasks.

Basil III (1505–33), son of Sofia and Ivan, begat Ivan IV (1533–84), who was only three years old when Basil died. In his later life this contemporary of Queen Elizabeth I, the Emperor Akbar, and Catherine de' Medici assumed the title of *Tsar*, probably derived

---

[2] Among the more perceptive general histories of Russia available in English are Michael T. Florinsky: *Russia: A History and an Interpretation* (2 vols., Macmillan, 1953); Sidney Harcave: *Russia: A History* (Lippincott, 1953); Dorsey D. Jones: *Russia: A Concise History* (Stackpole, 1956); V. O. Kluchevsky: *A History of Russia* (3 vols., Dutton, 1911); Alexander Kornilov: *Modern Russian History* (Knopf, 1943); Anatole G. Mazour: *Russia Past and Present* (Van Nostrand, 1951); D. S. Mirsky: *A History of Russian Literature* (Knopf, 1949); Sir Bernard Pares: *A History of Russia* (Knopf, 1953); Hugh Seton-Watson: *The Decline of Imperial Russia, 1855–1914* (Praeger, 1952); Ivar Spector: *An Introduction to Russian History and Culture* (Van Nostrand, 1954); B. H. Sumner: *A Short History of Russia* (Reynal, 1943); George Vernadsky: *Kievan Russia* (Yale University Press, 1948) and *A History of Russia* (Yale University Press, 1954). See also C. E. Black (ed.): *Rewriting Russian History: Soviet Interpretations of Russia's Past* (Praeger, 1955); Charles Morley: *Guide to Research in Russian History* (Syracuse University Press, 1955); and Warren B. Walsh: *Readings in Russian History* (Syracuse University Press, 1955).

from *Cæsar*, and became known as Ivan Grozny—"Ivan the Terrible" or "John the Dread"—because of his many crimes. These included the murder of his own child, the execution of the Metropolitan, the hideous punishment of the people of Novgorod for negotiating with Poland, and the callous torture and execution of any who opposed his will. Repin's famous painting in the Tretyakov Gallery in Moscow depicts him as horrified and grief-stricken as he clutches the bleeding body of his dying son, whom he, in a fit of rage, had fatally wounded. His recurrent sense of sin drove him to gestures of abdication and retirement to a monastery. Sergei Eisenstein's incomparable cinema portrayal of the tyrant in the 1930's was suppressed by the Politburo, after the release of Part I, on the ground that it presented Ivan not as a statesman but as a lunatic.

He was both. Only a species of madman, vicious and ruthless, could harry and hound the lethargic Muscovites into some image of the competence required to fulfill their historic mission. As their rulers defined it, that mission was to break out of the confines imposed by the still formidable power of the Tartars, often allied with the mighty Ottoman Turks; to recover the lost western lands; to make primitive Muscovy again a part of Europe; and to beat back successive invasions by more advanced Western Powers. Ivan the Terrible was unable to solve the problem. But he fashioned the means by which it was to be solved. He decimated the unruly boyars and compelled the survivors to obey. He gathered mercenary troops to buttress his power. He organized *streltsi*, or musketeers. He rewarded freebooters, or *Cossacks*, with new lands in exchange for fighting Tartars and Turks on the borders of the realm. (*Ukraine* then meant "beyond the frontiers" and came to be the name of the anarchic and dangerous wilds south of Muscovy.) He called into being a new nobility of *dvoryane* (courtiers) and *pomeshchiks,* sworn to fight for the Tsar in return for estates. That the estates might be profitable, he forbade the peasants to leave the land and reduced them to serfdom. Autocracy and feudalism were alike products of the needs of war.

The political fortunes of the dread Ivan were mixed. In 1552, bearing the cross of Dmitri Donskoi, he led 100,000 men to the storming of Kazan and the breaking of the power of the Tartars on the Volga. Astrakhan was annexed in 1556. The fantastic Church of St. Basil was erected in Red Square to celebrate the victory. All the East was now open. By 1582 the Cossack Yermak had reached the

Ob-Irtish and made West Siberia part of Muscovy. His successors pushed on to the Pacific, Kamchatka, the Aleutians, Alaska, the northwest coast of America, and down as far as California, following the route of the Amerindians out of Asia twenty thousand years ago. Only in 1824, following the promulgation of the Monroe Doctrine, did an overextended Russia, in agreement with the USA in the first Russian-American treaty, give up all claims in North America south of 54°40'. And only in 1867, by the sale of Alaska, did the "Third Rome" quit America and limit its imperialism to Eurasia.

In the West, Ivan had little success. During the grim centuries of the Mongols, most of the old Russian lands of the river road had been seized by western neighbors, since the Golden Horde paid little heed. Ivan in 1569 vainly proposed an alliance with Elizabeth I of England against Poland. His wars against German Knights, Swedes, Lithuanians, and Poles led only to the looting and burning of Moscow once more by the Turks and Tartars in 1571. Not yet was dark Muscovy capable of facing the West on equal terms.

The helplessness and hopelessness of this community, cursed by circumstances and benighted by its past, was vividly revealed in the aftermath of Ivan's demise. His moronic son, Fyodor—fitter, said his father, to be a bell-ringer in a convent than to be Tsar—came to the throne in 1584. Authority devolved upon his father-in-law, Boris Godunov, who in 1598, when Fyodor died, was elected Tsar by the *Zemsky Sobor* or Assembly of Landowners. Dissident boyars supported a "false Dmitri" pretending to be Fyodor's brother, who had expired by violence in 1591. Boris died in 1605. Cossacks and Poles brought the false Dmitri to Moscow, where he was slain in 1606. Basil Shuisky was named Tsar. Rebel serfs under Bolotnikov revolted in the south. A second "false Dmitri" tried to take power. Basil was deposed. The boyars offered the crown to the son of King Sigismund of Poland. Since politics abhors anarchy as much as nature abhors a vacuum, Russia's neighbors moved in. Sweden took Narva and Novgorod. Poland took Smolensk and, in 1610, occupied Moscow. Russia again seemed extinguished by its own disorders and the eager greed of its foes. Such was the melancholy "time of troubles."

Today, before the bulbous Church of St. Basil on Red Square stands a monument, formerly on a pedestal in the Square itself, to two national heroes. The figures represent Prince Pozharsky and a butcher of Nijni Novgorod, Cosmo Minin. These two led a popular

uprising that drove the Poles from Moscow in 1612. In the following year the *Zemsky Sobor* elevated to the Tsardom 17-year-old Mikhail Romanov. He and his successors never forgot that the cure for anarchy, among people unskilled in self-government, is Autocracy; that Autocracy requires Orthodoxy, as well as force, to command obedience, since the masses need mystery; that a cloudy mission of "saving the world" is an indispensable adjunct to the other *credenda* and *miranda* of power; that all foreigners should be viewed with suspicion as probable enemies; that "Westernization" is a precondition to fighting the West on equal terms; and that limitless aggrandizement is the best defense against foes always eager to despoil and, if possible, to destroy Muscovy at any sign of inner weakness or disorder. Such was the response of the Russian community of the 17th Century, and long thereafter, to the challenge posed by Russian backwardness in the face of neighbors possessed of superior technological and military skills.

Only the crises of the drama need be noted. During the reign of Alexis (1645–76), Polish overlords in the Ukraine were fought in hideous battle by rebel Cossacks under Hetman Bogdan Hmelnitsky, whose statue stands proudly in Kiev's largest square as the symbol of the reunion of Russia and the Ukraine. The event was elaborately celebrated in 1947 on the anniversary of the peace of 1667 whereby Russia recovered Kiev, Smolensk, and most of the east bank of the Dnieper.

Peter the Great (1682–1725), desperately bent upon "Westernization," built St. Petersburg on the Neva and made it a new capital as a "window to the West." He founded the Russian Navy and the Academy of Science. He traveled incognito abroad to learn science and technology. He butchered the *streltsi* and all others who resisted his innovations, took the title of "Emperor," cut off beards or heads with equal gusto, and long fought Sweden in the "Great Northern War" of 1699–1721. His forces were defeated at Narva in 1700, but triumphed over King Charles XII at Poltava in 1709. His saddle and Charles's are still to be seen in the Winter Palace, along with paintings depicting these memorable events. By the Peace of Nystadt (1721) Peter acquired much of Karelia and southeastern Finland and all of the south coast of the Gulf, including Estonia and what was then called Livonia. Great Peter, who, on horseback trampling a serpent, still stands in Leningrad looking out over the Neva, is the incarnation, like the Ivan before him and the Stalin of days to come,

of a ferocious passion to "modernize" Russia to enable it to resist and, if possible, "Russianize" the West.

Under Peter's daughter Elizabeth (1741–61) Russia joined the coalition against Frederick the Great in the Seven Years' War. In 1760 Russian troops occupied Berlin. But the victory was thrown away by Elizabeth's successor, the mad Paul III, who made peace on Frederick's terms. In the brilliant reign of the Great Catherine (1762–96), letter-writer, liberal, and libertine, public policy was shaped by the more influential of her lovers: Orlov, Potemkin, and Zubov, in succession. She was the first of the Romanovs to make Constantinople (Byzantium) the goal of her wars against the Turks. By the Peace of Kuchuk-Kainardji (1774) Catherine won Azov, Kuban, Terek, a protectorate over Moldavia, Turkish recognition of the "independence" of the Crimea, and what was later interpreted as a protectorate over all Christians in Turkey. In the second war, 1787–91, the Turks were again beaten by the military genius of General Alexander Suvorov. The peace of 1791 gave Russia the Crimea and the area between the Bug and the Dniester, including Odessa.

Catherine the Great also acquired Courland (Latvia) and joined Frederick in the first partition of Poland in 1772. In resistance to new Russian demands, Polish forces rallied under Kosciusko in 1794, but were defeated by Suvorov, who took Warsaw. A second partition followed in 1795. The third partition of 1796 put an end to the old Polish State.

In her last years Catherine was horrified by the French Revolution. She had looked with some sympathy upon the American Revolution, since it promised to weaken British power, but had refused to recognize the United States, from which Francis Dana came to St. Petersburg vainly seeking diplomatic relations. In 1773–4 another peasant revolt, led by Emilian Pugachev, swept the valley of the Volga before the rebels were crushed and Pugachev was executed in Moscow. Catherine, who called the Republican followers of Kosciusko the "Jacobins of the East," never permitted her "liberalism" to encourage social reform opposed by the landed aristocracy.

If the Muscovite Tsardom had become an executive committee of the landholding and serf-owning nobles, the Russian Church had become the spiritual bulwark of the State, inculcating obedience to Autocrat and landlord alike among dark multitudes steeped in poverty and ignorance. The attempted reunion of the Greek and Roman churches at the Council of Florence in 1439 had been repudiated

by the Russian clergy. Catholic attempts at reconversion failed, although in 1596, at the Union of Brest-Litovsk, the Jesuits had succeeded in attaching to Rome a large group of the Orthodox in the eastern provinces of Poland. The price paid by the Papacy for this victory was to permit the new "Uniat" church to retain its Greek rites and liturgy. The Russian Church became increasingly a national Church and an arm of the State. For a time the Patriarch Philarete, father of Mikhail Romanov, was, in fact if not in form, head of State as well as Church. But his successors were subordinated to the secular power, particularly after the resistance of the "Old Believers" to the corrections of ritual by the Patriarch Nikon (1653–66) led to a schism (*Raskol*) and to a later multiplication of dissident minority sects.

Peter abolished the Patriarchate (which was not restored until 1917) and substituted at the head of the Church a Holy Synod, the members of which were appointed by the Tsar. Said an Old Believer of the 19th Century: "The so-called orthodox faith is an appurtenance of the Crown and Treasury, an official badge. It rests on no basis of real life or sincere conviction, but merely does its duty as a government weapon for the defense of order." There was enough truth in this judgment to involve the Church in the ultimate ruin of the Autocracy.

5. THE END OF THE HOUSE OF RURIK

THE Tsar who died in 1598, Fyodor, son of Ivan, was the last direct patrilineal descendant of the Rurik of Jutland who founded the first Russian State. His mother, Anastasia, was Ivan's first wife. Her family stemmed from a German nobleman who had settled in Moscow two centuries earlier. Anastasia's father changed the family name of Koshkin to Romanov; her brother, Nikita, was chairman of a council of nobles which helped the feeble-minded Fyodor to rule. One of Nikita's sons, another Fyodor, had a son named Mikhail. Boris Godunov, fearing Romanov popularity, forced Mikhail's parents to separate and become monastics, in which role Fyodor took the name of Philarete and later became Metropolitan of Rostov. Until his death in 1633 this Philarete, as Patriarch of Moscow, ruled Russia jointly with his son. Mikhail, elected in 1613 as the first of the Ro-

manov Tsars, was thus related to Tsar Fyodor, cousin of Fyodor Romanov, and was accordingly deemed by the boyars the legitimate heir of the dynasty of Rurik.

During most of their rulership over Russia the Romanovs based their power on a feudal nobility and priesthood that perpetuated Autocracy and serfdom into an era of social change rendering both institutions obsolete. The Autocrats were adept in glorifying their precursors. In Leningrad can still be seen the statues of Peter I, erected by Catherine; of Catherine and her lovers and advisers, raised before the Pushkin Theater by Alexander III; and of Nicholas I on horseback, reared in Vorovsky Square, by Alexander II. The Autocrats were inept in meeting popular demands for reform, save for grudging and ultimately futile concessions in the wake of defeat in war. As late as the 1880's one of Alexander III's Ministers of the Interior, D. Tolstoy, could say: "Any attempt to introduce into Russia Western European parliamentary forms of government is doomed to failure. If the Tsarist regime is ever overthrown, its place will be taken by Communism, the pure undisguised Communism of Karl Marx." [3] That this prophesy was to prove self-fulfilling was doubtless due to the disposition of Russia's power-holders to equate all change in the *status quo* with subversion and to leave the discontented with no hope of reform save through political extremism and violent revolution.

Alexander I (1801–25), like Catherine, began as a liberal and ended as a reactionary. At first he played with ideas of limiting Autocracy and liberating the serfs. But nothing came of these proposals, nor of the later plans of his adviser, Mikhail Speransky, who urged a scheme of self-government based on elected local dumas which would choose delegates to district and provincial dumas which in turn would pick the members of a national duma or parliament. Alexander was more interested in war and diplomacy and in his ultimate mission as savior of Europe. He joined Austria, Prussia, and England in fighting Napoleon, but after the military disasters of 1805–6) he met the French Emperor at Tilsit (1807) and signed a peace pact. He was then free to pursue his wars with Sweden and Turkey, concluded respectively with Russian annexation of Finland in 1809 and of Bessarabia in 1812.

On June 23, 1812, Bonaparte invaded Russia with the largest land army thus far assembled for a single campaign. Alexander's

[3] Quoted in Carr, I, 14.

Marshall Mikhail Kutuzov, unlike Stalin's marshals of 1941, was unable to defend Moscow, but he fought skillful delaying actions and took full advantage of the onset of winter, the burning of the city, and the services of peasant partisans to bring about the destruction of the "Grand Army." The Corsican retired and recrossed the Niemen in November with 50,000 of his original force of 420,000. Alexander rallied the armies of the coalition, which defeated the French near Leipzig at the "Battle of the Nations" in October 1813. The Tsar, now a hero to all Europe, entered Paris in triumph at the end of the following March and subsequently dominated the Congress of Vienna and founded the "Holy Alliance." Within a month after his death those who were later called the "Decembrists" launched an unsuccessful uprising. It was the last palace *coup d'état.* It was also the first Russian revolutionary movement directly inspired by Western liberalism.

Nicholas I (1825–55) sought safety by the suppression of all critics. His early decision to establish a secret police—the "third section" of his personal chancery and predecessor of the dread *Okhrana* —typified the spirit of his regime, as did his crushing of the Polish insurrection of 1830–1 and his participation in the destruction of the Hungarian revolution of 1849. Although his war with Turkey (1827–9) led to the liberation of the Greeks, he aspired to be the policeman of Europe and the champion of legitimacy. His ambitions in the Near East led to war once more with Turkey in 1853. In order to halt the Russian drive to the Straits, Britain, France, and Sardinia declared war the following spring. Defeat in the Crimea hastened Nicholas's death.

His son Alexander II (1855–81) made the humiliating Peace of Paris and became the great "reforming Tsar" in recognition of the need for change and for concessions to popular demand. Serfdom— "better abolished from above than from below," said the Tsar—was at last ended by the law of March 3, 1861, with State compensation to the landlords for the small plots granted to the peasants and with heavy redemption dues owed to the State by the beneficiaries of emancipation. In 1864 elected county councils or *zemstvos* were established as agencies of local self-government, but on a basis that gave the landlords effective control. Public trial by jury in independent courts was likewise introduced (1864), as well as a measure of municipal self-government (1870) and a reform of the military service (1874).

In foreign affairs Alexander befriended the North in the American Civil War, partly out of fear of Anglo-French intervention in favor of the Polish rebellion of 1863; took advantage of the Franco-Prussian War to repudiate the provisions of the Treaty of Paris forbidding Russia to maintain a fleet in the Black Sea; balanced vanquished France against the newly united *Reich*; liberated Bulgaria through a new war with Turkey (1877); reacquired Bessarabia, annexed most of Transcaucasia, added Turkestan (1867) and Transcaspia (1874) to the Empire; acquired Sakhalin from Japan (1875); and obliged China (1858) to cede the Maritime Provinces, at the southern extremity of which Vladivostok was founded. But diplomatic successes abroad and reforms at home did not stem the tide of revolutionary Populism sweeping through the intelligentsia. On March 13, 1881, on the very day when he signed Loris-Melikov's project for a quasi-constitution, Alexander was killed by a terrorist bomb.

His dour son was the last Tsar but one. Alexander III (1881–94) proclaimed his devotion to absolutism and sought to restore the dwindling wealth and influence of the nobility. The press was muzzled, criticism was stifled, and national and religious minorities were persecuted. The alliance with France of 1892 was accompanied by an inflow of French capital but by no relaxation in the suppression of republican ideas. After living unhappily as a virtual prisoner, fearful of assassins and surrounded by policemen, the Tsar died unhappily at Livadia. His son, Nicholas II, inherited the whirlwind and lacked all talent for coping with it. He was weak and shy and therefore resolved to preserve the Autocracy intact. He dismissed plans for representative government as "senseless dreams." He was dominated by his wife, Princess Alix of Hesse, a superstitious woman who sought to save their only son, the hæmophiliac Alexis, by recourse to quacks, beginning with French spiritualists and ending with the degenerate and drunken monk Rasputin. Unsuccessful war with Japan (1904–5) led to the loss of southern Sakhalin and of Russian rights in Manchuria in the Treaty of Portsmouth. Defeat brought revolution. A decade later, defeat at the hands of the Central Powers brought catastrophe to the dynasty.

The Muscovite Autocracy which passed into the shades in March of 1917 was a divine-right absolutism whose subjects found it neither absolute, right, nor divine. Prior to 1905 its government was an arbitrary despotism, with no constitution, no parliament,

and virtually no public participation beyond the village *mir* and the provincial *zemstvos*. According to the Fundamental Laws, the Tsar was an "unlimited autocrat" to whom obedience was "ordained by God himself." The Sovereign administered his scores of provinces (*guberni* and *oblasti*) through Governors appointed on the nomination of the Minister of the Interior. In St. Petersburg sat the Council of Ministers, composed of department heads; the Imperial Council of a hundred appointed members, to whom were added in 1906 elected members in almost equal number, with both groups consisting chiefly of wealthy landowners; a Senate (established by Peter the Great), composed of Privy Counsellors and functioning as the highest judicial and administrative body; and the Holy Synod, dominated by its Procurator, who acted as a Minister for Church affairs. All these appointed officials were named by, answerable to, and removable by the Tsar alone. Legislation was prepared by the Imperial Council, but its members could merely advise and never control the Emperor and his Ministers. Earlier representative institutions, such as the *Duma* of the Boyars and the *Zemsky Sobor*, first called by Ivan the Terrible in 1550, had long since passed away.

This archaic political structure, like the feudal social hierarchy on which it rested, was placed in grave jeopardy when commerce and industry fostered the growth of cities. Urban capitalism, arriving belatedly in Russia, had social consequences similar to those it had produced in Western Europe a century earlier. A middle class of burghers grew in numbers and wealth, and shortly divided itself into an upper stratum of businessmen and a lower order of factory workers. As in the West, merchants and employers tended to embrace the ideals of liberalism and nationalism and to demand participation in government under a constitution. Workers lent willing ears to the agitators of radical internationalism, including various schools of revolutionary anarchism and socialism. Both new classes became the enemies of Tsarism and of the aristocracy.

The first opportunity for revolutionary mass action was provided by the results of the war with Japan. An eleven-point petition, drawn up at a conference of *zemstvos* representatives in November 1904, demanded civil liberties and constitutional government. On "Bloody Sunday," early in January 1905, a peaceful demonstration of workers, carrying ikons and singing hymns under the leadership of Father Gapon, was fired upon by troops before the Winter Palace with the loss of several hundred lives. Numerous

strikes, peasant disorders, mutinies, and acts of political terrorism ensued. By autumn a political general strike was under way in many centers under the direction of Councils or Soviets of Workers' Deputies. The Tsar's Ministers sought to appease the liberals and to suppress the revolutionary radicals. A black epoch of reprisals and punishments began in 1906 under the direction of Prime Minister Peter Stolypin. His assassination in 1911 did not alter the fact that the revolution had failed.

In the face of danger, however, the Tsar had issued the Manifesto of October 17, 1905, promising civil liberties and popular elections for a parliament that would have control over the Ministers and effective power over lawmaking and the purse strings. But in the final arrangement the new assembly or Imperial Duma was weakened by a second chamber in the form of a revamped Imperial Council. The franchise, moreover, was restricted in 1907 through a complex scheme of indirect class elections, with the result that the Third and Fourth Dumas were filled with conservatives and reactionaries. In practice the Duma was given no genuine authority over appropriations or legislation and none at all over the Ministry. The Tsar could veto all laws, could adjourn or dissolve the Duma at will, and could issue executive decrees (*ukaze*), having the force of law, without consulting the Duma. The Autocracy was no longer unlimited, but it was still an autocracy.

Its final disintegration and collapse was a direct result of the war with the Second *Reich*, which the Tsar's Ministers had done much to prepare and unleash. The military defeats of 1915–16 gave rise to "dark forces" at the Imperial Court, headed by the Tsarina and Rasputin, which sought to save the Autocracy through treasonable intrigues with the enemy. Toward the end the Tsarina told her husband: "Never forget that you are sovereign in your own right. Thank God, Russia is not a constitutional State. . . . . Don't yield. Be the boss. Obey your firm little wife and our Friend"—i.e., Rasputin. The mood of the last Tsar, always trivial, melancholy, and indifferent, was much the same as it had been after 1905 when he wrote in his diary, amid national upheavals shaking his throne: "Pretty doings! . . . Was quietly busy until dinner and all evening. Went paddling in a canoe. . . . Got dressed and rode a bicycle to the bathing beach and bathed enjoyably in the sea. . . . The weather was wonderful."

The assassination of Rasputin in December 1916 produced no

change in the blindness of the Tsar and his advisers in the face of mass misery and popular clamor for reform or revolution. In the midst of strikes, riots, and mutinies Nicholas II suddenly discovered that no one would any longer obey him. On March 15, 1917, he abdicated in favor of his brother, the Grand Duke Mikhail, who decided not to accept the throne unless the proposed Constituent Assembly should request him to. Thus was terminated the dynasty of despots who had ruled or misruled all the Russias during the three centuries since the accession of Mikhail Romanov—whose precursors, since Rurik reached the water road, had reigned for almost a thousand years.

CHAPTER THREE

Nineteen Seventeen

1. SHTO DYELAT?

INTO PETROGRAD's Finland Station puffed a train at 50 minutes before midnight on April 16, 1917. On board were Lenin and his wife, among other returning exiles, most of whom, like Lenin, had crossed Germany to Copenhagen in a sealed coach by agreement with the German authorities. Krupskaya and Lenin had been living in poverty only a week before in a rented room near a sausage factory in Zurich. He now wore a derby hat, a gray suit, and new shoes bought in Stockholm. A welcoming committee gave him a bouquet of red roses. He hurried to the Tsar's waiting-room, where he was met by Nikolai Chkeidze, Menshevik President of the new Petrograd Soviet.

"Comrade Lenin," said Chkeidze, "we welcome you to Russia. . . . But we consider that the principal task of the revolutionary democracy is to defend our revolution against every kind of attack, both from within and without. . . ." Lenin addressed the crowd: "Dear comrades, soldiers, sailors, and workers. I am happy to greet in you the victorious Russian Revolution, to greet you as the advance guard of the international proletarian army. . . . The war of imperialist brigandage is the beginning of civil war in Europe. . . . Any day may see the general collapse of European capitalism. The Russian Revolution has dealt it the first blow and has opened a new epoch. . . . Long live the International Social Revolution!"

Outside the station was a hubbub of shouting sailors and soldiers, red flags, searchlights, and a band playing "La Marseillaise." Lenin warned his hearers against trusting the Provisional Government. "The people needs peace. The people needs bread. The peo-

ple needs land. And they give you war, hunger, no bread—leave the landlords still on the land. We must fight for the social revolution!" The throng bore Lenin to an armored car (still on display in Leningrad), where another speech was called for. A cheering cavalcade moved westward, crossed Samson Bridge over a branch of the Neva estuary, and proceeded some blocks northeast of the Arsenal and the Fortress of Peter and Paul to a white brick mansion (today the Kirov Museum) which the Bolsheviks had seized and made their headquarters. Vain were the efforts of the owner to recover her property. She was Kshesinskaya, once a ballerina and mistress of the Tsar and now a little old lady. From a balcony overlooking the boulevard Lenin spoke again to the crowd below and then at length, far into the night, to the mob in the ballroom.

His message was strange: the imperialist war will turn into civil war and world-wide revolution. "We don't need any parliamentary republic. We don't need any bourgeois democracy. We don't need any government except the Soviet!" This was a weird gospel to all Marxists, Bolshevik and Menshevik alike, returning from exile: Kamenev, Muranov, Sverdlov, Molotov, and Stalin from Siberia; Maxim Gorky from Italy; Bukharin, Volodarsky, Tsereteli, Pyatakov from America; Trotsky from an apartment in the Bronx and from a British concentration camp at Halifax, where he had been detained during April. Among these and many others only Molotov had talked about the need of the Soviets assuming governmental authority—a view rejected by Stalin, who in 1925 wrote that his own "profoundly mistaken position, which I shared with other Party comrades," was "renounced completely only in mid-April when I adhered to Lenin's theses." [1]

"That," said Bogdanov, after hearing Lenin, "is the raving of a lunatic!" Wrote Plekhanov: "Deliriums are occasionally interesting." In *Pravda*, April 21, 1917, Kamenev asserted that Lenin's line was "unacceptable inasmuch as it proceeds from the assumption that the bourgeois democratic revolution has been completed and it builds on the immediate transformation of this revolution into a socialist revolution. . . . Let us remain the one and only party of the revolutionary masses of the proletariat without turning into a group of Communist propagandists." [2]

[1] Cf. Carr, I, 76–7.
[2] The texts of Lenin's speeches of April 16–17, 1917, are not available. The quotations here given are taken from N. Sukhanov: *Zapiski O Revolutsii*

After a decade abroad, Lenin thus returned with a doctrine that made him a leader without followers and a strategist with no forces to command. Every other Marxist knew that bourgeois democracy and capitalism must precede proletarian dictatorship and socialism. How could the Soviets become the "government" when they were controlled by SR's and Mensheviks who supported the existing government, when the Bolsheviks themselves (at first) repudiated any such thought, and when no one in his senses, in or out of the Soviets, ever dreamed that they could become a government? Lenin's genius consisted in so exploiting mass grievances and shifting circumstances that he finally won over his Party and many outside its ranks to a view which all at the outset dismissed as absurd. An understanding of how this came to pass requires a sampling of the ferment that was Russia in the spring of 1917.

In the beginning the Petrograd Soviet and the Provisional Government both met in the yellow, white-pillared Tauride Palace. The Government later moved to the Marian Palace and finally to the Winter Palace. The Executive Committee of the Soviet moved far off to Smolny Institute, once a convent and then a girls' school with a handsome church and bell-tower in its gardens. These two bodies had come into being simultaneously with the abdication of the Tsar.

On March 15 a Provisional Committee of the State Duma had established a "Provisional Government" headed by Prince George E. Lvov and composed of liberals and moderate socialists. All were agreed on the necessity of prosecuting the war and laying the foundations of a new democracy. The Minister of Justice was Alexander Kerensky, Social Revolutionary and leader of the group called "Populist Socialists" or "*Trudoviki*" in the Duma in March 1917. Paul Miliukov, Constitutional Democrat, was Minister of Foreign Affairs. Officials of trade unions and cooperatives had already formed a "Pro-

---

(7 vols., Z Grezhebin, Merlin, 1919–22), later translated into a one-volume condensation (cf. pp. 272–85) as *The Russian Revolution of 1917* (Oxford University Press, 1955), edited and translated by Joel Carmichael. The actual name of the author of these invaluable reminiscences was Nikolai Nikolayevich Himmer, a Menshevik who nevertheless worked for the Soviet regime as an economist and journalist. In 1931 he was tried for "treason" and "confessed" to plotting to promote armed intervention. Upon arriving at a concentration camp near Verkhne-Uralsk, he wrote an indignant appeal to the authorities, asking them to keep their promise "to release those willing to make untrue confessions." He was never heard of again.

visional Executive Committee of the Soviet of Workers' Deputies," which called upon the workers and soldiers of Petrograd to elect representatives to a new Soviet in the tradition of 1905. The deputies thus chosen, along with sundry invited Socialist leaders, had met as early as March 12 and organized the Petrograd Soviet with Chkheidze as President and Kerensky and M. I. Slobelev (Menshevik) as Vice-Presidents. The great majority of the members of the Soviet felt that they should support the Provisional Government but not participate in it. Other Soviets, first by scores and then by hundreds, emerged in other cities all over the land and soon assumed functions of local administration. Some 400 representatives of the provincial Workers' and Soldiers' Soviets met in conference in the capital, April 11–16, on the eve of Lenin's return. They elected an All-Russian Central Executive Committee as a national Soviet body.

Russia's political ambivalence in 1917 sprang from the coexistence of a Provisional Government, having the wish but not the means to govern, and a series of Soviet agencies, having the means but not the wish to govern. The new Ministers issued decrees, but lacked sufficient mass support to insure obedience. The Soviets had mass support, but preferred to issue demands and manifestoes rather than decrees. Responsibility without power confronted power without responsibility. The liaison between the two was, at best, tenuous. The formula that all accepted for resolving the dilemma was to prepare elections for a Constituent Assembly that would draw up a constitution on the basis of which a permanent government with both power and responsibility would presumably come into being.

It was in this situation that Lenin promulgated the "April Theses," which aroused contempt on all sides. His argument was simple: the Provisional Government must be repudiated; the workers and poorest peasants must seize power and end the war by ending capitalism; the Soviet is "the only possible form of revolutionary government"; it must therefore establish a Soviet Republic that would nationalize all land and assume control of the production and distribution of goods. The Bolsheviks must explain these necessities to the masses and meanwhile call a Party Congress to amend their own program, change the Party name to "Communist," and prepare for the creation of a Third International.

In speech and writing Lenin defended his "Theses" and denounced his critics:

The masses must be warned. Revolution is a difficult thing. Errors are unavoidable. . . . One must not fear to be in the minority. . . . We want the masses to rectify their errors by actual experience. . . . The art of government cannot be gotten out of books. Try, make mistakes, learn how to govern. . . . You fear to break with old memories. But in order to change one's linen, one must take off the soiled and put on the clean. . . . Outside of Socialism, there is no deliverance of humanity from wars, from hunger, from the destruction of millions and millions of human beings. . . . Mr. Plekhanov, the ex-Marxist, has absolutely failed to understand the doctrine of Marxism about the State. . . . The mistake of Comrade Kamenev is that in 1917 he sees only the past. . . . In reality, however, the future has already begun. . . . Comrade Kamenev has not grasped the fact, the significance of the existing Soviets, their identiy, as to their socio-political character, with the State of the Paris Commune. . . . Let us not imitate the woe-Marxians of whom Marx himself said, "I sowed dragons and I reaped fleas." . . . There is no other way out except a proletarian revolution. . . . We want to end this imperialist World War. We want to rebuild the world. . . .[3]

The political turmoil in the Russia of 1917 was less a struggle between those demanding socialism and those opposing socialism than a struggle among rival camps of socialists. It was likewise less a struggle between advocates of war and proponents of peace than one among rival groups of peace-seekers bidding for support in a nation already defeated and weary of war. The opponents of socialism, most of whom favored continuing the war, were divided against themselves. The liberal Cadets, speaking primarily for the business community and the lower middle class, stood for bourgeois democracy, a parliamentary republic, and solidarity with France, Britain, and America against the Central Powers. Various groups of conservatives and reactionaries, representing aristocrats, bureaucrats, and officers, deplored the fall of the Tsar and weighed all issues of

[3] *Collected Works of V. I. Lenin,* Vol. XX, *The Revolution of 1917,* Book I, pp. 93–157.

war and peace in the scales of their hopes at home. Both groups were progressively weakened and discredited by the fact that their conception of the future was widely at variance with the aspirations of most of the peasantry, the proletariat, and the soldiery. The men in the street, in the villages, and in the trenches were all "socialists" in varying degrees—and all clamant for peace. Miliukov informed Russian diplomats abroad that the new authority would "remain faithful to international engagements entered into by the fallen regime and will honor Russia's word." The USA, through Ambassador David R. Francis, granted the new Cabinet recognition as the Government of Russia on March 22, with the other Allied Powers following suit. The far-off but powerful voice of Woodrow Wilson asserted on April 2 that every American felt that "assurance has been added to our hope for the future peace of the world by the wonderful and heartening things that have been happening in Russia. . . . The great, generous Russian people have been added in all their naïve majesty and might to the forces that are fighting for freedom in the world, for justice and for peace. Here is a fit partner for a League of Honor."

But a government must govern. The Provisional Government was less and less able to govern because its Ministers evoked neither fear nor respect from the people. They could therefore command neither confidence nor obedience. The first crisis was caused by Miliukov's note of May 1 declaring the determination of the new Russia to continue the war by the side of the Allies until victory should be won. Mobs at once demonstrated in protest, shouting "Down with the Provisional Government!" The slogan was Bolshevik, but Lenin was not yet prepared for battle. The Central Committee of the Party endorsed the order of the Petrograd Soviet prohibiting street meetings. It also repudiated the slogan on the ground that power could pass to the proletariat only when the Soviets should see the need and purpose of taking power.

This time was not near. Minister of War A. I. Guchkov resigned on May 13 and Foreign Minister Miliukov two days later. On May 18 the Provisional Government was reshuffled into a greater semblance of a liberal-socialist coalition, with Kerensky becoming Minister of War, Tsereteli Minister of Posts, Skobelev Minister of Labor, and Chernov Minister of Agriculture. M. I. Tereshchenko, financier, sugar magnate, and friend of both Kerensky and British Ambassador Buchanan, became Foreign Minister. Popular longing for peace and

mass hopes for socialism made Prince Lvov and his colleagues the targets of constant criticism. These sentiments found expression in the Soviets, but the expression was garbled and the voice gave forth a many-tongued babel of discordant sounds. Not until autumn was a single nationwide Soviet organization to emerge. Meanwhile, the new freedom begot a profusion of conferences, congresses, and committees.

The first All-Russian Congress of Peasant Deputies, representing the village Soviets, met at Peoples' House from May 17 to June 2. Half of the thousand delegates were SR's, with most of the balance non-partisan. The SR's elected N. D. Avksentiev as chairman and controlled the Executive Committee of 30. The Congress voted support of the Provisional Government and the war. It rejected Lenin's proposal for immediate confiscation of land and transfer of political power to the Soviets. Its program was socialization of land after the meeting of the Constituent Assembly. A conference of factory-shop committees (June 12–16), on the other hand, voted approval of a resolution drafted by Lenin for workers' control of industry.

On June 16 the first All-Russian Congress of Soviets of Workers' and Soldiers' Deputies opened with 285 SR deputies, 248 Mensheviks, 105 Bolsheviks, and 144 divided among lesser groups. Lenin spoke again, denouncing those socialists who supported a war fought in the interest of capitalists and imperialists. When the Bolsheviks announced a demonstration for June 23 under the slogan "Down with the capitalist Ministers!" and "All power to the Soviets!" the Congress forbade all street meetings for three days and accused the Bolsheviks of an effort to overthrow the Government. The Bolshevik Central Committee again acquiesced—to the tune, however, of denials, protests, and plans for a later demonstration on July 1. This was the second occasion on which a Soviet body, though possessed of no formal governmental authority, had banned mass demonstrations in the capital for the sake of avoiding bloodshed. The nominal "Government," though fearing to act itself, was thus protected from mob pressure by the dislike and suspicion with which most of the Soviet deputies viewed the Bolsheviks. The All-Russian Central Executive Committee that the Soviet Congress elected on June 30 was strongly anti-Bolshevik. Soviet opposition to Bolshevism was matched by trade-union opposition to Bolshevism. At the third All-Russian Conference of Trade Unions, July 4–11, only 80 out of 220 delegates were Bolshevik sympathizers. The majority voted

down Bolshevik resolutions for class war and workers' control of industry.

Lenin and his followers refused to be discouraged by these rebuffs. At the beginning of the year the Party had some 23,000 registered members. By April it had 40,000. On May 7 the Party opened the five-day session of its Seventh Conference. It was the first to be held openly on Russian soil. In size, as well as in the importance of its decisions, it approached the proportions of a Party Congress. There were 151 delegates, representing 79,204 Party members. Numerous cleavages developed. A group from Moscow stood by the formula of 1905: "A dictatorship of the proletariat and the peasantry." Kamenev and Rykov opposed Lenin on the question of an immediate socialist revolution. Zinoviev opposed him on breaking with the Zimmerwald Union and forming a Third International. The Polish delegates, headed by Felix Djerzhinsky and supported by Bukharin and Pyatakov, opposed Stalin's proposals that national self-determination should include the right of secession. The resolutions adopted represented a compromise among divergent views. They nevertheless constitute a document remarkable alike for its sharp analysis of the current situation and for its formulation of the broad objectives that the Party of Lenin was to pursue during the months to come.

War and diplomacy remained the areas of most violent controversy between governmental intentions and popular aspirations. Out of the clash grew the crisis of July. On the first day of the month General Brussilov's weary soldiers, temporarily stirred to new fervor by Kerensky's oratory, launched an offensive against the Austrians which gained some initial successes. But a German counterattack soon led to defeat, disaster, and retreat for the poorly supplied Russian troops. The enemy halted his advance on the central front for political reasons, but took Riga in the north in September. The Petrograd garrison was already dominated by Bolshevist sympathizers. On July 15 the Cadet Ministers resigned from the Cabinet in protest against the intention of their socialist colleagues to grant autonomy to the Ukraine in advance of the Constituent Assembly. Mobs again paraded in the capital shouting "Down with the capitalist Ministers! All power to the Soviets!" On the morning of the 16th, delegates from the First Machine Gun Regiment called at the house of Kshesinskaya to ask Bolshevik direction of an armed demonstration

against the Provisional Government. The Party leaders refused on the ground that the effort was premature.

On July 17 the streets of Petrograd were thronged with scores of thousands of demonstrating workers. Armed troops paraded with banners used in the Bolshevik demonstration of July 1. Disorganized soldiers sought, with no success, to arrest the bourgeois Ministers. Others assembled near Tauride Palace, where the Central Executive Committees of the Soviet of Workers' and Peasants' Deputies were in joint session. The Bolshevik Central Committee had meanwhile decided to summon soldiers and civilians to take up arms and participate in a "peaceful" demonstration. In the confused rioting and random firing that followed in various parts of the city, a score of lives were lost and many score were wounded. In the Petrograd Soviet, in which the Bolsheviks already had a majority, the workers' deputies voted to seize power from the Provisional Government and named a committee to direct the new revolution.

Lenin, who had been in the suburbs for a week, returned and addressed the demonstrators from the balcony of Kshesinskaya House. Soldiers, sailors, and workers ("soldiers and hooligans," said Krassin) roamed the streets, took over the Fortress of Peter and Paul, clashed with Government troops, and sought to induce the Soviet Central Executive Committee to support their demands. The Menshevik and SR members of these bodies toured the factories and workers' districts to persuade the masses to refrain from violence. That there was a Bolshevik "plot" to seize power, as alleged by Sukhanov and denied by Trotsky, is doubtful, though some Bolsheviks sought to use the occasion for revolutionary purposes. But there was still no way of transferring power to Soviet authorities who had no desire for power. Lenin in a night session of the Party Central Committee approved an appeal to workers and soldiers to halt the demonstration. Fearing arrest, he decided to spend the night away from home.

On the 18th the press carried a story, obviously inspired, that Lenin was an agent of the German General Staff, which was said to have directed the demonstration. Some military units reaffirmed their loyalty to the Government and others adopted an attitude of "neutrality." Police raided the offices of the Bolshevik papers. Warrants of arrest were issued. Trotsky protested at his omission from

the list and demanded that he share the honor. Troops occupied Kshesinskaya House and the Fortress of Peter and Paul. The arrest of Lenin was ordered on the 19th. He opposed the general strike urged by some of his colleagues and went into hiding in the home of the worker, Sergei Alliluyev, whose only daughter was destined to become Stalin's second wife. Kamenev was apprehended on July 22, Trotsky and Lunacharsky on August 4. After much discussion with Krupskaya, Stalin, Zinoviev, and others, Lenin decided not to give himself up, despite his desire to appear in court to answer the charge that he was a German agent. He had moved into a stable garret in the suburbs. On July 23 he moved again—into a tent beside a haystack some miles from the Razliv Station. On August 3 he was formally indicted under the criminal code for treason and organization of an armed uprising.

Meanwhile, Prince Lvov had resigned as Premier and was succeeded (July 21) by Kerensky, who became a pseudo-dictator, sworn to save the country from Bolshevism. The new Cabinet, fully constituted by August 6, promised to call the Constituent Assembly on September 30 and asserted its resolve to fight all enemies at home and abroad. But it had no means of prosecuting the war successfully, and it failed to crush the Bolshevists. Lenin, in hiding, continued writing articles and declared that nothing short of an armed revolt of the workers could now save the Revolution from a military dictatorship.

The "July Days" thus amounted to a test of power between the Bolsheviks and the Government. The test had not been sought on either side, however, and was a result of spontaneous mob action. Its aftermath, moreover, was confusion worse confounded. On the surface the Government had crushed the Bolsheviks by closing their press and driving their leaders to jail or into hiding. But the "semi-insurrection" was followed by a "semi-dictatorship" that indulged only in a "semi-suppression" of its enemies. The balance of forces was such that only half-measures were possible. Each contestant feared that forthright action against the other would alienate the "neutral" groups which were wavering between them and thus strengthen the rival camp. From this time forward the new Provisional Government was increasingly dependent upon the support of reactionary military elements that were soon to become a threat rather than a protection. And from this time forward the Bolshevik leaders, now obliged to work more or less under cover, were the political bene-

ficiaries of growing sympathy for their position among the Soviets and were increasingly concerned with the preparation of an armed uprising.

2. THE DILEMMA OF LIBERALISM

SUKHANOV, a shrewd observer of the events in Petrograd in 1917, quotes Lenin as telling the First All-Russian Congress of Soviets in June: "The Citizen Minister of Posts and Telegraphs (Tsereteli) has declared that there is no political party in Russia that would agree to take the entire power on itself. I answer: there is. . . . Our Party is ready at any moment to take over the Government." Of the then head of the Government, Sukhanov comments:

> It was a heavy load that history laid upon feeble shoulders. . . . Kerensky had supernatural energy, amazing capacity for work, and inexhaustible temperament. But he lacked the head for statesmanship and had no real political schooling. Without these elementary and indispensable attributes, the irreplaceable Kerensky of expiring Tsarism, the ubiquitous Kerensky of the February-March days could not but stumble headlong and flounder. . . . Kerensky was really persuaded that he was a Socialist and a democrat. He never suspected that by conviction, taste, and temperament he was the most consummate middle-class radical. . . . This was why Kerensky saw himself not only as a Socialist but also as a little bit of a Bonaparte.[4]

A sorely tried populace was willing to continue fighting the war begun and lost by the Tsardom on condition that its purposes be redefined in terms consonant with the revolutionary vision of freedom and brotherhood, and on condition, further, that victory should appear attainable without intolerable new sacrifices in blood and misery. The masses were at the same time hungry for peace—not at any price but on condition that its terms should offer an opportunity to harvest the anticipated fruits of the Revolution. "The army," said Lenin, "voted for peace with its legs." By mid-1917 a million deserters had left the ranks. Few were prepared to continue fighting for

[4] Sukhanov, pp. 31–3, 380.

the "imperialistic" goals of Tsarist diplomacy. Few were prepared to stop fighting if the cost of peace should be the triumph of counter-revolution. Lenin proposed peace through proletarian revolt that should spread forthwith to enemy and Allied nations alike and end the war everywhere by overthrowing the governments and ruling classes that were waging it. If it could be realized, such a peace would end all danger of counter-revolution and open up millennial vistas of salvation. Kerensky proposed continued war in unity with the Allied and Associated Powers until the new Russia should share in the benefits of common victory.

Had the Provisional Government been able to make this prospect plausible to the multitude by demonstrating the possibility of victory and of new war aims, its deferment of land reform and of other economic and political changes until the meeting of the Constituent Assembly would probably have evoked acquiescence. Land and Bread could be had if Peace through victory were assured. But Bread and Land seemed unattainable so long as no Peace, with or without victory, was in sight. Kerensky and his aides were never able to resolve this problem.

Those who practiced high politics in Washington, London, Paris, and Rome could doubtless have saved the Provisional Government had they acted in such a fashion as to convince the Russian masses of Allied willingness to embrace new purposes and Allied ability to aid Russia effectively. Such action would have required a larger degree of understanding of Russian hopes and fears than was possessed by the foreign diplomats in Petrograd. It would also have required more flexibility and astuteness in the conduct of political warfare than the Western statesmen were capable of. The year 1917 was one of limited successes and costly reverses for Allied arms—Vimy Ridge, the Champagne, Ypres, Passchendaele, Caporetto—coupled with disaffection in the French and Italian armies, severe shipping losses, and relatively slow American mobilization. In war those seeking to win new friends or to retain old ones must either demonstrate that Might makes Right or, if they are weak, that Right makes Might. The Russians, who had already suffered the heaviest losses, were scarcely to be persuaded of the Might of their Allies by the record. What was done to persuade them that their allies were fighting for the Right proved to be too little and too late.

Allied officials were disturbed by the Provisional Government's espousal as early as May 18 of "a general peace . . . without annex-

ation, without indemnities and on the basis of the self-determination of peoples." They were alarmed by Soviet appeals for peace through international revolutionary action. In a note of May 26 to the Provisional Government President Wilson championed "liberty, self-government . . . and a common covenant to secure peace and justice in the dealings of nations with one another." But when Foreign Minister Tereshchenko asked the Allies in June for a conference to reconsider "the agreements concerning the ultimate aims of the war," he received little encouragement. During June and early July a special diplomatic mission from the United States toured Russia. It was headed by ultra-conservative Elihu Root and included three business leaders (Charles R. Crane, Cyrus H. McCormick, and Samuel R. Bertron), one ex-Socialist (Charles Edward Russell), and one labor leader (James Duncan). The report of the Root mission, like the dispatches of Ambassador Francis, was naïvely optimistic regarding the Russian war effort and the prospects of democracy. Late in June a Russian mission, headed by Ambassador Boris Bakhmetev, reached Washington and also bespoke solidarity and confidence. Under the War Loan Acts, credits of $325,000,000 were made available to the Provisional Government for the purchase of supplies and munitions. Against these, cash advances of $187,729,750 were extended between July and November, constituting the principal of the Russian war debt to the United States Government.

But payments of money, professions of virtue, and praise for unity were insufficient to persuade the Russian populace that the Provisional Government could provide peace through victory. After the July Days, Ambassador Francis protested to Tereshchenko at the failure of the authorities to take more severe measures against the Bolshevik leaders. He felt certain that the execution of Lenin and Trotsky for treason would make everything right. He feared that Kerensky was "weak," but did what he could to persuade him to stay in office after being assured by Miliukov that Kerensky was Russia's only hope. President Wilson sent greetings on August 26 to the State Conference that Kerensky convoked in Moscow, expressing "confidence in the ultimate triumph of ideals of democracy and self-government against all enemies within and without." On October 9 the British, French, and Italian Ambassadors (whom Francis declined to join in this *démarche*) presented a note to the much-annoyed Kerensky, asking that the war be prosecuted more vigorously.

As he saw his political fortunes passing into the shadows, Kerensky sought to strengthen his position by summoning a Provisional Council of the Republic (the "Pre-Parliament") and by encouraging high hopes for the promised Inter-Allied conference to redefine war aims. When Balfour and Bonar Law indicated that the conference would not discuss the aims of the war but only the methods of conducting it, the supporters of the Provisional Government began to despair of solving their problems. The Bolshevik press exulted in this new "proof" that the Allied Governments were determined to pursue "capitalistic" and "imperialistic" objectives. In an Associated Press interview of November 1, Kerensky opined that Russia was exhausted. When the *Washington Post* published an abbreviated version of the interview under the headline "Russia Quits War," the State Department issued a denial: "There has been absolutely nothing in the dispatches received by the Department of State from Russia nor in information derived from any other source whatever to justify the impression . . . that Russia is out of the conflict. . . . Our own advices show that the Provisional Government in Petrograd is attacking with great energy the problems confronting it." Kerensky was overthrown seven days later. That the leaders of the Western democracies should have been so ill-informed regarding realities was an evil omen for their future relations with the Russian Revolution.[5]

Lenin had meanwhile exhibited his customary skill in facing facts, drawing correct conclusions from them, and devising a strategy appropriate to the occasion and to the temper of his followers and his enemies. From his hiding-place he continued to write articles and to keep in close touch with the Central Committee. Between August 8 and 16 the Party held its Sixth Congress in Petrograd. A decade had elapsed since Congress V. Lenin, fearing arrest, did not attend, but was elected honorary chairman and guided the discussions through Stalin, Sverdlov, Molotov, and Ordjonikidze. Party members now numbered 240,000. There were 157 voting delegates and

---

[5] The most detailed, definitive, and brilliant account of the confused processes of American policy-making in meeting the challenge of the Russian Revolution is to be found in *Soviet-American Relations, 1917–1920*, by George F. Kennan, of which the first of 3 volumes, *Russia Leaves the War* (Princeton University Press, 1956), traces in meticulous and fascinating detail the sequence of East-West interactions between midyear of 1917 and March 1918, all of which are merely outlined, with the benefit of Kennan's insights, in the ensuing pages of the present work.

128 others with no vote. They met in secret, first in the Viborg district and later in a school near the Narva Gate.

Congress VI was at once an evaluation of the July Days and a preparation for the October Revolution. The delegates accepted Stalin's view, which reflected Lenin's, that the slogan "All power to the Soviets!" must now be temporarily withdrawn so long as the Mensheviks and SR's controlled the Soviets. The new Party line was based on the proposition that power had passed from the Provisional Government to military reactionaries and Bonapartists, and that only an armed uprising of the proletariat, in alliance with the poorest peasants, could save the Revolution and achieve socialism. The Congress admitted to the Party the *Mezhrayontsi* or Centrists led by Trotsky and including Volodarsky and Uritsky. The preparation of a new Party program was again deferred, but new rules were adopted: "All Party organizations are organized on the principles of democratic centralism"; members must accept the program, belong to a local organization, obey all Party decisions, and pay dues of at least 1% of their wages; new members pay an initiation fee of 50 kopeks, are admitted by Party locals on the recommendation of two members and confirmed by the next general membership meeting of the local; those delinquent in dues for three months "without sufficient cause" are dropped; members may be expelled by a general meeting of the local, with appeal to the district or regional conference and, in the last resort, to the Party Congress; all locals pay 10% of dues and other receipts to the Central Committee; "regular Congresses are convened annually" and elect the Central Committee. . . .

The resolutions of Congress VI are a lament over the degradation of the Soviets under Menshevik and SR leadership and an open declaration of war against the Provisional Government. Allied "imperialists" and "bankers" are accused of conspiring with counterrevolutionists against the Russian people.

> The liquidation of imperialist domination puts before the working class of that country which shall first achieve the dictatorship of the proletarians and semi-proletarians the task of supporting by every means (including armed force) the struggling proletariat of the other countries. This problem will become especially urgent for Russia, if, as is quite probable, a new inevitable upsurge of the Russian Revolution places the workers and the poorest peas-

ants in power before the revolution takes place in the capitalist countries of the West. The sole means for a really democratic liquidation of the war is the conquest of power by the international proletariat, and in Russia the conquest of power by the workers and poorest peasants. . . . The Soviets are passing through agonizing torture, disintegrating because they failed to take State power into their own hands at the proper time. . . . The correct slogan at the present time can be only complete liquidation of the dictatorship of the counter-revolutionary bourgeoisie. Only the revolutionary proletariat, provided it is supported by the poorest peasantry, is strong enough to carry out this task, the task of a new upsurge. . . . The Party must take upon itself the role of front line fighter against counter-revolution. . . . The proletariat must not permit itself to be provoked by the bourgeoisie which is very anxious to provoke the proletariat at the present moment into premature battle. . . .

The "Kornilov affair" of September paved the way for the Party's seizure of power. General Lavr G. Kornilov, son of a Siberian Cossack, had been forced to relinquish his command of the Petrograd military district in April on the demand of the Soviet. After the July Days, Kerensky named him Commander-in-Chief of the Russian Armies as successor to Brussilov. At his insistence, the Government reintroduced capital punishment at the front and sought to restore discipline by combating Bolshevik propaganda and reducing the authority of the soldiers' committees. He addressed the State Conference in Moscow on August 27 and became the idol of all who thirsted after "law and order." In the words of his friend, General Anton Denikin: "Kornilov became a banner—for some of counter-revolution, for others of the salvation of the Motherland." This simple-minded soldier regarded Kerensky as a windbag and argued that all political problems could be solved by hanging Lenin and all the members of the Soviets. Through various leaks and indiscretions in a tragic comedy of errors, Kerensky was soon convinced, and with justification, that Kornilov was plotting his overthrow through a military occupation of the capital. On September 9 the Premier dismissed the General as Commander-in-Chief. Kornilov breathed defiance and was supported by most of the higher officers, including

General Denikin, on the southwestern front. But the temper of the troops was such that the officers could send no aid to the Commander-in-Chief. In Petrograd, Boris Savinkov, then in charge of the War Ministry, urged Kornilov to resign as a means toward reconciliation, while Paul Miliukov urged Kerensky to resign in favor of General Alexiev. On September 11 Sir George Buchanan, on behalf of the representatives of the Allied Powers and the USA, offered to "mediate" between Kerensky and Kornilov in the cause of "averting civil war."

Kerensky was saved by the support of those who, a few weeks later, would destroy him. The Soviet leaders demanded the suppression of the Kornilov movement and asked the Bolsheviks to join them against the common enemy in a "Committee for the Struggle with Counter-Revolution." The result was the recruiting and arming in the capital of some 25,000 workers, constituting a popular militia that revived the half-suppressed Red Guard of the Bolsheviks. Kerensky spurned Miliukov's advice. Tereshchenko rejected Buchanan's offer. Kornilov remained in Moghilev. His detachments melted away before they reached Petrograd in the face of the energetic propaganda and military preparation of the new Committee. General Krymov, one of Kornilov's aides, committed suicide after Kerensky accused him of mutiny. Another aide, the Don Cossack Ataman Kaledin, sought safety in Novocherkassk. Kerensky assumed the post of Commander-in-Chief on September 12. Kornilov, Denikin, and their co-conspirators were arrested in Moghilev. Their movement collapsed without bloodshed. Kerensky presently released them, suspecting that he might soon need the aid of the Right against the Left. In reality, he was now the helpless prisoner of his saviors. The workers of Petrograd retained their arms. The sailors of the Baltic fleet denounced the Premier. Within a week the Bolsheviks for the first time secured a majority in the city Soviets of Petrograd and Moscow. Many provincial Soviets displayed a similar trend. Trotsky, who had been released from prison on September 17, was elected President of the Petrograd Soviet on October 8.

Lenin, still in hiding, decided early in September to go to Finland. Wearing a wig, bearing a worker's passport, and disguised as a fireman, he crossed the border on a locomotive. He lived for a time at Yalkala and then in Helsinki. Early in October he moved to Viborg. Not until October 22 did he return to the capital. But he remained the master strategist of the Party during his seclusion and

found time in Helsinki to write six chapters of a book that he had sketched out in Switzerland. These pages were not published until 1918 and were never completed because, as he said in a postscript, "it is more pleasant and useful to go through the 'experience of the revolution' than to write about it." But they still remain, a generation later, one of the most illuminating expositions of the political gospel of the ruling Party of the USSR. A few excerpts will suggest, however inadequately, the thesis of these chapters which Lenin entitled *State and Revolution: Marxist Teaching about the Theory of the State and the Tasks of the Proletariat in the Revolution:*

> The replacement of the bourgeois by the proletarian State is impossible without a violent revolution. The abolition of the proletarian State, i.e., of all States, is only possible through "withering away." . . . The proletariat needs State power, the centralized organization of force, the organization of violence, both for the purpose of crushing the resistance of the exploiters and for the purpose of *guiding* the great mass of the population—the peasantry, the petty-bourgeoisie, the semi-proletarians—in the work of organizing Socialist economy. By educating a workers' party, Marxism educates the vanguard of the proletariat, capable of assuming power and of *leading the whole people* to Socialism, of directing and organizing the new order, of being the teacher, guide and leader of all the toiling and exploited in the task of building up their social life without the bourgeoisie and against the bourgeoisie. . . . The form of bourgeois States are exceeding variegated, but their essence is the same: in one way or another, all these States are in the last analysis inevitably *a dictatorship of the bourgeoisie.* The transition from capitalism to Communism will certainly bring a great variety and abundance of political forms, but the essence will inevitably be only one: *the dictatorship of the proletariat.* . . .
>
> We set ourselves the ultimate aim of destroying the State, i.e., every organized and systematic violence, every use of violence against man in general. We do not expect the advent of an order of society in which the principle of subordination of minority to majority will not be observed. But, striving for Socialism, we are convinced that it will develop into Communism; that, side by side with this,

there will vanish all need for force, for the *subjection* of one man to another, and of one part of the population to another, since people will *grow accustomed* to observing the elementary conditions of social existence *without force and without subjection.* . . . The State will be able to wither away completely when society has realized the rule: "From each according to his ability; to each according to his needs," i.e., when people have become accustomed to observe the fundamental rules of social life, and their labor is so productive that they voluntarily work *according to their ability.* . . . What is generally called Socialism was termed by Marx the "first" or lower phase of Communist society. Insofar as the means of production become *public* property, the word "Communism" is also applicable here, providing we do not forget that it is *not* full Communism. . . .

3. RED REVOLUTION

KERENSKY felt his political support slipping out from under his feet and the rope of proletarian revolt tightening around his neck. He clutched at the device of summoning a "Democratic Conference" in Petrograd (September 27), composed of representatives of the Soviets, the co-operatives, the trade unions, and local legislative bodies. The delegates voted first in favor of a new coalition government, then in favor of excluding the Cadets, and finally against any coalition. On October 8 Kerensky revamped his Cabinet, in which posts were now awarded to the industrialists Konovalov and Tretyakov. The futile Democratic Conference was followed by the formation of a "Council of the Republic," including propertied and non-Socialist elements and intended to serve as a consultative "Pre-Parliament" pending the meeting of the often postponed Constituent Assembly. The Council assembled in Marinsky Palace. On Lenin's orders, the Bolshevik delegates walked out on the opening day, October 20. Real power—ability to command the masses—resided neither in Marinsky Palace nor in the Winter Palace, where the Ministers met. Its new locus was Smolny Institute. Here in bare classrooms and assembly halls the RSDLP (B) had set up new headquarters. Here also were the officers of the Petrograd Soviet.

Lenin told the Central Committee that the Party, now in control of the Petrograd and Moscow Soviets, must take power immediately by organizing an armed insurrection. "To delay is a crime. To await the Congress of the Soviets [the Second Congress of Workers' and Soldiers Deputies] is a shameful play at formality, treachery to the Revolution. . . ." To the objections that the Party could not retain power, he wrote that the 240,000 members could govern Russia in the interest of the poor against the rich as easily as 130,000 landlords had governed after 1905 in the interest of the rich against the poor. Lenin's call was voted down. He argued and stormed and asked to be allowed to resign from the Central Committee. He was still in hiding, living after October 20, when he returned to the capital, in a large workers' tenement building in the Viborg district in the apartment of Marguerita Fofanova, an ardent Bolshevik. A dozen members of the Central Committee gathered in secret at Sukhanov's apartment on the evening of October 23 to meet the leader whose advice they had thus far resisted. Lenin reproached them for waiting. After an all-night discussion, relieved by tea and sandwiches, they passed a resolution by a vote of 10 to 2, declaring that "armed insurrection is inevitable and the time is quite ripe for it." A Political Bureau of seven was chosen: Lenin, Stalin, Trotsky, Sokolnikov, Bubnov, Zinoviev, and Kamenev.[6]

There was controversy in the inner circle as to the best date for the uprising. Despite the resolution, controversy also continued as to whether the insurrection should be attempted at all. Kamenev and Zinoviev were the two who had voted against the majority. They now appealed to the Party against Lenin's view, arguing that an uprising would probably fail and that the Party should await the Constituent Assembly. They reiterated their objections on October 29 at a Party conference, which voted 19 to 2 in favor of Lenin's resolution for "intensified preparation for an armed uprising."

Russia's "ten days that shook the world" were, for the participants at the time, less a self-conscious exercise in "the science of revolution" than a period of confusion, wrangling, heart-searching, fa-

---

[6] Forty years later only one of these seven was still alive. In 1956 Andrei Bubnov, aged 72 and one of the few survivors of Stalin's purge of the "Old Bolsheviks," was rehabilitated and released from prison, to which he had been sentenced in 1937 as "an enemy of the people" (Moscow UP dispatch, March 21, 1956). The classic account of the events of the October Revolution in Petrograd is still John Reed: *Ten Days That Shook the World* (International Publishers, 1919), suppressed in Russia by Stalin, because it contained no mention of his name, but republished in the USSR in 1957.

naticism, skepticism, mistakes, and sheer luck, good and bad, all jumbled into a chaos of words and deeds out of which, somehow, Lenin and his aides ultimately evolved the strategy of victory. The shape of the chaos and the unfolding of the strategy have many times been portrayed in day-by-day, hour-by-hour, and almost minute-by-minute accounts.

In the issue of October 31 of Gorky's journal, *Novaya Zhizn*, Zinoviev and Kamenev denounced, and thereby publicly revealed, the plans of the Bolshevik Central Committee to seize power. Lenin called this a "crime" and demanded that such "strikebreakers" be expelled from the Party. Stalin in *Rabochii Put* offered excuses for them and sponsored reconciliation. On November 3 the Central Committee accepted Kamenev's resignation and warned him and Zinoviev against further breaches of discipline, but did not press Lenin's plea for expulsion from the Party. When Trotsky denounced Stalin, along with the two dissenters, the Georgian offered to resign from the editorial board of the paper where his piece had appeared. The Central Committee rejected his offer and dropped the issue. The incident was the first clash between Stalin and Trotsky since the latter had joined the Bolsheviks.

Despite such wrangles, the crucial decisions, at least in retrospect, were few and simple. The Second All-Russian Congress of Soviets of Workers' and Soldiers' Deputies was originally scheduled to meet on November 3 and then deferred to November 7—October 25 by the old Russian calendar. It was soon apparent that the Bolsheviks would have a majority of the delegates, since most of the local Soviets of workers and soldiers (although not yet of the peasants) had moved away from the Mensheviks and SR's into the Bolshevik camp. The Bolsheviks' slogan once more was "All power to the Soviets!" The Petrograd Soviet in Smolny established a "Military Revolutionary Committee," consisting of 4 Anarchists, 14 Left SR's, and 48 Bolsheviks. The function of the MRC was ostensibly to safeguard the Revolution against its enemies and actually to plan and lead the insurrection.

Each contestant—the Ministers of the Provisional Government on the one side, the Soviet and Bolshevik leaders on the other—sought to depict the other as the aggressor. The Government's effort to move the Bolshevized Petrograd garrison to the front was resisted, as was its project of moving the capital to Moscow. On October 30 the harassed Premier told John Reed that "the Russian people are suffering from economic fatigue and from disillusionment

with the Allies. The world thinks that the Russian Revolution is at an end. Do not be mistaken. The Russian Revolution is just beginning. . . ."

On November 3 Lenin urged that the blow be struck on November 7 in order that power could be transferred forthwith to the Soviet Congress. The 4th was the "Day of the Petrograd Soviet"—an occasion for gigantic parades and mass meetings at which Bolshevik orators pledged their frenzied auditors to come out in the streets in support of the Soviet power when the signal should be given. On the same day the MRC, whose guiding spirits included Trotsky, Antonov-Ovseenko, Podvoisky, and Chudnovsky, told the soldiers of the garrison that no orders addressed to them should be deemed valid unless they bore the Committee's signature. This was a major challenge to Kerensky. The Ministers concluded that they must reply or at once lose all respect and all possibility of retaining power.

The bulk of the populace, the soldiers of the garrison, and the sailors of the fleet all obeyed the MRC of the Petrograd Soviet, though the Soviet power was not yet vested with the magic of the State. They looked with contempt on the Ministers in the Winter Palace, who were masters of a magic that had lost its efficacy. The Ministers were obeyed only by a few policemen, by the yunkers or student officers, and by scattered detachments of troops. Their efforts to summon reinforcements from the provinces and the front were as vain as their attempts to send the disloyal local troops out of the capital. The soldiers summoned refused to come. The soldiers ordered out refused to depart.

On the evening of November 5 the Cabinet decided to suppress the Bolshevik newspapers, to arrest the members of the Petrograd Soviet and its MRC, and to call in troops from the suburbs. At 5:30 a.m. of November 6 a commissioner, backed by a detachment of yunkers, appeared at a printing plant where two Bolshevik papers were issued. He confiscated 8,000 copies, broke up the type plates, and put a seal on the door. Shortly afterward the crew of the cruiser *Aurora* received an order to put out to sea. The MRC at once sent Red Guards to reopen the printing plant and ordered the *Aurora* to remain in the Neva estuary. The sailors obeyed. The printing of the papers was resumed. The MRC commanded the garrison to mobilize on a war footing to defend the Petrograd Soviet and to await further orders.

Kerensky, having no other means of asserting his authority,

went to Marinsky Palace later in the day and made a speech to the Council of the Republic. He spoke like a prosecuting attorney marshaling evidence against the defense:

> Ulianov-Lenin, a State criminal . . . has invited the proletariat and the Petrograd garrison . . . to immediate insurrection. Particularly should be noticed the activity of the present President of the Petrograd Soviet, Bronstein-Trotsky. . . . Given the state of mind of the masses, any movement at Petrograd will be followed by the most terrible massacres which will cover with eternal shame the name of free Russia. . . . I place myself at the point of view of the Right, and I propose immediately to proceed to an investigation and make the necessary arrests. . . . Those who have dared to lift their hands against the free will of the Russian people must be liquidated with precision! . . . Let the population of Petrograd understand that it will encounter a firm power.

The hall was an uproar as Kerensky, pale and perspiring, departed. Gotz, for the SR's, denounced the Bolshevik policy as criminal, but also denounced Kerensky for doing nothing about land and peace. Martov, for the Mensheviks, condemned the Premier for insulting the populace. The Left carried its motion, demanding "a decree transmitting the land to the peasants' Land Committee . . . and an energetic course of action abroad in proposing to the Allies a proclamation of peace terms and a beginning of peace parleys." Kerensky, hoping for a vote of confidence, regarded the motion as an expression of lack of confidence. He threatened to resign and complained bitterly to Gotz, Dan, and Avksentiev, President of the Council. They asserted that no criticism of the Government was intended. . . .

Later in the day (November 6) the Bolshevik Central Committee met again to plan the uprising. Zinoviev and Lenin were not present. Lenin sent a message through Marguerita Fofanova urging the seizure of power at once. But he now decided to move to Smolny. He put on a wig and proceeded to his destination. Krupskaya followed him that evening. They moved into a small room on the second floor of the Institute building. Years later the room became a museum where visitors could still see the desk and chair where Lenin worked for some weeks, and the small iron bedstead (behind

a partition) where he slept, with an identical bedstead for his wife. That night, in accordance with the plans elaborated by Antonov-Ovseenko, Podvoisky, and Chudnovsky, the troops of the MRC occupied two of the railway stations, the Nikolai Bridge, the State Bank, and the Central Telephone Exchange. There was no resistance and no disorder. The MRC overestimated the resources of the Government and deferred the attempt to occupy the Winter Palace, awesome citadel of the vanished power of the Tsardom, until the belated arrival of the sailors from Kronstadt.

The morning of November 7 cured Kerensky of his last illusions. At 10 o'clock the MRC proclaimed the overthrow of his Government. At about the same hour he departed for the front in his touring car, followed (as an added assurance of safe passage) by a car from the U.S. Embassy flying the American flag and placed at his disposal by Ambassador Francis. Konovalov became Acting Premier —for a few hours. Shortly after noon, troops of the MRC surrounded the Marinsky Palace and told the members of the Council of the Republic to go home. They obeyed under protest. That afternoon Lenin made his first public appearance since July. He addressed the Petrograd Soviet at Smolny: "Comrades, the workers' and peasants' revolution, which the Bolsheviks always said must come, has been achieved. . . ." Peace would be made and land would be granted to the peasants. "Long live the world socialist revolution!"

Not until early evening was a demand presented for the surrender of the Winter Palace. No reply was forthcoming from the huge and somber red-painted building. At 9 p.m. the cruiser *Aurora* began firing blank shells. (This venerable vessel, commissioned in 1902, is still to be seen today anchored at its original station near the Kirov Bridge and used as a training ship and museum.) Soldiers and sailors in Palace Square (to be renamed Uritsky Square, but today Palace Square once more) opened fire with rifles and machine guns. A few windows were broken. The defenders were a handful of yunkers and the Women's Battalion. Several girls made a sortie and were captured. Three were alleged to have been raped. One killed herself after conceding "disappointment in her ideals." None of the defenders was slain. Of the attackers, one soldier and five sailors were killed and a few others wounded. Red Guards entered the Palace and persuaded the inmates to yield. Wearing a floppy hat and a pince-nez, Antonov-Ovseenko arrested the Ministers and escorted them to the Peter-Paul Fortress, where they were soon freed.

Bloodshed, arson, and terror were all conspicuous by their absence. Soviet Russia was born and the Provisional Government died with a calm casualness that was anti-climactic. There was no struggle because the Government had almost literally no supporters. Almost everybody hailed the new revolution. Those who did not had no program, no hope, no confidence, and no desire whatever to risk their skins on behalf of a political vacuum.

Meanwhile, the Second Congress of Soviets met in the great hall on the lower floor of Smolny at 10:45 in the evening of November 7. Kamenev was President. The Mensheviks and Right SR's protested at the day's events. Abramovich, leader of the Bund, angrily declared that his group would leave the Congress. Trotsky shouted that they were "so much refuse that will be swept into the garbage-can of history." The protestants withdrew to the city Duma and helped to form an anti-Soviet "Committee for the Salvation of the Country and the Revolution"—which accomplished nothing. The Congress adjourned at 6 a.m. It reassembled on the evening of November 8. For the first time Lenin appeared. He was, in John Reed's words, "a short, stocky figure, with a big head set down in his shoulders, bald and bulging. Little eyes, a snubbish nose, wide, generous mouth, and heavy chin: clean-shaven now, but already beginning to bristle with the well-known beard of his past and future. Dressed in shabby clothes, his trousers much too long for him. Unimpressive, to be the idol of a mob, loved and revered as perhaps few leaders in history have been . . ."

Some moments of confusion, occasioned by the goings and comings of a few Bundists and Menshevik Internationalists who could not decide whether to depart or remain, were followed by an ovation to Lenin. When it ceased, he spoke in a hoarse voice, simply and with no gestures: "We shall now proceed to construct the Socialist order. . . . The first thing is the adoption of practical measures to realize peace. . . ." He read a "Proclamation to the Peoples of All the Belligerent Countries," proposing immediate negotiations for a "just and democratic peace," without annexations or indemnities, to be preceded by a three-month general armistice. "This proposal," said Lenin, "will meet with resistance on the part of the imperialist governments—we don't fool ourselves on that score. But we hope that revolution will soon break out in all the belligerent countries. . . ." All spokesmen of all groups expressed approval. The vote was unanimous. Delegates rose to their feet. "The war is

ended! The war is ended!" exclaimed a workman to John Reed. A thousand voices chanted the "International":

> Arise, ye prisoners of starvation! Arise, ye wretched of the earth! For justice thunders condemnation, a better world's in birth. No more tradition's chain shall bind you. Arise, ye slaves! No more in thrall. The world shall rise on new foundations. You have been naught: you shall be all. . . .

After the singing of the Funeral March for the revolutionary dead, Lenin, with a sure political instinct, read a Decree on Land, abolishing without compensation all private ownership of land and transferring all estates and all Crown and Church holdings to the Land Committees and peasant Soviets "until the Constituent Assembly meets." After a confused discussion and a long recess, the Decree was put to a vote. Only one member voted against it. At 2:30 a.m. Kamenev read a Decree on the Constitution of Power. Lenin had discussed with Trotsky what the new Cabinet should be called. "From persecution and a life underground, to come so suddenly into power. . . . It makes the head swim! . . . What shall we call them? Anything but Ministers . . ." Trotsky had suggested Commissars and then Peoples' Commissars and finally a Soviet of Peoples' Commissars "The Soviet of Peoples' Commissars?" commented Lenin. "Splendid! Smells terribly of revolution!" The Decree listed the new Soviet of Peoples' Commissars, or Sovnarkom. Since the Left SR's were as yet unwilling to take posts, all the members were Bolsheviks:

President of the Council: Lenin
Foreign Affairs: Trotsky
Nationalities: Stalin
Interior: A. E. Rykov
Agriculture: V. P. Miliutin
Labor: A. G. Schliapnikov
Military and Naval Affairs—
a committee composed of
V. A. Antonov-Ovseenko,
N. V. Krylenko, and F. M.
Dybenko

Commerce and Industry: V. P. Nogin
Popular Education: A. V. Lunacharsky
Finance: E. E. Skvortsov (Stepanov)
Justice: G. E. Oppokov (Lomov)
Supplies: E. A. Teodorovitch
Post and Telegraph: N. P. Avilov (Gliebov)
Railroads: To be filled later

The debate that followed gave rise to protests and expressions of anxiety. Voices were raised for a coalition of all socialist groups. Warnings were issued that a general peace would prove impossible, that the outcome would be an Entente-German peace against Russia or a separate German-Russian peace. Trotsky was defiant: "Coalition doesn't always add to strength. . . . There are only two alternatives: either the Russian Revolution will create a revolutionary movement in Europe, or the European Powers will destroy the Russian Revolution!" The Decree was carried by a large majority. The delegates adjourned *sine die* and departed shortly before dawn to carry the tidings all over the land.

A brief and half-hearted clash between Kerensky's troops and the Red Guards southwest of the capital (November 12–14) clinched the Bolshevik victory and sent the former Premier into flight and exile. A yunker revolt in the capital was bloodily suppressed at the same time, with some 200 dead. In Moscow severe street fighting for control of the Kremlin took 500 lives and ended in Red triumph. Throughout the length and breadth of the realm the transition to Soviet rule was effected swiftly and with little disorder. The ease with which the Provisional Government vanished and the new rulers secured themselves in power was as surprising to the Party as to Kerensky's demoralized supporters and to the outside world.

CHAPTER FOUR

The First War of East and West

1. "THE DICTATORSHIP OF THE PROLETARIAT"

DURING ITS first 40 years the regime established in Russia by the October Revolution was "at war," less or more, with Western Powers for all or part of 15 years and in a state of "peaceful coexistence," more or less, with the West for 25 years. This calculus assumes that the "Cold War," difficult to date as to initiation or termination, may be regarded as having been well under way by 1947 and as having sharply diminished in intensity with the signing of the Korean armistice in 1953. Since this third encounter involved no fighting by Russian armed forces, even though Soviet-Western relations were anything but "peaceful," some readers may prefer to change the preceding figures to 8 years of war and 32 years of "peace." The second encounter, 1941–5, was the bloodiest and most destructive military conflict during a comparable span of time in all the gory annals of human violence. The first encounter, 1918–20, is our immediate concern, for it followed hard upon the Revolution and shaped decisively the design of the new State at home and the pattern of its relations with other States abroad.

The question of who first opened war upon whom is here peculiarly complex. The armed violence of 1918 was, as we shall see, initiated by the decision of Western policy-makers to embark upon blockade, invasion, and intervention in Russia in the hope (though motives were mixed to the point of total confusion) of "strangling at birth," in Churchill's later phrase, the menace of a Communism come to power for the first time in one of the "Great Powers."

Yet the menace was a reality and not a myth. Revolutionary Marxism had "declared war" on all bourgeois governments as long ago as 1847. Lenin and his comrades had been summoning the "proletariat" to destroy all "capitalist" regimes in 1916, 1915, 1914, and indeed long before. Once they had come to power in Russia, their appeals became more shrill, though couched in terms of revolution, which their dogma told them was "inevitable," rather than invasion, which the power at their disposal was wholly inadequate to launch. Their image of the world, seen through Marxist-Leninist lenses, convinced them that their own retention of power and their very survival depended upon the early advent of "world revolution." Their messianic duty was to hasten the inevitable, since its failure to materialize was equated with death. The policy-makers of the Western Powers, thus threatened with doom, so acted in the end, quite understandably, as to confirm the catastrophic convictions of the Marxist fanatics who had seized power in Muscovy. Had either side responded differently to the challenge posed by the other, the outcome of their early contacts would assuredly have been different, though no one now can say how or in what respects or whether for better or for worse.

Our task is to review the record of what men did, not of what they might have done. And in explanation, if not in justification, of Western responses to the Communist conspiracy, it is well to note at the outset the acts of the Commissars which persuaded Western statesmen that no coexistence with such a regime was possible. When the Allies failed to respond to Trotsky's overtures for general peace negotiations, he published, out of the Tsarist archives, the "secret treaties" of 1915–16, which even the most casual reader could interpret as meaning that the sanctimonious "war to end war" and "make the world safe for democracy" was in fact a war for markets, spheres of influence, annexations, and the other customary stakes of diplomacy of "capitalistic" power politics. The Commissars, moreover, formally repudiated (February 8, 1918) the war debts and pre-war obligations to foreign creditors, public and private, of previous Russian regimes. They also decreed the confiscation of all foreign-owned properties and investments as part of their program of "expropriating the bourgeoisie."

What most infuriated Western politicians was the constant Bolshevik appeal for global social revolution. Long before the Bolshevik seizure of power, such appeals had been made by anti-Bolshevik

Russian socialists. On March 27, 1917, a dozen days after the abdication of the Tsar and a score of days before Lenin's return, the Petrograd Soviet, in which Bolsheviks were then negligible, issued a proclamation calling for revolution in other countries as the only way to peace. "Proletarians of all countries, unite!" (*Izvestia*, March 28, 1917.) On May 14, 1917, M. I. Skobelev, then a Menshevik and later Minister of Labor in the Provisional Government, told the Petrograd Soviets that peace depended upon general revolution. A resolve, unanimously adopted with the Bolsheviks abstaining, denounced the "imperialists of all countries" and declared that "the Russian Revolution is not only a national revolution; it is the first stage of the world revolution which will end the baseness of war and bring peace to all mankind." [1]

Such subversive views, widely shared among all Russian socialists in 1917, were, for the Bolsheviks, meat and drink. *Pravda* declared on November 19, 1917:

> The army of the Russian Revolution derives its strength from countless reserves. The oppressed nations of Asia are as eager for the fall of the regime of capitalistic oppression as are the oppressed proletarian masses of Europe. To fuse these forces in a world revolution against the imperialistic bourgeoisie is the historic mission of the Workers' and Peasants' Russia. The flame of the Petrograd November Revolution will inevitably grow into a fiery hurricane that will strike to the ground the sword of this piratic war and turn the dominion of capital to ashes.

Early in December 1917 the Sovnarkom appropriated two million rubles "for the needs of the revolutionary internationalist movement, at the disposition of the foreign representatives of the Commissariat of Foreign Affairs." Such initial candor, later obscured behind a veil of dissimulation, was both refreshing and alarming to the West—although, paradoxically, early Soviet efforts to promote world revolution (through a "Bureau of International Revolutionary Propaganda," headed by Boris Reinstein of Buffalo, New York, aided by two other Americans, John Reed and Albert Rhys Williams) were publicly subsidized by the United States Treasury and pri-

---

[1] For these and other early appeals, see *Russian-American Relations*, edited by C. K. Cumming and W. W. Pettit (League of Free Nations Association, New York, 1920), pp. 7 f.

vately subsidized by millionaire William V. Judson in the hope of fostering revolt in Germany. On the larger stage of world affairs, despite this ambivalence, it was soon clear to the West that the new rulers of Russia were dangerous madmen. Who but lunatics would repudiate State debts, confiscate foreign property, and summon the "workers of the world" to destroy law and order everywhere? How to deal with such madmen, or, preferably, how to consign them to asylums or cemeteries was a problem that Western statesmanship never quite solved.

Lenin's new government during the first phase of the Soviet regime was a blend of expediency with the somewhat vague directives supplied by Marx, Engels, the Paris Commune, the earlier Soviets, and the precepts of *The State and Revolution.* The Bolsheviks claimed no monopoly of legality. The first Sovnarkom consisted exclusively of Bolsheviks. But the new Central Executive Committee chosen by the Second Congress of Soviets on the night of November 8–9 consisted of 61 Bolsheviks, 29 Left Socialist Revolutionaries, 6 Menshevik Internationalists, 3 Ukrainian Socialists, 5 peasant representatives, 2 Navy men, 1 trade-union spokesman, and 3 unaffiliated members. This CEC, like the Sovnarkom, was tentative, since the question of an All-Socialist coalition was unsettled. This became the burning political issue of the following weeks.

Amid much wrangling, there were almost no supporters for the idea of a one-party government. On November 14 (cf. *Izvestia,* November 15, 1917) the Bolsheviks asked an accord with other socialist groups on the basis of acceptance of the decrees on peace, land, and workers' control, and responsibility of the Sovnarkom to the CEC and of an enlarged CEC to the Soviet Congress. The Right SR's repudiated the *coup d'état* of November 7 and broke off negotiations. The Mensheviks held that agreement with the Bolsheviks was impossible save on condition of the release of political prisoners and restoration of civil liberties. Many Bolsheviks shared these views. Some resigned from the Sovnarkom and demanded a coalition of all parties on the ground that "a purely Bolshevik government can maintain itself only by political terror." On November 17 Kamenev, Zinoviev, Rykov, Nogin, and Miliutin took the extreme step of resigning from the Bolshevik Central Committee. A. Lozovsky denounced the majority of the Committee for trying to establish an arbitrary and undemocratic regime. Lenin threatened the dissent-

ers with expulsion from the Party. The always vacillating Zinoviev recanted, with the others later following suit. Lozovsky continued to protest and was expelled from the Party in January 1918 but re-admitted in the following year.

This intra-Party crisis was resolved only with the creation of a quasi-coalition regime. Inconclusive negotiations in Petrograd were paralleled by secret but futile efforts on the part of Victor Chernov, one of the founders of the SR's, to form a rival government at Moghilev, HQ of the *Stavka* or Army General Staff, in collaboration with military groups and the railwaymen's union. On the summons of the Left SR's, a special Congress of Peasant Soviets met in Petro-grad, November 23–December 8. Maria Spiridonova was elected chairman. The members included 195 Left SR's, 65 Right SR's, and 37 Bolsheviks. Almost all favored an all-socialist coalition. But quar-rels among the SR factions precluded this solution. On November 28 the Left SR's reached an agreement with the Bolsheviks, as did the railwaymen's union. The land decree of November 8 was approved by the Congress. The Peasant Soviets were united with the Workers' and Soldiers' Soviets. Four leaders of the Left SR's—Spiridonova, A. L. Kolegayev, A. Proshyan, and I. Z. Steinburg—became members of the Sovnarkom. The new Cabinet or Council of Peoples' Commis-sars thus remained an all-Bolshevik body for only three weeks. That the coalition was not broader was due to the refusal of the Right SR's and the Mensheviks to participate.

This regime was a species of non-dictatorial dictatorship. The elected Soviet deputies continued to meet in regular session, with the Third Congress convening in January 1918, the Fourth in March, and the Fifth in July. Neither the Sovnarkom nor the CEC "dic-tated" to local authorities. All over the vast expanse of Russia, power was exercised by local Soviets. On December 20, 1917, the Cheka (*Chrezvychainaya Komissiya*) or "Extraordinary Commission to Combat Counter-Revolution, Sabotage, and Speculation" was brought into being by a decree of the Sovnarkom and organized by Felix Djerzhinsky as a new political police. During the next six months it arrested a few thousand persons and executed an uncer-tain number, estimated at 884 by the bitterly anti-Bolshevik S. P. Melgunov in his book *The Red Terror in Russia* (London, 1926) and at 22 by Martin Latsis, himself a member of the Cheka. In any case, contrary to the impression that soon became current in the West, the Soviet Government between November and June, 1917–18, estab-

lished itself and pursued its program with less violence and with far fewer victims than any other social revolutionary regime in human annals.

During this period the practical meaning of the time-honored Marxist slogan of a "dictatorship of the proletariat," as defined and implemented by the Bolsheviks, was not that the Party alone should rule. At the Seventh Congress of the Party, held in March 1918, this conception was clarified. The Party name was changed from "RSDLP (B)" to "Russian Communist Party (Bolshevik)." It was decided to move the capital to Moscow. Here also further steps were taken toward a new Party program. The draft resolution asserted that "there can be no question of freedom for the bourgeoisie. . . . The Party must mercilessly suppress all attempts of the bourgeoisie to return to power. And this is what is meant by a dictatorship of the proletariat."

In practice most "bourgeois" newspapers were suppressed and most "bourgeois" meetings were forbidden, while all socialist groups, so long as they were not anti-Soviet, carried on their activities with a minimum of interference. Although determined to socialize all means of production, Lenin had no desire to deprive the propertied classes of their liberty or their lives so long as there was hope of enlisting their cooperation. The Party sought to persuade bankers, manufacturers, bureaucrats, engineers, and even landlords—all who had exercised managerial functions in the old society—to become salaried officials in the new order. Land was "nationalized" as a means of meeting peasant demands. In most factories and stores a loose and chaotic form of "workers' control" was instituted. But there was no sweeping nationalization of business property. By mid-May of 1918 only 304 plants had been nationalized, mainly in mining and heavy industry. Even foreign trade remained in private hands until April 22, 1918, when it was made a State monopoly. Lenin moved slowly toward socialism, hoping to lessen the cost in the initial disruption of production and distribution and to "liquidate the bourgeoisie as a class" by absorbing its members peaceably into the new bureaucracy. That he failed does not change the fact that the Soviet regime, within the limits of its ultimate goals, was at first characterized more by patience, moderation, and muddling than by the intolerance and ruthlessness associated with totalitarian tyranny.

The one action of the Soviet power during these months which

could be deemed arbitrary and dictatorial was the suppression of the Constituent Assembly. The great expectations of many decades seemed near to realization when delegates were finally elected on November 25, 1917, under a decree of the Sovnarkom signed by Lenin on November 9. Bolshevik candidates won a majority of the ballots cast in Petrograd, Moscow, and other urban centers. But in the country as a whole the Party elected only 175 representatives out of a total of 707, while the Left SR's elected 40. The Cadets secured 17 members, the Mensheviks 16, and the Right SR's 370. The election was thus an overwhelming popular endorsement of socialism but a heavy defeat for the Bolsheviks and Left SR's at the hands of those who were unreconciled to the October Revolution and the Soviet regime. The Party leaders showed no enthusiasm for permitting the Assembly to convene on the day originally set: December 11. When the day brought street demonstrations, the Sovnarkom accused the Cadets of plotting a coup, declared them "enemies of the people," and ordered the arrest of their leaders. Bolshevik plans to delay or dissolve the Assembly led some of the SR's to concoct feeble plots against the Sovnarkom, which, in turn, strengthened Bolshevik determination to insist that the Assembly must recognize the Soviets as the basis of the new State.

Despite military intimidation, accompanied by street riots and bloodshed, the deputies gathered in Tauride Palace on January 18, 1918, and defied Bolshevik threats. Had they yielded to the demand that a new charter of governance should be founded on the Soviets, things to come would have perhaps proved more favorable for the survival of democratic values, since the Bolshevik leaders at this stage were hoping for an all-socialist coalition Soviet regime. The deputies refused to yield.

Victor Chernov, leader of the Right SR's, was chosen chairman. Various resolutions approved the land decree, the demand for an immediate democratic peace, and certain other acts of the Sovnarkom. While Lenin sat in the gallery, telling Albert Rhys Williams how he should study Russian, the deputies rejected, 237 to 136, the proposition that the new constitution should accept the Soviets as the basis of government. At 1 a.m. the Bolshevik and Left SR deputies withdrew. At 5 a.m. a sailor in charge of the Red Guards policing the Palace asked the chairman to close the meeting on the ground that the Guards were sleepy. Adjournment was voted to the evening of January 19.

In the morning, however, the Sovnarkom proposed dissolution. The Left SR's proposed new elections or the establishment of a revolutionary convention. The issue was referred to the CEC which voted simple dissolution after hearing a two-hour speech by Lenin (*Izvestia*, January 20, 1918):

> The transition from a capitalistic to a socialistic structure of society must necessarily be accompanied by a long and stubborn struggle. . . . There will be all sorts of errors and blunders . . . [but] the Soviets have started us on a road which is leading the people to the building of a new life. . . . The transfer of all power to the Constituent Assembly is nothing but the old policy of "conciliation" with the malevolent bourgeoisie. . . . As long as the slogan "All Power to the Constituent Assembly" is used to cloak the slogan "Down with the Soviet Power," so long will there be no escape from civil war, for we will not give up the Soviet power for anything in the world! . . . The Constituent Assembly, which failed to recognize the power of the people, is now dispersed by the will of the Soviet power. . . . The Soviet Republic will triumph, no matter what happens.

The deputies were not molested. N. D. Avksentiev, Right SR deputy, was already under arrest, however, along with several of his colleagues and most of the Cadet delegation. The dissolution was not without violence. Two Cadet deputies, Shingarev and Kokoshin, were murdered in their beds by a mob of sailors in the Marinsky Hospital—a deed strongly condemned by *Izvestia* as "a blot on the honor of the Revolution." Several more lives were lost when a crowd, bearing banners inscribed "All power to the Constituent Assembly," was fired upon by Red Guards as it tried to reach Tauride Palace. Maxim Gorky compared the incident to "Bloody Sunday" and bitterly denounced the "Peoples' Commissars" for "crushing Russian democracy, destroying the conquests of the revolution."

These events were followed by the Third All-Russian Congress of Soviets, which adopted the first Soviet Constitution and formally made the Soviets the permanent political basis of the revolutionary State. No popular support of the Constituent Assembly materialized. Had the Right SR's accepted the Soviets and offered to enter the Sovnarkom, the "dictatorship of the proletariat" might well have become a broad-based coalition. It now remained a Bolshevik-Left SR

coalition. When this liaison was later dissolved, all the foes of the Bolsheviks, socialists and anti-socialists alike, took up arms against the Soviet power and thereby transformed it into the dictatorship of the Communist Party. This transition was less a consequence of irreconcilable differences over domestic questions than of the Peace of Brest-Litovsk.

2. BETWEEN TWO FOES

THE new rulers of a war-weary land were from the outset preoccupied with the peace they had promised to achieve, for without peace no regime in Russia could long endure. The proposal of November 8 for a three-month armistice and negotiation of a general settlement elicited no replies from abroad. On December 3 negotiations for a separate peace were opened in Brest-Litovsk between a delegation of the Central Powers, headed by General Max von Hoffmann, and a Soviet delegation that included Joffe, Kamenev, Sokolnikov, and Karakhan, all fated to die by violence. An armistice was signed on December 15. In the bargaining for a treaty, Trotsky resisted the demands of Hoffmann, Richard von Kühlmann, and Count Ottokar von Czernim and broke off discussions on February 10, declaring that his government would sign no such pact as the enemy proposed but regarded the war as ended. This formula of "no peace, no war" proved futile. German armies resumed hostilities on February 18, seized Dvinsk, penetrated the Ukraine, and moved toward Petrograd. On February 23, 1918 (later celebrated as the birthday of the "Red Army"), hastily gathered Soviet forces halted the foe at Pskov and Narva. But the Commissars were militarily helpless. In the face of new German threats, Lenin insisted on capitulation: "To carry on a revolutionary war, we need an army which we do not have."

On March 3, 1918, the Treaty of Brest-Litovsk was signed. Russia lost Erivan, Kars, Batum, the Ukraine, the western provinces, Finland, and the Baltic area, comprising 1,267,000 square miles, 62,000,000 people, a third of her best crop areas, half of her industrial plants, and three quarters of her coal and iron. Such terms evoked dissent. The Party leadership was split. The oppositionists or "Left Communists" (Bukharin, Uritsky, Lomov, and Bubnov) had quit the Central Committee and founded a paper, *The Communist*,

to oppose Lenin's views. At Party Congress VII, the first since the seizure of power, only 46 delegates for 145,000 members appeared in Petrograd (March 6–8), although the Party now had 270,000 members. After heated debate (a practice still possible in both Party and Government in the Soviet Russia of 1917–18), the delegates repudiated the "Left Communists" and upheld Lenin's plea for approval of the treaty, 30 to 12, with 4 not voting.

During the "Great Purge" of the 1930's, the "Left Communists" were accused retrospectively of "treason" in 1918, in accordance with Stalin's facile formula that all current rivals or critics had obviously been "enemies of the people" from the beginning and therefore deserved to be shot. In fact the "Left Communists" were loyal comrades who, for all their Marxism, were sufficiently patriotic to resist acceptance of an "imperialist" peace of conquest. That Lenin was right in arguing that no alternative was available, in the absence of massive military aid from the Allies, does not impugn the integrity of the Bolsheviks who disagreed. Bad judgment or espousal of minority opinion is equated with "treason" only in totalitarian regimes. The Soviet regime was not yet "totalitarian" in 1917–18.

Lenin, Trotsky, and many of their collaborators still hoped, through Western help, to risk rejection of the treaty already signed but not yet ratified. Their hopes proved vain. All the Allies, shocked by the separate peace, refused anew to recognize the Marxist regime. All their envoys (save only Sir George Buchanan, who perceived that Russia was unable to continue hostilities and should not be held to its "pound of flesh") were agreed that Muscovy must somehow be kept in the war and that its new rulers, bent upon peace at any price, should be overthrown and replaced by suitably loyal and belligerent democrats or monarchists. Despite these attitudes, unofficial negotiations were entered into between the Soviet power-holders and Western representatives—Captain Sadoul of the French Military Mission; General William V. Judson, U.S. Military Attaché until his recall in January 1918; Colonel Raymond Robins of the American Red Cross Mission, who went home in May; and Bruce Lockhart of the British diplomatic service. Kamenev, landing at Aberdeen on February 23, 1918, went to London, conferred with a few MP's, was denied an official reception, and was deported when the Quai d'Orsay refused to admit him to France.

The issue, before and after the signing of the Pact of Brest-Litovsk, was whether Russia could be helped to continue resistance

to the Central Powers. Robins and Lockhart thought so. Woodrow Wilson hailed Russian pleas for "no annexations, no indemnities, and self-determination" and in his "Fourteen Points" address of January 8, 1918, bade Russia "a sincere welcome into the society of free nations under institutions of her own choosing and, more than a welcome, assistance of every kind that she may need and may herself desire. The treatment accorded to Russia by her sister nations in the months to come will be the acid test of their goodwill." The Western Powers were destined to fail the test. Wilson sent greetings on March 11 to the Fourth Congress of Soviets, met in Moscow to debate ratification of the treaty. He expressed "sincere sympathy for the Russian people" and regret at the inability of America "to render the direct and effective aid it would wish to render."

Words were empty. Trotsky told Robins: "Colonel Robins, your Embassy sends you here with a big bag marked 'American help.' You arrive every day, and you bring the bag into my room, and you set it down beside your chair, and you keep reaching into it as you talk, and it is a powerful bag. But nothing comes out." On March 13, 1918, Trotsky gave up his post to become, prophetically, Commissar for War. His successor at the Narkomindel (Peoples' Commissariat for Foreign Affairs) was a neurotic aristocrat, George V. Ornatsky, alias Chicherin, who had resigned from the Tsarist diplomatic service in 1904 and joined the RSDLP. Long a Menshevik, he became a Bolshevik in 1915. Early in 1918 he was an inmate of Brixton Gaol for delivering a defeatist speech in Hyde Park. Trotsky, through Litvinov in London, wangled his release. Chicherin was to be Soviet Foreign Minister until 1930 and to be buried with honors and a handsome monument in the fabulous cemetery of the Novodevichy Convent in Moscow.

This change of chiefs in mid-March of 1918 effected no change of problems. A week before his shift of posts, Trotsky pleaded with Robins and Lockhart to secure from Wilson and Lloyd George some pledge of help. These unofficial "Ambassadors" did their best. On March 16, in the evening, Lenin spoke to the Congress of Soviets.

"At 11:20 he was sitting in a chair on the platform. Robins was sitting on the steps of the platform. Lenin waved to Robins to come to speak to him. Robins came. Lenin said: 'What have you heard from your Government?' Robins said: 'Nothing. . . . What has Lockhart heard from London?' Lenin said: 'Nothing.' Then Lenin said: 'I shall now speak for the peace. It will be ratified. . . .' He

spoke for a necessary peace, a preparatory peace, a peace of respite and return. Red cards rose up in hands all over the house to approve. Red cards rose up to disapprove. The count was held. Not voting, 204. Voting against ratification, 276. Voting in favor of ratification, 724." [2]

Russia was at peace. But, thanks to the peace, Russia was to be at war once more, at home and abroad, within a few months. Brest-Litovsk not only divided Communists against themselves, but produced an irreparable schism with the SR's, both Left and Right, and multiplied demands in Allied capitals for military intervention to keep Russia in the war. On March 21, 1918, with new divisions freed from the East, Ludendorff opened the first of the great "drives" on the western front which almost reached Paris and the Channel and almost won World War I for the Central Powers. Under these hazardous circumstances all proposals for restoring an eastern front were sympathetically received by Allied statesmen.

Intervention, depicted as a necessary step in the war against the *Reich*, was in fact begun before the conclusion of the Treaty of Brest-Litovsk and continued long after the end of the war in the West. Tokyo, supported by London and Paris but opposed by Washington, began pressing for occupation of Siberia in November 1917, and sent troops to Vladivostok early in April 1918. Meanwhile, in December at Rostov-Don, Generals Kornilov, Kaledin, and Alexiev successfully revolted against Soviet authority (the only such in-

---

[2] William Hard: *Raymond Robins' Own Story* (Harper, 1920), pp. 151–3. The final vote was 261 against and 784 for. In his autobiography Trotsky does not discuss this episode, but refers to similar parleys with Ambassador Noulens. Cf. G. Chicherin: *Two Years of Foreign Policy* (The Russian Soviet Government Bureau, New York, 1920); Alfred L. P. Dennis: *The Foreign Policies of Soviet Russia* (Dutton, 1924); Leon Trotsky: *From October to Brest-Litovsk* (The Socialist Publication Society, New York, 1919); and David R. Francis: *Russia from the American Embassy* (Scribner, 1921).

George F. Kennan, in his detailed analysis of these events (*Russia Leaves the War*, Princeton University Press, 1956), implies that there was no political possibility at any time of effective Allied aid to the Soviet regime against Germany or of Soviet rejection of a separate peace in return for such aid. His case is persuasive. Yet the very record he has given us so fully suggests that Western policy-makers were even more befuddled by ignorance and prejudice than Soviet policy-makers and thereby fumbled an opportunity to confound the Central Powers by fostering Soviet resistance to German demands. By a subconscious oversight to which none of us is immune, Kennan fails to mention either the crucial decision of the Constituent Assembly which provoked its dissolution or the "birthday of the Red Army" when Soviet forces did in fact fight and halt the Germans at Narva and Pskov.

stance during this period in any area outside of German control)
and set up a "United Government" and a "Volunteer Army" to
which, despite its monarchist orientation, support was pledged by
Paul Miliukov, Boris Savinkov, George Plekhanov, and other anti-
Bolsheviks. This flash on the Don meant nothing, for by mid-Febru-
ary 1918 the movement had collapsed, with Kornilov slain, Kaledin a
suicide, and Alexiev in flight after naming Anton Denikin as his
successor.

This feckless gesture of the Tsarist generals was, nevertheless, a
portent. London offered them £20,000,000 and Paris 100,000,000
rubles to fight the Soviet power. Downing Street contemplated a
"protectorate" over the Caucasus, and the Quai d'Orsay over the
Crimea, Bessarabia, and the Ukraine. The U.S. Consul General in
Moscow, Dewitt C. Poole, went to Rostov and Novocherkaask in December 1917, and reported to Ambassador Francis in January that
Washington should support the cause. All of this antedated by
months the Treaty of Brest-Litovsk, although it followed the armistice of December 15. The episode demonstrated who was willing
to line up with whom among the Russian foes of Lenin and what
manner of motivation was at work among Allied policy-makers.

After Brest-Litovsk, war came to Russia anew under circumstances almost grotesque. Some 45,000 Czechoslovak deserters from
the Hapsburg armies had joined the Tsarist hosts in fighting the
common enemy, hoping for independence for their fatherland. The
Revolution left them stranded in the Ukraine. Plans were made to
bring them to the western front by way of Siberia, the Pacific,
America, and the Atlantic. The Soviets were willing. But on May 14,
1918, at Chelyabinsk violence broke out between a Czech contingent and a group of liberated Austrian and German prisoners moving homeward. When Trotsky rashly ordered all the Czechs disarmed, they rebelled and, with Allied encouragement, speedily
overthrew Soviet authority throughout Western Siberia and in the
Urals, thus enabling anti-Soviet Russians to set up centers of pretended power and to appeal for native and foreign support against
the Moscow Commissars.

A brutal incident of these days of incipient civil war is noteworthy. Nicholas II, with his wife and children, had been shipped
from Tsarkoe Selo near Petrograd to Tobolsk and then to Ekaterin-
burg (Sverdlovsk), north of Chelyabinsk. When Czech and Russian
anti-Soviet troops moved on the town, the Ural Territorial Soviet

concluded that the royal refugees could not be permitted to fall into hostile hands. During the night of July 16–17, 1918, Red Guards took the Romanovs, with their doctor and servants, to the basement of the house where they resided and there shot them all to death, burning the bodies in a near-by mine and scattering the ashes in a swamp.

When the Left SR's broke with the Bolsheviks in protest against Brest-Litovsk, they resorted at once to their time-honored weapon. Maria Spiridonova and Boris Savinkov (who kept contact with a British agent, Captain Sidney Reilly, to whom he had been introduced by Winston Churchill) were adepts in organizing assassinations. On June 20 murder removed Moisei Markovich Volodarsky (Goldstein), who had lived, 1913–17, in the USA as a member of the Socialist Party and was now Commissar for Press and Propaganda. On July 6 Count von Mirbach, the German Ambassador, was dispatched.[3] An attempted SR *coup d'état* in Petrograd and Moscow on the same day was swiftly suppressed. General Eichhorn, German commander in the Ukraine, was next to be slain, July 30. A month later Mikhail Uritsky, President of the Petrograd Cheka, fell before an SR assassin. The same evening, August 30, 1918, Lenin spoke at the Michelson factory in Moscow. As he left the meeting, Fania Kaplan-Roid, an ex-anarchist and now a Right SR, opened fire with a revolver supplied by Boris Savinkov. Lenin was hit in the neck and shoulder, but soon recovered. His bullet-riddled overcoat is still to be seen in the Lenin Museum in Moscow. Why he was wearing an overcoat in August is a mystery.

The Soviet State, albeit still feeble in the means of violence, could easily, if left alone, have beaten down the terrorists and even suppressed the Czechoslovak revolt. But the combination of inter-

---

[3] For a full account of the murder of Mirbach by the SR assassins Blumkin and Andreyev, see the opening pages of Gustav Hilger and Alfred G. Meyer: *The Incompatible Allies: A Memoir History of German-Soviet Relations, 1918–1941* (Macmillan, 1953). Bukharin's role as secret villain in the attempt on Lenin is depicted in the Soviet film *Lenin in 1918*. Cf. the Marx-Engels-Lenin Institute: *V. I. Lenin: A Political Biography*, p. 213: "As subsequently proved at the trials of the Right-Trotskyite enemies of the people, Trotsky, Bukharin and their hangers-on took part in this villainous attempt on Lenin's life." This judgment may be dismissed as fiction. But there is no question of Savinkov's guilt. Trapped and arrested in 1924 while trying to enter the USSR, he was tried and condemned to death, but spared because of his full confession (in this case apparently authentic) and his then professed desire to work for the Soviets. He died in jail in 1925, allegedly a suicide. See Michael Sayers and Albert Kahn: *The Great Conspiracy* (Little, Brown, 1945).

nal rebellion and foreign intervention was almost fatal. Ambassador Francis, who went to Archangel from Vologda in July, had been urging military action since May and ignoring Chicherin's overtures for peace. Wilson reluctantly yielded to Allied pressure on July 17, knowing that other Powers would intervene in any case and hoping that American participation might influence the course of a dubious enterprise.

Following further inter-Allied parleys, Acting Secretary of State Frank L. Polk issued an "explanation" of what was about to be done, as did the authorities in Tokyo, on August 3, 1918. This ambiguous pronouncement began by condemning intervention on the ground that it "would be more likely to add to the present sad confusion than to cure it and would injure Russia rather than help her out of her distress." Intervention, moreover, would not aid the war against Germany. Nevertheless, military action is admissible "to render such protection and help as is possible to the Czechoslovaks against the armed Austrian and German prisoners who are attacking them, and to steady any efforts at self-government and self-defense in which the Russians themselves may be willing to accept assistance." American troops from Vladivostok and from Archangel and Murmansk would guard military stores and "render such aid as may be acceptable to the Russians." The United States would therefore cooperate with Britain and France at Archangel and had proposed to Tokyo a joint American-Japanese occupation of Vladivostok. All of this "contemplates no interference with the political sovereignty of Russia, no intervention in her internal affairs . . . and no impairment of her territorial integrity, either now or hereafter." The United States, after giving military assistance to the Czechoslovaks, would "send to Siberia a commission of merchants, agricultural experts, labor advisers, Red Cross representatives, and agents of the Y.M.C.A., accustomed to organizing the best methods of spreading useful information and rendering educational help of a modest kind . . . to relieve the immediate economic necessities of the people. . . ."[4]

What was about to be done, had it been boldly done with ample troops and funds, might have destroyed the Soviet regime as the

[4] This announcement differed in a number of respects from the secret communication to the Allies of July 17. Cf. *U.S. Foreign Relations, 1918, Russia,* II, pp. 288–9. The differences reflect little credit on the wisdom, candor, or honesty of American policy-makers of the time.

Paris Commune was drowned in blood by the soldiery of the National Assembly in 1871. What was in fact done was a frightful muddle, flowing from false premises to unworkable conclusions. It must be judged as an instance of the one deed in politics worse than a crime—namely, a blunder. Its consequences, so little considered by the authors of the adventure and then only in fear and ignorance, were to poison East-West relations forever after, to contribute significantly to the origins of World War II and to the later "Cold War," and to fix patterns of suspicion and hatred on both sides which even today threaten worse catastrophes in times to come. Few in the West recall the war of East and West of 1918–20. Every city, town, and village in Russia preserves mementoes of these tragic years. What was done therefore deserves recounting, if only in outline.

British troops, followed by French and American Marines, had come to Murmansk in March of 1918. On August 2 British forces landed at Archangel, as Chekists raided the British Embassy in Petrograd, killing the Naval Attaché, Captain Cromie. Bruce Lockhart was arrested in Moscow, and in October was exchanged for Litvinov, who had been arrested in London. On September 4 some 4,500 American troops reached Archangel. A day later a local "revolution" deposed the anti-Soviet regime of socialists headed by Nicholas V. Tchaikovsky and other members of the Constituent Assembly in favor of a cabal of monarchist officers led by a Captain Chaplin. Popular indignation compelled the restoration of a socialist-liberal coalition, dubbed the "Provisional Government of the North," but British General Poole and his successor, General Ironsides, who commanded the 15,000 Allied troops at Archangel, saw no point in such nonsense. Francis went home in November.

The sequence was similar elsewhere. Behind the Czechoslovaks, the SR leader Avksentiev set up a liberal-socialist regime in Ufa, Omsk, and Tomsk. But on November 18, 1918, Tsarist Admiral Alexander Kolchak arrested the socialist Ministers and made himself dictator, while British troops preserved "law and order" by shooting down objectors in Omsk. The Czechs, now disillusioned, refused all support to the Siberian "White Army" that Kolchak began to organize with Allied and American aid. General William S. Graves commanded the 7,000 U.S. troops who landed at Vladivostok in August and September to join British, French, and Japanese contingents. Very soon, in strict interpretation of his orders, he forbade his forces to fight Red troops and eschewed all political intervention. In July,

Washington and Tokyo had agreed to send not more than 12,000 men apiece into Siberia. By autumn Tokyo had poured 75,000 soldiers into Russia's easternmost provinces, followed by salesmen and concession-hunters. Germany's collapse averted a major American-Japanese crisis by moderating Tokyo's annexationist ambitions. But Japan's puppet, Ataman Gregory Semenov, defied Kolchak and pillaged the countryside. Aroused Red partisans resisted fiercely—with the sympathy of Graves, who described Semenov as "a murderer, robber, and a most dissolute scoundrel." British General Knox protested that Graves "was getting the reputation of being a friend of the poor and didn't he know they were only swine." [5] Of all the participants in a miserable business, only General Graves, as Russians later acknowledged, emerged with a reputation for honesty and decency.

In this befuddled enterprise, the publicly announced objectives of the Allied and Associated Powers were to rescue military stores at Archangel and Vladivostok from German seizure, to help the Czechoslovaks, and to aid Russians in "self-government" and "self-defense." The actual goal was to destroy the Soviet regime and replace it by a "respectable" government, whether socialist, liberal, or monarchist nobody much cared. The crusade almost succeeded. In the final reckoning, its failure was due to Western ignorance of the people of Russia. Among the poor and illiterate, those who abhor Bolshevism may yet prefer it, with all its abuses, if the only alternative is exploitation by feudal landlords and military martinets subsidized by alien Powers. These were the choices posed, half unwittingly, by the Allied interventionists of 1918.

3. FIGHT FOR SURVIVAL

DURING 1918 and 1919 the new Soviet State was blockaded, invaded from every point of the compass, and assailed by a formidable combination of domestic and foreign enemies bent upon doing it to death. The means of defense and counterattack adopted by the Commissars in the Moscow Kremlin (to which they moved from Petrograd in March of 1918) converted the semi-democratic, quasi-coali-

[5] Cf. William S. Graves: *America's Siberian Adventure, 1918–1920* (Cape & Smith, 1931).

tion government into a one-party dictatorship as the first
"totalitarian" regime of our time. Its power-holders outlawed all opponents, ruled by terror and a political police, abolished civil liberties, nationalized all industry, carried "class war" to the villages, and
in other respects devised the ways of arbitrary governance and economic planning which were to characterize the USSR for decades
thereafter. Given the Marxist formulas in their Bolshevik version,
these results, or some of them, might conceivably have ensued in
the peaceful development of the Soviet polity. In fact they were
Leninist responses not to the precepts of dogma but to the exigen-
cies of "total war" waged against Red Muscovy and evoking as the
price of life the ugly devices of the "Total State."

To reduce to order the frenzies of these years of chaos would be
to do violence to the facts. To retell an oft-told tale in full would require many volumes.[6] But we may note the nature of the menace
confronting the Communist Commissars and observe how the menace was met.

The "Whites" struck their first successful blows in the south.
Anti-Soviet elements proclaimed the "independence" of Georgia and
made their mountain land a German protectorate, only to be attacked by the Turks. With British aid, SR's and Mensheviks overthrew the Baku Soviet in late July 1918. The 26 Baku Commissars
who fled across the Caspian were seized by anti-Soviet forces and,

[6] The most useful works in English on the War of the Intervention are:
James Bunyan and H. H. Fisher: *The Bolshevik Revolution, 1917–1918* (Stan-
ford University Press, 1934); James Bunyan: *Intervention, Civil War and Com-
munism in Russia,* April-December 1918 (Johns Hopkins Press, 1936); John S.
Reshetar, Jr.: *The Ukrainian Revolution, 1917–1920* (Princeton University
Press, 1952); George Stewart: *The White Armies of Russia* (Macmillan, 1933);
G. R. Treviranus: *Revolutions in Russia* (Harper, 1944); Betty M. Unterberger:
America's Siberian Expedition, 1918–1920 (Duke University Press, 1956);
Elena Varneck and H. H. Fisher (editors): *The Testimony of Kolchak and
Other Siberian Materials* (Stanford University Press, 1935); Robert D. Warth:
The Allies and the Russian Revolution (Duke University Press, 1954).

For fuller accounts of the political and economic developments of the
Civil War, see: Edward Hallett Carr: *The Bolshevik Revolution, 1917–1923*
(4 vols., Macmillan, 1951–4); H. H. Fisher: *The Famine in Soviet Russia
1919–1923* (Stanford University Press, 1935); Robert K. Murray: *Red Scare:
A Study in National Hysteria, 1919–1920* (University of Minnesota Press, 1955);
Richard Pipes: *The Formation of the Soviet Union: Communism and Nationalism, 1917–1923* (Harvard University Press, 1954); Leonard Schapiro: *The
Origin of the Communist Autocracy, 1917–1922* (Harvard University Press,
1955); Allen S. Whiting: *Soviet Policies in China, 1917–1924* (Columbia University Press, 1954); William A. Williams: *American-Russian Relations, 1781–
1947* (Rinehart, 1952).

with British connivance, shot at Krasnovodsk on September 20, while Turkish troops took Baku and massacred 30,000 Armenians. On November 26 Anglo-French forces occupied Odessa, but were obliged to depart in April 1919 when the sailors of the French fleet, led by André Marty, unfurled the red flag, sang the "International," and compelled their officers to sail away. Meanwhile Denikin's White Army overran the North Caucasus, and a Don Cossack general, P. N. Krasnov, led other Whites in an assault on Tsaritsin (Stalingrad), which in the autumn of 1918 was successfully defended by Stalin and Voroshilov. The Volga and the Urals were restored to Soviet power by the Red Guard. But by early 1919 Kolchak's White Army, with Allied and American supplies, was moving westward out of Siberia. Allied troops from Archangel were pushing southward. Denikin's recruits—singing "God Save the Tsar," butchering Jews, torturing Communists, whipping peasants, and wielding British and French guns, tanks, and planes—were overrunning the Ukraine and advancing northward.

Bolshevik defensive measures took many forms: a vain quest for foreign aid, the Red Terror, the outlawry of opponents, the forging of the Red Army, the economics of "War Communism," the enlargement and consolidation of the Party, attempts at negotiation, new appeals for world revolution, etc. As regards the first of these, no foreign help against the Allies was to be had from any source save Germany. The Treaty of Brest-Litovsk pledged the signatories to refrain from revolutionary propaganda. "This article," said Chicherin publicly, "we really observe." "Yes, of course," said Lenin privately on the eve of ratification, "we have already violated the treaty 30 or 40 times." Violations continued, but on August 27, 1918, three supplementary accords were signed in Berlin. Germany agreed to evacuate Byelorussia. Moscow renounced Latvia, Estonia, and Georgia, agreed to pay an indemnity of six billion marks, and undertook to "employ all means to expel the Entente forces from north Russian territory in observance of neutrality," failing which it was secretly agreed that Germany would do so with the aid of Finnish troops and Moscow "would not regard such intervention as an unfriendly act."

In presenting the accords for ratification, Chicherin gave voice to an early version of "peaceful coexistence" by saying: "In spite of the great differences between the regimes of Russia and Germany, and the fundamental tendencies of both governments, the peaceful cohabitation of the two peoples, which has always been the object

of our Workers' and Peasants' State, is at present equally desirable to the German ruling class." [7] But Germany was now facing defeat in the West and could give no aid. The armistice of November 11, 1918, marked the collapse of the Central Powers, against whom the Allies had intervened in Russia. But the Allied war against Bolshevism was pressed with renewed vigor.

As for terrorism, many Marxists opposed it in any form, although Marx himself in 1848 had praised the Hungarian rebels for daring "to meet the cowardly rage of the counter-revolution with revolutionary passion, the *terreur blanc* with the *terreur rouge*." The SR assassinations and rebellions of the summer of 1918 brought into action the Cheka, which thus far had done little beyond suppressing an anarchist center in Moscow in April. In mid-July 10 officers of Boris Savinkov's terrorist group were shot in Moscow, while 350 rebels in Yaroslav were executed (*Pravda*, July 26, 1918). Said Latsis: "If you do not kill, you will be killed. Therefore, kill." (*Izvestia*, August 23, 1918.) On September 2, Zinoviev ordered the shooting of 500 hostages in Petrograd. The Sovnarkom ordered mass terror on September 5, involving the taking of hostages and the execution without formalities of all participants in White Guard activities. Allied diplomats protested in pious horror, although Allied troops were shooting all captured Communists, while White Terrorists were soon slaughtering wholesale all suspected Soviet sympathizers. Djerzhinsky's killers made short work of SR assassins and White supporters and ultimately decimated the aristocracy and bourgeoisie. How many scores of thousands were put to death in this double holocaust will never be known, for the Cheka records are incomplete and the White executioners kept no accounts.

Despite mass murder, the Communist leaders did not at once outlaw all other parties. On June 14, 1918, the Soviet Central Executive Committee ordered the expulsion of all Right SR's and Mensheviks from all Soviet bodies. At the Bolshoi Theatre, where the Fifth All-Russian Congress of Soviets met on July 4 under the chairmanship of black-bearded Jacob Sverdlov, there were 745 Bolsheviks and 352 Left SR's among the 1,132 delegates. But the murders of Mirbach and Uritsky and the desertion of SR General Muraviev to the enemy at Simbirsk put even the Left SR's beyond the pale. Nevertheless, despite the earlier outlawry of the party, the Cadet

[7] Quoted in Carr, III, 86.

paper *Svoboda Rossii* was still being published in the summer of 1918 and giving currency to an alleged decree of an "anarchist club" in Saratov making all women "State property." Menshevik and anarchist papers were still being printed. In October 1918 the Menshevik Central Committee held a five-day conference in Moscow. In February 1919 an SR conference met in Petrograd. As late as December 1919, Menshevik leaders, including Dan, were present at the Seventh All-Russian Congress of Soviets. Even in 1920 there was a Menshevik office and club in Moscow. Not until the spring of 1921 were all other parties completely suppressed and the Communists left with a monopoly of legality.[8]

The Red Army, based on conscription, took shape in the summer of 1918, with Trotsky as Commissar for War dashing from front to front in an armored train and developing remarkable administrative and military talents—all to be expunged from Soviet history as rewritten in the 1930's. Party commissars kept watch over the many Tsarist officers pressed into service. This ragged host, which at no time had more than 700 pieces of artillery, 2,800 machine guns, and 500,000 rifles, never amounted to more than 600,000 combat troops, although 5,200,000 men passed through its ranks. Half deserted to the Whites and half of these deserters returned to the Red ranks with the shifting fortunes of battle. Ultimate victory was due less to martial might than to popular support.

Armed violence was supplemented by the mobilization of all resources in the name of "War Communism." The Supreme Soviet of National Economy, headed by Rykov, was directed by the Sovnarkom on June 28, 1918, to take over all large-scale industry. Former owners and managers who acquiesced were made salaried employees of the State. Strikes were outlawed and labor duty made obligatory in October, a year after the victory of the "workers' revolution." Banks were nationalized, private trade was outlawed, and all foodstuffs were rationed, while a printing-press inflation soon reduced all paper money to worthlessness. "Committees of the Village Poor" aided agents of the Commissariat of Food to requisition grain from the middle peasants and kulaks ("fists"), often to the tune of fisticuffs or bloodshed. Without this thievery, called "class war in the villages" and a "State monopoly of grain-trading," the Red Army and the urbanites would have starved. The progressive paralysis of all production precluded any adequate exchange of rural

[8] For details, see Carr, I, 155–71.

crops for town-made goods and finally compelled the abandonment of this initial desperate venture in "total planning"—but not before it had enabled the regime to survive.

The Party meanwhile waxed as internal dissensions waned, despite Trotsky's quarrels with Stalin and other leaders over military strategy. All Communists knew that they would be shot if the Whites prevailed. Sverdlov died. In March 1919, at Congress VIII, 301 delegates representing 313,766 members accepted Lenin's proposals for a new Program, for conciliation of the middle peasants, for censure of the "Military Opposition" resisting strict discipline in the Army, and for a *chistka* or purge (i.e., expulsion) of unworthy members. A year later 554 delegates of 611,978 members met in Congress IX and endorsed one-man management of factories and Lenin's vision of electrification.

Those who are strong often risk war. Those who are weak usually seek peace. The Muscovite Commissars, facing defeat, repeatedly sought peace with the Allies and were as repeatedly rebuffed. Raymond Robins, come home to urge coexistence, was a voice in the wilderness. General Graves, whose men were denounced by Kolchak as "riff-raff" and "Jews," was far off in Siberia and without influence in the West. On the eve of the Peace Conference, Kolchak and Denikin named Sergei Sazonov, Tsarist warmonger of 1914, as their Foreign Minister in Paris. Around him rallied Lvov, Miliukov, Bakhmetiev, and sundry Cadets, socialists, and monarchists bent upon winning Allied aid for the destruction of the Soviet regime. Western leaders—above all, Winston Churchill—were eager to help. Into the U.S. *Congressional Record* Senator McCumber read as fact the fictitious "Decree of the Saratov Soviet" nationalizing Russian women. Elihu Root opined that the Red rulers of Russia were "a horrid group of cut-throats and assassins." The American Association for International Conciliation described them as "degenerates, drunkards, and sex-perverts." *The New York Times* (November 1, 1919) depicted them as "ravening beasts of prey, a large part of them actual criminals, all of them mad." Ambassador Francis urged extermination. Secretary of State Lansing concurred: "Bolshevism must be suppressed."

Given these attitudes, Chicherin's pleas for peace negotiations got nowhere. Wilson and Lloyd George to be sure, persuaded Clemenceau and Orlando on January 22, 1919, to agree to a conference of all Russian factions on Prinkipo Island in the Sea of Marmora, but

Sazonov and Lvov refused to meet with "murderers." In March, Wilson secretly sent William Christian Bullitt, Lincoln Steffens, and Captain Walter Pettit to Moscow, whence they brought back proposals that, so Bullitt believed, promised peace "on a just and reasonable basis." Wilson told Colonel House, however, that he was busy with the League Covenant and had a "one-track mind." House quibbled evasively until Bullitt resigned in disgust. The Paris "Big Four," while not yet willing to grant diplomatic recognition to Kolchak, were confident that his troops would take Moscow and butcher the Bolsheviks. When Chicherin named Ludwig C. A. K. Martens as first Soviet "Ambassador" to the USA, the luckless would-be envoy was hounded in New York and ordered deported (December 15, 1920), amid Attorney General A. Mitchell Palmer's "red raids" against "subversives," on the ground that he and his superiors "believe in, teach, and advocate the overthrow of the Government of the United States by force and violence."

So indeed they did—not only because of their Marxist dogma, which they and their successors have always been able to reinterpret with some modicum of realism, but because the grim events of 1919–20 convinced them anew that without "world revolution" their power in Russia was doomed to annihilation at the hands of the Western "capitalists" and "imperialists." In January 1918 Lenin incredulously rejoiced that his regime had endured longer than the Paris Commune. A year later its prospects were dismal. No hope remained save to do what Lenin had vainly tried to do in Switzerland in 1915 and 1916: rally the "workers of the world" to the revolutionary overthrow of their "exploiters," who otherwise seemed likely to liquidate the Marxists who had seized control of the realm of the Romanovs.[9]

Between the 2nd and 6th of March 1919, in response to a Bolshevik invitation of January, 32 voting delegates from Central and Eastern Europe, plus others from Asia and the Atlantic world, met

[9] Carr, III, 88–9: "The vital question whether the coexistence of capitalist and socialist states was possible had at any rate been left open by the first pronouncements of the Soviet Government. . . . Now it seemed irrefutably clear that this coexistence was impossible, at any rate with the countries of the Entente, and that revolutionary propaganda directed to the workers of these countries was the most effective, and indeed the only effective, weapon in the hands of a government whose military resources were still negligible. . . . World revolution, in form a logical, though extreme development of communist doctrine, was in fact imposed on the regime, not so much by doctrinal orthodoxy, as by the desperate plight of the civil war."

in Moscow to found the Third or Communist International. Its prolix Manifesto summoned the proletarians of all lands to overthrow all bourgeois governments and "erect in their place the structure of the Socialist world order" and the "International Republic of the Workers' Soviets." On July 18, 1920, the Second Congress of the Comintern, now described by Kamenev as the "General Staff of World Revolution," assembled in Petrograd. Ardent greetings were sent to the Red Army then advancing on Warsaw. Rigid conditions were imposed upon Marxist parties seeking admission, designed to insure the expulsion of "reformists" and "opportunists" and the dedication of all comrades to violent revolution. Zinoviev was named top man of the "open conspiracy." In September the "First Congress of the Peoples of the East" (no second ever met) assembled at Baku under Zinoviev, who, in a frenzy, preached a Holy War all over Asia against "British Imperialism."

No magic of political or social science can reveal with any precision what factors played what roles in determining the outcome of any such disorderly combat as raged over Russia between 1918 and 1921. Major elements in shaping the result were the ignorance and indecisiveness of Allied policy-makers and the atrocities perpetrated by the White Armies, which led many uncommitted Russians to support the Red cause. "World revolution" never materialized. Postwar ferment in Central Europe promoted the establishment in Budapest, on March 21, 1919, of a Soviet regime led by a Jewish journalist, Bela Kun. The "Sparticists" in Germany strove mightily to provoke proletarian revolution and were staunchly resisted by Ebert, Scheidemann, and their Social Democratic comrades—all "orthodox" Marxists now transmuted into conservatives and, as always among people of deep conviction, hating heretics more than infidels. Rosa Luxemburg and Karl Liebknecht were slain by the Berlin police in January of 1919. On April 7 a Soviet regime was nevertheless proclaimed in Munich.

Lenin, Chicherin, Zinoviev, and other Russian comrades sent greetings and promised aid. But, encircled as they were by invading armies, they could neither help, nor receive any help from, their fellow rebels on the Danube and the Isar. The *Reichswehr* crushed the Bavarian Soviet at the end of April. The Hungarian Soviet perished in July at the hands of Rumanian invaders and Admiral Nicholas Horthy's White terrorists. As his supporters were butchered, Bela

Kun fled to Muscovy, where years later he was himself to be miserably exterminated at the behest of the high priest of the cause he served.

Not by world revolution and not by arms alone did the Kremlin Commissars win victory in this chaotic war to the death. In the hot immediacies of the moment, however, the verdict was rendered through trial by battle.

The White Armies were well supplied by the West. Had their leaders known how best to use what they got, how to win popular support, how to restrain the excesses of their subordinates, how to avoid the appearance of being Tsarist reactionaries, they might well have won. Of these arts they were innocent. In their attitudes and acts they foreshadowed the "Fascism" of times to come, and were beaten thereby. Most men and women (always excepting the Germans and Japanese of 1935–45), if forced by the ineptitude of liberals to choose between a Fascist totalitarianism that is wholly destructive and a Communist totalitarianism that is partly constructive, will prefer the latter to the former. But this backward-looking wisdom was not available in 1919. In Washington the State Department, cooperating with Ambassador Bakhmetev, extended to Kolchak the U.S. war loans to Kerensky's regime and sent supplies of arms to the White Army in Siberia. Britain, according to Churchill, sent Kolchak 100,000 tons of goods in 1919 and supplied Denikin with 250,000 rifles, 200 guns, 30 tanks, "large masses of munitions and equipment," and sundry British advisers. France, Italy, Japan, and, in fact, all of the 14 nations actively engaged in the great crusade gave what they could to the cause. Such aid was expected to insure victory. It contributed to defeat, since most Russians were patriots and rallied to the support of a Marxist regime (which many of them detested) rather than submit to the rule of compatriots subsidized from abroad.

For the interventionists and their agents the battle went badly from the outset, despite occasional hopes of victory. The mysteries of the "Russian soul," like the heroism of the defenders of the Soviet Fatherland, baffled Western statesmen. Chaos was king in many areas of combat. In the Ukraine the peasant anarchist Nestor Makhno led partisans against, successively, Denikin's Whites, Trotsky's Reds, Wrangel's Whites, and finally everybody, until he fled to Rumania in 1921. Other "Green Guards" fought all efforts to establish any government of any kind. In Central Asia, Enver Pasha, emu-

lating Tamerlane, sought to found an Islamic empire until he was beaten and killed near the Afghan frontier in 1922. In Outer Mongolia, Baron Ungern-Sternberg, a Buddhist convert claiming descent from Ghenghis Khan, relished raids into Soviet territory and lavish banquets of many courses, at the end of which he enjoyed shooting his guests. After his capture by Red troops and on the eve of his execution, he protested eloquently against the absurdity of judicial proceedings.

Such vagaries, while typical of the disorder of these years, need not obscure the larger scene of conflict. Allied and American forces from Archangel vainly sought to reach Vologda during the Arctic winter. When the Red Army counterattacked at Shenkursk on January 25, 1919, in a temperature of 30° below zero, American and Canadian detachments fled and by March were in full retreat. At month's end, mutiny broke out in the 339th U.S. Infantry, since nobody knew what he was fighting for in the frigid wastes of North Russia. By the end of June 1919 the last of the American interventionists in this area had been withdrawn, after suffering 244 dead and 305 wounded. New British forces were helpless in the face of local revolts, bred by the daily execution of Soviet sympathizers and persistent attacks by Red forces from the south. Churchill finally accepted what he called "the difficult and painful alternative of withdrawal." The last of the British troops embarked for home in mid-October of 1919.

In the interim, Kolchak's White Army, driving westward, almost reached Kazan on the Volga in May of 1919 and there was beaten by the Red soldiery of General Mikhail Frunze and forced into swift retreat. The embittered Czechoslovaks, long since "neutral," denounced the atrocities perpetrated by Kolchak's troops—which aroused the peasantry to rebellion. Red forces took Omsk on November 15 and Tomsk on December 16. On Christmas Day 1919, Kolchak yielded his command to Semenov. Czechs at Irkutsk delivered the Admiral to Red partisans. On February 7, 1920, he was shot at dawn. On April 1 the last U.S. troops sailed from Vladivostok, which the Japanese immediately occupied.

Denikin's troops meanwhile moved on Moscow from the south in October of 1919 as General Nicholas Yudenich's White Army, based in Estonia with British naval support, tried to take Petrograd. Red forces beat back the assault on Peter's city. Other Soviet armies crushed Denikin's host at Orel and Voronezh in mid-October of

1919. Kursk, Kharkov, Kiev, Tsaritsin, and Rostov were soon in Red hands once more. On April 4, 1920, Denikin abdicated in favor of Baron Peter Wrangel and fled to Istanbul and thence to Malta, Paris, and America, where he died in Ann Arbor in 1953. These military operations were small-scale by the standards of World Wars I and II. They were nonetheless highly destructive of property (Kiev changed hands 19 times within 3 years) and hideously destructive of life. Unlike the combatants in America's Civil War, both sides were animated by a furious fanaticism that ignored all rules of international law and sanctioned massacre and pillage and the execution, often after torture, of all enemy commanders.

The defeat of Yudenich, Denikin, and Kolchak brought no peace to Russia. On December 5, 1919, the Seventh Congress of Soviets passed a resolution asserting its desire "to live at peace with all people, and to devote all its strength to internal constructive work, in order to perfect production, transport, and public administration on the basis of a Soviet regime, to the work which has hitherto been hindered by the pressure of German imperialism and subsequently by the Entente intervention and the starvation blockade." The resolution recalled the nine peace offers made since August 5, 1918, and expressed "an unchanging desire for peace by proposing once more to all the Entente Powers—to Great Britain, France, the United States of America, Italy, and Japan, to all together and to each separately—immediately to commence peace negotiations."

The Allied Supreme Council lifted the blockade in January 1920 and rejected the project of Foch and Clemenceau for an international army to renew the struggle. On February 24 the Council informed the border States that the Allies could not assume responsibility for advising them to continue war or to adopt aggressive policies toward Soviet Russia. The ultra-nationalistic leaders of resurrected Poland, headed by Marshal Josef Pilsudski, nevertheless waged war anew, having remained quiescent during 1919 lest White victory should lead to efforts at the reincorporation into Russia of Poland, whose independence Red Moscow had long since recognized.

The new quarrel was over frontiers. The Allied Supreme Council, with U.S. approval, proposed on December 8, 1919, that the Poles content themselves with an eastern boundary (the "Curzon Line") embracing all areas in which Polish-speaking peoples were a

RUSSIAN WAR FRONTS: 1919-1920

① *Farthest Southern Advance of Allied Troops in North Russia, January 1919*
② *Farthest Westward Advance of White Army of Kolchak, May 1919*
③ *Farthest Northward Advance of White Army of Denikin, October 1919*
④ *Farthest Eastward Advance of White Army of Yudenitch, October 1919*
⑤ *Farthest Eastward Advance of Polish Army, June 1920*
⑥ *Farthest Westward Advance of Red Army Into Poland, August 1920*
⑦ *Farthest Northward Advance of White Army of Wrangel, November 1920*

majority of the population. Pilsudski, Josef Beck, and the Warsaw Colonels insisted on the frontiers of 1772, whereby millions of Russians, Byelorussians, and Ukrainians along the ancient water road would become Polish subjects. Chicherin (December 22, 1919, February 2 and March 6, 1920) offered peace on the basis of a frontier midway between the "Curzon Line" and the boundary of 1772, and far to the east of the border of 1921–39. The policy-makers in Warsaw would have none of this. Already possessed of Vilna and Minsk, they demanded, at the end of March, Soviet abandonment of all lands west of the 1772 frontiers, payment of an indemnity, and Polish occupation of Smolensk as a "guarantee." London and Washington protested these "imperialist" claims. The Kremlin rejected them and made new proposals for peace.

On April 23, 1920, Pilsudski concluded a "treaty" with Ukrainian Hetman Simon Petlura, then a refugee in Poland, whereby the Hetman acknowledged Polish title to extensive Russian lands in return for aid in setting up an anti-Soviet regime in the Ukraine. On the same day Pilsudski ordered the Polish army to attack. On May 8 Kiev was taken, although it lay beyond the frontiers of 1772, while Petlura's men followed fast behind, killing Jews and carrying banners (still on exhibit in the Kiev Historical Museum) emblazoned with the anti-Semitic *Hakenkreuz*.

The men in the Kremlin responded as any rulers of Russia would have done. All patriots, including General Brussilov, rallied to the defense of the Motherland. Budenny's cavalry forced the Poles to quit Kiev on June 13. In the north the troops commanded by young General Tukhachevsky drove the invaders from Minsk (July 11), Vilna (July 14), Grodno (July 22), and Brest-Litovsk (July 31). By early August, Soviet armies were moving on Warsaw, while Zinoviev, Trotsky, and Lenin cherished dreams of Bolshevizing Poland and carrying revolution on bayonets into Central Europe ("a false political reckoning," said Lenin later).[1] But London

---

[1] Stalin opposed Lenin in May 1920 on the issue of trying to Sovietize Poland, arguing that most Poles, as patriots, would staunchly resist any such endeavor. Lenin insisted. Stalin yielded. A Polish puppet government followed the Red Army. Lenin later acknowledged his error. See Stalin: *Sochinenya* (*Collected Works*), IV, 323–4, 332–3; Lenin: *Sochinenya*, XVII, 334; and Isaac Deutscher: *Stalin: A Political Biography* (Oxford University Press, 1949), pp. 215–17. Cf. Aleksander W. Rudzinski: *Soviet Peace Offensives* (International Conciliation, No. 490, 1953, Carnegie Endowment for International Peace).

gave massive material aid to the hard-pressed Poles, while Paris sent General Weygand to direct the defense. Through the blundering that so often characterizes the waging of war, Budenny's horsemen failed to take Lvov or to move northward against the defenders of the Vistula. Eager to reach the German frontier, Tukhachevsky bypassed the Polish capital and pushed his forces toward the "Corridor," far beyond their lines of supply. From Warsaw an adroit counterblow in late August sent the invaders reeling back toward the east.

The Polish adventure and the Soviet counteradventure had both failed. An armistice was signed at Riga on October 11, 1920. The Treaty of Riga of March 18, 1921, established a frontier far to the west of the borders of 1772 and westward of what Moscow had been willing to concede in peace a year before. Millions of Great Russians, Byelorussians, and Ukrainians were nevertheless incorporated into Poland, creating an "Irredenta" that the Kremlin long accepted but promptly moved to rectify when opportunity offered in 1939.

The Western Powers, while deploring Polish annexationist ambitions, aided Warsaw to repel the Red hordes and ultimately acknowledged the new frontier. As the battle raged, U.S. Acting Secretary of State Bainbridge Colby, in reply to a question from Italian Ambassador Baron Avezzano, publicly asserted on August 10, 1920, that America championed Russian territorial integrity (sans Finland, ethnic Poland, and Armenia), regarded the Baltic States of Estonia, Latvia, and Lithuania as properly part of Russia, and would not recognize the Soviet regime because it espoused repudiation of debts, confiscation of foreign property, and revolutionary propaganda against other governments. On the same day Paris extended diplomatic recognition as the "government of Russia" to Baron Peter Wrangel, last of the White hopes, who had rallied the remnants of Denikin's army to occupy the Crimea and invade the Kuban and the Ukraine during the Polish war. Wrangel's "Foreign Minister" was Peter Struve, who had written the first program of the RSDLP in Minsk in 1898.

The last of the White Armies was crushed when Soviet troops stormed the Perekop Isthmus on November 7, 1920, swept through the Crimea, took Sebastopol on November 14, and compelled Wrangel and his surviving supporters to flee to Istanbul in British, French, and American warships. Aside from "mopping-up" operations in Central Asia, the final campaign of the Red Army in the

civil war was the reconquest, in February 1921, of Georgia, where a Menshevik regime had striven for independence and courted Western socialists against Moscow.

The first efforts of the West to destroy Bolshevism, and of the Bolsheviks to destroy Western "bourgeois" governments, had ended in a stalemate, leaving the West in doubt, Russia in ruin, and the two parts of a now divided world in a relationship of reciprocal suspicion and fear destined to persist for decades.

4. COEXISTENCE: 1921f.

IN the glorious and age-old game of violence known as war, murder is honorable instead of sinful and suicide is heroic instead of cowardly. The players are occasionally, in happy times and places, gentlemen fighting in a mood of chivalry for sport, booty, or real estate and dealing with one another as equals. In more miserable epochs, including our own, the players are fanatic crusaders who confound themselves with the angels of God and undertake, in the sacred name of nation, race, class, or creed, to exterminate enemies as agents of Lucifer. Such was the war between Whites and Reds, and between Russia and the West, in the aftermath of the First World War of the 20th Century—with the combatants, in a frenzy and fury of destruction, displaying many of the traits of murderous and suicidal intolerance which were to characterize the later "totalitarians" of the 1930's, Communist and Fascist alike.

But when violence is thwarted by counterviolence, even the most inflexible of fanatics are sometimes constrained, against all their "principles," to make peace lest more war prove not only futile but fatal. Thus, Christians and Moslems, after centuries of strife, finally stopped fighting. So also did Catholics and Protestants, first in the Peace of Augsburg of 1555 and later in the Peace of Westphalia of 1648, after generations of mutual butchery. Moved by similar considerations of expediency and in a comparable spirit of reluctant toleration of evil, Soviet Russia and the West made peace in 1921.

"Coexistence" is a formula not of the 1950's but of the 1920's. The unwillingness of both antagonists to accept it is attested by numerous public utterances on both sides. As late as December 1922 Trotsky wrote:

Rally closer to the mass reserves! Whatever storms—harbingers of proletarian victory—may come, the Soviet frontier is the trenchline beyond which the counter-revolution shall not pass and on which we shall remain at our posts until the reserves will arrive and the Red Flag of the European Socialist Union of Soviet Republics as forerunner of the World Federation of Proletarian Republics shall be hoisted to the mast. (*Izvestia*, December 29, 1922.)

Lenin, bespeaking catastrophe, told Party Congress VIII:

We are living not merely in a State, but in a *system of States;* and it is inconceivable that the Soviet republic should continue to exist for a long period side by side with imperialist States. Ultimately one or the other must conquer. Until this end occurs a number of terrible clashes between the Soviet Republics and bourgeois States is inevitable. (*Sochineniya*, XXIV, 122.)

This avowal of implacable combat has been quoted thousands of times throughout the West, particularly in America during the "Cold War," as evidence—coupled with Stalin's later marginal comment, "Clear, one would think!"—that no peace was possible between East and West. Few of the assiduous quoters reveal the context of Lenin's statement.[2] It was made in March 1919 when Allied armies were seeking to destroy the Soviet regime by violence, when Kolchak was moving on Moscow from the Urals, and when Denikin was preparing to move on Moscow from the Ukraine, with both White Armies subsidized and supplied by the Western Powers.

Circumstances alter attitudes. Desperate dogmatism in the minds of men often yields to the inexorable pressure of facts. Questions of sincerity are irrelevant as compared with considerations of necessity. Said Chicherin in the spring of 1920:

There may be differences of opinion as to the duration of the capitalist system, but at present the capitalist system exists, so that a *modus vivendi* must be found in order that our socialist State and the capitalist States may co-

---

[2] Even Merle Fainsod, in his admirably detailed and documented analysis of *How Russia Is Ruled* (Harvard University Press, 1953), fails to indicate the context of this famous quotation. Cf. p. 285 of his prize-winning book.

exist peacefully and in normal relations with one another. This is a necessity in the interest of all.[3]

At the same time the brilliant Austrian journalist Karl Radek, who for a time was a major figure in the Soviet regime, wrote:

> If our capitalistic partners abstain from counter-revolutionary activities in Russia, the Soviet Government will abstain from carrying on revolutionary activities in capitalist countries; but we shall determine if they are carrying on counter-revolutionary agitation. There was a time when a feudal State existed alongside capitalist States. In those days liberal England did not fight continuously against serf-owning Russia. We think that now capitalist countries can exist alongside a proletarian State. We consider that the interests of both parties lie in concluding peace and the establishment of the exchange of goods, and we are therefore ready to conclude peace with every country which up to the present has fought against us, but in future is prepared to give us in exchange for our raw materials and grain, locomotives and machinery. The guarantees which our enemies are demanding from us lie in the interests of both parties. (*Wireless News,* Moscow, March 3, 1920.)

Popular opposition in the West to continued interventionism helped to persuade Allied policy-makers to seek some basis of accommodation with the fanatics of Moscow. When Swedish industrialists accepted Soviet orders for goods worth 100,000,000 kronen, to be paid for in gold and short-term notes, Stockholm concluded an "unofficial" trade accord with the Kremlin in May 15, 1920. Lloyd George invited Krassin to London. He arrived on May 26, 1920. The parleys foundered on the rocks of the problems posed by the Polish War. Before another year had passed, however, Moscow had negotiated treaties with Iran, Turkey, and Afghanistan, concluded a provisional trade agreement with Germany (March 6, 1921), signed the final Treaty of Riga with Poland (March 18, 1921), and made peace with Finland, Latvia, Estonia, and Lithuania. Paris and Washington remained firmly opposed to any negotiations with the Mus-

---

[3] Quoted in A. L. P. Dennis: *The Foreign Policies of Soviet Russia* (Dutton, 1924), p. 384.

covite monsters. But when drought and disorder in 1921 brought famine to the Volga Valley, where two million peasants died of starvation, Maxim Gorky's appeal to Herbert Hoover for help led to massive aid, both public and private, through the "American Relief Administration," which saved the lives of another ten million *muzhiks*. The rich America of the 20th Century, while often blind to political realities, is never deaf to humanitarian appeals for mercy.

On March 16, 1921, Leonid Krassin and Sir Robert Horne concluded in London an Anglo-Soviet accord involving *de facto* British recognition of the Red regime, resumption of trade, repatriation of prisoners, deferment of a settlement of financial claims, and assumption of reciprocal obligations to refrain from hostile deeds of word or act. Soviet trade pacts were signed with Norway (September 2, 1921), Austria (December 7, 1921), and Italy (December 26, 1921). Moscow was unrepresented at the Washington Conference of 1921–2 save for a delegation, headed by Boris Skvirsky, from the "Far Eastern Republic," an early Soviet satellite set up at Chita in 1920 as a challenge to continued Japanese occupation of the Maritime Provinces. Under American pressure, Tokyo withdrew its troops from Vladivostok in October 1922. A fortnight later the "Far Eastern Republic" rejoined Mother Russia. Nipponese forces evacuated Northern Sakhalin on May 1, 1925.

Chicherin had meanwhile gone to Genoa, where delegates of 34 States met on April 10, 1922, in an economic and financial conference to further the reconstruction of Central and Eastern Europe. The United States refused to take part. By the Treaty of Rapallo, signed on April 16 by Chicherin and Walter Rathenau, the Kremlin obtained *de jure* recognition from the German Republic, a mutual cancellation of all financial claims, and a regulation of German-Soviet trade on the basis of the most-favored-nation clause. Rapallo was not, as indignant British and French commentators insisted, a Soviet-German "alliance." But it was a *rapprochement* between outcasts, each of which thereby enhanced, however slightly, its bargaining power in dealing with London, Paris, and Rome.

Efforts at Genoa to achieve a general settlement of financial claims were unsuccessful. Said Chicherin: "The British Premier tells me that if my neighbor has lent me money, I must pay him back. Well, I agree, in that particular case, in a desire for conciliation; but I must add that if this neighbor has broken into my house, killed my children, destroyed my furniture, and burnt my house, he must

at least begin by restoring to me what he has destroyed." Against Allied claims of thirteen billion dollars against Russia for Tsarist and Kerensky debts and confiscated properties, Chicherin posed Soviet counterclaims of sixty billion dollars for damages suffered from unlawful intervention. He offered to settle for a token payment plus new loans for reconstruction, but the Allied representatives refused to agree. The conference ended on May 19 in discord, mitigated by a temporary "peace pact" pledging abstention from aggression and subversive propaganda.[4] A meeting of experts at The Hague ended in July with no better results. Litvinov declared that his Government would pay none of the war debts, would insist on a reduction and moratorium for the pre-war debts, and would pay compensation for nationalized property only in return for new loans.

At Lausanne, where another conference met late in 1922 to consider the status of the Straits in the light of the defeat of the Greeks by the Turks in the Anatolian war-after-the-war, Chicherin clashed with Lord Curzon over the question of whether Turkey should or should not have full sovereignty over the waterways, including the right to close them to foreign warships. On May 8, 1923, during these protracted negotiations, London delivered a virtual ultimatum to Moscow threatening to terminate the trade agreement unless the Narkomindel should, within ten days, release certain British fishing vessels, disown and recall its agents in India, Persia, and Afghanistan for alleged anti-British propaganda, and meet certain other demands. Two days later Vaslav Vorovsky, Soviet delegate at Lausanne, was assassinated by Maurice Conradi, a Russian *émigré* of Swiss descent. The conference studiously ignored the murder, while the Swiss courts acquitted the assassin, who was praised by part of the Swiss press. Krassin flew to London with a conciliatory but firm reply to the British demands, which were settled or lost track of in later discussions. The Straits Convention signed at Lausanne, July 24, 1923, demilitarized the Dardanelles and the Bosporus, but limited foreign naval forces permitted to enter the Black Sea. Moscow adhered and became a member of the Straits Commission.

These complex and often acrimonious parleys led to the *de jure*

---

[4] For details, cf. Coates: *op. cit.*, pp. 71–102; F. L. Schuman: *American Policy Toward Russia Since 1917*, pp. 207–23; Louis Fischer: *The Soviets in World Affairs*, I, 300–54; Raymond L. Buell: *The Washington Conference* (Appleton, 1922); Alfred L. P. Dennis: *The Foreign Policies of Soviet Russia* (Dutton, 1924); Henry K. Norton: *The Far Eastern Republic of Siberia* (Allen & Unwin, 1923); and J. Saxon Mills: *The Genoa Conference* (Hutchinson, 1922).

recognition of the Soviet Government by many States during 1924: Britain, February 1; Italy, February 7; Norway, February 13; Austria, February 20; Greece, March 8; Sweden, March 15; China, May 31; Denmark, June 18; Mexico, August 1; France, October 28; and Japan, January 20, 1925. Among the Great Powers only the United States declined to enter into official relations with Moscow. The diplomatic and commercial boycott of the Soviet State was ended. The USSR was again a member of the family of nations.

The peace thus concluded between "irreconcilable" foes endured for two decades. America refused recognition, acquiesced in trade through the Amtorg Company incorporated in New York in 1924, and asked, in the words of Calvin Coolidge, for "works meet for repentance" and more "evidences of returning to the ancient ways of society" (December 6, 1923) before official relations were conceivable. After five years of championing the view of the Russian *émigrés* that the Baltic Provinces belonged to Russia, the State Department on July 27, 1922, announced recognition of the independence of Estonia, Latvia, and Lithuania. Kerensky's Ambassador, Boris Bakhmetev, retired on June 30, 1922, in favor of his financial attaché, Serge Ughet, who continued to be listed by the State Department as "representative of Russia" for another eleven years in accordance with the quaint American custom, later exemplified in dealing with Communist China, of declining to acknowledge the political facts of life. All other Western Powers, plus China and Japan, came to terms with the Kremlin during the 1920's. The settlement was a truce. For lack of its conversion into a genuine accord, all mankind was later to be plunged into tragedy. Yet there were real possibilities during the long armistice of an East-West bargain for the mutual benefit of both parts of a divided world. How and why this opportunity was lost will be later explored in these pages.

CHAPTER FIVE

Means and Ends

1. FROM LENIN TO STALIN

VLADIMIR ULIANOV, revered for his simplicity and modesty and heroized anew throughout Sovietland after Stalin's demise, was not granted a long life. He was nonetheless the chief founder of the Soviet State, as all the comrades of the late 1950's extravagantly acknowledged even as they ambivalently deplored the "cult of personality." He was likewise the leading architect of the new dispensation, abroad and at home, which he and his colleagues felt compelled to adopt in the face of the reduction of Russia to misery by six years of fighting and the planned chaos of "War Communism." By the end of 1920 only half of the pre-war farming area was still under cultivation. Unable to buy goods, the peasants refused to sow or reap beyond their own needs. Industrial production was down to 15% of its 1914 level and in iron and steel stood at 7%. Death by famine took its hideous toll along the Volga. Everywhere in Russia people were on the edge of starvation amid a general paralysis of production and distribution.

Workers struck in vain protest against the decrees of the would-be builders of the "workers' paradise." *Muzhiks* rebelled. Early in March 1921 the sailors of Kronstadt, Red heroes of the October insurrection, rose in revolt to demand civil rights, a "Third Revolution," and "Soviets without Communists." Trotsky's troops crossed the ice of the Neva estuary, stormed Kronstadt, and slaughtered the last of the mutineers on March 10, 1921. The day was the 50th anniversary of the proclamation of the Paris Commune.

Under these grim conditions, Lenin saw the need for a "strategic retreat" toward a limited "capitalism" whereby production and

exchange of goods might be restored. At Party Congress IX in March 1920, before 554 delegates representing 612,000 members, Lenin preached electrification as the way to socialism. A "State Commission for Electrification" (Goelro) was established and expanded in February 1921 into a "State Planning Commission" (Gosplan). But this was the stuff of dreams. People must eat. At Congress X, opening on March 21, 1921, with 694 delegates representing 733,000 members, Lenin put through, amid echoes of the Kronstadt rebellion, the "New Economic Policy" or NEP. Its essence was the abolition of the State monopoly in grain-trading, the abandonment of requisitions, and the substitution of a fixed tax in kind or currency, beyond which peasants could sell all they had by way of surpluses in a newly legalized "free market" for whatever prices the antique "capitalist" laws of supply and demand might dictate.

To permit peasants to bargain and barter as they liked, contrary to all sound Marxist principles, carried with it other implications and imperatives. A State Bank was authorized in 1922 to replace the valueless paper money of the Revolution with a *chervonetz* currency backed by gold. A system of taxation replaced simple robbery of the rich. Artisans and small-scale entrepreneurs or Nepmen were permitted to produce and trade, while the State kept control of the "commanding heights" of heavy industry, transport, and foreign trade. Said Lenin: "This capitalism is not dangerous to us because we will decide in what measure we shall grant concessions. . . . The extent of the ruin and the destitution caused by the War and the Civil War condemns us for a long time to come to the mere healing of our wounds."

This partial return to the freedom of the market was not matched by any restoration of political freedom. On the contrary, one of the resolutions of Congress VIII now became fact: "The Party must win for itself undivided political mastery in the Soviets and practical control of all their work." Power passed from the All-Russian Congress of Soviets and its Central Executive Committee to the Sovnarkom and the Party Central Committee, which now began issuing decrees jointly. The Party in turn became more centralized and less democratic. In the first *chistka* or mass purge, at the time of Congress X, a quarter of the members were expelled for unworthiness. The abolition of the Cheka in February 1922 and the transfer of its functions to a "State Political Administration" (GPU) within the Commissariat of Internal Affairs effected no change, de-

spite intent, for the GPU was soon as arbitrary and as much "above the law" as the Cheka had ever been. During the summer of 1922 some 47 SR leaders were arrested, tried, and sentenced to jail. All opposition was outlawed.

Until very late, Lenin expressed no fear of abuses under the monolithic system of oligarchy implicit in embryo in "democratic centralism" and born full-grown from the civil war. Congress XI in March 1922 was the last he attended. He reviewed the good results of the NEP and asserted on March 27 that it must be continued "in earnest and for long" until Communists should learn to become businessmen.

> By our side a Capitalist is busy, he acts as a robber, he grabs profits, but he knows his job. And you—you are trying new methods: you make no profits. Communist principles, excellent ideals, are written large on you, you are holy men, fit to go alive to Paradise, but do you know your business? . . . We must understand this simple thing—that in a new and unusually difficult task we must learn to begin anew again and again. If one start has led you into a blind alley, begin again, redo the work ten times; but attain your end, don't be self-important, don't pride yourself on being a Communist and no such thing as that non-Party commercial clerk; he may be a White (there is probably no doubt he is a White), but he knows his job . . . and you do not. . . . When an army is retreating discipline must be a hundred times greater than during an offensive, for then all ranks compete in pushing forward. But if during a retreat everyone were to begin to compete in pushing backward, that would be ruin, inevitable and immediate. . . . In the masses of the people we are as a drop in the sea and we can govern only if we adequately express what the people feels. . . . All the revolutionary parties that have hitherto fallen have fallen because they became proud and unable to see where their strength lay, and were afraid to speak of their weakness. We shall not fail, because we are not afraid to speak of our weakness and will learn to overcome our weakness.[1]

[1] Quoted by D. S. Mirsky: *Lenin* (Little, Brown, 1931), pp. 185–7.

In May 1922 a cerebral hemorrhage paralyzed Lenin's right arm and leg. He recovered and on November 20 spoke, for the last time, before the Moscow Soviet: "We have dragged socialism into everyday life, and here we must be able to keep our bearings. This is the task of our day. . . . Difficult as it may be, we shall all, not in one day, but in the course of several years, all of us together fulfill it, come what may; and NEP Russia will be transformed into Socialist Russia." [2]

Another stroke in March 1923, following a slighter one in December, left him incapable of any work beyond writing. "I have wound up my affairs," he wrote to Stalin, "and can leave with a quiet mind." But his mind was unquiet, particularly regarding Stalin, for he remained even in illness, in his country house in the village of Gorki near Moscow, a shrewd judge of character and an astute political analyst. On Christmas Day of 1922 he dictated the first of the several communications to the Party Central Committee collectively known as his "Testament." This document was read to Party leaders on May 22, 1924, and thereafter became well known in higher circles, although it was never published in the Soviet press until 1956. Max Eastman's translation appeared in *The New York Times* of October 18, 1926, and in Trotsky's *The Real Situation in Russia* (1928), even though Trotsky in 1925 had deemed it expedient to denounce the document as a forgery. Stalin himself seems to have quoted from it to the Central Committee in late October 1927 (cf. *Pravda*, November 21, 1927).

Having no hope of recovering his health and feeling anxiety over the succession, Lenin offered his judgment of his colleagues in the expectation that they would take heed. Kamenev and Zinoviev were "weak" and "not by accident" in 1917, but should not be condemned. Pyatakov is a poor politician but a good administrator. Bukharin is a fine fellow but more of a scholastic than a real Marxist. Stalin has "concentrated enormous power in his hands; and I am not sure that he always knows how to use that power with sufficient caution. On the other hand, Comrade Trotsky is distinguished not only by his exceptional abilities—personally he is, to be sure, the most able man in the present Central Committee—but also by his too far-reaching self-confidence and a disposition to be too much attracted by the purely administrative side of affairs."

[2] *V. I. Lenin: A Political Biography*, p. 269.

On December 27, 1922, Lenin commented to the Politburo on the treatment of Georgia, where Stalin had practiced harshness and Lenin had urged mildness. "I think that a fatal role was played here by Stalin's hastiness and administrative impulsiveness, and also by his resentment against the notorious 'social-chauvinism.' Resentment altogether plays the worst possible role in politics." On January 4, 1923, Lenin penned a postscript:

> Stalin is too rude, and this fault, entirely supportable in relations among us Communists, becomes insupportable in the office of General Secretary. Therefore, I propose to the comrades to find a way to remove Stalin from that position and to appoint another man who in all respects differs from Stalin except in superior ability—namely, more patient, more loyal, more polite, and more attentive to comrades, less capricious, etc. This circumstance may seem an insignificant trifle, but I think that from the point of view of preventing a split and from the point of view of the relation between Stalin and Trotsky . . . it is not a trifle, or it is such a trifle as may acquire decisive significance.[3]

Lenin's last letter was dated March 5, 1923, and was addressed to Stalin, breaking off "comradely relations" because of the Georgian's insulting attitude toward Krupskaya. On March 9 he suffered his third stroke, which left him helpless, as Woodrow Wilson was helpless in his last years. As dusk fell over Gorki on the wintry afternoon of January 21, 1924, Lenin's life flickered out. Woodrow Wilson died thirteen days later.

Both men left an indelible imprint upon posterity. Let historians dispute as to which imprint was the more enduring. One of Wilson's own comments is applicable to Lenin as well: "I would rather fail in an enterprise that will some day succeed than succeed in an enterprise that will some day fail." Early in 1943, when Americans and Russians were comrades in arms, the editors of *Life* captioned a picture of Lenin: "This is perhaps the greatest man of the 20th Century."

Josef Vissarionovich Djugashvili, whose father said he would make a good shoemaker and whose mother prayed he would be a

---

[3] Cf. Carr IV, 258–66. Carr's account, while supplemented by the publication of further documents in 1956, is not outdated or superseded.

priest, was not unimpressed, we may reasonably infer from the record, by Lenin's comments on his character. He could not bring himself, to be sure, to renounce the pleasures of power, nor is there any evidence that he ever contemplated such an abnegation. But for a decade after Lenin's passing he wielded the vast authority that he shrewdly concentrated in his hands with circumspection and even, by his own standards, with moderation. Only later, as he persuaded himself of his own infallibility (as Trotsky was to do and as Lenin had seldom done) and came to regard all rivals and critics as traitors, did he assume the now familiar guise of a moral monster comparable to Caligula or Cesare Borgia but far more comparable to Ivan Grozny and Peter I.

Stalin was Commissar of Nationalities in the first Sovnarkom. In March of 1919 he became a member of the Politburo and Orgburo of the Party Central Committee, and in April, Commissar of State Control, a new agency set up to combat bureaucracy and supervise public administration. On February 7, 1920, this Ministry was transmuted into the "Peoples' Commissariat of Workers' and Peasants' Inspection" (Rabkrim), which evidently achieved little in the fulfillment of its alleged purposes and was merged in 1923 into the "Central Control Commission" of the Party, marking a further identification of Party and State. Stalin remained its chief. Meanwhile, on Lenin's motion, the Plenum of the Party Central Committee, immediately after Congress XI in March 1922, had named Stalin General Secretary of the Central Committee, a post hitherto unimportant but destined to be adroitly used by Stalin, in conjunction with his governmental opportunities for patronage, favors, and deprivations, to make himself "Boss" or "*Vozhd*" of Party and Government alike.

The stormy course of intra-Party politics will be considered below. Here we may well ask: what manner of man and politician was Stalin at this period and how did he live his life, seek love, experience frustration, wield authority, and finally convince himself of his indispensability? Communist ethics forbid any public revelations about private lives. But Stalin's second marital adventure, about which something is known, is not unrevealing. In 1919 he married Nadezhda Sergeyevna Alliluyeva, youngest of the four children of his old comrade in conspiracy, Sergei Yakovlevich Alliluyev. She bore him a son, Vassily, who became a Colonel in the air force in World War II but remained otherwise obscure, and a daughter,

Svetlana, who became a Komsomol and in 1944 entered the Moscow University School of International Relations, setting down her father's vocation as "professional revolutionary."

Nadezhda in the 1920's pursued the study of chemistry at the University. On November 8, 1932, she died suddenly. Her passing was attributed to peritonitis. In post-Stalin Muscovy it was widely conceded that she was a suicide, said by some to have been driven to self-destruction by her husband's brutality against his alleged foes, including some of Nadezhda's friends who were banished to Siberia, and against the initial victims of collectivization and industrialization. She was buried in Moscow's famous cemetery of Novodevichy Convent. Over her grave Stalin erected a simple white marble column topped by a sculptured likeness of her head and right arm.[4] Whether Stalin subsequently married or lived with Rosa, sister of Lazar Kaganovich, the only Jewish member of the Politburo in the 1940's, is a mystery never resolved, nor indeed ever mentioned, in the Soviet press.

By the time of his 50th birthday, December 21, 1929, Stalin was already well on his way toward becoming a charismatic incarnation of all wisdom and virtue, depicted in the neo-Byzantine iconography of endlessly multiplied statues, busts, and portraits as an incomparable Hero and all-seeing Father of his people. Typical of thousands of similar utterances were the words, early in 1934, of his closest colleague, Sergei Kirov:

> Comrades, it is not easy to grasp the figure of Stalin in all its gigantic proportions. In these latter years, ever since we have had to carry on our work without Lenin, there has been no major development in our labors, no innovation,

---

[4] Whether the detailed account of her last days and suicide in *Notes for a Journal* (Morrow, 1955) ascribed to Maxim Litvinov (whose grave, near Chicherin's and Alexandra Kollontai's, is also to be seen in the Novodevichy cemetery) is accurate is a moot question, as is the authenticity of this entire work. E. H. Carr in his Introduction deems it partly authentic. Ernest J. Simmons in *The Nation*, November 19, 1955, writes: "Either the whole is authentic or the whole is spurious. . . . The bulk of the material has the ring of truth. Many of the facts recorded check with what we know. If the *Journal* is a forgery, then it is an extraordinarily skillful one and could have been perpetuated only by someone who was extremely intimate with Litvinov." Conversely, Philip E. Mosely in *The New York Times Book Review*, November 6, 1955, notes various falsehoods and discrepancies and suggests that the book may have been the work of Gregori Bessedovsky, Counselor of the Soviet Embassy in Paris, who defected in 1929.

slogan or trend of policy of any importance of which Comrade Stalin was not the author. All the major work—and this the Party should know—is guided by the instructions, the initiative and the leadership of Comrade Stalin. . . . The mighty will and organizational genius of this man insure our Party the timely accomplishment of the big historical turns involved in the victorious construction of Socialism. . . . All emanates from this man, and all that we have achieved in the period of the First Five Year Plan has been due to his direction.[5]

2. THE TRAGEDY OF TROTSKY

STALIN as an ex-theology student turned atheist was fully aware of the need for Miracle, Mystery, and Authority in driving the Russian masses along stony roads chosen for them by their new masters. He it was, in the face of ridicule and opposition within the Party leadership, who insisted on the permanent public display of Lenin's embalmed body in the sacred tomb on Red Square. And he it was who, after Lenin's funeral, pronounced religiously a curious kind of vow:

> We Communists are people of a special mold. We are made of special material. We are those who comprise the army of the great proletarian strategist, the army of Comrade Lenin. There is nothing higher than the honor of belonging to this army. . . . In departing from us, Comrade Lenin bequeathed to us the duty of holding aloft and guarding the purity of the great title of member of the Party. We vow to you, Comrade Lenin, that we will fulfill your bequest with honor. . . . In departing from us, Comrade Lenin bequeathed to us the duty of guarding the unity of our Party like the apple of our eye. We vow to you, Comrade Lenin, that we will also fulfill this bequest of yours with honor. . . . In departing from us, Comrade Lenin bequeathed to us the duty of guarding and strengthening the dictatorship of the proletariat. We vow to you,

[5] Marx-Engels-Lenin Institute: *Joseph Stalin: A Short Biography* (Foreign Languages Publishing House, Moscow, 1943), p. 53.

Comrade Lenin, that we will spare no effort to fulfill also this bequest of yours with honor. . . .[6]

At the time of the funeral Trotsky was recovering from illness in warm Transcaucasia. He attributed his fever to the effects of an autumn hunting trip. It may well have been psychosomatic. This authentic genius was already developing neurotic convictions of his own infallibility and paranoid fears that he was a victim of persecution. In these traits, as well as in many concrete policies, Stalin, his archfoe, was ultimately to pay him the sincerest form of flattery. But not yet was this the case. In the bitter winter of 1923–4, Trotsky, in Tiflis when Lenin died, was informed in time to attend his funeral. He went instead to Sukhum on the Black Sea shore, thereby committing the first of the major political mistakes that finally enabled Stalin (for whom he had all of the conceited intellectual's contempt toward anti-intellectual proletarians and stupid bureaucrats) to outmaneuver him completely and encompass his downfall. At Sukhum, Trotsky preferred to lie in the sun and spin fantasies: "Individual episodes emerged with the vividness of a dream. Gradually all of it began to assume increasingly sharp outlines. . . . As I breathed the sea air in, I assimilated with my whole being the assurance of my historical rightness in opposition to the epigones"—i.e., Stalin and his supporters.[7]

The schism that was to evoke "Trotskyism" and "Stalinism" was well developed before Lenin's passing. In April 1923, at Congress XII, attended by 408 delegates of 386,000 members, large majorities voted down appeals by Trotsky for squeezing the peasantry, by Sokolnikov and Bukharin for extending the NEP to foreign trade, and by Radek and Krassin for extensive concessions to foreign capital. With the approval of the Politburo, Trotsky expounded the "scissors crisis" (industrial prices stood at 140% of the 1913 level, while agricultural prices were only 80%) and proposed, as remedies, grain exports, reduction of costs of industrial production, and, ultimately, an end of the NEP in favor of full socialism and total planning. Given the difficulties of "primitive socialist accumulation," workers, he argued, must be content with only half of the value they produced. In this Stalin doubtless concurred. But he sensed a threat to his ambitions in October 1923 when Trotsky supported, even though

[6] V. I. Lenin: *A Political Biography*, pp. 276–7.
[7] *My Life*, p. 509.

he did not sign, a "Platform of 46 Oppositionists" wherein the NEP and the Party machine were both denounced and a demand was made for a conference between those supporting the majority of the Central Committee and their critics. In mid-January 1924 the 13th Party Conference, after hearing Stalin review the earlier discussion, rejected the views of the "Oppositionists."

At Congress XIII in May 1924, where 748 delegates spoke for 736,000 members, following the "Lenin enrollment" of 240,000 workers into the ranks, Trotskyism was condemned as a "petty bourgeois deviation from Marxism." When Zinoviev insisted that Trotsky recant or face expulsion, he did neither, but voiced a judgment, later repudiated, which was widely shared among Party leaders and was finally to bring many of them to humiliation and ruin: "The Party in the last analysis is always right because the Party is the single historic instrument given to the proletariat for the solution of its fundamental problems. . . . I know that one must not be right against the Party. One can only be right with the Party and through the Party." [8]

The issues between Stalin and the fluctuating group of his opponents were not only issues of intra-Party "democracy," Party "discipline," and the proper timing for a resumption of the "socialist offensive." They were also issues of the possibility of "socialism in one country" as against the doom of the regime which Trotsky and his confreres predicted if "world revolution" were not achieved. When, in the autumn of 1924, Trotsky published a volume of his speeches of 1917–18, he sowed the wind by gloating in his Introduction, "The Lessons of October," over his own support of Lenin's plan for an armed seizure of power which Zinoviev, Kamenev, and even Stalin had initially opposed. The harvest of the whirlwind was soon reaped. Trotsky was forced out of the Commissariat of War in January 1925 in favor of Mikhail Frunze, although he was at the same time made Chairman of the Concessions Committee and given other posts. Congress XIV, with 665 delegates of 643,000 members, adopted a famous resolve in December 1925, anticipating things to come and provoking a crisis. It declared that "in the sphere of economic development, the Congress holds that in our land, the land of the dictatorship of the proletariat, there is 'every requisite for the building of a complete socialist society' (Lenin). The Congress con-

[8] Merle Fainsod: *How Russia Is Ruled,* p. 139, quoting from the stenographic record of Congress XIII.

siders that the main task of our Party is to fight for the victory of socialist construction in the USSR."

Zinoviev and Kamenev favored the expulsion of Trotsky from the Party. Stalin opposed them: "Today we cut off one, tomorrow another, the day after tomorrow a third. But, by then, what will be left of the Party?" Zinoviev and Kamenev rejected the resolution for building "Socialism in One Country" and championed World Revolution. After the Congress adjourned, Zinoviev called a meeting of the Leningrad Provincial Committee of the Young Communist League (Komsomol), which passed a resolution refusing to abide by the decisions of the Congress. This flagrant breach of Party discipline brought Molotov, Kirov, Voroshilov, Kalinin, and other leaders to Leningrad, where they effected the endorsement of the work of the Congress by the Party local and the condemnation of the "New Opposition."

Trotsky, who spent the spring of 1926 doctoring in Berlin, formed a bloc with Zinoviev and Kamenev and demanded a new Party discussion. They were supported by Radek, Rakovsky, Pyatakov, Evdokimov, Smilga, Sokolnikov, and Smirnov in denying the possibility of socialism in a single country and insisting upon "permanent revolution," more intra-Party democracy, greater authority to the trade unions, and immediate steps to liquidate the kulaks, who had been permitted in 1925 to lease land and hire labor. Against this Left wing, formed in June 1926, a Right wing developed around Bukharin and Rykov, who then stood with Stalin against Trotsky but favored further concessions to the kulaks and an extension of the NEP. Trotsky's new colleagues were not towers of strength. Kamenev, who had married Trotsky's sister, was timid and vacillating. Both he and the loud-mouthed, faint-hearted Zinoviev "lacked that little thing called character," wrote Trotsky later. Stalin contended that collectivization and industrialization could build a socialist Russia, but only after production should be restored, by the methods of the NEP, to the pre-war level. After lively discussions at many Party gatherings, in which Left spokesmen made few converts, the new anti-Stalinist trio pledged itself in October to avoid any activities that might engender a split.

In 1927 Trotsky and his supporters seized upon several alarming events abroad to accuse Stalin of "betraying the World Revolution." The Comintern held its Third Congress in 1921, its Fourth in 1922, its Fifth in 1924, and its Sixth not until 1928. Revolutionary

hopes faded except in China, where Sun Yat-sen's Kuomintang had allied itself with the Communists and accepted Soviet aid through Mikhail Borodin and General Bluecher (Galen). But Sun died of cancer in 1924. Chiang Kai-shek, now victor in war, broke with the Communists in April 1927, deported his Russian advisers, and began the savage repression of all intellectuals, workers, and peasants suspected of Leftist sympathies. On May 26, 1927, the Soviet Minister in Warsaw, Peter Voikov, was assassinated by an *émigré*.[9] The Tory Cabinet in London, in protest against Soviet support of the General Strike of the preceding year, had meanwhile broken diplomatic relations with Moscow on May 26. Trotsky assailed Stalin anew and entered upon what he himself called "an open struggle" via "secret meetings" and "illegal means." [1]

Only later, as we shall see, did infractions of discipline or deviations from the Party "line" mean imprisonment or death. "Purge" still meant no more than demotion or expulsion from the brotherhood of oligarchs.[2] Zinoviev was dropped from the chairmanship of the Comintern. Kamenev and Trotsky were expelled from the Politburo. In September, in the "Platform of the 83," they demanded that their views be published and discussed in preparation for Congress XV. When the Central Committee refused, they secretly published and distributed their "Platform." On November 7 they organized street demonstrations in Moscow and Leningrad, leading to minor disorders. On November 14 the Central Committee voted to expel Zinoviev and Trotsky from the Party. When Adolf Joffe, Trotsky's deputy, killed himself on November 16, the Opposition demonstrated anew at the funeral.

That the Leftists should appeal to the Party membership and the general public against Stalin, Bukharin, and Rykov may seem quite legitimate to most Western liberals. But in terms of Lenin's conception (and Stalin's) of a disciplined, monolithic brotherhood, this was an intolerable offense. The Oppositionists justified their con-

[9] The assassin of Voikov, Boris Kowerda, was sentenced to life imprisonment, commuted to ten years at hard labor. He survived both World War II and the "Cold War," and in 1956 was admitted to the United States by a special Congressional dispensation. Cf. *NYT*, March 19, 1956.

[1] *My Life*, pp. 531–2.

[2] For details of the first instance (1923) of the arrest of a prominent Party member for a political offense—Sultan-Galiev, a Tartar Bolshevik of Kazan, who was exposed as a Moslem agitator against "Russianism," arrested by order of Stalin, Zinoviev, and Kamenev, tried, found guilty, expelled from the Party, and released after a brief detention—see Carr, IV, 286–9.

duct with the contention that Stalin had suppressed all free discussion within the Party. The argument was contrary to fact. In any event, the Leftists were less advocates of freedom of thought and talk than challengers of the Central Committee for the privilege of dictating thought and talk to the Party and the country.

Congress XV opened on December 2, 1927, with 898 delegates chosen by 887,000 members. In the voting, delegates representing 724,000 members supported the Central Committee. The Opposition received the vote of delegates speaking for only 4,000 members, with the balance abstaining. Stalin now urged collectivization and a Five Year Plan of industrialization. The Congress declared war on the kulaks, authorized the seizure of their grain surpluses, and offered the poorest peasants 25% of the confiscated crop. The Congress likewise expelled from the Party Trotsky, Zinoviev, Kamenev, Radek, Rakovsky, Preobrazhensky, Smirnov, Serebryakov, and several hundred lesser Oppositionists. It ruled that adherence to Trotsky's views was incompatible with Party membership. All the leading Oppositionists, save Trotsky, recanted and were readmitted on probation in June 1928 on condition of denouncing Trotskyism and accepting unconditionally Party decisions. In January 1928 Trotsky was exiled to Alma Ata in Turkestan.

Here he hunted, fished, lived comfortably, despite attacks of colitis, gout, and malaria, and carried on an extensive correspondence with little interference. Between April and October, by his own account, he sent out 800 political letters, "among them quite a few large works," and 550 telegrams, and received 1,000 political letters and 700 telegrams. He also carried on "secret" correspondence by courier. On December 16, 1928, an agent of the GPU arrived from Moscow with the demand that he cease his leadership of the Opposition. He refused in a long letter to the Central Committee and the Presidium of the Comintern. Stalin's supporters, he said, were "creatively impotent, false, contradictory, unreliable, blind, cowardly, inept" and were "executing the orders of the enemy classes. . . . The great historical strength of the Opposition, in spite of its apparent weakness, lies in the fact that it keeps its fingers on the pulse of the world historical process. . . . To abstain from political activity would mean to abstain from getting ready for tomorrow." On all points Trotsky was wrong. Being wrong, he was never able to forgive Stalin for being right. On January 20, 1929, he received the decision of the GPU:

Considered: the case of Citizen Trotsky, Lev Davydovich, under Article 58/10 of the Criminal Code, on a charge
of counter-revolutionary activity expressing itself in the organization of an illegal anti-Soviet Party, whose activity has
later been directed toward provoking anti-Soviet actions
and preparing for an armed struggle against the Soviet
Power. *Resolved:* Citizen Trotsky, Lev Davydovich, to be
deported from the territory of the USSR.

Trotsky with his wife and son were taken to his native Ukraine
and sent by sea from Odessa to Istanbul, where they arrived on
February 12. He tried to go to Germany or England, but could get
no visa. He finally went to France, then to Norway, and ultimately
to Mexico. His later role and that of his erstwhile followers belongs
to another chapter.

3. TOWARD SOCIALISM

THE transformation of Soviet society which began with the resumption of the "socialist offensive" in 1928, involving the end of the
NEP and the launching of the first of the "Five Year Plans," can
scarcely be regarded as an expression of the wishes of the masses of
peasants and workers. Most farmers and wage-earners, all Nepmen,
and some intellectuals, Communist and non-Communist alike, would
have preferred the relative prosperity of 1927 and a slow and painless "natural" growth of the economy, on the basis of a mixture of
"socialism" and "capitalism," to the frenzied tempo of directed development which Stalin, now undisputed leader of the oligarchs,
forced upon a sorely tried people. At most this "second revolution"
served the long-run interests of the populace, as distinct from its
own desires and definitions of its needs. It is arguable, moreover,
that without this compulsory mutation of town and countryside
Mother Russia would have succumbed to alien enemies in 1941–2.

But no mystique of Marxism can equate the process with "democracy" or "government by the people." As always in Russia's long
past, the sluggish and backward folk of the steppes, when unwilling
to do what was imperative for their own good, have given obedience, however reluctantly, to an Autocrat prepared to beat and

bludgeon them into doing what they otherwise would not have done. Such was the role of Ivan the Great, Ivan the Terrible, Peter the Great, and the Georgian cobbler's son, self-named Stalin or "Man of Steel." The name, chosen to indicate "strength of character" in the cause of proletarian revolution, is a symbolic paradox. Stalin's greatest claim to immortality, apart from the infamy of many of his deeds, was that he changed a country of wood into a country of steel.

The agonized striving of the "dark people" for modernity is the latest and most significant chapter of the age-old Russian effort to acquire Western science and technology, even though the Communist slave-drivers were so suspicious of the West as to seek at times to return to the most extreme forms of "Slavophile" xenophobia and isolationism. The process is also an aspect of the slow awakening of non-European peoples to the possibility of replacing ancient ignorance, poverty, filth, and squalor with some semblance of Western education, plenty, cleanliness, and welfare. This aspiration has been elevated in our time, among the yellow, brown, and black peoples of the world's slumlands, into a desperate passion to acquire steel mills, dams, power plants, and other components of a mechanized way of life. The dream first came to dramatic expression among the peoples of Red Muscovy. Although "white" in epidermal pigmentation and partially European in cultural heritage, they had lingered long on the dim periphery of Western civilization until their Marxist masters deferred messianic visions of "world revolution" in favor of a ruthless "Westernization" of Russia—albeit by ways that few Westerners could look upon without contempt and horror.

Industrialization is not unique. It has been experienced by England, Germany, and the United States and is now being experienced by China and India. What is unique in the USSR is that a single decade saw developments that required half a century or more elsewhere. Industrialization was achieved, moreover, without private capital, without foreign investments (save in the form of engineering skills and technical advice), without private ownership of any of the means of production, and with no unearned increment or private fortunes accruing to entrepreneurs or lucky investors. Resources were developed, labor was recruited, trained, and allocated, capital was saved and invested not through the price mechanism of a competitive market but through a consciously devised and deliberately executed national economic plan, drawn up by quinquennia,

by years, and by quarters for every segment of the economy. Politburo, Sovnarkom, and Gosplan supplied direction and coordination to the effort. But almost all Soviet citizens participated in planning, contributed to fulfillment in proportion to their abilities, and shared in the results. Nothing remotely comparable to this endeavor had ever been before attempted. Most outside observers were therefore certain that the effort would fail. But in all that was decisive for the future, Party and people carried through their self-imposed tasks to success.

This gigantic design for change can scarcely be depicted in statistics. It has tangible meaning only in terms of the experiences of millions, sharing in the excitement of achievement and in the deprivations required to translate fantastic blueprints into fabulous actualities. A staggering human reality is mirrored but faintly in the obvious generalizations: the adventure led from illiteracy to literacy, from the NEP to socialism, from archaic agriculture to collective cultivation, from a rural society to a predominantly urban community, from general ignorance of the machine to social mastery of modern technology.

Between the poverty-stricken year of 1924, when Lenin died, and the relatively abundant year of 1940, the cultivated area of the USSR expanded by 74%; grain crops increased 11%; coal production was multiplied by 10; steel output by 18; engineering and metal industries by 150; total national income by 10; industrial output by 24; annual capital investment (*c.* 40 billion rubles in 1940) by 57. During the First Five Year Plan, 51 billion rubles were invested; during the Second, 114; and during the Third, 192. Factory and office workers grew from 7,300,000 to 30,800,000, and school and college students from 7,900,000 to 36,600,000. Between 1913 (roughly comparable in most fields of production to the levels of 1927) and 1940, oil production increased from 9 to 35 million tons; coal from 29 to 164; pig-iron from 4 to 15; steel from 4 to 18; machine tools from 1,000 to 48,000 units; tractors from 0 to over 500,000; harvester combines from 0 to 153,500; electrical power output from 2 billion killowatt hours to 50 billion; and value of industrial output from 11 billion rubles to more than 100 billions by 1938. If the estimated volume of total industrial production in 1913 be taken as 100, the corresponding indices for 1938 are 93.2 for France; 113.3 for England; 120 for the United States; 131.6 for Germany; and 908.8 for the Soviet Union.

The human meaning of the last statistic is best suggested in personal terms. John Scott, who took part in the drama, puts the matter vividly:

> I arrived in Magnitogorsk, on the eastern slopes of the Ural mountains, in the fall of 1932 and went to work on blast-furnace construction. A week or so later, another young man came to work in the same gang. His name was Shaimat. Shaimat was a Tatar. He left his village because he had heard that in Magnitogorsk his bread ration would be larger than it was at home. When he arrived, he had never seen an electric light, a staircase, or a locomotive. He had seen a hammer but had never used one. The only hammering he had done was to drive a tent stake into the ground with a rock. . . . He did not wash and had many lice.
>
> Shaimat was sent to our gang by the plant personnel office in response to an urgent request by our foreman for an electrician. Shaimat had no such qualifications, of course, but he was a man. . . . Kolya, the foreman, cursed colorfully when he found Shaimat spoke no Russian—only his native Tatar—and was illiterate. But he put him to work in a booth where a half-dozen German AEC motor generators were grinding out direct current for welding. When the bulb in the ceiling went out, as it often did because of breakdowns in the power house or on the line, Shaimat was to turn off the motors, then switch them on again in two stages when the juice came back.
>
> During his first day Shaimat burned out two motors. He followed through with three more several days later. For a month or more he sat humming to himself some doleful Tatar tune or gaping up at the blast furnaces and coke ovens, without any comprehension at all of what it was all about. He had come to Magnitogorsk for that 1,000 gram bread card. He was getting it and seemed content.
>
> But then Shaimat began doing two things: first, he began to learn the Russian language by a sort of osmosis, and started to converse with the others in the gang and in the barracks at night; second, he was "organized" into a course for adult illiterates—nearly every barracks had such a course

—and he began to learn to read. As he struggled through his first simple newspapers and as he talked with those around him, his horizon suddenly broadened. . . . He learned that Magnitogorsk was one of the major construction jobs of the Five Year Plan, that its equipment had been bought in America and Germany in exchange for some hundred million dollars worth of Soviet butter and cloth and furs and wheat, which was why he, Shaimat, was frequently hungry and never well clothed. He learned that already the plant was producing half as much pig-iron as all of Russia in 1913. He was told—and believed—that the plant belonged to him and that ultimately he would get his steel in nails and rails and, perhaps, a bicycle.

And as he learned these things, Shaimat grew to like his work. He learned to curse the men in the power house when the juice went off and the gang stood idle. He learned that it was "cultured" to smear his spittle with his foot when he spit on the floor. He learned to attend the trade-union meetings and use his "activity" to get an extra meal card for the dining room. He also learned something of the nature of an electric motor.

As months became years, Shaimat changed rapidly. By 1937 he was going to night school, learning about amperes and ergs. He could rewind his motors when they burned out. He read books and magazines. He washed himself all over in the *banya* once a week. He had no lice and his clothes were neatly patched and fairly clean. He could solve quadratic equations, and he knew that Joseph Stalin, the Great White Father in Moscow, was responsible for these many blessings.

Of course Shaimat was crude, stubborn, and one-sided, but his way of life had changed more in his five years in Magnitogorsk than had that of his Tatar ancestors since the days of Tamerlane. He had been picked up by the scruff of the neck from a medieval village and dropped into a relatively modern industrial town with all the complicated technical and social problems one finds in such cities all over the world.

And Shaimat had survived. Many of his friends and fellow workmen did not survive. They died of typhus, froze

in the sub-zero temperatures in winter; they fell from scaffolds, dropped things on each other's heads. They ran afoul of the sleepless NKVD and got themselves shot. There were many hazards to which millions succumbed. But tens of millions, like Shaimat, survived and worked hard, excited with their new opportunities, hopeful of a better life in years to come.[3]

The political driving force behind the great offensive was the Communist Party and the Komsomol or League of Communist Youth. The battle was joined, though the full course of the campaign was not yet apparent, at Congress XV in December 1927. Stalin's endorsement of a Five Year Plan of industrialization and of the collectivization of agriculture was less a product of orthodox doctrine or of a desire to "steal the thunder" of the Trotskyites than of economic need, political necessity, and a lively apprehension of foreign attack.

The economic need arose from the fact that, although the NEP had raised rural production to something approaching its 1914 level, the marketed grain surplus available for urban consumption or export was only a third of its pre-war volume. Without a larger food supply, progress toward industrialized socialism was unthinkable. The situation, moreover, promised to become worse and to reproduce on a disastrous scale the "scissors crisis" of 1923–4 when agricultural prices were declining and industrial prices rising so sharply as to deprive the peasant of incentives to produce beyond his own needs. Most of the marketed grain came from the farms of the *kulaki,* or relatively well-to-do and efficient peasants, rather than from the *seredniaki* (middle peasants) or *bedniaki* (poorest peasants). The easiest means of increasing the food supply would have been to encourage the middle and poor peasants to become kulaks and to foster larger production by the kulaks through higher prices for grain, subsidies for increased output, and tax differentials in favor of the larger producers.

The political necessity which dictated a policy diametrically (and dialectically) opposed to any such course arose from the fact that such a policy would have established a large and growing class of prosperous "capitalist" farmers, producing for profit, owning

[3] John Scott: *Political Warfare: A Guide to Competitive Coexistence* (Day, 1955), pp. 158–61.

their own farms in fact if not in form, and inevitably serving as the nucleus of a new bourgeoisie. To relieve the food shortage by fostering any such development would have destroyed the class basis of the Revolution, dissolved the *smychka* or alliance between the proletariat and the peasantry, and rendered inevitable the evolution of the NEP into a full-fledged capitalism. The delegates at Congress XV were moved to reconsider the dicta of Lenin: "If peasant farming is to develop further, we must firmly assure also its transition to the next stage, and this next stage must inevitably be one in which the small, isolated peasant farms, the least profitable and most backward, will by a process of gradual amalgamation form large-scale collective farms." In the spirit of the Master, Stalin posed the question and gave his answer:

> What is the way out? The way out is to turn the small and scattered peasant farms into large united farms based on the common cultivation of the soil, to introduce collective cultivation of the soil on the basis of a new and higher technique. The way out is to unite the small and dwarf peasant farms gradually but surely, not by pressure but by example and persuasion, into large farms based on common, co-operative, collective cultivation of the soil with the use of agricultural machines and tractors and scientific methods of intensive agriculture. There is no other way out.

Congress XV "declared war" on the kulaks and took steps to "restrict the development of capitalism in the countryside and guide peasant farming toward socialism." In pursuit of these directives, the Soviet authorities empowered the courts to confiscate grain surpluses from kulaks who refused to sell them at low fixed prices, exempted a third of the poorest peasants from the land tax, and placed at their disposal a quarter of the grain confiscated from their more prosperous neighbors. Instructions were also issued for an increase in the number of *Sovkhozi* or State Farms and for the promotion of *Kolkhozi* or collective farms through the consolidation of individual holdings into large-scale enterprises.

Fear of foreign attack, prompted by the developments of 1927, contributed to this decision, for it was assumed that in the long run a socialist, collectivized agriculture would prove more productive than a capitalist agriculture. The Congress also directed the Gosplan to prepare the first of a series of Five Year Plans for the devel-

opment of socialized industry. Lenin had long ago anticipated such a program. The Red Army required a solid industrial base. Collective agriculture, moreover, presupposed the production of tractors, combines, and other machines for large-scale mechanized farming and of other manufacturers to be exchanged for foodstuffs. The engineer, V. I. Grinevetsky, in this book *Post-War Prospects of Russian Industry* (1919), had urged a systematic development of heavy industry and the location of new plants in the Urals and West Siberia. The Gosplan prepared its blueprints early in 1928. The first *Piatiletka* or Five Year Plan went into effect on October 1, 1928. In the following April the 16th Party Conference rejected the "minimal" variant of the Plan and adopted the "optimal" quotas. In a mood of crusading enthusiasm Congress XVI (June 1930) decided to "complete the Five Year Plan in four years"—by December 31, 1932.

What followed was a harrowing ordeal for the entire urban population and an embittered struggle throughout the countryside. The agrarian revolution of 1917–18, involving the expropriation of the aristocracy and the division of its estates among the peasants, had increased the number of family plots from roughly 16,000,000 to 25,000,000. The new revolution led finally to the consolidation of almost all of these individual farms into 250,000 *Kolkhozi*. Whether this radical transformation of Soviet agriculture could have been achieved by propaganda and material inducements in an orderly and economical fashion is debatable. It was in fact achieved by a resumption of "class war" in the villages and by a return to the conditions of 1918, when the "Committees of the Poor" terrorized and expropriated the more prosperous villagers. Stalin had urged collectivization by "example and persuasion." But by the autumn of 1929, when the program got fully under way, the slogan was: "Liquidate the Kulaks as a Class!" Their rights to hire labor and rent land were rescinded. The poorer peasants were allowed to pool all the possessions of the kulaks in the new collectives. In many districts enthusiastic Party leaders pushed the program far ahead of schedule and established "communes," in which all property was collectivized, instead of "artels," in which only land and tools became common assets.

The result was resistance and tragedy. The kulaks had been encouraged under the NEP to "get rich" and had contributed the larger share of the restoration of agricultural production. They were now forced into collectives and therewith lost not only their homes, land,

and equipment, but their horses, cattle, and even chickens. Their natural resentment led to punitive measures. Early in 1930 all village Soviets were dissolved and replaced by new Soviets elected exclusively by the poorest peasants. The "dekulakization" of the more prosperous took the form of denying them membership in the collectives and deporting hundreds of thousands to the far north and Siberia, where they were housed in GPU concentration camps and forced to work at lumbering, road-building, and the construction of canals and railways. Their fellows in the villages had no leadership, but decided as one man, with the unanimity and stubbornness of wronged farmers the world over, to oppose their oppressors. Their opposition took the initial form of slaughtering their cattle and horses in preference to having them collectivized. The result was a grievous blow to Soviet agriculture, for most of the cattle and horses were owned by the kulaks. Between 1928 and 1933 the number of horses in the USSR declined from almost 30,000,000 to less than 15,000,000; of horned cattle from 70,000,000 (including 31,000,000 cows) to 38,000,000 (including 20,000,000 cows); of sheep and goats from 147,000,000 to 50,000,000; and of hogs from 20,000,000 to 12,000,000. Soviet rural economy had not recovered from this staggering loss by 1941.

Stalin sought in vain to save the situation. In January 1930 he had resolutely endorsed the policy of eliminating the kulaks as a class (cf. *Krasnaya Zveszda*, January 21, 1930). In *Pravda* of March 2, 1930, however, he rebuked the more ardent comrades in an article entitled "Dizzy with Success." He noted that 50% of all farms had been collectivized—more than double the number envisaged in the Plan. "People are often intoxicated by such successes, they become dizzy with success, they lose all sense of proportion, they lose the faculty of understanding realities. . . . In such cases care is not taken to *consolidate* the successes achieved and systematically to *utilize* them for the purpose of advancing further. . . ." Collectivization should be voluntary. "Collective farms cannot be set up by force." Stalin condemned "distortions" and insisted upon the artel as the appropriate form of collectivization, with no pooling of houses, gardens, orchards, livestock, and poultry. Some "revolutionaries" are "disintegrating and discrediting" the movement. Some begin collectivization "by removing the church bells. How revolutionary indeed! Blockheads!" The Central Committee published resolutions. A halt was called.

But great damage had already been done. More followed. Many members now left the collectives. In the autumn 48 officials of the Commissariat of Agriculture were executed for sabotage, theft, and oppression of the peasants. In March 1933 the GPU announced that 35 more officials had been found guilty of counter-revolutionary acts and had been tried and executed. They included Feodor Konar, alias Polashchuk, Vice-Commissar of Agriculture, who confessed to having acted for years as a Polish spy and to having directed a conspiracy to reduce food output and to drive the peasants to desperation. Many indeed were desperate. In the Ukraine most of the kulaks appear to have become completely demoralized as a result of systematic persecution. Some murdered officials, set the torch to the property of the collectives, and even burned their own crops and seed grain. More refused to sow or reap, perhaps on the assumption that the authorities would make concessions and would in any case feed them.

The aftermath was the Ukraine "famine" of 1932–3. Its existence was never acknowledged by Soviet spokesmen. Lurid accounts, mostly fictional, appeared in the Nazi press in Germany and in the Hearst press in the United States, often illustrated with photographs that turned out to have been taken along the Volga in 1921. During the summer of 1933 Moscow barred foreign reporters from the Ukraine, although continuing, with bureaucratic inconsistency, to admit tourists by thousands—the present writer among them. The "famine" was not, in its later stages, a result of a food shortage, despite the sharp reduction of seed grain and harvests flowing from special requisitions in the spring of 1932 which were apparently occasioned by fear of war with Japan. Most of the victims were kulaks who had refused to sow their fields or had destroyed their crops. Observation in the villages suggests that this portion of the peasantry was left to starve by the authorities and the collective farmers as a more or less deliberate policy. Large numbers (again unspecified) were deported to labor camps, where some died of malnutrition and disease and others were rehabilitated into useful citizens. The human cost of "class war in the villages" was horrible and heavy. The Party appeared less disturbed by dead kulaks than by dead cows. The former were "class enemies."

The grim and brutal battle for collectivization was nevertheless crowned with ultimate victory. Congress XVI in June 1930 pushed the attack. Stalin called it "the Congress of the sweeping offensive of

socialism along the whole front, of the elimination of the kulaks as a class, and of the realization of solid collectivization." In January 1933 the Central Committee decided to organize "political departments" in the Machine and Tractor Stations serving the *Kolkhozi*. Some 17,000 Party members went out into the countryside to work for the cause. By 1933 over 200,000 tractors and 25,000 combines were in use. By the end of 1940, 99% of all arable land throughout the Union was included in the collectives. The balance represented State Farms and a scattering of individual holdings. The *Kolkhoz* members painfully learned to become mechanics and to make mechanized agriculture pay dividends to themselves and the State. Opposition and doubt gave way to confidence and energetic participation in the new agriculture, which had demonstrated its superiority over the old ways.

The ruthless struggle for rapid collectivization and industrialization was accompanied by arrests, executions, and various trials of obstructionists, saboteurs, and scapegoats. During the earlier years the GPU, "the unsheathed sword of the proletarian dictatorship," retained its power to make arrests, conduct secret trials, and impose sentences. In December 1930, in a spectacular public trial, eight engineers and intellectuals, headed by Prof. Ramzin, were sent to prison after confessing to a conspiracy, subsidized from abroad, to establish an "Industrial Party" for the purpose of replacing the Soviet power with a bourgeois regime.[4] In March 1931 a group of Mensheviks was sent to jail after confessing to a sabotage plot, allegedly planned at a secret meeting in Moscow in the summer of 1928 with Rafael Abramovich, Menshevik leader in exile. Abramovich published an "alibi," purporting to prove that he had resided in Germany and Belgium during the entire summer. In March 1933 Allan Monkhouse, Leslie Thornton, William MacDonald, and three other British subjects, plus various Russians, all employed by the Metropolitan-Vickers Company, were arrested for espionage and sabotage. Several confessed and received prison sentences in April. London imposed an embargo on Soviet goods. In July it was lifted when the jailed Britishers were released and deported. Other similar episodes marked these hectic years. Thousands of Soviet citizens suffered

[4] Ramzin and four other defendants were sentenced to death, but the sentences were commuted to 10 years' imprisonment. On July 7, 1943, Prof. Ramzin was awarded the Order of Lenin and the Stalin prize of $30,000 for the invention of the Ramzin turbo-generator.

even heavier penalties for theft of State property (made a capital offense by the law of August 7, 1933) and for interfering in other ways with the fulfillment of the Plans.

Within the Party the miseries and frustrations engendered by the great adventure found expression in the "Right Deviationists" who followed Bukharin and Rykov. In their concern for the kulaks and for the future of agriculture, those who had formerly supported the majority of the Central Committee against the Trotskyites now sought to make common cause with their erstwhile foes against Stalin. In July 1928 Bukharin secretly visited Kamenev, who jotted down the comments of his guest and sent the notes to Zinoviev, who dispatched them abroad to Trotsky's followers, by whom they were later published: "We [Bukharin, Rykov, and Mikhail Tomsky] consider Stalin's line fatal to the Revolution. . . . He is an unprincipled intriguer who subordinates everything to his appetite for power. . . . While giving way, he has kept hold of the leadership and later will strangle us. . . . What is to be done? . . . Stalin's policy is leading us to civil war. He will be forced to drown the rebellion in blood." Early in 1929 clandestine negotiations were apparently begun for the formation of a bloc of Right and Left Oppositionists. When Rykov, Tomsky, and Bukharin proposed to quit the Central Committee, they were condemned by their colleagues for "this saboteur policy of resignations." In November 1929, however, the Central Committee removed Bukharin from the Politburo, warned other Rightists, and ruled that propagation of the views of the Right Deviationists was incompatible with Party membership.

Not for another five years were the dissenters within the ranks to bring down upon themselves the full wrath of the Party and State. In the interim they recanted and professed obedience to Party decisions. The Party moved forward in its herculean task under a leadership that by 1931 included among the members of the Politburo such able administrators as Vyacheslav Molotov, successor to Rykov as Chairman (Premier) of the Sovnarkom; Valerian V. Kuibyshev, Chairman of the Gosplan; Y. E. Rudzutak, Commissar for Communications; G. K. Ordjonikidze, Commissar for Workers' and Peasants' Inspection; and Klementy E. Voroshilov, Commissar for Defense. By the time of Congress XVI, whose 1,268 delegates assembled on June 26, 1930, the Party for the first time had more than a million members (1,261,000) and over 700,000 candidates. Congress XVII, meeting in January 1934, had 1,225 delegates, speaking for 1,874,000

members and 935,000 candidates. At this "Congress of Victors," Bukharin, Rykov, Tomsky, Kamenev, and Zinoviev renounced their past mistakes and eulogized the Party leadership—with something less than full sincerity, as was soon to become clear. New Party rules were adopted. To all outward appearances, the crusading brotherhood that ruled the USSR was not only more successful than ever before in carrying out its program but was solidly united in the pursuit of its purposes.

Its central objective—to build a mammoth structure of heavy industry on socialist foundations—was carried far toward completion between Congresses XV and XVII. The machine age came swiftly. By millions the sons and daughters of illiterate *muzhiks* now learned to read and write, to handle modern tools, to understand motors and assembly lines and even in many cases to become technicians and engineers. These exhilarating experiences, opening out new vistas in every direction, overshadowed the incalculable wastage and wreckage and the incredible squalor and want of the new industrial centers. Whenever production fell amid the advances and retreats of the First Five-Year Plan, brigades of *Udarniki* or shock-workers were rushed to threatened sectors of the industrial front to hold the line. Factories sprouted like mushrooms on this strange battlefield. On the great bend of the Dnieper a new citadel arose, under the direction of Hugh L. Cooper, American engineer: the Dnieper River Power Station, with its gigantic dam and mighty turbines. Far to the east, Magnitogorsk sprang from the soil as a bastion of the Ural-Kuznetsk industrial combinat. Pipelines in Transcaucasia, railways in Turkestan, plants for manufacturing motor cars, tractors, and agricultural machinery in Gorky, Stalingrad, Rostov, Kharkov, and Chelyabinsk all were visible symbols of victory.

All difficulties were met by setting higher goals, by exhorting all to greater efforts, and by pouring millions of new proletarians into industry. Quality was sacrificed to quantity. Workers whose output was far below Western European and American standards were supplemented by other workers in endless numbers, equally inefficient but inspired by the new gospel and able to learn and produce results. Between 1929 and 1940 wage-earners worked five days and rested one in overlapping shifts with no regard to Sundays or holidays, so that many industrial establishments operated seven days a week and twenty-four hours a day with three daily shifts. Living standards, measured in consumers' goods and housing, although not

in social services and educational opportunities, declined during the first Plan. The result was a ceaseless migration of workers from district to district in search of more favorable conditions, with a labor turnover of amazing proportions. Under the second Plan, 1933–8, life became easier, if not less hectic, and the labor supply became more stable.

In 1935 a coal miner named Alexei Stakhanov stumbled upon some of the elements of "Taylorism," with its time-motion-and-efficiency methods of rationalizing production. Through teamwork he greatly increased his daily output and became the symbol of "Stakhanovism" in all industry. "Speed-up," piece-work, and bonuses became the order of the day. To "overtake and surpass America" in industrial production became the watchword. This goal was as yet beyond accomplishment. But in striving toward it the USSR was to become the second most powerful industrial State of the world.

4. IN QUEST OF SECURITY

THE *modus vivendi* achieved between Marxist Muscovy and its neighbors in the aftermath of the First War of East and West persisted throughout the 1920's to the tune of various vicissitudes and occasional crises, but with no renewal of violence. The post-Versailles "stabilization of capitalism" sent Communist dreams of World Revolution glimmering. The consolidation of the Soviet order, the success of the NEP, and the later "building of socialism" thwarted Western prayers for the downfall of the Red regime. On both sides hope continued to spring eternally from reciprocal suspicion. But in fact no practical alternative to peace was available.

For the men in the Kremlin, as for any group of policy-makers ruling a "Great Power" in a State System comprising a multiplicity of rival sovereignties, the gravest danger and the recurrent nightmare of all *Realpolitik* has always been the possibility of finding themselves alone in the face of a hostile combination of all other Powers. Since the USSR was the only "socialist" State in the world of "bourgeois" States during the long armistice between World Wars, this peril loomed large in the minds of the Communist power-holders who had inherited the Tsarist empire. Their prescription for minimizing the hazard was compounded of diplomatic support to

the vanquished and "revisionist" States of Europe against the dominant French bloc, championship of disarmament and outlawry of war, and sponsorship of bilateral non-aggression and neutrality pacts pledging the signatories to non-participation in any hostilities initiated by others. For more than a decade this formula served the purposes of Soviet security. To outline its application is our present concern.

The Narkomindel was ably directed by Chicherin, who later retired in ill-health and died on July 7, 1936, and by his shrewd helpmate Litvinov, who succeeded him as Commissar for Foreign Affairs on July 25, 1930. Both continued to seek recognition from the USA, but without success, for the America of the 1920's was as determined never to acknowledge the fact of Communist rule of Russia as the America of the 1950's was determined never to acknowledge the fact of Communist rule of China. This attitude, usually futile in relations among Great Powers, was a legacy of Woodrow Wilson's aberration in confusing diplomatic recognition (always a convenience and often a necessity) with moral or political approbation and in using non-recognition as a weapon to punish Evil and foster Good. When Litvinov in March 1921 sent a message from Kalinin to President Harding soliciting negotiations, Secretary of State Hughes replied that "this Government is unable to perceive that there is any proper basis for considering trade relations" pending "convincing evidence" of a restoration of "private property, the sanctity of contracts and the rights of free labor." Russia, said the Secretary, was "a gigantic economic vacuum" and would remain so as long as "the present political and economic system continued." Despite the anomaly of no official relations between the only two Great Powers that held the League of Nations in contempt and ardently championed disarmament and neutrality, Soviet-American trade flourished in a modest way, with Amtorg handling most of the exchanges of machinery, metals, cotton, and motor cars for furs, manganese, flax, and caviar.

The curious pattern of concords and clashes between Washington and Moscow during the '20's is worth recalling in view of later relationships. Although American policy-makers were eager for disarmament by international agreement, they were as shocked as were their Western European counterparts when the wily Litvinov, with tongue in cheek, appeared in Geneva in November 1927 at the fourth session of the League Preparatory Commission to arrange a

general disarmament conference and there slyly suggested that the
way to disarm was to disarm. He urged an immediate global accord
for the total demobilization of all land, sea, and air forces, the scrap-
ping of all weapons, the cessation of military training, and the abolition of general staffs, defense ministries, and military budgets. This
"breach of all the proprieties," as he himself said, was "received as
a sacrilege." His appeal for American support was rebuffed by Hugh
Gibson. When his plea was rejected, he proposed limited disarmament by degrees on a quota basis—which was also rejected. The
League's General Disarmament Conference did not meet until February 2, 1932, when the Japanese Navy was bombarding Shanghai.
In a maladjusted world again on the road to war, all such efforts
were doomed.

When a peace-seeking America sponsored the Kellogg-Briand
Pact of Paris of August 27, 1928, renouncing war as an instrument of
national policy and pledging the signatories to settle disputes by
peaceful means, Litvinov at once signed (August 31) and saw to it
that the USSR was the first Power to ratify. He further persuaded
Poland, Rumania, Estonia, and Latvia to sign the "Litvinov Protocol" (February 9, 1929), to which Lithuania, Danzig, Turkey, and
Iran soon adhered, putting the Pact into effect at once between
them and the USSR. This apparent parallelism of American and Soviet policies had a paradoxical sequel. Washington had protested in
vain to China against a Sino-Soviet accord of May 31, 1924, signed
by Wellington Koo and Leo Karakhan, whereby the USSR renounced all Russian concessions, privileges, and rights of extraterri-
toriality in China and agreed to joint control of the Chinese Eastern
Railway to the exclusion of other Powers. When the young Manchurian warlord, Chang Hsueh-liang, arbitrarily seized the railway
in the summer of 1929, Moscow sent troops across the frontier to
protect Soviet interests. Washington espoused "internationaliza-
tion" and "neutralization" of the line. Chang yielded to Soviet pressure and agreed on December 3 to a restoration of joint Russian-
Chinese management. On the preceding day Secretary of State
Henry L. Stimson had "invoked" the Kellogg Pact, with the implication that Moscow had violated its pledges. Litvinov at once denounced such "unjustified pressure" and unwelcome "advice and
counsel" from a government that refused to maintain diplomatic relations with the USSR.

The Kremlin meanwhile quarreled bitterly, albeit non-violently,

with Britain, where Churchill (November 28, 1925) said "the dark power of Moscow" was based upon "a band of cosmopolitan conspirators gathered from the underworld" and Lord Birkenhead described the Soviet regime as "a junta of assassins and thieves." On August 8, 1924, the first Labor Cabinet signed two treaties, subject to parliamentary approval, contemplating a loan to Moscow as a condition of compensation to British property-owners and bondholders for their losses in Russia. The Tories were outraged and the Liberals, under Asquith and Lloyd George, resentful. The Cabinet fell on October 8, 1924. Four days before the election set for October 29 the Foreign Office published a protest to Moscow against an alleged appeal by Zinoviev to British Communists for "armed insurrection." The "Zinoviev Letter" was a Tory device to discredit the Laborites. Ramsay McDonald, as usual, fumbled the ball. The polling reduced Labor from 191 to 151 seats in Commons, and the Liberals, who never recovered, from 159 to 40. The triumphant Tories named a Cabinet headed by Stanley Baldwin, with Sir Austen Chamberlain as Foreign Secretary. The treaties were dropped and an attitude of unyielding hostility was assumed in the face of repeated Soviet efforts to negotiate a settlement of all disputes.

On May 26, 1927, following a Home Office raid on the HQ of Arcos, Ltd. and the Soviet Trade Delegation, London severed diplomatic relations with Moscow, while Lord Birkenhead vainly strove to effect an Anglo-French-German coalition against the USSR. The election of May 30, 1929, returned the Laborites to power. A new pact of October 1, 1929, approved in Commons on November 5, provided for a resumption of diplomatic relations, subsequently effected with the exchange of Ambassadors Sir Esmond Ovey and Gregory Sokolnikov. A commercial accord of April 16, 1930, provided for most-favored-nation treatment and the restoration in London of a Soviet Trade Delegation with diplomatic immunities. For the first time, but by no means the last, the politics of a democratic Great Power had been set askew by fear of Red radicalism and by fabricated crises in relations with the USSR.

The men of Moscow, in the interim, had viewed with alarm the British proposals of 1924 for a Western European security pact, lest it presage an anti-Soviet coalition. During the 1920's the Kremlin cultivated Berlin in the "spirit of Rapallo" and enabled the Weimar Republic to evade the Treaty of Versailles by sending officers to Russia for training in military tactics and techniques. When a Treaty

of Mutual Guarantee was signed at Locarno, October 16, 1925, by Stresemann, Briand, Sir Austen Chamberlain, Benito Mussolini, and other Western statesmen, Chicherin pressed Stresemann to enter into Bismarckian "reinsurance" arrangements with Russia. The result was the German-Soviet treaty of April 24, 1926.

This agreement embodied the basic formula of all Soviet peace pacts during these years. It was foreshadowed by the treaty of December 17, 1925, signed in Paris by Chicherin and Tewfik Rushdi Bey, Foreign Minister of Turkey, who was smarting from the award of Mosul to Iraq by the League Council two days previously. Turkey and the USSR each agreed to remain neutral in any war involving the other and pledged themselves not to attack each other or to enter into any blocs, coalitions, or agreements against each other. The Soviet-German treaty, concluded for five years and subsequently extended, reaffirmed the Treaty of Rapallo and specified that "should one of the Contracting Parties, despite its peaceful attitude, be attacked by one or more third Powers, the other Contracting Party shall observe neutrality for the whole duration of the conflict" (Art. 2). If such a conflict should occur or a coalition be formed "with a view to the economic or financial boycott of either of the Contracting Parties, the other Contracting Party undertakes not to adhere to such coalition" (Art. 3). Stresemann further pledged his Government to oppose any anti-Soviet moves at Geneva and to decide for itself whether the USSR should ever be deemed an aggressor and to what extent, if any, the Reich would apply League sanctions. Moscow concluded similar non-aggression and neutrality pacts with Lithuania (September 28, 1926), Afghanistan (August 31, 1926), Iran (October 1, 1927), Estonia (May 2, 1932), Latvia (February 5, 1932), Finland (January 21, 1932), Poland (July 25, 1932, extended May 5, 1934, to December 31, 1945), and finally with France (November 29 1932).

Neutrality is the antithesis of collective security. The Soviet peace pacts of the 1920's were in principle and purpose the negation of the League Covenant. The latter sought to generalize war by obligating all States to join forces against aggressors. The former sought to localize war by obligating each signatory to remain aloof from any conflict in which the other might be involved. For Moscow, as for Washington, the formula for peace was not the Wilsonian precept of "making any war everybody's business," but rather the injunction of "keeping out of other people's wars." American isolation-

ism and Soviet fear of hostile coalitions led to a similar result in foreign policy. Moscow was in no sense "isolationist." But under the conditions of the time it correctly envisaged its security in terms of pledging as many other States as possible to refrain from aggression and to observe neutrality in any armed clash in which the USSR might be involved.

Litvinov crowned his structure of peace pacts by negotiating at the otherwise fruitless London Economic Conference of 1933 a "Convention for the Definition of Aggression," signed on July 4–6 by envoys of the USSR, Estonia, Latvia, Lithuania, Poland, Rumania, Czechoslovakia, Jugoslavia, Turkey, Iran, and Afghanistan. Aggression was defined as declaration of war, invasion, attack on territory, vessels, or aircraft, naval blockade, and support of armed bands invading another State. "No political, military, economic or other considerations may serve as an excuse or justification for aggression."

Peace was thus sought by legalistic formulas equally beloved by Soviet and American diplomats. The long armistice was, in fact, about to come to an end by virtue of a real, rather than imaginary, "collapse of capitalism," with political and military consequences wholly and horribly different from those forecast in the Marxist prognosis. Adolf Hitler became Chancellor of Germany on January 30, 1933. In the sequel the rulers and the ruled of Russia had desperate need of new devices for national survival.

CHAPTER SIX

The Reign of Fear

1. DEFENSE AGAINST FASCISM

To convert imperialist war into civil war was Lenin's favorite formula for international peace and global proletarian revolution. To convert civil war into imperialist war became the formula of Fascism in the 1930's for the solution of the problems posed by the catastrophic breakdown and prolonged stagnation of capitalistic economy. In none of the afflicted societies did the débâcle foreseen by Marx and Lenin create favorable conditions for the proletarian revolt which they and their followers anticipated. In several national communities it produced new despotisms brought to power by frightened industrialists and aristocrats, and fanatically supported in the name of anti-Bolshevism by the desperately insecure and neurotic masses of the lower middle class. The new tyrants restored production by programs of colossal rearmament. They kept peace at home by waging war abroad. First and last, the major target of their plans for aggression was the Soviet Union—as they never tired of boasting, once they discovered that those with wealth and influence in the "decadent" democracies were favorably impressed by such advertising. The anatomy of disaster is still fresh in many memories.

On "Black Thursday" in late October 1929 the American Dream of endless inflationary prosperity through stock speculation and installment buying came to an end with a panic-stricken fall of prices on the New York Stock Exchange. By month's end, the bottom had fallen out of the market. By year's end, corporate shares had declined in value by $15,000,000,000. Within two years the slump had wiped out $50,000,000,000 of paper values, bankrupted millions of

Americans, and reduced the richest country on earth to beggary, with 13,000,000 unemployed by 1933. At the close of the Hoover Administration every bank in the USA closed its doors. The American economy was prostrate. This "collapse of capitalism," hailed with joy by all Communists, was scarcely attributable to the "causes" alleged in the Marxist-Leninist analysis, but was rather due to the inability of statesmen in America and elsewhere to comprehend the sources of the disaster and to resort boldly to Keynesian measures of amelioration.

The ensuing "World Depression" grievously afflicted every community in the world save only the Soviet Union, whose totally socialized and planned economy was, for all its ills, immune to "business cycles." The USSR, to be sure, was adversely affected by the drastic decline of prices for raw materials coupled with a slower decline of prices for manufactures. More goods had to be exported to pay for the same amounts of imports. Otherwise the effects of the slump were negligible. Elsewhere they proved disastrous, with the political beneficiaries of mass misery everywhere sworn to Holy War against Bolshevism.

"Fascism" had already conquered Italy in 1922 under the leadership of an ex-Marxist turned demagogue and dictator. The burghers of Germany, facing bankruptcy and confronted by 6,000,000 jobless, cast 6,400,000 votes for Hitler's Nazis in the *Reichstag* election of September 14, 1930; 13,400,000 in the presidential election of April 10, 1932; and 13,745,000 (37% of the total) in the *Reichstag* election of July 31, 1932. Through a conspiracy of industrialists, bankers, and militarists, Hitler became *Reichskanzler* on January 30, 1933, and proceeded in six months to do what Mussolini had taken three years to accomplish: the suppression of all other parties, the creation of a totalitarian dictatorship on the Soviet model, and the restoration of prosperity through public spending on armaments in preparation for wars of conquest to come. The warlords of Japan effected, more slowly, a like transfer of power in Tokyo. Similar groups arose and flourished in Austria, Hungary, the Balkans, Spain, France, and elsewhere.

The crisis found all Communists, bewitched by their vision of "proletarian revolution" and absorbed in their war against Social Democrats as "traitors" to Marxism, totally incapable of comprehending political realities. In most of Europe political liberals did no better, for many among them agreed with conservatives that Fas-

cism was a bulwark against Bolshevism. The black magic of an evil time made politics a hopeless contest between the discouraged and the demented, with the former often regarding the latter as guardians of civilization against Communism. The outcome posed to the USSR a mortal threat of assault from abroad.

The masters of Muscovy, reduced to consternation by the demonstrated falsity of their own dogma, strove to meet the danger by abandoning the formula of "neutrality" and embracing the concept of "collective security" in the hope of somehow organizing a Grand Alliance against Fascism. Had this effort succeeded, World War II would never have been fought, for the aggregation of superior power confronting the Fascist Cæsars would have convinced them, for all their delusions and ambitions, that they had no chance of victory in their bid for world conquest. Even madmen in power do not unleash war unless they believe that their prospects of winning are good. The Soviet effort failed, partly because of continued Muscovite suspicion of the motives of the Western Powers but chiefly because Anglo-French policy-makers hoped, to the ghastly end, that Fascist aggression could be deflected against the USSR. The record of the failure of statesmen, in East and West alike, to meet the challenge of the new nihilists has elsewhere been recounted at length. It is enough for the task in hand to outline the responses of the Kremlin Commissars to the successive crises of a decade of disaster.[1]

On September 18, 1931, Lieut. Gen. Honjo's Imperial Japanese Kwantung Army, using as a pretext a bomb explosion on the tracks of the South Manchuria Railway near Mukden, began the seizure of China's rich northeastern provinces. A year later Henry Pu-yi, last of the Manchus, was set up as "Emperor Kang Teh" in the Japanese puppet state of "Manchukuo." Neither League resolutions at Geneva

[1] For detailed diplomatic histories of these years, based upon all the documentation available at the time of writing, see the present writer's *Europe on the Eve* (Knopf, 1939) and *Night over Europe* (Knopf, 1941). Cf. George D. Brodsky and F. L. Schuman: *Design for Power* (Knopf, 1942). See also the various annual and special volumes of the Royal Institute of International Affairs, Chatham House, London (Oxford University Press), dealing with these years, and Donald G. Bishop (ed.); *Soviet Foreign Relations: Documents and Readings* (Syracuse University Press, 1953); R. P. Browder: *The Origins of Soviet-American Diplomacy* (Princeton University Press, 1953); David T. Catell: *Communism and the Spanish Civil War* (University of California Press, 1955); Joseph E. Davies: *Mission to Moscow* (Simon & Schuster, 1941); Stefan T. Possony: *A Century of Conflict: Communist Techniques of World Revolution, 1848–1950* (Regnery, 1953); and Pauline Tompkins: *American-Russian Relations in the Far East* (Macmillan, 1950).

nor America's "Stimson Doctrine" of non-recognition of the results of aggression changed Tokyo's course. *Izvestia* (September 21, 1931) opined that Chinese inability to defend Manchuria revealed "the depths of the collapse and the degree of weakness to which China has been brought by the Kuomintang feudal-bourgeois reaction." Litvinov voiced "serious alarm." Molotov in December asserted that the League Powers had shown "complete lack of desire and ability" to end the conflict, which he termed "the most important problem of our foreign policy."

The Narkomindel's devices for countering the danger of Japanese aggression were several. A new offer of a neutrality pact was evaded by Tokyo. Chinese proposals for a resumption of diplomatic relations, severed in 1927, were accepted by Moscow in December 1932. When Geneva invited the USSR to become a member of the League Advisory Committee of February 1933 to seek acceptance of the proposals of the belated and futile Lytton Commission, Litvinov declined on the ground that the USSR was pledged to "strict neutrality" and that most of the other members "do not maintain any relations with the Soviet Union and consequently are hostile to it." Since Japanese interruption of traffic on the Chinese Eastern Railway was now chronic, Litvinov on May 2, 1933, proposed the sale of Russian rights in the line. After much Oriental haggling, "Manchukuo" (i.e., Japan) agreed on March 23, 1935, to pay 170,000,000 yen. A valuable Soviet property on Chinese soil was thus sacrificed at a fraction of its worth in the hope of minimizing friction with Tokyo. But it soon became apparent that the militarists of Japan understood only the language of force. Said Litvinov to the Central Executive Committee in December, 1933:

Along with infringing our rights on the railroad, political figures in Japan, including official representatives of the Japanese Government, began to discuss openly and even in the press the question of war against the Soviet for the purpose of seizing the Primore and the whole Far Eastern Krai. . . . In Manchuria near our border a large number of Japanese troops were concentrated, war materials were brought, railroads and highways were built, etc. In this way the danger not only of the seizure of our railroad by Japanese arms, but a direct danger to our frontier was created. Under these circumstances there was nothing left for our

Government to do but to begin to fortify our frontier, transferring the necessary forces for that purpose and taking
other military measures.[2]

Soviet-Japanese tension, coupled with American-Japanese friction, the rise of Hitler, and the advent of the "New Deal," contributed to Washington's belated recognition of the USSR. Senator
William E. Borah had long urged a facing of facts. Franklin D.
Roosevelt was favorably disposed. Business interests were sympa-
thetic, the more so as exports to the USSR had declined from $100,-
000,000 in 1931 to $9,000,000, in 1933. Raymond Robins, long an ad-
vocate of recognition, visited Moscow early in the year, traveled
through the Ukraine and Siberia, and had a long interview with
Stalin on May 13, 1933. In June, Raymond Moley and William C.
Bullitt conferred with Litvinov in London. Bullitt subsequently returned to Moscow, where Wilson had sent him in 1919. The Administration's course was much influenced by Robert F. Kelley, Chief of
the Eastern European Division of the State Department since 1926.
His memorandum of July 27, 1933, urged that recognition be withheld until Moscow should agree to a cessation of revolutionary propaganda, payment of repudiated debts, and compensation for confiscated property.[3]

On October 10, 1933, Roosevelt invited Kalinin to send an envoy "to end the present abnormal relations" between the two countries. Litvinov reached Washington on November 7, staying with
Boris Skvirsky, head of the Russian Information Bureau, and telling
newsmen that all questions could be settled in half an hour. His
prime purpose was to promote American-Soviet collaboration to
checkmate Japan and Germany. Roosevelt and Hull, unwilling and
unable to assume any such commitments, concentrated on the problems of propaganda, debts, and claims. Long discussions ensued, unhappily lacking in precision, as later controversies were to reveal. On
November 16, 1933, texts of accords were issued.

President and Commissar agreed to an exchange of Ambassa-

---

[2] Maxim Litvinov: *Against Aggression* (International Publishers, 1939),
pp. 76 ff. Cf. Arthur Upham Pope: *Maxim Litvinoff* (Fischer, 1943) and Harriet Moore: *Soviet Far Eastern Policy, 1931–1945* (Princeton University Press,
1945).

[3] See William Appleman Williams: *American-Russian Relations, 1781–
1947* (Rinehart, 1952), pp. 231–55, and Marshall Knappen: *An Introduction
to American Foreign Policy* (Harper, 1956), pp. 238 f.

dors (William C. Bullitt and Alexander Troyanovsky) and expressed
the hope that diplomatic relations would lead to cooperation for
"mutual benefit and for the preservation of the peace of the world."
Litvinov agreed that the USSR should refrain "from interfering in
any manner in the internal affairs of the United States"; should restrain all persons and organizations under its control from all agitation or propaganda aimed at "bringing about by force a change in
the political or social order of the whole or any part of the United
States, its territories or possessions"; and should not permit on its
territory any organization or group aiming at intervention in, or revolutionary propaganda against, the United States. Roosevelt accepted reciprocal obligations and included in the compact a guarantee (willingly accepted by Litvinov to the tune of relevant citations
from Soviet legislation) that Americans in the Soviet Union would
be granted complete and unqualified religious liberty and would enjoy most-favored-nation treatment in legal protection. Questions of
financial claims and counter-claims were deferred. But Litvinov expressly agreed to waive all counter-claims arising out of intervention in Siberia, thanks to his "examination of certain documents of
the years 1918 to 1921 relating to the attitude of the American Government toward the expedition into Siberia, the operations there of
foreign military forces and the inviolability of the territory of the
USSR."

The sequel was not cooperation against the rising tide of Fascism, equally menacing to Russia and America, but petty squabbling
over irrelevancies. Litvinov and Troyanovsky contended that it had
been agreed that new American loans to finance trade were to precede Soviet payments on old debts and claims. Hull and Bullitt
(who, when he discovered that his Soviet hosts ignored his advice,
soon became an ardent crusader against Communism) insisted that
Soviet payments must precede any new credit. Parleys over this issue
ended in deadlock on February 1, 1935, with no payment ever made
on either the Kerensky war debts and claims for nationalized properties or on Soviet counter-claims for damages arising out of an Archangel expedition of 1918. In July 1935, under the terms of the Reciprocal Trade Agreement Act of 1934, Moscow agreed to buy
$30,000,000 worth of American goods annually. When the Seventh
(and last) Congress of the Comintern met in Moscow, July 25–
August 20, 1935, to renounce "World Revolution" in favor of a "Peoples' Front" against Fascism, Earl Browder appeared on behalf of

the pathetic Communist Party of the USA. Hull at once ordered Bullitt to protest against Soviet violation of Litvinov's anti-propaganda pledge of 1933. The Narkomindel disclaimed all responsibility for the Comintern. Hull rejoined that in the event of continued propaganda "the friendly and official relations between the two countries cannot but be impaired." Said Litvinov, bitterly, to Bullitt: "No nation ever starts talking about the activities of the Comintern unless it wishes to have as bad relations as possible with us. The activities of the Comintern are merely an excuse for breaking diplomatic relations." [4]

Bullitt withdrew in the summer of 1936 to become Ambassador to France, where he had propagandized against any French-Soviet *rapprochement*. His wealthy successor, Joseph E. Davies, reached Moscow in January 1937 and compensated for Bullitt's embittered anti-Sovietism by a naïve pro-Sovietism. Both attitudes ill served the cause of American interests and of Soviet-American collaboration. Chargé Loy W. Henderson reported to Hull on May 14, 1937, that secret Soviet microphones had been discovered in both the office and the residence of Ambassador Davies. "The discovery of the wiring and other traces of eavesdropping is being kept secret and it is hoped that following the Ambassador's return it may be possible to ascertain whether or not the Soviet agents have actually been endeavoring from the attic to listen to the various important and frequently confidential conversations which have taken place in the Ambassador's office." In late 1938 a firm of naval architects, with FDR's approval, presented blueprints for a Soviet "super-battleship." They were rejected by the Kremlin in favor of a standard capital ship to be built in the USA. American suspicions that Moscow desired such a vessel only to copy American secrets of construction killed the contract.

Lawrence Steinhardt succeeded Davies [5] in March 1939, but did not arrive until August, by which time all hope of East-West collaboration against Fascism had waned. A major source of failure was symbolized by an utterance in mid-year 1935 of Rear Admiral Yates

[4] For full documentation on this and other aspects of American-Soviet relations see *Foreign Relations of the United States: Soviet Union, 1933–1939* (Government Printing Office, 1952).

[5] For a persuasive argument that Davies, then and later, came to the "right" conclusions for the "wrong" reasons, see Richard H. Ullman: "The Davies Mission and United States–Soviet Relations, 1937–1941," *World Politics*, January 1957.

Sterling, Jr., USN, echoing sentiments widely shared in America and Western Europe. He called for support of Hitler in a "great crusade led by Germany . . . not only forever laying the ghost of Bolshevism, but opening up the fertile land of Russia to a crowded and industrially hungry Europe."

Western hopes of turning Fascist aggression against the USSR frustrated all efforts to establish an anti-Fascist coalition and ultimately engendered Soviet hopes of turning Fascist aggression against the Western Powers—to the subsequent ruination of all the participants in a mad game of power played out to its tragic end. Said Stalin in Congress XVII on January 26, 1934:

> Some bourgeois politicians think that war should be organized against the USSR. Their plan is to defeat the USSR, divide up its territory, and profit at its expense. It would be a mistake to believe that it is only certain military circles in Japan who think in this way. We know that similar plans are being hatched in the leading political circles of certain States in Europe. Let us assume that these gentlemen pass from words to deeds. What may be the upshot? There can hardly be any doubt that such a war would be the most dangerous war for the bourgeoisie, not only because the peoples of the USSR would fight to the very death to preserve the gains of the Revolution . . . [but because] it would be waged not only at the fronts but also behind the enemy's lines. . . . Some German politicians say that the USSR has now taken an orientation toward France and Poland; that from an opponent of the Versailles Treaty it has become a supporter of that treaty, and that this change is to be explained by the establishment of the Fascist regime in Germany. That is not true. Of course we are far from being enthusiastic about the Fascist regime in Germany. But Fascism is not the issue here, if only for the reason that Fascism in Italy, for example, has not prevented the USSR from establishing the best relations with that country. Nor is it a question of any alleged change in our attitude toward the Versailles Treaty. It is not for us, who have experienced the shame of the Brest-Litovsk Peace, to sing the praises of the Versailles Treaty. We merely do not agree to the world being flung into the abyss

of a new war on account of this Treaty. The same must be said of the alleged new orientation taken by the USSR. We never had any orientation towards Germany, nor have we any orientation towards Poland and France. Our orientation in the past and our orientation at the present time is toward the USSR, and toward the USSR alone. And if the interests of the USSR demand *rapprochement* with one country or another which is not interested in disturbing peace, we take this step without hesitation. . . . Those who want peace and are striving for business intercourse with us will always receive our support. And those who try to attack our country will receive a stunning rebuff to teach them not to poke their pig snouts into our Soviet garden again.

The melancholy drama of aggression and appeasement proceeded, act by act, to its inevitable denouement through a dismal calendar of wasted years. On March 16, 1935, Hitler repudiated the disarmament clauses of Versailles and decreed the restoration of military conscription. Litvinov at Geneva (April 17) called for action, contending that the Nazi step was "a violation of the Covenant" and "a threat to peace." London and Paris consulted, sent notes, and did nothing. Sir John Simon and Sir Samuel Hoare negotiated with Ribbentrop and signed, June 18, 1935, an Anglo-German naval pact conceding the "right" to rearm and granting to Hitler's Reich parity with Britain in submarines, plus a new navy one-third the size of Britain's and easily capable of controlling the Baltic.

On October 3, 1935, Mussolini, carefully noting the success of Tokyo in conquest and of Berlin in treaty-breaking, invaded Ethiopia. Laval had approved in advance. Hoare had agreed with Laval in September that while League sanctions should be imposed for the sake of appearances, none should be contemplated which might halt the invasion or provoke Italian resistance. Baldwin's Tories won an overwhelming majority in the British election of November 14, 1935, by pledging full support of the League Covenant. A fortnight later Hoare and Laval agreed to restore "peace" by giving Mussolini Ethiopia. The American Congress, by the "Neutrality" Act of 1935, forbade Americans to sell arms to belligerents. Ethiopia was in desperate need of foreign arms. Italy needed none. *Il Duce* floated to

victory on a sea of American oil. The United States, in its befuddled anxiety to "keep out of other peoples' wars," helped to make the world safe for aggression.

Litvinov's appeals at Geneva for aid to Ethiopia were ignored. Black men died in agony from Fascist poison gas. Badoglio entered Addis Ababa in triumph on May 5, 1936. The farce of sanctions was abandoned. The League died at Geneva on the 4th of July. Blum and Halifax urged "peace." Haile Selassie spoke in bitterness: "God and history will remember your judgment. . . . What reply have I to take back to my people?" The answer was betrayal and desertion. Litvinov spoke to a hall of shame, pleading in vain for obligatory sanctions against aggressors or, at least, for European regional security pacts under the Covenant. No one listened.

Hitler had meanwhile (March 7, 1936) ordered the remilitarization of the Rhineland, in violation of Versailles and Locarno. London and Paris sent protests and passed resolutions. At the League Council meeting in London on March 17, Litvinov quoted *Mein Kampf* and declared: "One cannot fight for the collective organization of security without taking measures against the violation of international obligations. We, however, do not count among such measures collective capitulation to the aggressor, capitulation in the face of the violation of treaties, or the collective encouragement of such violations. . . . I declare on behalf of my Government that it is ready to take part in all measures that may be proposed to the Council of the League by the Locarno Powers and will be acceptable to the other members of the Council." The only answers were empty echoes, words without content, gestures without motion. Hitler began the building of the Siegfried Line. Belgium resumed neutrality. French power to aid France's eastern allies was at an end.

The next test was posed by the Fascist attack on the Spanish Republic, unleashed by Franco's rebellion of July 18, 1936. Blum proposed "non-intervention"—i.e., a common policy of forbidding the Spanish Republic to buy arms abroad for its own defense. The London "Non-Intervention" Committee did what it could to see that the Loyalists received no aid. It concealed and even promoted a steady flow of troops, planes, tanks, and guns to Franco from Lisbon, Rome, and Berlin. The Roosevelt Administration, obedient to Downing Street and the wishes of the Vatican, saw to it that Madrid could buy no American arms. Asserted Litvinov:

Here is an attempt at a forcible implantation in Spain from without of a Fascist system, an attempt to force upon the Spanish people a Fascist Government with the aid of bayonet, hand-grenade and bomb. If this attempt were to succeed, there would be no guarantees against its repetition on a wider scale in relation to other states. . . . I would like to express the confidence that the League Council, not only in the interests of Spain, but in the interests of international justice and the preservation of peace, and also in the interests of the League itself, will throw its word into the scale and render all possible support to the Spanish people.

The League Powers preferred to render all possible support to the aggressors. The USSR sought to save the Spanish Republic by counter-intervention. The effort failed in the face of the determination of the Western democracies that Fascism should conquer Spain. At the end of March 1939 the heroic resistance of the Loyalists, deserted and betrayed to the Axis by Paris, London, and Washington, was at last beaten down. At the funeral of Spanish democracy the voice of John Donne came singing down the centuries to Frenchmen, Britons, and Americans: "Send not to know for whom the bell tolls. It tolls for thee. . . ."

A further test was posed by the resumption of the Japanese attack on China in July 1937. *Pravda* (September 22) declared that "the blood of whole peoples" was being spilled and that aggression could be halted only by the "collective repulse of the Fascists by all the Governments interested in peace, the collective defense of indivisible peace." Once more the democratic Powers acted on the premises that peace was divisible, that aggression should be appeased, and that collective action would involve greater risks than inaction. In the apt words of Arnold J. Toynbee: "They made their momentous choice neither on the absolute criterion of morality nor on the relative criterion of expediency, but on that trivial distinction between this moment and the next which keeps the sluggard cowering between the blankets when the house is burning over his head."

The Fascist "Axis" and then the "Triplice" meanwhile took form under the guise of "protecting civilization from Communism," a theme always warmly endorsed by many persons of wealth and influence in the Western democracies. At the London Economic Con-

ference, Alfred Hugenberg had circulated a memorandum demanding the return of the German colonies and a "mandate" to the Reich to "reorganize" Russia through German "constructive and creative genius." Dr. Schacht told the Governor of the Bank of France, according to Pertinax (*Echo de Paris*, November 3, 1935), that "we have no intention to change our Western frontiers. Sooner or later Germany and Poland will share the Ukraine, but for the moment we shall be satisfied with making our strength felt over the Baltic provinces."

The shape and size of the menace to be met are best suggested by noting the milestones of Fascist diplomacy. Following the German-Italian quarrel over Austria in 1934, negotiations were initiated in search of a basis of cooperation. The Berlin-Vienna Accord of July 11, 1936, and the joint German-Italian attack on the Spanish Republic launched a week later, paved the way for the formation of the "Axis." Before massed thousands of goose-stepping fanatics and civilian hysterics, Hitler at Nuremberg declared in September that "if I had the Ural mountains with their incalculable store of treasure in raw materials, Siberia with its vast forests, and the Ukraine with its tremendous wheat fields, Germany under Nationalsocialist leadership would swim in plenty." Said Rosenberg: "The Soviet Union's Government is controlled by Jewish interests and it is money stolen from the Russian people by the Jews that is being used in an attempt to awaken the underworld in all nations to march against European culture." Added Göbbels: "Bolshevism must be annihilated." On October 25, 1936, Ciano and Ribbentrop signed a secret pact. Commented *Il Duce*: "It is no wonder if today we raise the banner of anti-Bolshevism. This is our old banner!" On November 18 the two Cæsars of Fascism took their first joint step in diplomacy: simultaneous recognition of Franco's rebels as the Government of Spain.

Less than a week later, on November 25, 1936, Ribbentrop and Mushakoji, Japanese Ambassador in Berlin, signed the five-year "Anti-Comintern Pact," pledging collaboration between their States against "Communist subversive activity." Italy adhered on November 6, 1937. Tokyo recognized Italian title to Ethiopia. Rome recognized Manchukuo. Trade agreements followed. On the first anniversary of the Pact, Matsuzo Nagai sent greetings to Göbbels: "The Sino-Japanese conflict is for us a holy war to free the Chinese people from the Red Peril." The Reich recognized Manchukuo on May 12,

1938. The German-Italian treaty of military alliance (May 22, 1939) and the Tripartite Pact (September 27, 1940), threatening the United States with war, were the capstones of the Fascist coalition.

Four days before the Anti-Comintern Pact was signed, *Izvestia* (November 21, 1936) declared that "the two most aggressive Powers in the world have formed a bloc" and are engaged in a "conspiracy against peace," directed as much against Britain and America as against the USSR. The answer must be "organization of collective security and real protection for peace." Moscow feared attack in the East from a Japan in control of Manchuria, Inner Mongolia, and much of China. Moscow feared attack in the West from an Axis in control of truncated Austria, feudal-Fascist Hungary, corrupt Rumania, helpless Bulgaria, and wavering Jugoslavia. Despite Warsaw's alliance with Paris and its peace pacts with the USSR, Poland veered toward the Axis camp. Pilsudski was less anti-German than anti-Russian. His friend, Josef Beck, became Foreign Minister, November 2, 1932. Warsaw and Berlin signed a ten-year non-aggression pact on January 26, 1934. At Pilsudski's funeral in Cracow, May 18, 1935, Laval, fresh from a hurried visit to Moscow, conferred at length with Göring. The orientation of Pilsudski's Colonels, who continued to rule Poland, is suggested by the widely circulated book of Wladimir Studnicki, *Poland's Political Aims* (1935): "Poland has the strongest interest in a victory of Japan over Russia. Participation in a Russo-Japanese war would be possible if Poland were to ally itself with Germany with this in view. No attention need be paid to France which occupies today a secondary position. Poland and Germany could lay the foundations of a great Central European bloc."

The Second and Third Five Year Plans made provision for a vast Soviet war industry capable of supplying a modern, mechanized defense force. In the Maritime Provinces a self-sufficient Red Banner Army of 250,000, under General Vasily Bluecher (Galen), was established to parry a possible Japanese attack from Manchukuo. A thousand bombing planes based at Vladivostok were calculated to impress Tokyo with the unwisdom of aggression. The Trans-Siberian was double-tracked. A new railroad was laid north of Lake Baikal to Komsomolsk on the lower Amur, with branches southward to Khabarovsk and eastward to the coast opposite Japanese Sakhalin. Frontier defenses were everywhere strengthened. Alone among European military forces, the Red Army kept pace with the growth of

the *Wehrmacht* by expanding its regular troops to a million men by 1935, to two millions by 1937, and to almost three millions by 1939, all equipped with guns, tanks, and planes turned out by the new heavy industries. Said Defense Commissar Voroshilov in 1936: "When the enemy attacks the Soviet Ukraine or Soviet Byelorussia or any other part of the Soviet Union, we will not only prevent his invading our own country but will defeat him in the territory whence he came."

Against the Japanese danger it was impossible to make even a beginning of organizing an effective coalition. America, Britain, and France, though all threatened by Tokyo, were paralyzed. While their diplomats appeased the aggressors, their exporters supplied the Japanese war machine with oil, rubber, scrap iron, and all else needed to continue aggression. *Izvestia* (May 21, 1937) endorsed the Australian project of a Pacific security pact, but warned that such a policy required "that the Powers do not refuse ahead of time to participate in a real struggle for peace in the Pacific, that they do not prefer their attempts to reach agreements with the aggressor, and that they do not retreat before his impudent demands."

China, the first victim of attack, was as helpless as the Western Powers. Rather than resist Japan, Chiang Kai-shek preferred to conduct annual crusades against the peasant Soviets of the northern provinces. Extreme measures were required to change his mind. When he visited Sian Fu in Shensi in December 1936 he was kidnapped by the troops of Chang Hsueh-liang, who freed him only on condition that he cease his war against Red China, work for anti-Japanese unity, and cooperate with the Communists and northern warlords against the invader. As a result of this prospect, and of their own defeat at the polls at home, the Nipponese militarists launched a new and murderous assault on China, beginning with the clash on the Marco Polo Bridge near Lukouchiao, southwest of Peking, on July 7, 1937.

The initial Chinese protest at Japanese aggression was sent to the USSR as well as to the signatories of the Nine Power Pact. An American squadron, for the first time since the Revolution, made a courtesy call at Vladivostok at the end of July. In pursuit of their new program of conquering all of China, Japanese forces machine-gunned the British Ambassador, bombed and sank the U.S.S. *Panay*, and raided Soviet Consulates at Tientsin and Shanghai. Now, if ever, a Four-Power coalition was called for to halt the madmen of

Tokyo. But the only result of the crisis was the signature of a five-year Sino-Soviet neutrality pact on August 21, 1937, by which the signatories renounced aggression and agreed "not to render assistance of any kind, either directly or indirectly," to any third Power which might attack the other. Litvinov's pleas at Geneva for effective League action against Japan came to nothing. The USSR accepted the invitation to attend the Brussels Conference of the signatories of the Nine Power Pact. But Litvinov soon left the Belgian capital and reported to his people what had happened:

China applies to the League of Nations for protection, referring to the corresponding points in the Covenant. The League forms a committee, the committee appoints a subcommittee, and the latter elects an editorial committee. A paper is drafted and addressed to Japan: "We do not approve of your offensive. Probably it is based on a misunderstanding. Please come to confirm this and, lest you feel lonely among us, we are inviting your kindred spirit and friend, Germany." From Japan comes confirmation that there is no misunderstanding at all, that she is on the warpath quite deliberately and agrees to discuss matters only with China and only on terms of the latter's surrender. Disarmed by this reply, the League decides to refer the question to the Powers most concerned in Far Eastern affairs, signatories to the so-called Washington Treaty which is violated by Japan for the second time. (It was violated the first time by the occupation of Manchuria.) And so the Brussels Conference is called, and the Soviet Union is also invited, although she is not a signatory to the Washington Treaty. What does this conference do? Its activity was very neatly hit off in a cartoon which I saw in a foreign newspaper. This shows the honorable delegates of eighteen States, not without great effort and strain, dragging a letter to the postbox for Japan. In this letter, as you know, they again demand Japan's confirmation whether she is deliberately committing her aggression in China and request her to stop and accept mediation. Confirmation is not long in coming. Japan, even with an inflection of resentment, replies that there is no need to bother her; she has repeatedly stated that she is attacking China quite deliberately and for

quite definite aims. She does not need anybody's mediation; she is ready to negotiate only with China—about capitulation, of course—and the only thing the conference can do is to make China agree to this capitulation. This reply disarmed the Brussels Conference, just as the first reply disarmed the League of Nations, and the Conference was closed.

Only in Outer Mongolia did it prove possible for Moscow to acquire an "ally" against Japan. After the Chinese Revolution of 1911, the ancient land of Ghenghis Khan, under the leadership of the Khutukhta or "Living Buddha," had broken away from Chinese control. Between 1921, when the regime of Baron Ungern-Sternberg was liquidated and a Soviet-Mongol treaty of friendship was signed, and 1925, Soviet troops had remained in Mongolia. With the death of the last Khutukhta in 1924, after twenty-three earthly incarnations, a popular revolution against the feudal-theocratic rule of the Lamas and princes led to the establishment of a "People's Republic" fashioned on Soviet models. The northwestern area of Tannu-Tuva had already become an "independent" Soviet protectorate in 1923. The People's Republic, with its capital at Ulan Bator, was still nominally under Chinese suzerainty, but looked to the USSR for protection against Japanese pressure, which became heavy in 1936. On March 1 Stalin told Roy Howard that "if Japan should venture to attack the Mongolian People's Republic and encroach upon its independence, we will have to help the Mongolian People's Republic. Stomoniakov, Litvinov's assistant, recently informed the Japanese Ambassador in Moscow of this and pointed to the immutable friendly relations which the USSR has maintained with the Mongolian People's Republic since 1921."

On March 12, 1936, at Ulan Bator, a Soviet-Mongolian Protocol was signed, putting into formal effect a "gentlemen's agreement" of November 27, 1934. For a period of ten years "the Governments of the USSR and of the Mongolian People's Republic undertake in the event of military aggression against one of the Contracting Parties to give each other every assistance, including military assistance" (Art. 2). Troops stationed by one State in the territory of the other by mutual agreement would be withdrawn, as in 1925, as soon as the necessity had passed (Art. 3). China protested on the ground that the Protocol violated Article 5 of the Sino-Soviet treaty of 1924. Lit-

vinov retorted that the pact did not "violate to the slightest degree the sovereignty of China." Moscow charged that Tokyo had inspired the protest. A Soviet-Japanese press war raged throughout the year and thereafter. But Japanese-Manchukuo forces were halted at the Mongolian border by the knowledge that the Red Army would resist any farther advance.

The militarists of Tokyo persistently refused to negotiate a non-aggression pact, arguing that all outstanding issues should first be settled. Involved negotiations over fisheries and frontiers pursued their tedious course. With the signature of the Anti-Comintern Pact, Moscow refused to revise or replace the fisheries convention of 1928 and made Japanese rights dependent upon annual agreements. The Kwantung Army and the soldiers of Henry Pu-yi indulged in cautious experimentation to test the will and the power of Moscow to defend the Soviet and Mongolian frontiers. This policy was safe since Tokyo knew that the Kremlin would not take the initiative in precipitating a full-scale war. This policy was also conclusive; all the experiments had the same outcome.

Soviet diplomacy was supplemented by force. Arms achieved that which diplomacy alone could not have accomplished: the prevention of open war. The major clashes which convinced the Sons of Heaven that war with Russia would be unwise were interspersed among hundreds of border incidents. During the spring and summer of 1937 Japanese units on the Amur River south of Blagoveshchensk sought to occupy various islands claimed by the USSR. The incident was publicized throughout the world out of all proportion to its significance. In January 1938 Zhdanov criticized the Narkomindel before the first session of the newly elected Supreme Soviet, contending that it "should be more resolute in its attitude toward the arrogant, hooligan and provocative conduct of the agents of Japan and of that puppet State called Manchukuo." At the end of July, in the region southwest of Vladivostok, a Japanese division occupied Chankufeng Hill and another eminence to the north, both west of Lake Hassan near the juncture of Korea, Manchukuo, and the Soviet hinterland of Possiet Bay. Early in August a Soviet division, aided by tanks and bombers, drove out the intruders with several hundred casualties on both sides. Litvinov and Ambassador Shigemitsu signed an armistice on August 11, 1938, restoring the *status quo*.

Early in May 1939 new hostilities began in the district of No-

monhan, southeast of Lake Bui-Nor along the Khalka River, easternmost point of Outer Mongolia. Moscow came at once to the defense of the People's Republic. Intermittent fighting continued
through the summer until Soviet-Mongol forces routed the invaders
at the end of August, destroying or capturing 8 tanks, 144 guns, and
600 planes. A truce of September 16 restored the *status quo*. Having
learned a costly lesson, the men of Nippon henceforth refrained
from challenging Red forces to battle. Less resistance was to be encountered in other directions.

If the geopolitics of Soviet strategy called in the Orient for that
which was unattainable—alliances with China, Britain, and America
to checkmate Japanese ambitions—it called in the West for allies on
Germany's flank and rear. The French post-Versailles alliance system already embraced Belgium, Poland, Czechoslovakia, Jugoslavia,
and Rumania. British and Soviet support of this bloc would have
rendered the Nazi Reich helpless. Moscow was willing and anxious
to effect such a combination. London, Paris, and Warsaw were be-
fogged in illusions and evasions. Yet the effort was persistent.

Soviet entry into the League of Nations was the point of departure for the attempts of the Narkomindel to organize collective security against aggression. Little progress was made until the coming
to the Quai d'Orsay of Louis Barthou in the wake of the Fascist riots
in Paris of February 6, 1934, and the ensuing resignation of the Daladier cabinet. Barthou, serving under Premier Gaston Doumergue,
was 72 years old and a staunch conservative. He was the only French
Foreign Minister during a fateful decade who understood the nature
of the Nazi menace and saw how it might be met. The French-Soviet
non-aggression pact of November 29, 1932, had paved the way for a
rapprochement, as had the visit of Litvinov to Paris in July 1933 and
the September journeys to Moscow of Edouard Herriot and Pierre
Cot. Barthou spent the spring of 1934 visiting Warsaw, Prague, Geneva (where he conferred with Litvinov), Bucharest, and Belgrade,
hoping to strengthen the French-Polish alliance and to weld the
"Little Entente" and "Balkan Entente" into a firm structure of security.

Litvinov, like Barthou, realized that the safety of France and
the USSR required an alliance. Without illusions, he had accepted
Nazi renewal (May 5, 1933) of the 1926 neutrality treaty. In September 1933 he concluded a non-aggression pact with Italy. But he
ignored overtures from the Wilhelmstrasse during his passage

through Berlin in December. He took it for granted that in the end nothing would halt the Axis drive to war save a counter-mobilization of superior force. He now endorsed the familiar French view that security must be organized in concentric circles, and argued (May 18, 1934) that in the first circle must stand France, the USSR, the Baltic States, Poland, and the Little Entente; in the second, the Mediterranean Powers; and in the third, the Pacific Powers. His fears of a German-Polish-Finnish bloc against Muscovy were enhanced by the Polish-German pact of January 1934 and German rejection of his proposals of March 28, 1934, for a joint guarantee of the four Baltic States. He therefore supported Barthou's project of a mutual-assistance pact on the Locarno model among France, Germany, Poland, Czechoslovakia, the Soviet Union, and the Baltic States.

But the project failed, despite the blessing of Sir John Simon in July. Berlin and Warsaw both refused to participate save on conditions that would have made the arrangement meaningless. The attempt at least demonstrated, even to the British Cabinet, that there was no workable alternative to a French-Soviet alliance. Soviet membership in the League, it was agreed, should be a first step. Chicherin had opposed the Geneva organization with what he called "absolutely undiluted, unmixed, unwavering, unswerving" enmity. But Stalin told Walter Duranty on Christmas Day, 1933, that "notwithstanding the withdrawal of Germany and Japan—or perhaps just because of this—the League may become something of a check to retard the outbreak of military actions or to hinder them. . . . If historical events should follow such a course, then it is not impossible that we should support the League of Nations despite its colossal defects."

Barthou had induced Prague and Bucharest to grant full recognition to Moscow on June 9, 1934. Bulgaria and Hungary did likewise, but not Jugoslavia, whose King Alexander had a horror of "regicides"—though his own father had come to the Serbian throne in 1903 through the murder of his predecessors. By the end of August, Barthou had secured general assent to an invitation to the Kremlin to join the League and to take a permanent seat on the Council. Swiss, Portuguese, and Irish objections could be ignored. Polish objections were more serious. Pilsudski's henchmen, already notorious for their oppression of the Byelorussians and Ukrainian populations of the eastern provinces, feared that Litvinov at Geneva might raise the question of the Polish treatment of minorities.

They distrusted Soviet disclaimers of any such intention. On September 13, 1934, at the 15th League Assembly, Josef Beck declared that "pending the introduction of a general and uniform system for the protection of minorities, my Government is compelled to refuse, as from today, all cooperation with the international organizations in the matter of the supervision of the application by Poland of the system of minority protection."

In the sequel the Western Powers acquiesced in Polish repudiation of the minority treaty as the price of Polish support of Soviet membership in the League. On September 12 Barthou had sent Litvinov a formal invitation from the Council. On September 15, despite De Valera's protest, letters were exchanged and the Council voted to invite the Assembly to approve. On September 18, 1934, third anniversary of the Mukden Incident, the Assembly voted to approve Soviet admission, 38 against 3 (Switzerland, Portugal, and the Netherlands), with 7 abstentions (Argentina, Belgium, Cuba, Luxembourg, Panama, Peru, and Venezuela). Marcel Houden of the League Secretariat sought to embarrass Litvinov and his colleagues by bringing them into the gloomy Bâtiment Electoral ten minutes before the Assembly President, R. J. Sandler of Sweden, had concluded his welcoming speech. (Such petty spite found later expression in assigning to Litvinov the chairmanship of the Committee on Seaweeds.) Josef Beck sneered at the whole proceeding. But Litvinov's words from the rostrum were a clarion call to a world that might have saved itself infinite suffering had its leaders listened and acted:

> The Soviet State has never excluded the possibility of some form or other of associating with States having a different political and social system, so long as there is no mutual hostility and if it is for the attainment of common aims. . . . The organization of peace! Could there be a loftier and at the same time more practical and urgent task for the cooperation of all nations? . . .
>
> One thing is quite clear to me, and that is that peace and security cannot be organized on the shifting sands of verbal promises and declarations. The nations are not to be soothed into a feeling of security by assurances of peaceful intentions, however often they are repeated, especially in those places where there are grounds for expecting aggres-

sion or where, only the day before, there have been talk and publications about wars of conquest in all directions, for which both ideological and material preparations are being made. . . . Far be it from me to overrate the opportunities and means of the League of Nations for the organization of peace. I realize, perhaps better than any of you, how limited these means are. I am aware that the League does not possess the means for the complete abolition of war. I am, however, convinced that, with the firm will and close cooperation of all its members, a great deal could be done at any given moment for the utmost diminution of the danger of war, and this is sufficiently honorable and lofty a task, the fulfillment of which would be of incalculable advantage to humanity.

The Kremlin was now fully committed to collective security. The enterprise was auspiciously begun. But the obstructionism of the Polish Colonels, who were to persist to the end in their anti-Soviet orientation, was an evil augury. Still more ominous was the tragedy which brought Pierre Laval to the Quai d'Orsay: on October 9, 1934, one Vlada Georgiev, a Macedonian terrorist in the pay of Ante Pavelich's Croatian *Ustaschi*, a revolutionary movement linked with Fascist conspirators in Budapest, Rome, and Berlin, perpetrated a double assassination in Marseilles. The victims were King Alexander of Jugoslavia and Foreign Minister Louis Barthou of France.

2. RULE BY TERROR

MURDER, both retail and wholesale, was a customary device of the Fascist gamblers for global hegemony. Murder, retail but not wholesale, had long been a weapon of the Russian Populists and SR's in their wars against Tsars and Commissars. Murder, wholesale but not retail, became, as we have seen, a Soviet weapon of defense in the days of White and Red terrorism. In the middle 1930's, in the bloody tradition of Ivan Grozny and Peter I, it was developed into a science of liquidation by Stalin and his tools and linked with a vast system of imprisonment, Siberian exile, and forced-labor camps. The victims of this monstrous machinery of torment and death were

no longer "class enemies," all of whom were long since gone, but Communist Party members, and particularly "Old Bolsheviks," alleged to be "enemies of the people" and co-conspirators with Fascist agents to betray the Socialist Fatherland.

This phantasmagoria of homicide, even in the perspective of the 1950's when much was made known which was hitherto unknown, still poses many mysteries. Yet the record of evil admits of summation. Be it noted, to begin with, that the killing of Barthou and Alexander in Marseilles was but one of a series of Fascist murders perpetrated to serve the purposes of Fascist politics. Among others slain were Chang Tso-lin, June 3, 1928; Ion Duca, Premier of Rumania, December 19, 1933; and Engelbert Dollfuss, Chancellor of Austria, July 25, 1934.

At 4:30 p.m., December 1, 1934, in Smolny Institute in Leningrad, Sergei Mironovich Kirov was shot to death by Leonid Nikolayev, a young Party member previously arrested for suspicious behavior but soon released. Born in Viatka in 1886, Kirov had joined the Party in Tomsk in 1904 and was four times arrested, jailed, or exiled before 1917. The Revolution found him a Bolshevik leader in Vladikavkaz. During the civil war he defended Astrakhan and helped restore Soviet authority in the Caucasus. He was elected a member of the Central Committee at Congress XI and then became Secretary of the Party's Leningrad Committee, a member of the Politburo (1930), a member of the Presidium of the Central Executive Committee of the USSR, and, with Kaganovich and Zhdanov, one of the three Secretaries of the Party Central Committee serving under Stalin. This able administrator, Party boss, and popular hero lived and worked in Kshesinskaya's House, which is now the Kirov Museum.

No foreshadowing of the frightful aftermath of Kirov's murder was evident at Party Congress XVII, the "Congress of Victors," which had met in January 1934. The 1,225 voting delegates spoke for 1,874,000 members. The ranks had been temporarily closed to new applicants in 1933, while members judged unworthy were expelled in large numbers. In his report on the work of the Central Committee, Stalin declared that the Party must be kept "in a state of mobilization for the fulfillment of the Second Five-Year Plan," on which Molotov, Kuibyshev, and Kaganovich presented reports. New Party rules were adopted, emphasizing discipline and duty, designating local cells as "primary organizations," and raising qualifica-

tions for admission in terms of the number of sponsors and years of probation required of candidates, with minimum requirements for industrial workers of five years' standing. Provision was also made for the establishment of "sympathizer groups" of non-Party people.

Stalin had emphasized the need of trained personnel and more efficient administration. The old Central Control Commission of the Party and the Commissariat of Workers' and Peasants' Inspection were replaced by a Party Control Commission under the Central Committee and a Soviet Control Commission under the federal Sovnarkom. Stalin also warned against dangers from bourgeois Powers and against "bourgeois survivals in men's minds": opportunism, deviationism, and local nationalism. Bukharin, Rykov, Tomsky, Zinoviev, and Kamenev all publicly flayed themselves as penitents and sought renewed grace by eulogizing the Stalinist leadership. There were no other hints of the tempest that was soon to break. On July 10, 1934, the GPU was abolished and replaced by a Commissariat of Internal Affairs (NKVD), headed by Henry Yagoda, a sinister figure who was later to confess to betraying the State of whose internal security he was the custodian.

Kirov's ashes were entombed in the Kremlin wall on December 6, 1934. On the same day the Soviet press published a list of 31 persons in Leningrad and 32 in Moscow who had already been shot. "A Circuit Session of the Military Collegium of the Supreme Court of the USSR . . . on December 5 *in camera*, for preparation and organization of terrorist acts against officers of the Soviet regime sentenced to death by shooting —— ——. The property of the condemned to be confiscated. The sentences have been carried out." [6] On the 7th, Radek denounced "imperialists" and "counter-revolutionaries" as 12 more "White Guards" were arrested in Minsk, of whom 9 were shot. On December 10 in Kiev 37 were arrested, of whom 28 were shot. Many of the victims of this initial blood-bath were already under arrest on December 1 as suspected subversives and clearly had no direct connection with the assassination. Stalin, who ordered these measures without even consulting the Politburo, was seeking not justice but the terrorization of all possible enemy agents and political dissenters.

By mid-December the Soviet press was writing of foreign plots against the Ukraine and linking the names of Zinoviev and Kamenev

---

[6] Cf. G. A. Tokaev: *Betrayal of an Ideal* (Indiana University Press, 1955), pp. 239–51.

with the conspiracy (cf. *Izvestia*, December 16–18, 1934). On December 21, Stalin's 55th birthday, 13 more arrests were made in Leningrad. All those apprehended were members or ex-members of the Party who were said to have participated, along with Nikolayev, in a "Leningrad Center" of terrorists composed of followers of Zinoviev and Kamenev. Two days later 15 more Party members were arrested in Moscow, including Zinoviev and Kamenev.

On December 26, 1934, an official announcement declared that the murder was part of a far-reaching plan to kill Stalin and other leaders and to destroy the Soviet regime by terrorism and intervention. One group of plotters was headed by Shatsky and another by Kotolynov, who had ordered Nikolayev to kill Kirov. The assassin was said to have received 5,000 rubles from a foreign consul who established contacts between the local conspirators and Trotsky. On December 29 Nikolayev and 13 other Party members were executed after a secret trial. On the last day of the year George Bissenieks, Latvian Consul General in Leningrad, was recalled. His Government denied any connection with Kirov's death. *Izvestia* and *Pravda* identified him as the Consul who had paid Nikolayev, and asserted that a "Great Power" (Germany) had aided him in his work. On January 16 Zinoviev and Kamenev were reported to have confessed to breaches of Party discipline. A week later Medved, head of the Leningrad NKVD, was sentenced to prison along with several of his subordinates for having known of the plot and done nothing to prevent its consummation.

Valerian Menzhinsky, former head of the GPU, had died on May 10, 1934; Maxim Peshkov, son of Gorky, on May 11; and Valerian Kuibyshev, originally head of the Gosplan and Vice-Chairman of the Sovnarkom, in October 1934. Maxim Gorky died in July 1936. All these deaths were apparently a result of illness. But Henry Yagoda later confessed to bribing and blackmailing the attending physicians into administering harmful drugs to their distinguished patients.

On January 17, 1935, Zinoviev was sentenced to 10 years in jail, Kamenev to 5, and other defendants to varying terms, all for knowing of the plot against Kirov and failing to act. Following this secret trial, Soviet "Justice" pursued its course in three dramatic and highly publicized open trials before the Military Collegium of Supreme Court of the USSR, headed by V. V. Ulrich as Presiding Judge with A. Y. Vyshinsky as State Prosecutor.

I. August 19–24, 1936: Zinoviev, Kamenev, I. N. Smir-
nov, G. Yedvodkimov, V. Ter-Vanganian, S. Mrachkovsky,
I. Bakayev, Y. Dreitser, V. Olberg, M. Lurye, N. Lurye,
T. Reingold, R. Pikel, E. Holtzmann, K. Berman-Yurie, and
F. David, all sentenced to be shot with confiscation of per-
sonal property.

II. January 23–30, 1937: Yuri L. Pyatakov, Leonid P.
Serebryakov, Nikolai I. Muralov, Yakov N. Drobnis, Yakov A. Livshitz, Mikhail S. Boguslavsky, Ivan A. Knyazev,
Stanislav A. Rataichak, Boris O. Norkin, Alexei A. Shestov,
Yosif D. Turok, Gavriil Y. Pushin, Ivan Y. Hrasche—to be
shot; Gregori Y. Sokolnikov, Karl B. Radek, and Valentin V. Arnold—imprisonment for 10 years and deprivation
of political rights for 5 years; Mikhail S. Stroilov—imprisonment for 8 years and deprivation of political rights for 5.
Confiscation of personal property of all the condemned.
"Enemies of the people, Lev Davydovich Trotsky, and his
son, Lev Lvovich Sedov, who were in 1929 deported from
the USSR and by the decision of the Central Executive
Committee of the USSR of February 20, 1932, were deprived of citizenship of the USSR, having been convicted
by the testimony of the accused Y. L. Pyatakov, K. B. Radek, A. A. Shestov and N. I. Muralov, and by the evidence
of V. G. Romm and D. P. Bukhartsev, who were examined
as witnesses at the trial, as well as by the materials in the
present case, of personally directing the treacherous activities of the Trotskyite anti-Soviet centre, in the event of their
being discovered on the territory of the USSR, are liable to
immediate arrest and trial by the Military Collegium of the
Supreme Court of the USSR."

III. March 2–13, 1938: Alexei I. Rykov (Lenin's successor as Chairman of the Sovnarkom, 1924–30), Nikolai I.
Bukharin, Henry G. Yagoda, Nikolai N. Krestinsky, Arkady P. Rosenglotz, Vladimir I. Ivanov, Mikhail A. Chernov,
Gregory F. Grinko, Isaac A. Zelensky, Armal Irkra-
mov, Faizulla Khodjayev, Vasily F. Sharangovich, Pro-
kopy T. Zubarev, Pavel P. Bulanov, Lev G. Levin, Ignaty N.
Kazakov, Benjamin A. Maximov-Dikovsky, and Pyoti P.
Kryuchkov—to be shot; Dmitry D. Pletnev—imprisonment
for 25 years; Christian G. Rakovsky and Sergei A. Bessonov

—imprisonment for 20 and 15 years respectively; confiscation of personal property of all the condemned; Pletnev, Rakovsky, and Bessonov to be deprived of political rights for 5 years after expiration of terms and to have terms counted from day of arrest.

The politics of purgatory reached far beyond these public trials in which all the defendants made detailed confessions. On June 11, 1937, after a closed trial by court-martial, Judge Ulrich sentenced to death on conviction of espionage and high treason Marshal Tukhachevsky, Gens. R. P. Eideman, I. E. Yakir, I. P. Uborevich, V. I. Putna, A. I. Kork, B. M. Feldman, and V. M. Primakov. Voroshilov asserted that General Yan Gamarnik, Assistant Commissar of Defense, who had taken his own life on May 31, had participated in the crime of seeking to overthrow the Soviet regime and restore "the yoke of the landlords and the industrialists." On December 19, 1937, it was announced that Karakhan, Yenukidze, and six other Party leaders had been executed. Many of Litvinov's Ambassadors, Ministers, and aides were dismissed, arrested, or executed. Among others who fell were Serbrovsky, successor to Pyatakov as Commissar for Heavy Industry; Milkhail Tomsky, long head of the trade union, who committed suicide in mid-August of 1936; Cherviakov, President of the CEC of the Byelorussian Republic, also a suicide; Liubchenko, President of the Ukrainian Sovnarkom; Admirals Orlov and Sivikov; and numerous diplomats, Union and Republican Commissars, industrial managers, etc.

The number of little people who were purged cannot be estimated. No public accounting was given. In the Ukraine one-quarter of the Party members were expelled, and throughout the Union one-fifth. Of these many were arrested, some were exiled, and a number were executed. In an atmosphere of universal suspicion, characterized by witch-hunting and a search for scapegoats, the Party leadership and the Soviet press may deliberately have exaggerated the scope and severity of the purge as a means of intimidating doubtful elements. It is probable that many of those who vanished, and some of those sentenced to death, were not in fact executed but were demoted and transferred to remote districts. When all allowable deductions are made, however, it is still certain that thousands lost their lives and that tens of thousands lost their liberties for varying terms of imprisonment or exile.

In the course of the slaughter the top leadership of the Party was reduced to a shambles and the chief purgers were themselves purged in late 1938 and 1939. On Stalin's order, Yagoda had been removed as head of the NKVD in September 1936 and replaced by N. I. Yezhov, who directed an unmitigated Reign of Terror or "*Yezhovshchina.*" In July 1938 Lavrenty Beria was named Yezhov's deputy and, in December, his successor. Yezhov vanished early in 1939. At the time of the second public trial, all of Ordjonikidze's deputies were arrested. It was reported in February 1937 that he had died of a heart attack. Not until 19 years later were the facts made known: after the liquidation of his brother, Ordjonikidze had killed himself. Of Stalin's closest associates in 1931, Chubar, Kassior, and Rudzutak were liquidated, while three candidate members of the Politburo, apart from Yezhov, disappeared: Postyshev, Eikhe, and Petrovsky. Of the 71 members of the Central Committee chosen at Congress XVII, 55 vanished, and of the 68 candidates, 60 were never heard of again.[7] Of the 115 who disappeared, 98 were shot. Of the 1,966 delegates and alternates to Congress XVII, 1,108 were arrested and many shot.

Contemporary efforts to explain this macabre drama, which to outsiders looked like *Le Grand Guignol* come to life, ranged from unqualified endorsement of Trotsky's own story to full acceptance of the official Kremlin version. The most popular explanation at the time in America and Western Europe was the one widely advertised by disillusioned ex-champions of Sovietism, eagerly seconded by Trotskyites, Socialists, Fascists, and many anti-Soviet conservatives and liberals. This thesis held that Stalin had betrayed the Revolution, made himself the "Bonaparte" of the "Thermidorian" reaction, and become a personal despot and a moral monster. To advance his personal power he had butchered the "Old Bolsheviks"— whose Society was in fact dissolved on May 25, 1935. He and his tools had given a façade of plausibility to part of the massacre by inventing accusations, "framing" the accused, extorting "confessions," and staging an elaborate criminal farce. By this logic all the accused, including Trotsky, were the innocent victims of a bloodthirsty tyrant vengefully bent upon exterminating all critics and possible rivals.

Against this thesis stands almost 2,000 pages of testimony in

[7] Cf. Merle Fainsod: *How Russia Is Ruled* (Harvard University Press, 1953), pp. 171, 267, 371 f.

the three public trials. The picture here painted by the defendants is one of a widespread conspiracy. The Left Oppositionists or Trotskyites and the Right Deviationists, led by Bukharin and Rykov, were allegedly linked in a secret bloc, in part directed from abroad by Trotsky. Their purposes included sabotaging Soviet industry and agriculture; promoting nationalist and secessionist movements; murdering outstanding Soviet leaders; preparing the way for a *coup d'état;* delivering military and economic information to the Polish, German, Japanese, and British intelligence services; securing Nazi and Nipponese assistance in return for promises of ceding Soviet territory; disorganizing the Red Army in the event of war; and seeking to seize power with the aid of foreign enemies. To these and similar charges all the accused in the public trials confessed in full, but no trustworthy evidence other than confessions was offered. Purported clandestine meetings of conspirators abroad turned out to be in hotels that did not exist or at airports unvisited by any foreign plane at the time alleged.

In the light of Khrushchev's revelations of February 24–5, 1956, in his scathing indictment of Stalin at Congress XX, the problem of which interpretation of the Great Purge is closer to truth may be deemed disposed of, even if some questions remain unanswered. Khrushchev himself hinted at remaining mysteries regarding the Kirov murder. It is still conceivable that some of the "confessions" of some of the victims of the public trials were partly true rather than wholly false, and that some of the fabricated confessions may have been inspired by "loyalty" to the Party even unto dishonor and death rather than by torture, as Khrushchev contended. It is still possible (nor did Khrushchev deny this) that some elements of a conspiracy existed among men morally sickened by Stalin's ruthlessness and patriotically convinced that his leadership would spell ruin for the Motherland in the war looming on the horizon. Tukhachevsky, Gamarnik, and other officers may indeed have conspired with Nazi agents, as Eduard Beneš and Winston Churchill earlier contended, or, with no such treasonable collaboration, may have planned a *coup d'état* to liquidate Stalin for the good of the country, as Isaac Deutscher and other anti-Stalinist commentators aver.[8]

[8] See Winston S. Churchill: *The Gathering Storm* (Houghton Mifflin, 1948), pp. 288–9; Isaac Deutscher: *Stalin: A Political Biography* (Oxford, 1949), pp. 378–80; and Joseph E. Davies: *Mission to Moscow* (Simon & Schuster, 1941), pp. 39–52. On motives for voluntary confessions to falsehoods, see Arthur Koestler's powerful novel *Darkness at Noon* (Macmillan, 1941).

Other evidence in support of the view that an actual conspiracy existed need not be ignored. Nazi "Fifth Columnists," "Trojan Horsemen," and "Quislings" sought to do in Denmark, Norway, the Low Countries, and France what their counterparts were alleged to have attempted in the USSR, although no subsequent light was thrown at Nuremberg or elsewhere on any details of such operations in Russia. Trotsky, moreover, was a professional rebel who was fanatically bent upon Stalin's removal; who repeatedly contended that no such overthrow was possible without conspiracy and a new and violent revolution; who had contacts with other anti-Stalinists in Russia; and who had few scruples about making common cause with strange bed-fellows against the traitor and monster in the Kremlin, of whom he said (January 26, 1937): "It is impossible to displace him except by assassination."

On August 21, 1940, Leon Trotsky died in Mexico City from wounds inflicted upon him the day before in his fortified house in Coyoacan by Ramon Mercader, alias Jacques Mornard van den Dresche, alias Frank Jackson, alias Leon Jacome, alias Leon Haikys, etc. The assassin, sentenced to a twenty-year prison term on April 16, 1943, was at once labeled by all Trotskyites and other anti-Stalinist groups a hired killer of the GPU. The murderer himself insisted that he was a Trotskyite who had slain Trotsky for "betraying" Trotskyism.[9]

When all is said and done, the fact is now established that Stalin in the 1930's, and indeed thereafter to the end, frequently ignored or threatened his colleagues and, with the aid of Yagoda, Yezhov, and Beria as managers of the machine of terrorism, put to death thousands of innocent persons, along with a few guilty, and erased all possible challengers to his one-man domination of the Party. His

[9] On Trotsky's views and probable role, see my *Soviet Politics* (Knopf, 1946), pp. 265–8. I then expressed the opinion (p. 264) that the Great Purge "produced shocking abuses and injustices," but that "the portrait of conspiracy spread on the Soviet court record appears . . . to be closer to reality than any alternative explanation." It is now clear that only some shreds and patches of this portrait were authentic and that the injustices and abuses were of gargantuan proportions. For accounts, partly factual and partly fanciful, of other aspects of the terror, see F. Beck and W. Godin: *Russian Purge and the Extraction of Confession* (Viking, 1951); Zbigniew K. Brzezinski: *The Permanent Purge* (Harvard University Press, 1956); Nathan Leites and Elsa Bernaut: *Ritual of Liquidation: The Case of the Moscow Trials* (Free Press, 1956); Klaus Mehnert: *Stalin Versus Marx* (Macmillan, 1953); Alexander Orlov: *The Secret History of Stalin's Crimes* (Random House, 1953); and Joseph Scholmer: *Vorkuta* (Holt, 1955).

mixed political and paranoid motives were infused with a twisted rationality akin to that of some of the barbarian kings, Oriental despots, and Byzantine Autocrats of long ago. Having no real faith in any alliances that might be concluded with Western Powers and no confidence in the durability of any bargains with the Fascist Cæsars, he foresaw the inevitability of a disastrous war in which, despite preparations and boasts, Russia would suffer invasion and experience such heavy losses as to jeopardize the very life of the regime and of the nation. Given this prospect, he deemed it his duty, as Deutscher has argued, to destroy in advance all potential "Fifth Columnists" and all possible leaders of an alternative regime. To accuse them of doing what in most cases they had not done but might conceivably try to do in the face of a future catastrophe, to extort confessions of crime, and then to have them shot was Stalin the Terrible's method of solving this problem. He could not see that the solution was almost fatal to Party and State alike. He did not care that it amounted to a most hideous and self-defeating idolatry of political immorality. In the end the Soviet State was to survive in spite of, rather than because of, Stalin's own survival.

Khrushchev's later arraignment of the dead dictator, based largely on the findings of an investigating commission named by the Party's Central Committee to explore the NKVD archives and other sources, is so fabulous a document as to require reading rather than résumé.[1] His point of departure is Stalin's warped character, illustrated by quotations from Lenin's "Testament," for the first time publicized in the USSR, and Krupskaya's bitter complaint over Stalin's "rude outbursts, vile invectives, and threats." Khrushchev's premise is that the ideological and political struggle against Trotskyism and Bukharinism had been won without violence long before Congress XVII and that Stalin's subsequent repressions at a time when the new social order was firmly established were needless, vicious, and horrible manifestations of Stalin's un-Leninist penchant for "brutal violence" and for the "moral and physical annihilation" of all who withheld "absolute submission" to his despotic will. Many "innocent people" and "honest Communists" were forced by "barbaric tortures" to sign false confessions that they were spies, wreckers, and "enemies of the people," and were executed in violation of all justice and "socialist legality."

[1] See the translation, as released by the State Department from a source unspecified, in *NYT*, June 5, 1956.

In 1936–7 Stalin prodded the NKVD into mass terror by denouncing it as being "four years behind" in unmasking the Trotsky-ite-Zinoviev bloc. Robert I. Eikhe, arrested on April 29, 1938, tormented into signing fabricated confessions implicating others, tried and shot February 4, 1940, is quoted at length in his agonized appeals for justice, all of which Stalin ignored. Rosenblum, Rudzutak, Postyshev, Kosaryev, Chubar, Kossior, and others are all shown to have been victims of similar "frame-ups" by the NKVD at Stalin's orders. In 1937–8 Yezhov sent to Stalin, who approved them all, 383 lists of persons to be arrested, with sentences prepared in advance. "From 1954 to the present the Military Collegium of the Supreme Court has rehabilitated 7,769 persons, many of them posthumously." Khrushchev implied regret that, although Stalin's victims could be "rehabilitated," they could not be resurrected from the dead.

Stalin was distrustful and "sickly suspicious." "Everywhere and in everything he saw 'enemies,' 'two-facers' and 'spies.'" He defended torture to extract confessions. He hired such judges as Rodos, "a vile person, with the brain of a bird, and morally completely degenerate." Stalin personally directed and supervised many of the "investigations" and gave advice on methods of securing confessions. "These methods were simple—beat, beat, and once again beat." Other items in the indictment are relevant to later phases of Stalinism. Sorrow and guilt, along with indignation, gleamed through Khrushchev's angry words, for, "in the past Stalin doubtless performed great services. . . . We cannot say that these were the deeds of a giddy despot. He considered that this should be done in the interest of the Party, of the working masses, in the name of the defense of the gains of the revolution. In this lies the whole tragedy!"

3. THE GREAT COALITION

ARNOLD J. TOYNBEE wrote that the Great Purge constituted "the self-erasure of the Soviet Union," which had become "a gigantic madhouse," for "the fact of Muscovy's madness in A.D. 1937 was not in doubt." [2] Many in the West concurred. Others doubted. Much was obscure. But Stalin's mania for decimating the leadership of the Party, the Army, and the Soviet Foreign Service was ill-calculated

[2] *Survey of International Affairs, 1937*, I, 11–22 (Oxford, 1938).

to inspire confidence abroad in the trustworthiness of the USSR as an ally against Hitler. The Narkomindel nevertheless pursued its goal and met with responses in other capitals, thanks to the onward march of the doubly demented Nazi madmen. That the effort finally foundered was due less to the madness of Stalinism than to the folly of the Western "appeasers" of Fascism, who managed, with secret shrewdness and public solicitude for "peace," to bring themselves and all the world to disaster.

Pierre Laval, among the more dishonorable members of this miserable company of muddlers, made a complex bargain with Mussolini in Rome on January 7, 1935, secretly blessing in advance *Il Duce*'s openly proclaimed plans for the conquest of Ethiopia. Sir John Simon, Laval's partner in error, was about to come to Berlin to yield to Nazi demands for arms when, on March 16, 1935, Hitler repudiated Part V of the Treaty of Versailles and began the conscription of a new army. On March 25 Sir Austen Chamberlain opined that "there is no doubt about the necessity of the cooperation of Soviet Russia in any complete system of European security."

On March 28, 1935, Anthony Eden, then Lord Privy Seal, reached Moscow in the company of Viscount Cranborne and Ivan Maisky, Soviet Ambassador in London. He was dined and wined by Litvinov. He conferred with Molotov and Stalin. The British Sovereign was toasted. "God Save the King" was played at the Bolshoi Theater. Eden visited the new subway and inspected aircraft factories. Devotion to collective security went so far that the butter on the table at Litvinov's *dacha* or country-house was stamped: "Peace is indivisible." When Eden boarded the Warsaw train, Litvinov said: "I wish you all success, for your success will be our success now." The long communiqué of March 31 championed collective security, asserted that "there is at present no conflict of interests between the two Governments on any of the main issues of international policy," and expressed hope of German and Polish participation in the proposed Eastern European mutual-assistance pact.

This hope proved vain. The result was the signature at the Quai d'Orsay on May 2, 1935, by Pierre Laval and Ambassador Vladimir Potemkin, of a Treaty of Mutual Assistance between France and the USSR. On May 16 at Prague, President Eduard Beneš and Ambassador Serge Alexandrovsky signed a similar pact between Czechoslovakia and the Soviet Union. Laval insisted that the agreement be limited to Europe and linked with the Covenant. Moscow and Paris

pledged themselves to come to each other's aid against unprovoked aggression by any European State "in application of Article 16 of the Covenant." They further agreed to act in the event of any failure of the League Council to reach a unanimous decision. A Protocol specified that the alliance would operate only in the event of aggression against the territories of the parties rather than against that of their other allies. Should the League Council fail to act against the aggressor, France and the USSR would nevertheless join forces for mutual defense. The pact of Prague was similar, but obligated the parties to come to each other's aid only "insofar as assistance may be rendered by France to the party victim of aggression." Beneš visited Moscow, where ratifications were exchanged on June 9, 1935. Laval also visited Moscow in mid-May, but hastened away to meet Göring in Cracow and returned to Paris with no visible intention of ratifying the French-Soviet alliance.

It had taken open Nazi rearmament to induce the slippery Laval to sign the Soviet pact. It required Nazi repudiation of the Locarno Treaties and remilitarization of the Rhineland, announced March 7, 1936, to bring about French ratification. Not until March 27 were ratifications exchanged at Moscow, putting the pact into effect for five years thereafter. Litvinov had come to London in January to attend the funeral of King George V. Moscow, moreover, was to reach a satisfactory compromise with Downing Street in the Montreux Convention of July 20, 1936, by which Turkey was permitted to refortify the Straits. Soviet war vessels were granted unqualified access to the Mediterranean in peace-time, in contrast to limited access to the Black Sea for naval forces of outside Powers. But the Anglo-German naval accord, signed June 18, 1935, by Ribbentrop and Sir Samuel Hoare (who had succeeded Simon), was a heavy blow to Soviet hopes. It granted the Reich 35% of British naval tonnage and parity in submarines, thereby giving Germany potential naval control of the Baltic. By 1936 the men of Moscow had long since begun to suspect that those most influential in shaping British and French policy had no intention of halting German rearmament or Fascist aggression in Asia, Africa, or Europe.

The Kremlin supplemented its diplomatic efforts to avert Armageddon by fostering a reorientation of Communist Parties throughout the world. This shift of the Comintern "line" promoted the conspirings of the Trotskyites within the USSR and led to their attempts abroad to form a "Fourth International." It constituted a further re-

pudiation by the Party leadership of the world-revolutionists within the ranks. It was dictated primarily, however, by the realization that the crisis of capitalism was not inaugurating a "Third Period" (following the post-1918 crisis and the recovery of the 1920's) in which proletarian revolution would become a possibility, but was instead initiating on a world scale an epoch of savage Fascist reaction which could be opposed only by a union of all anti-Fascist forces.

The German Communist Party, largest in the world outside of the USSR, went down to complete defeat before the Nazi assault. Such of its leaders as escaped execution or imprisonment continued for a time to echo Moscow in denouncing the Social Democrats as "Social Fascists" and in regarding Hitlerism as a passing episode. Only slowly was a new course charted. The heroic if futile resistance of the Socialist workers of Vienna to the clerical Fascism of Dollfuss (February 1934) helped to effect the transition, as did the revolt of the Spanish Socialists in Asturias in October. On February 12, 1934, French Communists joined French Socialists in a one-day general strike. For the first time since 1929 Communists sought a truce with Socialists in the face of a foe now recognized as formidable and fatal to both.

The new dispensation found expression in the Seventh Congress of the Comintern, held in Moscow from July 25 to August 20, 1935. The new General Secretary was Georgi Dimitrov, Bulgarian Communist-in-exile who had won world-wide admiration for his defiance of Göring during the *Reichstag* fire trial in Leipzig in 1933. From a "united front" of Communists and Socialists, the Comintern moved rapidly to the formula of a "People's Front," embracing bourgeois democrats and all other groups prepared to join forces against the common danger. World revolution was muted. Defense of democracy against war and Fascism became the watchword. In France the *Front Populaire* of Communists, Socialists, and Radical Socialists won the elections of April and May 1936 and brought Léon Blum to the Premiership in June. In Spain the *Frente Popular* won the election of February and brought to power a liberal coalition in which the Communist minority, contrary to widespread delusions abroad, played a moderate and even conservative role.

The Comintern now adapted its strategy to the purpose of the Narkomindel. Diplomatic and military coalitions among non-Fascist States were paralleled by efforts to promote political coalitions among all anti-Fascist forces within all States. Both devices were

destined to fail by 1939. The new program nevertheless marked a shift of Communist objectives away from global proletarian revolt and dictatorship to a defense of peace and democracy. In view of the past, inevitable skepticism prevailed abroad regarding the sincerity and permanence of the change. But the Soviet leaders and their Communist followers abroad were at least resolved that henceforth the vision of international working-class solidarity could be served only by making the security of the Soviet Union the paramount concern of all the comrades everywhere.[3]

American isolationism and British refusal to accept binding commitments on the Continent limited the efficacy of the Grand Alliance, as the implacable and understandable hostility of many Socialists and liberals toward Communists limited the prospects of "People's Fronts." Yet the coalition that had been built was adequate to its purpose if its members had had the wit and will to keep their pledges. France in alliance with the USSR, France in alliance with Poland, Czechoslovakia, Jugoslavia, and Rumania, and the USSR in alliance with Czechoslovakia and France could readily have checkmated the Axis Cæsars—if power had been held at Paris by a Poincaré, a Clemenceau, or a Barthou. But with the Quai d'Orsay guided by a Laval, a Blum, and later a Bonnet, with *La Grande Nation* hypnotized by the Maginot Line and riven by incurable schisms between Right and Left, and with Tory Britain inflexibly resolved to yield to Rome and Berlin in all matters of moment, even Litvinov's most adroit exertions were to prove futile.

4. THE DECLINE OF THE WEST

THE Communist conquest of Eastern and much of Central Europe in 1945 and thereafter has often been attributed to "betrayal" at Yalta, wickedness in Moscow, or incompetence or treason in Washington. In the long perspective of diplomacy and war, it was due to the strategy of the Western Powers in fighting the Axis in 1939–44. That strategy, in turn, was imposed upon the West because Western statesmen in 1935–8 surrendered all of Central and Eastern Europe to Hitler in the fatuous conviction that they were thereby "safe-

[3] Cf. Georgi Dimitroff: *The United Front: The Struggle Against Fascism and War* (International Publishers, 1938).

guarding civilization from Communism" and that Nazi aggression could be deflected against Russia while France and Britain remained at peace in the pleasant role of *Tertius Gaudens* or the "Happy Third." The course of this costly folly, almost sublime in the paradox and irony of its final result, is our next concern.

On March 12, 1938, the new *Wehrmacht* marched unresisted into Austria, followed by Hitler, the Austrian Corporal of 1914 and now *Führer* of the Nazi Reich, who proclaimed *Anschluss* in Vienna before madly cheering throngs while Jews and Slavs fled for their lives as best they could. Czechoslovakia was now outflanked, but Prague and Paris did nothing. Lord Halifax had visited Hitler in Berchtesgaden in the preceding November and convinced *Der Führer* that Britain would not oppose the Nazi *Drang nach Osten*. On February 20, 1938, Hitler had publicly demanded that Eden resign as Foreign Minister. In protest against Neville Chamberlain's appeasement policy, Eden resigned the same night. Halifax succeeded. When informed of the rape of Austria, he exclaimed: "Horrible, horrible, I never thought they would do it!" On March 17 Litvinov warned that Czechoslovakia was in danger and proposed a conference to discuss collective means of "checking the further development of aggression and eliminating an aggravated danger of a new world massacre." In a statement to the press he asserted: "Tomorrow might be too late, but today there is time yet, if all States, particularly great States, take up a firm, unambiguous stand on the problem of the collective salvation of peace." But the British Cabinet declined to assume any new commitments. The Soviet proposal was dismissed as "premature."

The next test was posed by the unleashing, through propaganda, diplomacy, and terrorism, of the Nazi campaign against Prague in the summer of 1938. Moscow was pledged to the defense of Czechoslovakia. Tukhachevsky had conferred with Beneš and General Sirovy—and then allegedly disclosed the plans of joint defense to Berlin. The revelation of his treason by Czech agents led to his speedy arrest, trial, and execution. Moscow remained pledged to the defense of Czechoslovakia. Paris was likewise pledged. The Quai d'Orsay and Downing Street, however, had other plans and hopes that required the betrayal and destruction of the Czechoslovak Republic. Chamberlain flew three times to Germany on the principle that "if you don't concede the first time, fly, fly again."

On September 19 the Prague Cabinet received an ultimatum

demanding that it surrender Sudetenland to Hitler, along with all the Czech border fortifications. The source of the ultimatum, incredibly, was not Berlin but Paris and London. Moscow offered to defend Czechoslovakia even after the French betrayal had released the USSR from any such obligations under the pacts of 1935. Amid the ruin of his hopes, Litvinov spoke with heavy heart at Geneva on September 21, 1938:

> The League was created as a reaction to the World War and its countless quarrels; its object was to make that the last war, to safeguard all nations against aggression, and to replace the system of military alliances by the collective organization of assistance to the victim of aggression. In this sphere the League has done nothing. Two States—Ethiopia and Austria—have lost their independent existence in consequence of violent aggression. A third State, China, is now a victim of aggression and foreign invasion for the second time in seven years, and a fourth State, Spain, is in the third year of a sanguinary war, owing to the armed intervention of two aggressors in its internal affairs. The League of Nations has not carried out its obligations to these States. At the present time a fifth State, Czechoslovakia, is suffering interference in its internal affairs at the hands of a neighboring State, and is publicly and loudly menaced with attack. . . .
>
> A fire-brigade was set up in the innocent hope that, by some lucky chance, there would be no fires. Things turned out differently, however. Fires have broken out in defiance of our hopes, but luckily not in our immediate vicinity. So (say some) let us dissolve the fire brigade—of course not forever, but merely temporarily. Directly the danger of any fire disappears, we shall reassemble the fire brigade without a moment's delay. . . .
>
> At a time when there is being drawn up a further list of sacrifices to the god of aggression and a line is under the annals of all post-war international history, with the sole conclusion that nothing succeeds like aggression—at such a moment, every State must define its role and its responsibility before its contemporaries and before history. That is why I must plainly declare here that the Soviet Govern-

ment bears no responsibility whatsoever for the events now taking place, and for the fatal consequences which may inexorably ensue.

The fruit of Anglo-French policy was the "Peace" of Munich of October 1, 1938, concluded at a Four-Power conference to which the USSR was not invited and from which the Czechs were excluded. Having consummated the ruin of Czechoslovakia, Prime Minister Neville Chamberlain concluded a non-aggression pact with Hitler and returned to London with happy words: "I have brought back peace with honor. I think it is peace for our time." In December, Foreign Minister Georges Bonnet, with the blessing of Premier Edouard Daladier, signed a non-aggression pact with Ribbentrop in Paris. With the reduction of the Czech army to helplessness, General Gamelin, top commander of the military forces of the French Republic, lost 45 divisions without lifting a finger to save them. London and Paris were now committed to the "localization" of future wars and to the deflection of Axis aggression eastward. Said Hugo Vavrecka, member of the Czech Cabinet: "It is a case without parallel in history that our allies and friends should impose conditions upon us which are usually imposed upon vanquished enemies. It is not a lack of courage that induced our Government to take the decision which grips our hearts. . . . God knows that more courage is needed for living than for committing suicide. . . . We shall not blame those who left us in the lurch, but history will pronounce a judgment about these days." Said Winston Churchill: "France and Britain had to choose between war and dishonor. They chose dishonor. They will have war."

The entire French alliance system was now destroyed. All Danubia and Balkania were at the mercy of the Axis. Czechoslovakia had been outflanked by the Nazi occupation of Austria. Poland was now outflanked by the Nazi victory at Munich. Far from appreciating the fact, the Warsaw Colonels joined Hitler in destroying Czechoslovakia through their armed seizure of Teschen on October 2. Two days later *Le Journal de Moscou* stated: "In effect France has with its own hands and without having consulted the USSR annulled the Soviet-Czech pact which was a corollary to the French-Soviet pact and one of the important elements of a regional eastern pact. . . . The loss of its allies and isolation—this is the price which France will have to pay for capitulation before the aggressor." The

great democracies had all but lost World War II before it had begun. No comparable instance of folly and perfidy on the part of the
responsible leaders of self-governing peoples is available in all the
past records of human weakness, stupidity, and crime.

The question of the motives and assumptions of the democratic
statesmen who thus condemned the world to war and their own people to hideous suffering is no longer open to serious controversy.
Millions of Americans, Britons, and Frenchmen had come to believe
that the way to have peace was to refuse to fight, meanwhile throw-
ing other peoples' children to the wolves. A large proportion of the
propertied classes in the Atlantic nations admired Fascism and supposed that their own interests would be served by maintaining and
extending Fascist power. A decisive group of democratic diplomats
and political leaders, moreover, fondly hoped and fervently believed
that a free hand for the Fascist Triplice on three continents would
eventuate in a German-Japanese attack on the Soviet Union, that
"civilization" would thereby be "saved from Bolshevism," and that
France, Britain, and America could remain neutral while Fascism
and Communism destroyed each other or the Fascist Powers fell to
fighting among themselves over the Soviet carcass. All these assumptions were tragically false. Democratic appeasement, like Fascist aggression, was the fever chart of the desperate sickness of a disor-
dered world.

A microcosm of this macrocosm is to be found in the political
situation in Prague on September 21, 1938, immediately before the
Cabinet reached its decision to accept the Anglo-French ultimatum.
President Beneš considered the advisability of risking war by welcoming Soviet aid and rejecting the demands of the Western Powers. Moscow could bring no public pressure to bear in favor of such
an outcome, since any such steps, leading inevitably to a break with
the Anglo-French leaders, would have played into the hands of the
appeasers and perhaps precipitated a Soviet-German war in which
the Western Munichmen would not only have stood aside but would
have blessed the Nazi crusade against Bolshevism. The Kremlin nevertheless offered armed assistance. When the issue was raised among
the Czechoslovak leaders, Rudolf Beran, head of the reactionary
Agrarian Party, declared that if Beneš summoned "Communist aid"
he and his followers would call in the Nazis and unleash civil war.
The People's Front Cabinet in France had faced similar threats from

those whose slogan was "Better Hitler Than Blum!" Beneš yielded The Nemesis of the West condemned its victims to suicide.

The attitudes and expectations of many British and French leaders, before they belatedly saw the light, are mirrored in numerous public utterances. A few examples will serve.

Winston Churchill in Rome, January 20, 1927:

> I could not help being charmed by Signor Mussolini's gentle and simple bearing and by his calm, detached poise in spite of so many burdens and dangers. . . . If I had been an Italian I am sure that I should have been wholeheartedly with you from the start to the finish in your triumphant struggle against the bestial appetites and passions of Leninism. . . . Your movement has rendered a service to the whole world. . . . Italy has shown that there is a way of fighting the subversive forces which can rally the masses of the people, properly led, to value and wish to defend the honor and stability of civilized society. She has provided the necessary antidote to the Russian poison. Hereafter no great nation will go unprovided with an ultimate means of protection against the cancerous growth of Bolshevism.

Lloyd George in Commons, November 28, 1934:

> In a very short time, perhaps in a year or two, the conservative elements in this country will be looking to Germany as the bulwark against Communism in Europe. . . . Do not let us be in a hurry to condemn Germany. We shall be welcoming Germany as our friend.

Leopold S. Amery in *The Forward View* (1935):

> The first condition of European peace today is the frank acknowledgment that Germany's armaments are now her own affair and nobody else's. . . . The doctrine of the inevitable contagion of war is of course pure nonsense. . . . It would be no concern of ours to prevent Japanese expansion in Eastern Siberia.

Ambassador William C. Bullitt to Secretary Hull, Paris, January 25, 1938:

Delbos said that he was convinced Germany desired genuinely to come to terms with France at the present time. He then related to me a conversation which he had had a few days ago with the Soviet Ambassador in Paris. The Soviet Ambassador had complained that the French Government seemed to be working for a reconciliation with Germany and had intimated strongly that if France should begin serious negotiations with Germany the Soviet Union would come to terms with Germany at once. Delbos said that he had replied that he was quite certain that Germany would much prefer to come to terms with France rather than with the Soviet Union and any such attempt on the part of the Soviets would be anticipated by France. He added that he felt a true statement of the situation was that the Soviet Union could not sell its friendship to anyone at the moment because there were no buyers for that commodity.[4]

Ambassador Robert Coulondre, reporting to Georges Bonnet from Berlin, December 15, 1938 (*French Yellow Book* of 1939, No. 33):

> The will for expansion in the East seems to me as undeniable on the part of the Third Reich as its disposition to put aside—at least for the present—any idea of conquest in the West; the one is a corollary of the other. . . . It has been as plain to me that Germany has no claims in the direction of France. . . . To secure mastery over Central Europe by reducing Czechoslovakia and Hungary to a state of vassalage and then to create a Greater Ukraine under German control—this is what essentially appears to be the leading idea now accepted by the Nazi leaders. . . . In order to achieve this, Rumania must be subdued, Poland won over, and Soviet Russia dispossessed. German dynamism is not to be stopped by any of these obstacles and in military circles they already talk of the advance to the Caucasus and to Baku. . . .

Soviet leaders had few illusions regarding the motives that led the great democracies to nourish the Frankenstein monster of Fas-

---

[4] This dispatch, not previously published, was introduced by the defense in the perjury trial of Alger Hiss. Cf. *NYT*, December 2, 1949.

cism. Conclusions were drawn. After a last vain effort to recapture collective security in the spring of 1939, Soviet policies were changed under circumstances to be reviewed in a later chapter. In the immediate aftermath of Munich, Soviet spokesmen saw clearly what was to come.

When the epigones of Pilsudski prepared to join Hitler in destroying Czechoslovakia, the Soviet press expressed itself in no uncertain terms. *Izvestia,* September 27, 1938: "Polish Fascist detachments have provoked a clash with Czech frontier guards. . . ." September 28, 1938: "New provocations of Polish Fascists on Czechoslovak frontiers. . . . *Gazetta Polska* has again come out with impudent attacks on Czechoslovakia and repeated demands for the immediate annexation of Teschen by Poland." October 3, 1938, in a dispatch by S. Moravan from Prague: "Reaction Lifts Its Head— With one hand Hitler has signed the Munich decision, and with the other he has unchained his Polish dogs for the purpose of provoking Czechoslovakia and driving her to full partition. . . ." October 6, 1938: "The campaign of the Polish Government press for the complete partition of Czechoslovakia continues. All official newspapers come out today with placards: 'Within a certain time there must be created a common Polish-Hungarian frontier.' . . . The organ of the Foreign Ministry, *Express Poranni,* supports the demands of the Hungarian Fascist *Magyarshag* for the annexation of Carpatho-Ukraine."

On the broader issue *Izvestia,* reflecting the prevailing views in the Sovnarkom and Politburo, was no less explicit. In the issue of September 29, 1938, its Geneva correspondent asserted that it was not a question of a "fight for Czechoslovakia but of a fight against German hegemony in Europe. In asking Rome to join in the solution of the problem, Chamberlain is simply strengthening the bargaining power of the aggressor." The Prime Minister was accused of paying homage to Hitler by his visits. September 30, quoting the Czech journal *Narodni Osvobozeni:* "We remind the Western nations once again that they are making a fatal error in trying to decide questions of a general European peace without the peoples of Central Europe and the East." A dispatch from Geneva in the issue of October 2 asserted that the ultimate purpose of Hitler was not reflected in the Munich accord, for it envisaged the full partition of Czechoslovakia. In the same issue Ilya Ehrenburg, under the title of "The Second Sedan," wrote from Paris:

The Parisian brokers have observed a "minute of silence": on the steps of the Bourse they prayed for the four "peace-makers." Finishing their prayers, they again cried out: "Royal Dutch," "Rio Tinto," etc. Organized parades greet the "peace-makers." The people of France are not to blame either for the partition of Czechoslovakia or for this tragic vaudeville. . . . Now, as I am dispatching these lines, the celebrating crowd rejoices on the Champs Élysées. Hitlerite bands at this moment are occupying towns and villages of Czechoslovakia. With what pride I now think: I am a Soviet citizen! There is no people which loves peace more than my people, but they know also what is their Fatherland—truth and honor. . . . Besides the four "peace-makers," there is still on this earth the Red Army.

The official Soviet verdict on Munich found expression in a long editorial in *Izvestia* on October 4, 1938, entitled "The Politics of Pacifying the Aggressor":

Official British and French circles are now attempting by means of loud exultation on the occasion of the attainment of a "peaceful triumph" to mask the base and vile character of the Munich deal. Nevertheless, illusions pass and facts remain. It remains an evident, prosaic fact that the capitulation of the so-called democratic nations before the aggressors has to the eye postponed war but in actuality has brought war nearer and with it immeasurably disadvantageous conditions for England and France. . . .

The Soviet Union occupies a plain and unmistakable position. It is a complete stranger to the politics of pacifying the aggressor, which the ruling circles in England and France are trying to pass off under the label of "consolidation of European peace." . . . If in the words of the Soviet representative (Litvinov at Geneva, September 21) the straightforward and honorable policy of the Soviet Union is clearly declared—a policy of defending peace and observing fidelity to international obligations, then the Munich conference, leading to the partition and spoliation of Czechoslovakia, casts a clear light on the policy of the present ruling circles in England and France who have gone over to the cause of the Fascist aggressors.

CHAPTER SEVEN

The Polity of Oligarchy

1. UNION OF SOVIETS

IN EACH of the major capitals of the world the student of politics, if he looks knowledgeably at the public buildings where affairs of State are transacted, will find in the architecture and arrangement of such structures some symbolic, and often unwitting, expressions of the realities of power. On Moscow's Okhotny Read ("Hunters' Row"), west of Sverdlovsk Square with its flowerbeds and fountains facing the façade of the Bolshoi Theater, stands a small domed hall, green with white pillars, called "Soviet House." It is old and squat and modest. Here the major Soviet bodies met during the early years of the regime. Towering over it to the west and facing the Moscow Hotel is the new 12-story, streamlined, modernistic citadel of the Council of Ministers, housing many of the secretarial staffs of the members of the national Cabinet, called "Peoples' Commissars" until 1946 and "Ministers" since. To the east, beyond Teatralny Proyezd, where the street turns at Lubyanskaya Ploshchad, looms the large, block-like building of the Lubyanka, HQ and central prison, successively, of the dread Cheka, OGPU, NKVD, and MVD or political police.

In Red Square the eye is first caught by the crimson flag flying day and night over a green dome on a yellow building behind the Kremlin battlements. This is the old Tsarist "Senate" building (1775–84), long the locus in early Soviet days of the Central Executive Committee of the All-Russian (later All-Union) Congress of Soviets and the meeting-place of the Soviet deputies. The more recent "Supreme Soviet of the USSR" meets far off on the river side of the Kremlin in St. Andrew's Hall of the Great Palace. The Krem-

lin itself is again a public museum and no longer a barred fortress
wherein the top oligarchs hide and whence Stalin, under heavy
guard, makes occasional secret exits or entrances on journeys to or
from his country *dacha*. Yet the Square, called "Red" or "Beautiful"
from time immemorial (*krasnya* has both meanings in Russian), is,
on closer inspection, focused on the "Holy of Holies"—the red marble tomb before which on all open days, rain or shine, thousands of
people patiently wait in the longest queue on earth for a brief
glimpse, in the awesomely lighted crypt, of the mortal remains of
Lenin and Stalin.

In the Soviet system of power, elected law-makers have long
been dominated by executive policy-makers named by the Party,
with the shadow of terror never remote. In turn, the Party—and State
and nation as well—have been dominated during most of four decades by the Leader, even though the great and good Lenin and the
great and bad Stalin are now both dead and the "cult of the individual" has given way to *Kollectivnost*: collective or collegial leadership. Here, as elsewhere among men, the naked and ugly realities
of power have been suitably garbed in seemly raiment to persuade
those from whom obedience is expected that the regime is not a
mere aggregation of arbitrary and self-chosen despots but is a dedicated group of guardians of a Supreme Law, devoted to Political
Truth, Civic Virtue, and the Common Good. The devices of bourgeois "constitutionalism" have often fulfilled this function in the
West. They were borrowed early by the Marxist rulers of Muscovy
to serve this need and were elaborated into "the most democratic
constitution in the world" precisely during the bloodiest years of
the terror.

This paradox involves a sequel: the Soviet State, which remains
an oligarchy of a self-perpetuating elite, could become in another
decade or next year or tomorrow a completely liberal polity, based
on a fusion of federalism and representative parliamentary democracy, without changing a single phrase or word of the Constitution
of 1936. The disparity between the theory and the practice of Soviet
governance seems to some Westerners conclusive proof of Communist hypocrisy, to others a curious product of trial-and-error fumbling with the puzzling tasks of ruling an ambivalent people, and to
still others a symbol of aspiration, of hope, and of the libertarian potentialities of times to come. Leaving for later consideration the
question of which of these views is the more nearly correct, it will

prove useful at this point to review the development of Soviet "constitutionalism."

During the first two months of Soviet rule, there was no "constitution," unless the early decrees—e.g., the Lenin-Stalin "Declaration of the Rights of the Nationalities" (November 15, 1917)—deserve to be so regarded. All agreed that the preparation of a basic law was the task of the Constituent Assembly. But this body suffered the fate anticipated as long ago as 1903 by Plekhanov, who then said: "If the safety of the revolution demanded the temporary limitations of such and such a democratic principle, it would be criminal to hesitate. . . . It is an admissible hypothesis that we, Social Democrats, might be against universal suffrage. . . . If elections should turn out ill, we should have to try to dissolve (the delegates) at the end of two weeks." The dispersal of the Assembly on January 19, 1918, in less than two days, created a vacuum in popular expectations which had somehow to be filled. The Party leaders concluded that the appropriate authority to prepare a constitution was the Third All-Russian Congress of Soviets, which had convened simultaneously with the Constituent Assembly.

This assumption of constituent powers by a legislative body, which is frowned upon in American (but not in British) political practice, eventuated in two documents: "A Declaration of the Rights of the Laboring and Exploited People" and a resolution on "The Federal Institutions of the Russian Republic." In February 1918 a committee of deputies formulated a draft charter of 25 articles, in which the term "Russian Socialist Federated Soviet Republic" (RSFSR) was used for the first time. The mechanics of government here sketched out reflected current practice: an All-Russian Congress of Workers', Soldiers', and Peasants' Deputies, meeting every three months, would exercise "supreme power" and choose a Central Executive Committee (CEC) and a Council of Peoples' Commissars (Sovnarkom). A drafting committee named by the existing CEC, and including Stalin, Sverdlov, and Bukharin, met on April 8, 1918, to perfect the blueprint.

The first Soviet Constitution, ratified by the Fifth Congress of Soviets on July 10, 1918, was the work of this group. In 90 articles, grouped in 17 chapters, the purposes and principles of the Soviet power were set forth (cf. *Izvestia*, July 19, 1918). A preamble charged the local Soviets to reprint the document and display it prominently in public places, while the Commissar for Education

was instructed to introduce "into all schools and educational institutes, without exception, the study of the basic principles of the present Constitution and their explanation and interpretation." The first section, echoing in much of its language the original Communist Manifesto, consisted of the Declaration of the Rights of the Laboring and Exploited Peoples:

1. Russia is declared a Republic of Soviet of Workers', Soldiers' and Peasants' Deputies. All central and local authority is vested in these Soviets.

2. The Russian Soviet Republic is established on the basis of a free union of free nations, as a federation of national Soviet Republics.

For the purpose of "suppressing all exploitation of man by man, of abolishing forever the division of society into classes, of ruthlessly suppressing all exploiters, of bringing about the socialist organization of society and the triumph of socialism in all countries," the Constitution (§3) proclaimed the socialization of all land, forests, mineral wealth, waterways, banks, "livestock and appurtances"; the ratification of the law on workers' control of industry; the repudiation of pre-revolutionary debts "as a first blow at international financial capitalism" and as a step toward "the complete victory of the international revolt of the workers"; the introduction of compulsory labor; the disarmament of the propertied classes; and the development of the Red Army.

In its allocation of authority to public agencies, the Constitution of 1918 vested "supreme power" in the All-Russian Congress of Soviets, meeting semi-annually and composed of one representative of urban Soviets for every 25,000 voters and one representative of provincial (rural) Congresses of Soviets for every 125,000 inhabitants (§25). The ratio of over-representation of the proletariat, as compared with the peasantry, was not 5 to 1, as often stated, but perhaps 2 to 1, assuming an average of 2½ non-voting inhabitants to each voter. The Congress elected a Central Executive Committee of not more than 200 members, described (§31) as "the supreme legislative, administrative, and controlling organ of the RSFSR." The CEC, in turn, appointed the Cabinet or Sovnarkom, comprising 18 Commissariats. Like the Congress of the United States, the All-Russian Congress of Soviets and its CEC were vested with enumerated powers (§§49–52), but since they were of very broad scope and

included "altering and supplementing of the Constitution," this legislature resembled more closely the British Parliament, which, in theory, possesses unlimited sovereignty.

Among the more striking features of the national legislature under the 1918 Constitution was the mode of its election. Soviet deputies were not elected by voters but chosen by other elected deputies —from the city Soviets directly and from the village Soviets indirectly through a hierarchy of Congresses of Soviets in rural districts (*Volosts*), counties (*Uezeds*), and provinces (*Gubernias*), with each body sending delegates to the next higher body, as in the traditional form of American political-party organization. This system of indirect representation, supplemented by a right of recall (§78), involved a choice of law-makers by voters only at the lowest level— city and village Soviets. Only here were there any elements of functional or occupational (as distinct from geographical) representation. "Elections are conducted according to established practice" (§66)—openly and orally and not by secret ballot. The right to vote and be elected was granted, with no residence requirements, to all citizens over 18, "irrespective of sex, religion, or nationality," provided they were engaged in productive work, domestic pursuits, or military service, or were incapacitated for work (§64). Both rights were expressly denied (§65) to employers hiring labor for profit, persons living on unearned incomes, private businessmen, monks, clergymen, former agents of the Tsarist police, members of the former dynasty, lunatics, imbeciles, and "persons convicted of infamous or mercenary crimes for a period fixed by law or judicial sentence."

The Communist Party is nowhere mentioned in this Constitution, which went into effect on the eve of terrorism, rebellion, and foreign intervention, in the sequel to which all other parties were suppressed. The Constitution of 1918 was limited to the RSFSR. It was adopted at a time when the Ukraine, the Caucasus, and other frontier regions were not under Moscow's authority. By 1921 other Soviet Republics had been set up in these areas and had entered into treaty relationships with the RSFSR. In December, 1922, at the Tenth All-Russian Congress of Soviets, Stalin introduced a resolution proposing the creation of a "Union of Soviet Socialist Republics." A commission of delegates drew up a "Treaty of Union" (December 30, 1922) among the RSFSR, the Byelorussian SFR, the Ukrainian SSR and the Transcaucasian SFSR. The Tenth Soviet Con-

gress of the RSFSR became the First Congress of the USSR. A Union Constitution was ratified by the new CEC of the USSR on July 6, 1923, and given final approval by the Second Congress of Soviets of the USSR on January 31, 1924. This Federation of four Republics became a Union of six in 1925 with the establishment of the Uzbek and Turkmen Republics. The elevation of Tadjikistan to the status of a Republic brought the member States to seven. By 1936 the same process in the Kazak and Kirgiz areas, coupled with the dissolution of the Transcaucasian SFSR into its component units (Georgia, Armenia, and Azerbaijan), brought the total of the federated Republics to eleven.

The Union Constitution of 1924 followed closely the RSFSR model of 1918. A preliminary section, taken from the Treaty of December 30, 1922, emphasized "mutual confidence and peace and the brotherly collaboration of peoples" in "the camp of socialism," in alleged contrast to "national enmity and inequality, colonial slavery and chauvinism, national oppression and pogroms, imperialist brutalities and wars" in "the camp of capitalism." The USSR was described as "a voluntary union of equal peoples," "a trustworthy bulwark against world capitalism, and a new decisive step along the path of the union of the workers of all countries in a World Socialist Soviet Republic." The Constitution itself, a document of 72 articles grouped in 11 chapters, begins with an enumeration of some two dozen federal powers, with all other powers reserved to the member Republics, each of which "retains the right of free withdrawal from the Union," subject to approval by all the Republics. Art. 2 specified that the ratification and amendment of the Constitution "comes exclusively within the competence of the Congress of Soviets of the USSR."

This body was made the supreme organ of federal authority. Like its local counterparts in the RSFSR and the other Republics, it consisted of deputies not elected directly but chosen by urban Soviets, with one deputy for each 25,000 voters, and by provincial and district Soviet Congresses (or, in Republics not having such Congresses, by Republican Congresses) with one deputy for every 125,000 inhabitants (§§8–10). Union Congresses met in ordinary session biennially (annually prior to 1927) and in extraordinary session on the call of the federal CEC or of either of its chambers or of any two Republics. The Congress, however, had less the character of a parliamentary body than that of a large mass meeting, con-

sisting of almost 2,000 members convened for only a week at a time. The Soviet analogue of a federal parliament under the 1924 Constitution was the Union CEC, chosen by the Congress and divided into two chambers: a Soviet of the Union, chosen in proportion to population from the delegates of the Republics to the number (by 1936) of 451, with 300 from the RSFSR, 75 from the Ukraine, 30 from Transcaucasia, 13 from Byelorussia, etc.; and a Soviet of Nationalities, consisting of 5 delegates for each Republic and one delegate for each Autonomous Region within the Republics, to the number of 136 members. The CEC met in ordinary sessions three times a year and in extraordinary sessions on the call of its Presidium or of the CEC of any one of the Republics. The federal CEC was vested with authority to enact legislation (§§16–20) by a majority vote of both chambers.

The executive agencies of federal government were headed by the Presidium of the CEC and the Union Sovnarkom. The former body, consisting in final form of 27 members chosen by the two houses of the CEC, was described (§29) as "the supreme legislative, executive, and administrative organ of authority of the USSR" between sessions of the CEC, to which it was "responsible." The Presidium was charged with carrying out the Constitution and all resolutions of the CEC and of the Union Congress of Soviets (§30) and empowered (§§31–3) to "suspend and repeal the resolutions of the Sovnarkom and individual Commissariats of the USSR and also of the CEC's and Sovnarkoms of the Republics"; to "suspend resolutions of the Congresses of Soviets of the Union Republics and subsequently to present such resolutions for examination and confirmation" by the federal CEC; to "issue decrees, resolutions, and ordinances" and to examine and confirm draft decrees submitted by the Union Sovnarkom and by federal and Republic CEC's, "their Presidia and other organs of authority."

The Union Sovnarkom or federal Cabinet, identified (§37) as "the executive organ of the CEC of the USSR," consisted of the heads of executive departments or Commissariats. The 10 Commissariats originally established by the Constitution embraced 5 All-Union Commissariats (Foreign Affairs, War and Marine, Foreign Trade, Communications, Post and Telegraphs), functioning throughout all the territory of the federation through their own officials, and 5 United or joint Union-Republican Commissariats (National Economy, Food, Labor, Finance, and Workers' and Peasants' Inspec-

tion), functioning through the corresponding Commissariats of the Republics. Each Commissar presided over a departmental Collegium, appointed by the Sovnarkom as a whole, to which he was obliged to report all decisions and from which, in the event of dissent, he might expect complaints to the Sovnarkom.

This apparently cumbersome structure of national government was even more intricate than has been suggested, since the basic law of the USSR embraced the Constitutions of the Union Republics and of the constituent parts of the RSFSR. From observation limited to scanning the documents, British students could read into it the parliamentary principle of executive responsibility to the legislature. American observers could find a plausible facsimile of the doctrine of separation of powers and of federal-state relations in the USA. Such projections of Anglo-American experience onto the Soviet scene are unwarranted. Despite surface resemblances to alien systems, and potentialities of development toward Western practices, the Soviet hierarchy was *sui generis*. It has never functioned, moreover, save within the controlling discipline and dynamism of the Party. These considerations are equally applicable to the Constitution of 1936.

Between 1929 and 1935 the economic and social order of the USSR underwent the most drastic transformation that has ever occurred in a similar period in any major community. In the Soviet Union, as elsewhere, political practices deeply imbedded in the habits of rulers and ruled change less rapidly than the texture of social living and the activities by which men and women earn their daily bread. Political vocabularies, with their sacred stereotypes and highly emotionalized symbols and slogans, are modified even more slowly. Political man, even when a citizen of a revolutionary State, is a conservative animal. Communists, however, pride themselves on their energy as innovators and swear by the Marxist dictum that political institutions are but the superstructure of class relations flowing out of prevailing modes of production. The collectivization of agriculture and the tremendous upsurge of industrialization, accompanied by the crises and convulsions already reviewed, transformed Soviet society and economy almost beyond recognition. The Party leadership therefore concluded in the course of the Second Five Year Plan that the constitutional structure dating from the early period of the NEP was no longer appropriate to the needs of a new epoch.

The Seventh All-Union Congress of Soviets voted on February 6, 1935, to appoint a Constitution Commission to draw up an amended text embodying equal suffrage, direct election, secret ballot, and recognition of "the present relation of class forces" in the light of the growth of socialist industry, the end of the kulaks, and the triumph of collectivization. On the next day the CEC named a Commission of 31 to draft a new document. Stalin became its president. In June 1936 the completed draft was published in hundreds of thousands of copies and in all languages of the USSR. General discussion was encouraged and almost demanded by the Party leaders. Over half a million meetings were held, attended by no less than 36,000,000 people. After many thousands of proposed changes were sifted out, 150 were given serious consideration and 43 were adopted.

At the Extraordinary Eighth Congress of Soviets on November 25, 1936, Stalin delivered a lengthy address on the revised draft. He dwelt first on the changes of recent years which had "eliminated all the exploiting classes"; "transformed the proletariat into the working class of the USSR, which has abolished the capitalist economic system, has established the socialist ownership of the instruments and means of production, and is directing Soviet society along the road to communism"; converted the peasants into collective farmers, "emancipated from exploitation"; and established a new Soviet Intelligentsia, serving the masses. The new Constitution, continued Stalin, must not be a program of the future—e.g., the achievement of communism—but a "summary of the gains already achieved"—e.g., socialism.

I must admit that the draft of the new Constitution does preserve the regime of the dictatorship of the working class, just as it also preserves unchanged the present leading position of the Communist Party of the USSR. If the esteemed critics regard this as a flaw in the Draft Constitution, that is only to be regretted. We Bolsheviks regard it as a merit. As to freedom for various political parties, we adhere to somewhat different views. A party is a part of a class, its most advanced part. Several parties, and consequently freedom for parties, can exist only in a society in which there are antagonistic classes . . . say, capitalist and workers, landlords and peasants, kulaks and poor peas-

ants, etc. . . . In the USSR there are only two classes, workers and peasants, whose interests—far from being mutually hostile—are, on the contrary, friendly. Hence there is no ground in the USSR for the existence of several parties, and consequently for freedom for these parties. In the USSR there is ground only for one party, the Communist Party. . . .

They talk of democracy. But what is democracy? Democracy in capitalist countries, where there are antagonistic classes, is, in the last analysis, democracy for the strong, democracy for the propertied minority. In the USSR, on the contrary, democracy is democracy for the working people, i.e., democracy for all. But from this it follows that the principles of democracy are violated not by the draft of the new Constitution of the USSR, but by the bourgeois constitutions. That is why I think that the Constitution of the USSR is the only thoroughly democratic constitution in the world.

On December 1, 1936, the deputies unanimously adopted a Resolution (*Izvestia*, December 2, 1936) approving the draft and appointing an Editorial Commission of 220 members to put it in final form. This body included such Party leaders as Andreyev, Beria, Vyshinsky, Zhdanov, Kaganovich, Kalinin, Litvinov, Mikoyan, Molotov, and Ordjonikidze; such military figures as Blucher, Budenny, Voroshilov, Zhukov, and Shaposhnikov; such intellectual celebrities as Alexandrovich, Bogomolets, Burdenko, Korchagina-Alexandrevskaya, Lysenko, and A. N. Tolstoi; and such prospective purgees as Yegorov, Yezhov, Tukhachevsky, Uborovich, and Yakir. The mandate commission of the Congress, which was the last to meet under the 1924 Constitution, compared the Eighth Congress with the Second, which had ratified the earlier charter (cf. *Izvestia*, December 2, 1936). In 1924 there had been 1,535 delegates, in 1936, 2,016, reflecting the representation of the new industrial cities and an increase in population "six times as great as that achieved by Germany in the same period." Of the 2,016 deputies, the RSFSR had 1,310, the Ukraine 370, Kazakistan 75, Uzbekistan 65, Byelorussia 62, Azerbaijan 42, Georgia 37, etc. In 1924, 90% of the delegates were Party members, in 1936 only 72%. In 1924 there were 58 women delegates, in 1936, 419. In the Eighth Congress, workers (of whom 97%

were Stakhanovites) comprised 42% of the total, peasants (all from collective farms) 40%, and intellectuals 18%. For these gains, declared Y. A. Yakovlev, "we are obliged to the best Leninist, the creator of the new Constitution, the great son of the Soviet people of whom our nation is proud, who in the family of every worker and peasant is called the father of toilers—our leader, Comrade Stalin!" (Ovation.)

In addressing the Congress on the same day, Nikita S. Khrushchev, a member of the Politburo, declared (*Izvestia*, December 2, 1936):

> The Fascists, especially the German, are now shouting about their triumph over Marxism, but this "triumph" is one of jesters and clowns of the Middle Ages. And here we are accepting our Constitution and celebrating the victory of Marxism-Leninism-Stalinism, a victory which is not only ours but is also that of toilers the world over. . . . The German Fascists have illusions about the breakdown of our Socialist State and they rave about seizing lands to the East. . . . If the Fascists attack us, we, our Red Army, together with the German working class, will drown Fascism not in glory but in their own blood. . . . All the toilers of our country know that the brains of the Revolution and the cement strengthening the forces of the Revolution is our Bolshevik Party, the Party of Lenin-Stalin. . . . In the Stalin epoch, the epoch of victorious socialism, the working class under the leadership of our great leader [*Vozhd*] will conduct a far-reaching battle for the final victory of communism and for its triumph the world over.

Headlines in the Soviet press spoke of "Unforgettable Days," "Great Charter for Liberated Humanity," "The Stalinist Constitution Lights Our Way," "For Strengthening the Peace and Security of the USSR." On December 5, 1936, which was made a national holiday, the Eighth Congress unanimously adopted the Constitution as finally revised by the Editorial Commission.

The new charter, the full text of which will be found in the Appendix, abolished class discriminations in voting, indirect elections, and balloting for candidates by a public show of hands. Provision was made (§§134–42) for "universal, direct, and equal suffrage by secret ballot." All persons over 18, save lunatics and

criminals deprived of electoral rights by a court sentence, were granted the right to vote and to be elected, "irrespective of race or nationality, religion, educational and residential qualifications, social origin, property status, or past activities." All deputies in all Soviets —Union, Republican, and local—were to be chosen by direct election in single-member constituencies. All voting was henceforth to be confidential and by ballot. All deputies were subject to recall by a majority of their electors. The right to nominate candidates (141) was secured to "public organizations and societies of the working people: Communist Party organizations, trade unions, cooperatives, youth organizations, and cultural societies." These provisions were made applicable to all elections throughout the territory of the Union. In contrast to the United States, where citizenship is defined by the federal Constitution and suffrage by the States within the limits of federal constitutional restrictions, both citizenship and suffrage in the USSR are defined in the Union Constitution.

Major changes in the structure of federal government were also introduced. The old Congress of Soviets, with its CEC of two houses, was replaced by a bicameral national legislature, the Supreme Soviet of the USSR, elected for four years. The Soviet of the Union, corresponding to the U.S. House of Representatives, consists of deputies chosen from districts of 300,000 population each. It had 569 members at the outset, and 647 by 1941 as a result of the annexations of 1939–40. The Soviet of Nationalities in the original draft was to have been appointive, like the U.S. Senate prior to the 17th Amendment. In response to popular proposals, which Stalin expressly approved, this upper chamber was made elective on the basis of 25 deputies for each Union Republic, 11 for each Autonomous Republic, 5 for each Autonomous Region, and 1 for each National Region. Its membership was 574 at the outset and 713 by 1941. All federal legislation requires a majority vote in each house. The two chambers, meeting jointly, choose a Presidium of 42 members, headed by a President (Kalinin). The Presidium has 15 (originally 11) Vice-Presidents, one for each Union Republic. The Supreme Soviet is normally convened by its Presidium twice a year, with special sessions meeting on the call of the Presidium or of any one of the Republics. The Supreme Soviet appoints the Union Sovnarkom, consisting at the outset of 25 Union Commissariats and 15 Union-Republican Commissariats.

On paper this design for power establishes a completely demo-

cratic system of government by all modern definitions of democracy. It was currently hailed in the USSR as "the most democratic constitution in the world." To what extent and in what sense, if any, it has been a vehicle of democracy in its actual operation will be considered below. Here cognizance may usefully be taken of the general principles of governance which are stated or implied in the document.

The Soviet Constitution, unlike that of the United States, does not purport to establish what is generally termed a "presidential" system of government. Its scheme (on paper) comes closer to a "parliamentary" system, comparable to that of the United Kingdom, the French Republic, the Weimar Republic, and other Continental democracies. Stalin (November 25, 1936) rejected the proposal that the President of the Presidium of the Supreme Soviet be popularly elected: "According to the system of our Constitution there must not be an individual President in the USSR, elected by the whole population on a par with the Supreme Soviet, and able to put himself in opposition to the Supreme Soviet. The President in the USSR is a collegium, it is the Presidium of the Supreme Soviet, including the President of the Presidium, elected not by the whole population, but by the Supreme Soviet and accountable to it. Historical experience shows that such a structure of the supreme bodies is the most democratic, and safeguards the country against undesirable contingencies." The responsibility of the executive (here the Sovnarkom and the Presidium) to the legislature is the antithesis of the American system and the essence of the parliamentary system.

2. THE SOCIALIST STATE

THE manifold contradictions between theory and practice, law and fact, ideology and reality, in the public life of the USSR have counterparts in all the schemes that men have devised for the ordering of their common concerns. The "Electoral College" of the USA, the forms of "democracy" masking the forces of dictatorship in many Latin American republics, and the magic and mythology of the powers of the British Crown come at once to mind—along with memories of the "Holy Roman Empire," wherein Hohenstaufens and Hapsburgs wielded shadowy authority as universal rulers of Chris-

tendom on the basis of the tangible lands of local principalities, and, still earlier, of the Roman Empire, in which a divine despot commanded obedience in the name of the "Republican" sovereignty of "Senate and People." These paradoxes of politics, however, were products of generations of groping efforts by the political animal to meet the needs of the present and anticipate the demands of the future without sacrificing the sacred symbolism of the past. The paradoxes of Soviet politics emerged full-blown, like Minerva from the brow of Jove, within a single year after the adoption of the Constitution of 1936. They persisted with little change for two decades and more and surpassed by far all parallels in other times and climes. These antitheses moved many Soviet citizens to confusion and to alternating despair and hope, and stirred many Western commentators to cynical contempt for a system of power characterized by such gross discrepancies between what politicians said they were doing within a government of laws and not of men and what in truth they were doing in a government of men and not of laws.

Here the fiction of the "dictatorship of the proletariat" confronted the fact of rulership by a managerial elite. Here the juridical theory of a government by Soviets, local, regional, and national, faced the practice of the monolithic and monopolistic oligarchy of the Party. Within the Party, Lenin's concept of "democratic centralism," postulating the responsibility of the leaders to the led, gave way to Stalin's totalitarian machine, ruthlessly exacting obedience from the led to the leaders. Within the leadership, collective deliberations and decisions often gave way, prior to Stalin's demise, to a species of Cæsarism.

Any account of government in the USSR must, if it is to do justice to reality, simultaneously take account of the paradoxes and avoid their exaggeration into the totality of Soviet political experience. Whether the comments to follow will achieve this goal is doubtful, but they will at least be directed toward its attainment.[1]

[1] Among the more useful Western studies in English on the structure and function of Soviet Government (with an asterisk [*] indicating Great Books), those which emphasize theory at the expense of the realities of power include: Hewlett Johnson: *Soviet Russia Since the War* (Boni and Baer, 1947); Corliss Lamont: *Soviet Civilization* (Philosophical Library, 1952); B. J. Stern and S. Smith (eds.): *Understanding the Russians* (Barnes & Noble, 1947); Sidney and Beatrice Webb: *Soviet Communism: A New Civilization?* * (2 vols., Longmans, Green, 1936).

Those which emphasize Soviet oligarchy or dictatorship at the expense of

As regards the "federal" character of the Soviet Union and of its largest unit, the Russian Socialist Federated Soviet Republics, Communist publicists claimed from the outset that Soviet federalism represented the final resolution of the "nationality problem" of the Tsarist Empire, with its scores of ethnic groups and its pogroms, oppressions, and efforts at "Russification." A new day allegedly dawned, suffused with the light of tolerance, equality, and brotherhood

---

the theory of "Soviet Democracy" include: George S. Counts and Nucia Lodge: *The Country of the Blind* (Houghton Mifflin, 1949); David J. Dallin: *The Real Soviet Russia* (Yale University Press, 1944) and *The Changing World of Soviet Russia* (Yale University Press, 1956; H. S. Dinerstein and L. Goure: *Two Studies in Soviet Controls* (Free Press, 1955); Merle Fainsod: *How Russia Is Ruled* * (Harvard University Press, 1953); Louis Fischer: *The Life and Death of Stalin* (Harper, 1952); George Fischer: *Soviet Opposition to Stalin* (Harvard University Press, 1952); Michael M. Florinsky: *Toward an Understanding of U.S.S.R.* (Macmillan, 1951); Igor Gouzenko: *The Iron Curtain* (Dutton, 1948); Waldemar Gurian (ed.): *The Soviet Union: Background, Ideology, Reality* (University of Notre Dame Press, 1951); George B. de Huszar and Associates: *Soviet Power and Policy* (Crowell, 1955); Alex Inkeles: *Public Opinion in Soviet Russia* (Harvard University Press, 1950); Alex Inkeles, Raymond A. Bauer, and Clyde Kluckhohn: *How the Soviet System Works* (Harvard University Press, 1956); W. W. Kulski: *The Society Regime: Communism in Practice* * (Syracuse University Press, 1954); Robert Magidoff: *The Kremlin vs. the People* (Doubleday, 1953); Boris Meissner: *The Communist Party of the U.S.S.R.* (Praeger, 1956); Barrington Moore, Jr.: *Soviet Politics: The Dilemma of Power* (Harvard University Press, 1950) and *Terror and Progress: U.S.S.R.* (Harvard University Press, 1955); Bertram D. Wolfe: *Six Keys to the Soviet System* (Beacon Press, 1956).

Those which strike a reasonable balance, as I see it, between theory and practice include: Harold H. Fisher: *The Communist Revolution* (Stanford University Press, 1955); Samuel N. Harper: *Civic Training in Soviet Russia* (University of Chicago Press, 1929); John N. Hazard: *Law and Social Change in the U.S.S.R.* (Carswell, 1953); Maurice Hindus: *Crisis in the Kremlin* (Doubleday, 1953) and *Mother Russia* * (Doubleday, 1944); Hans Kelsen: *The Political Theory of Bolshevism* (University of California Press, 1948); Sir John Maynard: *Russia in Flux* * (Macmillan, 1948); Sir Bernard Pares: *Russia* * (Mentor Books, 1949); W. W. Rostow and Alfred Levin: *The Dynamics of Soviet Society* (Norton, 1953); Julian Towster: *Political Power in the U.S.S.R., 1917–1947* * (Oxford University Press, 1948).

Among recent Soviet publications, all of which glorify "Soviet Democracy" and ignore the reality of oligarchy, the most comprehensive is Andrei Y. Vyshinsky's *Soviet State Law* (Moscow, 1938), translated as *The Law of the Soviet State* under the auspices of the American Council of Learned Societies and published in New York by Macmillan in 1948. See also the following monographs, all published by the Foreign Languages Publishing House, Moscow: A. Y. Vyshinsky: *The Soviet Electoral Law: Questions and Answers* (1955); G. Glezerman: *The Soviet Socialist State* (1955); and V. Karpinsky: *How the Soviet Union Is Governed* (1954). See also John S. Curtiss: *The Russian Revolutions of 1917* (Van Nostrand, 1957) and John L. Stipp (ed.): *Soviet Russia Today* (Harper, 1956).

among equals—reflected, as of 1941, in the formal existence within the RSFSR of 15 "Autonomous Soviet Socialist Republics (ASSR), of 6 "autonomous regions" (AR), and 9 "National Districts," plus 2 ASSR's (Adzhar and Abkhazian) and 1 AR (South Ossetian) in Georgia, 1 ASSR (Nakhichevan) and 1 AR (Nagorno-Karabakh) in Azerbaijan, 1 ASSR (Kara-Kalpak) in Uzbekistan, and 1 AR (Gorno-Badakhan) in Tadjikistan.

Within these far-flung Eurasian areas of mixed populations and many national minorities, peace and harmony were officially declared to be assured by autonomy and "self-determination" for all, each enjoying its own language and culture "national in form, but proletarian in content," and all united in a federation of "Union Republics"—ultimately 16 in number, including Estonia, Latvia, Lithuania, and Moldavia, annexed in 1940, and reduced to 15 in July 1956 with the absorption of the Karelo-Finnish SSR, the smallest in population, into the RSFSR.

Before considering the truth or falsity of such claims, a digression is in order on the puzzling problem of the size and distribution of the population of the USSR and its constituent parts. Great Russian is the native language of half the inhabitants and the second language of most of the remainder, comprising some 200 ethnic groups (many of them tiny cultural curiosities), of which the most numerous are Ukrainian, Byelorussian, Kazak, Uzbek, and Georgian. Eleven years after 1945, for obviously absurd "security" reasons, no major Soviet city possessed a street plan, guidebook, or even telephone directory. (Only two street maps of Moscow were to be found in the Soviet capital in the spring of 1956, both in offices of foreign representatives and both printed in Washington, D.C.) Russian street maps began to appear, however, during the summer of the same year. No population statistics were published between 1939 and 1956. The census of December 17, 1926, reported a total population of 147,028,000. The census of January 17, 1939, tallied 170,468,000. No subsequent census had been taken by 1957. Planners and policemen kept tab on population growth, since the necessary data were available through the internal-passport system and registrations of birth and deaths. Western estimates commonly postulated a total between 210,000,000 and 220,000,000 by 1955, with no confirmation or denial from Soviet sources.[2]

[2] In calculating Soviet population in 1954 for Funk & Wagnall's *New International Year Book* (article on USSR, edition of 1955), I compared the

In July 1956 the Central Statistical Board of the Soviet Council of Ministers issued, for the first time since 1939, a handbook on *The National Economy of the USSR (Narodnoye Khozyaistvo SSSR)*, giving the total of Soviet population as 191,700,000 in 1940 and 200,200,000 in April 1956. By this estimate, according to which Soviet war losses were vastly greater than anyone in the West previously supposed and subsequent population growth was far smaller than hitherto assumed, the Soviet population in 1956 was distributed as follows among the Union Republics:

	1940	APRIL 1956
R.S.F.S.R.	107,900,000	112,600,000
Ukraine	41,000,000	40,600,000
Byelorussia	9,200,000	8,000,000
Uzbekistan	6,200,000	8,500,000
Kazakhistan	6,200,000	8,500,000
Georgia	3,600,000	4,000,000
Azerbaijan	3,200,000	3,400,000
Lithuania	2,900,000	2,700,000
Moldavia	2,500,000	2,700,000
Latvia	1,900,000	2,000,000
Kirgizia	1,500,000	1,900,000
Tadjikistan	1,500,000	1,800,000
Armenia	1,300,000	1,600,000
Turkmenistan	1,200,000	1,400,000
Estonia	1,000,000	1,100,000
Karelo-Finnish	500,000	600,000

To what degree has "Soviet federalism" been a reality and to what degree a fiction among the national groups of the USSR? The letter of the law is clear. Art. 123 of the Constitution of 1936 asserts:

Equality of rights of citizens of the USSR, irrespective of their nationality or race, in all spheres of economic, State, cultural, social, and political life, is an indefeasible law. Any direct or indirect restriction of the rights of, or, con-

published totals of registered voters in the election of 1937 (93,639,458), 1946 (101,717,686), and 1953 (120,750,816) with the published totals of population for 1937 and 1939 and concluded that the inhabitants of the USSR in 1954 numbered about 217,198,000. Comparable estimates were common in the West at this time. Harrison E. Salisbury of *The New York Times* first cast serious doubt on such figures (issue of March 11, 1956) on the basis of his inferences from Warren W. Eason's calculation from other sources, and concluded that the total Soviet population in 1956 was only 200,500,000—a figure remarkably close to that published in the later Soviet statistical handbook of July 1956.

versely, any establishment of direct or indirect privileges for, citizens on account of their race or nationality, as well as any advocacy of racial or national exclusiveness or hatred and contempt, is punishable by law.

In pursuit of this aspiration, Soviet policy-makers brought literacy to the "backward peoples" of the Caucasus and Central Asia, often in Latin alphabets to begin with and later in Cyrillic alphabets. The forgotten men of Transcaucasia, Turkestan, and remote Siberia not only learned how to read and write their own tongues but came into possession of schools, libraries, hospitals, and factories, with resulting living standards far above those of other Asian peoples beyond the Soviet frontier. In all the ordinary social and civic relationships among human beings, Soviet society—in this respect, at least, conforming to the highest ideals of Christianity and liberalism—achieved at times an approximation to complete freedom from racial and national prejudice and discrimination.

But if the question be posed as to whether "federalism" in the Western sense—i.e., a formula for uniting separate sovereignties into a union in which each yields certain powers to a common authority and retains all others in local autonomy—is a reality of political life in the USSR, the only possible verdict must be a negative one. Even among the citizens of true federations—such as the USA, Canada, Mexico, Brazil, Australia, South Africa, and Switzerland—the formula is ill understood save among constitutional lawyers and judges and the few advocates of Atlantic or world federation. For present purposes it is enough to distinguish between "federal" governments and, on the one hand, "unitary" governments (e.g., Britain, France, Italy, and each State of the USA) wherein central authorities decide the division of powers between the local and central agencies and, on the other hand, "confederations" (e.g., the USA, 1781–9, the CSA, 1860–5, the League of Nations, 1920–39, and the United Nations Organization, 1946 f.) wherein the local units decide what powers the central agencies shall wield. In a genuine federation the allocation of authority between public agents of the local units and those of the whole community is made by means of a written constitution that can be altered only by the joint consent of both—for example, in the USA by two-thirds of each chamber of the federal Congress and by three-quarters of the State legislatures. Federalism presupposes two spheres of law, with federal law in its

limited area prevailing over local law wherever the two are in conflict (cf. Art. VI of the Constitution of the USA), dual citizenship, federal power to tax and to legislate, and enforcement of federal authority not through the coercion of States by States or by the central government but through the application of federal law to individuals on the local level by local policemen and judges. Whether the member States of a federal union have a right to secede is always a moot point, decided definitively for the USA at Gettysburg and Appomattox.

The Soviet scheme of government embodies on paper many of the attributes of federalism. The 1936 Constitution describes the USSR as "a federal State formed on the basis of the voluntary association of Soviet Socialist Republics, having equal rights" (§13). Twenty-three federal powers are enumerated, with all others left to the Republics (§§14–15). The Soviet equivalent of Article VI of the American Constitution is found (cf. Appendix) in §§19, 20, 105, and 130, by which the primacy of federal law is assured. Amendments to the Union Constitution (§146) require a two-thirds vote of each chamber of the Supreme Soviet but do not, as in the United States, require ratification by state legislatures—i.e., the Supreme Soviets of the Union Republics. These, however, are equally represented in the Soviet of Nationalities and in theory (§17) could secede if dissatisfied with a constitutional amendment. In a semantic *tour de force,* Stalin and his collaborators, in framing the Union Constitution of 1936, provided for an unqualified right of secession. "Of course," commented Stalin (November 25, 1936) in a masterpiece of understatement, "none of our Republics would actually raise the question of seceding from the USSR."

In practice Soviet "federalism" has been, from beginning to end, a pretense. Repeatedly over the years boundaries have been changed (e.g., the transfer of the Crimea from the RSFSR to the Ukraine in February 1954, and the absorption of the Karelo-Finnish SSR into the RSFSR in July 1956), the division of powers has been altered, and whole populations have been uprooted not through any "federal" procedure of decision-making but by joint decrees of the Union Sovnarkom or Council of Ministers and the Central Committee of the Party. In his indictment of Stalin (February 24–5, 1956), Khrushchev noted indignantly that in 1943–4, on the order of the *Vozhd,* all the people of the Karachai AR, and of the Kalmyk, Chechen-Ingush, and Kabardino-Balkar ASSR's were deported to

Asia, along with the inhabitants of the Crimean Tartar and Volga German ASSR's, both unmentioned by Khrushchev.

> The Ukrainians avoided meeting this fate only because there were too many of them and there was no place to which to deport them. . . . Not only a Marxist-Leninist but also no man of common sense can grasp how it is possible to make whole nations responsible for inimical activity, including women, children, old people, Communists, and Komsomols, to use mass repression against them, and to expose them to misery and suffering for the hostile acts of individual persons or groups of persons.

In Stalin's last years, moreover, anti-Semitism and other forms of discrimination against minority peoples became a marked feature, despite semantic disguises, of the official conduct of Soviet policy-makers. In happier days to come, federalism may be given practical meaning in the public law and political life of the USSR. During most of the unhappy past it has been a fiction or a fraud.[3]

A like judgment is warranted by the record on many other aspects of the theory of Soviet governance in contrast to the practice of the arts of power by the oligarchs. On paper the Soviet Constitution establishes a "parliamentary" system on the British and Continental model. Cabinets in both the USSR and the Union Republics are chosen by, and from, the freely elected members of legislative bodies and may, in principle, be altered or displaced by the deputies who appoint them. In fact any such relationship is wholly contrary to reality. The persisting pattern of Soviet public life, still unaltered in 1957 despite hopes and prospects of change, was firmly established by the oligarchs in 1937. Its genesis therefore merits review.

[3] Joshua Kunitz, in his otherwise perceptive and illuminating essay "The Jewish Problem in the USSR" (*Monthly Review,* March and April 1953), argues that *popular* anti-Semitism was widespread after 1945 but that no *official* anti-Semitism existed. It is doubtless true that no individuals were persecuted or discriminated against because of Jewish origin *per se,* provided that they were willing to renounce their Jewish religious and cultural heritage. But Party and Government alike, prior to Stalin's demise, savagely attacked not only political Zionism, or even the slightest suspicion thereof, but suppressed all manifestations of Hebrew or Yiddish culture, even to the extent of executing, on trumped-up charges, numerous Yiddish writers and artists. Amends have since been made. The realities of 1948–53, however, suggest that Kunitz's dichotomy is a distinction without a difference. Cf. Solomon M. Schwarz: *The Jews in the Soviet Union* (Syracuse University Press, 1953).

The first election held under the 1936 Constitution took place on December 12, 1937, for the new Supreme Soviet. In preparation for the event the old federal CEC appointed a Central Electoral Commission, which directed a hierarchy of local commissions in registering voters and candidates, conducting propaganda, supervising the preparation of ballots, envelopes, and ballot boxes, counting the ballots, and announcing the results. Electoral districts, established at least 45 days before the election, were to be fixed by the CEC and subsequently by the Supreme Soviet itself. For purposes of registering voters and casting and counting ballots (but not for purposes of representation) the RSFSR was divided into 93,927 precincts, of which 2,047 were on boats. The population of some of the urban precincts was as large as 150,000, while districts in the lesser Republics varied between 5,000 and 20,000 inhabitants.

Candidates were proposed in the constituencies by trade unions, cooperatives, Komsomol units, cultural societies, army regiments, collective farms, and the primary organizations of the Party, with the latter in most instances advising other groups in areas where it was decided not to nominate a Party member. No candidate could be nominated by an individual, but all voters were entitled to attend meetings where nominees were proposed. Efforts of church congregations to propose candidates were disallowed by the Electoral Commission. Procedure conformed closely to the Election Regulations later issued by the Supreme Soviet. Voting lists were compiled by agents of city and rural Soviets on the basis of house rolls, membership lists of collective farms, and personal canvassing. In the absence of any residence requirement, all temporary and permanent inhabitants were listed alphabetically in each precinct. Those moving before election day or engaged in travel were granted certificates by local Soviets, entitling them to vote wherever they might be. The lists thus compiled were posted in local Soviet HQ 30 days before the election. All citizens were entitled to complain of omissions or errors, with each complaint to be dealt with inside of 3 days by the Soviet Executive Committee, with appeal to the People's Courts, which were required to reach a decision in open hearings within 3 days in the presence of the complainant and a representative of the Soviet.

Qualifications for candidates were the same as those for voters, except that no candidate could be a member of an Electoral Commission and each was required to consent in writing to be a nom-

inee. The names of proposed candidates were to be published in the local press 25 days before the election. Ballots were to be printed 15 days before the election. In most districts several candidates were proposed, usually by acclamation in the various nominating groups. But in all districts only one candidate for each seat in the Soviet of the Union and the Soviet of Nationalities (1,143 in all) appeared on the ballot. Of the total thus nominated, 37 were dropped and replaced by others, on the order of the Central Electoral Commission. This elimination of all but one candidate normally took place within the 10 days between the publishing of names and the printing of ballots. The procedure was nowhere set forth by law or decree. It amounted to a highly informal "primary," inevitably guided by the local Party members. The choice of deputies was thus made not at the election but during the campaign in the name of a "bloc of Party and non-Party people." Of the 569 candidates for the Soviet of the Union, 81% (and of the 574 candidates for the Soviet of Nationalities, 71%) were members or candidates of the Party. Others were designated as "non-Party Bolshevists."

Soviet theory continued to anticipate multiple nominations for membership in the Supreme Soviet. The statutes provided for "run-off" elections two weeks after the original polling if less than half of the registered voters cast ballots or if no candidate received an absolute majority. While it does not appear that this familiar democratic device, or the constitutional right of popular recall, has ever been applied to federal offices, the possibility of at least 3 candidates for a single seat was clearly contemplated. Mayors of cities were at this period elected by popular choice through secret ballot from among four or five candidates. The same was true for members of village and urban Soviets, in which non-Party members usually constitute two-thirds or three-quarters of the deputies.

If the first federal election day was a gala occasion, the preceding nation-wide campaign to get out the vote had all the earmarks of an educational crusade. Scores of millions of copies of election pamphlets and books on the records and qualifications of candidates were published. "Delegate Campaigners" were elected in pre-election conferences in all precincts to organize campaign workers and act as official electioneers. Most urban precincts had *Agitpunkts* for reading, lectures, and entertainments. The Soviet press teemed with slogans and resolutions: "All to the polls!" "Let us transform Election Day into a great holiday in celebration of the unity of So-

viet youth around Stalin!" "Comrade Communists: Vote for the Non-Party candidates in the same friendly manner as for Communist candidates! Comrade Non-Party Voters: Vote for the Communist candidates in the same friendly manner as for Non-Party candidates!" "Party and people are indivisible!" "Long live the Invincible bloc of Communists and Non-Party people!" Wrote *Pravda*, December 10, 1937:

> As a result of the Stalin policy the Soviet people has for 16 years been delivered from war-clashes and lives a peaceful life and has the opportunity to continue without hindrance its peaceful labors. . . . The Party is going to the elections with a program: peace . . . , extensive strengthening of the industrial might of the Fatherland . . . , securing gains in the Stakhanovite record . . . , increasing the successes of collective farms . . . , attainment of new heights of cultural creativeness. The people know that in the Party of Bolsheviks there is no dichotomy of word and deed. . . . Stalin can reckon on our good faith. . . .

In expressing his appreciation to those who had nominated him in a Moscow district, Stalin, in an address broadcast over the Union from the Bolshoi Theater on election eve (cf. *Pravda*, December 12, 1937), touched on many matters dear to Bolshevik hearts:

> What can be added to the speeches of our leading comrades, Kalinin, Molotov, Voroshilov, Kaganovich, Yezhov, etc.? . . . I could have prepared some light speech about everything and nothing. It is possible that such a speech would amuse the public. It is said that masters of such speeches reside not only in capitalist countries but also here in the Soviet State. But first of all, I am not a master of such speeches. . . . I know the meaning of confidence. It naturally confers upon me new and additional duties and responsibilities. . . . Among us Bolsheviks it is not the accepted thing to shirk responsibility. I accept it willingly. . . . It is more than an election; it is really a public holiday for our workers, our peasants and our intellectuals.

Sunday, December 12, 1937, was a day of singing, dancing, and merrymaking. It was also a day of earnest dedication to civic duty by all Soviet citizens, very few of whom shared the view abroad

that an election whose results were predetermined must be a mockery. To a people who were voting by secret ballot for the first time in 20 years, this was a minor detail. Oldsters could recall elections to the impotent Duma in Tsarist times, but the suffrage had been narrowly restricted. Now all could vote. No matter that the unsuccessful candidates had already retired and that the new parliament would do the Party's bidding. From the Party had come the new Constitution and the new life which, for all its rigors, was infinitely better for the masses than the old. The goals were unanimity now now and solidarity forever. Polls were open from 6 a.m. until midnight. Moscow and other cities were aglow with bunting, garlands, and flags. Stalin, Molotov, and Voroshilov voted in precinct 58 of the Lenin election district of the capital. Others voted by millions in town and countryside, in lonely villages and remote valleys, in Arctic outposts and desert oases, on ships at sea, and even at railway stations, where booths were set up for passengers in transit.

Of the 93,639,458 enfranchised Soviet citizens, 90,319,436, or 96%, cast ballots. Of the ballots for deputies to the Soviet of the Union, 636,808 were invalid and 632,074 had names crossed out. In electing the members of the Soviet of Nationalities, the voters cast 1,487,582 invalid ballots and crossed out names in 562,402 instances. "Invalid" ballots were those spoiled by incorrect marking or by the writing in of names. Even the overenthusiastic voter who wrote in Stalin's name in districts where he was not a candidate rendered the ballot invalid. Apart from refusing to vote, the only means of final protest in the privacy of the voting booth was to cross out candidates' names or write in the names of others. But protestants were few. In only three Union Republics did less than 95% of the registered electors vote: Turkmenistan, 94.2%; Uzbekistan, 93.5%; and Kirgizia, 94.3%. In the Ukraine 97.8% voted and in the RSFSR 96.8%. The participants in only one Republic (Kirgizia, 97.2%) cast fewer than 98% of their ballots for the "Bloc of Party and Non-Party People" (cf. *Pravda*, December 17, 1937). The "victors" who filled the 1,143 seats comprised 855 Party members and 288 non-Party members. Of the total, 354 were workers or peasants, 120 Red Army or Navy men, 78 non-official intellectuals, and 51 members of the NKVD. Women elected numbered 184.

With the coming of war, the second federal election, scheduled for December 1941, was indefinitely postponed, as were Republican and many local elections. Supreme Soviets of the Union and Au-

tonomous Republics had been elected in June 1938, and local Soviets in December 1939. In both instances the form and substance of the ceremonies were similar to those of the first election under the 1936 Constitution. The federal Supreme Soviet first met in January 1938, again in August, and twice annually thereafter. All the Supreme Soviets chose new Presidia and Sovnarkoms at their first sessions. These executive bodies, like their parent legislatures, carried on with little change during hostilities and thereafter.

The pattern thus established was followed undeviatingly up to the 40th anniversary of the October Revolution. To Western liberals, it is a travesty of representative democracy, since there can plainly be no effective freedom or representation or democracy in ritualistic exercises in unanimity. To many Russians, unfamiliar with Western ways or disposed to regard them as "bourgeois frauds," the ceremonials perhaps recall with nostalgia and gratitude the age-long search of the Slavs for unity in the face of schisms within and hostility from without—reflected paradoxically in the *liberum veto* in the Diet of the old Kingdom of Poland and in the requirement of unanimity for major decisions in the ancient Russian *Veche* or Assembly. As recently as 1956, when portents of a new dispensation were numerous, only one name for each office appeared on Soviet ballots, even in neighborhood "elections" of judges of the local People's Courts and of their two lay assistants, all chosen for two-year terms and most of them, incidentally, women.[4]

Given this system of polling, no light can be thrown on the realities of power or the processes of decision-making by reviewing the voluminous official statistics of subsequent Soviet "elections." A few notations are enough. On February 10, 1946, 101,450,936 Soviet voters (out of a total of eligible voters of 101,717,686) cast ballots, 99% affirmatively, for 682 deputies to the Soviet of the Union and 657 deputies to the Soviet of Nationalities, with Party members numbering 1,085 out of the total of 1,339, "Non-Party Bolsheviks" 254, and women deputies 277. On March 12, 1950, 111,090,010 Soviet voters (out of a total of 111,116,373 eligible) did likewise in "electing" 671 members of the Soviet of the Union and 631 of the Soviet of Nationalities. On March 14, 1954, the ritual was repeated, with 120,727,826 voters (out of 120,750,816) choosing 708 and 639 deputies, respectively, for the two chambers of the Supreme Soviet, of

[4] Cf. George D. Carson: *Electoral Practices in the U.S.S.R.* (Praeger, 1955).

whom 1,050 were Party members, 297 were non-Party, and 348 were women, with the proportions of non-Party deputies and women deputies almost identical in the two houses.

Soviet legislative procedure has, thus far, followed a comparable pattern. Soviet "law-makers" are not salaried officials but part-time deputies with other jobs, paid travel expenses and *per-diem* allowances out of public revenue. On the federal, Republican, and local levels, they hear and consider legislative proposals presented by the Ministers, listen to reports and speeches, rarely advance proposals of their own, discuss bills in committees, but in their final "decisions" always vote unanimously in favor of whatever projects the Party leadership has resolved to adopt as public policy. Their function, not unlike that of Western parliamentarians in this respect, is to reflect local expectations, demands, grievances, and hopes, and to act as *liaison* agents between the Party leadership and administrative bureaucracy, on the one hand, and their constituents on the other. But they have possessed, thus far, no powers of decision, save insofar as their advice may influence the judgment of the top-level oligarchs whose ultimate conclusions have long been sacrosanct on the premise (long unquestioned but vaguely acknowledged to be dubious and dangerous since Stalin's demise) that the Party is infallible and therefore above criticism or challenge. The reality of executive responsibility to the legislature during the 1940's and early 1950's is well put, albeit unwittingly, by V. Karpinsky:

> The Council of Ministers of the USSR is formed at a joint sitting of both Chambers of the Supreme Soviet of the USSR. At the first session of the Supreme Soviet, held in March, 1946, the Government of the Soviet Union was formed in the following way: J. V. Stalin, the head of the outgoing government, submitted a written statement to the Chairman of the joint sitting of the Chambers declaring that the Government "considers its duties at an end and surrenders its powers to the Supreme Soviet." This statement was read to the Assembly by the Chairman. The floor was then taken by one of the Deputies who, amidst general approval, said that the Supreme Soviet was unanimous in its complete confidence in the outgoing government. The Supreme Soviet accepted the Government's statement and unanimously commissioned J. V. Stalin to submit proposals

for a new government. At the next joint sitting of the Chambers, the Chairman read the list of members of the new Government as proposed by J. V. Stalin. After statements by Deputies, the Chairman announced that no objection had been raised to any of the candidates for government office and that none of the Deputies insisted on a roll-call vote. The composition of the Council of Ministers of the USSR as proposed by J. V. Stalin was then voted on as before and unanimously adopted. J. V. Stalin was elected Chairman of the Council of Ministers of the USSR. This illustrates the manner in which the Council of Ministers of the USSR is formed.[5]

3. THE RIGHTS OF MAN

WITHIN the limits of oligarchy, what are the realities and what are the fictions of the "constitutional rights" of Soviet citizens as elaborately set forth (see Appendix) in Chapters X and XI of the Charter of 1936? The answer is less simple than many Western commentators have assumed. "Real liberty," declared Stalin to Roy Howard (cf. *Izvestia*, December 8, 1936), "can be had only where exploitation is destroyed, where there is no oppression of one people by another, where there is no unemployment and pauperism, where a person does not shiver in fear of losing tomorrow his job, home, bread. Only in such a society is it possible to have real, and not paper, liberty, personal and otherwise."

This "reality" proved meaningless over many years to the millions of Soviet citizens arrested by agents of the OGPU, NKVD, or MVD and consigned to forced-labor camps in Siberia and the Far North, where only the hardiest survived the rigors or arduous work, meager diet, miserable living conditions, and systematic terrorization and exploitation—pending the amnesties, relaxations, and "mellowing" of the police-state regime since Stalin's death.[6]

[5] *How the Soviet Union Is Governed* (Moscow, 1954), p. 154.

[6] No official Soviet figures have ever been published regarding the number of persons confined at any one time, or *in toto* over the years, to so-called "correctional labor camps," despite the downgrading of Stalin, the execution of Beria, and the acknowledgment of gross abuses, fabricated confessions, and wholesale incarcerations of the innocent. A decade ago (cf. *Soviet Politics*, pp.

Many other rights solemnly guaranteed by the Supreme Law of Sovietland remained "dead letters" during most of the two decades after 1936. Freedom of speech, press, assembly, and association (§§125, 126) and inviolability of persons, homes, and correspondence (§§127, 128) were often honored more in the breach than in the observance, as was acknowledged at Party Congress XX and thereafter. The same was true of intellectual, scientific, and academic freedom, particularly in the black years of Stalin's posturing as the infallible source of all truth and taste—when the *Vozhd* and his agents felt in duty bound to impose "Socialist Realism" on writers, artists, and musicians, Lysenko's fantasies on biologists, "Marxist physics" on other scientists, etc. Political privileges (§§134–42) have been less rights than duties, and have, in any case, only a tangential relationship to public policy-making and the selection of representatives. The independence of the courts (§112) and the protection of the individual against arbitrary arrest, imprisonment, or execution (§§111, 127, 128) remained fictitious so long as the MVD possessed the right to punish alleged political offenders without public trial, so long as the criminal code permitted penalization "by analogy" of acts not defined as crimes but held dangerous to the State, so long as the death penalty was prescribed (as in the act of August 7, 1932) for theft of public property, and so long as the full rigors of the criminal code were made applicable (as in the act of April 7, 1935) to juvenile delinquents.

Freedom of conscience and worship (§124), or the lack thereof,

340–3) I regarded Western estimates of 15,000,000 to 20,000,000 persons condemned to forced labor as exaggerations or mere guesses. I know of no current reason for altering this judgment. But the moral enormity of this institution and the unreality of personal "freedom" for the Soviet citizenry during an entire generation are not functions of arithmetic but of the admitted fact that many guiltless persons were thus dealt with. For estimates of numbers, descriptions of the system, and, in some instances, eye-witness accounts by former inmates, along with discussions of its place in Soviet penology as a whole, see Harold J. Berman: *Justice in Russia* (Harvard University Press, 1950) and, with Boris A. Konstantinovsky: *Soviet Law in Action* (Harvard University Press, 1955); David J. Dallin and Boris I. Nicolaevsky: *Forced Labor in Soviet Russia* (Yale University Press, 1947); Elinor Lipper: *Eleven Years in Soviet Prison Camps* (Regnery, 1951); and Joseph Scholmer: *Vorkuta* (Holt, 1955). Cf. also *NYT* April 4, 5, 6, 7, October 17, and October 19, 1955, for accounts by John H. Noble, an American inmate, of the Vorkuta camps north of the Arctic Circle, of the strike of prisoners against intolerable conditions in the summer of 1953, followed by a wholesale massacre of those who refused to work, and of the closing of the camps in the fall of 1955 as related by another inmate, Mrs. Erika Glaser Wallach, adopted daughter of Noel and Herta Field.

have undergone many vicissitudes during the four decades of Soviet power. The sequence began with open persecution by a regime of atheists of many churchmen and believers during the years when the established Orthodox Church, smarting from Soviet disestablishment and dispossession of most of its wealth, championed Autocracy and the cause of the White Armies. The charter of 1936 re-enfranchised the clergy. The "League of the Militant Godless," founded in 1925 and directed by Emilian Yaroslavsky, claimed 10,000,000 members by 1932 but had declined to 3,000,000 by 1940. When Communist efforts to extirpate religion had clearly failed and the new Church patriotically rallied to the defense of the State against the Nazi invaders, the League was dissolved and its publishing facilities were transferred to the Orthodox priesthood. On September 12, 1943, an officially sponsored *Sobor* elected Metropolitan Sergei of Moscow Patriarch of all Russia. Upon his death a new *Sobor* in January 1945 elected Metropolitan Alexei as Patriarch. Meanwhile, in October of 1943 a State Council on Church Affairs, headed by Georgi Karpov, was set up to promote "genuine religious freedom."

Any congregation willing to pay the salary of a cleric and the costs of building maintenance may conduct services in church, mosque, or synagogue. But religious instruction of the young outside of home is still (1957) forbidden. No church receives any financial aid from the State save for the restoration and upkeep of ecclesiastical structures of historic or artistic importance—most of which, however, are without congregations and have been converted into museums. Under these circumstances religious life languishes despite formal freedom of worship.

Soviet citizens enjoy certain other "constitutional rights" that are more substance than shadow. Individual and collective property rights, along with rights of ownership and inheritance of income, personal property, savings, and private houses (§§7–10), appear to be well respected within the limits already indicated. The major social gains of the Revolution are embodied (§§118–20) in the rights to work, to paid vacations, to insurance against illness and old age, and to free dental and medical service, including access to hospitals and sanatoria. The social-insurance system, administered by the trade unions, and socialized medicine, directed by the Ministry of Health, are among the significant contributions of the Soviet State to the welfare of the people. The number of physicians increased from 20,000 in 1913 to 63,000 in 1928, 141,000 in 1941 (January 1), and

299,000 in 1955 (July 1), with lesser health workers, including *feld-shers* (medical aides) and nurses, increasing from 393,200 in 1941 to 731,100 in 1955. Death rates declined from 18.3 per thousand population in 1940 to 9.6 in 1950, 9.0 in 1953, and 8.4 in 1955, while birth rates for the corresponding years were reported as 31.7, 26.5, 24.9, and 25.6.[7]

Equality of rights for women, including equal access to all vocations and identical status with men as to salaries, vacations, social insurance, and education, plus "pre-maternity and maternity leave with full pay" (§122), is also a fact and not a fiction. Early Soviet legislation made marriage and divorce simple civil formalities, costing only a few rubles at the Registration bureaus (*Zags*), recognized no distinction between legitimate and illegitimate children, and permitted free abortions in public clinics. In a change of "line," decrees and laws of 1936 forbade abortions except for reasons of health. Under the impact of the fearful blood-letting of World War II, new legislation of 1943–4 made divorce expensive and difficult, imposed special taxes on the unmarried and the childless, and offered monetary rewards and honors to mothers of many children. While these statutes are still in force, abortion was again legalized in 1955. Any Soviet woman, married or unmarried, may by her own decision have an abortion without cost. Meanwhile, Western travelers in the USSR are often shocked to see women sweeping streets, working in construction gangs, building houses, and performing other heavy tasks. But this phenomenon is merely visual evidence—along with many policewomen and numerous female bus-drivers, subway-operators, taxi-drivers, etc.—that equality of the sexes is a reality. By 1955, according to the handbook issued in Moscow by the Central Statistical Board, women comprise the following percentages of sundry vocations: health services, 85 (over two-thirds of Soviet physicians are women); restaurant workers, 83; teachers, 68; public administration, 49; industry, 45; transport and communications, 33; and construction, 31.

Amid so mixed a record of failures and successes, of pledges broken and of promises carried out, of rights betrayed and rights

[7] See *Narodnoye Khozyaistvo SSSR* (*National Economy of the USSR*), issued in 1956 by the Central Statistical Board of the Council of Ministers, Moscow. See also *Health and Medical Care in the U.S.S.R.* (National Council of American-Soviet Friendship, 1956). For references to earlier, but still useful, studies of Soviet medicine, see my *Soviet Politics at Home and Abroad* (Knopf, 1946), p. 626, n. 22.

achieved, it is fitting to conclude our evaluation with the one duty of the State which has been most adequately fulfilled and is bright with hope for the future. §121: "Citizens of the USSR have the right to education. . . ." Freedom from ignorance through the abolition of illiteracy has been achieved via the nation-wide network of ten-year public schools, combining elementary and secondary grades in one sequence and raising the number of pupils in attendance from 7,900,000 in 1914 to 34,800,000 in 1940. Falling birth rates and the decline of population during the years of war reduced the total to 28,200,000 in 1955. All Soviet children were going through seven grades by 1956. All would go through all ten grades by 1960, thus universalizing high-school education even more completely than in the USA. Coeducation, introduced in 1918 and abolished in 1943, was restored in 1956–7. Early experimentation in "progressive" education gave way in the 1930's to an exacting discipline, which has never since been much modified, despite complaints in recent years that school children are overworked.

Mathematics and the natural sciences are the "core" of Soviet education in the upper grades. All pupils are required to choose English, French, or German in the fifth grade (Latin, Greek, Spanish, Italian, and other tongues are not taught below the university level) and to study their choice for six years—with graduates of the ten-year schools usually acquiring a good reading knowledge, though seldom an adequate speaking knowledge, of the language thus selected. German was the most popular choice before 1939. English has been the favorite since 1945. A new network of highly selective "boarding schools" was established in 1956–7 on the model of English "public" and American private schools.

Beyond the ten-year schools Soviet higher education has taken flourishing form in a galaxy of trade schools, technical institutes, research centers, and universities, with the latter planned not for the few, as in Western Europe, but for the many, as in America. Small tuition fees were introduced in 1940 but were abolished in 1956–7. All Soviet youths with the requisite talents are encouraged to attend universities, granted scholarships and living stipends whenever their needs call for such support, and generously rewarded for outstanding achievement with honors, prizes, and vocational opportunities. Between 1940 and 1955 the graduates of institutes and universities waxed from 908,000 to 2,184,000, with engineers increasing from 289,000 to 585,900, economists and business specialists from 59,300

to 113,800, and teachers, librarians, and other "cultural workers" from 300,400 to 906,400. In 1955, 1,230,000 young people were full-time students at universities, as compared with 850,000 in 1950 and 590,000 in 1940 (USA, 1954: 2,499,750). In 1955, 54,700 books were published in almost a billion copies, with even the most abstruse scientific works, however large the printing, being snatched up by an insatiable public within a few days in the innumerable bookstores and sidewalk stalls throughout the USSR. Public libraries numbered 277,000 with 527,000,000 books in 1940, and 392,000 with 1,351,000,-000 books in 1955.

In short, Russia since 1917 has become educated as well as in-dustrialized and urbanized. Stalin's totalitarian police state brought into being a community that can no longer be governed by the police methods of totalitarianism. In sundry ways, not yet altogether clear in 1957, the "dead letters" of the Constitution of 1936 were in painful process of having some breath of life infused into their empty sym-bols by the post-Stalin "collective" leadership. It is not fortuitous that, apart from the nearby Kremlin, the most impressive building in central Moscow, 40 years after 1917, is the Lenin State Library, claiming to be, with its 18,000,000 books, pamphlets, and periodicals, the largest library in the world, though singularly devoid of anti-Soviet works in any language. Neither is it accidental that the visitor who comes to Moscow by plane obtains his first glimpse of the So-viet capital, on the horizon of the Lenin Hills between the airport and the city, in the form of the 37-story tower (surrounded by a gi-gantic "suburban" development of huge apartment blocs, planned to house 200,000 people) of the new building of Moscow State University, opened in 1953. This imposing edifice, along with its adjuncts, is dedicated to physics, chemistry, biology, and allied sciences, with social studies and the humanities housed elsewhere in older academic structures within the city proper. The central citadel of learning, unquestionably the largest university building in the world, contains classrooms, lecture halls, laboratories, gymnasi-ums, and apartments for all of the faculty and much of the student body of 22,000. The Stalinist State, having in some measure expiated the crimes committed in its name by educating Russia, was in proc-ess, four decades after 1917, of ceasing to be a Stalinist State.[8]

[8] Amid the voluminous literature in English on Soviet education, religion, family life, intellectual and æsthetic activities, and kindred subjects, the most useful of recent books, it seems to me, are: Raymond A. Bauer: *Nine Soviet*

4. THE GUARDIANS

IN the cave of images and signs depicted in Plato's *Republic* (Book VII), the prisoners mistook shadows for realities and echoes for voices, an experience common to mankind since the Garden of Eden. In the 1930's some Soviet citizens and many sympathizers abroad mistook the "Stalin Constitution" for the literal law of the land instead of recognizing it as a piece of propaganda, a statement of aspirations, or, at best, a charter of governance susceptible of meaningful application only in some remote and happier time. The complex forms of federalism, popular election, judicial bodies, parliaments, executive councils responsible to law-makers, etc., were also mistaken by the naïve for a new version, Soviet style, of government of the people, by the people, and for the people. They were in fact a series of devices whereby the oligarchs could more effectively test and control "public opinion," promote an illusion of wide participation in decision-making, administer more adroitly the vast enterprises of the socialized economy, and enlist the support of mass organizations in the tasks set for the nation by its actual rulers.

The Party's "monopoly of legality" remained unaltered. The internal structure of this secular priesthood became ever more cen-

Portraits (Wiley, 1955); John R. Baker: *Science and the Planned State* (Macmillan, 1945); Harriet Borland: *Soviet Literary Theory and Practice, 1928–1932* (Columbia University Press, 1950); Ruth C. Christman: *Soviet Science* (American Association for the advancement of Science, 1952); John S. Curtiss: *The Russian Church and the Soviet State, 1917–1950* (Little, Brown, 1953); Joshua Kunitz (ed.): *Russian Literature Since the Revolution* (Boni & Gaer, 1948); Elizabeth Moos: *Higher Education in the Soviet Union* (National Council of American-Soviet Friendship, 1956); Gerhert Neimeyer and John S. Reshetar, Jr.: *An Inquiry into Soviet Rationality* (Praeger, 1956); Pierre van Paassen: *Visions Rise and Change* (Dial Press, 1955); Maurice J. Shore: *Soviet Education* (Philosophical Library, 1947); Ernest J. Simmons (ed.): *Through the Glass of Soviet Literature: Views of Russian Society* (Columbia University Press, 1953); John Somerville: *Soviet Philosophy* (Philosophical Library, 1946); Timothy Sosnovy: *The Housing Problem in the Soviet Union* (Research Program on the U.S.S.R., 1954); Matthew Spinka: *The Church in Soviet Russia* (Oxford University Press, 1956); Gleb Struve: *Soviet Russian Literature, 1917–1950* (University of Oklahoma Press, 1951); and Alexander Vucinich: *The Soviet Academy of Sciences* (Stanford University Press, 1953). For earlier studies of these facets of Soviet life, see my *Soviet Politics* (Knopf, 1946), pp. 625–6. For a Marxist travesty of some of the matters dealt with above, see Y. Umansky: *Constitutional Rights of Soviet Citizens* (Foreign Languages Publishing House, Moscow, 1955).

tralized and less democratic as Stalin—abetted now by this group and now by that among the members of the Politburo and aided always by his self-effacing private secretary, Alexander Poskrebyshev—gathered more and more authority into his own hands and used it in an ever more arbitrary and dictatorial fashion. The *Vozhd* increasingly overshadowed the Politburo, the Central Committee, and the Party Congress, which met less and less frequently. Five years elapsed between Congress XVII (January 1934) and Congress XVIII (March 1939). These were the years of the Terror and the Blood Purge, when tens of thousands, rendered helpless against the murderous decrees of a paranoid despot by their loyalty to the Party, were done to death while millions were sent to the jails or labor camps of the NKVD.

Apart from Stalin's colleagues who died or killed themselves in despair or were put to death by his *ukase*, the top ranks of the Party leadership exhibited an extraordinary degree of continuity, persisting through several decades. The major figures among the survivors of the purge are therefore worthy of study, since the quality and direction of any system of leadership are functions of the skills and character of the personalities elevated to its highest posts of authority. The loftiest among the oligarchs in 1939 were, with few exceptions, already prominent in 1934 and even earlier, and were destined, again with few exceptions, to lead the nation through the dismal swamps of disastrous diplomacy, through the inferno of invasion and defeat, and then through victory to peace and to war once more, although cold rather than hot.

To anticipate a future implicit in the past, on March 22, 1939, the new Central Committee held its first plenary meeting and elected from its members the three principal executive organs of the Party: the Politburo (Andreyev, Voroshilov, Zhdanov, Kaganovich, Kalinin, Mikoyan, Molotov, Stalin, and Khrushchev, with Beria and Shvernik as alternates); the Secretariat (Andreyev, Zhdanov, Malenkov, and Stalin); and the Organization Bureau (Orgburo), comprising Andreyev, Zhdanov, Kaganovich, Malenkov, L. Mekhlis, N. Mikhailov, Stalin, Shvernik, and Shcherbakov. The chairmanship of the important Party Control Commission of the Central Committee, charged with discipline and training of the membership, went to Andreyev.

The Politburo in 1934 also included Y. E. Rudzutak, P. P. Postyshev, S. V. Kossior, G. I. Petroski, V. Y. Chubar, and R. I. Eikhe. *Pravda* (January 19, 1938) reported that Postyshev had been re-

moved. *Izvestia* (January 29, 1938) said the same of Kossior, but added (February 9, 1938) that Petrovski had been awarded the Order of Lenin. None was mentioned in the Soviet press after February of 1938. All were acknowledged in 1956 to have been shot at Stalin's behest. Among older leaders, Ordjonikidze committed suicide February 18, 1937, and Krupskaya died February 27, 1939.

If we begin our survey of the political elite in the late 1930's and early 1940's with the newest and youngest recruits, rather than with surviving "Old Bolsheviks," we may first consider the ill-fated Nikolai A. Voznesensky and the able but unfortunate Georgi M. Malenkov. Both, along with Alexander S. Shcherbakov, joined Beria and Shvernik as alternate members of the Politburo in February 1941, at the time of the 18th Conference. Here also new members were named to the Central Committee, including Ivan Maisky, V. G. Dekanosov (Ambassador in Berlin), Otto Kuusinen, and General Georgi K. Zhukov. The youthful Voznesensky was born near Tula, December 3, 1903, into the family of an office worker. He joined the Party in 1919 and became a leader of the Komsomols in his native Chernsky County. He was a classmate of Shcherbakov at the Sverdlov Communist University, 1921–4. After several years of Party work in the Don Basin, where he distinguished himself in economic planning, he graduated in 1931 from the Moscow Institute of Red Professors, where he became an instructor. By 1935 he was head of the Leningrad City Planning Commission and presently Vice-Chairman of the Leningrad Soviet. The year of Munich found him, at the age of 35, in the high post of Chairman of the Gosplan, in which capacity he played a leading role in the drafting of the Third Five Year Plan. In March 1939 he became a member of the Central Committee and in April a Vice-Chairman of the federal Sovnarkom. Early in 1942 he joined the State Committee on Defense (War Cabinet). In recognition of his writings in economics, he was elected a member of the Academy of Sciences in October 1943.

Malenkov was born in Orenburg (now Chkalov), January 8, 1902. As a young volunteer in the Red Army he worked his way up to the post of Political Commissar of the Eastern and Turkestan fronts and became a Party member in April 1920. In the 1920's and the 1930's he served as a Party functionary on the staff of the Central Committee and in the Moscow city organization. Like Voznesensky, he was made a member of the Central Committee at the time of Congress XVIII. He was the youngest of the original five members

of the State Committee on Defense. With his "card-index brain" and his managerial talents, he was equally useful as a member of the Orgburo in supervising Party personnel and as a Vice-Chairman of the Sovnarkom in directing heavy industry. For his services in the production of planes, motors, and tanks he was awarded (October 1943) the title of Hero of Socialist Labor, the Order of Lenin, and the Hammer and Sickle Gold Medal.

Molotov, son of a salesman, was born March 9, 1890, in Vyatka Province in the town of Kukarsk (now Sovietsk). He joined the Party in 1906. After being arrested in 1909 and spending two years in exile in Vologda, he entered the Polytechnical Institute of St. Petersburg, contributed to the Bolshevik paper *Zvezda*, and became secretary of *Pravda*. He became a member of the Central Committee shortly before the fall of the Tsardom. By 1926 he was a member of the Politburo. He became chairman of the federal Sovnarkom in December 1930 and Commissar for Foreign Affairs in May 1939. His wife established the Soviet perfume industry, became the head of the cosmetic trust, and for a time was an alternate member of the Central Committee—until February 1941. On Molotov's fiftieth birthday the Presidium of the Supreme Soviet conferred on him the Order of Lenin and renamed the city of Perm "Molotov" and the town of Nolinsk "Molotovsk." In October 1943 he was awarded the title of Hero of Socialist Labor. His various books and articles during his earlier years dealt principally with agrarian and industrial problems.

Andrei Andreyevich Andreyev, small, prosaic, but gifted in the skill of power, was born into a peasant family near Smolensk on October 30, 1895. After only two years of school in his native village, he became a factory worker in Moscow and later in southern Russia. He first became acquainted with Marxist literature and with Party members at the age of 15, but did not join the brotherhood for another four years, at a time when he worked in a Petrograd cartridge factory whence he moved to the offices of the Putilov (now Kirov) steel works. He organized the Petrograd Metal Workers' Union and played an active part in the Revolution. In 1920 he became a secretary of the All-Union Central Council of Trade Unions and served from 1922 to 1928 as Chairman of the Central Committee of the Railwaymen's Union. He was elected to the Party Central Committee in 1920 and to the Politburo in 1932, after serving as an alternate for six years. He also served as Chairman of the Control

Commission (1930 and again after 1939), Commissar of Workers' and Peasants' Inspection, Vice-Chairman of the Sovnarkom, and Commissar of Transport until March 1935, when he was replaced by Kaganovich. In December 1943, Andreyev succeeded Ivan A. Benediktov as Commissar for Agriculture.

Lazar Moiseyevich Kaganovich, the only Jewish member of the Politburo, is tall, vigorous, and vastly efficient. He was born November 22, 1893. Trained as a tanner, he joined the Bolsheviks in Kiev when he was 18 and spent the years before the Revolution in underground work in the Ukraine, including direction of an illegal trade union of shoemakers. During the civil war and immediately thereafter he played a leading role in organizing the Red Army and in directing Party activities in various places, from Nizhni-Novgorod (Gorky) to Tashkent. In 1924 he became a member and secretary of the Central Committee and from 1925 to 1928 he served as General Secretary of the Central Committee of the Party in the Ukraine. Kaganovich became Secretary of the Central Committee of the CPSU(B) in 1928 and was elected to the Politburo two years later. As secretary of the Moscow Regional and City Committees of the Party, he directed the construction of the Moscow subway and subsequently, as head of the agricultural and transport departments of the Central Committee, supervised the organization of political departments on State Farms and in machine and tractor stations serving the collectives. As Commissar of Railways (1935-7 and again 1938-42) he was credited with major improvements in railway transport. He has likewise served as Commissar of Heavy Industry, Commissar of the Fuel Industry, Assistant Chairman of the federal Sovnarkom, deputy to the federal Supreme Soviet and to several Republican Supreme Soviets. On February 20, 1942, the Presidium of the Supreme Soviet made him a member of the State Defense Committee. On April 6, 1932, Kaganovich was transferred from the post of Commissar of Railways to that of Vice-Chairman of the Committee for the Coordination of Transport. He holds the Order of Lenin and the Order of the Red Banner of Labor.

Anastas Ivanovich Mikoyan, born of Armenian working-class parents in Tbilisi, November 25, 1895, joined the Party in his 20th year. In 1918 he was arrested by British forces in Transcaucasia and barely escaped execution along with the twenty-six Baku Commissars. In the final phases of the civil war he helped to restore Soviet authority in Azerbaijan. As Commissar of the Food Industry (1934-

8), he visited the United States in the summer of 1936 to study mass-production methods of food-manufacturing, and later was awarded the Order of Lenin for introducing similar methods in the USSR. As early as 1926 Mikoyan was named Commissar of Foreign and Domestic Trade. In 1937 he became Vice-Chairman of the federal Sovnarkom and in 1938 Commissar of Foreign Trade. He has been a member of the Politburo since 1935. In 1942 he joined the State Defense Committee. For his work in organizing the supply services of the Red Army in food, fuel, and clothing he was again awarded the Order of Lenin and named Hero of Socialist Labor in 1943.

Nikita Sergeyevich Khrushchev, a miner and son of a miner, was born in a mining camp near Kursk, April 17, 1894. He joined the Party in 1918, fought in the civil war, and completed his neglected education in the Moscow Industrial Academy, which he entered on a Party assignment in 1929. During the middle 1930's he was a Party leader in the Moscow district and shared honors with Kaganovich for initiating the construction of the subway. Khrushchev served as a member of the Central Committee (since 1934), first secretary of the Party in the Ukraine (1938), alternate member of the Politburo (1934), and full member since his election in March 1939. He is a deputy in the federal Supreme Soviet and a member of its Presidium, as well as a deputy to the Supreme Soviet of the Ukraine. With Timoshenko he shared responsibility for military operations in the Ukraine in 1941–2 and helped to organize guerrilla warfare against the invaders. In 1943 he was named a Lieutenant General and awarded the Order of Suvorov, second class. In the following year he became Chairman of the Ukrainian Sovnarkom and received the Order of Lenin on his fiftieth birthday.

Klimenti Efremovich Voroshilov, son of a railroad watchman and a scrubwoman, is one of the older Party leaders, having been born February 4, 1881, in the Ukraine. Sent to work in a mine at the age of seven, he did not learn to read or write until he was twelve. At the age of 15 he was employed in the metal works at Lugansk (now Voroshilovsk) and at 18 was already a revolutionary organizer and strike-leader. He joined the Party in 1903, suffered imprisonment for his activities in 1904–6, and met Lenin and Stalin in 1907, after which he was almost continuously in prison or exile until the Revolution. With Djerzhinsky he helped to organize the Cheka. With Stalin he led the defense of Tsaritsin and later commanded various armies against Denikin, Pilsudski, and Wrangel. With the death

of Frunze (1925), Voroshilov became Commissar of Defense and joined the Politburo in the following year. After 1940 he was Vice-Chairman of the Sovnarkom and Chairman of its Committee on Defense. For his services he was awarded two Orders of Lenin, four Orders of the Red Banner, and many other honors. He served as an original member of the State Defense Committee of 1941, but was replaced by Bulganin and transferred to other duties on November 22, 1944.

Mikhail Ivanovich Kalinin, the most venerable member of the old elite, was singularly blessed in his choice of parents, birthday, and vocations. Born of poor peasants in the province of Tver (now Kalinin), November 7, 1875, he was first apprenticed to a landlord and then became a youthful worker in the Putilov works in St. Petersburg, where he was repeatedly arrested and exiled as a revolutionary agitator. He was one of the original Bolsheviks of 1903. By 1916 he had been arrested 14 times. As one of Lenin's closest colleagues, he became President of the All-Russian Central Executive Committee in 1919, a post which in its various transformations he continued to hold thereafter—as Chairman of the CEC of the USSR (1923 f.) and Chairman of the Presidium of the federal Supreme Soviet (1938 f.). Kalinin became a member of the Politburo in 1925. He was awarded the Order of Lenin on his 60th birthday and the title of Hero of Socialist Labor in 1944 on the twenty-fifth anniversary of this election as Chairman of the CEC. At 70 he remained the prototype of the shrewd but simple peasant, short, bearded, kindly, and tough. He still spent much time among peasants, hearing complaints, receiving petitions, and serving generally as a highly respected collective grandfather.

Other life histories of the highest-ranking Party leaders serve to confirm the pattern already suggested. Lavrenti P. Beria, Georgian chief of the NKVD; Nikolai M. Shvernik, Chairman of the Presidium of the RSFSR and Kalinin's successor as Chairman of the federal Presidium; and the late Alexander S. Shcherbakov (Zhdanov's brother-in-law), who died May 10, 1945,—all in varying degree share with Stalin and their colleagues those traits and experiences which, until the 1950's, were the prerequisites of political eminence in the USSR: peasant or proletarian origin, poverty-stricken youth, little formal education (only Zhdanov had university training and could be deemed an intellectual), much informal education in the school of hard knocks, early conversion to the cause,

fame won in revolutionary agitation and organization, and a generous measure of vision, courage, unflagging energy, relentless determination, and genius for holding many jobs simultaneously and for directing and inspiring subordinates to perform the impossible.[9]

The culminating political ritual of the oligarchy in the grim, bloodstained, anxious, and yet hopeful years prior to the catastrophe of World War II was Party Congress XVIII, meeting in Moscow March 10–21, 1939. Little was "decided" here, despite Lenin's contention that the Congress must be the decision-making organ of the Party, and much of what appeared to be decided turned out later not to have been decided. The occasion was nonetheless notable, as are all Congresses, for sundry promulgations of the Party "line" by the leaders. Stalin's and Manuilsky's prophetic contributions in the field of foreign affairs are best reserved for the following chapter. Meanwhile, be it noted that in 1938 all Party locals had again chosen officers, a quarter of them new. Voting delegates at Congress XVIII numbered 1,567, representing 1,600,000 members, a reduction of 270,000 since Congress XVII. "But," said Stalin, "there is nothing bad in that. On the contrary, it is all to the good, for the Party strengthens itself by clearing its ranks of dross. Our Party is now somewhat smaller in membership, but on the other hand it is better in quality, this is a big achievement."

The opening address and the longest speech at the Congress was made by Molotov, who devoted himself to evaluating the Third Five Year Plan—not in his usual dry role as a bureaucrat but as a visionary, impelled to praise Stalin's atrocities in double-talk, yet inspired by the Marxist dream:

> A new society has been established equipped with the most modern technique. There has taken shape a Socialist State of workers and peasants which is mounting aloft, is marching onward to the complete victory of communism along the tried and true road of Bolshevism. . . . As you know, the machinations of the class enemy abroad, in the camp of capitalism, particularly the camp of Fascism, have been completely frustrated by us. Their new espionage

[9] Sketches of some of these leaders are to be found in Edgar Snow: *The Pattern of Soviet Power* (Random House, 1945). Most of the data given above, however, are taken from the *Soviet Desk Calendar,* published annually in Moscow (in Russian). Published commentaries on the "private lives" of Soviet leaders are virtually nonexistent in the USSR.

methods of intervention, in which all these Trotskys, Rykovs, Bukharins, Zinovievs, Tukhachevskys, Radeks, Ikramovs and Lubchenkos played the contemptible role of wreckers, stool-pigeons and filthy agents of foreign espionage services, have suffered complete shipwreck. . . . No enemy can now break down our Soviet Union. . . . Whomever our frank warnings do not suffice, will get to know this at the appropriate hour. . . .

Capitalism has accumulated no little store of material and cultural values, but it is no longer able to use them, even in its own interests. It has already in many respects begun to strangle progress, science, art and culture. That is a fact; but, then, all the worse for capitalism. There is now somebody to take over the heritage of capitalism. Communism grows out of what capitalism has created, out of its numerous fine achievements in the sphere of economy, material life and culture. Communism reassesses all these values and achievements in its own way—not in the interests of the "elite" of society, but in the interests of the whole people, of all mankind. We must spare no efforts to study this cultural heritage. We must know it thoroughly and profoundly. We must utilize everything produced by capitalism and the earlier history of mankind, and from the bricks made by the labor of man in the course of many centuries build a new edifice, a bright, spacious and sunlit edifice suited to the life of the people. (Loud and general applause.) [1]

Stalin, vaingloriously justifying his paranoia and displaying complete blindness to the fearful and almost fatal havoc wrought by his suspicions and vengefulness, asserted:

In case of war, the rear and front of our army, by reason of their homogeneity and inherent unity, will be stronger than those of any other country, a fact which people beyond our borders who love military conflicts would do well to remember. Certain foreign pressmen have been talking drivel to the effect that the purging of the Soviet or-

[1] The full text of speeches, reports, and resolutions is available in English in *The Land of Socialism Today and Tomorrow* (Foreign Languages Publishing House, Moscow, 1939).

ganizations of spies, assassins and wreckers like Trotsky,
Zinoviev, Kamenev, Yakir, Tukhachevsky, Rosengoltz, Bukharin and other fiends has "shaken" the Soviet system and
cause its "demoralization." One can only laugh at such
cheap drivel. How can the purging of Soviet organizations
of noxious and hostile elements shake and demoralize the
Soviet system? . . . To listen to these foreign drivellers one
would think that if the spies, murderers and wreckers
had been left at liberty to wreck, murder and spy without
let or hindrance, the Soviet organizations would have been
far sounder and stronger. . . . What, for instance, do the
events at Lake Hassan show, if not that the weeding out of
spies and wreckers is the surest means of strengthening our
Soviet organizations?

The longest speech at the Congress, next to Molotov's, was
made by corpulent, cherubic Andrei A. Zhdanov (born February 26,
1896), Leningrad leader, son of a Ukrainian school inspector of
Mariupol, member of the Party since 1915, of the Central Committee since 1930, secretary of the Central Committee since 1934, and
chairman of the Supreme Soviet of the RSFSR since the summer of
1938. Zhdanov's address was in part a commentary on the new
Party rules, which he had played a large role in formulating, and in
part a denunciation of the mistakes and tragedies of the recent past
which the new rules were intended to correct. Like all the speeches
of March, 1939, it concluded with a eulogy of Stalin—"the genius,
the brain, the heart of the Bolshevik Party, of the whole Soviet people, of the whole of progressive and advanced humanity." But its
gist was "self-criticism," embellished with numerous examples of
abuse of authority. By unwritten law, the "self" was never Stalin,
never colleagues in good standing, and seldom the speaker, but
merely "the Party" and sometimes "we," garbed in the anonymity
of collective responsibility. Thus Zhdanov on March 18, 1939:

> Experience has shown that in practice the rights of
> Party members are often violated. There have been fre-
> quent cases of bureaucratic and hostile elements hounding
> and persecuting members for criticism and self-criticism.
> There have been frequent cases of decisions concerning the
> activities or conduct of Party members being adopted in
> their absence. We know of quite a number of cases of hos-

tile and bureaucratic elements forbidding the Party members to address certain given statements to the higher Party bodies. . . . There have also been cases of infringement of the rights of Party members to elect and be elected. . . . It has been repeatedly pointed out by Lenin and Stalin that a bureaucrat with a Party card in his pocket is the most dangerous and pernicious kind of bureaucrat, because, possessing a Party card, he imagines that he may ignore Party and Soviet laws and the needs and interests of the working people. By inscribing the rights of Party members in the Rules we shall place in the hands of the Party a powerful weapon for combatting swelled-headedness, bureaucratic self-importance and conceit, and for improving the contacts between leaders and led. . . .

Mass purges . . . are attended by many mistakes, primarily by the infringement of the Leninist principle of an individual approach to people. . . . There were numerous cases of unwarranted expulsion from the Party, and of hostile elements who had wormed their way into the Party taking advantage of the purges to persecute and ruin honest people. . . . During the purge of 1933 the largest group of persons expelled from the Party comprised the so-called passive elements. It was in respect to them that most mistakes were committed. . . . The slandering of honest people under the guise of "vigilance" is at the present time the most widespread method used to mask and screen hostile activities. If you want to discover still unexposed enemy wasps' nests, look for them above all among the slanderers. . . . In some organizations the slanderers lost all sense of restraint and simply put their feet on the table. . . .

We must get an iron broom and sweep our Party house clean of this garbage. (Loud applause.) The refusal to be worried about human beings, the reluctance to investigate the charges brought against a man on their merits, is a malady which still ails a good many leaders of our Party organizations. There are still quite a number of people in our organizations who like to insure themselves and be on the safe side. . . . These people forget that our whole work of building socialism, our whole educational work, is designed to remold the minds of men. That is what our Party exists

for, that is why we strove for and achieved the victory of socialism, that is why we are undertaking the tasks of communist development, namely, to remold people, their ego. If there are some who think that remolding the minds of men does not apply to Party members, that Communists are born free of all prejudices and absolutely require no reeducation, this is nothing but an idealistic and schematic view of people. This way of judging people abstractly, in accordance with a ready-made standard, instead of studying them in all their connections and manifestations, condemns one to passivity, to a pessimistic view of people. This pessimistic view looks back on the past. This way of judging people has nothing in common with Bolshevism. . . . All this is a Menshevik backsliding. . . . If you scratch these pseudo-moralists, you will find plenty of hypocrites and humbugs among them. You'll never cook your porridge with a lot of grave-diggers like this. (Loud applause.) . . .

The new rules were designed to remedy these and other abuses. They abolished the four grades of applicants (industrial workers, non-industrial workers, peasants, and others), with their varying requirements of probationary periods and endorsements by members, established at Congress XIV. Henceforth anyone 18 or over could apply for membership on the basis of recommendations from three Party members of three years' standing, with a uniform probation period of one year. All members were now guaranteed the right to criticize any Party worker at Party meetings; to elect, and be elected to, all Party organs; to be present at all meetings making decisions regarding their conduct and activities; and to address statements and questions to any Party body, including the Central Committee. Mass purges were abolished. Expulsions would in future be dealt with as individual cases, with elaborate safeguards against unjustified action. In the election of all Party bodies, voting must now be by secret ballot and by individual candidates rather than by lists, with an unlimited right of challenge and criticism. All Party meetings should be "not for parade and the formal and ceremonial approval of decisions" but for "genuine discussion."

Other changes introduced Military Departments in each Party local or primary organization, in all district, city, area, regional

(*rayon*), and territorial (*oblast*) committees, and in the Central Committees in each Republic. Their function was to assist in the registration and convocation of recruits, mobilization, air defense, etc. The old institution of the Party Conference was put into the rules, with the stipulation that it must be summoned at least once a year and composed of elected representatives of local organizations, with the basis of representation and the election procedure determined by the Central Committee of the CPSU(B). The Conference was empowered to replace as many as one-fifth of the members of the Central Committee elected at the preceding Congress by new members chosen from among the alternates, and to elect a corresponding number of alternates. Other decisions of the Conference would be binding on all Party organizations only with the endorsement of the Central Committee.

The Komsomols (Young Communist League) would henceforth be subordinated to, and guided by, the Party, with their Central Committee under the orders of the Party Central Committee and all locals under the orders of corresponding Party units. Congresses must in future meet not less frequently than once every three years. Party dues were fixed at 20 kopeks per month for members earning 100 rubles a month or less, up to 2 rubles for those earning 250–300 rubles, 2% of earnings up to 500 rubles a month, and 3% over 500 rubles. Entrance fees were set at 2% of monthly earnings.

These rules indicated the resolve of the leadership to parallel the governmental arrangements of the 1936 Constitution by a restoration of intra-Party democracy and, in Zhdanov's words, "to put an end to the violations of the principles of democratic centralism which formerly prevailed in the Party." Lenin's original conception of a free brotherhood of comrades, settling differences through discussion, electing their own leaders, and carrying out majority decisions with iron discipline, had been respected during the years of fear more in shadow than in substance. Members might propose or even oppose, at considerable risk, but the Politburo disposed and reposed in the seats of power. All this was now to be changed by making the Party a truly representative and democratic organization of the membership.

These decisions, however were carried out only in part. No Conference met in 1939 or 1940, though Conferences were to be annual. The 18th Conference met in February 1941. Its *leitmotif* was expressed by young Nikolai A. Voznesensky, chairman of the Gosplan:

"Keep your powder dry and do not stint means for the production of aircraft, tanks, munitions, warships and shells." Congress XIX, which would have met in 1942, was deferred. These departures from the rules, like the suspension of Soviet elections, were attributed to the outbreak of war. Precarious neutrality, defensive aggrandizement, and resistance to invasion all called for unity and discipline rather than for government by talk. The course charted on the eve of hostilities was to prove impossible of realization.

Zhdanov's hopes and resolves were to prove meaningless. Whether they might have been given meaning in the absence of war is an academic question. Doubt would seem warranted by Stalin's predilection for suppressing all criticism and for jailing or shooting all critics. In fact, no democratization of the Party was achieved. The Soviet polity remained an oligarchy dominated and terrorized by an Autocrat. His errors and outrages condemned millions of Soviet citizens to death at the hands of domestic inquisitors and alien invaders. His slyness and shrewdness, to be sure, were to contribute substantially to the survival of the State in a fearful time of trouble—partly of his own making and partly engendered by the decline of the West into a hideous miasma of irresponsibility, barbarism, and homicidal madness. How the tragedy of the 1940's came to pass is our next concern.

CHAPTER EIGHT

The Diplomacy of Disaster

1. NINETEEN THIRTY-NINE

THE PARANOID suspicions that motivated the Great Purge, even as Soviet statesmen were elaborating the new Constitution and striving paradoxically for some semblance of the "rule of law," were paralleled in the late 1930's in the arena of *Realpolitik*. As the diplomats of East and West, confronted with a comman danger, sought to build a common front, each side privately attributed to the other the basest of motives and secretly dreamed of safety through the role of "Happy Third." The sickness of the soul which bred foreign policies of paralysis and suicide in the Western nations and converted Soviet internal politics into a nightmare of terror had already brought murderous psychopaths to power in Japan, Italy, and the *Reich*. With the Anglo-French Munichmen concluding non-aggression pacts with the Nazi madmen and eagerly seeking a *rapprochement* at the prospective expense of Russia, the policy-makers of Moscow were eager to reorient themselves and their people in an ever more dangerous world.

At Congress XVIII, Dmitri Manuilsky, in the name of the Party delegation to the Executive Committee of the Comintern, spoke bluntly and grandiloquently of the war to come:

> The plan of the British reactionary bourgeoisie is to sacrifice the small States of southeastern Europe to German Fascism so as to direct Germany eastward—against the USSR; to attempt, by means of such a counter-revolutionary war, to retard the progress of socialism and the victory of communism in the USSR; to buy off Germany,

with her imperialist claims on British colonies. At the same time the British reactionaries would like to use the USSR to draw the fangs of German imperialism, to weaken Germany for a long time to come, and to preserve the dominant position of British imperialism in Europe. . . .

But the British reactionary bourgeoisie are digging their own graves with their predatory plans. . . . The moribund capitalist world will not save itself by a counter-revolutionary war on the Soviet Union, but will only hasten its own destruction. The armed resistance of the great Soviet people will stir up the whole world of labor, all those whose right to liberty, work, a better life, and an independent country has been trampled under foot by Fascism. It will rouse proletarians and working people in all corners of the globe, who will realize that the hour of retribution for their centuries of suffering is at hand. It will let loose throughout the world a mighty movement of anti-Fascist forces, heartened by the tremendous power of resistance offered by the Soviet people to Fascism. It will spur on to struggle peoples who have hitherto avoided coming to grips with Fascism. It will turn against Fascism the peoples of the Fascist States, who will have arms placed in their hands. For the Fascist governments it will be a war not only against the Soviet Union, but also against their own peoples. For the Soviet people, for the working people of the world, for all advanced and progressive mankind, it will be the most just and sacred war ever waged in the history of humanity. . . .

Stalin, speaking on March 10, 1939, hinted at the devices he proposed to employ to avoid involvement in Armageddon:

It is a distinguishing feature of the new imperialist war that it has not yet become universal, a world war. The war is being waged by aggressor States, who in every way infringe upon the interests of the non-aggressive States, primarily England, France and the USA, while the latter draw back and retreat, making concession after concession to the aggressors. . . . Incredible, but true. . . . To what then are we to attribute the systematic concessions made by these States to the aggressors? . . .

The chief reason is that the majority of the non-aggressive countries, particularly England and France, have rejected the policy of collective security, the policy of collective resistance to the aggressors, and have taken up a position of non-intervention, a position of "neutrality." . . . The policy of non-intervention means conniving at aggression, giving free rein to war, and, consequently, transforming the war into a world war. The policy of non-intervention reveals an eagerness, a desire, not to hinder the aggressors in their nefarious work: not to hinder Japan, say, from embroiling herself in a war with China, or, better still, with the Soviet Union; not to hinder Germany, say, from enmeshing herself in European affairs, from embroiling herself in a war with the Soviet Union; to allow all the belligerents to sink deeply into the mire of war, to encourage them surreptitiously in this; to allow them to weaken and exhaust one another; and then, when they have become weak enough, to appear on the scene with fresh strength, to appear, of course, "in the interests of peace," and to dictate conditions to the enfeebled belligerents. Cheap and easy! . . .

The hullabaloo raised by the British, French and American press over the Soviet Ukraine is characteristic. . . . The gentlemen of the press there shouted until they were hoarse that the Germans were marching on Soviet Ukraine, that they now had what is called the Carpathian Ukraine, with a population of some 700,000, and that not later than this spring the Germans would annex the Soviet Ukraine, which has a population of over 30,000,000, to this so-called Carpathian Ukraine. It looks as if the object of this suspicious hullabaloo was to incense the Soviet Union against Germany, to poison the atmosphere and to provoke a conflict with Germany without any visible grounds. . . .

Even more characteristic is the fact that certain European and American politicians and pressmen, having lost patience waiting for "the march on the Soviet Ukraine," are themselves beginning to disclose what is really behind the policy of non-intervention. They are saying quite openly, putting it down in black on white, that the Germans have

cruelly "disappointed" them, for instead of marching farther east, against the Soviet Union, they have turned, you see, to the west and are demanding colonies. One might think that the districts of Czechoslovakia were yielded to Germany as the price of an undertaking to launch war on the Soviet Union, but that now the Germans are refusing to meet their bills and are sending them to Hades.

Far be it from me to moralize on the policy of non-intervention, to talk of treason, treachery and so on. It would be naïve to preach morals to people who recognize no human morality. Politics is politics, as the old, case-hardened bourgeois diplomats say. It must be remarked, however, that the big and dangerous political game started by the supporters of the policy of non-intervention may end in a serious fiasco for them. . . .

The foreign policy of the Soviet Union is clear and explicit.

1. We stand for peace and the strengthening of business relations with all countries. That is our position; and we shall adhere to this position as long as these countries maintain like relations with the Soviet Union, and as long as they make no attempt to trespass on the interests of our country.

2. We stand for peaceful, close and friendly relations with all the neighboring countries which have common frontiers with the USSR. That is our position; and we shall adhere to this position as long as these countries maintain like relations with the Soviet Union, and as long as they make no attempt to trespass, directly or indirectly, on the integrity and inviolability of the frontiers of the Soviet State.

3. We stand for the support of nations which are the victims of aggression and are fighting for the independence of their country.

4. We are not afraid of the threats of aggressors, and are ready to deal two blows for every blow delivered by instigators of war who attempt to violate the Soviet borders. . . .

The tasks of the Party in the sphere of foreign policy are: (1) To continue the policy of peace and of strengthen-

ing business relations with all countries; (2) To be cautious and not allow our country to be drawn into conflicts by warmongers who are accustomed to have others pull the chestnuts out of the fire for them; (3) To strengthen the might of our Red Army and Red Navy to the utmost; (4) To strengthen the international bonds of friendship with the working people of all countries, who are interested in peace and friendship among nations. . . .

Five days after these words were spoken in Moscow, Hitler in Berlin, having sponsored the "independence" of a Nazi puppet regime in Slovakia and browbeaten helpless President Emil Hácha and Foreign Minister Frantisek Chvalkovsky into agreeing to the annexation of Bohemia and Moravia to the Reich, ordered the *Wehrmacht* to occupy Prague. The remnant of Czecho-Slovakia was expunged. Bonnet, Daladier, Halifax, and Chamberlain noted that the Anglo-French guarantee to Prague promised at Munich had never materialized, and that London and Paris consequently had no duty to act. But on March 16 Hitler permitted Hungary to annex Carpatho-Ukraine, long groomed as the nucleus of the "Great Ukraine" that *Der Führer* had pledged himself to carve out of the USSR. The Munichmen now registered shock and dismay. Ambassador Robert Coulondre in Berlin reported to Bonnet that "the Reich, before carrying out its vast program in the east, will first turn against the Western Powers," precisely as forecast in *Mein Kampf.*

Chamberlain and Daladier, thoroughly alarmed by the bankruptcy of their previous policies, belatedly sought to rebuild an anti-Fascist coalition. Moscow rejoiced and responded, only to be rebuffed. Chamberlain preferred to negotiate first with Poland, whose bitterly anti-Soviet regime would never consent to any viable alliance with the USSR. Litvinov's proposal of a conference to plan joint action was rejected as "premature." On March 22, thus encouraged, Hitler threatened Lithuania with invasion and compelled Vilna to cede Memal to Germany and to sign a non-aggression pact. The devious and tragic course of Tory diplomacy in 1939 eventuated in a British guarantee of Polish "independence" (March 31), a pledge on April 6 of an Anglo-Polish pact of mutual aid (not actually signed, however, until August 25), a unilateral British guarantee, following Mussolini's seizure of Albania on April 8, of the "independence" of Greece and Rumania (April 13), and an Anglo-Turkish

accord of May 12, which, in turn, led to no treaty of alliance until October 19 and was followed by Turkish neutrality until February 23, 1945.

Without Soviet participation this house of cards was worthless or, as Lloyd George put it, "sheer madness." Hitler replied to Roosevelt's plea for peace by denouncing (April 15, 1939) the German-Polish non-aggression treaty of January 1934 and the Anglo-German naval pact of June 1935. Ciano and Ribbentrop in Berlin signed on May 22 a German-Italian treaty of military alliance. Pompously dubbed the "Pact of Steel," it was actually a fraud since *Il Duce* secretly declared his unreadiness for war for another three years, pathetically pleaded with *Der Führer* to avoid hostilities, and was henceforth treated by his Nazi allies with contempt.[1] "A Prince," observed Machiavelli, "ought to take care never to make an alliance with one more powerful than himself for the purpose of attacking others . . . because if he conquers, you are at his discretion." This advice Mussolini ignored. This advice Stalin was likewise to ignore. The results in both cases were calamitous.

Since the Nuremberg trials it has been known (although how many outsiders knew at the time is uncertain) that Hitler & Co. secretly reached their decision to attack Poland in April of 1939. Keitel's April 3 directive for the *Wehrmacht* outlined "Case White," the strategic plan for the invasion of Poland on or after September 1, 1939. Hitler on May 23 opined: "There is no question of sparing Poland. . . . There will be war. If there were an alliance of France, England, and Russia, I would attack England and France with a few annihilating blows." [2] This decision was reported in the "Friends of Europe Information Service" bulletin (London) for June 20, 1939, and reflected during the spring and summer in the diplomatic dispatches from Berlin contained in *The French Yellow Book of 1939*.

---

[1] See Hugh Gibson (ed.): *The Ciano Diaries, 1939–1943* (Doubleday, 1946) and Dino Alfieri: *Dictators Face to Face*, translated by David Moore (New York University Press, 1956).

[2] See my article "The Nazi Road to War, I" in *Current History,* January 1953. In Moscow in May 1956 I attempted to gain entry to the Foreign Ministry, handsomely housed in the city's first skyscraper (1951) on Smolenskii Boulevard, and to secure answers to questions as to when Soviet policy-makers first knew of this Nazi decision, when they first learned of the Nazi decision of 1940 to attack the USSR, why Molotov took a large delegation to Paris in July 1947 to discuss participation in the Marshall Plan, and what the Soviet role in Korea was in June 1950. My efforts elicited no response of any kind from Mr. Molotov, his successor, Dmitri Shepilov, or any of their aides or subordinates.

It is therefore highly improbable that Nazi intentions were unknown in the inner counsels of Downing Street, the Quai d'Orsay, and the Narkomindel.

What is now known disposes of two myths long entertained and endlessly repeated: (1) that Hitler invaded Poland on September 1 because of the "green light" of the Nazi-Soviet pact of August 23; and (2) that an Anglo-French Soviet alliance in the spring or summer of 1939 would have "contained" or "deterred" the Third *Reich* and thus averted hostilities. War was already inevitable by the will of the Nazi policy-makers. But an alliance, if seriously meant and honored by all signatories, offered the only possibility of defending Poland, preventing the Nazi conquest of Europe, and bringing Germany to defeat at minimum cost. Churchill opined, correctly, that such an alliance was "a matter of life or death." Litvinov concurred and was eager to negotiate a strategically viable pact with the West.

The enterprise foundered on various rocks: Polish refusal to accept Soviet military aid, since acceptance might at best have placed in jeopardy the Treaty of Riga frontier of 1921 and at worst have led to a Sovietized Poland (both calamities were, nevertheless, to come to pass); Anglo-French evasiveness, procrastination, and equivocation; and Stalinist suspicions, well nourished by the words and deeds of London and Paris, that the Western Powers had no purpose other than to embroil the USSR in war with the Reich while they stood aloof. The final result was disaster for all.[3]

[3] Full diplomatic documentation regarding the Anglo-Soviet negotiations of 1939 is still not available, since neither London nor Moscow has seen fit to publish or release the whole record, probably because it casts little credit on either party. Readers of Russian, however, would do well to consult V. M. Khvostov and I. I. Mints (V. P. Potemkin, ed.): *Istoriya Diplomatii (History of Diplomacy)* (State Publishing House for Political Literature, Moscow, 1945) and, on diplomatic problems in another area, Y. M. Zhukov (ed.): *Mezhdunarodyne Otnosheniya na Dalnem Vostok 1870–1945 (International Relations in the Far East, 1870–1945)* (State Publishing House for Political Literature, Moscow, 1951). For background, foreground, hindsight, and foresight, always bearing in mind the available documentation at the time of writing, see: Max Beloff: *The Foreign Policy of Soviet Russia, 1929–1941* (2 vols., Oxford University Press, 1947); Donald G. Bishop: *Soviet Foreign Relations: Documents and Readings* (Syracuse University Press, 1955); E. H. Carr: *German-Soviet Relations: Between the Two World Wars* (Johns Hopkins University Press, 1951); Jane Degras (ed.): *Soviet Documents on Foreign Policy* (3 vols., Oxford University Press, 1951–3); Louis Fischer: *The Soviets in World Affairs* (2 vols., Cape & Smith, 1930); Gustav Hilger and Alfred G. Meyer: *The Incompatible Allies* (Macmillan, 1953); John A. Lukacs: *The Great Powers and Eastern Europe* (American Book Co., 1953); Bronislaw Kusnierz: *Stalin and*

Not until mid-April did Downing Street undertake discussions with the Narkomindel through Halifax and Ambassador Ivan Maisky in London and through Ambassador Sir William Seeds and Litvinov in Moscow. The Kremlin asked a binding alliance. Westminster preferred a more "flexible" formula that would leave Warsaw and Bucharest free to decide whether they desired Soviet aid in case of war and would leave Paris and London free to abstain should Hitler, after all, attack the USSR and leave the West in peace. On May 3, 1939, Maxim Litvinov, genial Jewish genius of the Narkomindel for nine years, resigned his post on grounds of "ill-health" and was succeeded as Foreign Minister by Premier Molotov. The meaning of this portent was lost on Western statesmen. Litvinov was the incarnation of "collective security" against Fascist aggression. His retirement was a reflection of the view in Stalin's secret counsels that the West was not negotiating in good faith and that Soviet safety might better be sought by some alternative prescription.

Yet Molotov pursued the parleys, simultaneously dickering in private with Berlin for a bargain. He was prepared to accept the "best bargain" offered. Such cleverness was its own reward. At the same time, the Western policy-makers (who were by no means unaware of the alternate possibility, despite their later "astonishment") were bound by the circumstances of the situation to "outbid" Berlin or at least to demonstrate to the Kremlin that their intentions were honorable and their statesmanship practical. This they never did. When Molotov urged commitments whereby France, Britain, and the USSR would take up arms together against aggression directed toward any of the border States between their countries and the Reich (The Netherlands, Belgium, Luxembourg, Finland, Estonia, Latvia, Lithuania, Poland, and Rumania), Chamberlain piously replied that the Western Powers could not "guarantee" States unwilling to be guaranteed. Molotov told the Supreme Soviet on May 31 that "as yet it cannot even be said that France and Britain are seriously desirous of abandoning the policy of non-intervention, the policy of non-resistance to the further development of aggression." The USSR, said he, would sign no pact without a binding alliance, a

---

the Poles (Hollis, 1949); Ivan M. Maisky: *Before the Storm* (Hutchinson, 1940); F. L. Schuman: *Europe on the Eve* (Knopf, 1939) and *Night over Europe* (Knopf, 1941); Leonard Shapiro (ed.): *Soviet Treaty Series* (2 vols., Georgetown University Press, 1955); and Gerhard L. Weinberg: *Germany and the Soviet Union, 1939–1941* (Brill, Leyden, 1954).

joint guarantee of all European States bordering on the Soviet Union, the concrete accords for joint defense. Chamberlain refused to go to Moscow, and instead went fishing in Hampshire with a bitterly anti-Soviet diplomat, Sir Francis Lindsey.

These talks were doomed less by perfidy on either side than by a long legacy of reciprocal fear and suspicion which could have been overcome only by the warmth and imagination of a Churchill, a Roosevelt, or a Khrushchev. Churchill, as a bitter foe of "appeasement" of the Fascist Cæsars, was in the Tory "doghouse." FDR was leader of a nation paralyzed by its passion for "keeping out of other people's wars." Khrushchev as yet played no role in matters of such moment. With the business in the hands of Stalin and Molotov, Chamberlain and Halifax, Daladier and Bonnet, mutual distrust vanquished confidence. All were left adrift in shallows and in miseries because all alike were unable to take the tide which leads on to fortune. In June, Chamberlain sent Munichman William Strang to aid Seeds in Moscow and to offer "consultation" should the USSR be threatened in the Baltic. Andrei Zhdanov in *Pravda* (June 29, 1939) opined that the Western Powers had "artificially invented a stumbling block" and had "no wish for an equal treaty with the USSR." On July 31 Chamberlain dispatched an Anglo-French military mission to Moscow. Consisting of nonentities, it traveled by slow boat, not reaching the Soviet capital until August 11, and then announced that it had no authority to sign any agreement. Stalin and his aides, doubtless knowing Hitler's timetable, drew the conclusions they deemed necessary.

2. FROM ALLIANCE TO APPEASEMENT

THE rulers of Russia make all major decisions in secret. Some secrecy is essential in all politics and diplomacy, since the essence of such operations is flexibility and compromise. Both are precluded by publicity. Soviet secrecy in such matters, however, is a psychic disease far older than the Red regime and attributable to a thousand years of suspicion of the purposes of foreigners in dealing with Mother Russia.

The men of Moscow secretly decided in midsummer of 1939 that a workable alliance with Britain and France was unobtainable,

that Soviet security might better be served by peace than by war, and that non-involvement in the war to come could best be achieved by a "deal" with Hitler. Their more subtle calculations, which proved to be tragically mistaken, can only be guessed at. They were not unaware that on March 16 the Federation of British Industries and the *Reichsgruppe Industrie* concluded various Anglo-German cartel accords; that in May the British Cabinet approved the transfer to Berlin of £6,000,000 in Czech gold; that in July, Westminster was contemplating a loan of £1,000,000,000 to Hitler's Reich; that Sir Nevile Henderson in Berlin was suggesting an Anglo-German alliance; and that "Perfidious Albion" under its Tory leaders of 1939 did not inspire confidence in either its desire or its capacity to act effectively against Fascist aggression.

It is likely, though documentary proof is currently unobtainable, that the Anglo-Russian deadlock and the Nazi-Soviet bargain of 1939 were due in some measure to Soviet "irredentist" aspirations. In the *modus vivendi* of 1921 the Kremlin, out of weakness, had given up all claim to Finland, the Baltic States, Western Byelorussia, the Western Ukraine, and Bessarabia. In the negotiations of 1939 Muscovite spokesmen may well have hinted at an alteration of the *status quo*. Even if they did not, the implications of Soviet "protection" of the old *cordon sanitaire* against Nazi aggression, however disguised as a tripartite alliance, were obvious. Western statesmen recoiled in horror from violating their "principles" and, in effect, made clear their preference: better let Hitler take over the borderlands, which the West could in no way defend, than accept their "mutual defense" at the possible price of Soviet aggrandizement. The Kremlin's own revisionist "imperialism," whether overtly expressed or tacitly implied, reinforced this view and nourished the perennial hope of the Munichmen that the two totalitarian colossi might yet be turned against each other to their mutual destruction.

In the sequel Stalin and Molotov outchamberlained Chamberlain in a masterly super-Munich. Cynical Machiavellian astuteness in planning and executing the bargain was surpassed only by the excruciating Mephistophelean penalties exacted in the end by the tempter. Parleys between Berlin and Moscow began tentatively in mid-April 1939, with a mutual view toward "improving relations." By the end of May, after discussion of an economic accord, consideration was being given to a possible political agreement. Not until late July did the discussions become serious. On August 10 Dr.

Karl Schnurre, Counsellor of Legation at the *Wilhelmstrasse,* told Soviet Chargé Georgi Astrakhov that war with Poland was probable, that German interests were limited and in no way incompatible with Soviet interests, and that the latter might better be served by a German-Soviet understanding than by any Anglo-French-Soviet alliance to guarantee "megalomaniac Polish aspirations." Molotov responded favorably. Within a fortnight the bargain was struck.[4]

The terms are now well known, even if the interpretations to be placed upon them will long remain in controversy. The German-Soviet trade accord was signed in Berlin on August 19, contemplating exchanges of goods to the value of almost 200,000,000 marks on each side during 1939–41. Ribbentrop and his aides landed at Moscow airport at 1:00 p.m., August 23. Following lunch and conferences, they proceeded to the Kremlin, met with Stalin and Molotov, and, an hour after midnight, signed a ten-year non-aggression and neutrality pact, plus a secret protocol. There was much drinking of toasts, including Stalin's: "I know how much the German nation loves its *Führer*; I should therefore like to drink to his health." In the preliminary exchanges of views and drafts, the Nazi envoys emphatically made clear that war was imminent. Moscow, having failed to obtain from the Western Powers any commitments to a strategically viable coalition, contracted out of the impending hostilities by selling its neutrality to Hitler for a price far higher than London or Paris was prepared to pay for an alliance: control of the Baltic States and Eastern Poland, and all of this with no involvement in the war, which an alliance with the West would have entailed. The bargain, seen from Berlin, was magnificent, for it ensured the

[4] Moscow, understandably, has published (as of 1957) no useful documentation regarding these secret *pourparlers*. A partial record is available in the Department of State's "Cold War" propaganda booklet of 1948, *Nazi-Soviet Relations 1939–1941: Documents from the Archives of the German Foreign Office*, edited by Raymond James Sontag and James Stuart Beddie. This publication, while not without its uses, may well be deemed an instance of American imitation of the worst Stalinist methods of historical distortion. The selections and omissions are so devised as to convey the impression, widely echoed in the U.S. press, that Hitler's invasion of Poland was the result of the Nazi-Soviet agreement and that Hitler's later decision to attack the USSR was the consequence of Molotov's "demands" in Berlin in November 1940. The Nuremberg documents, as well as other sources, show conclusively that the sequence of decision-making implied in this compilation bears no relation to the facts. For comments, see Walter Lippmann: "Propaganda That Backfired," February 12, 1948; *Falsificators of History*, Embassy of the USSR, Washington, February 1948; and my own "Diplomacy by Falsehood," *Soviet Russia Today*, April 1948.

benevolent neutrality of the USSR in whatever conflict might develop. The bargain, seen from the Kremlin, was superb. Only two things were ignored by the Politburo: the *Wehrmacht* was to prove temporarily invincible and capable of conquering Europe; Hitler and his confreres were scoundrels and madmen. Mistakes of judgment on both sides by Soviet policy-makers were almost to cost the USSR its life.[5]

[5] The texts of the agreements, dated August 23, 1939, were as follows:

TREATY OF NONAGGRESSION BETWEEN GERMANY AND THE UNION OF SOVIET SOCIALIST REPUBLICS, AUG. 23, 1939

Guided by the desire to strengthen the cause of peace between Germany and the Union of Soviet Socialist Republics, and basing themselves on the fundamental stipulations of the neutrality agreement concluded between Germany and the Union of Soviet Socialist Republics in April, 1926, the German Government and the Government of the Union of Soviet Socialist Republics have come to the following agreement:

1. The two contracting parties undertake to refrain from any act of force, any aggressive act and any attacks against each other undertaken either singly or in conjunction with any other Powers.

2. If one of the contracting parties should become the object of warlike action on the part of a third Power, the other contracting party will in no way support the third Power.

3. The Governments of the two contracting parties will in future remain in consultation with one another in order to inform each other about questions which touch their common interests.

4. Neither of the two contracting parties will join any group of Powers which is directed, mediately or immediately, against the other party.

5. In case disputes or conflicts on questions of any kind should arise between the two contracting parties, the two partners will solve these disputes or conflicts exclusively by friendly exchange of views or if necessary by arbitration commissions.

6. The present agreement is concluded for the duration of ten years with the stipulation that unless one of the contracting partners denounces it one year before its expiration, it will automatically be prolonged by five years.

7. The present agreement shall be ratified in the shortest possible time. The instruments of ratification are to be exchanged in Berlin. The treaty comes into force immediately it has been signed. SECRET ADDITIONAL PROTOCOL:

On the occasion of the signature of the Nonaggression Pact between the German Reich and the Union of Socialist Soviet Republics the undersigned plenipotentiaries of each of the two parties discussed in strictly confidential conversations the question of the boundary of their respective spheres of influence in Eastern Europe. These conversations led to the following conclusions:

1. In the event of a territorial and political rearrangement in the areas belonging to the Baltic States (Finland, Estonia, Latvia, Lithuania), the northern boundary of Lithuania shall represent the boundary of the spheres of influence of Germany and the U.S.S.R. In this connection the interest of Lithuania in the Vilna area is recognized by each party.

2. In the event of a territorial and political rearrangement of the areas belonging to the Polish state the spheres of influence of Germany and the U.S.S.R.

The immediate aftermath of Stalin's pact with Hitler threatened no such doom, but, on the contrary, appeared highly advantageous to the national interests and military security of the Soviet State. At dawn of Friday, September 1, 1939, the *Wehrmacht* roared into Poland. Hitler and Ribbentrop, as well as Stalin and Molotov (but not Mussolini and Ciano), expected Paris and London to abandon Warsaw as they had abandoned Addis Ababa, Madrid, Vienna, and Prague. Bonnet at the Quai d'Orsay spent two days of earnest effort to achieve precisely this result, but was overruled by Downing Street. Britain and France declared on the Reich on September 3, despite their total inability to aid the Poles in any way. Within two weeks the Polish Army was destroyed, Warsaw was surrounded, and *Panzer* columns were plunging far to the east amid the chaotic debris of the Polish state. Molotov congratulated Berlin, but displayed surprise and anxiety. Ribbentrop offered to ameliorate Soviet-Japanese relations and pressed Moscow to use its influence to assure Turkish neutrality and, above all, to invade Eastern Poland and occupy Polish territories up to the demarcation line. Molotov pleaded unpreparedness and proposed, in embarrassment, that the Soviet military move be publicly depicted as anti-German. Berlin objected.

shall be bounded approximately by the line of the rivers Narew, Vistula, and San.

The question of whether the interests of both parties make desirable the maintenance of an independent Polish state and how such a state should be bounded can only be definitely determined in the course of further political developments.

In any event both Governments will resolve this question by means of a friendly agreement.

3. With regard to Southeastern Europe attention is called by the Soviet side to its interest in Bessarabia. The German side declares its complete political disinterestedness in these areas.

4. This protocol shall be treated by both parties as strictly secret.

Moscow, August 23, 1939.

For the Government of the German Reich:	Plenipotentiary of the Government of the U.S.S.R.:
v. RIBBENTROP	V. MOLOTOV

David J. Dallin (David Yulievich Levin, originally a Right Menshevik and an *émigré* from Russia in 1921) deserves credit for reporting, substantially correctly, the content of the Secret Protocol in his *Soviet Russia's Foreign Policy, 1939–1942* (Yale University Press, 1942), despite factual inaccuracies and passionate prejudices manifested in this and his many other anti-Soviet volumes. The Secret Protocol and its supplement of September 28, 1939, were first published in the *St. Louis Post-Dispatch* of May 22, 1946, by Richard L. Stokes, correspondent at the Nuremberg war-crimes trial. Both were officially published for the first time in *Nazi-Soviet Relations 1939–1941*, pp. 78 and 107.

An alternative formula was devised. "The Polish State and its Government have virtually ceased to exist," Ambassador Grzybowski was told at 3 a.m., September 17. "The Soviet Government cannot remain indifferent when its blood brothers, Ukrainians and Byelorussians in Polish territory, having been abandoned to their fate, are left without protection. . . ."

At 4 p.m., September 17, Soviet troops crossed the Polish frontier. A few of the defeated and scattered Polish units fought back. Among the new invaders, 737 were killed and 1,862 wounded. But 180,000 Polish soldiers became Soviet prisoners of war, with a macabre sequel to be noted later. Besieged Warsaw fell to the *Wehrmacht* on September 27, as Ribbentrop arrived again in Moscow to sign a "Border and Friendship Treaty." Another Secret Protocol reassigned Lithuania to the Soviet sphere and Central Poland to the Nazi sphere. In this fourth partition of the Polish nation, the Reich acquired 70,000 square miles with 22,000,000 people, and the USSR 80,000 square miles with 13,000,000 people—most of whom, however, were not Poles but Ukrainians, Byelorussians, and Jews, all annexed in October following "elections" (Soviet style) to "People's Assemblies."

The Kremlin agreed to support Berlin's "peace offensive." *Izvestia* (October 9) opined that "Hitlerism is a matter of taste. But to undertake war for 'annihilation of Hitlerism' is criminal folly." Molotov told the Supreme Soviet on October 31: "One swift blow to Poland, first by the German Army and then by the Red Army, and nothing was left of this ugly offspring of Versailles. . . . We have always held that a strong Germany is an indispensable condition for a durable peace in Europe." On November 29 Stalin asserted that Britain and France "attacked Germany. . . . The Soviet Union openly supported Germany's peace proposals because it believed that the earliest termination of the war would fundamentally alleviate the position of all countries."

Meanwhile the new course of Soviet foreign policy evoked feigned shock among Anglo-French policy-makers, most of whom well knew that the alternative to an Anglo-French-Soviet alliance would be a Nazi-Soviet bargain. Ambassador Sir Nevile Henderson had told Hitler on August 23 that he preferred a German-Soviet agreement to an Anglo-Soviet agreement, as did most of his colleagues and superiors. The new course created consternation among Communists abroad, who (in Louis Fischer's apt phrase) were

"caught with their dialectics down." They had been preaching for years, in slavish worship of Moscow, that the USSR was the great champion of collective security against Fascist aggression. In a new mood of reverence, echoing the early Church father who held that the true test of faith is to believe what is absurd, they now discovered abruptly that France and Britain were "imperialistic aggressors" and that peace with Hitler was the *sine quo non* of salvation. The men of the Kremlin had demonstrated anew that whenever they were confronted with a painful choice between promoting global Communism at the cost of Russian national interests and serving such interests as they defined them (however mistakenly) at the expense of Communists abroad, their choice was never in doubt. The point was best put by Churchill, speaking to Commons on October 1, 1939, and hopefully making the best of a currently hopeless situation:

> I cannot forecast to you the action of Russia. It is a riddle wrapped in a mystery inside an enigma; but perhaps there is a key. That key is Russian national interest. It cannot be in accordance with the interest or the safety of Russia that Germany should plant itself upon the shores of the Black Sea, or that it should overrun the Balkan States and subjugate the Slavonic peoples of southeastern Europe. That would be contrary to the historic life-interests of Russia. . . . That the Russian armies should stand on this line was clearly necessary for the safety of Russia against the Nazi menace.

In quest of greater safety, the Red rulers of Muscovy moved swiftly to buttress their defenses. The ancient Russian formula for security through aggrandizement could be fairly risked, since the Western Powers, locked in war among themselves, were helpless to act. By threats of force the Kremlin imposed mutual-assistance pacts on Estonia (September 28), Latvia (October 5), and Lithuania (October 10, 1939), involving Soviet bases and garrisons in the Baltic States and the forcible expulsion of the Baltic Germans to the Reich. Hitler fumed, but acquiesced. Turkey resisted Soviet pressure, but specified in its belated and empty alliance treaty with Britain and France that Ankara would do nothing "having as its effect of involving as its consequence entry into armed conflict with the USSR." To

Finland, Moscow proposed a 30-year leasehold on the port of Hanko, with a Soviet garrison and naval base, plus the cession to the USSR of various islands in the Gulf, a segment of land near Petsamo in the Far North, and part of the Karelian Isthmus northwest of Leningrad, all in exchange for a Soviet cession to Finland of part of Central Karelia, almost double the size of the proposed Finnish cessions to the USSR. The objective was to buttress the defenses of Leningrad and assure Soviet naval control of the Gulf of Finland. The Finns, whose leaders came to Moscow (October 11–November 13, 1939), refused to yield, since the Russian proposals would have involved abandonment of the costly Mannerheim Line of fortifications 20 miles from Leningrad.

The Politburo's response exemplified the worst features of Stalinism: political inflexibility, callous unconcern for suffering, misinformation, miscalculation, and blind violence in pursuit of a secondary objective. On November 26 Molotov alleged Finnish aggression and demanded a 25-kilometer withdrawal of Finnish troops. Helsinki denied the charge and refused the demand. As the Finnish leaders were about to make concessions, Molotov severed diplomatic relations and denounced the Finnish-Soviet non-aggression pact. On November 30, 1939, Red troops attacked and Soviet planes bombed Finnish cities. A day later Moscow announced a "People's Government of the Democratic Republic of Finland" in the border village of Terioki (actually in Moscow), headed by Otto Kuusinen, a Finnish Communist who had lived in the USSR for twenty years. When Helsinki tried to resume negotiations, the Narkomindel "recognized" this puppet regime as the "Government of Finland" and signed a pact with Kuusinen granting all the Soviet demands. The Soviet press resounded with appeals for the "liberation" of the Finns from the "White Guards." [6]

The premise of these mad antics was that no war would need to be fought, since the Finnish "masses" would rally to Kuusinen, overthrow their own "bourgeois" government, and joyfully accept all Soviet proposals. Seldom have so few been so wrong about so much. All Finns rose as one man to the defense of their Fatherland. The Red Army, whose use on a large scale the Politburo had never contemplated, was halted and humiliatingly defeated. Washington

[6] The Soviet action was in flagrant violation of numerous treaty obligations to which the USSR had solemnly subscribed. See my letter in *NYT*, December 10, 1939.

was thrilled and offered aid, albeit non-military. London and Paris engineered the expulsion of the USSR from the League of Nations as an "aggressor" on December 14. In January and February the statesmen of Britain and France, fatuously unconcerned with their own apparently "phony" war with Hitler's Reich, sent arms to Finland (in Lloyd George's immortal phrase, all "too little or too late") and made plans to attack the Soviet Union. In alarm, Stalin belatedly realized that he had unwittingly invited a catastrophe. In February 1940 troops and guns were hastily assembled under Gen. Gregory Stern to smash the Finnish defenses. Marshal Mannerheim, despairing of effective help from abroad, yielded. Moscow abandoned Kuuisnen and opened negotiations with Helsinki on March 8.

On March 12, 1940, Molotov, Zhdanov, and Commander Vasilevsky signed a peace treaty. By its terms Finland ceded without compensation the entire Karelian Isthmus, including Viborg and the islands; the northern and western shores of Lake Lagoda; territory east of Merkjarvi; and part of the peninsula near Petsamo, which, with its port and nickel mines, was restored to Helsinki. Hanko was leased as a naval base at an annual rental of $330,000. Moscow claimed a right of free transit across the Petsamo district to Norway and Sweden. By Article 3: "both contracting parties undertake mutually to refrain from any attack upon each other, not to conclude any alliances and not to participate in any coalition against one of the contracting parties." This peace was widely, though mistakenly, regarded as a defeat for France and Britain no less than for Finland. Chamberlain's political position was weakened. Daladier was forced on March 19 to yield the French Premiership to anti-Munichard Paul Reynaud, who remarked: "I have come too early." In fact he had come much too late.

Finland had lost between 15,000 (Mannerheim's figure) and 60,000 (Molotov's) dead, all to no avail, since Moscow had asked for considerably less in October 1939 and had offered a net enlargement, rather than a diminution, of Finnish territory. The USSR had lost between 48,745 (Molotov) and 200,000 (Mannerheim) dead and had gained little that could not have been obtained in December had the border incidents and the disastrous Kuusinen experiment not been concocted. On July 10 Kuusinen became Chairman of Presidium of the Supreme Soviet of the new Karelo-Finnish Republic, the 12th of the Union Republics. In his address to the federal Supreme Soviet on March 29, Molotov declared:

. . . Inasmuch as the Soviet Union did not wish to become the tool of British and French imperialists in their struggle for world hegemony against Germany, we have encountered at every step profound hostility of their policy toward our country. . . . If Finland had not been subject to foreign influences, the Soviet Union and Finland would have arrived at a peaceful understanding last autumn. . . . The Soviet Union, having smashed the Finnish army and having every opportunity of occupying the whole of Finland, did not do so and did not demand any indemnities for its expenditures in the war as any other Power would have done, but confined its desires to a minimum and displayed magnanimity towards Finland. . . . We pursued no other object in the peace treaty than that of safeguarding the security of Leningrad, Murmansk and the Murmansk Railway. . . . The task of our foreign policy is to ensure peace between nations and the security of our country. The conclusion must be drawn from this that we must maintain the position of neutrality and refrain from participating in the war between the big European Powers.

A grisly postscript to these events is in order. Among the Polish prisoners of the USSR in 1939 were 15,000 officers, the elite of the defunct Polish Army. After confinement in three camps, Kozielsk, Starobielsk, and Ostashkov, they were transferred in the spring of 1940 to destinations unknown. All vanished. Following resumption of diplomatic relations between Moscow and the Polish Government-in-Exile in July 1941, all prisoners were released. The officers were never found, nor did Soviet officialdom throw any light on their fate. On April 15, 1943, Göbbels announced with much fanfare the "accidental" discovery of a mass grave in Katyn Forest near Smolensk containing 10,000 or 12,000 bodies of Polish officers (actually about 4,000, although the rest were never located), all shot through the head by the "Jewish executioners of the GPU." On April 30, 1943, a Nazi-selected international medical commission, after exhumations and autopsies, reported that the officers were killed in the spring of 1940. The Kremlin now declared, for the first time, that they had been captured by the *Wehrmacht* in 1941 and massacred that summer by the Nazis. After Soviet reoccupation of the area a Special Commission of the Soviet Extraordinary State Committee on Ger-

man-Fascist Crimes investigated anew and "conclusively" confirmed Nazi guilt in its report of January 24, 1944, holding that the officers had been butchered by a Nazi murder unit, that the bodies had been carefully prepared for Göbbel's "revelation" by removal of most letters and documents postdated 1940, and that the 500 Russian prisoners who worked on these initial exhumations were all shot and secretly buried. Testimony was heard at Nuremberg, but the Soviet prosecutor failed to press the case. No verdict was rendered. The Nazi murder unit was never identified. The slain Russian prisoners were never found.

This atrocity later became a weapon of the "Cold War" and gave rise to mountains of "documentation." German guilt was never definitely established, despite the Nazi mass murder of millions of other victims of racial paranoia and megalomania. Soviet innocence can no longer be presumed in the absence of answers to a long series of evidential questions. Beria cryptically told Lieut. Col. Berling in October 1941: "We have committed a great blunder." It is possible that Stalin ordered the camps "liquidated" and that his henchmen in terrorism, misconstruing his intent, liquidated the prisoners instead. In any case, the weight of currently available testimony suggests that the Polish officers were slain in 1940 by agents of Beria's NKVD.[7]

[7] Published material on Katyn is far too voluminous for review or even for listing. It should be noted that in point of time Göbbels's original revelation coincided with, and was designed to deflect attention from, the heroic uprising against the Nazis of the Jews of the Warsaw ghetto, who preferred collective death in battle to individual extermination in gas chambers. The rebellion was followed by the Nazi massacre of every surviving man, woman, and child among the Jews of the Polish capital. Only later did the full story of this horror become known to the outside world. My own original conclusion on Katyn was based in part on analyses of the original Nazi propaganda treatment of the "discovery" while I was employed in Washington in 1943 as a Political Analyst for the Foreign Broadcast Intelligence Service of the Federal Communications Commission. See also Göbbels's diary for May 8, 1943. The bullets found in the bodies were unquestionably of German manufacture. Cf. William H. Standley and Arthur A. Edgeton: *Admiral Ambassador to Russia* (Regnery, 1955), pp. 257 f., 403–11.

In its Interim Report of July 2, 1952 (82nd Congress, 2nd Session, Union Calendar No. 762, House Report No. 2430), the Select Committee to Conduct an Investigation and Study of the Facts, Evidence, and Circumstances of the Katyn Forest Massacre, headed by Congressman Ray J. Madden, Democrat, of Indiana, concluded (p. 28), after exhaustive and expensive hearings in Washington, London, and Frankfurt: "This Committee unanimously finds, beyond any question of reasonable doubt, that the Soviet NKVD committed the mass murders . . . as a calculated plot to eliminate all Polish leaders who subse-

3. NEMESIS

AMERICAN abstention from the war of 1939 in the name of "isolationist neutrality" was compatible with American security so long as the belligerents were stalemated. Soviet abstention by way of a bargain with the Reich was consonant with Soviet safety on the same supposition. The precondition disappeared in the frightful spring of 1940 amid the dust of the *Panzer* Divisions and the vapors of the *Luftwaffe*. Europe's democracies, immune to the débâcle forecast by Marx and Lenin, succumbed to the doom predicted by Mussolini, Franco, and Hitler. Denmark and Norway were taken on April 9. A month later the *Wehrmacht* poured into Luxembourg, Belgium, and The Netherlands while the discredited Chamberlain made way in London for the indomitable Churchill. In mid-May the invaders broke through the Ardennes, destroyed the French Ninth Army, outflanked the Maginot Line, and headed for the Channel and Paris. In the calendar of catastrophe, to the tune of a ghastly obligato compounded of the screams of the dying and the thunder of world-shattering detonations, the British Expeditionary Force quit Dunkirk (June 3), Mussolini declared war (June 10), Paris fell (June 14), and Pétain capitulated to Hitler (June 22). The Axis Powers, now masters of Western Europe, concluded their Tripartite Pact with Japan, September 27, 1940, in a joint bid for global hegemony.

Every rational consideration of national survival now dictated American and Soviet entry into the war as allies of Britain and China in order that the Fascist Triplice might be crushed in least time and

quently would have opposed the Soviets' plans for communizing Poland." This attribution of motives is debatable, and the conclusion is identical with the premise with which the Committee began. Yet the testimony is impressive, particularly since Soviet authorities, who no longer have any reason to defend Beria's NKVD, have to date ignored it, save for indignant denunciation.

A more cautious judgment, based on a detailed examination of all Polish, German, and Soviet sources and upon conclusive evidence that the NKVD initially tried without success to "re-educate" and indoctrinate these Polish officers, is rendered by Janusz K. Zawodny in "Responsibility for the Katyn Forest Massacre" (unpublished M.A. thesis, Department of Political Science, State University of Iowa, 1951), p. 55: "The evidence points strongly, if not irrefutably, to the conclusion that the police (NKVD) of the Soviet Union perpetrated the Katyn Massacre. The Communist conception of the class struggle and the Communist attitude toward class enemies suggests an explanation of the crime."

at smallest cost. Both super-Powers were irrationally inhibited from any such course—the USA by the devotion of Congress, press, and public to a sterile anti-Communism and an obsolete "avoidance of foreign entanglements," and the USSR by the fanatical and fatuous anti-capitalism of the Party and the futile resolve of the Politburo to maintain "neutrality" in the "imperialist war" among the "bourgeois States." Both Washington and Moscow left the fateful decision to Berlin, Rome, and Tokyo, even though Roosevelt achieved "aid to Britain short of war" and Stalin countered Hitler by further defensive measures and fostered a tepid *rapprochement* with the Atlantic Powers. Sir Stafford Cripps arrived in Moscow as new British Ambassador in June 1940, but could effect no accord for Anglo-Soviet collaboration. Laurence Steinhardt, who had succeeded Ambassador Joseph E. Davies in June 1938, was absent from his post during the summer of 1940 and achieved no more in the autumn than the opening of a consulate in Vladivostok and a relaxation of the American embargo on the export to Russia of strategic goods, imposed during the Finnish war. Sumner Welles in Washington held many conferences with Ambassador Konstantin Oumansky, who had replaced Troyanovsky in 1939, but with no immediate results.

The Stalinist formula for defense against the power-drunk *Führer* was, again, annexation of territory. There is no evidence that even the most daring of Soviet politicians or generals (save possibly Marshal Shaposhnikov) proposed an attack on the Reich in the interest of saving France, maintaining a "second front," and sparing the USSR the agony to come. After a fortnight of military disasters France was beyond salvation. Now as always the Russian masses, moreover, could generate no enthusiasm for war unless the Motherland was directly attacked. Moscow, ever cautious to avoid provocation, acquiesced in German domination of Finland during the summer of 1940. To the south the Kremlin moved more boldly. Between June 14 and August 8, through military invasion, political pressure, and coerced referendums, Estonia, Latvia, and Lithuania were annexed to the USSR—amid moralistic indignation and "non-recognition" in Washington, where it had been insisted, between 1917 and 1922, that the Baltic States were properly part of Russia. During the same weeks Moscow wrested Bessarabia and Northern Bukovina from Rumania, which was already under Nazi domination and would be occupied by German troops in October.

The Reich, preoccupied with the "Battle of Britain," acquiesced.

But the megalomaniac *Führer,* hypnotized by Napoleon's fatal vision of 1812, soon came to the conclusion that the way to vanquish an unconquerable Britain was to conquer a vulnerable Russia. On July 29, 1940, Gen. Jodl told Walter Warlimont of "Plan Barbarossa" for the invasion of the USSR. In August, Keitel, with Ribbentrop's approval, vainly sought to dissuade Hitler from his folly. By September detailed plans for the attack were already being elaborated and the decision had been made, with elaborate precautions to keep it secret and with the date of the proposed assault left open.[8]

What was to come was clearly unknown to Molotov when he arrived with his aides in Berlin on a dark and rainy day: November 12, 1940. He remained three days, spent six hours with Hitler, saw Göring, Göbbels, Hess, Ley, and Keitel, and wined and dined with Ribbentrop amid much ostentatious cordiality. The visit was, pro forma, a return for Ribbentrop's two visits to Moscow. In fact it was inspired by frictions arising out of the Triplice Pact, Nazi infiltration of Finland, German occupation of Rumania, Berlin's designs on Bulgaria, and Mussolini's ill-fated attack on Greece in late October. The dour Molotov, not knowing that his hosts had already decided to attempt the annihilation of the USSR, sought to negotiate a new bargain. Ribbentrop, pending the forthcoming "conquest of Russia," sought to frighten England and intimidate America by inducing Moscow to join the Triplice in a Four-Power Pact and a proposed partition of the British Empire, which he held was already defeated. "Why, then," asked Molotov at one conference, "are we meeting in an air-raid shelter?" He expressed willingness to join but only for a *quid pro quo.* Would Berlin agree to withdraw troops from Finland and Rumania? To accept a Soviet protectorate over Bulgaria? To agree to Soviet bases "within the range of the Bosporus and the Dardanelles"? To concede that the region between the Caucasus and the Persian Gulf was "the center of the aspirations of the Soviet Union"? To help persuade Japan to renounce its coal and oil concessions in Northern Sakhalin?

[8] Documentary evidence of the timing of the decision is to be found in the voluminous records of the *Trial of the Major War Criminals Before the International Military Tribunal, Nuremberg, November 14, 1945–October 1, 1946.* Cf. my article "The Nazi Road to War, II" in *Current History,* April 1953. The established facts refute the contention of James F. Byrnes in *Speaking Frankly* (Harper, 1947) that the Nazi decision to attack the USSR was the result of Molotov's "demands" in Berlin in mid-November 1940, and the implication of *Nazi-Soviet Relations, 1939–1941* that the Nazi decision to attack Russia was reached in December.

Molotov received smiles but no answers to his questions. He went home a puzzled man. Cynicism is an attribute of all totalitarians. But the Soviet leaders of 1940-1 were as incredulous of the true intentions of the Nazi fanatics as their Western counterparts had been in earlier years. At November's end Hitler induced the helpless rulers of Hungary, Rumania, and Slovakia to adhere to the Triplice Pact. A Tass communiqué of November 23 protested that a German report that Magyar signature had been approved by the USSR "does not correspond to fact." Another communiqué of January 12, 1941, objected to German-Bulgarian "negotiations" without consultation with Moscow: "If German troops are in Bulgaria, this has taken place without the prior knowledge or consent of the USSR." On March 1, 1941, Bulgarian Premier Philov signed the Triplice Pact in Vienna. German divisions at once occupied his country. Moscow complained to Sofia and plaintively to the Wilhelmstrasse that Bulgaria was within the Soviet "security zone."

Hitler had already (December 18, 1940) issued secret directives to the *Wehrmacht* that it "must be prepared to crush Soviet Russia in a quick campaign," with preparations to be completed by May 15, 1941, for the annihilation of Soviet forces in "daring operations" and the establishment of "a defense line against Asiatic Russia running from the Volga to Archangel." Rumania and Finland would participate. "It may be expected that Swedish railroads and highways will be available for the concentration" of invasion forces in the north. The Nazi timetable was delayed by events in the Balkans. Berlin pressed Belgrade in February to sign the Triplice Pact. Moscow, London, and Washington, for the first time acting in unison, encouraged the Jugoslavs to resist. On March 21, however, the Belgrade Cabinet yielded to an ultimatum and signed the Pact in Vienna the next day. But on March 27 Gen. Dusan Simovich arrested the Ministers and Prince Regent Paul and formed an anti-Axis Cabinet under young King Peter. Moscow at once gave all possible support short of a promise of defense. On April 5 Molotov and Minister Gavrilovich, in Stalin's presence, signed a five-year Soviet-Jugoslav non-aggression pact, pledging mutual respect for the independence, sovereignty, and integrity of the parties and "friendly relations" should either be attacked by a third Power.

The Nazi reply was swift and crushing. *Wehrmacht* units were already poised in Austria, Rumania, and Bulgaria. Hungary—whose Premier, Paul Teleki, had committed suicide on April 3—was forced

to join in what was about to be done. On April 6, 1941, the *Luft-waffe* blasted Belgrade while armored columns breached the fron-tiers, reached the Ægean through Thrace, took the ruined capital on the 13th, and compelled the shattered remnant of the Serb army to capitulate on the 17th. Athens fell to the invaders ten days later. Parachute troops took Crete. Jugoslavia and Greece were conquered in three weeks.

The men in the Kremlin now began to fear the worst. Trapped in a pattern of Nazi-Soviet "friendship" of their own devising, they had recourse to futile diplomatic gestures. The Narkomindel (April 12) reproved Budapest for participation in the assault on Jugo-slavia. In Ankara, Ambassador Sergei Vinogradov joined Anthony Eden, Sir Stafford Cripps, and Col. William J. Donovan in efforts to frustrate Franz von Papen's courtship of Turkey. On March 25 the Narkomindel had pledged non-aggression and benevolent neutrality should Turkey be attacked. The Turks, although allied with Britain, refused to aid Greece and Jugoslavia and strove for neutrality be-tween Berlin and Moscow. On June 17, 1941, Ankara signed a neu-trality and non-aggression pact with the Reich, thus contracting out of the Anglo-German war already under way and the German-Soviet war about to begin.

Moscow's only victory of the spring was the Japanese-Soviet five-year neutrality pact of April 13, concluded with Molotov by Foreign Minister Yosuke Matsuoka, following his conferences in March with Hitler and Mussolini. An attached declaration pledged reciprocal respect for the frontiers of Manchukuo and Outer Mon-golia. Three years later Moscow revealed that Matsuoka was so eager to avoid involvement in the new war that he had agreed, as part of the bargain, to the surrender of Nipponese concessions in Northern Sakhalin. The warlords of Tokyo, while contemplating par-ticipation in the eventual conquest of the USSR, were convinced that the defeat of Britain and America must precede the enterprise. Hence the urgent need of "peace" with Moscow until London and Washington should be beaten down. In the sequel, when Hitler nevertheless assaulted Russia, Matsuoka vacillated, reconsidered the wisdom of a Japanese invasion of Siberia, was overruled, and then resigned. "Now that I am a free man," he commented, "I shall de-vote myself to reading." The Kremlin had won peace in the Far East.

In all else Soviet policy-makers in the menacing spring of 1941

conducted themselves like men in a dream, unable to comprehend that their Nazi friends, toward whom their conduct was consistently "correct" and even cordial, had already resolved upon their doom. From January onward, ample warnings of the Nazi decision had come from Sumner Welles, Winston Churchill, Soviet intelligence reports, and other sources. Stalin and Molotov, unable to grasp their import because unwilling to face the inevitable, were inflexibly committed to peace with Hitler and to avoidance of any "provocation," including adequate military preparations for defense. Appeasement to the end was deemed imperative.

On May 6, 1941, the Presidium of the Supreme Soviet decreed Molotov's retirement as Premier, Stalin's appointment to the post, and the designation of Molotov, still Foreign Minister, as Vice-Premier. The Narkomindel protested against scores of violations of Soviet frontiers by German planes, but denied all rumors of German "demands" on Moscow, while Hitler secretly assembled 170 divisions in the East. There were no demands. *Der Führer's* goal was not negotiation, but annihilation. On May 10 Nazi No. 2, Rudolf Hess, flew to Scotland, where he was interned; with him he carried a German "peace" offer: Berlin would "guarantee" the British Empire if London would acquiesce in the contemplated partition of Russia. A week later the Narkomindel barred foreign travel in the border zones, but continued "business as usual" in commercial relations with the Axis and, by way of recognizing the Nazi "New Order," denied diplomatic status to the envoys of the Governments-in-Exile of Norway, Belgium, Jugoslavia, and Greece. The Soviet press denied all reports of friction with Berlin. Foreign journalists (e.g., John Scott) who interpreted Soviet policies as "anti-German" were expelled. A Tass release of June 13 flatly denied all rumors of German-Soviet tension and reiterated Soviet adherence to the non-aggression pact. Solomon Lozovsky, Vice-Commissar of Foreign Affairs, lamely explained on June 28 that this statement was designed "to elicit from Germany her precise attitude." Since the Nazi press ignored it, the necessary conclusions were, allegedly, drawn by the Soviet policy-makers.

No conclusions were drawn. On June 21 Ribbentrop instructed Ambassador Schulenberg (who, along with most professional German diplomats, knew nothing of the mad resolves of the Nazi elite) to inform Molotov that the USSR had adopted an anti-German policy, had violated its treaties, and was "about to attack Germany

from the rear," and that "the *Führer* has therefore ordered the German Armed Forces to oppose this threat with all the means at their disposal." On the same day Vladimir G. Dekanosov, Soviet Ambassador in Berlin, delivered another protest at German aerial violations of the Soviet borders. Later in the evening Molotov summoned Schulenberg to ask, pathetically, in what respects Germany was dissatisfied with Soviet conduct. Schulenberg replied, honestly, that he did not know. At 4 a.m., June 22, Ribbentrop received Dekanosov —who had requested an interview to "pose a few questions requiring clarification"—and handed him a memorandum alleging Soviet "hostility," culminating in the Soviet-Jugoslav neutrality pact, the failure of efforts at understanding, and the regrettable necessity of military counter-measures.

At the same hour (precisely 129 years, short of a day, since Napoleon had crossed the Niemen at the head of the Grand Army) the massed might of the *Wehrmacht* and the *Luftwaffe* embarked upon the destruction of the Soviet Union.

CHAPTER NINE

The Second War of East and West

1. INVASION

D URING THE morning of June 22, 1941, Molotov broadcast an address to the people of the USSR:

Today at 4 a.m., without any claims having been presented to the Soviet Union, without a declaration of war, German troops attacked our country, attacked our borders at many points and bombed from their airplanes our cities, Zhitomir, Kiev, Sevastopol, Kaunas and some others, killing and wounding over 200 persons. There were also enemy air raids and artillery shelling from Rumania and Finnish territory.

This unheard of attack upon our country is perfidy unparalleled in the history of civilized nations. The attack on our country was perpetrated despite the fact that a treaty of non-aggression had been signed between the USSR and Germany and that the Soviet Government most faithfully abided by all provisions of this treaty. The attack upon our country was perpetrated despite the fact that during the entire period of operation of this treaty the German Government could not find grounds for a single complaint against the USSR as regards observance of this treaty. Entire responsibility for this predatory attack upon the Soviet Union falls fully and completely upon the German Fascist rulers. . . .

This war has been forced upon us not by the German

people, not by German workers, peasants, and intellectuals, whose suffering we well understand, but by the clique of bloodthirsty Fascist rulers of Germany who have enslaved Frenchmen, Czechs, Poles, Serbians, Norway, Belgium, Denmark, Holland, Greece and other nations. . . .

This is not the first time that our people have had to deal with an attack of an arrogant foe. At the time of Napoleon's invasion of Russia our people's reply was War for the Fatherland, and Napoleon suffered defeat and met his doom. It will be the same with Hitler, who in his arrogance has proclaimed a new crusade against our country. The Red Army and our whole people will again wage victorious War for the Fatherland, for our country, for honor, for liberty. . . .

The boast was to be fulfilled, but only after four years of unprecedented slaughter and devastation in which the USSR suffered heavier losses than the costs and casualties of all other belligerents of World War II combined. In a report to the Reparations Commission in September 1945, Soviet statisticians estimated that their country had sustained property damages totaling 679,000,000,000 rubles, including the wrecking of 1,700 towns, 70,000 villages, 6,000,-000 buildings, 84,000 schools, 43,000 libraries, 31,000 factories, 13,-000 bridges, 40,000 miles of railway track, etc., in addition to the loss of 7,000,000 horses, 17,000,000 cattle, 20,000,000 pigs, and 27,000,000 sheep and goats.

As for human losses no official figures were released, apart from the mythological claims of both sides during hostilities, until Stalin, in bitter comment on Churchill's speech of March 5, 1946, indicated that the USSR had lost 7,000,000 war dead. This figure must be regarded as a vague approximation of the appalling total of fatal casualties in battle. Other items on the ledgers of death must be added: Nazi extermination of most of the 4,000,000 Russian war prisoners who fell into German hands; the liquidation or starvation of millions of civilians in occupied territories; and the rise of mortality rates and the decline of birth rates in the population at large during the war years. It is probable that 25,000,000 Soviet citizens lost their lives before their time by violence, malnutrition, and disease, and that 15,000,000 babies who would otherwise have been conceived and born must be added to the roles of the missing.

Since all politics is a pragmatic art and all policies must be weighed in terms of who gets what when and how, the incredible holocaust that decimated the inhabitants of the USSR during these years of blood and fire constitutes a judgment of their political leadership before and during the disaster. Westerners are entitled to no self-righteousness in the matter, since the leadership they followed in the 1930's brought them also to the brink of a total military débâcle. Only the accidents of geography spared Britons and Americans a trauma comparable to that suffered by the Russians. Yet the agony of Muscovy between 1941 and 1945 raises numerous questions, most of which admit of only tentative or speculative answers, regarding the competence of the Communist oligarchs.

In the face of pre-war boasts of martial capacity to defend the frontiers and beat any aggressor on his own soil, the initial defeats of the Soviet armies and the frightful price of ultimate victory were not unrelated to Stalin's paranoid purging of the officers' corps in the late 1930's; to his refusal to heed numerous warnings of the impending assault; to his failure to prepare for it; to his initial incredulity when it came; and to his subsequent insistence on posing as a "military genius," dictating the strategy of operations, often with ghastly results, and seeking to claim personal credit for all successes (cf. Khrushchev's indictment of February 24–5, 1956). Stalin's rule by terror, moreover, had produced such widespread fear, despair, and disaffection as to promote extensive desertions to the enemy and cause many civilians to hail the invaders as "liberators." Only the sadistic madness of the Nazis, insanely bent upon the enslavement or butchery of all *Untermenschen,* among whom Slavs rated scarcely higher than Jews, convinced the steppe-dwellers that, in a choice of evils, Stalinism was preferable to Hitlerism.

Much too late, Hitler, Rosenberg, and Göbbels sought to make military and political capital out of potential assets they had hitherto wasted. Captured Lieut. Gen. Andrei A. Vlasov was set up, quisling-wise, as leader of a "Russian Army of Liberation," along with a "Ukrainian Liberation Committee," a "Ukrainian Liberation Legion," and sundry anti-Soviet groups in the Baltic States. But the time was March 1943, when Hitler had already lost the war on the Volga after convincing most Russians, including the most reluctant, that they could expect nothing from his henchmen save robbery, torture, and death. Vlasov's troops committed atrocities in Jugoslavia and Southern France. His "movement" in Russia was a total failure.

In August 1946 (when Ataman Gregory Semenov and five of his associates, all captured in Manchuria, suffered a like fate) Vlasov and ten of his aides, taken by American forces in Czechoslovakia and surrendered to the USSR, were hanged for treason.

The central source of Russia's long misery was a fatal miscalculation in foreign policy, comparable to those made earlier in Paris, London, and Washington but with infinitely more hideous consequences for the people of the plains. The false assumption was that peace was possible with the demented Germans of the Third Reich and that, if not, they would direct their aggressions against others. If successful, they would be satiated. If unsuccessful, they would be checkmated. So Moscow hoped and believed. But, like the Assyrians of old, the Macedonians and Romans of a later time, the Mongols of the 13th Century, and the French who followed Bonaparte, the Nazis had devised an invincible war machine which their compulsions drove them to use to "conquer the world." The moderation which Romans and Mongols displayed in sufficient measure to ensure the long survival of their empires was missing from the Nazi mentality. Militarism pursued as an end *per se*, as Arnold J. Toynbee has shown, is self-destructive and may well be deemed a prime source of the downfall of nations and of civilizations. The Nazi cult of violence doomed the Nazi leaders, in the end, to death. But in the interim they conquered Europe and almost conquered Russia, thanks to their proficiency in the use of force.

The USSR was assaulted in 1941 not only by the Reich but by all its allies and satellites. Italy, Slovakia, and Rumania declared war on June 22, Finland on the 25th, and Hungary on the 27th. Pétain's France, Franco's Spain, and most of the satrapies of Hitler contributed troops to the great crusade. Russia, with fewer than 200,000,000 people and an annual steel production of 18,000,000 tons, was attacked by a Fascist coalition with 240,000,000 inhabitants and a combined steel production of almost 50,000,000 tons, with 68,000,000 other subjugated Europeans forced to supply food, manufactures, and labor power to Germany. Berlin possessed at the outset a 3:2 advantage over the Red Army in manpower and a 5:2 superiority in machines of battle. Western military experts, with the exception of the late Max Werner and Col. Philip Faymonville (U.S. Military Attaché in Moscow, 1934–9), gave the USSR no chance of escaping total defeat within six weeks (General Marshall) or, at most, three months (the British General Staff). Under these circumstances,

coupled with Anglo-American inability to supply the USSR with substantial aid until 1943 or to open a "second front" until 1944, the survival of the Soviet Union, despite the help of time and space and mud and frost, was a miracle of heroism, mass sacrifice, and administrative and military competence, regardless of Stalin's blunders and crimes.

Whether the fruits of Soviet diplomacy in 1939–41 contributed significantly to survival is a moot point. Almost all the territories annexed as defenses against the Reich were lost within a fortnight. Yet it is probable that had the *Wehrmacht* been able to launch its assault 200 miles farther eastward, or two weeks earlier, Moscow would have fallen to the invaders. Hitler in Moscow in 1941, however, might have been no more able to win his war than Napoleon in Moscow in 1812. Farther speculation on this theme is pointless. At frightful cost in lives and treasure, Russia was to endure, survive, and emerge, bled white and ruined in victory, as the second greatest Power of the world.

The military history of the most gigantic and destructive war of all time cannot here be essayed.[1] Soviet politics and diplomacy are here our main concern. For a few sickening hours in the Sabbath dawn of June 22, 1941, Stalin and his colleagues, thanks to their sus-

---

[1] Although monographs, articles, contemporary reports, reminiscences, and novels about the "Great Patriotic War" are innumerable, I have been unable to discover, perhaps for lack of diligence in the search, any comprehensive, analytical, and adequate one-volume treatment of the strategy and tactics of the conflict in Russian, English, German, or any other language. Some light is shed on the matters here in hand, however, in Gen. Wladyslaw Anders: *Hitler's Defeat in Russia* (Regnery, 1953); John A. Armstrong: *Ukrainian Nationalism, 1939–1945* (Columbia University Press, 1955); Harold J. Berman and Miroslav Kerner: *Soviet Military Law and Administration* (Harvard University Press, 1955); John R. Deane: *The Strange Alliance* (Viking, 1947); Maurice Dobb: *Soviet Planning and Labor in Peace and War* (Routledge, 1942); Heinrich von Einsiedel: *I Joined the Russians* (Yale University Press, 1953); Raymond L. Garthoff: *Soviet Military Doctrine* (Free Press, 1953); Ihor Kamenetsky: *Hitler's Occupation of Ukraine* (Marquette University Press, 1957); George Lenczowski: *Russia and the West in Iran, 1918–1948* (Cornell University Press, 1950); William Hardy McNeill: *America, Britain, and Russia: Their Cooperation and Conflict, 1941–1946* (Oxford University Press, 1954); John Stuart Martin: *A Picture History of Russia* (Crown, 1945; 2nd ed., 1956); Albert Parry: *Russian Cavalcade: A Military Record* (Ives Washburn, 1944); George von Rauch: *A History of Bolshevist Russia*, translated by Peter Jacobsohn (Praeger, 1956); Samuel L. Sharp: *Poland: White Eagle on a Red Field* (Harvard University Press, 1953); N. A. Voznesensky: *The Economy of the USSR During World War II* (Public Affairs Press, 1948); and Alexander Werth: *The Year of Stalingrad* (Knopf, 1947).

picions and their dogmas, must have feared the worst: Anglo-American desertion and a hopeless prospect of fighting the Reich alone, with Japan attacking Siberia. This nightmare was soon dispelled. A Cabinet crisis in Tokyo resulted in Matsuoka's resignation and Nipponese dedication to "neutrality" in preparation for the assault to come on Britain, The Netherlands, and America in Southeast Asia and the Pacific. On Sunday evening Winston Churchill went to the microphone to broadcast one of his most moving addresses:

> At 4 o'clock this morning Hitler attacked and invaded Russia. All his usual formalities of perfidy were observed with scrupulous technique. . . .
>
> All this was no surprise to me. In fact I gave clear and precise warnings to Stalin of what was coming. I gave him warnings as I have given warnings to others before. I can only hope that these warnings did not fall unheeded. . . .
>
> Hitler is a monster of wickedness, insatiable in his lust for blood and plunder. Not content with having all Europe under his heel or else terrorized into various forms of abject submission, he must now carry his work of butchery and desolation among the vast multitudes of Russia and of Asia. The terrible military machine which we and the rest of the civilized world so foolishly, so supinely, so insensately allowed the Nazi gangsters to build up year by year from almost nothing; this machine cannot stand idle, lest it rust or fall to pieces. It must be in continual motion, grinding up human lives. . . .
>
> So now this bloodthirsty guttersnipe must launch his mechanized armies upon new fields of slaughter, pillage and devastation. Poor as are the Russian peasants, workmen and soldiers, he must steal from them their daily bread. . . .
>
> The Nazi regime is indistinguishable from the worst features of communism. . . .
>
> No one has been a more consistent opponent of communism than I have for the last twenty-five years. I will unsay no words that I've spoken about it. But all this fades away before the spectacle which is now unfolding. . . .
>
> We have but one aim and one single irrevocable pur-

pose. We are resolved to destroy Hitler and every vestige of the Nazi regime. From this nothing will turn us. Nothing. We will never parley; we will never negotiate with Hitler or any of his gang. We shall fight him by land; we shall fight him by sea; we shall fight him in the air, until, with God's help we have rid the earth of his shadow and liberated its people from his yoke.

Any man or State who fights against nazism will have our aid. Any man or State who marches with Hitler is our foe. . . . That is our policy and that is our declaration.

It follows, therefore, that we shall give whatever help we can to Russia and to the Russian people. We shall appeal to all our friends and Allies in every part of the world to take the same course and pursue it as we shall, faithfully and steadfastly to the end.

We have offered to the Government of Soviet Russia any technical or economic assistance which is in our power and which is likely to be of service to them. We shall bomb Germany by day as well as by night in ever-increasing measure, casting upon them month by month a heavier discharge of bombs and making the German people taste and gulp each month a sharper dose of the miseries they have showered upon mankind. . . .

The Russian danger is therefore our danger and the danger of the United States just as the cause of any Russian fighting for his hearth and home is the cause of free men and free peoples in every quarter of the globe.

Let us learn the lessons already taught by such cruel experience. Let us redouble our exertions and strike with united strength while life and power remain.

In Washington, after conferences with Roosevelt, who had exchanged views with Churchill and Halifax, Sumner Welles told the press on Monday that the events of the week end were further proof of Hitler's "hostile and murderous intent" in his quest for "world domination." "In the opinion of this Government, any defense against Hitlerism, any rallying of the forces opposing Hitlerism, from whatever source these forces may spring, will hasten the eventual downfall of the present German leaders, and will therefore redound to the benefit of our own defense and security."

Other Americans had other views and were free to give them voice. Senator Robert A. Taft: "A Victory for Communism would be far more dangerous to the United States than a victory for Fascism." Senator Burton K. Wheeler: "Just let Joe Stalin and the other dictators fight it out." Herbert Hoover: "Collaboration between Britain and Russia makes the whole argument of joining the war to bring the Four Freedoms a gargantuan jest." Charles A. Lindbergh: "I would a hundred times rather see my country ally herself . . . with Germany with all her faults than with the cruelty, the godlessness, and the barbarism that exists in Soviet Russia." George E. Sokolsky: "Soviet Russia has bluffed the world for a quarter of a century, and the bluff has been called. Soviet Russia will soon be eliminated." Martin Dies: "Hitler will be in control of Russia within thirty days." Senator Harry S. Truman: "If we see that Germany is winning we ought to help Russia and if Russia is winning we ought to help Germany and in that way let them kill as many as possible . . ." (*NYT*, June 24, 1941).

What was of paramount importance to the frightened men in the Kremlin, faced with a national catastrophe worse than the Mongol conquest, was that Churchill and Roosevelt pledged themselves to Anglo-American aid to the USSR. A preliminary alliance was signed by Sir Stafford Cripps and Molotov on July 12, 1941, in the form of an accord for mutual aid against Hitlerite Germany. On August 2, following numerous transatlantic consultations and Harry Hopkins's first visit to Moscow, Welles and Oumansky exchanged letters whereby the USA agreed to grant "unlimited licenses" for export to the USSR, priorities identical with Britain, and "all economic assistance practicable for the purpose of strengthening the Soviet Union in its struggle against armed aggression." A fortnight later Churchill and Roosevelt, in the first of their many meetings, concocted on shipboard off the coast of Newfoundland the "Atlantic Charter" of August 14, to which the USSR subscribed in a statement of September 24, emphasizing the sanctity of "self-determination of nations." Another fortnight found Harriman and Beaverbrook in Moscow. Following an initial British credit of £10,-000,000, Roosevelt by October 30 had promised $1,000,000,000 in lend-lease aid to the Soviet Union. On August 25 British and Soviet troops jointly began the occupation of Iran to keep open a vital supply route. Anglo-American-Soviet solidarity at long last seemed assured.

On July 1, 1941, by joint action of the Presidium, the Party Central Committee, and the Sovnarkom, a "State Committee on Defense" was created with Stalin as Chairman, Molotov as Vice-Chairman, and Voroshilov, Beria, and Malenkov as members. All authority was concentrated in this War Cabinet. Stalin assumed control of the Commissariat of Defense, while Marshals Voroshilov and Timoshenko took command, respectively, of the northern and central fronts. On July 2 the Commissariats of Internal Affairs and National Security, recently separated, were again merged into the United NKVD under Beria. On July 3 Stalin addressed the country—to explain military reverses, to promise ultimate triumph, to justify the pact that the foe had broken, and to appeal for guerrilla warfare and "scorched earth" in defiance of the invader:

> A grave danger hangs over our country. How could it have happened that our glorious Red Army surrendered a number of our cities and districts to the Fascist armies? . . . History shows that there are no invincible armies, and never have been. Napoleon's army was considered invincible, but it was beaten. . . . The fact of the matter is that troops of Germany, as a country at war, were already fully mobilized, and 170 divisions hurled by Germany against the USSR and brought up to the Soviet frontiers were in a state of complete readiness, only awaiting the signal to move into action, whereas Soviet troops had little time to effect mobilization and move up to the frontiers. Of no little importance in this respect is the fact that Fascist Germany suddenly and treacherously violated the non-aggression pact she concluded in 1939 with the USSR, disregarding the fact that she would be regarded as an aggressor by the whole world. Naturally, our peace-loving country, not wishing to take the initiative of breaking the pact, could not resort to perfidy.
>
> It may be asked: How could the Soviet Government have consented to conclude a non-aggression pact with such treacherous fiends as Hitler and Ribbentrop? Was not this an error on the part of the Soviet Government? Of course not! . . . I think that not a single peace-loving State could decline a peace treaty with a neighboring State even though the latter was headed by such fiends and canni-

bals as Hitler and Ribbentrop. . . . We secured for our
country peace for a year and a half and the opportunity of
preparing its forces to repulse Fascist Germany should she
risk an attack on our country despite the pact. . . .

The enemy is cruel and implacable. He is out to seize
our lands watered with our sweat, to seize our grain and
soil secured by our labor. He is out to restore the rule of
landlords, to restore Tsarism, to destroy national culture. . . . Thus the issue is one of life or death for the
Soviet State, for the peoples of the USSR: the issue is
whether the peoples of the Soviet Union shall remain free
or fall into slavery. The Soviet people must realize this and
abandon all heedlessness, they must mobilize themselves
and reorganize all their work on new, wartime lines, when
there can be no mercy to the enemy. . . .

In this war of liberation we shall not be alone. In this
great war we shall have loyal allies in the peoples of Europe and America, including German people who are enslaved by Hitlerite despots. . . . The State Committee of
Defense has entered into its functions and calls upon all our
people to rally around the Party of Lenin-Stalin and around
the Soviet Government so as self-denyingly to support the
Red Army and Navy, demolish the enemy and secure
victory.

All our forces for the support of our heroic Red Army
and our glorious Red Navy! All the forces of the people—
for the demolition of the enemy! Forward, to our victory! [2]

These words of the *Vozhd* were to prove, in the short run,
empty, as were the solemn pledges of collaboration among London,
Washington, and Moscow. Britain, in the end, was to extend substantial and invaluable help. America, in the end, was to grant, out
of a total by V-E Day of $39,000,000,000 to all the "United Nations,"
almost $11,000,000,000 of lend-lease aid to the USSR, including
6,800 tanks, 13,300 planes, 406,000 motor vehicles, 1,000 locomotives,
2,000,000 tons of steel, 150,000,000 yards of cloth, 11,000,000 pairs

---

[2] Text in *Soviet War Documents, June, 1941–November, 1943* (Soviet
Embassy, Washington, D.C.). This publication includes other addresses, statements, and Orders of the Day by Stalin, Molotov, and the Extraordinary State
Committee on Nazi Atrocities. Cf. Joseph Stalin: *The Great Patriotic War of
the Soviet Union* (International, 1945).

of shoes, etc. But in 1941 no significant Anglo-American aid was available, nor did supplies from the West amount to more than a trickle during 1942 and much of 1943. Soviet Muscovy was obliged to defend itself out of its own resources during the first two years of the deadly combat that raged across the steppes. Anglo-American support of the USSR, both material and strategic, was too little and too late to play any decisive role in the desperate defense of the Soviet Union against the invaders, although this was its primary purpose. But, by the politics of paradox so characteristic of the 20th Century, it became a major factor in the counter-attack and in the later subjugation of all of Eastern and much of Central Europe by Soviet armies—which was no part of the purposes of the Atlantic Powers. Why and how this came to pass will be considered in proper place below.

2. ORDEAL BY FIRE

THE first five months of war in the dark summer and black autumn of 1941 were a time of unrelieved disaster for the USSR. On every segment of the 2,000-mile battle front, Soviet troops were infiltrated, outflanked, annihilated, or forced to surrender in droves by the invincible Juggernaut that had vanquished in weeks or days every other army on the Continent. In the north, Mannerheim's Finns and Falkenhorst's Nazis encircled Leningrad, save for a tenuous supply route across Lake Lagoda, and long besieged the City of Peter, although never quite able to take it. Half a million of its people were to die of hunger. In the south, Antonescu's Rumanian troops, supported by Rundstedt's armies, invaded the Ukraine and aimed at Rostov-Don. In the center, the *Blitzkriegers* commanded by Leeb and Bock drove ever eastward toward Moscow. Timoshenko's soldiers lost Smolensk on July 17 and checked the invaders only briefly near the headwaters of the Dnieper during September. In October, Budenny's forces were driven from Odessa, Kiev, and Kharkov.

The main bulk of the *Wehrmacht* meanwhile drove so far toward the Soviet capital and inflicted such astronomic losses on the defenders that Hitler proudly proclaimed victory on October 3 and fatuously ordered a "cut-back" of German war production. In mid-October the tank columns commanded by Bock and Guderian were

temporarily halted. On October 20 all foreign diplomats and correspondents and many Commissariats were evacuated to Kuibyshev (Samara). Stalin remained in the Kremlin—whether because of courage or (as Khrushchev alleged 15 years later) because of a despairing belief that all was lost is unclear. On November 6 he addressed the Moscow Soviet, piously disclaiming, with moderation bred of desperation, all annexationist ambitions and preaching: "Death to the German invaders!" Ten days later the foe opened his final offensive to pierce the heart of Muscovy.

Georgi Konstantinovich Zhukov was entrusted with command of the apparently hopeless defense. This son of peasants, born in 1895 some 50 miles southwest of Moscow, was early apprenticed to a furrier and was doubtless familiar as a boy with the military traditions of his native village of Strelkova and the nearby town of Maloyaroslavets, whence Kutusov in 1812 had launched the counterattack that helped to turn the retreat of Napoleon's Grand Army into a rout. Zhukov was drafted into the Novgorod Dragoons in 1915 and served as a private in World War I. He joined the Red Army in 1918 and the Communist Party in 1919. In the course of his military career, he brought Soviet tanks to Madrid in 1936 and commanded the forces that crushed the Japanese at Nomonhan in 1939.

In the bitter battles of 1941 he was a close colleague of Bulganin, Konev, and Khrushchev, and of Timoshenko, his predecessor in command of the central front. He was later to be called *Spasitel* ("Savior") of Moscow. He had become Chief of Staff in February 1941. His earlier and later honors included close association in 1945 and thereafter with Eisenhower, who found him a reasonable man; the St. George's Cross, won in the Tsarist army; the rank of General, one of three to be granted the title upon its restoration in the Red Army in 1940; the Marshal's Star; Order of Suvorov; Order of Lenin; Hero of the Soviet Union; Stalingrad Medal; Order of Victory; and demotion by Stalin after 1945 to a garrison post in Odessa.

This man was entrusted by Stalin and Chief of Staff Shaposhnikov with the defense of Moscow in the grim autumn of 1941. His troops held fast, even when enemy detachments came within 13 miles of the capital. Zhukov ordered a counter-attack on November 27. What followed was the first defeat of the *Wehrmacht* in World War II. Rostov-Don was retaken on November 28. A general offensive in Central Russia in December drove the invaders back week

after week in killing cold. *Der Führer*, fearing a repetition of Bonaparte's disaster, ordered all lines held at all costs, even though his troops, expecting imminent victory, had no winter equipment and died by scores of thousands from frost, hunger, and enemy fire. By March of 1942 Zhukov had regained a fifth of the vast regions lost to the foe and had driven the Nazi divisions, despite their tenacious "hedgehog" defenses, 100 miles from Moscow. Douglas MacArthur's description of this victory (February 23, 1942) as "the greatest military achievement in all history" was a rhetorical exaggeration. Yet the battle, in retrospect, was "decisive" throughout Nazi-held Europe and inspired thousands of patriots, hitherto hopeless, to risk their lives in guerrilla warfare against their conquerors. But Russia's torment, far from ended, had only begun.

Things to come were a consequence of Anglo-American inability, for months and years, to extend any appreciable help to the USSR in its fight for life, in the form of either material aid or effective military operations against Nazi *Festung Europa*. In the long perspective of power politics, this impotence, like Russia's agony, was the result of the folly of West and East alike in permitting Hitler to conquer the Continent between 1938 and 1940. In the short run, it was the consequence of the decision of the warlords of Japan in November 1941. The complex miscalculations of policy-makers in Tokyo, Berlin, and Rome, which led them to open war on the USA in the face of Nazi defeat before Moscow, cannot here be analyzed. On November 26 Hull informed Nomura and Kurusu in Washington that the USA would lift its trade embargoes against Japan only if Tokyo would quit China and Indochina, a condition that Washington knew Nippon could not possibly accept. A Japanese naval task force left Etorofu Island in the Kuriles on November 27 on a secret mission. On December 3 Ambassador Toshio Shiratori told Mussolini that his Government had decided to attack America and expected Italy and Germany to declare war.[3] In the sequel, American "intelligence" and statesmanship proved no better than those of the USSR at their worst. The task force was never spotted. Japanese strategy was never suspected.

On December 7, 1941, Japanese bombers destroyed or put out of action five of the eight battleships of the U.S. Pacific Fleet anchored in Pearl Harbor. Other bombers sank the *Prince of Wales* and the

---

[3] Cf. *The Diary of Count Ciano*, December 3, 1941.

Repulse off Malaya. Japan declared war on America, Britain, and The Netherlands. Germany and Italy declared war on the USA on December 11. Tokyo's *Blitzkriegers* swiftly conquered Hong Kong, Malaya and Singapore, the Philippines, Guam, and Indonesia. The war was now "global" even though Japan and the USSR, Finland and America, and Bulgaria and the USSR remained "at peace." On December 11, 1941, a new Triplice Pact pledged combat to the death against America, Britain, and Russia. Hitler promised the conquest of the Soviet Union in 1942. Litvinov, now Soviet Ambassador to the USA, reached San Francisco a day before the Pearl Harbor débâcle and was received by Roosevelt in Washington on December 8. "We are all in the same boat now," he commented, "and will either perish together or together triumph over the greatest evil of our time." Eden, Cripps, and Maisky conferred with Stalin and Molotov in Moscow. Churchill came to America. On January 1, 1942, a "Declaration by United Nations," pledging military and economic cooperation and no separate peace or armistice, was signed in Washington by Roosevelt, Churchill, Litvinov, T. V. Soong, and 22 other envoys, many of them representing Governments-in-Exile. The Grand Alliance, which embraced 50 States by 1945, was at last a reality.

But Russia for long gained little from the coalition, not for lack of Anglo-American wit or will but for lack of power to do anything beyond staving off defeat. Admiral William H. Standley succeeded Steinhardt as U.S. Ambassador on February 9, 1942. Litvinov in Washington and Maisky in London pleaded for a "second front" in 1942. Molotov and Arkady Sobolev flew to London on May 20, then to Washington and back to London, and then home. On June 11 the results of their journey were made known: an Anglo-Soviet twenty-year alliance against German aggression, signed May 26, 1942; a new American-Soviet lend-lease agreement; and "a full understanding with regard to the urgent tasks of creating a second front in Europe in 1942." The "understanding" was a fiction designed to reassure Russians and alarm Germans. All that the Western Allies could do in 1942 was to launch an invasion of North Africa in November which, said London and Washington, "will divert German strength from the attack on Russia." The facts were otherwise. In August, Churchill, Brooke, Wavell, and Tedder flew to Moscow via Cairo and Teheran to assure Soviet leaders that they were doing their best.

The discussions in the Kremlin were acrimonious, thanks to the

conviction of Stalin and his colleagues that the Western Powers were eager to see Russia "bled white" before they assumed their share of the burden of defeating the foe. Said Churchill to Commons:

> The Russians do not think we or the Americans have done enough to take the weight off them. . . . It is difficult to make the Russians comprehend all the problems of the sea and of the ocean. We are sea animals and the United States are to a large extent ocean animals. The Russians are land animals. Happily, we are all three air animals. . . . But I am sure that we made their leaders feel confidence in our loyal and sincere resolve to come to her aid as quickly as possible. . . . [I found Stalin] a man of massive outstanding personality, suited to the somber and stormy times in which his life has been cast; a man of inexhaustible courage and willpower and a man direct and even blunt in speech. . . . Stalin also left upon me the impression of a deep, cool wisdom and a complete absence of illusions of any kind. I believe I made him feel that we were good and faithful comrades in this war—but that, after all, is a matter which deeds not words will prove.[4]

The Dieppe raid of August 19–20, 1942, with heavy casualties and failure, seemed calculated to demonstrate to Moscow that the Atlantic Powers could not yet invade the Continent. Wendell Willkie, while visiting the USSR, opined that "we can best help Russia by establishing a real second front in Europe with Great Britain at the earliest possible moment our military leaders will approve, and perhaps some of them need some public prodding. Next summer might be too late." Henry C. Cassidy of the AP was told by Stalin via letter on October 3 that "as compared with the aid which the Soviet is giving to the Allies by drawing upon itself the main force of the German-Fascist armies, the aid of the Allies to the Soviet Union has so far been little effective. In order to amplify and improve this aid, only one thing is required: the full and prompt fulfillment by the Allies of their obligations."[5]

---

[4] September 1942. Cf. W. P. and Zelda K. Coates: *A History of Anglo-Soviet Relations* (Lawrence and Wishart, 1943), pp. 726 f.

[5] Cf. Henry C. Cassidy: *Moscow Dateline* (Houghton Mifflin, 1943), pp. 269–83.

On November 6, twenty-fifth anniversary of the October Revolution, Stalin declared that the enemy had 240 divisions on the Russian front and only 4 German and 11 Italian divisions in Libya and Egypt because of the lack of a second front in Europe. On the same day Eisenhower's forces landed in Morocco and Algeria and opened the campaign that was to drive Axis armies from North Africa. There ensued in the summer of 1943 the invasion of Italy which led to the fall of Mussolini in July. These operations, while decisive for the final outcome of World War II, nevertheless deflected few *Wehrmacht* divisions from the East. In 1942–3, as in 1941, the USSR fought alone against a formidable foe.

In the second year of its trial, the Soviet Union once more faced total defeat and survived by the narrowest of margins. Hitler's campaign plan envisaged the conquest of the Caucasus, including the major Soviet oil fields, and an offensive to the Volga at Stalingrad to be followed, *à la* Ogdai Khan, by an advance northward and eastward along the river to outflank Moscow and encircle and annihilate the Muscovites. Timoshenko's troops delayed the invaders east of Kharkov in May and June, as did the defenders of Sebastopol in the Crimea, which the Nazis were unable to take until July 3 after 250 days of siege. The *Wehrmacht* meanwhile pushed eastward, retaking Rostov-Don in July, occupying the Maikop oil fields and reaching the Caucasus in early August, and driving simultaneously southward and eastward toward Transcaucasia and the Volga valley. On August 23, 1942, 80 Nazi tanks, followed by motorized infantry, broke through Soviet defenses and reached the Stalingrad tractor factory, while hundreds of bombers rained death on the far-flung city, stretched for 70 kilometers in a narrow band along the river.

The high tide of Triplice victory was reached near Midway Island in the Central Pacific, at El Alamein in Western Egypt, and at Stalingrad on Europe's longest and easternmost waterway. At Midway in early June 1942, U.S. task forces under Admirals Fletcher and Spruance inflicted a major defeat on the Japanese Navy in the first sea battle fought by carrier-based aircraft. At El Alamein in late October, Montgomery's Eighth Army vanquished Rommel's tankmen and began the long advance through the sands of the *Maghreb* to join Eisenhower's forces. At Stalingrad was fought the longest, bloodiest, most destructive, and most decisive battle of the most stupendous contest by arms in all the tragic annals of human violence.

Gen. Friedrich von Paulus's Sixth Army of 330,000 men in 22 divisions, amply equipped with tanks, guns, and planes, sought to destroy or compel the withdrawal of Gen. V. I. Chuikov's 62nd Army —which was supplied only by boat across the unbridged mile-wide river. By all past precedents, the outcome was obvious. By a miracle of courage, the soldiers and factory workers of Red Muscovy, aided by the women and even children of Stalingrad, turned every street, every block, every house of the city into a fortress. Month after month the ferocious struggle surged and swayed amid the ruin and rubble as the invaders strove to cut the metropolis into segments and drive to the water front. Much of the city was taken. At September's end Hitler proclaimed: "We have taken Stalingrad. . . . Nobody will remove us from this spot." But the defenders clung to Mamaiev Hill and to a narrow belt of wreckage wherein they spat defiance and death at the foe from every shattered building and crumbling ruin. Maj. Gen. Alexei Rodimtsev ferried his Guards from the east shore to reinforce Chuikov's forces. The Verdun of World War II was not to fall.

On November 8, proclaimed "Stalingrad Day" by Mayor La-Guardia, 20,000 Americans gathered in Madison Square Garden in a "Congress of American-Soviet Friendship," with Corliss Lamont as Chairman and Joseph E. Davies as Honorary Chairman. Roosevelt and Eisenhower sent greetings. Among many distinguished speakers, including bankers and labor leaders, Governors and Senators, Generals and writers, Vice-President Henry A. Wallace spoke for a new democracy. Maxim Litvinov declared that the words of admiration and support "will go straight to the hearts of the fighters in the Red Army among the ruins of Stalingrad and on other fronts, and will also be deeply felt by all the Soviet people, working as one man for the cause of freedom of humanity, amidst hardships which defy description."

Strategic genius soon came to the aid of incredible valor. Stalin, Shaposhnikov, Zhukov, and Voronov, Marshal of Artillery, made plans that were entrusted to stocky Col. Gen. N. F. Vatutin, broad-faced Col. Gen. A. I. Yeremenko, and tall Col. Gen. Konstantin Rokossovsky. Around the vortex of death on the Volga, a huge trap was set and sprung. On the misty morning of November 19, 1942, while the hell within Stalingrad flamed and thundered without surcease, Rokossovsky's divisions north of the city opened an attack that drove through the German lines to Kalach, near the Don. At the same time

Red tanks south of Stalingrad smashed the enemy lines and reached Kalach. On November 23 the forces met amid rejoicing, and proceeded to forge an unbreakable ring around the German Sixth Army still fighting for the city. Hitler ordered Paulus to hold fast while reinforcements from Rostov were rushed to Kotelnikovo. The Soviet High Command, anticipating precisely such a move, threw in sufficient forces to check Mannstein's advance and then to send his troops reeling back toward Rostov under the blows of the Guards Divisions. Zhukov opened other offensives near Leningrad, in the center, in the south, and along the Don.

The mad *Führer* refused to permit Paulus to withdraw while his troops might still have broken westward out of the ring. Relief by land was impossible. Supply by airlift proved futile. As the ring tightened, Voronov and Rokossovsky on January 8 delivered an ultimatum demanding surrender. Holed up in his HQ in the basement of the ruined Univermag department store near the center of the city, Paulus refused. Soviet troops then proceeded to hammer the Sixth Army to pieces, until the survivors were squeezed into two small pockets of rubble. At the end Hitler made Paulus a Marshal while Göbbels organized Wagnerian heroics and lamentations in the name of "strength through gloom." On February 1, 1943, Paulus capitulated and crawled out of his basement. The 91,000 survivors became prisoners, along with 24 Generals, 2,500 other officers, 750 planes, 1,550 tanks, 6,700 guns, and 61,102 motor vehicles.

Of killing, burning, and blasting there was to be no end for another two years and more. But the nature of the end was now foreordained. Barred from Saratov and the road to Astrakan and Baku, the invaders lost Rostov, the North Caucasus, Kharkov, Kursk, and Velikiye Luki south of Lake Ilmen, all in the first two months of 1943. In a local counter-action in March they retook Kharkov. On July 5 the *Wehrmacht* opened its third summer offensive, seeking to smash the Kursk salient and resume its advance eastward from Orel and Belgorod with 17 tank divisions, 3 motorized divisions, and 18 infantry divisions. In the greatest tank battle of the war Vatutin and Popov checked the enemy, counter-attacked a week later, wrecked or captured 1,000 Nazi guns and 3,000 tanks, retook Belgorod and Orel on August 5, and stormed Kharkov on August 23. In reward for these victories Gen. Ivan S. Konev was granted the Order of Suvorov, First Class, and, on February 20, 1944, the Marshal's Baton.

The shattered *Wehrmacht* was yet to exact an appalling price

before being driven from Soviet soil. But its defeat was henceforth inevitable, thanks in no small measure to what Soviet soldiers found as they advanced westward. Half of Kharkov's buildings were wrecked and all of its 430 factories were rubble. Only a third of its population of a million remained. 100,000 had been taken to the Reich as slaves. Another 100,000 had died of hunger and disease. All of the city's 30,000 Jews had been slaughtered. All the rest were refugees. Of Kiev's 900,000 people, only 65,000 remained, starving and in rags amid the ruins. Orel, Smolensk, and other liberated communities were ghost cities. The worst atrocities of Ghenghis Khan and Tamerlane paled beside the systematic horrors of Hitlerism.

The totality of the Nazi débâcle to come was due less to the misfortunes of war than to political and diplomatic events that ensured the annihilation of the Nazi Empire and made the USSR its residuary legatee in the East. Soviet policy-makers, in a combined warning to the Western Powers, a *riposte* to Nazi efforts at subversive and psychological warfare, and a serious attempt to shatter the monolithic unity of the Reich, established among German prisoners and Communist refugees a "National Committee for Free Germany." At its first session, held in Moscow, July 12–13, 1943, a Committee of 38 was formed with Erich Weinert as President and Major Karl Hetz and Count Heinrich von Einsiedel, a great grandson of Bismarck, as Vice-Presidents. On September 11, 1943, a "Union of German Officers" emerged from the ranks of the Nazi commanders taken at Stalingrad. Under Gen. Walter von Seidlitz, it endorsed the program of the Free German Committee. Paulus joined belatedly early in 1945, though, apart from testifying at the Nuremberg trial of Nazi war criminals in 1946, he played no subsequent public role. In marked contrast to 1918, the program and propaganda were not couched in terms of "proletarian revolution" and the Sovietization of the Reich, but called for democracy, equality, free enterprise, and national dignity *sans* Hitler and the Junkers and industrialists who had put him in power.

This effort failed to evoke any consequential response. The officers and businessmen who organized the plot to kill Hitler on July 20, 1944, in a desperate effort to save Germany from total catastrophe, may in some degree have been influenced by Soviet appeals for reconciliation with a reformed Reich. But the enterprise foundered in a series of accidents. All involved were shot or hanged. All other Germans, to the dismal end, were blindly obedient to the madman

who ruled them, and were thus condemned to complete disaster. Meanwhile, Anglo-American inability to assault Nazi Europe from the west until very late in the course of the Red Army's defeat of the foe laid the foundations of the new "Cold War" between East and West which was to follow hard upon the common victory over Fascism.

3. THE SHAPE OF VICTORY

ALLIES cooperate best when faced with the prospect of common defeat. Allies frequently quarrel once victory appears possible. The coalition of the USSR, the USA, and Britain against the Axis functioned well in 1941 and 1942. When military success loomed on the horizon of 1943, the alliance almost disintegrated. Efforts to preserve it led to a series of ambiguous bargains that were to bedevil East-West relations for years thereafter. Statesmen in London and Washington feared, with reason, a Muscovite effort to Sovietize Europe in the wake of Fascist collapse. Statesmen in Moscow feared, with reason, a Western effort to organize a post-war anti-Soviet Europe designed to cheat the USSR of the fruits of victory and, if possible, to resume the Great Crusade against Communism.

Out of these suspicions, coupled with the vicissitudes of war, diplomacy, and domestic politics, emerged a pattern of apparent solidarity which was soon revealed for what it was: an illusion and a potential nightmare. The Anglo-American invasion of Italy in the summer of 1943 effected the fall of Mussolini (July 25) and the capitulation of the Badoglio regime, but left the invaders stalled well south of Rome by a few German divisions while the bulk of the *Wehrmacht* continued its work of death all across the steppes. Roosevelt and Churchill at Casablanca in mid-January 1943 had publicized their respect for the Soviet war effort and their regret at Stalin's inability to leave the USSR for a conference. "The President and Prime Minister realize up to the full the enormous weight of the war which Russia is successfully bearing along her whole land front, and their prime object has been to draw as much weight as possible off the Russian armies by engaging the enemy as heavily as possible at the best selected points. Premier Stalin has been fully informed of the military proposals. . . ." The Western leaders sought to meet

Muscovite suspicions by pledging themselves to accept only "unconditional surrender" from the enemy.

This formula was widely condemned in later years, with the wisdom of hindsight, on the ground that it subordinated the political
objectives of the war to military victory as an end in itself. At the
time, however, it represented the only assurance of mutual confidence among allies. Ambassador Standley aroused a minor storm by
alleging (March 8, 1943) that the Kremlin was concealing from the
Russian people the scope and magnitude of American aid. On April
25, 1943, in the sequel to Göbbels's revelation of the horror of Katyn,
Molotov severed diplomatic relations with Sikorski's Polish Government-in-Exile, ostensibly because it had followed Berlin in asking
the International Red Cross for "an impartial investigation," but actually because the Polish leaders in London were resolved to restore
the *status quo ante bellum*, including the frontiers of 1921–39. In
May, Roosevelt sent Joseph E. Davies as special envoy on a second
"mission to Moscow," bearing a secret message for Stalin.

On May 22, 1943—whether as a result of Davies's mission or because of other considerations is still unclear—the Executive Committee of the Comintern proposed the dissolution of the "Third International" as obsolete and irrelevant to current tasks. Stalin wrote
to Reuter reporter Harold King on May 28 that this decision was
"proper and timely" and "exposes the lie of the Hitlerites that Moscow intends to intervene in the life of other nations and 'Bolshevize'
them. . . . It facilitates the work of patriots of all countries for uniting all freedom-loving peoples into a single international camp for
the fight against the menace of world domination by Hitlerism, thus
clearing the way to the future organization of a companionship of
nations based upon their equality."

This gesture of inter-allied unity did not change the fact of dis-
unity. Downing Street and the State Department, still unable to
launch a second front, gave the Narkomindel the impression that
they were wooing Pétain in France, Franco in Spain, King Victor
Emanuel and Badoglio in Italy, and comparable "reactionary" elements elsewhere in the hope of reconstituting a new *cordon sanitaire*,
based upon the slogan: "Come weal, come woe, my status is quo."
Eden came to Washington in March 1943 and Churchill in May. In
August, Roosevelt, Churchill, and T. V. Soong conferred in Quebec.
Moscow was "informed" of the decisions, but the information
brought cold comfort. The Kremlin told the world that the USSR

had not been invited to Quebec and that Litvinov would be recalled from Washington and Maisky from London, both to serve as Vice-Commissars of Foreign Affairs.

With the coalition thus falling apart, Under-Secretary of State Sumner Welles, fearing at worst a separate Nazi-Soviet peace and at best unilateral Muscovite policies in Central Europe and the Balkans, sought to "liberalize" the orientation of the Administration and to arrange a tripartite conference of Foreign Ministers. In the latter endeavor he was successful. In the former he failed, since the complex political genius of Franklin Delano Roosevelt consisted, among many other ingredients, in constantly confusing, compromising, and confounding "liberals" and "conservatives" alike and alternately paying lip service to the former (or latter) while pursuing the purposes of the latter (or former).[6]

Such subtlety contributed to a "crisis" in Washington in late August of 1943. Cordell Hull, deemed politically indispensable in his post by FDR, hotly resented Welles's intimacy with the President and, under a threat of his own resignation, forced Welles out of office. Drew Pearson, who accused the Secretary of anti-Soviet attitudes inspired by Leo Pasvolsky and Adolf Berle, was denounced by FDR as "a chronic liar" and by Hull as a perpetrator of "monstrous and diabolical falsehoods." Welles was succeeded by Edward R. Stettinius, Jr., destined briefly to become Secretary of State with Hull's retirement in November 1944. Ambassador Standley in Moscow was soon replaced by W. Averell Harriman. Berle meanwhile resigned and Hull reluctantly went to Moscow, as Welles had urged, and, to his surprise, came back a hero and a symbol of interallied unity.

Such unity remained fictitious, thanks to Stalin's determination to maximize Soviet power in the wake of Axis defeat plus the resolve of Anglo-American officialdom (with the exception of Churchill, as we shall see) to ignore the facts of life and to strive for a restoration of pre-Nazi Europe in the name of "freedom," "democracy," and "self-determination." These words, in their operational as distinct from their metaphysical significance, meant that the USSR, having borne the brunt of Teutonic aggression, should content itself with a restoration of the European and global balance of indulgences and

[6] Cf. the masterly evaluation of the 20th Century's most complex political leader by my colleague James MacGregor Burns: *Roosevelt: The Lion and the Fox* (Harcourt, Brace, 1956).

deprivations prevailing during the long armistice of 1921–39. Such magnanimous abnegation, it is arguable, might well have served Soviet interests best in the decade to come.

But Stalin and his aides, motivated by their own life experience as Marxists in fighting the "bourgeoisie" and by the painful record of Russian dealings with the West, were wholly incapable of any such renunciation. Their definition of "victory" at no point coincided with Anglo-American definitions of the terms. That all such definitions were to prove meaningless and self-defeating is irrelevant to the matters here in hand. The task of diplomacy in 1943–5 was to create a public appearance of concord to disguise a private knowledge of discord. How this was accomplished, and with what consequences, can be suggested by an outline of inter-allied negotiations. The actual result, as is commonly the case in the playing of the game of power, reflected not the verbal formulas of politicians, concerned with images of unity, but the hard realities of relative military might —of which the Kremlin policy-makers were prepared to take full advantage, and toward which Western policy-makers were long obtuse.

Between October 19 and 30, 1943, Hull, Eden, and Molotov, held a dozen meetings in Spiridonovka House in the Soviet capital, aside from numerous informal gatherings with one another and with Stalin and other Soviet leaders. For the first time the three Super-Powers were met as equals for the elaboration of a joint program of victory and peace. At the conclusion of their deliberations there were issued on November 1 a Joint Communiqué, a Four-Nation Declaration (signed for China by Ambassador Foo Ping-Sheung), a Declaration regarding Italy, a Declaration on Austria, and a Statement on Atrocities signed by Roosevelt, Churchill, and Stalin. Two joint agencies were established, both on Moscow's suggestion: a European Advisory Commission and an Advisory Council for Matters Relating to Italy.

Anglo-American anxieties regarding Soviet intentions toward the Reich were allayed by a joint pledge of unconditional surrender and disarmament. A new League of Nations, rather than a mere alliance or a world federation, was envisaged in the proclaimed recognition of "the necessity of establishing at the earliest practicable date a general international organization, based on the principle of the sovereign equality of all peace-loving States, and open to membership by all such States, large and small, for the maintenance of

international peace and security." This formula reappeared in the Connally Resolution, passed by the American Senate, 85–5, on November 5. American isolationists were thus assured against any "surrender of sovereignty." Small States were given at least verbal protection against "domination" by the Big Three, who agreed to act only "on behalf of the community of nations." The non-intervention pledge of the Anglo-Soviet alliance was reiterated in generalized form.

If all of these assurances represented Anglo-American projects accepted by Moscow, the Declaration on Italy was a Soviet project accepted by Washington and London. Its ringing phrases condemning Fascism and championing Italian democracy took cognizance of Soviet criticisms of Anglo-American policy in Italy since the Badoglio armistice of September 3. The pledge of Austrian independence, already anticipated by Churchill in the summer of 1942, was a limited compromise between Western proponents of the dismemberment of the Reich and Soviet champions of German unity. The broader issue was left open, but Austria at least (to which Moscow had been addressing appeals for revolt through a "Free Austria Committee") would be detached from Berlin. The final statement on atrocities, pledging punishment of war criminals in the lands where their crimes were committed, was in intent and even phraseology an Anglo-American acceptance of the Kremlin's views.

The results of the Moscow conference were hailed throughout the United Nations as a heartening assurance of victory and peace. In the USA the only important voices of dissent were those of Senator Burton K. Wheeler, the Hearst press, and the McCormick-Patterson newspapers, all of whom shouted that Hull had "sold out" the Atlantic Charter to Stalin. The ten Bishops and Archbishops of the Administrative Board of the National Catholic Welfare Conference expressed similar doubts, but described the accord as "a definite step in the right direction." Secretary Hull told Congress on November 18:

> It has never been my fortune to attend an international conference at which there was greater determination on the part of all the participants to move forward in a spirit of mutual understanding and confidence. . . . Mr. Molotov arranged for the business of the conference in a most efficient manner. Both as Chairman and participant he mani-

fested throughout the highest order of ability and a profound grasp of international affairs. . . . I found in
Marshal Stalin a remarkable personality, one of the great
statesmen and leaders of this age. I was deeply impressed
by the people of Russia and by the epic quality of their patriotic fervor. A people who will fight against ruthless aggression, in utter contempt of death, as the men and women
of the Soviet Union are fighting, merit the admiration and
good will of the people of all countries.

The first meeting of Stalin, Roosevelt, and Churchill soon followed. At Cairo, November 22–5, 1943, the President and Prime Minister met with Chiang Kai-shek to concert plans against Japan, leading to unconditional surrender: "It is their purpose that Japan shall
be stripped of all the islands in the Pacific which she has seized or
occupied since the beginning of the First World War in 1914, and
that all the territories Japan has stolen from the Chinese, such as
Manchuria, Formosa and the Pescadores, shall be restored to the Republic of China. . . . In due course, Korea shall become free and
independent." The Anglo-American leaders then proceeded to the
capital of Iran, where they conferred with Stalin, November 28–
December 1, after which they met President Ismet Inonu and Foreign Minister Numan Menemencioglu at Cairo, December 4–6, to
reaffirm the Anglo-Turkish alliance and proclaim firm friendship
between Turkey, the Soviet Union, and the United States.

To Teheran, to which all the delegations proceeded by plane,
Stalin brought only Molotov and Voroshilov among the top Soviet
leaders. Roosevelt was acompanied by Hopkins, Harriman, Marshall,
King, Leahy, Arnold, Somervell, and John Deane, Chief of the American Military Mission in Moscow. The planning of war was the
prime concern. Preparations were discussed for the Normandy invasion of the following June and for a Soviet offensive to be co-
ordinated with the long-awaited second front. Only two documents
were made public. One was a Three-Power Declaration on Iran,
promising economic aid and participation in the establishment of
post-war peace, security, and prosperity "in accordance with the
principles of the Atlantic Charter to which all four governments
have continued to subscribe" and expressing a common "desire for
the maintenance of the independence, sovereignty and territorial integrity of Iran." The second document, signed by the three leaders

of the Super-Powers, was less informative than hortatory and prophetic, but was eloquent testimony to the human significance of the gathering for all the world.[7]

Anecdotes regarding the personal relations of the three chief participants are endless. Roosevelt spent his first night in the American Legation, a mile away from the Soviet and British HQ, and then accepted Stalin's invitation to stay, for the sake of safety and convenience, in the yellow brick palace housing the Soviet Embassy. Its outer walls enclosed wide parks and gardens of chrysanthemums, roses, and sycamores, interspersed with quiet pools, smiling in the autumn sunshine. Despite the need of interpreters, the Squire of Hyde Park, with his unflagging ebullience, was soon on the most cordial terms with the son of the Georgian cobbler in his stiff

---

[7] ROOSEVELT-STALIN-CHURCHILL DECLARATION

We, the President of the United States of America, the Prime Minister of Great Britain, and the Premier of the Soviet Union, have met in these four days past in this capital of our ally, Teheran, and have shaped and confirmed our common policy.

We express our determination that our nations shall work together in the war and in the peace that will follow.

As to the war, our military staffs have joined in our round-table discussions and we have concerted our plans for the destruction of the German forces. We have reached complete agreement as to the scope and timing of operations which will be undertaken from the east, west, and south. The common understanding which we have here reached guarantees that victory will be ours.

And as to the peace, we are sure that our concord will make it an enduring peace. We recognize fully the supreme responsibility resting upon us and all the United Nations to make a peace which will command good will from the overwhelming masses of the peoples of the world and banish the scourge and terror of war for many generations.

With our diplomatic advisers we have surveyed the problems of the future. We shall seek the cooperation and active participation of all nations, large and small, whose peoples in heart and in mind are dedicated, as are our own peoples, to the elimination of tyranny and slavery, oppression and intolerance. We will welcome them as they may choose to come into the world family of democratic nations.

No power on earth can prevent our destroying the German armies by land, their U-boats by sea, and their war plants from the air. Our attacks will be relentless and increasing.

Emerging from these friendly conferences we look with confidence to the day when all the peoples of the world may live free lives untouched by tyranny and according to their varying desires and their own consciences.

We came here with hope and determination. We leave here friends in fact, in spirit, and in purpose.

Signed at Teheran, December 1, 1943.
Roosevelt, Stalin, Churchill

Marshal's uniform. The President softened the occasional asperities between Stalin and Churchill.

Although the Marshal brought no relatives, the gathering had at times the atmosphere of a family reunion through the presence of Randolph and Sarah Churchill, and of Elliott Roosevelt and John Boettiger, the President's son-in-law. Churchill's birthday was celebrated on November 30 in the British Legation, adjacent to the Soviet Embassy, with 69 candles on the cake and innumerable toasts on all sides. On the preceding day Churchill ceremoniously presented to Stalin a sword of honor from King George VI to the people of Stalingrad. Roosevelt and Stalin reportedly discussed the mutual ignorance of Americans and Russians of one another's customs. The Marshal expressed interest in the details of American federalism, perhaps with an eye to the forthcoming amendments to the Soviet Constitution promulgated in February. The President expounded the Good-Neighbor Policy and welcomed Stalin's assurance that he had no desire to "own Europe."

Cooperation among allies is a continuous process, calling for incessant vigilance and effort, not a problem to be solved at a stroke by verbal formulas. Teheran was a mighty contribution to the success of the process but in no sense a final solution. The crisis of the summer had been met and surmounted. The gathering in Iran, however, was followed by new friction—due in part to delays in carrying out what had been agreed upon, which in turn were partially attributable to the illnesses of both Roosevelt and Churchill after their journey. The Prime Minister's pneumonia obliged him to remain in Morocco until early January. The very success of the conference moved Göbbels to new frenzy. Earlier in the year he had said, accurately, that many Anglo-Americans looked upon the advances of the Red Army "with one rejoicing eye and one weeping eye." Isolationists and Russophobes in both Britain and America now redoubled their efforts to create doubts and fears.

The immediate diplomatic aftermath of Teheran was the conclusion in Moscow on December 12, in the presence of President Eduard Beneš, of a twenty-year treaty of alliance against Germany by the USSR and the Czechoslovak Government-in-Exile. This project had long been entertained by the Narkomindel as an alternative to the schemes of the Polish Government-in-Exile for a Czech-Polish federation, which the Kremlin equated with a new anti-Soviet *cordon sanitaire*. London and Washington had indicated opposition. Church-

ill and Roosevelt were presumably persuaded by Stalin to give their consent. An appended Protocol invited Polish participation. But the unresolved questions of the Polish frontiers and of the status of the London Poles prevented the fulfillment of this intention. Stalin and Molotov at Teheran undoubtedly received assurances that Churchill would not only make a public statement on the second front but would also endorse the Soviet view regarding the future western frontiers of the USSR and the identity of friends and foes within Jugoslavia. When weeks passed with no such statement, Moscow applied pressure not only through diplomatic channels but through various gestures in the press.

On January 5, 1944, David Zaslavsky in *Pravda* harshly assailed Wendell Willkie as "a political gambler" because he had asked "what Russia intended to do about the political integrity of Finland, Poland, the Baltic and Balkan States" in an otherwise friendly article ("Don't Stir Distrust of Russia") in *The New York Times Magazine*. When Soviet troops a few days later drove across the old Polish frontier, Moscow spokesmen suggested that comment abroad about the Red Army entering "Poland" was in error, since Poland lay west of the frontier of 1941. Public Anglo-American offers in January to "mediate" the issue were resented. Soviet denunciations of Franco and criticisms of the Pope for alleged Fascist sympathies stirred further resentment in certain Western circles. A minor storm burst when *Pravda* on January 17 published a dispatch from Cairo to the effect that "trustworthy Greek and Jugoslav sources" had reported "a secret meeting of two leading British personalities with Ribbentrop not so long ago in one of the coastal towns of the Iberian Peninsula . . . to clarify the conditions of a separate peace with Germany. It is supposed that the meeting was not without results." Downing Street and Lord Halifax at once branded the story as a lie. Tass broadcast the denial, but asserted that the Ankara correspondent of the London *Sunday Times* had reported German peace offers to Britain at Russia's expense. *War and the Working Class* (January 19) alleged that plans for a second front were being hindered by Anglo-American defeatists and appeasers.

Matters mended somewhat in February. Eisenhower was awarded the Order of Suvorov, First Class, on the 18th and other high honors were granted to many of his fellow officers. On the 26th anniversary of the Red Army, Roosevelt congratulated Stalin "on the great and significant victory of the armed forces of the So-

viet Union. . . . The magnificent achievements of the Red Army under your leadership have been an inspiration to all. . . . Together with the collaboration and cooperation which was agreed upon at Moscow and Teheran, they assure our final victory over the Nazi aggressors." Churchill sent an "expression of my profound admiration to you and all ranks. . . . They will go forward to victory and through victory to peace with honor." On February 22 the Prime Minister told Commons that Anglo-American forces would invade Europe "before the leaves fall." He also asserted that British support in Jugoslavia would henceforth go to the partisan forces of the National Committee of Liberation under Tito (Josip Broz). As for Poland, "I cannot feel that Russian demands for reassurance about her western frontiers go beyond the limit of what is reasonable and just."

The ensuing complexities of inter-allied relations were productive of billions of words of documentation, commentary, accusations, and counter-accusations.[8] The grand themes of the drama were simple enough. By June of 1944, when Anglo-American armies under Eisenhower at last poured across the Channel to invade Nazi Europe through Normandy, westward-moving Soviet forces, opening a

[8] For more detailed accounts, see *Soviet Politics at Home and Abroad* (Knopf, 1946), pp. 473–571, and, for a brilliant military and diplomatic history based on post-war documentation, Chester Wilmot: *The Struggle for Europe* (Harper, 1952). The reader who wishes to pursue these matters further would be well advised to begin his search with the following volumes: Dean Acheson: *The Pattern of Responsibility* (Houghton Mifflin, 1952); Max Beloff: *Soviet Far Eastern Policy, 1944–1951* (2 vols., Oxford University Press, 1953); James Byrnes: *Speaking Frankly* (Harper, 1947); Richard N. Current: *Secretary Stimson* (Rutgers University Press, 1954); Raymond Dennett and Joseph E. Johnson (eds.): *Negotiating with the Russians* (World Peace Foundation, 1951); Stanton Griffis: *Lying in State* (Doubleday, 1952); Cordell Hull: *The Memoirs of Cordell Hull* (2 vols., Macmillan, 1948); William Hardy McNeill: *Survey of International Affairs 1939–1946: America, Britain, and Russia: Their Cooperation and Conflicts, 1941–1946* (Oxford University Press, 1953); Walter Millis and E. S. Duffield: *The Forrestal Diaries* (Viking, 1951); F. Nemec and V. Moudry: *The Soviet Seizure of Sub-Carpathian Ruthenia* (Anderson, 1955); Hugh Seton-Watson: *The East European Revolution* (Praeger, 1951); Robert E. Sherwood: *Roosevelt and Hopkins* (Harper, 1948); Walter Bedell Smith: *My Three Years in Moscow* (Lippincott, 1950); William H. Standley and Arthur A. Edgeton: *Admiral Ambassador to Russia* (Regnery, 1955); John L. Snell *et al.*: *The Meaning of Yalta* (Louisiana State University Press, 1956); Edward R. Stettinius, Jr.: *Lend-Lease, Weapon for Victory* (Macmillan, 1944) and *Roosevelt and the Russians* (Doubleday, 1949); and Henry L. Stimson and McGeorge Bundy: *On Active Service in Peace and War* (Harper, 1948).

simultaneous offensive in the East, had reached the line of Narva, Pskov, Vitebsk, Brest-Litovsk, Cernauti, and Kishenev. "It is the Russian Army," said Churchill on August 2, "that has done the main work of tearing the guts out of the German Army." Six months later, with France free of the foe but with the Western Allies checked short of the Rhine in the Belgian "Battle of the Bulge," Soviet divisions stood before Warsaw, were besieging Budapest, and were in control of all the Balkans north of Greece. In Poland, with Red troops pausing at the Vistula, Gen. "Bor" (Tadeuz Komorowski) had launched a Warsaw revolt against the *Wehrmacht* on August 1, 1944, on behalf of the London Government-in-Exile—whose parleys with Moscow were doomed by Polish determination to restore the *status quo* and Soviet resolve to change the frontiers and impose a Communist-controlled regime. Moscow gave no aid and, amid bitter recriminations, impeded all efforts at Anglo-American assistance. By early October the rebels were forced to surrender after suffering 300,000 casualties and the almost complete destruction of the Polish capital.

The dark dialectics of war proceeded from thesis to antithesis to synthesis with inexorable logic, in defiance of all the efforts of Western diplomacy to change the result. The outcome was Communist control of most of Eastern and much of Central Europe and a restoration, after a thousand years, of the ancient line from the Elbe to the Adriatic as the frontier between *Deutschtum* and Slavdom. This consequence of the vicissitudes of battle was implicit in the calendar of combat. Rumania surrendered on August 25, 1944, as Anglo-American forces entered Paris. On the same day Finland asked Moscow for an armistice, which was signed in September. Red troops occupied Sofia on September 16 as Eisenhower's armies pushed eastward through France and Belgium. Zhukov's forces stormed Warsaw on January 17, 1945, and took Danzig on March 30. Budapest fell on February 13 and Vienna on April 13, the day after Franklin D. Roosevelt died at Warm Springs, Georgia. Western divisions were unable to cross the Rhine until March 8 at Remagen. In the south, Genoa was taken on April 27, and Milan and Turin on April 29–30. In the north, on April 25, 1945, the 58th Guards Division of Konev's First Ukrainian Army met the 69th Division of Gen. Courtney H. Hodge's U.S. First Army at Torgau on the Elbe.

On the same day Soviet forces encircled Berlin. Patton's troops

took Munich on September 30 and reached Braunau-am-Inn, Hitler's birthplace, on May Day—when fighting ceased in Italy, after Mussolini and his mistress had been slain by partisans on April 28. Two days later Hitler and his mistress committed suicide in their Berlin bunker. All fighting ceased on May 2 in the ruined German capital, with the red flag flying over the wreck of the *Reichstag* building. On May 7–8, 1945, documents of unconditional surrender were signed by Nazi generals in Rheims and Berlin. Moscow celebrated victory on May 9 with 1,000 guns firing 30 salvos and Stalin proclaiming the triumph of Slavdom over German tyranny. All day long huge throngs cheered before the U.S. Embassy, then on Mokhovaya Street, west of the Hotel National, until Chargé George F. Kennan felt obliged to greet them briefly in Russian from a balcony—to Stalin's chagrin and resentment. In a great celebration in Red Square on June 24, in which Swastika flags were dragged in the dirt, Zhukov, while bespeaking triumph, warned against conceit or complacency.

"Solidarity Forever" among the victors for the building of a better world could not alter the fact that the USSR was now master of half of Europe, having moved into the vacuum left by the Nazi débâcle and occupied all the lands ignominiously surrendered to Hitler by the Western Powers in 1938–40. This unexpected outcome of Armageddon the West was unwilling to accept and Moscow was unwilling to renounce. How this clash of wills precipitated the "Cold War" we shall consider later in our inquiry. Here we may note the extent to Soviet aggrandizement in the wake of victory, from north to south: the USSR, by the armistice terms of September 19, 1944, annexed Petsamo, restored Hanko to Finland, secured a 50-year lease on the Porkkala Peninsula near Helsinki, and restored the frontiers of 1940; Muscovy re-annexed Estonia, Latvia, and Lithuania and moved Poland westward by making the "Curzon Line" the new Soviet-Polish border and extending Poland to the Oder-Neisse line at Germany's expense; northern East Prussia, including Koenigsberg (Kaliningrad), became Soviet territory, while southern East Prussia went to Poland; to the south Carpatho-Ukraine was incorporated into the USSR by "agreement" with Prague (June 29, 1945) along with Bessarabia and Northern Bukovina (the Moldavian SSR) by "agreement" with Bucharest (September 12, 1944). Apart from these annexations, coupled with Soviet occupation of Eastern Germany and Eastern Austria, the men of Moscow, by threats and trickery, imposed Communist-controlled

regimes on Poland, Czechoslovakia, Hungary, Rumania, Bulgaria, and Albania—with a Communist regime also in control of Jugoslavia, although not by Muscovite fiat but by the victory of Tito's partisans.

Inter-allied policy during the final year of World War II centered upon unsuccessful Western efforts to frustrate or prevent this all-but-inevitable concomitant of the new facts of *Realpolitik*, and upon successful Soviet efforts to realize and perpetuate an age-old Slavic dream, now suffused with Marxist messianism. American policy-makers, bent upon "unconditional surrender" of the enemy and blinded by "legalistic moralistic abstractions," were unable to face the issue until too late. Churchill early perceived what was at stake and hoped to limit Soviet aggrandizement by invading Nazi Europe through Austria and the Balkans rather than through Northern France. Since the "soft underbelly" had already proved painfully hard in Italy, Washington vetoed his proposals on grounds of military practicality. As a statesman of sound sense, he then sought to restrict Soviet expansionism through a bargain as a second-best alternative to military action. In October of 1944 he went to Moscow with Eden and sundry colleagues to discuss the sequel to the three-month accord of June whereby the USSR was to enjoy predominance in Rumania while Britain occupied the same position in Greece. To this provisional arrangement Roosevelt had assented, over the objections of Hull and the State Department. In Moscow, by use of a quaint arithmetic, it was agreed that the Soviet Union should enjoy 90% predominance in Rumania and 75% in Bulgaria, Britain 90% in Greece and 25% in Bulgaria, and each 50–50 in Jugoslavia and Hungary.[9]

This bargain, which was "realistic" despite its fantasies of mathematics, evoked objections in Washington, where victory was envisaged not in terms of barter among the victors but in terms of the universal application of sacred principles of "democracy," "free elections," and "self-determination." That Stalinist versions of these terms, which the Muscovite leaders were quite willing to accept, would have nothing in common with Anglo-American versions was obvious to all well-informed observers—save the Western policymakers, who solicited Soviet lip service to the magic words and later accused the USSR of shamelessly violating its pledges. They

[9] Cf. Winston S. Churchill: *Triumph and Tragedy* (Houghton Mifflin, 1954), pp. 227, 232 f.

thereby established a persuasive legal case for virtue against vice but changed in no respect whatever the realities of power.

Sunny Yalta, a vacation resort on the pleasant southeast coast of the Crimea, was the site of the second and, as it turned out, final conference among Stalin, Roosevelt, and Churchill, each with numerous aides and advisers. The conferees met in a Tsarist palace at Livadia, near the war-wrecked town, between February 4 and 11, 1945. FDR, gray and aged and weary, was not long for this world, though there is no reliable evidence that he was befuddled or incompetent or "taken in" by either of his peers. Josef Djugashvili, hard-boiled but accommodating in the flush of victory, was genial and adaptable, provided that Soviet interests and ambitions were well served. Churchill, as anti-Communist as ever, was confident that a viable bargain could be struck between East and West.

The 17 complex accords and communiqués agreed upon at Yalta (two-thirds of which were kept secret for more than three years) were to give rise to endless disputation, marked by voluminous publications of supplementary minutes, records, and memoirs, allegations of "violation" by London and Washington against Moscow, and wild accusations of "betrayal" and "treason" in the USA. These controversies need not detain us. They are evidence neither of Muscovite villainy nor of Anglo-American bad faith, but only of semantic confusion, Soviet realism, and Western naïveté.

The conferees agreed, seriatim and *inter alia*, that envoys should gather in San Francisco on April 25, 1945, to establish a UN organization, limited in participation to States declaring war on the common enemy by March 1. London and Washington agreed to support the membership of the Ukraine and Byelorussia in the projected world agency, and all agreed that in the proposed Security Council all non-procedural or substantive decisions should require the concurrence of all the permanent members (the USA, the USSR, Britain, France, and China); that the peoples of liberated Europe should enjoy "democratic institutions of their own choice" and "free elections of governments responsive to the will of the people"; that Germany should be disarmed, demilitarized, and dismembered; that France should share with the Big Three a German occupation zone; that Germany (with the USA and the USSR agreed, and Britain dissenting) should pay $20,000,000,000 in reparations in the form of removals of equipment and annual deliveries from current production, of which "50% should go to the USSR"; that the Polish Pro-

visional Government should be democratized and broadened, with
the Curzon Line as the eastern frontier, and western and northern
territorial accessions to be finally determined by the Peace Conference; that a new Jugoslav Government should be based on the Tito-
Subasich agreement; that the Big-Three Foreign Ministers should
meet together "probably every three or four months"; and that
within "two or three months after Germany has surrendered . . .
the Soviet Union shall enter into the war against Japan" on the understanding that "the *status quo* in Outer Mongolia shall be preserved" and that the USSR would acquire Southern Sakhalin, a
naval base at Port Arthur, and equal rights with China in the operation of the Manchurian railways. "The Kurile Islands shall be
handed over to the Soviet Union. . . . The heads of the three Great
Powers have agreed that these claims of the Soviet Union shall be
unquestionably fulfilled after Japan has been defeated." Roosevelt
undertook to obtain Chiang Kai-shek's concurrence in these terms.
Stalin agreed to conclude "a pact of friendship and alliance between
the USSR and China in order to render assistance to China with its
armed forces for the purpose of liberating China from the Japanese
yoke." [1]

This bargain "made sense" at the time in terms of the common
purposes of East and West. Anglo-American military authorities anticipated another year or more of bloody struggle to defeat Japan
and regarded Soviet participation as essential to hasten victory and
reduce its cost. Moscow's price—a restoration, with embellishments,
of the pre-1904 Russian position in the Far East—was deemed a reasonable recompense. As for "democracy" and "free elections" in
Eastern Europe, Churchill certainly, and Roosevelt probably, had
no illusions that these formulas would or could prevent effective Soviet control of the marchlands which the Western Powers had abandoned in 1938. A few weeks after Yalta, Vyshinsky in Bucharest imposed a Communist-dominated regime on Rumania, thus anticipating

---

[1] The full texts of these accords will be found on pp. 228–33 of the fourth
edition of my *International Politics* (McGraw-Hill, 1948) and in many other
readily available documentary sources. It should be noted that Stalin had
promised Soviet participation in a war against Japan to Hull in Moscow in
October 1943, to Roosevelt in Teheran in November 1943, and to Churchill in
Moscow in October 1944. In December 1944 he presented to Ambassador
Harriman the Soviet "price" of such participation. It was cabled to Roosevelt
on December 15, accepted, and incorporated almost verbatim in the Yalta
agreement. See Herbert Feis: *The China Tangle* (Princeton University Press,
1953) and William D. Leahy: *I Was There* (McGraw-Hill, 1950).

the Soviet conception of "friendly governments" in all the Baltic-to-Balkan borderlands, soon to become "satellites" of Moscow.

Subordinate policy-makers in London and Washington, still hoping to forestall by legalism the aggrandizement of the USSR which their governments were helpless to forestall by power, protested at this "violation" of the Yalta pledges. Later allegations by ex-isolationists in the USA that Roosevelt at Yalta "betrayed" China, Poland, Rumania, etc., need not here be discussed. When one Power lacks power to prevent the ascendancy of another Power in a given area, its diplomats can either do nothing or propose formulas that the other Power will usually interpret as it pleases. The vexed question as to whether the Yalta accords superseded the Churchill-Stalin agreement on "spheres" in October of 1944 (to which the USA was not a party and about which Americans long knew nothing and cared less) may well be deemed disposed of, after Yalta, when FDR opined that "the Rumanian situation did not offer the best test of relations" with Moscow. Churchill to Roosevelt, March 8, 1945 (as first revealed by James F. Byrnes [*NYT*, October 18, 1947] in rebuttal to a British Foreign Office spokesman who denied any agreement on "spheres"), asserted anent Rumania:

> We have been hampered in our protests against these developments by the fact that, in order to have the freedom to save Greece, Eden and I at Moscow in October recognized that Russia should have the largely preponderant voice in Rumania and Bulgaria while we took the lead in Greece. Stalin adhered very strictly to this understanding during the thirty days' fighting against the Communists and Elas in the city of Athens, in spite of the fact that all this was most disagreeable to him and those around him.

In the dawn of victory increasing East-West frictions, prophetic of things to come, continued through the spring of 1945, although Roosevelt in his last days made light of these disputes. Their primary source was the resolve of Soviet policy-makers to subject East Europe and the Balkans, north of Greece, to Communist control as a means of preventing forever any repetition of the consequences, as in 1914 f. and 1941 f., of German control of these regions. Their secondary source was the equal determination in many Western circles to "roll back" Soviet power to the line of 1941, or better 1938, or still better 1918. The work of winning the war and making the

peace nevertheless went forward with an apparent concord of purposes.

The San Francisco Conference (April 25–June 26, 1945) hammered out the UN Charter. The process was painful, the more so as President Truman, almost at once upon taking office, began quarreling with Moscow over many matters. He sought to use American economic power as a weapon to obtain political concessions. Admiral William D. Leahy, Averell Harriman, James Forrestal, and other consultants favored a "strong stand." Stalin did not at first plan to send Molotov to San Francisco. Truman at one point contemplated a conference without Soviet representation: "If the Russians did not wish to join us, they could go to hell." As matters turned out, Stalin agreed to send Molotov to the Golden Gate while Truman sent Harry Hopkins back to Moscow to "talk things out."

Hopkins found Stalin disturbed at Washington's abrupt termination of lend-lease aid—in its manner, said he, "unfortunate and even brutal." If designed as pressure, this decision "was a fundamental mistake." Discussion of the Polish question, as usual, got nowhere. The San Francisco Charter postulated a world organization based upon a concert of power among Great Powers, each of which, as a member of the Security Council, could "veto" any enforcement action of which it disapproved and, indeed, any decision at all (save purely procedural rulings), including a decision as to whether any given question was "procedural" or "substantive." The sacred principle of national sovereignty was thus preserved, to the equal satisfaction of the USSR and the USA, at the expense of any prospect of an effective Parliament of Man or Federation of the World.

This curious coincidence of American and Soviet views found fresh expression at the Potsdam Conference of July 17–August 2, 1945. Stalin and Molotov, Truman and Byrnes, Churchill and Eden (later Clement Attlee and Ernest Bevin, following Labor victory in the British election of July 5), and innumerable aides met in the faded and war-damaged palaces of the Hohenzollerns. They agreed to the establishment of a Council of Foreign Ministers "to do the necessary preparatory work for the peace settlement"; to the governance of Germany, jointly and severally in their occupation zones, through the Commanders-in-Chief of the USA, the USSR, Britain, and France for the purpose of promoting disarmament, demilitarization, de-Nazification, decentralization, and democratization, plus reparations and the punishment of war criminals; to Soviet provi-

sional annexation of northern East Prussia; to Polish "democracy" and provisional Polish occupation of German lands up to the Oder-Neisse line; and to the "humane and orderly" expulsion of German inhabitants from Poland, Czechoslovakia, and Hungary.[2]

A joint warning was addressed to Japan by the conferees. On April 5 Molotov had informed Ambassador Naotake Sato of the Kremlin's decision to denounce the neutrality pact of 1941 on the ground that it had "lost its meaning," since Japan had aided Germany in aggression and was waging war on America and Britain, both Russia's allies. On July 26, 1945, the Allied leaders at Potsdam issued an appeal to Tokyo to surrender, under dire threat of "prompt and utter destruction." Truman confidentially revealed, although it is possible that Stalin did not immediately grasp the point, the successful test on July 16 at Alamagordo, New Mexico, of a new weapon: the atomic bomb. This harnessing to human purposes of the cosmic fire of the gods rendered all power politics obsolete, if mankind were to survive. This elementary fact, however, was beyond the imagination of any of the men at Potsdam or of any of their successors for another decade. The warlords of Tokyo, knowing nothing of such matters, ignored the Potsdam plea in a vain hope of arranging a peace of compromise through Soviet mediation.

What followed in the last weeks of World War II inaugurated a wholly new epoch in human affairs, even if few humans glimpsed its implications. Against the advice of many physicists who urged a test demonstration on an uninhabited island, Harry S. Truman and his political and military aides decided to use the new weapon against Japan—partly as a means of obviating the need of Soviet aid against Tokyo and, if possible, restricting Soviet gains in the Far East. On August 6, 1945, the crew of Superfortress *Enola Gay* dropped an atomic bomb on Hiroshima. 60% of the city was vaporized. 66,000 people perished. Another 60,000 died of incurable burns. 118,000 were wounded. 10,000 were "missing." On August 8 the USSR declared war on Japan. On August 9 the crew of Superfortress *Great Artiste* dropped a second atomic bomb on Nagasaki. 40,000 died. 18,000 buildings vanished. All the remaining 33,000 were wrecked or damaged. Other multitudes of victims later succumbed. The appalled policy-makers in Tokyo, not knowing that the USA had no more atomic bombs available, surrendered on August 14.

[2] Full texts will be found in *International Politics* (McGraw-Hill, 4th edition, 1948), pp. 233–46.

In the interim, as Eisenhower was wined and dined in Moscow as Zhukov's guest, Soviet armies commanded by Marshal Alexander N. Vasilevsky poured into Manchuria and, in a one-week *Blitzkrieg*, crushed Nippon's Kwantung Army, took half a million prisoners, and occupied Southern Sakhalin, Northern Korea, and the Kuriles. Hirohito capitulated and advised his subjects to cultivate the ways of rectitude. On September 2, aboard the U.S.S. *Missouri* in Tokyo Bay, Soviet representatives took part, with agents of the other major Allied Powers, in General MacArthur's ceremonial signature of articles of Japanese surrender with General Yoshijiro Umezh and Foreign Minister Mamoru Shigemitsu. A fortnight previously, on August 14, 1945, six Sino-Soviet accords were signed in Moscow by Molotov and Foreign Minister Wang Shih-chieh, with Stalin and Premier T. V. Soong in attendance. They included a 30-year alliance between the USSR and the Kuomintang regime against future Japanese aggression; a pledge of reciprocal non-intervention and respect for sovereignty and territorial integrity; Soviet moral and material support to China; Soviet recognition of Chinese title to Singkiang and Manchuria; Chinese respect for the independence of Mongolia, subject to a plebiscite (in which the voters voted unanimously for "independence"); joint ownership and management of the Manchurian railways; and conversion of Dairen into a "free port" and of Port Arthur into a joint naval base to be administered by China and defended by the USSR.

Stalin spoke over Radio Moscow on September 2:

> Comrades, Compatriots, Men and Women: . . . Two hotbeds of world Fascism and world aggression formed on the eve of this World War—Germany in the west, and Japan in the east. It was they who unleashed the Second World War. . . . The Second World War has come to an end. Now we can say that conditions necessary for the peace of the world have already been won. . . .
>
> We have a special account of our own to settle with Japan. Japan began her aggression against our country as far back as 1904. . . . Unexpectedly and treacherously, without declaring war, Japan attacked our country and assaulted the Russian squadron in the Port Arthur area. . . . Thirty-seven years later, Japan repeated exactly the same treacherous device against the United States when in 1941

she attacked the United States Naval Base at Pearl Harbor. . . . As is well known, Russia suffered defeat in the war with Japan, and Japan took advantage of Tsarist Russia's defeat to wrest southern Sakhalin from Russia, to strengthen her hold over the Kurile Islands, thus locking all outlets to the ocean in the east and consequently also the outlet for our country to the ports of Soviet Kamchatka and the Soviet Sea of Okhotsk. . . .

For forty years have we, men of the older generation, waited for this generation, waited for this day. . . . Southern Sakhalin and the Kurile Islands will pass to the Soviet Union, and from now on will not serve as the means for isolating the Soviet Union from the Ocean and as a base for Japanese attacks on our Far East. They will serve instead as a means of direct communication of the Soviet Union with the Ocean and as a base for the defense of our country against Japanese aggression. . . .

We have lived through hard years. But now every one of us can say: we have won. . . . Eternal glory to the heroes who fell in the battles for the honor and victory of our Motherland! May our Motherland thrive and prosper!

The high hopes of a new time found expression in the words of Ilya Ehrenburg (*Pravda*, May 10, 1945):

Shoulder to shoulder with us fought our gallant Allies, and fidelity triumphed over perfidy. . . . A new era has begun, an era of plowmen and masons, doctors and architects, of gardeners and schoolteachers, of printers and poets. Washed by the tears of spring, Europe lies wounded. Much labor, persistence, audacity and determination will be required to heal all the wounds, so that the 20th Century—saved from the bloody pit into which the Fascists had cast it—may again stride toward happiness. The boldness, talent and conscience of our people will help the world to rise to its feet.

4. COEXISTENCE, 1945 f.

IN considering the tangled and soon embittered relationship between East and West as they grappled with the problem of peace-
making, future historians, no less than contemporary participants,
will have difficulty in deciding when and why and how the Grand
Alliance dissolved by imperceptible degrees into the "Cold War"
after the war. Earlier sources of tension have been dealt with in previous pages. The new roots of conflict between 1945 and 1947 are
best reserved for a later chapter. Meanwhile, despite frictions over
matters large and small and an ever spreading cloud of hostility, the
victors of 1945 managed for a time to reconcile their differences and
get on with the work of peace. How the labor proceeded is our immediate concern.

If the statesmen of these years appear in retrospect to be singularly devoid of qualities of magnanimity and imagination and to be
prisoners of fear and prejudice, this condition may fairly be attributed less to personal defects than to a long legacy of reciprocal suspicion of motives, muted in the roar of battle and once more vocal in
the silence of peace. The result may further be ascribed to the persisting popular delusion, long rendered obsolete by the economic
realities of the 20th Century, that those who are "victors" in war are
entitled to the fruits of victory. This imperative of *Vox Populi* is
inescapable for all policy-makers in democracies. It is no less imperative, despite the processes of dictatorships, in despotisms and oligar-
chies. Here the few who wield power have even less freedom to
depart from the dogmas, demands, and expectations in the name of
which they win obedience. In such beds of Procrustes the diplomats
of East and West alike in 1945–6 were compelled to lie and toss and
turn in their maneuverings for advantage.

Under these circumstances the political achievements of the
months immediately following upon Armageddon are more remarkable for successes than for failures. At Lancaster House in London,
between September 11 and October 3, 1945, the Council of Foreign
Ministers, as proposed at Potsdam, met to consider peace-making.
The delegations were headed by Molotov, Byrnes, Bevin, Bidault,
and Wang Shih-chieh. Molotov pleaded for "Big-Three" control of

Balkan treaty-drafting. Byrnes and Bevin insisted on French and Chinese participation. Molotov assented and then discovered that the French and Chinese spokesmen, dependent upon Anglo-American aid for the survival of their governments, sided with London and Washington against Moscow on all controversial issues. He then revoked his assent. The result was deadlock, with no agreement even on a communiqué registering disagreement.

The Council, now limited to Molotov, Bevin, and Byrnes, reconvened in Moscow, December 16–26, 1945, and agreed that treaties with enemy states should be drafted only by participants in the accords of surrender, to be followed by a general advisory conference of all States which "actively waged war with substantial military forces against European enemy States." Final texts of treaties should thereafter be drawn up by the signatories of the various armistice agreements. It was further elaborately specified that a "Far Eastern Advisory Commission" should be established (its later role was inconsequential) and that an "Allied Council for Japan" should be created (it exercised no visible influence on U.S. governance of vanquished Nippon). Measures were proposed for a unified and democratic Korea and for a unified and democratic China "under the National Government" and for "a cessation of civil strife." Other steps were agreed upon for the "democratization" of Rumania and Bulgaria and for the setting up of a UN Commission for Control of Atomic Energy which should recommend proposals "for the elimination from national armaments of atomic weapons and of all other major weapons adaptable to mass destruction" and "for effective safeguards by way of inspection and other means to protect complying States against the hazards of violations and evasions."

Many of these worthy resolves came to nothing. The Council of Foreign Ministers nevertheless reconvened in London (April 25–May 16, 1946) and in Paris (June 15–July 12, 1946) and worked out terms of peace treaties, discussed at a huge Paris Peace Conference in Luxembourg Palace (July 29–October 15, 1946), where envoys from 21 States debated, and made recommendations regarding, innumerable proposals. Delegates and secretaries numbered 1,385, journalists 2,000, and guards 1,040. Five tons of paper were used up on busy days. In New York's Waldorf-Astoria the Council met once more (November 4–December 12, 1946) to put into final form the

voluminous peace treaties with Italy, Bulgaria, Hungary, Rumania, and Finland—all formally signed at the Quai d'Orsay on February 10, 1947.[3]

This not inconsiderable diplomatic accomplishment suggested the possibility of a general East-West *modus vivendi* in Europe, Asia, and the world at large. Such hopes were to be frustrated by Soviet ambitions and threats, as seen from London and Washington, and by Anglo-American threats and ambitions, as seen from Moscow. When the Council of Foreign Ministers reassembled in Paris (March 10–April 24, 1947) to discuss treaties for Germany and Austria, the pattern of conflict to come was soon manifest. Molotov asked for Four-Power administration of the Ruhr and $10,000,000,000 in German reparations to the USSR, to be paid out of current production over 18 years. Marshall rejected the Soviet proposals "categorically" and urged that part of the Polish-administered areas be restored to the Reich. Molotov categorically rejected such suggestions. The deadlock thus achieved was confirmed at the London meeting of the Council (November 25–December 15, 1947), by which time the "Cold War" was already well under way.

Coexistence between the Soviet Union and the Western Powers was thus short-lived after World War II, despite agreement on peace terms for four minor, and one major, enemy belligerents. During the years to come no accords between East and West proved possible regarding the balance of power in Central Europe and Eastern Asia, since each giant antagonist was more concerned with imposing its will on the other than with the possibilities of an accommodation. Both failed in their purpose. Before we consider the course of this hazardous venture, it will be helpful to look at internal developments in the USSR after 1945.

[3] Summaries of the terms will be found in *International Politics* (4th edition, McGraw-Hill, 1948), pp. 253–4. For full texts see Department of State: *Treaties and Other International Acts*, Series 1947. The texts were reprinted in *NYT*, January 18, 1947, and in *Current History*, March and April 1947.

CHAPTER TEN

Toward Communism

1. RECONSTRUCTION

T HE RUSSIA of 1945–6 was a war-blasted land of grief and ruin. Of those who survived the catastrophe, 25,000,000 were homeless. Many of the rest were in rags. From the western frontiers to the gates of Leningrad and Moscow, and far off to the North Caucasus and the right bank of the lower Volga, a vast region—comparable in expanse, and also in relative population density and productivity, to all of the USA east of the Mississippi—was a wasteland of wrecked cities, shattered towns, and burned villages. In many centers dwelt only pitiable wraiths of broken and famished people. Some cities, such as Stalingrad and Sebastopol, were totally demolished. In others—Kiev, Kharkov, Minsk, Orel, Odessa, Rostov-Don, etc.—a third to a half of all buildings had been reduced to rubble. So fearful was the toll taken by the Horsemen of the Apocalypse that even in 1956 the Ukraine, Byelorussia, and Lithuania had fewer inhabitants than in 1940. So appalling was the devastation of homes and lives and livelihoods that no alien observer could reasonably imagine any recovery within less than a generation. When asked by Hugh Baillie (October 28, 1946) how long a time would be required to rebuild western Russia, Stalin replied: "Six or seven years, if not more."

A decade later the USSR was a land transformed. Stalingrad was a handsome new metropolis, with its tractor factory and Red October steel works going full blast; with its Volga water front now a gracious boulevard surmounted by Greek colonnades; with its central "Square of Fallen Fighters" a minor glory of striking theaters, public buildings, and apartments; with the Volga-Don canal open to the south and a gigantic dam and hydroelectric plant under

construction to the north; and with innumerable new buildings going up everywhere in a municipality of busy and prosperous citizens, all fascinated by a 25-year building plan designed to achieve the Heavenly City on earth.

In Rostov-Don only two war ruins remained: the modernistic opera house on Engels Street (with architects disagreeing as to the appropriate style of its reconstruction) and the Palace of Soviets, in process of reconversion into an office building. Kiev's impressive Kreshchatik Boulevard, where only one structure had been intact in 1944, was a fanfare of ornate apartment blocks, stores, theaters, and public buildings, with all the rest of the city restored. In Moscow, cleanest and most varicolored of the world's great capitals, sundry skyscrapers reached toward the clouds, beginning with the HQ of the Ministries of Foreign Affairs and Foreign Trade on Smolenskii Boulevard (1951) and culminating in the 37-story tower (1953) of Moscow State University on Lenin Hills, surrounded by miles of huge residential blocks. The Donets Basin was once more a beehive of industry. Everywhere else in the devastated areas, and far beyond them, sights were similar. In the outskirts of Stalingrad, Rostov-Don, and elsewhere many still lived in cottages, shacks, or hovels ("private houses"), but all aspired hopefully to new apartments.[1]

This miracle of restoration, unlike its counterpart in West Germany, Normandy, and other battle-scarred regions, was achieved without foreign aid. Lend-lease was abruptly terminated with the cessation of hostilities. Help from UNRRA, ending in June 1947, was minimal: Byelorussia received only $60,400,000 and the Ukraine $188,302,000 worth of goods out of total expenditures of $3,500,000,-000. The USA lent $4,400,000,000 to Britain in 1945–6. Moscow applied for a loan of $6,000,000,000. The application was "misplaced"

[1] Forty years after the October Revolution, Soviet citizens, if so minded or compelled by austerity, could still build, buy, and sell "private houses," with aid from the State Bank. Most such houses, often lacking utilities and usually ranging in selling price from 5,000 to 15,000 rubles, would be regarded by Western Europeans and Americans as "slums." The Soviet ideal of suburban living, well exemplified in the Lenin Hills development southwest of Moscow, consists of enormous 8- or 10-story apartments, each a hollow square around a huge garden courtyard and containing a thousand two-, three-, or four-room apartments. Rents are nominal. Details of masonry, woodwork, décor, plumbing, and other niceties are still below American standards. These structures nevertheless constitute, despite continued scarcities and overcrowding, a vast improvement over Soviet housing standards of the past.

in Washington for six months. On March 1, 1946, the State Department announced that it had invited Moscow to open negotiations for a credit of $1,000,000,000. Nothing came of the discussions. Whatever chance remained for aid under the "Marshall Plan" of 1947 was lost by the Kremlin's own decisions. During the decade after victory the USSR was among the few countries in the world denied American largess. Soviet Muscovy, out of its own resources, nonetheless restored and further developed a rapidly expanding economy, and this more swiftly and effectively than did Britain, the Western nations of the Continent, and other beneficiaries of Yankee charity.

The "secret" of this achievement has never been adequately explained by Soviet or Western "experts." Some clues will be suggested in the following section. Meanwhile, it is well to note the major changes in the public life of the USSR under the impact of war and reconstruction.

On February 1, 1944, the Supreme Soviet amended Art. 18 of the Constitution to give each Union Republic the right to maintain its own "military formation" and to "enter into direct relations with foreign States, to conclude agreements with them, and exchange diplomatic and consular representatives." Arts. 77 and 78 were revised to convert the federal Commissariats of Defense and Foreign Affairs into joint Union-Republic Commissariats. Each Republic was granted the right to maintain its own Commissars of Defense and Foreign Affairs. The purpose of this change of arrangements was to foster local pride and an illusion of autonomy, particularly in Byelorussia and the Ukraine, whose peoples had borne the heaviest burdens of battle and enemy occupation. By the terms of the Yalta accords, both were granted separate representation in the UN. Both, along with Armenia, set up their own Commissariats of Foreign Affairs and concluded various agreements with neighboring States. This gesture toward decentralization otherwise effected no meaningful change, during the ensuing decade and beyond, in the central determination of military and foreign policy by the Politburo of the Party.

The Party in turn experienced no "democratization," despite the pledges at Congress XVIII. No Congress or Conference met during hostilities or for years thereafter. Many members lost their lives at the front. Large numbers, as many as 100,000 a month in late 1943, were admitted as new members. By V-E Day, candidates and mem-

bers totaled 5,000,000, plus 15,000,000 Komsomols. The pre-war oligarchy was dominated by carefully indoctrinated industrial workers and by surviving "Old Bolsheviks"—whose ratio to "New Bolsheviks" had already declined, however, from 4 to 1 in 1930 to 1 to 4 in 1941. The post-war oligarchy was a fellowship of newly recruited young people, two-thirds of all members and candidates in 1946 having been admitted during the preceding five years. Managers, intellectuals, and collective farmers, most of them in the Red Army, outnumbered "proletarians." But this change in composition effected no immediately visible transformation in the realities of power and policy-making. Lines of command continued to flow from top to bottom and lines of responsibility and obedience from bottom to top, as in all armies and in the pre-war Soviet polity.

Frictions between Party and Army, eagerly anticipated and often forecast abroad, failed to develop. Most Party leaders held military rank. Most high officers were Party members. The vicissitudes of war, the ordinary misfortunes of life, and the extraordinary hazards of Soviet politics took their toll of persons once prominent among the elite. Stalin relegated Zhukov to obscurity after 1945, and in 1949 savagely liquidated Voznesensky and various of his aides in the "Leningrad Case," for reasons and under circumstances still obscure. Chief of Staff Shaposhnikov died of illness in 1943. Gen. Nikolai F. Vatutin, hero of Kiev, expired April 14, 1944. Gen. Ivan D. Cherniakhovsky, brilliant Jewish commander of the First Byelorussian Army which first invaded Germany, succumbed to wounds February 18, 1945. Konstantin Oumansky perished in a plane crash near Mexico City, January 25, 1945. Among the members of the pre-war Politburo, three died from natural causes: Alexander S. Shcherbakov (May 10, 1945); Mikhail A. Kalinin (June 3, 1946); and Andrei A. Zhdanov (August 31, 1948).

Subtle changes meanwhile came to pass in Soviet conceptions of proper patterns of relationships among human beings. "Political Commissars" in the Army were abolished in August 1940, restored in July 1941, and demoted in October 1942 to "political instructors" subordinate to Army commanders. Generals, admirals, and diplomats, long ignored as deplorable relics of "bourgeois" culture, were now blessed with ornate uniforms, medals, honors, and large salaries. In industry, commerce, and agriculture a comparable process was manifest in rich rewards for able executives and highly productive workers and farmers.

The *credenda* and *miranda* of power whereby rulers ruled the ruled shifted slowly but unmistakably during a decade of mass sacrifice and heroic defense from the symbols of Marxist revolutionary "internationalism" to the older and more hallowed symbols of Russian patriotism. The *Rodina* ("native land") was again *sviashchenniya* ("sacred") and charged with the memories of Kutusov, Suvorov, Pozharsky and Minin, Dmitri Donskoi, and Alexander Nevsky. In December 1943 the Sovnarkom abandoned the "International" as the national anthem in favor of a new "Hymn of the Soviet Union" singing the praises of "Russia" and glorifying the ancestral *Otechestvo* ("Fatherland"). Martyred young partisans became national heroes. All Germans, with no distinction between "bourgeois" and "proletarian," were widely regarded as evil beasts, fit only to be killed. An exalted new nationalism, suffused with Great Russian ethnocentrism and a far-ranging Pan-Slavism, but also embracing the non-Slavic minorities (despite Stalin's mass reprisals against groups whose enthusiasm for the cause was insufficient), inspired millions to crush the foe and embark energetically on rebuilding the ruins of war.

The transition from war to peace, always difficult in all the modern nation-states where war is "total" and peace is dubious, was managed by the Party leadership with minimal dislocation and maximal incentives to get ahead with the work of restoration. Demobilization laws of June 23, 1945, released to civilian life some 7,000,000 older members of the armed forces. A decree of March 20, 1946, released 4,000,000 younger men. All were given transport home, food and clothing, graduated cash bonuses, and a pledge of re-employment. A decree of September 4, 1945, ended the "War Cabinet" or State Committee for Defense, even though Stalin was given the permanent title of "Generalissimo" of the USSR on July 27. Another decree, March 22, 1946, unified the armed forces under Stalin as Minister of Defense and Supreme Commander, with Bulganin as Vice-Minister and Marshal Alexander M. Vasilevsky as Chief of Staff. Federal Commissariats, numbering over 50 by the end of the war, were reshuffled and renamed "Ministries" by a constitutional amendment of March 15, 1946. The "Red Army" at the same time became the "Soviet Army."

Other signs and portents of a new era were short-lived gestures by the Politburo to ease the harsh conditions of Soviet life and to relax the rigid regimentation of previous years. But this trend gave

way almost at once to a new intolerance under the mounting tensions of the "Cold War" and to intensified efforts to hasten the tempo of further industrialization and enhance the military might of the nation through further mass sacrifice. By mid-year of 1946 Zhdanov was warning writers and artists to shun "bourgeois culture." By order of the Party Central Committee, Anna Akhmatova and Mikhail Zoschenko, both accused of addiction to "alien ideologies," were expelled from the Union of Soviet Writers—whose President, Nikolai Tikhonov, was dismissed and replaced by a governing board dominated by Alexander Fadayev and sworn to undeviating political orthodoxy. "Bourgeois" and "anti-Soviet" plays and films were banned. Sergei Eisenstein, having suffered the suppression of Part II of his cinema masterpiece *Ivan Grozny* as "anti-historical and anti-artistic," confessed his sins and agreed that "everything we do must be subordinated to the struggle against the corruptive ideology of the bourgeois world." In a new purge of incompetents, careerists, and addicts of "bourgeois nationalism," over half of the Party leaders and administrative executives in the Ukraine were replaced within 18 months, according to a statement by Khrushchev, August 23, 1946.

Early in March 1947, in one of his rare expressions of modesty, Stalin in the journal *Bolshevik* deplored "panegyrics in his honor," which "grate upon the ear" and are "really uncomfortable to read." At the same time he yielded his post as Minister of Defense to Bulganin, who also became a Vice-Premier. But on the 30th anniversary of the October Revolution, Stalin, who remained on the Black Sea coast during the festivities, was hailed as "leader of genius, teacher, wise father, and friend of Soviet youth" and as "the sun of the entire earth" in a testimonial signed by 26,475,000 young people. Militant defense against American "war-mongers" was demanded with increasing vehemence by all Party spokesmen.

Gen. Walter Bedell Smith had replaced Harriman as American Ambassador in February 1946, while Nikolai Novikov succeeded Andrei Gromyko in Washington and was followed in turn by Alexander S. Panyushkin in December 1947. On February 18, 1947, Bedell Smith reminded Molotov that none of the U.S. proposals of 1946 for enlarged cultural relations had been acted upon. When Ernest C. Simmons of Columbia sought during a summer visit to foster exchanges of students and scholars, he gained only insult for his efforts (cf. *Izvestia*, October 17, 1947). Returning veterans, hav-

ing discovered in Central Europe that the world of "capitalism" was wholly different from Party descriptions of it, were already a source of anxiety to the leadership. The "Iron Curtain" swiftly became a reality as a means of insulating the Soviet citizenry from contacts with the West. Paradoxically, the Supreme Soviet on May 26, 1947, abolished the death penalty in peace-time (it was restored January 13, 1950, for "traitors, spies, and saboteurs") on the ground that "peace can be considered secure for a long time."

The tide of intolerance and totalitarian repression flowed steadily in the late 1940's and early '50's as East-West relations became ever more exacerbated, with the process hastened by Stalin's progressive paranoia and megalomania. In December 1947, Fadayev, now President of the Writers' Union, Stalin Prize winner, and author of *Young Guard* (which had sold over a million copies), humbly agreed, following criticism in Party journals, to rewrite his novel to glorify the Party rather than the Komsomols. Economist Eugene Varga, demoted in 1947, continued to be assailed for his "false Marxist-Leninist views"—i.e., his insistence that no "capitalist crisis" was imminent and that public planning against depression was possible in bourgeois States. In February 1948 the Party Central Committee hurled accusations of "formalistic distortions," "æsthetic individualism," and "smelling strongly of the spirit of the bourgeois music of Europe and America" against the "Big Three" of Soviet music: Dmitri Shostakovich, Aram Khatchaturian, and Sergei Prokofiev. In April, Stalin Prizes of 100,000 rubles went to Reinhold Glière ("*Red Poppy* Ballet") and Josef Tallat-Kepsha (*Cantata about Stalin*) for "classicism" and "realism." In August 1948 the Central Committee, at Stalin's directive, "decided" the biological controversy over alleged inheritance of acquired characteristics in favor of Trofim D. Lysenko, with various dissident biologists demoted and penalized and all others warned to embrace "Bolshevik partisanship" and to eschew "Darwin's Malthusian errors" as used by "the ideologists of modern imperialism." H. J. Muller, Nobel Prize geneticist of the University of Indiana, resigned in protest from the Soviet Academy of Sciences, accusing Lysenko of "charlatanism" and "naïve and archaic mysticism."[2]

By midyear of the 20th Century Stalinist "reconstruction" had

[2] Cf. Conway Zirkle (ed.): *The Death of a Science in Russia* (University of Pennsylvania Press, 1949) and Julian Huxley: *Heredity, East and West: Lysenko and World Science* (Schuman, 1949).

assumed the form of furious campaigns against embezzlers, spies, deviationists, bad composers, poets guilty of ideological errors, free-thinking scientists and artists, psychiatrists who preferred Freud to Pavlov, "Jewish cosmopolitans," and other scapegoats. Elinor Lippert, German ex-Communist who survived 11 years in Soviet slave camps, told the International Rescue Committee at the Waldorf on November 1, 1951, that 98% of the Russian people had "tremendous hatred" toward their rulers but that revolt was "inconceivable" because of "the deliberate program of the Soviet regime to terrorize the entire population by filling prison camps with representatives of all types of people." Other reports, subsequently confirmed, told of systematic persecution of Zionists, suppression of Yiddish culture, including the judicial murder of writers and artists, and mounting economic discrimination against Jews. All spontaneity and freedom of expression, even in the most "non-political" realms of human activity, were stifled into silence and sullen conformity.

2. THE ECONOMICS OF MARXISM

MOST Americans are tempted to see other nations and international issues in simple terms of black or white. When told that the world is gray, they see red. This color-blindness is peculiarly baffling in contemplating Soviet society which, *ex hypothesi*, must be either all good or all evil. That its mosaic of paradox displays fragments of virtue and pieces of vice is always hard to grasp.

The foreign observer at mid-century could quite justifiably regard Sovietland as a kind of mad-house, echoing Toynbee's comment of 1937. If he limited his attention to the events recorded in the pages immediately preceding, he could come to no other conclusion than that the Red Empire was well on its way toward becoming a facsimile of George Orwell's *1984*. Yet the oligarchy that sponsored fierce fanaticism, outrageous injustices, and arrant nonsense in the arts and sciences, all in the name of ideological unanimity, at the same time devised the means (and elicited enthusiastic mass support for their effective application) to achieve the extraordinarily rapid rebuilding of the wreckage of war and to create within a decade after 1945 a vastly productive and flourishing economy, expanding at an unprecedented rate and offering each year

not only an ever brighter promise of a life of abundance but an ever greater measure of fulfillment.

This antithesis was a fact, not a mirage in the eye of the witness. It might therefore seem to call for no "explanation," save in the minds of Western liberals whose own historical experience led them to believe that freedom and democracy are prerequisites of economic progress. In the twisted mind of Stalin, and of the co-workers who gladly or reluctantly or fearfully followed his "line"—suffused into a curious synthesis of Byzantine hypocrisy, Georgian vendettas, Muscovite obscurantism, and a weird version of Marxism—the explanation was clear: industrialization in Russia was a product of revolution, Red terror, and the victory in the "class war" of the "proletariat" over the "bourgeoisie"; therefore, further economic development presupposed, and depended upon, further terrorism and regimentation, quite apart from real or imagined threats from abroad. How many Soviet Communists and bureaucrats believed this in their hearts or even supposed that it "made sense" we cannot know except by the light of their post-Stalin "revisionism." During the years we are here concerned with, they had no choice but to accept the formula or face demotion, exile, imprisonment, suicide, or execution. All save a handful conformed, thus becoming accessories in crime but also participating in the realization of their highest hope: the further industrialization and urbanization of the USSR as a contribution to "socialism" and a preparation for "communism." [3]

Within this contradiction is contained another, with far-reaching implications for the destinies of mankind during the second half of the 20th Century. The historical function of Marxism, as conceived by its founders and followers, was to rectify social injustice through proletarian revolution and the socialization of the means of production in mature "capitalistic" economies, thereby achiev-

[3] According to *Narodnoye Khozyaistvo CCCP* (*National Economy of the USSR*), Statistical Handbook (Moscow, 1956), Russia's "urban" population, as part of the total, increased from 17.6% in 1913 to 17.9% in 1926 to 32.9% in 1939 to 43.4% in 1956, when 87,000,000 Soviet citizens were classified as "urban" and 113,200,000 as "rural." Population of the 140 chief cities in April 1956 (cf. pp. 24–5) was given as: Moscow, 4,839,000; Leningrad, 3,176,000; Kiev, 991,000; Baku, 901,000; Kharkov, 877,000; Gorki 876,000; Tashkent, 778,000; Kuibyshev, 760,000; Novosibirsk, 730,000; Sverdlovsk, 707,000; Tblisi, 635,000; Stalino, 625,000; Chelyabinsk, 612,000; Odessa, 607,000; Dnepropetrovsk, 576,000; Kazan, 565,000; Riga, 565,000; Rostov-Don, 552,000; Molotov, 538,-000; Stalingrad, 525,000; Saratov, 518,000; Omsk, 505,000; Minsk, 412,000, etc., down to Voroshilov, 101,000.

ing the "cooperative commonwealth" in the most advanced and productive segments of modern industrialism. In no highly urbanized industrial nation of the contemporary world has anything of the kind ever taken place—save through the subtle osmosis (totally un-Marxist) of the Welfare State with its leveling income taxes, social insurance, full employment through public spending, and other devices to overcome the iniquities and instabilities of "free enterprise" economics. The historical function of Marxism, in fact, has been to devise a scheme of human relations, rewards, penalties, and resultant activities having no relevance whatever, save as a goad to "social reform," in already industrialized communities but having vast relevance to the problems and hopes of poor, primitive, rural, illiterate, and otherwise "backward" societies, still unhappily comprising more than half of the human race.

Marxism in its Leninist-Stalinist exegesis has long since become meaningless as an indictment of, or a substitute for, "capitalism," except in those areas where the evils of the 19th Century or the older evils of feudalism still persist. But Marxism as a *modus operandi* for lifting poverty-stricken nations by their bootstraps to some semblance of Western living standards is of enormous import to much of humankind. The method was first invented by the Communist oligarchs of the USSR. For the great mass of those who endured and survived the internal Inferno of the Purges and the external Hell of Hitlerism, the horrors of the 1930's and '40's and the abuses of the '50's are of small moment in everyday experience as compared with the central fact of Soviet life: the metamorphosis of the rural, miserable, illiterate, filthy, incompetent, and impoverished Russia of the NEP into the urban, hopeful, educated, clean, efficient, and prosperous Russia of the Sixth Five Year Plan.

How this transformation was brought about has been expounded in many volumes of analysis, description, and commentary, some by Marxists who mystically find the clue in "Marxism," and some by non-Marxists who although puzzled, have grappled valiantly with the problem.[4] Here we may usefully return to the bare

[4] The three comprehensive economic histories of the USSR, each with its special merits, are Alexander Baykov: *The Development of the Soviet Economic System* (Macmillan, 1946); Maurice Dobb: *Soviet Economic Development Since 1917* (International, 1949); and Harry Schwartz: *Russia's Soviet Economy* (Prentice-Hall, 1950). Among the more useful specialized studies in English are the following: A. Arakelian: *Industrial Management in the USSR*, translated by Elsworth Raymond (Public Affairs Press, 1949); Abram Bergson

bones of economics and depict the process in the simplest terms, while recognizing that its operational problems and imperatives and its decision-making and managerial aspects are of great complexity —so much so as to foster confusion, bewilderment, and initial disbelief in the viability of the enterprise even among the participants.

The industrialization of a major national community is obviously not a phenomenon unique to the USSR. This social mutation, beginning in England in the late 18th Century, took place on a huge scale in Germany and America in the 19th Century and is in progress today in China, India, and elsewhere. Soviet industrialization, however, differs from all earlier counterparts in three respects: (1) its enormously rapid tempo, which telescoped a half-century of change in the Atlantic communities into a single decade, 1929–39, in the USSR; (2) the absence of investments of foreign capital; and (3) the pursuit of the goal in a context of totalitarian socialism and total national planning, with no private ownership of any significant means of production and no incentives of private profit derived from property to spur the process. Since nothing of the kind had ever before been attempted, most Western observers were confident at the outset that the effort must fail. When confounded by its striking success, they often sought to "explain" what was clearly incredible in ways indicative of confused resentment rather than of accurate insight.

The essence of the matter, concerning which Marx offered little guidance apart from what he borrowed from pre-Marxist econ-

---

(ed.): *Soviet Economic Growth* (Row-Peterson, 1953), *Soviet National Income and Product in 1937* (Columbia University Press, 1953), and, with Hans Heymann, Jr.: *Soviet National Income and Product, 1940–1948* (Columbia University Press, 1954); G. Bienstock, S. Schwarz, and M. Yugow: *Management in Russian Industry and Agriculture* (Oxford University Press, 1944); Clark, M. Gardner: *The Economics of Soviet Steel* (Harvard University Press, 1956); M. V. Condoide: *The Soviet Financial System* (Ohio State University, 1951); Walter Galenson: *Labor Productivity in Soviet and American Industry* (Columbia University Press, 1955); David Granick: *Management of the Industrial Firm in the USSR* (Columbia University Press, 1954); Donald R. Hodgman: *Soviet Industrial Production, 1928–1951* (Harvard University Press, 1955); Oleg Hoeffding: *Soviet National Income and Product in 1928* (Columbia University Press, 1954); Franklyn D. Holzman: *Soviet Taxation* (Harvard University Press, 1955); Naum Jasny: *The Socialized Agriculture of the USSR* (Stanford University Press, 1949), *The Soviet Economy During the Plan Era* (Stanford University Press, 1951), *The Soviet Price System* (Stanford University Press, 1951), and *Soviet Prices of Producers' Goods* (Stanford University Press, 1952); Alexander Vucinich: *Soviet Economic Institutions* (Stanford University Press, 1952).

omists, comes to this: no society, unless aided from outside by loans or gifts, can accumulate capital for investment save through persuading or coercing its members to produce more than they consume or consume less than they produce. Without such a surplus of production above consumption, nothing is available for expanding the means of production, whether they are privately or publicly owned. The basic differences between Western "capitalism" and Soviet "socialism" as systems of business can best be envisaged in terms of how capital is accumulated and how capital is invested. The crucial questions are: Where does the capital come from? And where does the capital go to? In a free-enterprise economy, capital is garnered from the profits of corporations and from voluntary savings by the mass of the populace. Such capital finances the growth of the economy through the decisions of bankers, corporation directors, or individual savers to buy corporate bonds or stocks, with the current prices of such shares varying with collective guesses as to what returns on the investment may be expected.

In the USSR such choices are unavailable. Soviet citizens, if they save money from their incomes, may open bank accounts which earn interest or buy State lottery bonds on which they will receive nothing or little or much in the way of dividends, depending upon accidents of chance, with 4% in prizes paid back to the investors *in toto*. But these sources of capital are relatively unimportant, nor are any major contributions derived from income taxes (limited to 10% even in the top brackets), from customs duties, from taxes on the profits of collective farms and industrial enterprises, from the planned profits of industry, or indeed, until recently, from all of these combined.[5]

In the totally socialized Soviet economy all capital is derived from public revenue, the principal source of which has long been the "turnover tax." This device is comparable to a sales tax, except that it is included in the prices of all goods, rather than being added as an identifiable impost. It commonly comprises one-third to one-half of the price over and above the calculated cost of production and distribution. Consumers are thus "squeezed," relatively painlessly, into paying far more for commodities than the price which would cover the expense of fabrication, processing, and sale. This

[5] With all land and almost all buildings socialized, there are, of course, no property taxes save a nominal tax, usually 25 rubles a year, on privately owned dwellings.

margin does not flow, as in the West, into the profits of farmers, manufacturers, wholesalers, and retailers, but into the public treasury, along with all other sources of revenue. Out of this undifferentiated pool of currency the running expenses of government are met and capital is allocated for investment in State-owned agricultural, industrial, and commercial enterprises.

The allocation is not made, as in any competitive system of "capitalism," by the price mechanism of the free market, which, in principle, determines the exchange value of goods and services, the profit or loss of producers and distributors, and the fluctuating quotations of corporate shares in the money market. This familiar system, albeit increasingly modified by monopoly, oligopoly, public fiscal policies, and an ever larger volume of governmental taxing and spending, is ideally designed to result, through the beneficent manipulations of the "invisible hand," in the most efficient allocation of capital. In the Soviet economy the forces of the market are replaced by the Economic Plan. Decisions regarding the volume, the direction of flow, and the distribution among recipients of investment capital are not products of the buying and selling of millions of producers, consumers, lenders, and borrowers in the impersonal bartering of the market place. They are conscious choices of the members of the Gosplan, or State Planning Commission, who, on the basis of detailed analyses of resources, needs, and productive potentialities plus the current directives of the "Party line," draw up, by quinquennia, by years, and by quarters, target goals for all branches of business activity—each of which in turn is broken down, regionally and locally, into specific objectives for every farm, forest, fishery, factory, mill, mine, office, and store throughout the USSR.

The question of whether such a system can "work" to satisfy needs has long since been answered. As of today (and, so far as can be foreseen, for endless tomorrows) the Soviet scheme of socialized enterprise works extraordinarily well. In waste of goods and lives, the cost of early mistakes and trial-and-error experimentation was staggering. The price, material and psychic, of coercion, exploitation, regimentation, and ceaseless propaganda to increase production was almost intolerable in the 1930's and again in the late '40's. But with ultimate mastery of the techniques of planning and managing, the Soviet economy, four decades after October, was buzzing and booming in an ever more ample outpouring of goods and services ranging from steel mills and schools to motor cars and cosmet-

ics. Before considering other facets of this achievement, it will be well to take cognizance of a preliminary phase of reconversion from the demands of war to the tasks of peace.

Unlike other belligerent governments, the USSR financed its war effort on a pay-as-you-go basis with budgets balanced during the years of conflict, as before and after. Annual sales of State bonds were kept near peace-time levels: 13 billion rubles in 1942, 20 in 1943, 28 in 1944, and 25 in 1945. At the cost of a drastic reduction of living standards, alleviated through rationing, two customary concomitants of war financing were avoided: a sharp inflation of price levels and a huge public debt. Corporate or individual "war profits" were theoretically impossible in a socialized economy. Much new currency nevertheless poured into circulation by way of grants to war enterprises and generous bonuses and other rewards to individuals as incentives to martial ardor and to increased labor productivity in industry—much of which was bodily transported from Western Russia to the Urals in 1941–2. With all prices fixed and with all goods rationed, this excess purchasing power could not, in theory, raise price levels and depress the buying power of money. In practice, it fostered "black markets," which the planners sought to combat not only by shooting black-marketeers but by a system of "open stores" where goods were sold without ration points at prices much higher than those prevailing in the regular government stores. Much speculative and unrationed buying and selling for gain at inflated prices was winked at by officialdom as a means of preventing a too desperate impoverishment of the masses. War's end found the economy at once water-logged by excessive currency, much of it hoarded, and by a thirst for scarce goods—with results incompatible with sound accounting and effective planning.

A drastic solution of these problems was decreed on December 14, 1947. In anticipation, many possessors of currency had transformed their cash into goods. Despite wide publicity about this "buying panic" on the Voice of America, the U.S. Embassy was reported to have been "caught short" with a million rubles in cash. The decree abolished all rationing, put an end to "open stores" and extra-legal inflationary transactions, and established uniform prices for all commodities. It also revalued the ruble through the issue of new currency exchanged for old in a ratio of 1:10 for cash in hand, 1:1 for bank deposits up to 3,000 rubles, 2:3 for deposits from 3,000 to 10,000 rubles, and 1:2 over 10,000. Lottery bonds of 1938 and 1947

were exchanged at parity for new 3% lottery bonds. All other bonds were exchanged in a ratio of 1 new ruble for 3 old rubles. The effects of this "last sacrifice" were to deprive most bond-holders of two-thirds of the value of their certificates, to cause hoarders of currency to lose nine-tenths of their holdings, and to take from large bank depositors a third to a half of their savings. Small depositors suffered no loss. Recipients of low incomes gained from reduced prices and the maintenance of all wage and salary payments in new rubles at the old level.[6]

So much done, the work of restoration and economic expansion could proceed without the embarrassments of rationing, double price levels, and excess currency. The annual consolidated State Budget of the USSR, embracing the budgets of all the Republics and all their provinces, municipalities, and economic enterprises, comes close to representing, in the absence of private business, a national balance sheet of total income, savings, spending, and investment. Each year, for many recent years, it has been submitted annually to the Supreme Soviet by Finance Minister Arsene Zverev and unan-

---

[6] A decree of the Council of Ministers of February 28, 1950, declared that after March 1, 1950, the ruble would be exchanged for foreign currencies not on the basis of 5 rubles, 30 kopeks to the dollar, as previously, but on the basis of a theoretical gold content of the ruble (which, like all other currencies, remained inconvertible into gold) of 0.221168 grams, equivalent to 4 rubles to the U.S. dollar and 11.20 rubles to the £. The diplomatic rate of 8 rubles to the dollar was changed to 6 and then abolished altogether on July 1, 1950, thus doubling the cost of operating the U.S. Embassy in Moscow. Official Soviet exchange rates long remained purely arbitrary. Prior to the summer of 1956, Americans in the USSR, while well rewarded for their Intourist coupons purchased in dollars in the USA and covering meals, hotels, guides, cars, and other transport, were obliged, in buying "incidentals" in rubles at the rate of 4 to a dollar, to pay $1.25 for a pack of cigarettes or a bottle of beer, $1.75 for a package of the cheapest pipe tobacco, $6.25 for a bottle of the least expensive vodka, $7.50 for opera, theater, and ballet tickets, and wholly prohibitive prices for gifts, souvenirs, and *objets d'art*. At the same time West Germans were granted 0.90 rubles for one West German mark and East Germans 1.80 rubles for 1 East German mark, although in Germany 1 Westmark was worth 5 Eastmarks. Since midsummer 1956, all U.S. tourists in the USSR receive a "gift" of 25 rubles per day for "spending money." Any inferences from these exchange rates regarding the "cost of living" to Soviet citizens, however, is unwarranted, since the ruble prices cited are by no means exorbitant in terms of average ruble wages of Soviet workers. An exchange rate of 12 or 15 rubles to the dollar would have made most commodities available to American visitors at prices comparable to those prevailing in the USA. Prior to 1935, when the institution was abolished because it contributed to "black-market" operations in currency and goods, Russians and foreigners alike could purchase many commodities at moderate prices at "Torgsin" stores for foreign currency or "*valuta.*"

imously voted by the deputies, sometimes after minor changes. It provided in 1933 for total revenues of 40 billion rubles, of which 23 billions came from the turnover tax. By 1948, after a roughly ten-fold increase of the productivity of the Soviet economy, revenues were planned at 429 billion rubles, of which 281 billions came from the turnover tax, and expenditures at 388 billions, of which 149 were allocated to the "National Economy," 66 to "Defense," and 116 to "Social and Cultural" activities. Not until 1953, when revenues were 543 billion rubles and expenditures 530 (156 to National Economy, 110.2 to Defense—a reduction from 114 in 1952—and 140 to Social and Cultural purposes), did all other revenues combined (303 billions) exceed those from the turnover tax (240). In 1955, of total revenues of 590 billion rubles, 222 came from the turnover tax and 368 from all other sources. In 1956 total revenues were tabulated at 593 billion rubles and expenditures (102.5 for Defense) at 570 billions. The budget for 1957, voted by the Supreme Soviet on February 9, contemplated revenues of 617 billion rubles and expenditures of 604.6 billions, of which 96.7 billions were allocated for Defense.[7]

Since this central juggling with astronomical sums of money does not represent "make-believe" but is in fact an annual accounting of the Soviet economy, the tangible results of taxing, spending, and investing are as impressive as the progression of figures given above. The Fourth Five Year Plan (1946–50) contemplated an annual steel output of 25,000,000 metric tons by mid-Century (15 in 1946), 19,000,000 tons of pig iron (11 in 1946), 250,000,000 tons of coal (166 in 1946), and 35,000,000 tons of oil (31 in 1946). In an address broadcast from Moscow on the 32nd anniversary of the Revolution (November 6, 1949), Georgi M. Malenkov sang the praises of these achievements:

> Three years and ten months have elapsed since the So-
> viet people, led by the Bolshevik Party, proceeded to carry

[7] Detailed budgetary statistics would here be meaningless in the absence of a total analysis of the complex and often obscure processes of Soviet budget-making and economic planning. Gross revenues and their sources, plus gross expenditures and their broad allocation, year by year since 1945, will be found in my annual articles on the USSR in Funk & Wagnall's *New International Year Book*. Much more data on the annual Soviet budget will be found in the *Current Digest of the Soviet Press*, weekly since January 1949. It should be noted that under the grim circumstances of the war years receipts from the turnover tax in 1943 fell to 71 billion rubles as compared with 139 billions from other sources.

out the first Stalin post-war Five Year Plan. Our national economy has not only attained its pre-war level but surpassed it. We have every reason to believe that the first post-war Five Year Plan will be completed ahead of time. . . . The total volume of industrial output of the USSR in 1950 was to exceed the output of 1940 by 48%. In October of this year gross industrial output was over 50% above the average monthly output in 1940. . . . The gross output of the whole of the industry of the Soviet Union in the first ten months of the current year was 20% higher than in the corresponding period of last year. In the first three years and nine months of the post-war Five Year Plan, upwards of 4,600 state owned industrial plants, not counting cooperative and other small plants, have been either rehabilitated or newly built and put into operation. In the first nine months of 1949 the productivity of labor in industry was 14% higher than in the corresponding period of last year. In the first nine months of 1949 the cost of industrial production declined, in comparable prices, by 7.2%. . . .

In sober truth the Soviet economy since 1945 has been expanding at an annual rate of at least 7% and possibly as much as 9% as compared with a normal yearly expansion of less than 4% in America and most of Western Europe. The major targets of the Fourth and Fifth (1951-5) Five Year Plans were attained or exceeded in most lines of industry, despite lags in agriculture, housing, and some consumers' goods. The scope of accomplishment is best indicated by noting the volume of production in key commodities (all in millions of metric tons) attained in terminal years as compared, in parentheses, with the goals set five years previously.[8]

	1950	1955
Steel	27.3 (25)	45.3 (44.2)
Pig-iron	19.2 (19)	33.3 (33.9)
Coal	261.1 (250)	390 (377.5)
Oil	37.9 (35)	70.8 (69.5)

[8] See the voluminous data in *Pravda* and *Izvestia* on targets and achievements in all lines of industry and agriculture, much of it translated in the *Current Digest of the Soviet Press*, and the figures offered in *Narodnoye Khozyaistvo CCCP* (Central Statistical Board, Moscow, July 1956).

At the opening of the 40th year of the Soviet regime the original goals of the Sixth Five Year Plan (1956–60)—steel, 68.3 million tons; pig-iron, 53; oil, 135; coal, 593; etc.—seemed likely to be somewhat reduced in the interest of more consumers' goods through a slowing of the tempo of industrialization. The annual report of the Central Statistical Administration, issued on January 30, 1957, estimated that Soviet industrial output in 1956 was 11% above 1955 and that capital investments, although 6% below the targets originally set, were 17% above 1955. Production in 1956, in millions of metric tons, was calculated at 48.6 for steel, 35.8 for pig-iron, and 78 for oil. Pervukhin's report to the Supreme Soviet in February 1957 on the revised economic goals indicated that the planned increase of industrial production during 1957 would be less than 8% above the level of 1956. Even at this reduced rate of expansion, however, the Soviet economy in its fifth decade was growing more rapidly than any of its Western counterparts.

The vehicle of planning was meanwhile modified to take account of short-range and long-range targets. On May 26, 1955, the Gosplan was bifurcated into a State Commission for Future Planning, headed by Nikolai K. Baibakov, an oil expert, and a State Commission for Current Planning, still headed by Maxim Z. Saburov —who had been awarded the Order of Lenin on his 50th birthday, February 19, 1950. The Soviet economy had long since become a flourishing system for the abundant production of goods and services, even if the ideal of overtaking and surpassing America was still remote. Its output of the products of heavy industry in 1957 was approaching that of all Western Europe combined and moving from one-third toward one-half of the output of the USA.

Lincoln Steffens' ecstatic comment on his return from Moscow in the spring of 1919—"I have seen the future, and it works!"—was a delusion. He had not seen the future. What he saw was unworkable, for the Russia of 1919 was in chaos. The USSR of the 1950's was in no sense "the future" even for the third of mankind under Communist rule. But it worked very well indeed. The implications of the Soviet economy for the people of Sovietland, for the West, and for the rest of the world are best deferred in our inquiry, pending a survey of the processes of politics in the final years of Stalin's dictatorship.

3. THE POLITICS OF STALINISM

THE structure of power in the Soviet State was defined by its founders in 1917 as a "dictatorship of the proletariat." By 1928 it had become an oligarchy of the Party leaders. By 1938 its lines of arbitrary authority and fear-inspired obedience had begun to resemble an Autocracy, albeit never legitimized, embodied in a *Vozhd* who was the son of a Georgian cobbler. By 1948 and thereafter, in ever greater measure until his passing, Stalin's despotism was rigidly superimposed upon the oligarchs and in the fashion of its functioning had little in common, apart from semantic continuity, with the regime that emerged from the October Revolution.

Most Western observers of these transitions have long seen the essence of the political process in the USSR in terms of "struggles for power" at the apex of the hierarchy. Here is a tale of sound and fury, highlighted by Stalin's ruthless expunging of rivals, the Party's tyrannical imposition of doctrinal uniformity, and the progressive concentration of lawless command in the hands of a despot and his hirelings, all drunk with the wine of omnipotence and selfishly seeking the preservation of their privileges. This portrait is not inaccurate. But it is incomplete and therefore misleading as a picture of the relations between rulers and ruled in the Russia of mid-Century.

The rulers, including Stalin, were pursuing a vision transcending the usual imperatives of power and privilege in politics. The vision, in theory, contemplated the "building of socialism" in preparation for "communism," which, once attained, was expected, nebulously and miraculously, to create a happy society of prosperous freemen united in equality and brotherhood. The vision, in practice, called for the industrialization, urbanization, and education of all Russia, with "defense" against "bourgeois imperialists" and "warmongers" given first place in the order of priority. The mass of the ruled, in turn, had little interest in the interpersonal rivalries and Byzantine dialectical disputations among the great and powerful, but enormous interest in peace, in prices and wages, in better housing, and in improved living standards. All looked forward to the fulfillment of the promise of their rulers: a highly productive industry and agriculture offering comfort and "culture" as a reward for sacrifice and numerous opportunities for social advancement to those who worked harder than their neighbors.

Rulers, if they wish to continue to rule, can never ignore the mass expectations of the ruled even in the most repressive and arbitrary of regimes. In the USSR, thus far, the vision of those in command and the hopes of those who obey coincide in considerable measure, although the motives differ. Soviet politics is thus inseparable, in a special sense, from Soviet economics. To reduce the drama of Stalin's last years to a survey of interpersonal feuds is to ignore the realities of the daily experiences and aspirations of the vast multitudes of the USSR. Under total socialism, "politics" and "economics" are identical. So much said as a necessary prologue, let us proceed to consider the course of Soviet politics at home (leaving politics abroad for later discussion) between 1945 and 1952.

On August 19, 1945, the Central Committee of the Party and the Council of Peoples' Commissars jointly instructed the Gosplan to prepare directives for a new *Piatiletka* or Five Year Plan designed to repair the ruin of war by 1950, double electric-power output, and increase productivity and living standards beyond the level of 1940. On October 5 the Presidium of the Supreme Soviet fixed February 10, 1946, as the date of "election" of a new federal parliament. The "campaign" proceeded in pre-war style (see pp. 225 f. above). Its culminating ritual was Stalin's broadcast address of February 9 to a meeting of voters in the "Stalin Electoral District" of Moscow. After attributing World Wars I and II not to mistakes of statesmanship but to the "crises" and "catastrophes" bred by "capitalism," the Soviet Premier took pains to distinguish between the two disasters. World War II, "the most bitter and arduous of all wars in the history of our Motherland," was an anti-Fascist war of liberation and a triumphant testing-time of the Soviet system. After celebrating the pre-war economic achievements and the military victories of the Red Army ("during the last three years of the war our tank industry produced an annual average of more than 30,000 tanks, self-propelled guns, and armored cars . . . our aircraft industry up to 40,000 planes per year . . . our ordnance industry 120,000 guns of all calibers, 100,000 mortars, 240,000,000 shells and bombs," etc.), Stalin promised the early abolition of rationing and concentration on consumers' goods to raise living standards.

> As regards the plans for a longer period ahead, the Party means to organize a new mighty upsurge in the national economy, which would allow us to increase our

industrial production, for example, three times over as compared with the pre-war period. We must achieve a situation where our industry can produce annually up to 50 million tons of pig-iron (prolonged applause), up to 60,000,000 tons of steel (prolonged applause), up to 500,000,000 tons of coal (prolonged applause) and up to 60,000,000 tons of oil (prolonged applause). Only under such conditions can we consider that our homeland will be guaranteed against all possible accidents. (Stormy applause.) That will take three more Five Year Plans, I should think, if not more. But it can be done and we must do it. (Stormy applause.)

The new goals were widely interpreted by Western commentators, including Walter Lippmann, as a "declaration of war" against the capitalist world. Given the appalling devastation and bitter impoverishment occasioned by World War II, they could better have been interpreted as an elementary requirement of political prudence, dictating intensive effort to repair the ravages of battle and restore living standards, as soon as possible, to pre-war levels. Concentration of labor and resources once more on heavy industry rather than on consumers' goods was not indicative of a preference for guns over butter. On the contrary, as later developments were to show, it was a prerequisite for an ultimately abundant output of butter and bread and all other necessities and amenities of life. Crop failures and semi-famine in the Ukraine and elsewhere deferred the promise. The post-war upsurge of the Soviet economy did not get fully under way until 1948. Politics, Soviet-style, meanwhile pursued its devious course.

In the absence of any Congress or Conference of the Party, the Central Committee filled its own vacancies by appointment and in March 1946 added Malenkov and Beria to the members of the Politburo, with Bulganin and Kosygin as new alternates. The other members were: Stalin, Molotov, Zhdanov, Kalinin, Mikoyan, Khrushchev, Andreyev, Voroshilov, and Kaganovich, with Shvernik and Voznesensky as alternates. The new Supreme Soviet met on March 12, 1946, and again in June and September to approve the budget and hasten further demobilization to supply labor for the new tasks of industry. On August 28, 1946, Radio Moscow announced that "in view of drought in a number of regions and the diminution of State food reserves" rationing would have to be continued into 1947.

Shortages of foodstuffs and the deplorable disposition of collective farmers to concentrate their labors on their private plots—the produce of which was salable in "free markets" and "commercial stores" at prices far higher than those paid by government purchasing agents—were countered by Soviet planners through complex manipulation of price levels and sundry incentives to increase agricultural output. In industry the eight-hour day was restored early in 1946, after the war years of nine or ten hours of daily toil. Strenuous efforts were made, not without success, to recruit and train new technical personnel, increase labor efficiency, and enlarge production while reducing costs.

The year 1947—marked by the "currency reform," an end of rationing, and an intensification of the already latent "Cold War"—found Moscow's May Day Parade dominated by military fanfare. In the September celebration of the 800th anniversary of the founding of Moscow, Stalin described the city as "the capital of a great peace-loving Power and a mighty bulwark of peace" in the struggle against "imperialists" and the "incendiaries of a new war," a theme redramatized on the 30th anniversary of the Revolution. On New Year's Day of 1948 *Izvestia* opined that the "consolidation" of the forces of "world democracy" would discomfort "the dark forces of reaction assembled under the banner of Wall Street. . . . The struggle will continue. . . . We shall win because the peoples do not want to serve the god of war and gold."

Zhdanov's demise on August 31, 1948, at the age of 52, removed from the scene the Party leader widely regarded as Stalin's successor-designate. Stalin, ever suspicious of "plots" against him among his colleagues, launched the still obscure "Leningrad Case," secretly culminating in 1949 in the deposition and liquidation of Voznesensky and various subordinates, all of whom were probably "guilty" of nothing more than occasionally questioning Stalin's infallibility. Saburov replaced Voznesensky as Chairman of the Gosplan. Economic rehabilitation proceeded apace. On April 9, 1948, the Cabinet decreed a further reduction of retail prices, to be repeated annually for years thereafter. A decree of the federal Presidium (August 29, 1948) took cognizance of what was already an established practice by authorizing all citizens to build or buy for their own use private houses of not more than five rooms. Industrial construction and productivity waxed mightily to the tune of intensive campaigns to enlarge the labor force and train specialists.

In agriculture a good crop year was made better by the bringing of 27,000,000 new acres under cultivation, by higher rewards to collective farmers, and by penalty taxes to discourage undue attention to private garden plots at the expense of collective agronomy. On October 24, 1948, the Council of Ministers and the Central Committee of the Communist Party jointly announced a 15-year reclamation and conservation program in the heart of the country, contemplating protection from desiccation and erosion of the central "black-earth" lands between the North Caucasus and the Southern Urals through reforestation, shelter belts, reservoirs, irrigation projects, and crop rotation. The scheme was not limited to blueprints. Years later the traveler by plane in south central Sovietland could see in the countryside below many visible evidences of accomplishment.

On April 19, 1949, another joint decree of Cabinet and Central Committee proclaimed a general "offensive all along the front of agricultural development," aiming at a 50% increase of output by 1951 of meats, fats, milk, butter, eggs, and leather and a large increase in cattle, sheep, goats, pigs, and poultry. Red Muscovy's rural dilemma nevertheless proved difficult of solution. With all allowances for differences in rainfall, temperature, soil, and growing seasons, Russia's peasantry, thanks to ancient ways of indolence and incompetence, remained far less productive per acre, per man, and per hour of labor than the farmers of Western Europe and America. Individual output could best be enhanced by returning to individual "free-enterprise" farming. But this un-Marxist restoration of a rural class of kulaks or "bourgeois" cultivators was unthinkable to the Marxist oligarchs, the more so as such farmers, while living better by the produce of their labor, would probably dispose of less of a marketable surplus to feed the cities than could be squeezed out of a collectivized peasantry. How to extract a maximum output from the kolkhozes has always been a baffling problem. In 1950 Andreyev, hitherto top Party expert in agriculture, was publicly criticized and soon demoted and relegated to obscurity for espousing small, rather than large, working teams on the collectives and fostering rural productivity from private garden plots. Khrushchev emerged as the new agronomic Messiah, dedicated to "giantism"—the merging of collective farms into ever larger units and the planning of "Agrogorods" or "industrial cities" of tillers of the soil.

Khrushchev's program was more successful in form than in

fact. The Russian lands in 1957 still consisted, as from time immemorial, in scattered villages, more often than not strung along single streets, from which the *muzhiks* went out as in olden times to farflung fields—using twice or thrice the manpower to produce the same harvests as Western farmers reap, despite the aid of the Machine Tractor Stations and the services of skilled agronomists. Khrushchev's "reform" reduced the total number of collective farms through consolidation from 252,000 to 94,000 between 1950 and 1956, by which time the process had been halted. That this operation did not result in the expected increase of output is clear from the sequel.

Beginning in 1951 Khrushchev pushed through an ambitious program of opening new lands in Siberia, for the most part organized as "State Farms" (*sovkhozi*) rather than "Collectives" (*kolkhozi*); 70,000,000 new acres were brought under cultivation between 1951 and 1954. This campaign in its later phases was accompanied by a nation-wide drive, in emulation of America, to foster the cultivation of maize (*kookoorooza*) in pursuit of an Iowan corn-hog economy. Since the climate in most of Russia's best farming regions is unfavorable to corn-growing, this venture produced results disproportionate to the capital and labor devoted to its success. Nevertheless, despite waste and excessive cost, Soviet agriculture by the middle 1950's was producing and marketing enough in the way of foodstuffs to make possible a steady rise of living standards for the rural and urban populations alike.[9]

Meanwhile, on March 4, 1949, Andrei Y. Vyshinsky succeeded Molotov as Foreign Minister and M. A. Menshikov replaced Mikoyan as Minister of Foreign Trade—for reasons unexplained but doubtless related to the pending North Atlantic Treaty. Other shifts of Party and Governmental personnel (see *New International Year*

[9] The appalling costs of the "collectivization" of the 1930's and of the Nazi invasion of the 1940's (previously acknowledged by Khrushchev in various public utterances) and the scope of the restoration achieved in subsequent years are strikingly indicated in the figures released in *Narodnoe Khozyaistvo CCCP* (Moscow, 1956) regarding total livestock on Soviet farms in millions of heads:

	COWS	HOGS	SHEEP AND GOATS
1928	33.2	27.7	114.6
1940	22.8	22.5	76.7
1946	22.9	10.6	70.0
1950	24.6	22.0	93.6
1955	29.2	52.2	142.6

Book, Events of 1949, p. 562), including an apparent purge of the aides of the departed Zhdanov, displayed no obvious relationship to changing problems and policies among the Soviet power-holders.

At long last in 1952, after an interval of 13 years, a Party Congress met, not to arrive at decisions through debate and voting (a procedure long since abandoned by the oligarchs) but to hear expositions of the new "line" and to register unanimous approval thereof. On January 8, 1952, Malenkov was honored on his 50th birthday with the Order of Lenin and praised in the Soviet press as "a true pupil of Lenin and a coadviser of Comrade Stalin." On August 20 the Central Committee called a new All-Union Congress for October 5 and published a new Party statute proposing sundry organizational changes. Local Party Congresses met in most of the Union Republics during September.

On October 2, 1952, in the magazine *Bolshevik,* Stalin published a 50-page article on "Economic Problems of Socialism." He argued that World War II had put an end to the world market of "capitalism." The Communist bloc was self-sufficient and would soon have surpluses for export. A war of "capitalism" against "socialism" was far less likely than eventual war among the bourgeois States themselves. The basic "law" of monopoly capitalism is super-profits, and of socialism "uninterrupted growth of production." In moving toward communism, Soviet society must strive to reduce the working day to six or even five hours, improve housing, raise wages, and foster a direct exchange of goods between factories and farms.

Congress XIX opened on October 5 in the Great Palace of the Kremlin, with delegates cheering the members of the Politburo and the opening address by Malenkov. Representatives of 44 foreign Communist parties attended. All speakers triumphantly celebrated past achievements and future prospects, hailed "Popular Fronts for Peace," and cheered national and colonial revolts against "American Imperialism." After adopting the new rules and dropping the old label "Bolshevik" from the official name of the Party, the Congress closed on October 14, following a 25-minute address by Stalin in which he re-emphasized the themes of peace and international proletarian solidarity and the pledges of Communists abroad that they would never fight against the USSR.

The newly chosen Central Committee of 125 members and 110 alternates announced on October 17 the membership of the new "Presidium," formerly Politburo and now comprising 25 members

and 11 alternates. The former group included Stalin, Beria, Bulganin, Voroshilov, Kaganovich, Malenkov, Molotov, Mikoyan, Khrushchev, and Shvernik (all members of the old Politburo), while Andreyev was dropped and Kosygin became an alternate. A committee headed by Stalin was charged with revising the Party program—for the first time since 1919.[1]

This enlargement of the Politburo, now combined with the Orgburo in the new "Presidium," was, as we shall see, to be temporary. Stalin in the twilight of his life could evidently not foresee any of his colleagues succeeding to his unique role of *Vozhd*. Malenkov, his obvious heir apparent, he did not trust, for he trusted no one in his last lonely years. Hence the need for paving the way for a return to the "collective" or "collegial" leadership that had preceded the consolidation of Stalin's personal despotism in the 1930's. The expansion of the Presidium and of the Central Committee (which was given the functions of the now abolished institution of the Party "Conference") was clearly a step in this direction, comparable to Lenin's enlargement of the Central Committee in 1922. Of the four resolutions of Congress XIX—On the Preparation of New Program, On Change of Name, On the Fifth Five Year Plan, and On New Party Rules—the last-mentioned was the most significant, at least in prior intention if not altogether so in subsequent performance.

The Party now had 6,882,145 members (October 1, 1952), including 868,886 candidates, represented at Congress XIX by one delegate for each 5,000 members. Its junior auxiliaries, the Komsomols and the Pioneers or Communist boy and girl scouts, had, respectively, 10,000,000 and 7,000,000 members. The new rules, expounded by Khrushchev, were designed, like the long-neglected rules of 1939, to promote intra-party democracy. The Party was defined as "a voluntary militant union of Communists holding the same views, formed of people of the working class, the working peasantry, and the working intelligentsia." Members must be 18 years old, must be sponsored by 3 members of 3 years' standing, and must remain on

[1] For full details and documents of Congress XIX, see the speeches published in various Western tongues by the Foreign Languages Publishing House, Moscow, 1952; *Current Digest of the Soviet Press*, November 1952; Leo Gruliow (ed.): *Current Soviet Policies* (Praeger, 1953); and James H. Meisel and Edward S. Kozera: *Materials for the Study of the Soviet System* (George Wahr Publishing Co., Ann Arbor, Mich., 1953). Cf. John N. Hazard: "A Political Testament for Stalin's Heirs," *International Journal* (Toronto), Spring 1953, and Merle Fainsod: *How Russia Is Ruled*, pp. 209–64.

probation as candidates for one year, to which the local Party unit might add another year for those deemed inadequately prepared. Expulsion of members of the Central Committee, including in extreme cases their expulsion from the Party, required a majority vote of the Party Congress or a two-thirds vote of the Central Committee, with similar procedures provided on the lower levels of the hierarchy for the removal of unworthy members of lesser eminence. Members were enjoined anew to practice unity, discipline, responsibility, criticism, and self-criticism. Party Congresses must henceforth meet at least every four years. The Central Committee, which chooses the Presidium, the Party Control Commission, the Central Inspection Commission, and the Secretariat, must meet at least every six months.

The motifs stressed by Stalin and by Malenkov were designed to assure Party and people that fears of war were unwarranted and that the long-promised transition from "socialism" to "communism" was still the ultimate aim of the oligarchs. Further increases of production and further assimilation of townsmen and countrymen would allegedly hasten the advent of the classless and stateless cooperative commonwealth, whose precept must be: "From each according to his ability; to each according to his need." In criticizing the open markets wherein the *kolkhozi* sold their surpluses beyond required deliveries to the State, Stalin declared that "commodity exchange must be replaced by product exchange" and hinted at a goal seldom mentioned since 1919: the abolition of money. Such fantasies were later to be ridiculed by Stalin's successors. But the far-off, divine event of a Utopia of abundance was to remain a dream of the leadership, perhaps never to be attained but never to be abandoned. The "brotherly union" of the Soviet nationalities was said to be paralleled by the global solidarity of the "workers of the world," manifested at the Congress by the presence of foreign Communists and by the singing of the "International." Whether, after years of the embittered "Cold War" in which Stalin had involved his subjects, all his listeners were fully reassured by his promises of peace was problematical.

CHAPTER ELEVEN

The Third War of East and West

1. CHALLENGE AND RESPONSE

WITHIN TWO years after V-E Day of World War II, many American policy-makers and not a few simple citizens, all aglow with prosperity and a new sense of national power, had persuaded themselves of the "inevitability" of World War III. Numerous Europeans and Asians shared this view, but with horror rather than with the confidence displayed by some Americans. Soviet policy-makers revealed in word and deed that they were no less convinced of the probability of another Armageddon, although they were obliged to bespeak "peace" by their knowledge that their long-suffering subjects would find a new war unendurable. The supposed sources of a third irrepressible conflict between East and West were plain and simple to the shapers of policy and opinion in West and East alike, even if unacknowledged realities were neither simple nor plain and were altogether different from what great masses of mankind believed them to be.

The tyranny of words lay heavily upon all the actors in the drama. The reigning Marxists of Muscovy, as prisoners of their creed, were certain that the collapse of "capitalism" and the universal triumph of "Communism" were written in the stars and that bourgeois "imperialists" and "Fascists," in the future as in the past, must seek to delay their doom by launching another murderous assault upon the Socialist Fatherland. Hence the necessity, in the time-honored Muscovite formula, of defending the *Rodina* by speeding the salvation of the West by the East through all means at hand

and by recourse to ruthless Autocracy, intolerant ideological orthodoxy, crusading messianism, limitless territorial aggrandizement,
and unswerving efforts to overtake and surpass the foe in technology
and the arts of war. Most Westerners were equally certain that the
devils in the Kremlin were inflexibly dedicated to conquering and
enslaving all the human race; that the dynamics of all totalitarian
systems were identical; that Communism was "Red Fascism," driving inexorably toward aggression; and that sheer self-preservation
required that the menace be met and halted and that its source, if
possible, be expunged with fire and sword as a precondition of
security.

How this all came about and how its strange *dénouement* confounded the expectations, fears, and hopes of both contestants is our
present concern. The cosmic context of the new battle of the Titans
suggested a different result and revealed anew that all historical
analogies are hazardous. According to the Toynbeean exegesis—foreshadowed by Nikolai Danilevsky, Brooks Adams, and Oswald
Spengler—every civilization in its "time of troubles" is riven by frat-
ricidal warfare among parochial national societies until the most
potent among them puts an end to intolerable anarchy by establishing, after a suitable series of wars of annihilation, a Universal State
and a *Pax Œcumenica*. Such indeed was the self-appointed mission
of all Communists and of some Western apostles of "Manifest Des-
tiny" and the "American Century" in the late 1940's and early '50's.
On a more mundane level of discourse, it has more often than not
been the case in past State Systems resembling our own that all rival
Powers are finally reduced to two—e.g., Egypt and Assyria, Athens
and Sparta, Macedonia and Persia, Rome and Carthage—and that
one then "knocks out" the other and founds a World Imperium.
Why the contemporary contest of two Super-Powers for global hegemony had a wholly different outcome may be suggested by a brief
review of the record of their rivalry.[1]

[1] No detailed and documented account of this contest of wills is yet available or, indeed, possible. Kenneth Ingram's *The History of the Cold War* (Philosophical Library, 1955) is nevertheless a useful pioneer effort. I know of no
Soviet sources or studies that throw any light on the inner processes of decision-
making in the USSR or even undertake any narrative or analysis of the conflict
beyond reiterating the clichés of the current Party "line." Leaving for later nota-
tion the more imaginative, hysterical, and bellicose American literature of the
period, the following serious Western studies of U.S. policy-making, Soviet
policy-making, and other aspects of the "Cold War" will be found helpful:
Gabriel A. Almond *et al.*: *The Appeals of Communism* (Princeton University

Unlike other struggles of similar import, the combat here in hand has no neatly defined initial encounter and no precise terminal point, although future historians, if possessed of full documentation of policy-making on both sides, may achieve more precision and neatness in such matters than is now possible. Earlier sources of frictions and tensions, during and long before Hitler's bid for world mastery, have been surveyed in previous chapters. Here we may usefully begin by noting the controversies that evoked maximum diplomatic and public attention in 1945–7.

The matrix of the "Cold War" was forged in the heat of battle in the resolve of the rulers of Muscovy to impose their power upon all of Europe north of Greece and east of the Stettin-Trieste line and

Press, 1954); American Friends Service Committee: *The United States and the Soviet Union* (Yale University Press, 1949); Thomas A. Bailey: *America Faces Russia* (Cornell University Press, 1951); Frederick C. Barghoorn: *The Soviet Image of the United States* (Harcourt, Brace, 1950); Rhul J. Bartlett: *The Record of American Diplomacy* (Knopf, 3rd ed., 1954); C. E. Black (ed.): *Challenge in Eastern Europe* (Rutgers University Press, 1954); Chester Bowles: *The New Dimensions of Peace* (Harper, 1955); W. A. Brown, Jr., and R. Opie: *American Foreign Assistance* (Brookings Institution, 1953); Camille M. Cianfarra: *The Vatican and the Kremlin* (Dutton, 1950); Edward Crankshaw: *Cracks in the Kremlin Wall* (Viking, 1951); Vera M. Dean: *The United States and Russia* (Harvard University Press, 1947); Martin Ebon: *World Communism Today* (McGraw-Hill, 1948); Harold H. Fisher: *America and Russia in the World Community* (Claremont College, 1946); Michel Gordey: *Visa to Moscow* (Knopf, 1952); John Gunther: *Behind the Curtain* (Harper, 1949); Joseph M. Jones: *The Fifteen Weeks* [1947] (Viking, 1955); Marie N. Kelly: *Mirror to Russia* (Country Life, 1952); Marshall Knappen: *An Introduction to American Foreign Policy* (Harper, 1956); Drew Middleton: *The Defense of Western Europe* (Appleton-Century-Crofts, 1952); *The Nation*, 85th Anniversary Number, December 16, 1950: "Peace with Russia: Can It Be Negotiated?"; National Council of the Arts, Sciences, and Professions: *Speaking of Peace* (1949); J. P. Nettl: *The Eastern Zone and Soviet Policy in Germany, 1945–50* (Oxford University Press, 1951); B. Newman: *Soviet Atomic Spies* (Hale, 1952); Harry B. Price: *The Marshall Plan and Its Meaning* (Cornell University Press, 1955); Leslie Roberts: *Home from the Cold Wars* (Beacon Press, 1948); Joseph S. Roucek et al.: *Central-Eastern Europe: Crucible of World Wars* (Prentice-Hall, 1948); Frank Rounds, Jr.: *A Window on Red Square* (Houghton Mifflin, 1953); D. A. Schmidt: *Anatomy of a Satellite* [Czechoslovakia] (Little, Brown, 1952); Philip Selznick: *The Organizational Weapon: A Study of Bolshevik Strategy and Tactics* (McGraw-Hill, 1952); Sir John Slessor: *Strategy for the West* (Morrow, 1954); Leslie C. Stevens: *Russian Assignment* (Little, Brown, 1953); T. H. Tetens: *Germany Plots with the Kremlin* (Schuman, 1953); James P. Warburg: *How to Coexist without Playing the Kremlin's Game* (Beacon Press, 1952), *Germany: Key to Peace* (Harvard University Press, 1953) and *The United States in a Changing World* (Putnam, 1955); Doreen Warriner: *Revolution in Eastern Europe* (Turnstile Press, 1950); and Theodore H. White: *Fire in the Ashes* (Sloane, 1953).

in the determination of Western statesmen to thwart or undo this program lest any such vast enhancement of Soviet power should leave all the Atlantic communities at the mercy of the Kremlin. The frictions and bargains of 1943–5 have already been recounted. Pending victory over Japan, quarreling was muted. But on August 18, 1945, Secretary of State Byrnes announced that he was "not satisfied that the existing provisional Bulgarian Government is adequately representative of the important elements of democratic opinion." Two days later, in his first speech to Commons as Foreign Secretary, Ernest Bevin declared that "the Governments which have been set up [in Bulgaria, Rumania, and Hungary] do not, in our view, represent the majority of the people, and the impression we get from recent developments is that one kind of totalitarianism is being replaced by another. . . . The question of secret police in Poland has still got to be cleared up." The Soviet press responded with a sharp *tu quoque* concerning Allied supervision of elections in Greece. This initial Anglo-American challenge to Soviet domination of Danubia and Balkania had no immediate effect. Deadlock was registered at the September meeting of Foreign Ministers in London. A temporary *détente* was achieved at their December meeting in Moscow.

Winston Churchill, out of power but still a mighty man in all the councils of the West, returned to the fray in his memorable address of March 5, 1946, in Fulton, Missouri, delivered in the presence of President Truman. In his plea for an Anglo-American alliance, he borrowed (without acknowledgment) and immortalized a favorite phrase of the late Dr. Paul Joseph Göbbels:

> From Stettin in the Baltic to Trieste in the Adriatic an iron curtain has descended across the Continent. All these famous cities and the populations around them lie in the Soviet sphere and are subject, in one form or another, not only to Soviet influence but to a very high and increasing measure of control from Moscow. Athens alone, with its immortal glories, is free to decide its future at an election under British, American and French supervision. . . . If the Western democracies stand together in strict adherence to the principles of the UN Charter, their influence for furthering those principles will be immense, and no one is likely to molest them. . . . If the population of the Eng-

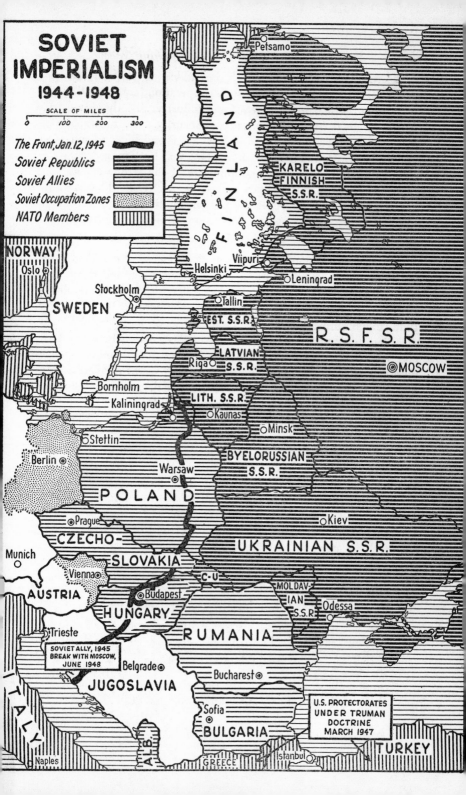

SOVIET IMPERIALISM
1944-1948

SCALE OF MILES

0   100   200   300

The Front, Jan. 12, 1945
Soviet Republics
Soviet Allies
Soviet Occupation Zones
NATO Members

NORWAY
Oslo

SWEDEN
Stockholm

FINLAND

Petsamo

KARELO FINNISH S.S.R.

Helsinki
Viipuri
Leningrad
Tallin
EST. S.S.R.
Riga
LATVIAN S.S.R.

Bornholm
Kaliningrad
LITH. S.S.R.
Kaunas
Minsk

R.S.F.S.R.

MOSCOW

Stettin
Berlin
Warsaw
POLAND

BYELORUSSIAN S.S.R.

Prague
CZECHO-SLOVAKIA

Munich
Vienna
AUSTRIA
Budapest
HUNGARY

Kiev

UKRAINIAN S.S.R.

C·U
MOLDAVIAN S.S.R.
Odessa

Trieste

**SOVIET ALLY, 1945
BREAK WITH MOSCOW,
JUNE 1948**

Belgrade
JUGOSLAVIA

RUMANIA

ITALY

Naples

ALB.

Sofia
BULGARIA

Bucharest

**U.S. PROTECTORATES
UNDER TRUMAN
DOCTRINE
MARCH 1947**

GREECE
Istanbul
TURKEY

lish-speaking Commonwealth be added to that of the
United States, with all that such cooperation implies in the
air, on the sea, and in science and industry . . . there will
be an overwhelming assurance of security. . . . Fraternal
association requires not only growing friendship and mutual understanding between our two vast but kindred systems of society, but the continuance of the intimate relations between our military advisers. . . . It should carry
with it a continuance of the present facilities of all naval
and airforce bases in the possession of either country all
over the world.[2]

Pravda condemned this plea as "poisonous." *New Times* accused Britain of fostering Fascism in Greece, Italy, and Spain and
perpetuating colonialism in India and Indonesia. Stalin (March 13,
1946) called Churchill a "war-monger" comparable to Hitler. By
June, to be sure, Churchill, with no sense of inconsistency, was
pleading in London for a negotiated *modus vivendi* between East
and West and saying: "It is better to have a world united than a
world divided. But it is also better to have a world divided than a
world destroyed." His earlier words made a deeper impression on
a receptive America.

On July 23, 1946, former Vice-President Henry A. Wallace, now
Secretary of Commerce, submitted a memorandum to President Truman. "I have been increasingly disturbed by the trend of international affairs since the end of the war, and I am even more so by
the apparently growing feeling among the American people that another war is coming. . . ." He pleaded for an atomic accord that
would obligate the USA to destroy its bombs at a specific time or
under specific conditions. He argued for agreement with Russia,
"even at the expense of risking epithets of appeasement," on the

---

[2] That the apprehension here expressed by Churchill long antedated
the Marxist conquest of Muscovy is shown by an article in the *Neu Oderzeitung*
of April 1855: "Panslavism is a movement which endeavors to undo what a
thousand year old history has created. It cannot achieve its aim without sweeping Turkey, Hungary, and half of Germany off the map of Europe. Should this
result ever be accomplished, it could be made to last by no other means than
the subjugation of Europe. Panslavism has now transformed itself from an
article of faith into a political program. By now, it is no longer only Russia,
but the whole Panslavistic plot which threatens to found its realm on the ruins
of Europe. This leaves Europe only one alternative—subjugation through slavery
or the lasting destruction of the center of its offensive strength." The writer of
the article was Karl Marx.

basis of reciprocal respect for security requirements. The President appeared to concur. On September 12, 1946, Wallace spoke in Madison Square Garden: "The real peace we now need is between the U.S. and Russia. On our part we should recognize that we have no more business in the political affairs of Eastern Europe than Russia has in the political affairs of Latin America, Western Europe, and the USA. . . ." (On the same day in New Orleans, John Stelle, National Commander of the American Legion, asserted: "We ought to aim an atomic bomb right at Moscow—and save one for Tito, too!")

Truman had endorsed Wallace's speech in advance. When a storm of controversy broke out, he explained that he had not meant that he approved the speech but merely supported the Secretary's right to deliver it. Byrnes in Paris fumed. Several days later, after long conferences at the White House, Wallace said that he had agreed to make no more speeches on foreign policy during the Paris Peace Conference. Byrnes made it clear by transatlantic phone that he would resign if Wallace remained in the Cabinet. Truman telephoned Wallace and asked for his resignation on September 20. There was, explained the President, a "fundamental conflict" between Wallace's views and those of the Administration. "No change in our foreign policy is contemplated."

Meanwhile, the first major crisis in post-war East-West relations had blossomed in Iran, poisoned the UN at its inception, and then withered away with Soviet acquiescence in defeat, leaving behind, however, new roots of mutual suspicion destined to bear bitter fruit. Allied troops were scheduled to end their joint occupation on March 2, 1946. When Moscow in January indicated its intention of prolonging the occupation and supporting a puppet regime in Iranian Azerbaijan until Teheran should grant the USSR oil concessions in the north comparable to those enjoyed by British and American corporations in the south, Iran, with Anglo-American support, appealed to the UN Security Council, meeting for the first time. The UN thus became, at the outset, not a vehicle of inter-allied concord, as it was intended to be, but an arena of East-West discord.

In retrospect, Soviet policy-makers, however clumsy and perverted their methods may have been, were not seeking, as London and Washington feared, to partition or subvert or annex Iran to the USSR. They were asking what they believed was justified by Soviet war losses and contributions to common victory: a position of equality with the Western Powers in access to Iranian oil reserves. After

much wrangling, Soviet troops left Iran in May 1946, on the basis of an oil agreement—which the Iranian Parliament later repudiated, leaving Iran as an Anglo-American protectorate designed in Muscovite eyes to play a major role, thanks to its proximity to the Soviet oil fields of Transcaucasia, in what the Kremlin regarded as an Anglo-American "plot" to encircle and threaten the USSR.[3]

Who was the more justified in attributing to whom the most dastardly of motives in these and other controversies, major and minor, cannot here be decided. The central facts are clear. Muscovite aggrandizement, coupled with Marxist messianism in support of the post-war mass Communist parties of Italy, France, and China, soon convinced politicians in Washington, London, Paris, Rome, and elsewhere in the West that they were confronted with the fearful menace of a revived Russian imperialism, rendered all the more dangerous by its liaison with a creed of "world revolution." Western efforts to "contain" the tide of Muscovite advance convinced politicians in Moscow that they were confronted with the frightful threat of another Western attempt to destroy the USSR. Maximum hopes on each side amply nourished the most dismal fears of the other. In this counterpoint of suspicion, rising in a steady crescendo, there could be no emotionally satisfying climax short of total war to the death. And this in fact was the prospect in the middle years of the 20th Century.

Probability was brought measurably closer to certainty by the American and Soviet responses to the challenge of the atomic era. When the UN Atomic Energy Commission met for the first time on June 14, 1946, the rulers of the USSR had already accused the USA of "brandishing the atomic weapon for purposes which have little in common with the peace and security of nations" (*New Times,*

---

[3] Current Western attitudes were admirably reflected in *The New York Times,* which is, by a large margin, the most accurate, authoritative, and reliable newspaper in the world. The *Times's* distortion of Russian news in 1917–20 was fully revealed by Walter Lippmann and Charles Merz in the *New Republic* of August 4, 1920, "A Test of the News." When Byrnes (March 12, 1946) released a statement, which proved to be false, regarding Soviet troop movements in Iran, the *Times* ran eight-column banner headlines: HEAVY RUSSIAN COLUMNS MOVE EAST IN IRAN; TURKEY OR IRAQ MAY BE GOAL (March 13); SOVIET TANKS APPROACH TEHERAN (March 14); RUSSIANS PRESS ON (March 16). On the latter date Frederick Kuh reported in *PM*: "British authorities have admitted that there is no evidence whatever indicating that Red Army forces have moved beyond the Soviet area in Iran." On March 23 Premier Ahmed Ghavam in Teheran officially asserted that no additional Soviet troops had entered Iran since March 2 and that some contingents previously in Iran had been withdrawn.

March 20, 1946). The Truman Administration had endorsed, and then in effect repudiated, the statesmanlike Lilienthal-Acheson proposals of March 16, 1946, for a UN Atomic Development Authority to own and operate all nuclear installations throughout the world as an international public corporation. On March 18 Truman named multimillionaire "elder statesman" Bernard Baruch as U.S. representative to the UNAEC. On June 14 he presented the Administration's program. He supported in principle a global ADA, but insisted, as a condition of American renunciation of atomic weapons, that a "fool-proof" system of inspection and control must be agreed upon to prevent any other nation from acquiring nuclear weapons, and that the "veto" in the UN Security Council must be abolished in atomic matters to insure "condign punishment" for any State violating the pact. On June 19, 1946, Andrei Gromyko for the USSR proposed a multilateral treaty for the renunciation of the production and use of all atomic weapons and the destruction of all stockpiles within three months. A UN committee should later consider the problem of inspection and control.

The lines thus drawn were never much modified during the decade to come. Washington's goal was to perpetuate America's monopoly of the bomb by offering proposals for "international control" which Baruch and all his colleagues knew would never be accepted by Moscow. The hoped-for result was that the USSR could be blamed for "obstructionism," the USA could continue to stockpile nuclear weapons, and the Russians would be indefinitely delayed in acquiring the bomb. Moscow's goal was to break the American monopoly as soon as possible, via Soviet espionage, science, and technology, while offering proposals that Gromyko and all his superiors knew would never be accepted by Washington. Seldom in the practice of diplomacy do envoys deliberately present plans that they know the other side will reject. Never in the human adventure, since the discovery of fire, have men and statesmen faced a life-or-death challenge comparable to that posed by man-made nuclear fission and fusion.

Neither the USSR nor the USA possessed the requisite resources of creative imagination to grapple constructively with the issue. In pursuit of the ancient objectives of *Realpolitik*, now rendered obsolete, both sides envisaged the fearful wonderwork wrought by the physicists as merely another weapon in the arsenals of power. The men of Moscow assumed—correctly, as events turned out—that the

USSR could soon acquire the bomb and—more dubiously—that its acquisition would assure Soviet security. The men of Washington assumed—incorrectly—that the American monopoly could be long protracted and used as a threat against the USSR. They further assumed that 100% security for America was theoretically attainable if only the Russians could somehow be persuaded or coerced into accepting American demands—and that, if not, the partial security of a limited accord should be spurned in favor of no agreement at all and no security whatever. Both positions in the long run were to prove irrelevant and highly hazardous. In the short run, Moscow was to triumph over Washington.

The game of thrust and parry was, almost by happenstance, transferred to the Eastern Mediterranean and then extended to all of Europe during the fateful year of 1947. Soviet efforts in late 1945 and 1946 to secure bases on the Dardanelles in the name of "joint defense" of the Straits by the Black Sea Powers and to obtain Turkey's retrocession to Russia of Kars, Ardahan, and adjacent territories encountered firm resistance from Ankara, supported by London and Washington. Negotiations ended inconclusively in October 1946 with the Kremlin abandoning or deferring its ambitions and Washington asserting that any attack on Turkey should be "a matter for action on the part of the Security Council." In Greece during the winter of 1944–5 British troops had enabled the Monarchists, amid much bloodshed, to defeat the Communist-led Republican forces of the EAM. Stalin, abiding by his Balkan bargain with Churchill, acquiesced and made no move to aid the Red guerrillas in the Greek mountains until after Bevin and Byrnes began challenging Soviet hegemony in Danubia and Balkania. Athens charged in the autumn of 1946 that the rebel partisans were receiving support from Bulgaria, Albania, and Jugoslavia. The UN Commission named to investigate the accusation had made no report by March of 1947. Its later report of May was inconclusive. Contrary to the impression given to the world by the American President, neither Turkey nor Greece was at the time a "democracy" (Turkey was ruled by a one-party dictatorship and Greece by a Fascist-Royalist oligarchy) nor was either in any visible danger of Soviet invasion or Communist subversion.

On March 12, 1947, President Truman nevertheless asked Congress for $400,000,000 to "defend" Greece and Turkey, and enunciated his memorable "doctrine" as a clarion call to freemen every-

where to resist the Red Menace. As usual in all politics, motives were mixed. On February 24 London had advised Washington that Britain's steadily worsening economic and financial plight necessitated the withdrawal of its troops and subsidies from Greece. Massive American aid to all of Western Europe was swiftly looming as the only alternative to insolvency, impoverishment, and political chaos. Aid to Greece and Turkey, however incongruous and irrelevant to the larger issue, might pave the way in Congress to a bolder program. But even so small a step could scarcely be rendered politically palatable to the America of 1947 unless it could be spiced and flavored as "defense against Communism." Contrary to the advice of George F. Kennan, who later was to indict U.S. policy-makers for preoccupation with unrealistic and dangerous "legalistic-moralistic abstractions," Truman seized upon the occasion to rally his countrymen once more against the beast of Bolshevism.

. . . The very existence of the Greek State is today threatened by the terrorist activities of several thousand armed men, led by Communists, who defy the Government's authority. . . . Greece must have assistance if it is to become a self-supporting and self-respecting democracy. . . . Turkey has sought financial assistance from Great Britain and the U.S. for the purpose of effecting that modernization necessary for the maintenance of its national integrity. That integrity is essential for the preservation of order in the Middle East. . . . We shall not realize our objectives unless we are willing to help free people to maintain their free institutions and their national integrity against aggressive movements that seek to impose upon them totalitarian regimes. This is no more than a frank recognition that totalitarian regimes imposed on free peoples by direct or indirect aggression undermine the foundations of international peace and hence the security of the U.S. . . . The U.S. has made frequent protests against coercion and intimidation, in violation of the Yalta agreement, in Poland, Rumania, and Bulgaria. . . . I believe that it must be the policy of the U.S. to support free peoples who are resisting attempted subjugation by armed minorities or by outside pressures. . . . We must take immediate and resolute action. . . . The free peoples of the world look to

us for support in maintaining their freedom. If we falter in our leadership, we may endanger the peace of the world—and we shall surely endanger the welfare of our own nation.

The appeal was successful. During the Congressional hearings, Representatives Fred L. Crawford of Michigan and Walter H. Judd of Minnesota opined (March 31, 1947) that the USA should present the USSR with an ultimatum demanding disarmament and, if rebuffed, should atomize Russian cities. The Senate endorsed the "Truman Doctrine" on April 23, 67 to 23, and the House on May 22, 287 to 107. Missions and money flowed to Athens and Ankara to enrich Greek speculators and prepare bases in Turkey from which American bombers could threaten the oil fields of Soviet Transcaucasia. Thousands of Greeks, shocked by the corruptions and repressions of the Athens regime, rallied to the rebel cause—which was ultimately to be doomed not by American aid to the Monarchy but by the quarrel of 1948 between Tito and Stalin. The net effect of the "Truman Doctrine," coupled with the "containment" program that presently emerged, was to convince the Politburo that America was a major menace to Soviet security and to condition Americans to prepare for the next "Great Crusade" against foreign sin.[4]

Hard upon this American formula of "anti-Communism" followed a far more hopeful and constructive program of aid to the war-shattered economies of Europe. Its outlines were sketched in public addresses by Dean Acheson in Cleveland, Mississippi, May 8, 1947, and by George C. Marshall at Harvard, June 5, 1947. Said the Secretary of State:

> . . . Europe's requirements for the next three or four years of foreign food and other essential products—principally from America—are so much greater than her present ability to pay that she must have substantial additional help, or face economic, social and political deterioration of a very grave character. . . .

[4] The formula of "containment" was first set forth, as a means of thwarting Soviet expansionism and ultimately bringing about a "breakdown" or a "mellowing" of Soviet power, by George F. Kennan, writing in *Foreign Affairs*, July 1947, as "Mr. X," on "The Sources of Soviet Conduct." Kennan, as he many times later explained, did not envisage "containment" as primarily a military problem, into which shape it was soon distorted by Pentagon, Truman, Marshall, Acheson, Congress, and the prevailing temper of American opinion. For contemporary criticisms of this conception, see my letter in *NYT*, October 6, 1947, and Walter Lippmann: *The Cold War* (Harper, 1947).

It is logical that the United States should do whatever it is able to do to assist in the return of normal economic health in the world, without which there can be no political stability and no assured peace. Our policy is directed not against any country or doctrine but against hunger, poverty, desperation and chaos. Its purpose should be the revival of a working economy in the world so as to permit the emergence of political and social conditions in which free institutions can exist. Such assistance, I am convinced, must not be on a piece-meal basis as various crises develop. Any assistance that this Government may render in the future should provide a cure rather than a mere palliative. Any government that is willing to assist in the task of recovery will find full cooperation, I am sure, on the part of the United States Government. Any government which maneuvers to block the recovery of other countries cannot expect help from us. Furthermore, governments, political parties or groups which seek to perpetuate human misery in order to profit therefrom politically or otherwise will encounter the opposition of the United States.

It is already evident that, before the United States Government can proceed much further in its efforts to alleviate the situation and help start the European world on its way to recovery, there must be some agreement among the countries of Europe as to the requirements of the situation and the part those countries themselves will take in order to give proper effect to whatever action might be undertaken by this Government. It would be neither fitting nor efficacious for this Government to undertake to draw up unilaterally a program designed to place Europe on its feet economically. This is the business of the Europeans. The initiative, I think, must come from Europe. The role of this country should consist of friendly aid in the drafting of a European program and of later support of such a program so far as it may be practical for us to do so. The program should be a joint one, agreed to by a number, if not all European nations.

Here again the UN, which might have been made the vehicle of such a program, was bypassed in favor of unilateral American

action. What the Marshall proposal portended in detail was unclear. But within a fortnight Bevin and Bidault had hailed it with enthusiasm and met in Paris to name committees to study European needs. On June 18, 1947, Molotov was invited by Bevin to join in the consideration of prospects. Had the USSR agreed to participate in things to come, it is probable that the American Congress, in a new upsurge of anti-Communist fervor, would have repudiated the whole enterprise—a result that would have served Communist purposes better than the actual result. But the members of the Politburo revealed themselves anew to be victims of the delusions of their doctrines to the detriment of their own interests and aims. Warsaw and Prague expressed willingness to share in the benefits of the "Marshall Plan." The Soviet Union, as the most fearfully devastated of all the belligerent countries, had most to gain and least to lose by sharing. Molotov arrived in Paris on June 27, accompanied by an impressive staff of economists, to confer with Bidault and Bevin. He at once asked to know what the United States was offering and on what terms, apparently hoping to submit a "shopping list" that Washington would fulfill. No one could answer, since no one then could know, least of all American policy-makers, what was politically possible in the execution of the proposal. Bevin pleaded for a pan-European draft program as an incentive to American action.

The Marxists of Moscow could not conceive of American "capitalism" aiding in European reconstruction without sinister ulterior motives. When they hinted that the USA was seeking "imperialist" control over the recipients, Marshall (July 1) denounced them for "a malicious distortion." A day later the Paris meeting broke up amid recriminations. Molotov's departing comments, which Bevin called "a complete travesty," held that Washington was threatening "the economic independence and sovereignty" of the nations of Europe and seeking to "make use of some European countries against others in whatever way certain strong Powers, seeking to establish their domination, should find it profitable to do so." Moscow held aloof and compelled Prague and Warsaw to do likewise. Stalin and his aides, bewitched by their dogmas, thus rejected an opportunity for constructive East-West collaboration in deference to their deep-seated suspicions of the "bourgeois" world.

What followed is well known. European envoys conferred from July through September 1947 and finally asked $19,330,000,000 in US assistance through 1951. The Harriman Committee (November

8) urged $17,000,000,000 in aid to "prevent World War III" and "win the first major battle" of liberty against totalitarianism through a "European Recovery Program" (ERP). Reluctantly and with many reservations and conditions, the American Congress ultimately appropriated almost $20,000,000,000 for ERP with more to follow in economic and military subsidies in the name of a "Mutual Security Program." By abstaining, the men of the Kremlin facilitated the rehabilitation of Western Europe under the banner of "anti-Communism." At the same time Byrnes urged action through the UN to expel the Russians from East Germany under threat of "measures of last resort." *The Times* of London (October 16, 1947) opined that these proposals were "little better than a simple recipe for war." The *Daily Mirror*: "Mr. Byrnes is so frank as openly to advocate war with Russia. Is this wickedness, idiocy, or a mixture of both?" The Council of Foreign Ministers, meeting in London (November 25–December 15, 1947), broke up in discord halfway through its agenda, on Marshall's motion to adjourn, when Molotov, although offering minor concessions to Western views, questioned U.S. motives in dealing with Germany.

America's Grand Design for renewed defense against Bolshevism was woven of many strands. The restoration of Western Europe was envisaged as a means of thwarting Soviet aggression or Communist revolution and contributing toward an ultimate liberation of Eastern Europe. In May 1947 Communists were expelled from the coalition Cabinets of both France and Italy. "Containment" was pursued via diplomacy, psychological warfare, massive military expenditures, and the steady stockpiling of atomic bombs. The UN was induced to accept the American program for international control of nuclear weapons and was increasingly used by Washington to roll up anti-Soviet majorities, evoking scores of Soviet vetoes in the Security Council. Marshall succeeded in bringing into being the "Little Assembly," the UN Balkan Commission, and the UN Korean Electoral Commission—all boycotted by the USSR and its satellites. On only two major issues did the USA and the USSR see eye to eye in the UN: confirmation of the U.S. Pacific Mandates (so devised as to be indistinguishable from annexation), accepted by Moscow as a *quid pro quo* for hoped-for American approval of Soviet annexation of Southern Sakhalin and the Kuriles; and the partition of Palestine into projected Arab and Jewish states, voted by the Assembly on November 29.

Muscovite maneuvers to thwart the allegedly monstrous purposes of the American colossus were equally manifold and multi-
tudinous. All bore the imprint of the Georgian despot Djugashvili,
whose political genius consisted in taking infinite pains in the arts
of intrigue and liquidation. Initial measures in 1947–8 were aimed
at reactivating the Communist word conspiracy and compelling the
satellites, through force and fraud, to accept all-Communist regimes
in which the local comrades would be obedient agents of the Kremlin. At a secret meeting in Poland in late September of 1947, eighteen delegates of various Communist parties—including Zhdanov and
Malenkov, Edvard Kardelj of Jugoslavia, Josef Refai of Hungary,
Anna Pauker of Rumania (soon to become Foreign Minister), Vice-
Premier Wladyslaw Gomulka of Poland, Jacques Duclos of France,
Rudolf Slansky of Czechoslovakia, and Luigi Longo of Italy—conferred on the restoration of a regional facsimile of the Comintern.
Their conclusions, along with the new propaganda line, were announced in Warsaw and Moscow on October 5. A "Communist In-
formation Bureau" (Cominform) of representatives of C.P. Central
Committees of nine countries, including Italy and France, would
be set up in Belgrade to publish a journal and co-ordinate Communist activities. A long manifesto declared, *inter alia:*

> . . . Two opposite political lines have formed:
> On the one side the policy of the USSR and democratic
> countries directed toward undermining imperialism and
> strengthening democracy, on the other side is the policy of
> the USA and England directed toward strengthening im-
> perialism and strangling democracy.
> Since the USSR and countries of the new democracy
> became a hindrance in carrying out imperialistic plans for
> the struggle for world domination and the smashing of
> democratic movements, there was proclaimed a campaign
> against the USSR and countries of the new democracy,
> reinforced also by threats of a new war on the part of most
> zealous imperialistic politicians in the USA and England.
> In such a way, two camps formed—the imperialistic
> and anti-democratic camp, which has as a main aim the
> establishment of world domination of American imperial-
> ism and the smashing of democracy, and the anti-imperial-

istic and democratic camp, which has as a main aim and undermining of imperialism and the strengthening of democracy and the liquidation of the remnants of Fascism. . . .

The Truman-Marshall plan is only a constituent part, the European section of the general plan of world expansionist policy carried on by the United States in all parts of the world. The plan of economic and political enslavement of Europe by American imperialism is supplemented by plans for the economic and political enslavement of China, Indonesia and South America.

The aggressors of yesterday—the capitalistic magnates of Germany and Japan—are being prepared by the USA for a new role—to become the instrument of the imperialistic policy of the USA in Europe and Asia.

The arsenal of tactical measures utilized by the imperialistic camp has very many forms. Here are combined the direct threat by force, blackmail and extortion, all measures of political economic pressure, or bribery, of utilization of internal contradictions and controversy for the reinforcement of their positions—and all this which is covered by the liberal-pacifist mask designed for deceit and fooling people who are not experienced in politics.

A special place in the tactical arsenal of imperialists is occupied by the utilization of the treacherous policy of Right-wing Socialists of the type of [Leon] Blum [former French Premier and Socialist party leader] in France, [Prime Minister] Attlee and [Foreign Secretary Ernest] Bevin in England, [Dr. Kurt] Schumacher [head of the Social Democratic party] in Germany, [President Karl] Renner [Socialist] and Schaerf [Vice-Chancellor, Adolf Schaerf, Socialist] in Austria, [Right-wing Socialist Giuseppe] Saragat in Italy, et cetera. . . .

The day-to-day and month-to-month conduct of Soviet policy toward the USA was shaped and colored at every point by the bitter rivalry already reviewed. When Kiril Alexeev, employee of the Soviet Trade Representative in Mexico, deserted his post and fled to the U.S., Moscow early in January requested his extradition as

an "embezzler." The State Department refused. When Washington a few days later requested Soviet restoration of Dairen to Chinese control, Moscow equivocated.

On February 15 Molotov protested at Dean Acheson's statement to a Senate committee that Soviet policy was "aggressive" and "expansionist," while Eugene Tarlé, Soviet historian, accused John Foster Dulles of "plotting war." Washington's reply rejected the protest on the ground that Acheson's statement was due to "frankness," not "unfriendliness." Molotov rejected the reply and reiterated that the statement was "a base slander."

Harold E. Stassen's interview with Stalin in Moscow on April 9 was featured by mutual expressions of hope for the peaceful coexistence and fruitful collaboration of the two systems. But by year's end the Republican aspirant was as vocal as his political rivals in denouncing the USSR and demanding punitive restrictions on American-Soviet trade, which had already fallen to a ten-year low —though it increased somewhat in the fall. Numerous Congressmen likewise urged an economic embargo against Russia, as did Arthur Hays Sulzberger, publisher of *The New York Times*, in an interview in London on July 3, 1947.

In resigning on April 16 as cultural attaché to the U.S. Embassy in Moscow, Armond D. Willis charged that anti-Soviet members of the staff had obstructed his work and sought to block all efforts at American-Soviet reconciliation. As the anti-Soviet *leitmotif* of the American press rose in a constant crescendo, Soviet journalists indulged in increasingly bitter denunciations of American policies.

When Washington asked Moscow to intercede to prevent the execution of Nikola Petkov, Bulgarian opposition leader, the Soviet Foreign Ministry on August 26 dismissed the premise of the proposal as false and rejected it as unwarranted interference. A second U.S. note of September 3 produced a like reply, as the State Department rejected Soviet protests against Anglo-American plans to raise the level of industry in Bizonia. On September 19 Andrei Vyshinsky, in a long address before the UN Assembly, presented a comprehensive and documented indictment of U.S. foreign policy, war profits of American corporations, and American "war-mongers," all of which was indignantly dismissed by U.S. spokesmen and pressmen as "demagogery," "insult," and "slander."

The State Department felt obliged, however, to modify its originally inflexible opposition to the Soviet proposal of a UN resolution

condemning propaganda for war and finally accepted such a resolution in much diluted form. A visitor from Mars would have had difficulty during 1947 in deciding which of the Super-Powers had the edge on the other in its professions of peace, preparations for war, and accusations of aggressive intent on the part of the other.

When Boris Gorbatov in the *Literary Gazette* published a long article on "Harry Truman," belittling the President, condemning "dollar diplomacy," and asserting that the Chief Executive "vies for the laurels of the little corporal from Munich," the State Department protested sharply at this "gratuitous personal insult," which was described in Ambassador Smith's note of September 25 as "libelous," "slanderous," "incendiary," "shocking," and worse than Göbbels at his worst. Molotov at once rejected the protest with a barbed *tu quoque.*

A week later Molotov refused visas to Assistant Secretary of State John E. Peurifoy and ten Senators who desired to "inspect the U.S. Embassy." Violent attacks in the Soviet press on leading American personalities reached new levels of invective, particularly with reference to James F. Byrnes's book *Speaking Frankly,* which was described as an appeal for war—a judgment in which most of the British press concurred.

More fuel for the flames was provided when Chile ousted two Jugoslav attachés in October, accused Soviet agents of instigating a coal strike, and joined Brazil on October 21 in severing diplomatic relations with the USSR—and with Czechoslovakia. Both Rio de Janiero and Santiago suppressed local Communist parties. The Brazilian action in breaking relations was explained in terms of Moscow's failure to reply to protests over accusations in the Soviet press that President Dutra was under U.S. influence and had accepted Nazi decorations. Such charges were the more intolerable for being true.

By the turn of the year, American-Soviet relations had deteriorated to their lowest point since recognition in 1933, and perhaps since 1919, when American troops were fighting the Red Army on Soviet soil. Each government blamed the other for the situation. On October 24 Moscow announced the replacement of Ambassador Nikolai Novikov by Alexander S. Panyushkin, who was coolly received by President Truman in December. On November 9 a group of 16 Protestant churchmen, including Bishop Charles Gilbert of New York, Dr. John R. Mott, and Rev. Ralph Sockman—alarmed at

"the shocking amount of suspicion, hatred, and hysteria" in American-Soviet relations—called for "a great spiritual crusade" for peaceful cooperation. Such appeals had no immediately visible effects, except to expose their proponents to charges of "Communist sympathies."

Meanwhile, Muscovy proconsuls in the marchlands made short work of "unreliable" political elements in favor of 100% Stalinists. Petkov in Bulgaria was executed on September 23, 1947. Subasich resigned from Tito's government. Dragoljub Jovanovich, Serb Agrarian follower of Tito, was sentenced to nine years of hard labor, October 8, 1947. In Hungary, Bela Kovacs, Secretary-General of the Smallholders Party, which won a majority in the election of November 4, 1945, was arrested by Soviet authorities on February 26, 1947, and, despite U.S. protest, was later jailed on the basis of a patently bogus "confession." Many of his aides were shot. Premier Ferenc Nagy was forced into exile in late May as Matyas Rakosi, a Soviet citizen and long-term Magyar Communist-in-exile, became Stalin's "boss" in Budapest. Father Bela Varga, Nagy's colleague and President of the National Assembly, fled to Germany on June 2.

In famine-stricken Rumania, Juliu Maniu and Ion Mihalache, leaders of the National Peasant Party, were sentenced to life imprisonment on November 11. King Michael abdicated, December 30, 1947, in favor of a "People's Democracy" run by Moscow-trained Peter Grozu and Anna Pauker. In Poland, where Ambassador Arthur Bliss Lane fretted and fumed in helpless rage at Communist violation of the Yalta agreement for "democracy," a rigged "election" was held on January 19, 1947. The Government-sponsored "left" bloc obtained 9,000,000 votes as against a little more than 1,000,000 for Stanislaw Mikolajczyk's Polish Peasant Party. In the new regime of February 5 Boleslaw Bierut became President of the Republic, while Joseph Cyrankiewicz was named Premier and Wladyslaw Gomulka Vice-Premier in a coalition Cabinet (in which Communists were a small minority but, as it turned out, the ruling group)—from which Mikolajczyk's followers were excluded. He fled to London in mid-October. In November the new parliament declared him "guilty of treason," expelled him from the Assembly, and deprived him of citizenship.[5]

[5] Further details of these developments will be found in the annual articles on the satellite countries in Funk & Wagnall's *New International Year Book*; in C. E. Black's section on "The People's Democracies of Eastern Europe"

Stalin's grim resolve to have all of Russia's allies ruled by Communists sworn to unswerving obedience to Moscow reached its culmination in Prague, where democracy, Western-style, still flourished in the Muscovite shadow. The Czech Communists won 38% of the popular vote in the free elections of May 26, 1946, but suffered a decline in 1947 and prospective defeat in the election scheduled for 1948. When, already in control of the Ministries of Interior and Information, they sought to take over command of the Prague police force against the orders of the Cabinet, a dozen non-Communist Ministers resigned on February 20, 1948. Whatever hopes they may have entertained of preventing the inevitable were dashed by mass demonstrations of Communist "action committees" which compelled President Eduard Beneš to accept a new Communist-dominated Cabinet on February 25. A fortnight later Foreign Minister Jan Masaryk lost his life—some said by murder, others by suicide. More probably he perished from a psychosomatic heart attack induced by the death of all his hopes. Beneš died on September 3. In an "election" of May 30, 1948, the Communists won 89% of the vote.

Everywhere in the marchlands—save only in Finland, where Moscow's desire to preserve Swedish neutrality dictated respect for Finnish freedom—post-war coalition regimes were swiftly replaced by "People's Democracies." These governments, however embellished with "elections" and new Constitutions, were in every case dictatorships of Stalin's stooges. The immediate result was Soviet victory and Western defeat. The ultimate result was to be the disintegration or devolution of the new Red Empire because it is forever true in all politics that, in Napoleon's phrase, "you can do everything with bayonets except sit on them."

The new conflict of East and West reached its first climax in Germany. Here in the ruined Reich the original inter-allied objectives of democratization, decartelization, de-Nazification, and demilitarization in a united nation soon gave way to Soviet efforts to use East Germany against the West and Anglo-American efforts to use West Germany against the East. The spring meeting (London) and the fall meeting (Moscow) of the Council of Foreign Ministers in 1947 to frame treaties for Germany and Austria foundered on Soviet demands for Four-Power control of the Ruhr and $10,000,000,000 in

in Taylor Cole (ed.): *European Political Systems* (Knopf, 1953), pp. 188–265; and John A. Lukacs: *The Great Powers and Eastern Europe* (American Book Co., 1953).

additional reparations out of current production over 18 years, and Western demands for revision of the Polish-German frontier in Germany's favor. Since each set of demands was wholly unacceptable to the opposite side in this contest of wills, no accord was possible. Soviet policy-makers persuaded themselves that the Western Powers were aiming at a reunited Reich to be used for further aggression against the USSR. Western policy-makers persuaded themselves that Moscow was aiming at a Sovietized Germany to be used against the West. Washington, London, and Paris thereupon decided in the spring of 1948 to set up a West German government in their occupation zone.

Following a Soviet walk-out, the Allied Control Council in Berlin ceased to function in March 1948. In June a currency reform in the West replaced each 10 Reichsmarks with 1 new Deutsche Mark. Comparable anti-inflationary measures were long overdue in the Soviet zone. Thanks to mutual suspicions, no serious effort was made to effect a common monetary policy. On June 24, 1948, Soviet authorities cut off all land and water transport between the Western zone and West Berlin, ostensibly to prevent the introduction of the new currency into this Western-controlled enclave of the Soviet zone. The actual purpose of the "Berlin blockade" was to see whether the Western Powers could either be forced out of Berlin or deterred from setting up a Western State in "Trizonia." By July 1948 the West Berliners, who were completely dependent for sustenance on trade with West Germany or with the circumambient Soviet zone of East Germany, were wholly isolated, besieged, and facing starvation.

General Lucius Clay at one point proposed to reopen the highways with tank columns, but was overruled by President Truman. If local Soviet commanders proposed any comparable resort to force, they were overruled by the Kremlin. The Western Powers organized a costly "airlift" of supplies to West Berlin—with no Soviet interception, even though this device was destined in the end to defeat Moscow's purposes. A Bonn Assembly drafted a "Basic Law" that became effective May 20, 1949, and established the *Bundesrepublik Deutschland* or German Federal Republic, in which foreign military administrations gave way to an "Occupation Statute" and an Allied High Commission. In the elections of August 14, 1949, Konrad Adenauer's Christian Democrats won 139 seats, the Social Democrats 131, and the "Free Democrats" 52 in the new *Bundestag*—out of which emerged a government headed by Adenaur as Chancellor and

Theodore Heuss (Free Democrat) as President. Moscow reluctantly followed suit in the East by setting up a "German Democratic Republic" with Wilhelm Pieck as President, Otto Grotewohl as Premier, and Walter Ulbricht as Vice-Premier (October 11, 1949). All were Soviet agents, ostensibly legitimized by the forcible suppression of the Social Democratic Party and its fusion with the Communists in the "Socialist Unity Party" or SED. By the close of 1949 two Germanies confronted each other across the Elbe, with 50,000,-000 Germans in the West and 18,000,000 in the East, with each regime a creature of the Super-Powers of East and West in their struggle for mastery of the globe.

The Kremlin in the interim acknowledged defeat in the cold "Battle of Berlin." UN consideration of the issue led to private parleys in New York in January 1949 between Philip Jessup and Jacob Malik. In the sequel the USSR lifted the blockade on May 11, 1949, on condition that Western Powers would lift the counter-blockade of the Soviet zone and that a new meeting of the Council of Foreign Ministers would be scheduled. The original currency question was ignored. The new meeting, as usual during these years of frustration, got nowhere. The net effect of this phase of the combat of the giants was the partition of Germany in an apparently permanent bifurcation, and a vast enhancement, despite the "settlement" of 1949, of reciprocal fear and hatred.

2. THE CRUSADERS

In the long and lamentable history of man's inhumanity to man the most monstrous crimes of cruelty and rapine have been perpetrated by those persuaded that the triumph of their creed was equivalent to cosmic salvation and that any toleration of heretics or infidels meant eternal damnation. Ample witness is borne by the hideous atrocities attending the Christian Crusades against Islam, the Moslem "Holy Wars" against Christendom, the European "Wars of Religion," the French and Russian Revolutions, the horrors of Hitlerism, and the conflicts of Arabs and Israelis. This age-old pattern of consecrated frenzy and devout ferocity reappeared in the relations of East and West in the middle years of the 20th Century and threatened disaster to all mankind. The Czech coup and the Berlin block-

ade convinced many Westerners, among whom Americans were the most eloquent, that their very survival as freemen required the annihilation of all Communists everywhere in the world. Western counter-measures led most Communists to the renewed conviction that nothing less than the total destruction of "capitalism" and "bourgeois imperialism" could assure the security of the Socialist Fatherland and the accomplishment of its sacred mission of saving all humanity from sin.

These attitudes found expression in innumerable utterances in both halves of a divided world. Why they did not result in an orgy of mutual butchery we shall consider in due course. Here we must note the pattern of Western response to the Red challenge and of the Soviet response to the Western challenge. Both were suffused with widely shared belief in the inevitability of a war to the death. The men of Moscow disguised their fears and hopes by incessant propaganda for "peace" and endless denunciation of Western "war-mongers." Many in the West, most notably in the USA, prepared for war in the expectation that the menace they faced could be removed only by violence.[6]

[6] See James Burnham: *The Coming Defeat of Communism* (Day, 1950) and *Containment or Liberation?* (Day, 1953); William C. Bullitt: *The Great Globe Itself* (Scribner, 1946); E. Day Carman: *Soviet Imperialism: Russia's Drive for World Domination* (Public Affairs Press, 1950); William Henry Chamberlin: Introduction to *Blueprint for World Conquest* (Human Events, Chicago, 1946); Whittaker Chambers: *Witness* (Random House, 1952); David J. Dallin: *The New Soviet Empire* (Yale University Press, 1951); George Fielding Eliot: *If Russia Strikes* (Bobbs-Merrill, 1949); Louis Fischer (ed.): *Thirteen Who Fled* (Harper, 1949); C. Grove Haines (ed.): *The Threat of Soviet Imperialism* (Johns Hopkins Press, 1954); Frank Howley: *Your War for Peace* (Holt, 1953); Lydia Kirk: *Postmarked Moscow* (Scribner, 1952); Walter Kolarz: *Russia and Her Colonies* (Praeger, 1953) and *The Peoples of the Soviet Far East* (Praeger, 1953); Arthur Bliss Lane: *I Saw Poland Betrayed* (Bobbs-Merrill, 1948); Nathan Leites: *The Operational Code of the Politburo* (McGraw-Hill, 1951) and *A Study of Bolshevism* (Free Press, 1953); Clarence A. Manning: *The Forgotten Republics* (The Baltic States) (Philosophical Library, 1952) and *The Ukraine under the Soviets* (Bookman Associates, 1953); Stanislaw Mikolajczyk: *The Rape of Poland* (McGraw-Hill, 1948); Fulton J. Sheen: *Communism and the Conscience of the West* (Bobbs-Merrill, 1948); Leland Stowe: *Conquest by Terror* (Random House, 1952); Nicholas S. Timasheff: *The Great Retreat: The Growth and Decline of Communism in Russia* (Dutton, 1946); and Edmund A. Walsh: *Total Empire: The Roots and Progress of World Communism* (Bruce, 1951). The American mood during the height of the "Cold War" is suggested by the circumstance that at the Williams College Commencement of June 20, 1948, Dwight D. Eisenhower, then President of Columbia University and later destined to make indispensable contributions to peace, gave warm praise as

Fear of Soviet aggression inspired Western efforts to build a new coalition capable of checkmating the Muscovite colossus. In retrospect, it is arguable that a simple unilateral U.S. guarantee of independence and territorial integrity would have protected any State in the world from any possible danger of Communist attack. It is equally arguable, as many able Europeans and Americans argued at the time, that the safety and welfare of the "Free World" could best be promoted by a Western European federation and/or a Federal Union of the Atlantic democracies. But the power of parochial loyalties proved too potent to permit any such daring departure in statesmanship. Under the circumstances of 1948 the problem of Western security was envisaged by policy-makers in conventional terms of armaments and alliances.

On June 11, 1948, the U.S. Senate approved the Vandenberg Resolution, modeled on the Pan-American "Act of Petropolis," which reaffirmed hope of "international peace and security through the UN" but urged "progressive development of regional and other collective arrangements for individual and collective self-defense . . . based on continuous and effective self-help and mutual aid" as permitted under Art. 51 of the UN Charter. On March 4, 1947,

---

"a magnificent fighting speech" to a Phi Beta Kappa student address ending with the words: "Last month Secretary Marshall said, 'Russian leaders must be convinced that the Soviet Union can live side by side in peace with the Western Powers in the United Nations.' I wonder if we ought to convince ourselves that we are able to live in peace beside the modern police state. I suggest that we cannot negotiate or compromise with the uncompromisable without surrendering our souls. War and its suffering are not as damnable as the living death of slavery by default. When freedom and human decency are at stake, we should not ask whether war is inevitable, or whether it is desirable. When freedom and decency are at Stake, for those of us who are free men war is imperative."

Such sentiments were multiplied in extent and intensity after the outbreak of the Korean war and may be regarded as having attained their culminating literary expression in *Collier's* magazine of October 27, 1951. Here in 130 pages, lavishly illustrated in color, 22 able and responsible writers—including Robert E. Sherwood, Edward R. Murrow, Hal Boyle, Hanson W. Baldwin, Lowell Thomas, Arthur Koestler, Stuart Chase, Allan Nevins, Harry Schwarz, Erwin Canham, and Senator Margaret Chase Smith—depicted in fiction form "Russia's Defeat and Occupation, 1952–1960" in a "Preview of the War We Do Not Want." With the aid of nuclear bombs and atomic artillery, US and UN forces crush the USSR and "liberate" the grateful people of Russia, who at once adopt the American way of life. Thomas J. Hamilton, reporting in *The New York Times*, November 11, 1951, on the UN Assembly session in Paris, wrote: "The October 27 issue of *Collier's* . . . is providing Communist delegates with material for constant attacks on the alleged aggressive aims of the USA."

Britain and France had signed at Dunkirk a 50-year alliance treaty pledging mutual aid against renewed German aggression or "any infringement by Germany of her obligations with regard to disarmament and demilitarization" to the end of "insuring that Germany shall not again become a menace to peace." On March 17, 1948, Britain, France, and the Benelux States concluded the 50-year Brussels alliance treaty, establishing a "Western Union" against any "armed attack in Europe," origin unspecified but obviously directed, after the Communist coup in Prague, against the Soviet bloc.

In the sequel to complex negotiations, the USA, Canada, Britain, France, Italy, and seven other Western European States (to which Greece, Turkey, and West Germany were subsequently added) signed the 20-year North Atlantic Treaty of April 4, 1949. Under Art. 5 of this defensive pact or "regional security arrangement," the parties agreed that an armed attack against any should be deemed an attack upon all, and that each would assist the victim of such attack "by taking forthwith, individually and in concert with the other parties, such action as it deems necessary, including the use of armed force, to restore and maintain the security of the North Atlantic area."

Moscow contended that NATO was not only incompatible with the Anglo-Soviet and French-Soviet treaties of 1942 and 1944, but was a violation of the UN Charter as well. The Soviet note of protest of April 1, 1949, stated, *inter alia:*

> To justify the conclusion of the North Atlantic Treaty, references are being made to the fact that the Soviet Union has definite treaties with the countries of the People's Democracies. These references, however, are utterly untenable. All the treaties of the Soviet Union . . . of mutual assistance with the countries of the People's Democracies are of a bilateral nature, and they are directly solely against the possible repetition of German aggression, of which danger no single peace-loving State can be unaware. The possibility of interpreting them as treaties which are in any degree aimed against the Allies of the USSR in the late war . . . is absolutely precluded.
>
> Moreover, the Soviet Union has similar treaties . . . not only with the countries of the People's Democracies, but also with Great Britain and France.

In contradistinction to this, the North Atlantic Treaty is not a bilateral but a multilateral treaty which creates a closed grouping of States, and—what is particularly important—absolutely ignores the possibility of German aggression. . . .

Participants in the North Atlantic Treaty are effecting extensive military measures which can in no way be justified by interests of self-defence of these countries. The extensive military measures carried out by the United States in co-operation with Great Britain and France under the present peacetime conditions, including the increase in all types of armed forces, the drafting of a plan for the utilisation of the atomic weapon, the stockpiling of atomic bombs—which are purely offensive weapons—the building of a network of air and naval bases, etc., by no means bear a defensive character.

The preservation in Washington of the combined Anglo-American staff, organised during the Second World War, the recent establishment of the Military Staff of the so-called Western Union at Fontainebleau, as well as the intention immediately to set up the Defence Committee envisaged by the North Atlantic Treaty, is by no means an indication of the peace-loving or defensive aims of the participants of the Treaty, but together with other numerous military preparations, contributes to an intensification of anxiety and alarm and to the whipping up of war hysteria in which all sorts of instigators of a new war are so interested. . . .

The Parties to the North Atlantic Treaty maintain that this Treaty allegedly represents a regional arrangement envisaged by Article 52 of the United Nations Charter. But such references are utterly groundless and untenable. There can be no question whatsoever of any regional character in this Treaty, inasmuch as the union provided for by the Treaty embraces States in both hemispheres of the globe, and has not as its aim the settlement of any regional issues. . . .

Nor can the establishment of the North Atlantic grouping of States be justified by the right of each Member of the UN to act in individual or collective self-defence, in

conformity with Article 51 of the Charter. Suffice it to say
that such a right . . . can arise only in the case of armed
attack against a Member of the [UN] Organisation. Yet,
as is known to all, neither the United States, Britain,
France, nor the other parties to the pact, are threatened by
any armed attack.

Whatever the cogency or logic of these arguments, the Western
Powers were neither convinced, intimidated, nor deterred from their
enterprise. With NATO once established, the signatories might well
have taken the view that the immense global resources at the disposal of the new coalition, now including all the wealth and power
of the USA (still enjoying its monopoly of nuclear weapons), would
prove sufficient to deter any Muscovite disposition toward aggression. A different view nevertheless prevailed—that Western security
depended upon massive European rearmament aimed at the difficult, if not impossible, goal of checkmating on the Continent the local
superiority of Soviet air and land power by accumulating sufficient
guns, tanks, planes, and divisions to make feasible, in the event of
war, the effective "defense" of Western Europe rather than its costly
"liberation" after another prolonged occupation.

Progress in this direction, desperately hurried after the outbreak of hostilities in Korea, soon led to a blind alley. In January
1951 Prime Minister Attlee announced a program for spending £4,-
700,000,000 on rearmament over the next three years. Bevin died,
April 14, and was replaced by Herbert Morrison as Foreign Secretary. On April 22, 1951, Aneurin Bevan and Harold Wilson quit the
Cabinet in protest at this proposal, which, said "Nye" Bevan, was
"fantastically wrong" and "already dead" since it was an economic
and fiscal monstrosity certain to wreck the social services of the
Welfare State and was, moreover, a product of "hysteria, intolerance, hatred, and witch-hunting" and of British dependence on
"American capitalism, unable to restrain itself at all." The Labor
Cabinet survived this defection but, by a narrow margin, lost the
election of October 25, 1951. Churchill, back in power, conceded
that Bevan had "by accident" been right and that the projected
arms program was "utterly beyond our economic capacity to bear."
The Continental nations of the West were no more able to carry the
burden that the needs of "defense" allegedly required, despite massive American subsidies and the merging in December 1950 of

"Western Union" with the NATO command under SHAPE (Supreme Headquarters of the Allied Powers in Europe), headed by Gen. Eisenhower until June 1, 1952.

Since Western policy-makers—Democrats and Republicans, Laborites and Tories, Leftists and Rightists—were all committed to "defending" Western Europe by arms, thanks to fears inspired by Soviet conduct, and since this objective was clearly incapable of accomplishment with the resources available, the idea soon emerged that the impossible might be made possible through the rearmament of Germany. This dangerous dispensation originated in Washington in 1949. It evoked no enthusiasm among Britons, Frenchmen, Scandinavians, or Lowlanders, but nonetheless became the avowed common aim of Western policy after the beginning of war in Korea. In September 1950 Secretary of State Acheson induced the NATO Council to endorce, formally and officially, the rearming of the Reich. This resolve, although a response to Soviet threats, evoked the most acute anxieties in the Kremlin—reflected, as we shall see, in almost panic-stricken reactions profoundly affecting internal politics in the USSR, Soviet relations with the satellites, and Moscow's dealings with the West. Given these consequences of the NATO decision, it will be well to review the devious course of the Western program, even at the cost of departing momentarily from the chronological order of events.

Under treaties signed in Paris, May 26, 1952, German armed forces were to be incorporated into an international army of a "European Defense Community" (EDC). Despite heavy pressure from Dean Acheson and even heavier pressure from his successor, John Foster Dulles—who in January 1953 threatened an "agonizing reappraisal" of U.S. defense policy in the event of West European rejection of the American formula—the French Assembly, after long and anxious debate, repudiated the EDC treaties in August 1954. Premier Pierre Mendès-France felt obliged, however, to yield to demands from Washington for a new formula for German rearmament: a new *Wehrmacht* (rechristened *Bundesheer*) as a contingent of a "Western Union" Army, with West Germany to enter NATO and be subject to sundry restrictions and controls on its armaments, all of which were demonstrably meaningless by all past experience. These complex arrangements were embodied in treaties signed in Paris on October 23, 1954, and ratified by large majorities in Commons and Congress. Mendès-France, still hoping against hope to

forestall German rearmament, urged upon London and Washington an inter-allied arms pool, West European Federation, and a Big Four conference—all in vain. On December 24, 1954, the French Assembly rejected the pact for German rearmament, 281 to 257, despite the Premier's appeal for overwhelming endorsement. When Mendès-France posed the issue of "confidence," the deputies, sullenly and reluctantly, accepted the pact, 287 to 260, on December 30 with many abstentions. Then, after Washington, London, and Bonn had turned down all the Premier's safeguarding proposals, the Assembly voted his Cabinet out of office, 319 to 273, on his North African policy, February 5, 1955, but with no reversal of French endorsement of the rearming of the Reich.

Western hopes and Soviet fears regarding German rearmament were both unwarranted by the new facts of power. The projected German force of 12 divisions, including 6 motorized divisions, 2 mechanized divisions, and 4 *Panzer* divisions, would constitute, to be sure, the most formidable army in Western Europe. But it promised to be wholly useless, either defensively or offensively, against the Communist bloc (now including a rearmed East Germany), which could easily, if need be, match the *Bundesheer,* tank for tank, gun for gun, division for division, in a ratio of 2 or 3 to 1. The industrialization of Russia may well be deemed to have ended forever Germany's role as a "Great Power."

In December 1954 the NATO Council decided to compensate for the obvious and irreversible preponderance of Soviet land and air forces on the Continent by using tactical atomic bombs at the outset of any new war. The *Frankfurter Allgemeine Zeitung* in February 1955 published two articles by Liddell Hart, contending that any such strategy would be suicidal. In March, Col. Bogislaw von Bonin was dismissed from his post in Bonn by Defense Minister Theodore Blank for saying in public, and contrary to orders, that Germany could not be expected to raise an army in the service of a strategy which would make the total destruction of the Reich inevitable in the event of hostilities. NATO air maneuvers of June 1955, code-named "Carte Blanche," indicated that 335 small atom bombs dropped between Hamburg and Munich would kill 1,700,-000 and wound 3,500,000 Germans, not counting casualties from radiation.

It is self-evident, from the reported results of other tests, that ten hydrogen bombs, properly placed, could annihilate all of West

Germany and all of its inhabitants. Given these facts, the new *Bundesheer* could play no military role against the USSR. Its only possible role, quite unintended by its Anglo-American sponsors, might be to dominate Western Europe—with possible Soviet connivance. This prospect was not changed by the appointment (announced by U.S. Gen. Lauris Norstad, February 6, 1957) of Nazi Gen. Hans Speidel as commander of NATO land forces in Central Europe as of April 1, 1957.

If men were rational in politics, the policy-makers in Moscow would have looked upon the resurrection of German military forces with indifference or perhaps with satisfaction as a meaningless waste of Western resources. But if men were rational in politics, the policy-makers in Bonn, Paris, London, and Washington would never have embarked in the first place on Germany's military revival. The members of the Politburo ("Presidium" after Congress XIX) regarded Western efforts to rearm the Reich as conclusive proof of "bourgeois" wickedness and of the resolve of "imperialist warmongers" to organize a new attempt to destroy the USSR. In defense or counter-attack they resorted to a multiplicity of devices, some successful and some self-defeating. In so confused a jumble of responses, any neat ordering of tactics and strategy would be highly unrealistic. Any full treatment of all of the gambits would require many volumes. A few salient features of Marxist Muscovy's new war against the West are nonetheless deserving of note.

The eternal hope of "world revolution" was revived once more. The "exploited proletariat" of Britain and America remained staunchly anti-Marxist. Many workers in France and Italy were loyal to their mass Communist parties, but with no possibility and no desire to "overthrow the bourgeoisie." The Cominform, unlike the Comintern in its early years, was not, and could never be, a "General Staff" of global proletarian rebellion. Yet the ferments stirring among dark multitudes of Asians and Africans offered opportunities to strike at the Western Powers and to extend the Red Empire by subversion and guerrilla warfare. In Indonesia local Communists seized the city of Madiun in September 1948, suffered failure and partial suppression, and then in 1952 switched to a tactic of "united front from above" and won over 20% of the votes in subsequent elections. In India the C.P. at its Second Congress in 1948 made violent revolution its official policy, sought to set up in the Telengana district a revolutionary base, which government

troops destroyed, and in 1950 espoused legal political and parliamentary action.

In the Philippines, Luis Taruc's "Hukbalahaps," perhaps on orders from Moscow, launched civil war in 1948, but were never able to win over the mass of the peasantry or to enlarge hostilities beyond guerrilla proportions. (The remnants surrendered in May 1954.) Similarly, in Malaya the Communist-led "People's Liberation Army" unleashed anti-colonial rebellion and social revolution in 1948, but achieved nothing against the British forces beyond ambushes and the occasional murder of rubber planters and the robbery or destruction of plantations. Matters turned out quite otherwise in China, Korea, and Indochina with results, as well be shown below, decisive for the world balance of power—some of them to Muscovy's advantage. In these ancient Oriental lands, however, Stalin capitalized upon forces and events beyond his effective control rather than "master-minding," as some Westerners assumed, a vast conspiracy directed from the Kremlin.

Moscow made adroit use during the "Cold War" of the time-honored Communist device of ostensibly non-partisan or "united-front" organizations whereby many non-Communists and even anti-Communists were enlisted in causes that often served the purposes of Soviet propaganda or foreign policy. Among many others, the most widespread and perhaps the most effective (efficacy in such enterprises, as in all "psychological warfare," is seldom measurable) was the "Partisans of Peace," launched in 1949 and eventuating in the "World Peace Council." In March 1950 the "Partisans," meeting in the Swedish capital, formulated the "Stockholm Appeal" demanding the prohibition of atomic weapons. Within the next five years the Council claimed that the Appeal had obtained 482,482,198 signatures throughout the world, many of them in non-Communist countries. The Council convoked in Vienna in December 1952 a "World Congress of Peoples for Peace" and in Helsinki in June 1955 a "World Assembly for Peace." Its Appeal for a Five-Power Peace Pact allegedly obtained 612,522,504 signatures and its "Vienna Appeal" for a top-level diplomatic conference 655,963,811. Such activities, unwittingly aided by the bellicose utterances of some American politicians and publicists, doubtless persuaded some people, hitherto uncommitted, that the USSR stood for "peace" and the USA for "war." That the dichotomy was false or meaningless is

a tribute to Communist cleverness in using words to befuddle thought.[7]

Stalin's prime concern in the face of what he pretended to believe was a mounting menace of Western attack was to tighten Soviet military, political, and economic bonds with the European satellites of the USSR, constituting a *glacis* or *cordon sanitaire* in reverse against the West, and to insure that the power-holders in each should be totally subordinate to Moscow's will. His ends, as usual, were well conceived in terms of Soviet interests, Muscovite security, and Communist ambitions. His means, as usual, were those of a despot afflicted with delusions of omnipotence and wholly incapable of comprehending that relationships of charity, trust, and voluntary cooperation forge stronger links of unity than relationships of dictation and savage intolerance towards any dissent. Local Communist regimes in Danubia and Balkania were expected, moreover, to ape Red Muscovy in ideological regimentation, forced collectivization of agriculture, and grandiose schemes of industrialization—all of which, coupled with various forms of economic exploitation for the benefit of the Soviet economy, bred hot resentments seething beneath the surface of allegedly monolithic regimes of "liberation" and "socialism."

In Tito's Jugoslavia, firmly bound to the Soviet bloc by the heroic exploits and final triumph of the Communist-led partisan fighters of 1943–5, the first signs of friction became public knowledge on March 20, 1948, when Tito published a letter to Molotov expressing "amazement" at the notification, two days previously, that Moscow was withdrawing all military and civilian advisers on the ground that they were "surrounded by hostility." Earlier friction had been kept secret: Jugoslav complaints over the conduct of Soviet troops and resentment at Moscow's agreement with the West that Tito's forces should quit Trieste. And now the world was to know that all was not well in the relations between Moscow and Belgrade. The Central Committee of the CPSU declared on March 27, 1948, that Soviet emissaries in Jugoslavia were denied information and "trailed" by local policemen; that the Jugoslav C.P. had only a quasi-legal status in the "People's Front" and was "undemocratic"; that

[7] See Bernard S. Morris: "Communist International Front Organizations: Their Nature and Function," in *World Politics*, October, 1956 (Princeton University Press).

Belgrade was fostering "capitalism" and "nationalism"; and that some Jugoslav spokesmen were "slandering" the USSR.

Tito and Kardelj replied on April 15, expressing "surprise" and denying the allegations. "We regard it as improper for the agents of the Soviet Intelligence Service to recruit in our country, which is going towards Socialism, our citizens for their intelligence service. We cannot consider this as anything else but detrimental to the interests of our country. This is done in spite of the fact that our leaders have protested against this and made it known that it cannot be tolerated. . . . We cannot allow the Soviet Intelligence to spread its net in our country."

The Jugoslav Communist leaders, in short, felt themselves entitled to autonomy and non-intervention from Moscow. Despite their allegedly overriding loyalty to the creed of Marxist-Leninism, their sense of national dignity and patriotism precluded submission to Stalinism. On May 4, 1948, the Central Committee of the CPSU rebuked the Belgrade comrades for "immodesty" and "deviationism" and threatened to withdraw Soviet aid. Tito and Kardelj replied to Stalin, May 17: "It would be superfluous to write of the discouraging impression created on us by this letter. . . ." Following further exchanges, the Cominform (June 28, 1948) issued a long statement expelling the Jugoslav C.P. from membership and accepting the view of the C.C. of the CPSU "which assumed the initiative in unveiling the wrong policy of the C.C. of the C.P. of Jugoslavia and especially the wrong policy of Comrades Tito, Kardelj, Djilas, and Rankovitch." They were accused of "a hateful policy in relation to the Soviet Union"; discrediting, and spying upon, Soviet military specialists; "identifying the foreign policy of the USSR with that of the imperialistic Powers"; disseminating "slanderous propaganda borrowed from the arsenals of counter-revolutionary Trotskyism"; fostering "capitalist elements" and "kulaks" in the villages; relying on the peasantry rather than on the proletariat; subordinating the Party to the People's Front; ignoring the principles of intra-party democracy and self-criticism; choosing members of the Central Committee by co-optation instead of elections; displaying "exaggerated ambition, megalomania, and conceit" in spurning earlier criticism; and indulging in "adventurism," "opportunism," "anti-Marxism," and "nationalism." Cominform HQ were transferred from Belgrade to Bucharest. In predicting Tito's downfall, *Pravda* on July 1 accused him of "Bonapartism" and his followers of "idolatry."

This excommunication of the Jugoslav schismatics was expected to bring about Tito's disappearance, which Stalin, according to Khrushchev (February 25, 1956), forecast as follows: "I will shake my little finger—there will be no more Tito. Tito will fall." Every resource of propaganda, diplomacy, and economic pressure was brought to bear from the Kremlin to consummate Tito's political demise, to the tune of reiterated accusations that were palpably false. Only one measure Stalin, fearful of global war, refrained from taking: military aggression. Tito's regime not only survived but flourished and accepted economic and military aid from the West.

This result, incredible to the members of the Politburo, stirred new fears that "Titoism" might spread to other satellites and undermine all of the Red Empire. The consequence was a series of barbarous "purges" of alleged Titoists or "deviationists," none of whom, it was later conceded in the post-Stalin era of "rehabilitations" (many of them posthumous), was guilty of anything other than a hope for some degree of local autonomy for their countrymen. This sordid record of intolerance in the marchlands, comparable to the most savage cruelties at home of Ivan Grozny, Peter the Great, and Stalin the Terrible, is better tabulated than described:

ALBANIA. Enver Hoxha's Soviet-sponsored and Communist-controlled regime quarreled with Greece, Italy, Britain, and the USA during 1946. In 1947 London and Washington severed diplomatic relations when a Tirana court (September 29) condemned 16 persons to death for sabotage, subversive activities, and allegedly treasonable collaboration with agents of Western Powers. In a purge of "Trotskyites and Titoists" in October 1948, Koci Xoxe, Pandi Christo, and other top Communist leaders were ousted from office. A year later Hoxha flew to Moscow to appeal for aid in his increasingly hopeless efforts to support the Red guerrillas in Greece, stranded by Tito's defection. On June 10, 1949, Xoxe was sentenced to death as a "Titoist." Many other opponents of the regime or scapegoat victims of its insecurities were arrested, jailed, or executed while Hoxha strengthened his ties with the USSR and the other Soviet satellites. The grim processes of "Russification" and "Stalinization" were completed during 1950 under the guidance of Vice-Premier and Police Chief Mehmet Shehu.

BULGARIA. Nikola Petkov, leader of the Agrarian Party opposition to the "Fatherland Front" regime, was increasingly assailed by offi-

cial spokesmen during 1946. Dr. Georgi M. Dimitrov, a refugee in the USA, was sentenced *in abstentia* to life imprisonment, July 10, 1946. Premier Georgi Dimitrov, hero of the *Reichstag* fire trial in Leipzig in 1933 and no relation to his namesake, consolidated his power during 1947 as Petkov was arrested, tried, and executed (September 22) in what the U.S. State Department called "a gross miscarriage of justice." Repression of opponents continued during 1948. Dimitrov died in Moscow July 2, 1949. He was succeeded in the Premiership by Vassil Kolarov, with V. Chervenkov as Vice-Premier. Forced collectivization bred bitter peasant resentment. Purges and executions became routine. Former Vice-Premier Traicho Kostov was hanged December 16, 1949. Since the prosecution had implicated Minister Donald R. Heath in his "Titoist" and "subversive" activities, the USA severed diplomatic relations on February 21, 1950. Meanwhile, Kolarov died on January 21 and was succeeded as Premier by Chervenkov ("Little Red Wolf"), who continued to liquidate presumptive "Titoists" to the accompaniment of peasant unrest and renewed convulsions among the oligarchs, leading to further arrests, imprisonments, and executions.

RUMANIA. Petru Grozu's "coalition" regime won a handsome victory in the election of November 19, 1946, despite protests from London, Washington, and the local opposition that the outcome was fraudulent. During 1947 Maniu and Mihalache were jailed, King Michael was deposed, and all opposition was crushed. In new "elections" of March 1948 the Red-led "Popular Democratic Front" won 90.8% of the votes, after which critics of the regime were further purged, forced to flee, or liquidated. During 1949 the country was thoroughly Sovietized and its government converted into a pliable tool of Stalinism. Anna Pauker, daughter of a rabbi, assumed leadership during 1950 in a violent anti-Zionist campaign, *à la* Muscovy, often indistinguishable from anti-Semitism. In 1951 Rumania embarked on its first Five Year Plan, promising ultimate plenty and freedom but immediate poverty and terrorism.

HUNGARY. On June 28, 1946, Lieut. Gen. V. P. Sviridov demanded of Premier Ferenc Nagy the suppression of the Boy Scouts and three Catholic youth organizations, and the dismissal of various officials for "Fascist" activities. Despite support from Cardinal Mindszenty and from London and Washington, the Premier yielded on July 11, 1946. Early in January 1947 sundry army officers and other right-wing members of the Smallholders Party were arrested

on orders of Gen. Palffy Oisterreicher and Interior Minister Lazlo Raijk, both Communists. As the purge of "plotters" proceeded, Ferenc Nagy was forced out of office and into exile in late May 1947. On July 30, 1948, President Zoltan Tildy resigned when his son-in-law, Victor Csornoky (later found "guilty" and hanged), was arrested for espionage and high treason. He was succeeded by Arpad Szakasits, Chairman of the (Communist) "United Workers' Party," with Istvan Dobi replacing Lajos Dinnyes in the Premiership in December, amid new repressions culminating in the arrest for treason, espionage, and speculation of the courageous anti-Communist Josef Cardinal Mindszenty on December 27.

The Cardinal, accused of plotting a Hapsburg restoration with Archduke Otto and forced by torture to plead "guilty" to most of the accusations against him, was sentenced to life imprisonment on February 7, 1949. Widespread indignation in the Western world was reflected in innumerable notes of protest and UN resolutions. All were rejected or ignored by the Budapest regime dominated by Communist boss Matyas Rakosi, whose "People's Front" won 95.6% of the vote in the "election" of May 15, 1949.

The new Cabinet included Erno Gero (Minister of State), Janos Kadar (Interior), and Josef Revai (Culture). A new Constitution made Hungary a "People's Republic." On June 15, 1949, the Workers' Party expelled Lazlo Raijk and Tibor Szoenyi as "imperialist spies" and "Trotskyite agents." Four days later both were arrested, along with many others. Raijk, a veteran Communist, had fought in the Spanish war and later become a hero of the anti-Nazi underground. He "confessed" to fantastic charges and, along with Szoenyi and Andrai Szalai, was hanged on October 15. On Stalin's birthday, December 21, 1949, President Szakasits opined that the Soviet Premier had "soared to staggering heights . . . so high human eyes can scarcely follow him, but we still feel we are close to this hard and cheerful, wise and simple man." Rakosi waged verbal war on Tito and ruthlessly pressed on with the Stalinization of Magyarland.

CZECHOSLOVAKIA. During 1947 Prague, under President Beneš, Premier Klement Gottwald, and Foreign Minister Jan Masaryk, maintained its freedom, Western-style, and hoped to remain a "bridge" between West and East. The tragic events of 1948 have already been noted (p. 367). In December, Premier Zapotocky visited Stalin in Moscow. During 1949 the C.P. waged war upon,

and then made a peace of sorts with, the Catholic Church, while the Party purged its ranks of "unreliables" and rooted out sundry army officers and bureaucrats accused of "plotting" with Western agents against the regime. On March 14, 1950, Foreign Minister Vladimir Clementis was dismissed, and soon accused of "bourgoeis nationalist deviationism" and anti-Stalinism. He recanted and was briefly spared. In September 1951 Rudolph Slansky, Secretary General of the C.P., was removed and demoted. The purging of the purgers ensued, on the Stalinist model, with more and more potential dissidents linked with Clementis and Slansky—who, after a show trial, were hanged December 3, 1952, along with various "confederates."

POLAND. The "Government of National Unity" of June 1945, under President Boleslaw Bierut and Premier Edward Osubka-Morawski, encountered increasing opposition from Vice-Premier Stanislaw Mikolajczyk's Polish Peasant Party, leading to rural guerrilla warfare in 1946. The "left bloc" triumphed in the "election" of January 19, 1946. In the new Cabinet of February 5 Joseph Cyrankiewicz, Secretary-General of the Socialist Party, became Premier and Communist leader Vladyslaw Gomulka Vice-Premier, with all the "London Poles" excluded from the government and the "Moscow Poles" now ruling the roost. Following the disintegration of the guerrilla forces opposing the regime, partly through an amnesty and partly through the bloody suppression of the remnants, Mikolajczyk fled abroad in October 1947. When in August and September 1948 Gomulka opposed complete subservience to the Cominform line of anti-Titoism, compulsory collectivization, and forced industrialization, he was ousted as Secretary-General of the C.P. In December 1948 the Socialist Party and the Workers' Party were merged, under Communist control. Gomulka was dropped from the Cabinet in January 1949, and expelled from the Party in November along with Gen. Marian Spychalski and Zenon Klisco. On November 7, 1949, Soviet Marshal Konstantin Rokossovsky, born in Warsaw in 1896 and now assuming Polish citizenship, was named "Marshal of Poland," Minister of National Defense, and, on May 12, 1950, a member of the Party Politburo. By 1951 Gomulka, Spychalski, and numerous other "anti-Stalinists" were in jail.

The common denominator of these scattered and confused political events in the Soviet marchlands is too obvious to require elaboration. In 1945–6 Stalin and his colleagues were prepared to

tolerate more or less democratic "bourgeois" coalition regimes in the countries of the carapace, providing their governments should be "friendly" (i.e., pro-Soviet) and allied with the USSR. With the rising challenge from London and Washington to the whole Soviet position in East Europe, Moscow moved toward the suppression of all "bourgeois" parties and the imposition of all-Communist regimes on the satellites. With the rise of Titoism, the consolidation of Stalinist power in all the "People's Democracies" was sought by means of the bloody liquidation of all Communists suspected of anti-Stalinism. The politicians of Muscovy were unable to devise any method of holding together their new empire other than the method perfected by Stalin in the USSR in the 1930's—the jailing or killing, behind a façade of carefully staged "judicial" proceedings, of all prominent opponents, schismatics, heretics, and potential dissidents.

As in Russia itself, this political device—which is by no means unique in the building of empires—was paralleled by the economic "building of socialism" in the name of justice, plenty, and freedom. To all Westerners, save those bewitched by the Marxist dialectic, the politics of Stalinism was the negation of the economics of Stalinism. This judgment was to be proved false by developments in the USSR. It was partially valid in the satellites, thanks to Muscovite exploitation of the labor of Albanians, Hungarians, Bulgarians, Rumanians, Czechoslovaks, and Poles. Even in these communities, however, some semblance or promise of prosperity, despite material sacrifices and an ever-present terror so long as Stalinism endured, induced years of acquiescence in the new dispensation. The result was the failure of Western efforts to achieve any significant disintegration of the Red Realm or any "liberation" of its subject peoples.

3. THE SHOW OF VIOLENCE

THE greatest apparent victory for the USSR and the greatest apparent defeat of America's "containment" policy during the 1940's was the Chinese Revolution, which delivered the most populous community of mankind, comprising almost a quarter of the human race, into the hands of new rulers who were disciples of Marxism-Leninism, although not, as we shall see, of "Stalinism." The Communist Empire herewith assumed the menacing proportions of the Mongol

realm of Ogdai and Kublai Khan. To many Americans it seemed to threaten the conquest of all the world, in accordance with Sir Halford J. Mackinder's false dictum that "who rules East Europe commands the Heartland; who rules the Heartland commands the World Island; who rules the World Island commands the World." [8]

Communist mastery of China was widely interpreted in the West as a Muscovite conquest of Cathay and therefore as a monstrous menace to the security of the "Free World." The conspirators in the Kremlin were now assumed to have at their disposal all the vast human and material resources of the ancient "Middle Kingdom" for their war against the West. This interpretation of the meaning of the victory of Mao Tse-tung and his comrades was widely at variance with the facts. The actual course of events was quite different from what American policy-makers assumed them to be. [9]

In a century of irony and paradox, we are here in the presence of the greatest paradox and irony of all. The American statesmen who later were to be bitterly accused of "betraying" China at Yalta and subsequently "surrendering" China to Russia at no time had any effective control over the course of events in China. There was no possibility of their betraying or surrendering to anyone something they did not possess. The Soviet statesmen, who later won blame or praise for "Communizing" China, had no more control over events. Indeed, they mistakenly strove to prevent the Communist conquest of China. When the deed was done by the Chinese, against the will of Moscow, the men in the Kremlin became temporary beneficiaries of the *fait accompli* only because of the mistaken American conviction that Russia had "conquered" China. Here on a colossal scale

[8] *Democratic Ideals and Reality* (Holt, 1943, originally published in 1919). This point of departure for all the imposing literature of "geopolitics," productive of some wisdom and much nonsense during the long armistice, was, of course, a fallacy in terms of all past human experience and promised to remain a fallacy for the future.

[9] Assistant Secretary of State Dean Rusk, addressing the China Institute in New York, May 18, 1951, declared: "The Peiping regime may be a colonial Russian government—a Slavic Manchukuo on a larger scale. It is not the Government of China. . . . It is not Chinese. It is not entitled to speak for China. . . . The National Government of the Republic of China [Formosa] more authentically represents the views of the great body of the people of China." Uncritical acceptance of such mythology, endlessly reiterated in the USA of 1950 and after, was a precondition of social and political respectability in a country whose Congress, every year for many years, unanimously and solemnly resolved that the Communist Government of China must never be recognized or allowed to represent "China" in the UN.

was the most sardonic vindication in our time of the despairing comment of the Chancellor of Sweden, Count Axel Oxenstierna (1583–1654): "With how little wisdom is the world ruled!"

Stalin, here as tightly trapped in the Marxist dogma as were the Russian Mensheviks in the early 1900's, could not conceive of the possibility of "proletarian revolution" (without which, by definition, no "socialist" regime was possible) in a semi-feudal peasant country where "capitalism" was in its infancy and where the "proletariat" was insignificant. In his role as a Machiavellian practitioner of *Realpolitik*, he calculated, moreover, that a weak and disorderly China, under an incompetent and corrupt regime, was preferable as Muscovy's Asian neighbor to a strong and united China ruled by people of purpose—the more so as the latter possibility, unlike the former, would sooner or later jeopardize the tangible fruits of the Yalta bargain and of Russia's second war with Japan: economic privileges in Manchuria, control of Dairen and Port Arthur, and the "independence" of Outer Mongolia. In Asia, as in Europe, he took it for granted in 1944–6 that only "bourgeois" governments were possible. He urged the Communists of the satellites to tolerate quasi-democratic coalitions. He urged French Communists to support De Gaulle and Italian Communists to accept King Victor Emanuel and Badoglio. He urged Tito to accept the monarchy and cooperate with Britain. By the same logic, he urged Mao Tse-tung to compromise with Chiang Kai-shek. The Chinese Revolution said the *Vozhd* to Mao in 1945, "has no prospects." Mao should therefore "seek a *modus vivendi*" with the Kuomintang, join Chiang's Government, and dissolve the Chinese Communist army.

Mao assented, or implied assent by silence, and then did what he thought best for his own purposes. By February 1948 Stalin admitted to Kardelj that he had been "mistaken" about China. Yet half a year later he was advising Mao to limit his campaigns to guerrilla warfare and abstain from any effort to take the major cities. Mao smiled once more and did what he deemed best. The final result was the antithesis of what Stalin desired, although he promptly faced facts and turned them to Soviet advantage with an adroitness conspicuous by its absence among Western policy-makers.[1]

[1] At the time of writing only shreds and patches of these aspects of Soviet policy in China are available from published sources. But see Isaac Deutscher's perceptive observations in *Russia What Next?* (Oxford University Press, 1953), pp. 91–117, and particularly his comments on the evidence offered by Kardelj

With the defeat of Japan, the Chinese Communist armies flowed into Manchuria and secured substantial stores of Japanese arms, with or without Soviet connivance, while local Muscovite agents were looting the northwest provinces, making terms with Chiang, and giving Chinese Red leaders bad advice. American efforts to mediate between the Kuomintang and the Communists, through the mission of Marshall (November 27, 1945–January 7, 1947) and the ensuing Wedemeyer mission in the summer of 1947, failed of their purpose, thanks to Chiang's delusion that he could crush the Communists by force. Huge U.S. subsidies in money and arms to Chiang were wasted in the ubiquitous graft and irresponsibility of the Nationalist regime. The events of 1949 decided the issue. Red forces, joined by throngs of deserters from the Kuomintang armies and hailed as "liberators" by millions of peasants and townsmen alike, took Nanking on April 20 and Shanghai on May 25. On September 21, 1949, the "People's Republic of China" was proclaimed at Peiping. Canton fell on October 15. In December of 1949 Chiang and the remnants of his soldiery and bureaucracy fled to Formosa, where they survived only because of subventions and protection by the United States.

This *bouléversement* of the global balance of power confronted policy-makers in East and West with the problem of how to deal with an undesired and unforeseen innovation. The American response was to swear undying enmity toward the new rulers of China and to pursue the will-o'-the-wisp of Chiang's return to the mainland to "liberate" China from Communist tyranny. The Soviet response was to strike a bargain with the victors, who were, after all, Marxists and Leninists even if not Stalinists. On February 14, 1950, in Moscow Vyshinsky and Chou En-lai signed a 30-year treaty of friendship and alliance, pledging the parties to mutual aid and immediate military support of each other in case of renewed aggression by Japan or "any other State which, directly or indirectly, would unite with Japan in acts of aggression." Moscow agreed to extend 10-year

---

and by V. Dedijer (*Tito Speaks*) and on *The Times* (London) report of June 27, 1950. Useful background data will be found in Gerard M. Friters: *Outer Mongolia and Its International Position* (Johns Hopkins Press, 1949); Robert C. North: *Moscow and the Chinese Communists* (Stanford University Press, 1953); Michel N. Pavlovsky: *Chinese Russian Relations* (Philosophical Library, 1948); and B. A. Romanov: *Russia in Manchuria* (American Council of Learned Societies, 1952).

credits to China to the amount of sixty million dollars annually for 5 years at 1% interest for the purchase of Soviet machinery and railway equipment; to restore to China all Manchurian properties acquired from Japanese owners; and to return Port Arthur, Dairen, and the Manchurian railways to Chinese control not later than the end of 1952.

The sequel was implicit in the premises of the Sino-Soviet alliance. Following negotiations in Moscow (August 17–September 16, 1952), Chou En-lai and Vyshinsky publicly agreed—amid pledges of "friendship and collaboration" for "the preservation and strengthening of peace and international security"—to Soviet surrender to China by December 31, *sans* compensation, of all Russian rights in the Manchurian railways and a prolongation of Soviet control of Port Arthur "until such time as peace treaties between the Chinese People's Republic and Japan and between the USSR and Japan are concluded." In fear of American folly and out of respect for American power, Moscow subsequently strove to restrain Peiping from rash adventures in Formosa and Indochina. After parleys in Peiping, the two allies announced, October 11, 1954, that the USSR would grant credits and machinery to China to the value of almost a billion rubles, evacuate Port Arthur by January 1, 1955, yield to China all Soviet shares in mixed companies in return for compensation in goods over a span of years; promote scientific and technical cooperation; and collaborate in the building of railways from Lanchow via Urumchi to Alma-Ata and from Tinmin via Ulan Bator to Soviet territory.

The partners further agreed to "help in consolidating peace and security in the Far East and the whole world in accordance with the aims and principles of the U.N.," to oppose U.S. policies of "aggression" in protecting Formosa and barring China from the UN, to promote Korean unification and Japanese "independence," and to base their policies on "a strict observance of the principles of mutual respect for sovereignty and territorial integrity, of mutual non-aggression, mutual non-interference in domestic affairs, equality and mutual advantage and peaceful coexistence which opens wide possibilities for the development of fruitful international cooperation."

Such rhetoric was belied by intervening events. In the context of the Sino-Soviet entente of February 1950, the global "Cold War" became, four months later, a localized hot war in Korea. At dawn of June 24, 1950, the troops of Kim Il-sung's North Korean Communist

regime at Pyongyang, amply equipped with Soviet guns, tanks, and planes, embarked upon the invasion and projected conquest, in the name of "unification," of South Korea, where Syngman Rhee's anti-Communist government had been declared by the UN, on the initiative of the USA, to be the only lawful government of Korea. American subsidies in money and arms to the South Korean authorities in Seoul had been generous, although stopping short of such equipment as might enable Rhee to do what he had long promised to do—invade and conquer North Korea in the name of "unification."

Moscow's role in these events is still obscure.[2] That the invasion was in any literal sense "ordered by Stalin," as most Americans at once assumed, is doubtful. Soviet policy-makers, to be sure, had armed and trained the North Korean troops and presumably controlled, or believed they controlled, decision-making in Pyongyang as in the capitals of the other Soviet satellites. Yet events in China had demonstrated that such "control" was sometimes fictitious. The relations in the spring of 1950 between Peiping and Pyongyang are equally obscure. If the Politburo in the Kremlin initiated, by proxy, the Korean hostilities, then it is strange that the USSR, currently engaged in boycotting UN gatherings in protest against the denial of Peiping's right to represent "China," should have had no envoy on hand to cast the inevitable veto when the Security Council in late June and July resolved on armed resistance to the North Korean aggression.

It is arguable that any such veto would have been a blatant confession of Soviet "guilt" for inaugurating war and that Stalin, Molotov, & Co., with Machiavellian cleverness, deliberately refrained from vetoing UN military action—perhaps on the even more

---

[2] My efforts in the Soviet capital in the spring of 1956 to secure enlightenment on the fateful decisions of 1950 (and of some other crucial periods in foreign policy) were unsuccessful. Available documentation answers none of the central questions of policy-making. At present, therefore, the investigator must largely rely on inference and a weighing of probabilities. The world-wide "Communist line" to the effect that the Korean War was instigated by South Korean aggression, supported by the USA, must be relegated to the realm of mythology or prevarication in the light of U.S. and UN documentation. See, however, I. F. Stone: *The Hidden History of the Korean War* (Monthly Review Press, 1952), which raises many searching and disturbing questions of motives and purposes. Compare with Robert T. Oliver: *Why War Came in Korea* (Fordham University Press, 1951). The most plausible version of Soviet-Korean relations in 1950 is offered by a former member of the U.S. Military Government in Korea, Wilbur H. Hitchcock, in "North Korea Jumps the Gun," *Current History*, March 1951.

Machiavellian assumption that in the ensuing conflict the Soviet policy-makers, at little cost and with no risk to themselves, could enjoy the pleasant spectacle of the UN (at this point almost wholly subordinated to the purposes of American foreign policy) becoming totally discredited through defeat and failure while the USA wasted its resources in an endless and hopeless war on the Asian mainland. Such calculations cannot be excluded from the realm of possibility. The precepts of the Florentine are still relevant to world politics in a world community lacking world government. Most super-Machiavellian interpretation of *Weltpolitik*, however, deserve to be viewed with skepticism. In such affairs Soviet power-holders, like their counterparts elsewhere, are less frequently engaged in subtle and devious conspirings, despite their messianic fanaticism, than in trial-and-error fumblings, bumblings, and blunderings. In the course of such endeavors the actual results of plans and plots, if any, bear little resemblance to anticipated results amid the inexorable vicissitudes and confusions of high politics in a State System that is anarchic rather than orderly.

The best guess presently possible regarding Muscovite motives in the matter is this: Stalin and his agents had armed North Korea to a point at which Kim Il-sung was confident of the ability of his soldiery to overrun South Korea in a *Blitzkrieg*. All Communist policy-makers involved in the drama interpreted, quite understandably, the various public utterances in January 1950 of Dean Acheson, President Truman, Louis Johnson, Omar Bradley, *et al.*, putting Korea outside the "defense perimeter" of the USA in the Pacific, as meaning that the colossus of the West would not defend South Korea. Pyongyang may well have launched its assault without consulting Moscow. If consulted, Muscovite politicians must have said in effect: make the attempt, if you choose to, but do not count on us to "bail you out" with more tanks, planes, guns, or troops if you fail, for we shall stand aside and run no risks of global war. What, if anything, was said from Peiping by way of encouragement or discouragement is presently unknown. Under such circumstances Kim Il-sung embarked upon his tragic gamble.

America's response to this challenge was immediate and vigorous. At noon of July 27, 1950, after consultation with the Cabinet, authorization to Gen. MacArthur to give aid to Syngman Rhee, and recourse to the UN Security Council for a "cease-fire" resolution, President Truman issued a public statement:

In Korea the Government forces, which were armed to prevent border raids and to preserve internal security, were attacked by invading forces from North Korea. The Security Council of the UN called upon the invading troops to cease hostilities and to withdraw to the 38th parallel. This they have not done but, on the contrary, have pressed the attack. The Security Council called upon all members of the UN to render every assistance in the execution of this resolution.

In these circumstances I have ordered U.S. air and sea forces to give the Korean Government troops cover and support.

The attack upon Korea makes it plain beyond all doubt that Communism has passed beyond the use of subversion to conquer independent nations and will now use armed invasion and war. It has defied the orders of the Security Council of the UN issued to preserve international peace and security. In these circumstances the occupation of Formosa by Communist forces would be a direct threat to the security of the Pacific area and to U.S. forces performing their lawful and necessary functions in that area.

Accordingly I have ordered the Seventh Fleet to prevent any attack on Formosa. As a corollary of this action I am calling upon the Chinese Government of Formosa to cease all air and sea operations against the mainland. The Seventh Fleet will see that this is done. The determination of the future status of Formosa must await the restoration of security in the Pacific, a peace settlement with Japan, or consideration by the UN. I have also directed that U.S. forces in the Philippines be strengthened and that military assistance to the Philippine Government be accelerated.

I have similarly directed acceleration in the furnishing of military assistance to the forces of France and the associated States in Indo-China and the dispatch of a military mission to provide close working relations with those forces.

I know that all members of the UN will consider carefully the consequences of this latest aggression in Korea in defiance of the Charter of the United Nations. A return to the rule of force in international affairs would have far-reaching effects. The United States will continue to uphold

the rule of law. I have instructed Ambassador Austin, as the representative of the United States to the Security Council, to report these steps to the Council.

Decision-makers in Washington, embittered by the "loss" of China and by the endless frustrations of "Cold War," thus seized upon the occasion not only to defend the Republic of Korea with U.S. forces available in Japan but to enlist the UN, in the name of "collective security," in a "police action" against aggression, to make Formosa an American protectorate, to support Paris in its fore-doomed efforts to perpetuate colonialism in Indochina, and to in-dict "Communism" for resorting to armed violence as a means to-ward world conquest. All these decisions were to have results quite contrary to those expected. The pretended monolithic unity of the "Communist bloc" was already a myth in 1950, although no staunch Communist could admit the fact and not many Western statesmen were aware of it. As for the central generalization in the Truman pronouncement, there had never been, and there was never to be, any instance of Communist military aggression against any area that the USA had plainly declared its intention to defend. Had Washing-ton made clear in January what was made clear in June—American resolve to protect South Korea—there would in all likelihood have been no attack. American blunders were matched by Soviet blun-ders. But in the balance sheet of cast accounts the USSR emerged, by happenstance, in a more powerful position than the USA—and this without firing a single gun or losing a single life while America, in a war never to be "won," was to see 25,000 of its sons done to death in Korea. All the vast resources of the USA were to prove in-capable of achieving any settlement beyond a stalemate on the basis of the *status quo ante bellum*. If the illusion of American omnipo-tence was thus shattered, Muscovite interests were in some other re-spects ill served by this enterprise in bloodshed and destruction, for the war brought new unity, inspired by fear, to the "Free World" coalition and caused the Atlantic Powers to embark upon a gigantic rearmament program.[3]

[3] At no time during these troubled years did the policy-makers of Moscow contemplate armed aggression against the West. This fact was appreciated by some Western statesmen, even though the whole pattern of Western policy was predicated on the opposite assumption. On March 8, 1949, John Foster Dulles told the 3rd National Conference on Churches and the World Order: "So far as it is humanly possible to judge, the Soviet Government, under conditions

The melancholy sequence of mutual miscalculations in Korea is familiar to all: how the UN Security Council recommended military aid (June 27, 1950) and voted (July 7) to establish a unified UN Command "under the USA"; how 15 other States sent token forces; how Jacob Malik returned to the Council in August and vetoed further condemnation of North Korea for defiance; how Red forces swept down the peninsula and by September had pinned the defenders into a small pocket around Pusan; how Gen. MacArthur's masterly amphibious operation at Inchon, launched September 15, retook Seoul, trapped many of the invaders, and forced the rest to beat a hasty retreat; how the UN Assembly on October 7 authorized the "liberation" of North Korea, despite Chinese and Indian warnings of intervention by Peiping (all dismissed by MacArthur as "bluff") and on November 3 adopted a "Uniting for Peace" resolution, contemplating the permanent conversion of the UN into a military coalition to wage war on aggressors; how UN divisions crossed the 38th parallel and drove toward the Yalu in October and November; how they were overwhelmed in December by vast masses of Chinese "volunteers," who captured many, pushed the rest into the sea, retook Pyongyang and Seoul, and again drove southward; how Attlee flew to Washington in December to warn Truman against any use of atomic weapons or any waging of war on China outside of Korea; how the Assembly (February 2, 1951) held Red China

---

now prevailing, does not contemplate the use of war as an instrument of its national policy. I do not know any responsible high official, military or civilian, in this Government or any Government who believes that the Soviet Government now plans conquest by open military aggression." George F. Kennan, writing in *Harper's Magazine*, August 1956, on "Overdue Changes in Our Foreign Policy," commented on "a rather common impression that Stalin was a man of war, aiming to launch a military onslaught against the non-Communist world, whereas his successors are men of peace. Proceeding from this assumption people argue that whereas it was right for us, several years ago, to orient our policies exclusively to the danger of war, we now no longer need to do so. This is a great oversimplification. Stalin was not what you would call a nice man, and his intentions toward ourselves were strictly dishonorable. But these intentions, I am convinced, did not conclude the determination to unleash a third world war in the grand manner. The image of a Stalinist Russia poised and yearning to attack the West, and deterred only by our possession of atomic weapons, was largely a creation of the Western imagination, against which some of us who were familiar with Russian matters tried in vain, over the course of years, to make our voices heard. In this respect the change that has recently come about has been more a change in the American interpretation of external reality than in that reality itself." See also the closing pages of Kenneth Ingram: *History of the Cold War.*

guilty of "aggression" and urged "additional measures," which no one was prepared to take; how "negotiations" between Truman and MacArthur failed to shake the General's conviction that the war could be "won" by bombing Manchuria, invading China, and risking conflict with the USSR; how the President dismissed the General on April 11, 1951; and how hostilities bogged down in the spring, near the original line of demarcation, into a costly and hopeless stalemate of trench warfare reminiscent of the Western Front of 1914–18.[4]

The pattern of Soviet policy, here as in other matters, cannot be analyzed by reference to any available records of debates in the Politburo over alternative courses of action (such records are either non-existent or are "top secret"), but can only be inferred from public words and deeds. The Stalinist "Party Line," slavishly followed by all Communists save those in Jugoslavia, held that the war, in the customary Billingsgate of the comrades, was the work of South Korean "Fascists" who were "puppets" of American "militarists," "capitalists," "imperialists," and "war-mongers" hellishly bent upon destroying the "free" and "democratic" Utopia of Kim Il-sung, "enslaving" China and all of Asia to enhance the profits of American "monopolists," and destroying "socialism" everywhere by violence—including hideous atrocities in Korea, among them alleged recourse to "germ warfare." The circumstance that this version of events bore no relationship to the truth obligated all Stalinists to insist with redoubled vehemence upon its veracity. But here, as always, Stalin and his aides in their dual roles as visionary missionaries of the millennium and as responsible power-holders in Muscovy displayed ability to temper mysticism with realism and to draw the necessary operational conclusion from stubbornly irreducible facts.

Malik, who in January at Lake Success accused the USA of seeking to enlarge the war in Asia and sought in vain to show a "documentary" film of American atrocities, hinted in a radio broadcast of June 23, 1951, at the desirability of a Korean cease-fire. A conference in Moscow four days later between Ambassador Allan G. Kirk and Acting Foreign Minister Andrei A. Gromyko led to truce

---

[4] The voluminous documentation and political and military literature of the Korean War are here beyond our purview. In *The Commonwealth of Man* (Knopf, 1952), pp. 368–402, I have dealt at some length with these events as a further demonstration of the unworkability of the gospel of "collective security" in its classical form.

negotiations between Communist envoys and agents of Gen. Ridgway at Kaesong and Panmunjom—since it was evident to Western leaders, as to policy-makers in Moscow, Peiping, and Pyongyang (if not in Seoul), that no "victory" was possible in the Korean conflict unless it should be enlarged into a world war, in which, even more clearly, no victory would be possible. The negotiations broke down and were prolonged over weary months and years on the issue of whether prisoners should be forcibly repatriated against their wishes. Among some 15,000 Allied soldiers in Communist hands, only a "brain-washed" handful (about 350) finally opted to remain in the Red Empire. Among North Korean and Chinese prisoners in Allied custody, numbering almost 100,000, some 75,000 accepted repatriation, while 23,000 declared they would resist it to the death. This moral defeat of the Communist cause long seemed to preclude an armistice, since each side, with an eye to the "next war," was concerned, anxiously or hopefully, with prospective defections of its troops to the enemy. Shooting ceased in Korea only after Stalin's death and Communist acquiescence in the UN position. But the military reality of an unbreakable stalemate was obvious by June of 1951.

Recourse to violence in dealing with problems of power is self-defeating when neither side can impose its will on the other. Korea was the microcosm of the global macrocosm of "Cold War" in the early 1950's. A comparable lesson had been learned, on both sides, from the "Battle of Berlin" of 1948-9 and was to be learned in Indochina, where Ho Chi Minh's Vietminh armies, in an eight-year war of independence, fought the French and their reluctant Vietnam allies to a standstill. In the larger arenas of conflict no other outcome was possible, despite the hopes and fears of East and West. Anglo-American efforts to enlist the Arab States with the West against the USSR were to prove disastrous. The Western policy of allying a rearmed Reich with the Atlantic Powers perpetuated the partition of Germany. American dreams of alliance with a rearmed Japan appeared, superficially, more attainable.

At San Francisco (September 5-8, 1951) another major conference assembled, with China and Korea unrepresented; India, Burma, and Jugoslavia refusing to attend; and the USSR, Poland, and Czechoslovakia rejecting the outcome: a Peace Treaty of 29 articles, signed by 49 States, restoring Japanese sovereignty and providing for an end of "occupation," with Nippon renouncing title to Korea, For-

mosa, the Kuriles, South Sakhalin, the mandated islands, etc., and accepting a U.S. trusteeship over the Ryukus, including Okinawa. Moscow had proposed in May a summer meeting of the Council of Foreign Ministers to prepare a treaty. Washington refused and warned that the San Francisco meeting "is not a conference to re-open negotiations on the terms of peace" and that the USSR had no choice but to sign or refuse to sign the text already drafted and published. Gromyko's proposed 13 amendments were not permitted to come to a vote. He condemned the pact as unjust to China, as a façade for American aggression via the militarization of Japan, and as certain to promote war, not peace, in Asia. Acheson and Premier Shigeru Yoshida simultaneously signed (September 8, 1951) a Japanese-American Security Treaty, making Japan an ally and protectorate of the USA. But even here no decisive gains were scored by West against East, since Japan, like Germany, had no possible future role as a "Great Power" and would sooner or later be obliged for its own safety and welfare to come to terms with the new China and the USSR.

4. COANNIHILATION?

ON Friday morning, September 23, 1949, following a solemn Cabinet meeting, Charley Ross distributed to newsmen at the White House a brief release by President Truman announcing that the USSR had exploded an atomic bomb. America's closely guarded "secret" (which many physicists had insisted from the outset was no secret) herewith vanished. The Atomic Age, which began in secret at Stagg Field at the University of Chicago on December 2, 1942, with the achievement for the first time on earth of a self-sustaining chain reaction in nuclear fission, and opened in public with the vaporization of Hiroshima and Nagasaki on August 6 and 9, 1945, now entered upon a new epoch. The Metropolitan Life Insurance Company announced that premiums would not be increased. Some property-owners in Rome at once offered for sale, at bargain prices, their holdings near Vatican City. Congressman Rankin proposed that the capital of the USA be transferred from the District of Columbia to Kentucky. Consternation gripped the West, since the American monopoly of nuclear weapons had been widely expected to endure for another

decade at least. Official spokesmen in Washington and Moscow announced no change of policies toward international control of atomic energy—which policies, being wholly incompatible, had precluded, and would continue to preclude, any East-West accord. Vyshinsky spoke vaguely of Soviet use of atomic power to move mountains, irrigate deserts, and otherwise contribute to sweetness and light.

On the grim calendar of nuclear tests, Washington announced further American detonations of atomic weapons July 1 and 26, 1946, at Bikini; spring of 1948 at Eniwetok; January and February 1951 at Las Vegas, Nevada; April and May 1951 at Eniwetok; October and November 1951 at Las Vegas; spring of 1952 at Las Vegas; autumn of 1951 at Eniwetok; spring of 1953 at Las Vegas; March and April 1954 at Eniwetok (the H-Bomb on March 1, 1954); spring of 1955 at Las Vegas; spring of 1956 at Bikini and Eniwetok (H-Bomb, May 21, 1956). The Kremlin kept silent while Washington announced all of the earlier Soviet tests or series of tests: September 23, 1949; October 3 and 22, 1951; August 20, 1953; August 31, 1953; October 26, 1954; August 4, 1955; September 24 and November 20, 1955; November 23, 1955 (H-Bomb); and March 21, August 26 and 31. The tests of September 3 and 10 and November 17, 1956, were announced in Moscow before American detectors broke the news. Other tests followed during 1957.

Some experts contended and others denied that such tests were dangerously poisoning the earth's atmosphere with strontium 90 and other radioactive by-products of nuclear fission and fusion, and thus threatening all mankind with bone cancer and genetic deterioration. This is a problem which ignorant laymen must leave to the "experts," however fallible their *expertise* and however hazardous their possible errors of calculation. Our immediate concern is with the import of the Soviet bomb for the grand strategy of the "Cold War." Since neither Washington nor Moscow acknowledged any change of tactics and policies after September 1949, it might appear that the breaking of the American monopoly was without effect on decision-making. But this conclusion would be mistaken. The evidence upon which it rests is merely further proof that men and statesmen are creatures of habit and that ancient ways in politics yield only slowly to revolutionary innovations in science and technology. The advent of the bomb, possessed in 1957 by America, Russia, and Britain and certain to be soon possessed by more and more lesser Powers, ren-

ders all "power politics" obsolete, despite human reluctance to grant the conclusion, and human bewilderment as to what to do, operationally, on the basis of the conclusion.

Nuclear fission and fusion made armed hostilities unthinkable as a method of resolving problems of power between East and West [5] —unless men and statesmen should prove sufficiently insane to prefer mutual national suicide, and conceivably the self-extermination of the human species, to a pacific *modus vivendi*. Quite apart from the A-Bomb and H-Bomb, the arms race and the rivalry of the coalitions had effected by mid-Century, with no one planning such an

---

[5] The shift of public attitudes in the USA before and after the advent of the Soviet bomb is well illustrated by the following items. *Newsweek*, May 17, 1948, in commenting on an address by Gen. George C. Kenney, Commander of the U.S. Strategic Air Command, observed: "American strategists are thinking . . . in terms of closing the circle of air bases around Russia, making it smaller and smaller, tighter and tighter, until the Russians are throttled. This means getting bases through combined air, sea, and ground operations ever closer to Russia's heartland, then using the bases for sustained bombing and guided missile attack." Moscow vainly protested to Washington against the article, June 9, 1948, as a violation of the UN resolution against war propaganda. Cf. *Look*, June 22, 1948: Ben Kocivar, "Air Force Plans for Bombing Russia"; *Life*, August 16, 1948: Gen. Carl Spaatz on the need for overseas bases to bomb Russia; and *Saturday Evening Post*, September 11, 1948: Joseph and Stewart Alsop, "If War Comes—": "From Baku north to Leningrad, from Smolensk east to Novosibirsk, the vitals of the Soviet State will be scorched and destroyed with the terrible fire of the atomic bomb." Following Soviet acquisition of the bomb, the *American Magazine*, February 1951, published an article by Ellsworth Raymond, who served for six years as translator and political analyst in the U.S. Embassy in Moscow. It was entitled "Why Doesn't Somebody Kill Stalin?" In August 1951 Farrar, Strauss, and Young published a novel by Sterling Noel: *I Killed Stalin*. In September 1951 Congress passed the Mutual Security Act, setting aside $100,000,000 annually to finance activities of "selected persons who are residing in or escapees from" the USSR and other Communist countries, "either to form such persons into elements of the military forces supporting NATO or for other purposes." This legislation was sponsored by Congressman Charles J. Kersten of Wisconsin, who in October 1951 protested to Warren Austin that the proposed UN code of international law condemning terroristic acts might prevent liberation of Eastern Europe. In November, Moscow vainly protested that the Mutual Security Act was a violation of the Roosevelt-Litvinov agreements of 1933.

Both before and after the advent of the Soviet bomb, however, many Americans were convinced that no safety was to be had without the destruction of the USSR, whether by atomic war or by subversion and terrorism. Cf. Standley, *Admiral Ambassador to Russia* (p. 506): "I have been wrong about the Soviet Government and its leaders, but I have never been wrong about Communism. Communism is a religion of the devil; it is a distillation of evil; it is the very anti-Christ. We will never be safe from this evil faith until it is driven back to the hell from which it came."

outcome, an equipoise or balance of forces between East and West of so unprecedented and peculiar a character as to preclude any overt and total recourse to armed violence by either contestant against the other.

World Wars, like other cataclysmic phenomena, have their pre-conditions and prerequisites. From the tragically abundant experience of the first half of the 20th Century, and of earlier centuries in our own and previous State Systems, we may say that World Wars are possible, and indeed probable, when five sets of circumstances simultaneously coincide: (1) all or most of the "Powers" are aligned in rival alliances; (2) the coalitions are engaged in an arms race in which each strives to acquire potential military superiority over the other; (3) incidents and episodes of violence and local conflict offer occasions for a "showdown" and sparks to set off the explosion; (4) one side or the other makes demands for control of components or positions of power which the "enemy" cannot and will not yield, unless vanquished in battle, lest by yielding it should so weaken its own posture and capabilities of future fighting capacity as to insure prospective victory to its rival; and (5) diplomats and strategists on one side or the other—or, more commonly, both—have persuaded themselves, however erroneously, of the martial supremacy of their own coalition and have devised a plausible plan of campaign which offers reasonable promise of victory.

If space permitted, it could readily be shown that all five conditions existed in 1914 and again in 1939. During the "Cold War" of 1947 and after, the first three conditions were plainly present. But the fifth was lacking. Because it was lacking, the fourth never materialized, since national policy-makers, including those touched with madness, never make "demands" of the type required to precipitate general hostilities unless they are convinced of their probable invulnerability and invincibility and of their prospective capacity to defeat the enemy. Whenever during the decade of "Cold War" either antagonist moved, in Mr. Dulles's phrase, to the "brink" of open combat, wiser counsels prevailed, either within the ranks of national decision-makers or from the warnings and pressures of allies. This repeated pattern can be traced in detail from available sources for policy-making in Washington. Given Soviet secrecy in such matters, no comparable analysis is possible for policy-making in Moscow, but the result was the same. In Berlin, Korea, and Indochina each side pressed the other to the verge of widespread and total warfare and

then retreated and accepted the implications of a local stalemate rather than run the incalculable risks of another Armageddon.

This reiterated recourse to moderation was in no sense due to any "reasonable" mitigation of inordinate fears, hopes, and ambitions on either side, since attitudes of fanatical detestation of the "enemy" were abundantly present on both sides. Neither is it plausible to contend, as Churchill so often argued, that only the American monopoly of atomic weapons "deterred" the men of the Kremlin from invading and conquering Western Europe. Were this thesis true, Marxist Muscovy would have essayed the enterprise once its stockpiles of atomic and hydrogen bombs were sufficient to counterbalance those of the West. Stalin and his confederates, blissfully believing that Western Europe was in any case doomed to decay by the "contradictions of capitalism" and the shifting of the centers of world power, never contemplated any such military adventure. Each side abstained, despite extreme provocation, from a "showdown" because of a few elementary facts of global power.

The "Communist bloc," prior to its partial disintegration in 1956–7, comprised one-third of the human race, solidly occupying the Eurasian "Heartland" and having at its disposal ample human and material resources for the conquest in war of all of Europe and all of Asia in the face of any possible resistance that might be mobilized by the local inhabitants or the Atlantic Powers. The "Free World," prior to its partial disintegration in 1956–7, possessed, conversely, well over half of all the industrial plants in the world, a naval force vastly outnumbering all other navies combined, some 400 atomic air bases ringing the Red Empire, and a demonstrated capacity to fight and win protracted wars of attrition under circumstances initially deemed hopeless. Given this balance of forces, encompassing overwhelming Communist superiority in local infantry, tanks, guns, and planes and overwhelming Western superiority in global naval and air power and in industrial productivity, no strategists in Moscow or Washington, however adroit or self-deceived, could entertain any delusions of "superiority" of power or figure out any way to win the "inevitable" war. The arms race, moreover, closely resembled the famous race of Alice and the Red Queen in Wonderland wherein both remained under the same tree the whole time. The war therewith ceased to be inevitable and, instead, became inconceivable, with each side cautiously refraining from pressing to the full any demands—whether for "liberation" of the satel-

lites, unification of Germany, "emancipation" of Western Europe from "capitalism," restoration of Formosa to China, etc.—which might have caused the other to offer all-out armed resistance.

The "geopolitical" result of this equipoise of power, coupled with the reluctance of each antagonist to challenge the other to mortal combat, was the consolidation of the coalitions, followed, as we shall see, by the beginnings of dissolution on both sides in 1956— after the verdict of "Cold War" had confirmed the fact of deadlock and vastly reduced, if not eliminated altogether, the likelihood of trial by battle. The West was successful in "containing" powerful Communist parties in France and Italy, maintaining the Stettin-Trieste line as the European frontier between the "Free World" and the Red Empire (with Jugoslavia neutralized by the Tito-Stalin schism), temporarily frustrating Marxist machinations in the Near and Middle East, thwarting Communist ambitions in Latin America, and retaining effective control of two-thirds of Germany and of half of Korea and Indochina.[6] The East was successful in maintaining its mastery of the European marchlands, including a third of the former Reich, defending North Korea and Northern Vietnam, capitalizing upon native "anti-colonialism" in Asia and Africa, and exploiting universal aspirations for "peace" and "disarmament." The stalemate thus achieved pointed toward either a general thermonuclear war or a quest for a *modus vivendi*. Since the former solution of the problem promised to result not in one Rome but in two Carthages, each reduced to irreparable ruin by the weapons of the other, the latter alternative, though highly distasteful to both sides, ultimately appeared preferable to mutual suicide.

Other considerations, more subtle but no less persuasive, led reasonable people in both halves of a divided world to opt for peace rather than war despite (or because of) mounting public hysteria in

---

[6] The USA demonstrated in Guatemala in the spring of 1954 that it was no more prepared to tolerate a pro-Communist regime near its frontiers than the USSR was prepared, in Hungary in the autumn of 1956, to tolerate an anti-Communist regime on its borders. The overthrow of the government of President Arbenz by rebel forces under Castillo Armas was effected with neatness and dispatch, and with a minimum of killing and destruction, by the USA, Honduras, and Nicaragua—all acting in the service of "national interest" and in flagrant violation of customary international law, the UN Charter, and the Charter of the Organization of American States. For details and documentation, see Philip B. Taylor, Jr.: "The Guatemalan Affair: A Critique of United States Foreign Policy," *American Political Science Review*, September, 1956, pp. 787–806.

each camp. In the USSR and its satellites the costs of "Cold War," as we have seen, included a reversion to political terrorism involving regimentation and repression on an immense scale and the grim dedication of Communist oligarchs everywhere in Marxland to the seizure, jailing, torture, and execution of thousands of alleged or potential dissidents. This hideous *reductio ad absurdum* of the vaunted humanitarian goals of "socialism" gave pause in the end, after frightful abuses and atrocities, to such comrades as still took their "socialism" seriously. West Europeans endured the tensions of a troubled time without sacrificing their heritage of freedom. In America the "Cold War" begot "McCarthyism" on a vast scale, national and local, and threatened for a time to submerge all standards of decency and sanity in a miasma of suspicion, fear, and hate. Save for suicides, few victims of the national hysteria were killed—apart from Ethel and Julius Rosenberg, executed as "atomic spies" on June 19, 1953. But hundreds were defamed and thousands lost their livelihood, in and out of public service, under accusation of being "Communists" or Soviet sympathizers. A Russia whose power-holders, in the name of defense, were reducing all the ideals of "socialism" to a travesty and an America whose policy-makers, in the name of defense, were steadily subverting many of the ideals of "democracy" and the "rule of law" were ultimately summoned by this tragic erosion of all the deepest beliefs and hopes of their peoples to reconsider their course in the "Cold War." [7]

[7] See Eric F. Goldman: *The Crucial Decade: America, 1945–1955* (Knopf, 1956), pp. 112–33 and 249–78. Perhaps the best one-sentence characterization of "McCarthyism" was written by Arnold J. Toynbee in *A Study of History* (Oxford University Press, 1954), IX, p. 451: "In this odious atmosphere [i.e., Fascist Italy, Nazi Germany, and the America of the early 1950's, although here Toynbee hoped that "this spiritual malaria" might be cured by "counterattack"] a villain could count on being able to win popularity and power for himself by making preposterously false charges against the innocent, since it was an atmosphere in which the innocent had only to be accused of impiety against the current idols of the market-place to find themselves permanently under a cloud, however conclusively they might have proved their integrity, while the unscrupulous had only to launch such accusations to find themselves heroes of the hour, even when they had been convicted of having known their charges to be false before they had launched them." For a detailed and disturbing analysis of the "evidence" in many of the Canadian and American "spytrials" of the "Cold War," see William A. Reuben: *The Atom Spy Hoax* (Action Books, 1955).

AN ADDENDA ON
DEFECTORS, DETECTORS, DEFENDERS,
AND DIPLOMATISTS, 1946–56

THE tangled and troubled course of East-West hostilities during the "Cold War" was marked by numerous incidents and episodes that cannot be fully discussed in such a survey as this. None of these dramatic "crises" can reasonably be regarded as having influenced decisively the formulation of high policy on either side. All of them, taken together, shaped the "climate of opinion" during these hectic years, as did innumerable similar outrages and controversies in the satellites and in Chinese-Western relations—all outside the scope of our narrative. Newspapers and periodicals devoted millions of words to these events. Some are dealt with in detail, although not always with detachment, in such books as Michael Bialoguski: *The Case of Colonel Petrov* (McGraw-Hill, 1955), David J. Dallin: *Soviet Espionage* (Yale University Press, 1955), F. Bowen Evans (ed.): *Worldwide Communist Propaganda Activities* (Macmillan, 1955), Marguerite J. Fisher: *Communist Doctrine and the Free World* (Syracuse University Press, 1953), Otto Heilbrunn: *The Soviet Secret Service* (Praeger, 1956), John Scott: *Political Warfare* (Day, 1955), and Harrison E. Salisbury: *American in Russia* (Harper, 1955).

A chronicle of major episodes may have its uses, since space is lacking for any full treatment of these incidents. Their leitmotifs are disloyalty (on both sides), "cloak-and-dagger" operations, espionage, aerial reconnaissance, destruction of planes, and reciprocal defections by, and accusations against, members of the diplomatic and consular services.

1946: Canada arrests and brings to trial sundry participants in a "Soviet spy ring," first exposed by Igor Gouzenko, a former staff member of the Soviet Embassy. Walter Bedell Smith replaces Averell Harriman as U.S. Ambassador in Moscow, February 14, and Nikolai Novikov replaces Gromyko as Soviet Ambassador in Washington April 10. Truman asserts, May 30, that he has twice invited Stalin to visit the USA but that the Premier has declined for reasons of health. Molotov makes a friendly social call on the President at

the White House on November 7. On March 26 the F.B.I. arrests Naval Lieut. Nikolai G. Redin in Portland, Oregon, on charges of espionage. He is tried in Seattle, found innocent on July 17, and released. In the spring Ilya Ehrenburg, Konstantin Simonov, and Maj. Gen. Mikhail Galaktionov spend two months touring the USA at the invitation of the State Department. Among well-known Americans visiting Moscow later in the year are Ernest C. Ropes, Lewis L. Lorwin, Earl Browder, and Elliott Roosevelt.

1947: Field Marshal Montgomery is cordially received by Stalin in January, but Stalin accuses Bevin of "abandoning" the Anglo-Soviet alliance. For other developments of the year see pp. 356 f.

1948: Annabel Bucar (February) and James M. McMillan (May), both of the U.S. Embassy staff in Moscow, desert their posts and refuse to return to the USA. In August, Oksana Stepanova Kosenkina and Mikhail L. Samarin, two Soviet teachers in the USA, refuse to return to the USSR and are "rescued" by the Tolstoy Foundation, Victor Kravchenko, Vladimir Zenzinov, and the F.B.I. Molotov and Panyushkin protest such "kidnapping" and demand the return of both to the Soviet Consulate in New York. Amid furious charges and counter-charges in Washington arising out of "revelations" of Communist "spy rings" by Elizabeth Bentley, Whittaker Chambers, *et al.*, against Alger Hiss, Harry Dexter White, *et al.*, Mrs. Kosenkina, back in the Soviet Consulate, jumps out of a window on August 11 and is taken to a hospital by local police as Moscow accuses Washington of violating consular immunities. Marshall (August 19) repudiates the protests and demands the recall of Consul General Jacob M. Lomakin for "abusing" his position. Moscow (August 25) closes its two consulates in the USA (New York and San Francisco), abolishes the U.S. Consolate at Vladivostok, and cancels plans for a U.S. Consulate in Leningrad. Mrs. Kosenkina writes and sells her memoirs and, like Elizabeth Bentley and Louis Budenz, becomes a convert to Roman Catholicism.

On April 15 the Soviet Foreign Ministry expels Robert Magidoff as a "spy." On May 4 Ambassador Smith presents a note to Molotov denying any American "hostile or aggressive designs" against the USSR and soliciting negotiations. Molotov replies favorably (May 11), while Bedell Smith goes fishing in Normandy and Henry A. Wallace, in an "Open Letter to Premier Stalin" (who replies favorably), calls for a diplomatic settlement of all outstanding issues. Truman and Marshall deny any intention of negotiating or changing U.S.

policy. Marshall (May 26) in a letter to the Senate Foreign Relations Committee lists 37 Soviet "violations of agreements." During the summer the Soviet press features new attacks on "American war-mongers." In October, Truman considers sending Chief Justice Fred M. Vinson to Moscow on a special mission, but is dissuaded by Marshall and Lovett. American exports to Russia approach the vanishing-point as Washington refuses to license the sale of "strategic" goods to Eastern Europe. The Secretary of State reiterates U.S. recognition of the "independence" of Latvia, Estonia, and Lithuania.

1949: Stalin in January bids Truman to negotiate. The State Department admits Communist delegates to a "Cultural and Scientific Congress for World Peace," arranged at the Waldorf in March by the National Council of the Arts, Sciences, and Professions, bars non-Communist delegates, and then accuses the Congress of being "Communist-dominated." Moscow sponsors "peace." Smith resigns, March 25, and is replaced by Alan G. Kirk, who is well received, while Truman (September 1) expresses confidence that the "Cold War" will end in Soviet unconditional surrender. New U.S. embargoes reduce trade to negligible proportions. Judith Coplon and Valentin A. Gubitchev of the UN staff are arrested, March 5, on suspicion of espionage. Acheson denies Gubitchev's diplomatic immunity. He is found guilty, March 7, 1950, is sentenced to fifteen years, but, on the State Department's motion, is deported to the USSR.

1950: *Literary Gazette* (March 16) calls Acheson a "Fascist-minded diplomat," an "incorrigible liar," and a "hired lackey of the war-mongers." Vyshinsky, April 11, protests to Kirk that a B-29 has fired, over Latvia on April 8, on Soviet fighter planes, which returned the fire and drove the intruder out to sea. The State Department, April 18, in its own version of the incident, accuses the USSR of shooting down an unarmed Navy Privateer over the Baltic and vainly demands apology and reparation. The plane is never found. On September 4, U.S. naval forces shoot down a Soviet plane over the Yellow Sea off the west coast of Korea. Moscow vainly demands apology and reparation.

1951: Vyshinsky warns in January that German rearmament will be a major threat to peace. The Deputy Foreign Ministers of the Big Four hold 74 meetings (March to June) in the Palais Rose in Paris and dissolve in discord after the Western Powers refuse to discuss NATO and U.S. bases abroad as "threats to peace." All American-Soviet "negotiations"—in reality, no more than propaganda blasts

—over a lend-lease settlement, trade relations, U.S. moves to "liberate" the satellites, the arrest as "spies" of 4 U.S. fliers forced down in Hungary, and other matters, are ritualistic exercises in invective and insult.

1952: George F. Kennan is named Ambassador to the USSR, February 7, and arrives in Moscow, May 6. On October 8 the USSR declares him *persona non grata* and demands his recall because newsmen quote him as comparing the Soviet Union to Nazi Germany in an "interview" at the Berlin airport. Georgi N. Zarubin succeeds Panyushkin in Washington in June. In October, Washington protests against Soviet machine-gunning of a U.S. hospital plane near Berlin and the shooting-down of a B-29 near the Kuriles. Moscow counter-protests and refuses any reparation. The Kremlin continues to champion "peace." On April 1 Stalin answers 4 questions posed by James L. Wick, U.S. publisher. Is World War III approaching? "No, it is not." Would a meeting of heads of States be helpful? "Possibly it would be beneficial." Is the moment opportune for the unification of Germany? "Yes." Is coexistence possible? "Fully possible, given the mutual desire to cooperate . . . and non-interference in the internal affairs of other States."

On December 24 Stalin replies to four questions by James Reston of the *NYT*. Is peace possible between the USA and the USSR? "I still believe that war between the USA and the Soviet Union cannot be considered inevitable, and that our countries can continue to live in peace." Wherein lies the source of tension? "Everywhere and in everything wherever the aggressive actions of the policy of 'Cold War' against the Soviet Union find their expression." Would you welcome a meeting with Eisenhower? "I regard this suggestion favorably." Would you cooperate to end the Korean War? "I agree to cooperate because the USSR is interested in ending the war in Korea."

Maj. Gen. Robert W. Grow, U.S. Military Attaché in Moscow, July 1950–January 1952, has his diary stolen in Frankfurt and published, March 6, by British Communist Richard Squires in East Germany: "Communism must be destroyed! . . . War! As soon as possible! Now! The time is ripe for a blow this year. . . . We must start by hitting below the belt. . . . We must employ every subversive device to undermine the confidence and loyalty of Soviet subjects for their regime. . . ." The General is reprimanded for carelessness and indiscretion.

1953: The State Department in January asks the recall of Yuri V. Novikov, 2nd Secretary of the Soviet Embassy, as a co-conspirator with spies. Moscow in February accepts Charles E. ("Chip") Bohlen as Kennan's successor. President Eisenhower asks Congress to indict the USSR for perverting war-time agreements and enslaving free peoples. The U.S. Air Force in March alleges that a Soviet Mig has tried to shoot down a U.S. RB-50 reconnaissance plane 25 miles east of Kamchatka. Washington demands "discipli-nary action." Moscow charges that the plane twice violated Soviet territory and opened fire on Soviet planes. Senator Ralph E. Flan-ders opines that the U.S. Air Force story is "preposterous" and a "falsehood." Pearl Mesta tours Russia and finds it "strange." Moscow in June allows the Russian wives of newsmen Eddy Gilmore, Rob-ert Tucker, Thomas P. Whitney, Henry Shapiro, Andrew J. Steiger, and George Adkins to leave the USSR and join their husbands. Washington denies as "fantastic" Soviet charges that the USA para-chuted "four spies" into the Ukraine. At July's end the United States protests in "strongest terms" against the shooting-down by Migs of another RB-50 bomber 40 miles off the coast of Siberia. Moscow al-leges violation of Soviet territory and protests the shooting down of a civilian Ilyushin 12 over Manchuria by U.S. fighter planes from Korea. Each side, as usual, refuses to pay damages asked by the other.

1954: Vyshinsky in May deposits Soviet ratifications of the UN conventions outlawing genocide and sponsoring equality of rights for women, both of which the USA refuses to ratify. He announces Soviet membership in UNESCO and the ILO. He dies of a heart attack, November 22, and is succeeded at UN by Jacob Malik. Mos-cow on June 24 protests seizure of the Soviet tanker *Tuapse* off For-mosa. Washington denies responsibility. Soviet jets, September 4, shoot down a U.S. Navy bomber off Cape Ostrovnoi, 125 miles from Vladivostok. Washington protests this "wanton and unprovoked at-tack" and appeals to the UN. On November 7, Migs shoot down a U.S. B-29 off Hokkaido over Habomoi Island, claimed by the USSR as part of the Kuriles. Charges and countercharges, as usual, get no-where, although Eisenhower is conciliatory and Moscow expresses "regret." The Foreign Ministry accuses Mrs. Karl Sommerlatte, wife of the 3rd Secretary of the U.S. Embassy, of "hooliganism" and de-mands her recall as *persona non grata*. Senators Jenner and McCar-

ran on May 13, and Knowland on September 5, urge a diplomatic rupture with the USSR.

Yuri A. Rastvorov, Soviet intelligence agent, defects in Tokyo and receives U.S. asylum in February. On August 13, following Otto John's spectacular defection to the Communists in Germany, Washington "unveils" Rastvorov, who allegedly reveals important espionage secrets and says he has sought asylum because he "wants to live like a decent human being." In May, Capt. Nikolai E. Khoklov, MVD agent, tells the Jenner Committee that he defected rather than obey orders to kill Georgi Oklovich, anti-Soviet leader of Russian *émigrés* in Germany. East and West expel sundry attachés as "spies," while an Australian Royal Commission sensationally exposes Soviet espionage and sabotage with the aid of defector Vladimir M. Petrov.

1955: On June 24, with Molotov in San Francisco, the White House announces that a Navy patrol plane over Bering Strait has been the victim of "an inexplicable and unwarranted attack" by Soviet Migs, leading to a crash landing on St. Lawrence Island. Washington later suspends air patrols in the Bering Sea and accepts a Soviet offer to pay for half the cost of the wrecked plane. On July 4 Khrushchev, Bulganin, *et al.* attend the American holiday reception in Spaso House and speak hopefully of pending negotiations. . . .

By 1956–7, despite the crises of October–November 1956 in Hungary and the Middle East, the "tone" of American-Soviet relations was no longer what it had been in 1948–50, even though some symptoms had recurred of a return to the "normal" pattern of uncompromising hostility and recrimination.[8] The circumstances and

---

[8] With regard to the "cloak-and-dagger" episodes here touched upon, a fuller catalogue will be found in David J. Dallin: *Soviet Espionage.* Thanks to Communist skill in the arts of deception, conclusive proof of Red wickedness in such matters is often difficult to come by. It is noteworthy that Dallin (pp. 353–5), who is not gullible regarding Soviet accusations against the USA, concurs, with ample evidence, in the Muscovite charge that on April 26, 1953, a four-motored U.S. plane flew over the Ukraine and dropped four agents: Alexander V. Lakhno, Alexander N. Makov, Sergei I. Gorbunov, and Dmitri N. Remiga, all parachuted with firearms, poison, short-wave radio sets, large sums of Soviet currency, false documents, etc. All were Russian *émigrés* who had served against the USSR in the Nazi *Wehrmacht* during World War II. All had been trained in espionage and sabotage at Bad Wiessee, near Munich, and had been supplied at Athens by U.S. Intelligence Major Harold Irving Fidler, who had visited the USSR three times in 1951 as a U.S. diplomatic courier.

problems of the new time are best reserved for discussion after consideration is given to the end of the long reign of Stalin.

All were allegedly betrayed by a Soviet defector and "double agent," Capt. Nikita Khorunzhi, who infiltrated the U.S.-supported "counter-intelligence" school at Bad Homburg maintained by the NTS or "National Toilers' Union" or "Solidarists," an anti-Soviet *émigré* group in Germany financed by the USA. Late in 1953 Khorunzhi was caught, tried by a U.S. military court, and sentenced to jail. Meanwhile, the four agents were all apprehended on April 27, tried by the Military Collegium of the Supreme Court of the USSR, and sentenced to execution.

CHAPTER TWELVE

New Horizons

1. A TIME TO DIE

JOSEF VISSARIONOVICH DJUGASHVILI, born in Gori, December 21, 1879, and dead in the Kremlin, March 5, 1953, earned his immortality by his genius for inspiring men to murder, not by his talent for moving them to compassion. The ultimate "verdict of history" may yet hold that the enduring results of his dictatorship—the industrialization, urbanization, and education of Russia—counterbalance his inhumanity in the cast accounts of eternity and place him in the category of such precursors as Ivan the Terrible and Peter the Great, who also committed hideous cruelties in their earlier efforts to "modernize" a backward and benighted nation. Whatever the verdict, it is clear that the aging Stalin in the last months of his life did not mellow into a "benevolent despot," but, on the contrary, became even more than before a suspicious and evil-minded paranoiac whose mad directives his subordinates, filled with fear for their lives, felt obliged to obey.

During Stalin's final year he was, apparently, alert and well. Two of his old diplomatic helpmeets departed this life, Maxim Litvinov, aged 75, on December 31, 1951, and Alexandra Kollontai, aged 80, on March 9, 1952. Both were buried in the fabulous Moscow Cemetery of Novodevichy Convent. At Congress XIX (see p. 344) Stalin sought to lay down the "line" for times to come and, in effect, designated Malenkov as his successor. His 73rd birthday was celebrated with no more than the usual fanfare and the customary distribution of "Stalin Peace Prizes" to those whom he deemed most worthy of reward for serving the purposes of Soviet foreign policy. But a new horror was soon to materialize—concocted, almost certainly, at Stalin's own initiative.

The Soviet press on January 13, 1953, burst forth with the fantastic tale of the "Jewish Doctors' Plot"—perhaps attributable to Stalin's senility, although quite consonant, save in its *Grand Guignol* elements, with Stalin's political technique in his prime. The story held that nine doctors, mostly Jewish and all in league with American, British, and Zionist spies—including Prof. P. I. Yegorov, top Kremlin physician, and Prof. V. N. Vinogradov, holder of the "Order of Lenin"—had confessed to killing Andrei Zhdanov (d. 1948) and Alexander Shcherbakov (d. 1945) through wrong diagnoses and treatment, and had plotted the deaths of military leaders Vasilevsky, Konev, Shtemenko, Govorov, and Levchenko. *Izvestia* accused Soviet security agencies (presumably Beria's MVD) of "laxity," while other official organs were filled with demands for "death" for the "traitors."

New Times excoriated Zionists as paid agents of "American imperialism." *Ukrainian Pravda* held that "American bosses" had long sought to murder Communist leaders through "Jewish" and "Masonic" agents. *Izvestia* on February 8 reported the "liquidation" of a "nest of American spies" in Vladivostok. When terrorists bombed the Soviet Legation in Tel Aviv on February 9, Moscow severed diplomatic relations with Israel (February 12). Despite anti-Semitic tirades in the Soviet press, Jewish Lev Z. Mekhlis, former Minister of State Control and Vice-Commissar of Defense, who died on February 13, was publicly praised and given a state funeral. *Pravda* revealed on February 20 that the "doctors' plot" had been exposed by Dr. Lydia Timashuk, who was awarded the "Order of Lenin" for her revelations.

The dictum of the ancient wise men that "these things too shall pass away" applies even to nightmares. On March 4 the Central Committee of the Party and the Council of Ministers jointly announced that Stalin had suffered a paralytic stroke during the night of March 1–2. Successive medical bulletins ended with the news that Stalin died at 9:50 p.m., March 5, 1953. The Soviet and world press were filled for days with obituaries and descriptions of the state funeral. Amid colorful ceremonies on March 9, eulogies of the dead leader were delivered by Malenkov, Molotov, and Beria. The films of the occasion were later suppressed because of Beria's participation.

On November 19 Stalin's embalmed body in military attire, laid to rest next to Lenin in the marble tomb in Red Square, was exposed

to public inspection by the curious and the reverent. Visitors reported that he looked "serene" and "relaxed." Indeed, in 1956 he looked quite "healthy," although not much like any of his heroized portraits and statues. His mien was more that of a stunted and twisted son of a Georgian cobbler—in contrast to Lenin, who after 32 years of sepulchral repose appeared pale and waxy but still exuded an aura of immense intelligence, intense energy, human sympathy, and nobility of spirit.

The exact circumstances of Stalin's demise may never be publicly known. His last decisions, obviously, threatened a new "blood purge" in which none of his colleagues could be sure of survival. Andrei A. Andreyev, agricultural specialist, had been dropped from the Politburo in 1952. (In 1955, while not readmitted to the *sanctum sanctorum*, he was awarded his third "Order of Lenin" on his 60th birthday and praised in the press for foresight.) According to Khrushchev, Molotov and other leaders were threatened with liquidation. The hypothesis that Stalin may have been murdered is not implausible. For his speculations in print on this possibility Harrison E. Salisbury of *The New York Times* was denied a visa to reenter the USSR. Another tale current in Moscow in the aftermath held that Stalin, at a meeting of the Party Presidium, proposed the deportation to Siberia of all Jews in European Russia; that Kaganovich (whose son, Mikhail, had married Stalin's daughter, Svanidze, in 1951) threw his Party card on the table and declared he would resign if any such decision were adopted; and that Stalin, livid with rage, then suffered the stroke that was to end his life. Available evidence admits of no definitive conclusion. It is probable that his final resolves, threatening a repetition of the atrocities of 1936–9, evoked dissent among his colleagues and contributed to his collapse, since he had long since convinced himself of his infallibility and of the impossibility of tolerating any alternative views. At all events, he remained in death as strange a figure as he had always been in life— for decades revered by all the faithful as an incomparable genius and charismatic idol, soon to be denounced as a devil by his closest associates, and widely regarded in the non-Communist world as the incarnation of Beelzebub.

None of these judgments is likely to stand the test of time. Few men, and still fewer statesmen, can be neatly classified as angels or demons. Statesmen are compelled by their vocation, in dictatorships and democracies alike, to regard the "interests" of their States as

paramount over all considerations of law and morality. Politics seldom poses a choice between good and evil, but usually a choice between the lesser evil and the greater evil. Stalin's choices were often monstrous, even by the debased standard of the Marxist eschatology. Yet the Soviet State, at appalling cost, was somehow preserved, enriched, and enhanced during his reign. Insofar as these achievements can be deemed fruits of his policies, his leadership, despite his evil deeds, may come to be regarded in the perspective of the future as having been more constructive than destructive.

2. THE EPIGONES

ON March 6, 1953, the Central Committee of the Party, the Council of Ministers, and the Presidium of the Supreme Soviet jointly announced that Georgi Maximilianovich Malenkov, aged 51, would assume the Premiership. Beria, Molotov, Bulganin, and Kaganovich would be First Vice-Premiers, with the first three being named, respectively, Ministers of Internal Affairs (MVD), Foreign Affairs, and Defense. The watchwords of the new order were "Unity," "Calm," "Vigilance," "Civil Liberties," and "Peace." The Politburo or Party Presidium was again reduced from 25 to 10 members: Malenkov, Beria, Molotov, Voroshilov, Khrushchev, Bulganin, Kaganovich, Mikoyan, Maxim Z. Saburov, and Mikhail G. Pervukhin, with Shvernik, Ponomarenko, Melnikov, and M. G. Bagirov as alternates. On March 20 Malenkov retired as Secretary of the Central Committee in favor of a Secretariat of five: Nikita S. Khrushchev, N. A. Suslov, T. N. Pospelov, N. M. Shatalin, and S. D. Ignatiev. A broad amnesty decree of March 27 freed from prisons and labor camps all serving sentences of 5 years or less, and reduced by half the sentences of many serving for more than 5 years.

On April 4 an official announcement proclaimed the release of the "Jewish doctors" as having been arrested wrongly and "without any legal grounds," and the annulment of the "Order of Lenin" to Dr. Timashuk. The "confessions" were said to have been obtained by "impermissible" means. *Pravda* now accused the "gullible" leaders of the Ministry of State Security of having "fallen down on the job," "forgotten they are servants of the people and guardians of Soviet legality," and "fabricated provocations against honest Soviet

people and outstanding leaders of Soviet science." Ignatiev was removed from the Party Secretariat and transferred to Leningrad. Deputy Minister of State Security Ryumin was arrested. The "plot" of January was abruptly dismissed as a fiction.

Other signs of a new era included emphasis in official utterances on "collective leadership" and repudiation of "hero-worship," shifts of personnel in Party and Government posts in many Republics, stressing of "civil rights" for Soviet citizens, and new appeals for "peace" with the "capitalist" world. The apotheosis of Stalin ceased in the Soviet press. A smooth transition of power had apparently been effected in the direction of a more humanized and liberalized regime.

The calm of springtime was broken on July 10 with the announcement that Beria had been dismissed on June 26 as head of the MVD and was being held for trial as "an enemy of the people," charged with "criminal" and "anti-state" activities in the interests of "foreign capital." *Pravda* asserted that Beria, through "ignominious machinations" and "crafty schemes," had sought to make the MVD superior to Party and Government and had plotted to stir up hatred among the national minorities, acted as a "bourgeois renegade," and become "an agent of international imperialism."

Sergei N. Kruglov succeeded Beria as Minister of Internal Affairs. Vladimir G. Dekanozov, former diplomat and Georgian Minister of Internal Affairs, was expelled from the Party on July 15. M. D. Bagirov, former Premier of Azerbaijan, was expelled three days later. Other removals of Beria's followers ensued, although some were later reconsidered.

Foreign speculation as to the causes of Beria's downfall were largely fruitless, since outsiders cannot know what goes on within the secret councils of an alien oligarchy. Insofar as the Malenkov regime was seeking to minimize the "police-state" aspects of the Soviet polity, the chief of the political police doubtless resisted the process. The rest of the official story may well be set down as fiction. Rumors in September, publicized by Senator Joseph McCarthy, that Beria had escaped to the West were never verified. During the next four months there was no mention of his name in the Soviet press. The anniversary of the Revolution was celebrated with keynote addresses by Bulganin and Voroshilov, bespeaking unity, strength, economic progress, and peace.

On December 16 Radio Moscow broadcast a statement by the

Soviet State Prosecutor alleging, in the best Stalinist manner, that Beria and his accomplices (V. N. Merkulov, V. G. Dekanozov, S. A. Goglidze, P. Y. Meshik, L. E. Vladzimirsky, and B. Z. Kobulov) had confessed to "subversive activities," involving "sabotage" of the collective-farm system, fostering of "bourgeois nationalism," conspiracies with "imperialists" dating back to 1919, espionage, treason, "lawlessness," "criminal intrigue," "terrorist murders," etc. All were to be tried before a special session of the Supreme Court under the law of December 1, 1934.

Expectations that this indictment foreshadowed a spectacular public trial were disappointed. Press and radio carried a brief announcement on December 23 that the accused had been tried before a tribunal headed by Marshal Ivan Konev, had all been found guilty, and had all been shot. Beria's fate was thus identical with that of most of his predecessors at the head of the Soviet political police, and with that of many other guardians of orthodoxy through terrorism in other times and climes.

The new leadership appeared during 1954 to be in process of consolidating its power in the name of "liberalization," but with no visible democratization as yet of either Party or Government. On March 14, 1954, Soviet voters went to the polls to approve unanimously the slate of the "People's Bloc of Party and non-Party" candidates for the two houses of the Supreme Soviet. The new Council of the Union had 700 deputies (170 of them women), of whom 565 were Party members. The Council of Nationalities had 639 deputies (178 women), of whom 485 were Party members. The deputies met in mid-May to hear speeches by leaders and to give unanimous approval to the decisions of the Party Presidium and the Council of Ministers. Other public events of the year included a reshuffling of *oblast* boundaries announced in January, involving the abolition of 5 provinces in Byelorussia and the redistribution of the territories among the remaining 7, and the creation of 6 new provinces (Arzamas, Balashov, Lipetsk, Belgorod, Kamensk, and Cherkassy) in the RSFSR and the Ukraine; the transfer (February 26) of the Crimea from the RSFSR to the Ukraine; and an elaborate celebration in late May of the 300th anniversary of the Union of the Ukraine with Russia.

The departed *Vozhd*, long damned with faint praise in the Soviet press, was praised with faint damns on his birthday. The dead Beria continued to be execrated. The trial and execution of several

of his alleged accomplices was announced on December 24: Viktor S. Abakumov, former Minister of State Security, and his aides, A. G. Leonov, V. I. Komorov, and M. I. Likhachev. A 25-year sentence was imposed upon Y. M. Broverman and one of 15 years on I. A. Chernov. Local leaders in various Republics were demoted, many of them apparently under suspicion of being protégés of Beria. Mikoyan's aide, Alexei D. Krutikov, named a Deputy Premier in 1948, was expelled from the Party in August for allegedly doing favors for relatives and friends.

During 1955 a major reshuffle of top Party personnel in public posts—effected without accusations, arrests, trials, or executions—evoked voluminous speculation abroad, ranging from the view that a Khrushchev-Bulganin-Zhukov faction had engineered the "downfall" of a Malenkov faction to hypotheses that the shift was due to an alleged "collapse" of Soviet agriculture or to a neo-Stalinist Party resolve to "downgrade" consumers' goods once more in favor of heavy industry and militarization. None of these "explanations" squared with the facts. Motives were mixed, as usual in politics, but the central, albeit unspoken, consideration was plain enough. Acts of Western governments early in the year made German rearmament a certainty. The prospective resurrection of this *bête noir*—still viewed, honestly even if mistakenly, by Soviet policy-makers as a mortal threat—dictated a closer liaison of Party and Army and a vigorous diplomatic offensive, conducted by the heads of Party and Government rather than by Molotov, designed to strengthen the power of the Communist coalition and to win friends and influence people among the millions of the uncommitted. What followed the reshuffle of 1955 in the realm of foreign policy, to be surveyed later in these pages, amply confirms this interpretation of its purposes.

In a New Year's message Premier Malenkov said that in order to remove tensions between the USSR and the USA "it is necessary to put an end to re-creating German militarism, to stop the arms race, and drop the policy of encircling the peace-loving States with military bases." On January 2 the USA put 27% of its territory "out of bounds" to Soviet citizens in retaliation for the banning of foreigners from 30% of the area of the USSR. Moscow's campaign to thwart ratification of the Paris Accords for German membership in NATO was unsuccessful.

On February 8 Malenkov informed the Supreme Soviet of his resignation as Premier, pleading insufficient experience as well as

responsibility for the unsatisfactory state of agriculture. He was succeeded by Marshal Nikolai A. Bulganin. On February 9 Marshal Georgi M. Zhukov became Minister of Defense, while Malenkov was named Vice-Premier and Minister of Electric Power Stations.

Shvernik, who became chairman of the All-Union Council of Trade Unions, had already (1953) been succeeded by Voroshilov as chairman of the Presidium of the Supreme Soviet or "President" of the USSR. Nikolai A. Mikhailov succeeded Georgi F. Alexandrov as Minister of Culture on March 21, 1955. Vassily V. Kuznetsov was named 1st Deputy Foreign Minister on March 22, and Vladimir S. Semyenov and M. T. Fedorenko Deputy Foreign Ministers. Dmitri V. Pavlov replaced Mikoyan as Minister of Domestic Trade. Mikoyan, Pervukhin, and Saburov had already been named Vice-Premiers on February 28, this rank being shared with Molotov and Kaganovich.

The Party Presidium continued to consist of Khrushchev, Bulganin, Malenkov, Molotov, Voroshilov, Kaganovich, Pervukhin, Saburov, and Mikoyan. At its semi-annual meeting, July 11, 1955, the Central Committee elected Mikhail A. Suslov and Alexei I. Kirichenko to the Presidium; named Dmitri T. Shepilov, Nikolai I. Belyayev, and Averky B. Aristov as Party Secretaries, and fixed February 14, 1956, as the date for convening Congress XX, to consist of one delegate for every 5,000 members.

Before we consider the import of Congress XX, it will be well to notice some of the broader lineaments of Soviet society as it appeared to outsiders, and as it was experienced by its members, in the 40th year after the October Revolution.[1]

---

[1] Further data on the politics of the post-Stalin era will be found, for readers of Russian, in the Soviet newspapers and periodicals of the period, in the invaluable translations provided by the *Current Digest of the Soviet Press* (weekly since January 1949), and in the following books in English: Isaac Deutscher: *Russia: What Next?* (Oxford University Press, 1953); Walter Duranty: *Stalin & Co.* (Sloane, 1949); Martin Ebon: *Malenkov: Stalin's Successor* (McGraw-Hill, 1953); Leo Gruliow: *Current Soviet Policies* (Praeger, 1953); George B. Huszar *et al.: Soviet Power and Policy* (Crowell, 1955); Marshall MacDuffie: *The Red Carpet* (Norton, 1955); George Shueller: *The Politburo* (Stanford University Press, 1951); Hugh Seton-Watson: *From Lenin to Malenkov* (Praeger, 1953); Budu Svanidze: *My Uncle Josef Stalin* (Putnam, 1953); and Gordon Young: *Stalin's Heirs* (Verschoyle, 1953). See also John N. Hazard: *The Soviet System of Government* (University of Chicago Press, 1957).

3. CLASSES AND MASSES

THE problem of how to describe any human society, without distortion of reality as experienced by insiders and with meaningful communication of reality to outsiders, has puzzled social scientists from Plato to Pareto and beyond and has become a central concern of all contemporary anthropologists and sociologists. The problem is far from solution—nor is its solution, for the USSR, likely to be achieved in these pages. Certain general considerations, applicable to all the literate or "civilized" communities devised by men, may nevertheless be helpful in approaching the mystery of the uniqueness of Soviet society (insofar as it is unique) at the end of the fourth decade of the Red regime.

Whatever his disservices, Marx performed a service in calling attention to the circumstance that all hitherto existing societies of human beings possessed of written language and enjoying (or suffering from) urban life have been sharply hierarchical in structure, with a few at the top receiving maximum per-capita shares of available satisfactions and the many at the bottom receiving minimum shares. His corollary premises—that all people in such societies are divided into antagonistic "classes" of exploiters and exploited, that ultimate bipolarity of class structure is inevitable, and that all history (meaning all politics) is the history of "class struggles"—are far more questionable. Still more dubious is the Marxist conclusion that this alleged state of affairs is attributable to private ownership of the "means of production" and that the "socialization" of economic enterprise will somehow eventuate in a society which will not only be "classless" but also "stateless," since the "State" has already been defined as having no function save the organization of force, fraud, and favors for the oppression of ruled classes by ruling classes.

At all events, the USSR in 1957 bore no resemblance to this prescription. The State was ubiquitous. The society was more sharply stratified into classes than the mature "capitalistic" societies of Atlantica. Aside from remaining vestiges of "slave labor," receiving nothing for work aside from meager rations and miserable shelter, the poor comprised unskilled workers and the less fortunate collective farmers, paid from 300 to 500 rubles a month, housed in shacks or in tiny, overcrowded apartments, and living on black bread, *kasha,* and potatoes, with only occasional meat, fruit, or any beverage beyond

milk, tea, kvass, and beer. The rich consisted of a new managerial and intellectual elite,—a few of whose members (e.g., popular novelists, dramatists, actors, and musicians) were receiving from 20,000 to 40,000 rubles per month in stipends and royalties; many of whose members (e.g., top business executives) could count on from 6,000 to 10,000 rubles monthly in salaries and bonuses; more of whose members (e.g., Army Marshals, Cabinet Ministers, and some lesser executives) were assured of 5,000 rubles a month or more in take-home pay and expense accounts; and the majority of whom (e.g., top engineers and technicians, aircraft pilots, architects, professors, scientific workers, the better-paid journalists, some physicians, a few lawyers) were earning from 2,000 to 4,000 rubles monthly. In between was a large and growing "middle class" of lesser technicians and engineers, skilled workers, teachers, storekeepers, physicians in general practice, minor bureaucrats, directors of kolkhozi, and a few of the more prosperous collective farmers, all earning from 800 to 2,000 rubles each month, with living standards proportionate to income.

Those in the top brackets could afford cars—not very often the Zim or Zis, retailing at 40,000 rubles, but easily the tiny Moskvich (8,000 rubles), often the standard Pobeda (16,000), and increasingly the new Volga (12,000). Many prizes, medals, and other honors earned by successful executives entailed exemption from taxes. In any case, no income tax took more than 10% of income. The rich could also afford comfortable apartments, country dachas, good food and clothes, candy, caviar, vodka, and champagne.

Available Soviet statistics, unfortunately, admit of no quantitative estimate of the proportion of Soviet citizens in each of these "classes," all reduced to a meaningless jumble in the Marxist jargon of "workers," "peasants," and "intelligentsia." We know only that "urban" populations in 1956 comprised 87,000,000 people and "rural" 113,300,000; that birth rates declined from 31.7 per thousand in 1940 to 25.6 in 1955 and death rates from 18.3 in 1940 to 8.4 in 1955; that "manual laborers" numbered 8,300,000 in 1940 and 14,300,000 in 1955; "engineers and technicians" 900,000 and 1,500,000, and "domestic servants" 770,000 and 750,000 in the same years; that women in 1955 comprised 45% of all employed persons (45% in industry, 31% in construction, 33% in transport, 58% in "distribution," 83% in restaurants, 68% in education, and 85% in health services); that "specialists with higher education" numbered 908,000 on January 1, 1941,

and 2,184,000 on July 1, 1955, with "teachers, librarians, cultural workers" trebling in numbers as against a doubling in the number of physicians, lawyers, economists, agronomists, and engineers; and that "scientific workers" waxed from 95,900 in 1939 to 223,900 in 1955. Such data are useful, but offer no clear portrait of the distribution of income and social status among the 200,000,000 people of the USSR.[2]

The steeply hierarchical structure of Soviet society at midcentury differed, to be sure, in its genesis from its counterparts in the West. All Soviet incomes were, allegedly, "earned." No one lived on so-called "unearned income" derived from private ownership of rent-producing or profit-making properties or from interest and dividends on corporate bonds or stocks—all non-existent in the USSR, save for State lottery bonds and bank accounts. The elaborate organization of Soviet trade unions, moreover, had no direct means, as in the West, for enhancing the incomes of members through "collective bargaining" and the right to strike. No such right was acknowledged in Soviet law. At most, under new legislation of February 1957, grievances could be arbitrated, with a right of appeal to the courts. Union functions were limited to management of the social-insurance system and to efforts to raise productivity. Inequalities in the distribution of income were nevertheless comparable to those prevailing in "bourgeois" Europe and America. Here crushing taxes on high incomes of corporations and individuals (albeit sometimes evaded by adroit devices) tended to produce for most of the population a greater degree of egalitarianism in "take-home pay" than prevails in the USSR, even if all orthodox Marxists are obliged by their creed to deny the fact and to juggle statistics to prove their point.

For the present, and perhaps for a future whose duration cannot currently be calculated, a more important consideration is the problem of social mobility as related to the rate of economic expansion. How do the prospects of Western workers, businessmen, and professional people for improving their economic and social status compare with those of their Soviet counterparts? Here, thus far, the USSR has a definite "edge" over the Atlantic communities, to say nothing of the miserable masses of most of Asia, Africa, and Latin America. Where a national economy is growing at an annual rate of 8% (as in the USSR for many years) instead of at 3% or 4% (as in

[2] See *Narodnoye Khozyaistvo S.S.S.R.*, Central Statistical Board of the Council of Ministers, Moscow, 1953.

Western Europe and the USA), opportunities to rise in the social scale are, roughly, doubled. During the past two decades many millions have raised themselves from *muzhiks* to workers, from workers to technicians, and from technicians to membership in the managerial elite. So long as this process continues, Soviet social classes will remain fluid and mobile, with little prospect of their crystallizing into rigid "castes," despite some evidence to the contrary.[3]

This society, contrary to all Marxist prognoses, was afflicted with problems of psychic estrangement, deviation, and dissent not different in kind or degree from those of concern to the world of the West. "*Blat*"—meaning sometimes merely exercise of influence or exploitation of friendships to circumvent the bureaucracy, and othertimes graft and embezzlement—was widespread. Many of the young, particularly the "gilded youth" of the middle and upper classes, displayed less dedication to the ideals of Communism, as championed by the Komsomols, than determination to defy all the conventions, to the horror of their elders. Some became *stilyagi* or "zoot-suiters,"

[3] For other useful commentaries by American visitors on the Soviet society and economy, see Joseph A. Livingston, Financial Editor, "The Business Outlook," *The Philadelphia Bulletin*, in a series beginning June 3, 1956, and widely syndicated in other U.S. papers; Morris H. Rubin: "The New Soviet Challenge," *The Progressive* (Madison, Wisconsin), September 1956; F. L. Schuman: "Notes on a Russian Journey," *The Berkshire Eagle* (Pittsfield, Mass.), a series beginning in the issue of May 29, 1956, and four articles in *The Nation* of July 14 ("Moscow: Symbol of Change"), July 28 ("Miracle at Stalingrad"), August 4 ("Ivan's Take-Home Pay"), and August 11, 1956 ("Heirs to the Despot"). Cf. William Benton: "Now the 'Cold War' of the Classrooms," *NYT Magazine*, April 1, 1956; John Hersey: "Soviet Business Executives," *Life*, January 15, 1945; and Peter F. Drucker: "Stalin Pays 'Em What They're Worth," *Saturday Evening Post*, July 21, 1945.

See also *The Soviet Union Since World War II*, Annals of the American Academy of Political and Social Science, May 1949; R. A. Bauer: *The New Man in Soviet Psychology* (Harvard University Press, 1952); Fedor Belov: *The History of a Collective Farm* (Praeger, 1955); Harold J. Berman: *The Russians in Focus* (Little, Brown, 1953); Georges Bissonnette: *Moscow Was My Parish* (McGraw-Hill, 1956); Lief Bjork: *Wages, Prices, and Social Legislation in the Soviet Union* (Dobson, 1953); W. P. and Zelda K. Coates: *The Soviets in Central Asia* (Philosophical Library, 1951); Isaac Deutscher, *Soviet Trade Unions* (Royal Institute of International Affairs, London, 1950); M. I. Kalinin: *On Communist Education* (Foreign Languages Publishing House, Moscow, 1950); Beatrice King: *Russia Goes to School* (Heinemann, 1948); Czeslaw Milosz: *The Captive Mind* (Knopf, 1953); Jules Monnerot: *Sociology and Psychology of Communism* (Beacon Press, 1953); Rudolf Schlesinger: *The Spirit of Post-War Russia* (Dobson, 1947) and *Changing Attitudes in Soviet Russia: The Family in the U.S.S.R.* (Routledge, 1949); and Solomon M. Schwarz: *Labor in the Soviet Union* (Praeger, 1952).

aping their Western counterparts. Others, including the "jet-set" adolescents of the new aristocracy, affected even more bizarre behavior, often verging on "hooliganism." Still others, again recruited from the children of the new rich rather than from the poor, became delinquents and often acted as had their precursors, the *besprizorni* or homeless orphans of a previous generation—gathering in gangs to steal, destroy, and sometimes to kill. *Trud* acknowledged in February 1957 that prostitution had not, after all, disappeared in the USSR. The old question *Shto Dyelat?* puzzled Soviet militiamen, jurists, and reformers. Such problems, *ex hypothesi*, were phenomena of decadent "capitalism." How could they reappear in the Socialist Fatherland? Their presence suggests that the "proletarian" heaven had somehow come to approximate the "bourgeois" hell of the West, to the bewilderment and consternation of the Marxist masters of Muscovy.[4]

The implication of these conditions and transitions for "politics" has been the central concern of Soviet politicians since Stalin's demise, even if Marxist-Leninist terminology forbade them to pose the problem in the terms here suggested. Stalin, ambiguously acknowledging reality in his glosses on the Constitution of 1936 while giving this reality no recognition whatever in his practice of politics, sought to perpetuate a Byzantine-Mongol-Romanov Autocracy by means of terrorism, and succeeded in so doing despite the metamorphosis of Soviet society effected by his earlier policies. His successors, released from his tyranny, were obliged to grapple as best they could with the economic and social transformation of a new nation bearing little resemblance to the primitive community over which Stalin had made himself despot in the 1930's. Their efforts by trial-and-error fumbling, and by muddled attempts to reconcile past dogmas with present facts, are our next concern.

4. THE THAW

DMITRY KOROTEYEV, engineer; Ivan Juravliov, factory manager; Lena, his unhappy wife, who finally leaves him in disgust at his bureaucratic obsessions and deceptions; Andrey Pukhov, schoolteacher;

[4] See Edward Crankshaw: *Russia Without Stalin* (Viking, 1956).

Nadya, his wife; Sonya, their student daughter; Volodya, their artist son, doomed to frustration by his refusal to conform to orthodox canons of "Socialist Realism"—these and others live out their bored and tangled lives in a provincial city in a time of change. In the end the best among them find happiness in breaking with the bleak past. All are fictitious characters in Ilya Ehrenburg's story *The Thaw*, written in 1953 and published early in 1954.[5]

This is not a "great" novel, nor is it even comparable to defector Igor Gouzenko's bitter satire on Maxim Gorky, *The Fall of a Titan*. It is merely a shrewd essay in disenchantment and renewed hope, delicate in its subtle irony and in its efforts to promote a new "humanism." For his pains Ehrenburg was rebuked for "deviationism" late in 1954 by the Second Congress of the Union of Soviet Writers, although his book continued to enjoy a large sale.

The spring thaw, which covers the steppes of Russia with turgid flood waters, is a symbol of a new time. Ice is gone. Snows are melting. But the leaves and flowers of the season to come are still nascent and, to all appearances, implausible amid the dark puddles and shifting mud and slime left in winter's wake. Yet they will come into being, inexorably, if only the weather-gods will grant warm winds and bright sun from blue skies.

Sergei Prokofiev, who died March 4, 1953, was officially praised for his 7th Symphony, despite earlier Party criticism of alleged "bourgeois" defects in his music. Voices were raised in the press in favor of "love," not "work," in films; against "chauvinist ignorance" of foreign cultures; for more circuses and genuine "humor" by clowns; against "idealizing" Tsarist heroes in literature and the cinema; in favor of French and Italian painting, long banned or neglected in Russian museums; and even against Trofim Lysenko, Stalin's anti-Mendelian geneticist. In the November 1953 issue of *Soviet Music* Aram Khatchaturian spoke out eloquently against political regimentation of art and in favor of creative initiative and individual originality.

The thaw continued far beyond the springtime of Stalin's passing and promised to become permanent. Contacts of all kinds with the West were vastly enlarged. Jack Begon, NBC broadcaster, was admitted to Moscow in June 1955, the first foreign broadcaster to be received since 1948. Foreign newsmen became more numerous than

[5] Translated by Manya Harari (Regnery, 1955).

at any time since 1947. Hotel building was rushed. Some 2,000 Soviet vacationists were allowed to go abroad. Intourist resumed plans for a large tourist influx, with Gabriel Reiner of the Cosmos Travel Bureau of New York becoming its agent in the USA.

During 1955 the number of Soviet publications exportable abroad was greatly increased. Pianist Emil Gilels and violinist David Oistrakh toured America. An accord was reached on October 27 for the exchange of publications between major libraries in the USA and the USSR. Numerous exchange visits with Western countries took place, including far-flung tours by Soviet and American farm delegations. In December an agreement between Washington and Moscow provided for resumption of publication in the USSR of the U.S. Russian-language journal *Amerika,* and in the USA of *USSR,* an illustrated monthly distributed by the Soviet Embassy in Washington. By late summer of 1956 both publications were being widely sold, while scores of professional delegations and thousands of tourists traversed frontiers that were no longer an "Iron Curtain."

The import and implications of the thaw for the processes of politics in the Soviet Union, and for Soviet relations with the "satellites," were by no means clear to the "collective leaders" who inherited the structure of power bequeathed by the dead despot. Amid much agonizing and bickering, they agreed easily enough upon some "reforms." All education would henceforth be free of tuition fees and be generously subsidized by the State, both as to stipends for university students and as to faculty salaries and research projects. Voluntary abortions, at no cost to the women involved, were re-legalized in 1955. The law of 1940, penalizing workers who quit their jobs, had already lapsed and was formally repealed in 1956, along with comparable statutes subjecting to criminal prosecution collective farmers not fulfilling their quotas and business executives selling surplus equipment or otherwise evading inflexible bureaucratic edicts. Many forced-labor camps were closed. The remainder were subjected to new regulations, holding directors to criminal responsibility for abuses. Those accused of political crimes, although still to be tried in military courts, were granted public trials, right of counsel, and other procedural safeguards. The "Special Boards" or *troikas* of the MVD, hitherto authorized to pass secret sentences on "subversive" and "socially dangerous" persons and functioning as

the chief tribunals of terrorism, were abolished, with such proceedings transferred to regular civil or military courts. Sweeping revisions of the Soviet civil and criminal codes were initiated in the name of restoring "socialist legality" and the "rights of citizens." [6]

Such steps as these, along with many others of like import, created a new "climate" and evoked, for the first time in years, a large measure of public approbation toward the purposes of the oligarchs of Muscovy. But they offered no guidance, except by implication, as to how the new leaders might best grapple with the problems of breaking the spell over the Soviet multitudes of the now repudiated "cult of personality," of "liberalizing" and "democratizing" Party and Government, and of evolving a new pattern of relationships between the USSR and its "allies." All these problems would have been difficult enough if those charged with their solution could have approached them with "open minds"—a condition never possible in human affairs. Fettered by the chains of their doctrine, fastened tightly upon them by life experiences that (save for the oldest of the elders) had transpired exclusively in the context of totalitarian socialism, their problems of repudiating "Stalinism" and charting a new course consonant with changed realities were extraordinarily difficult. The ancestral directives of Marxism-Leninism were useless for the purpose except as they might be reinterpreted and selectively applied to the needs of a new time on the basis of a fresh revelation. Such revelation was slow in emerging. The policy-makers in Moscow, albeit obliged by their cult to couch all new departures in old jargon, at least tried to strike out boldly in new directions. In their trial-and-error experimentations, they enmeshed themselves in sundry dilemmas, resolved a few, reduced others to tragedies of frustration and brutal aggression, and failed, as of 1957, to evolve any over-all pattern of adaptation applicable to all their puzzles. Their ventures abroad will be discussed in the section to follow. Their devices at home came to dramatic, although confused and ambiva-

[6] For details of Soviet legal and judicial innovations since 1953, see Harold J. Berman: "Soviet Legal Reforms," *The Nation*, June 30, 1956; John N. Hazard: "Soviet Commentators Re-evaluate the Policies of Criminal Law," *Columbia Law Review*, June, 1955, and "Governmental Developments in the USSR Since Stalin," *Annals of the American Academy*, January 1956; and the numerous and invaluable other articles and books of recent vintage on Soviet law by Hazard and by Berman, the two outstanding contemporary authorities in the USA in this field. For background see I. T. Golyakov: *The Role of the Soviet Courts* (Public Affairs Press, 1949) and Vladimir Gsovski: *Soviet Civil Law* (2 vols., University of Michigan Law School, 1948–9).

lent, expression in Party Congress XX, meeting in St. Andrew's Hall of the Great Kremlin Palace, February 14–25, 1956.[7]

This gathering of 1,355 voting delegates, plus 81 with "consultative" voices—representing the candidates for Party membership—bore no resemblance to early Congresses where, in the Leninist tradition, debate was free, decisions were arrived at by majority vote, and all differences were expressed, discussed, and resolved by ballot. It conformed closely to the Stalinist tradition of the preceding quarter of a century. Speeches were heard and applauded. No debate took place. All votes were unanimous. Decisions were reached in secret by leaders and uncritically approved by followers. The monologues and resolves nevertheless reflect, at least on the level of public expression, the best wisdom of the oligarchs as to how the problems facing them could best be dealt with. The 7,215,505 Party members (February 1, 1956), including 419,609 candidates, listened and obeyed.

Apart from dramatic expositions of economic progress, the themes of Congress XX were the repudiation of arbitrary government and the "cult of personality" in favor of "collective leadership" and the restoration of "socialist legality." Suslov eloquently denounced the evil results of hero-worship. Mikoyan questioned the correctness of Stalin's analysis in "Economic Problems of Socialism," urged a revision of Party history, condemned Stalin's retroactive denunciation and liquidation of early Party leaders, and ridiculed Stalin's solemn "vow" of 1924. Mikoyan further hinted at Lenin's "testament," which was finally to be published in *Komsomol* of June 30, 1956. Molotov, who had earlier confessed his "error" in asserting that the USSR had achieved the "basis" of socialism instead of acknowledging the fulfillment of socialism, was downgraded. Dmitri Shepilov, editor of *Pravda*, who was to succeed Molotov as Foreign Minister on June 1, 1956, denounced "Western imperialism." Malenkov acknowledged "mistakes." Zhukov emerged as a major figure. Much

[7] Merle Fainsod, author of by far the best American analysis of the Soviet polity in the early 1950's, *How Russia Is Ruled*, concluded, perhaps rightly, that the problem of transition to a "democratic" regime was insoluble. His closing sentences (p. 500) are: "The governing formula of Soviet totalitarianism rests on a moving equilibrium of alternating phases of repression and relaxation, but its essential contours remain unchanged. The totalitarian regime does not shed its police-state characteristics; it dies when power is wrenched from its hands." Given the flourishing condition of the Soviet economy in 1957, there is no possibility of the wrenching of power from the hands of the Soviet rulers. But the shedding of "police-state characteristics" was already far advanced.

was said about future economic plans; about the need of "democratizing" the Party and recruiting its membership more carefully; about "peaceful coexistence" and renunciation of world-revolutionary ambitions ("It is not true," declared Khrushchev, "that we regard violence and civil war as the *only way* to remake society"); about the inevitable and universal triumph of socialism, now envisaged in terms of "negotiation" and of "popular fronts" with anti-Communist Marxists, liberals, and peace-seekers; and about many other aspects of Soviet policies at home and abroad.

Khrushchev's concluding indictment of Stalin and Stalinism (see p. 191), addressed to a "closed" session of the Congress, was not published but was subsequently read, in whole or in part, by Party spokesmen to millions of Soviet citizens gathered in thousands of meetings during the spring of 1956. Its apparent purpose was to shock Party delegates, members, and non-Party citizens out of their habitual lethargy, indifference, helplessness, and uncritical acquiescence in the infallibility of the leadership (endlessly reiterated for almost three decades) in the hope of somehow fostering initiative, spontaneity, criticism, and "self-criticism." The intent was to promote a broadening participation of the Soviet masses in the formulation of a relatively "free" public opinion and, if possible, in the processes of policy-making. Much of the Soviet public was shocked. Whether the shock would produce the other hoped-for results was still an open question in 1957.[8]

The resolutions of Congress XX, running to 100 pages, verbosely endorsed the Reports of the Central Committee and the Central Auditing Commission; amended the rules to require more frequent meetings of local Party committees and to "extend the rights of local Party organs"; commented at length on the Sixth Five Year Plan; and instructed the Central Committee to draw up, prior to Congress XXI, a new Draft Program of the Party. All this verbiage, most of it reiterating *ad nauseam* the traditional clichés of Marxism-

[8] Since the epigones were all actively or passively implicated in Stalin's crimes and were indeed the political beneficiaries of his ruthless liquidation of all possible competitors for power, the problem of public confidence in the new "collective leadership" is a puzzling one. According to one tale, perhaps apocryphal. Khrushchev on the platform at Congress XX, in the midst of his memorable indictment of the departed *Vozhd,* received an anonymous written query: "Where were you when Stalin was doing these things?" He asked the delegate who had sent up the question to rise, identify himself, and come forward. No one responded. When a second request was also met with silence, Khrushchev declared: "Now you know where I was!"

Leninism, was in part reminiscent of the futile semantics of 1934 and 1939, which effected no change whatever in the realities of power, and in part suggestive of hopeful, though confused, gropings toward a new and more "democratic" ordering of decision-making.

On February 27, 1956, the new Central Committee announced changes of personnel in the directing organs of the Party, although it does not appear from the published records that any of these were voted on, or even discussed, at the Congress. The eleven members of the existing Party Presidium were re-elected without change. Six "alternates" were added: Shvernik; Zhukov; Shepilov; Ekaterina A. Furtseva, the first woman to attain such eminence; Leonid I. Brezhnev, Party leader in Kazakistan; and Nikolai A. Mukhitdinov, former Premier of Uzbekistan. The new Secretariat comprised Khrushchev, Brezhnev, Suslov, Shepilov, and Furtseva, plus Averky B. Aristov, Nikolai A. Belyayev, and Pyotr N. Pospelev, all relative newcomers in the ranks of the political elite.[9]

5. COEXISTENCE, 1953 f.

DURING the entire life span of the Soviet regime no previous period of comparable scope on the calendar was so sharply characterized by intensive, ubiquitous, energetic, imaginative, and, on the whole, successful diplomatic activity as the years following Stalin's decease. Molotov's role in initiating and directing this far-flung diplomatic

[9] The texts of the many and lengthy addresses at the Congress were published (with the exception of Khrushchev's concluding indictment of Stalin) in Russian, English, French, and German by the Foreign Languages Publishing House of the USSR, 1956, and are individually available in pamphlet form. No single-volume record of Congress XX had been compiled at the time of going to press, although such a volume is in preparation. Among the more incisive Western commentaries and interpretations, see Charles D. Kenney: "The Twentieth C.P.S.U. Congress: A Study in Calculated Moderation," *American Political Science Review,* September 1956, pp. 764–86; Merle Fainsod: "Russia's 20th Party Congress," *Foreign Policy Bulletin,* May 1, 1956, Foreign Policy Association, New York; "After the Twentieth Congress," *Monthly Review,* June 15, 1956; Philip E. Mosely: "Soviet Foreign Policy: New Goals or New Manners?" and Bertram D. Wolfe: "Stalin's Ghost at the Party Congress," both in *Foreign Affairs,* July 1956; and the chapter on Congress XX by John S. Reshetar, Jr., in Boris Meissner: *The Communist Party of the Soviet Union* (Praeger, 1956). Cf. also Helene and Pierre Lazareff: *The Soviet Union after Stalin* (Philosophical Library, 1957), C. L. Sulzberger: *The Big Thaw* (Harper, 1956), and Bertram D. Wolfe: *Khrushchev and Stalin's Ghost* (Praeger, 1957).

"offensive" was major in 1953–4 and minor thereafter, although we may assume that he was usually consulted by his colleagues if only because of his *expertise* acquired at innumerable conference tables over many years. Khrushchev, Bulganin, Malenkov, and, to a lesser degree, Zhukov were, jointly and at times severally, the movers and shakers in these matters. The objectives were to win friends and influence people; to soften past rigidities in the interest of bargaining and compromise; to weaken the Western bloc by replacing a Soviet posture of menace and fear with one of confidence, hope, and earnest solicitude for peace; to liberalize, somehow, Muscovy's relations with the "satellites"; to cultivate all neutrals and to persuade all Asians, Arabs, and Africans that the USSR was their valiant champion against the "colonial" Powers. Although much of the "inside story" of the diplomacy of coexistence in the middle 1950's is still unrevealed, a full account of these endeavors, limited to the public records, would fill many volumes. We must here limit ourselves to the bare bones of the business.

In pursuit of "peace" Soviet policy-makers, like their American counterparts, were not unmindful of the ancient Roman adage: *Si vis pacem, para bellum.* During 1953 "armed vigilance" against "capitalist encirclement" continued to be urged on Soviet holidays: February 23 (Red Army Day), May 1 (when the Moscow military parade was greatly curtailed and Bulganin, though demanding "preparedness," spoke in conciliatory fashion), August 23 (postponed Aviation Day, when 600 jet fighters and bombers, the largest number ever displayed, took part in Moscow's aerial demonstration), and November 6.

On March 16 the First Lord of the Admiralty, J. P. L. Thomas, told Commons of a "very remarkable" increase in Soviet naval construction, making the Soviet Navy second only to that of the U.S.A. The *Sverdlov,* prototype of a class of 10,000-ton cruisers, represented the Soviet fleet at the British Coronation naval review in June. The Soviet submarine force was estimated abroad at 354 U-boats, with 120 under construction and a goal of 1,000. Military aircraft were estimated at 20,000, with an equal number in reserve and an annual output of 19,000.

On August 8 Malenkov, while disclaiming all territorial ambitions and bespeaking "peace" with America, told the Supreme Soviet that "the USA no longer possesses a monopoly of the hydrogen bomb." It was generally believed in the West by year's end that the

USSR was stockpiling hydrogen or fusion bombs as well as plutonium or fission bombs.

On December 31, 1953, the USSR yielded to Red China its partnership and property rights in the Manchurian railways. Vassili V. Kuznetzov, former head of the Soviet trade unions, had been named Ambassador to Peiping in March. Soviet economic aid continued to be extended to China and North Korea. When Iran canceled the recently expired 25-year Soviet-Iranian contract establishing a joint caviar-fisheries company, Moscow made no threats, but proposed negotiations.

In February 1953 the USSR donated $252,000 to flood relief in The Netherlands, and in July offered 4 million rubles to the UN Technical Assistance Fund. On March 12, near the Elbe, Soviet Migs shot down a British bomber, allegedly violating the Soviet zonal frontier. British protests evoked "regrets" and proposals for avoiding such incidents in the future. Soon afterward Moscow effected the release of 10 British civilians long imprisoned in North Korea. In April, 14 Frenchmen were similarly released.

Churchill's plea of May 11, 1953, for a negotiated settlement of the "Cold War" elicited a warm response in the Soviet press. In June, Moscow resumed diplomatic relations with Jugoslavia, and in July with Greece and Israel. Also in July, Moscow, in a note to Turkey, withdrew its claims of 1945 for the cession of Kars, Ardahan, and Artvin, and for participation in defense of the Straits. In November the Kremlin moved to join the International Labor Organization and proposed economic and territorial concessions to Finland.

Exchanges of notes during the year paved the way for possible negotiations in 1954 over Germany and Austria. Eisenhower's plea of December 8 for a UN pool of atomic materials for peaceful purposes elicited negative responses in the Soviet press. But on December 21 Moscow, while reiterating long-standing Soviet pleas for the outlawry of atomic weapons, expressed willingness to discuss the new proposal. The "Cold War" had become less warlike. Whether a new recourse to diplomacy might achieve some facsimile of peace remained to be demonstrated.

Moscow's role in the termination of hostilities in Korea is still unclear. Within weeks after Stalin's death the Communist negotiators at Panmunjom indicated willingness to exchange sick and wounded prisoners, to resume parleys for a truce (suspended in early October 1952), and to reconsider their insistence on the forci-

ble repatriation of all P.O.W.'s. Truce talks were resumed on April 26. Further delays were due less to Communist intransigence than to Syngman Rhee's demands that China must withdraw all its troops, the North Korean Communists must surrender unconditionally, and all Korea must be united under his rulership. Such proposals were wholly visionary, in the light of the military stalemate. The armistice signed on July 26, 1953, established a line of demarcation and a "neutral" zone along the existing battle front, running 20 miles north of 38° in the center and east and 10 miles south of the parallel in the west.

On New Year's Day of 1954 Malenkov appealed for peace and friendship with the USA. On March 31 he conceded that the consequence of an atomic war would be the destruction, not of "capitalism," but of "world civilization." Meanwhile, on January 25, 1954, for the first time since June 1949, four of the five members of the Council of Foreign Ministers reassembled. The Council was established at the Potsdam Conference of 1945 as a "Big Five" agency, including Nationalist China, "to do the necessary preparatory work for the peace settlements." Vyacheslav M. Molotov, Georges Bidault, Anthony Eden, and John Foster Dulles were chiefs of impressive delegations. Sessions met during alternate weeks in the Allied Control Authority building in West Berlin and the Soviet Embassy on Unter den Linden. Molotov at the outset urged a conference with Communist China and proposed a broad agenda, including questions of European security, global tensions, world disarmament, and East-West trade. The Western ministers envisaged the gathering as a "Big Four" meeting limited to the problems of treaties for Germany and Austria. After preliminary sparring, these problems became the major topics of discussion.

On January 29 Western spokesmen offered a plan for German unification through free elections supervised by the Big Four, with the reunited Reich free to join the Western coalition. Molotov countered with a draft treaty for German neutralization, restriction of German armaments, withdrawal of occupation troops, and dismantling of Allied bases in West Germany. He further proposed an all-German referendum on a peace treaty vs. German membership in EDC.

Neither set of proposals was acceptable to the other side. Basic hopes and fears remained unstated. Western leaders knew that they

lacked means to induce the USSR to accept the unification of a re-armed Reich aligned with the Atlantic Powers. They were unwilling to pay the price of German demilitarization and neutralization for German unity, the more so as a reunited Reich would have a Protestant majority in religion and, probably, a Social Democratic majority in politics, marking the end of Adenauer's Christian Democratic regime. Soviet representatives knew that free elections meant the end of the Communist-controlled regime in East Germany. Such a sacrifice of Soviet power was conceivable only in exchange for guarantees of German neutrality. But these alternatives were obscured in evasive verbiage. The East-West deadlock over Germany therefore remained unchanged.

On February 10 Molotov proposed military evacuation of Germany and a general European treaty of non-aggression and collective security, to which both West and East Germany should be signatories, pending unification. When these and other suggestions on both sides effected no alteration of the stalemate, the Foreign Ministers of the West and of Austria offered to accept the Soviet version of all of the remaining articles of the Austrian treaty. Molotov, however, insisted on new provisions which, pending a German treaty, would have left occupation forces indefinitely in Austria. He rejected an Austrian proposal to extend the occupation to June 30, 1955.

The delegates finally turned their attention to the possibility of a Far Eastern conference. On February 18 the Berlin sessions closed with an agreement to call a conference in Geneva, to begin April 26, of the Big Four plus Communist China, North and South Korea, and other participants in the Korean hostilities, to seek "a peaceful settlement of the Korean question" and discuss "the problem of restoring peace in Indochina." The final communiqué also pledged a further exchange of views on disarmament.

All participants expressed regret at their failure to come to terms, satisfaction over a better understanding of opposing views, and hopes for future concord. An Anglo-French-American communiqué of February 19 asserted that "the Soviet Government is not now ready to permit free all-German elections, or to abandon its control over Eastern Germany," that progress toward an Austrian treaty "depends upon the Soviet Union's modifying its attitude" and that Soviet proposals "would have involved the dissolution of the Western security system, while the military power of the Soviet bloc remained

intact. The three Powers do not intend to be deflected from their efforts to develop the system of defense upon which their survival depends."

By bringing to an end eight years of warfare in Indochina, the largest and most prolonged international conference of 1954 marked a new phase in the slow achievement of a *modus vivendi* between East and West. On April 26, as agreed at the Berlin Conference, the delegates gathered in the old League of Nations building, under the chairmanship of Prince Wan Waithayakon, Foreign Minister of Thailand. They included the Foreign Ministers of the USA (Dulles), Britain (Eden), France (Bidault), the USSR (Molotov), Communist China (Chou En-lai), the Vietminh regime (Pham Van Dong), Vietnam (Tran Van Do), Laos, Cambodia, North Korea (Nam Il), South Korea (Pyun Yung Tai), and other participants in the Korean War.

The context of the negotiations was complex. Ho Chi Minh's Vietminh armies, with Chinese aid, were winning their war against the French, as demonstrated by their capture of Dienbienphu on May 7. They appeared capable, in time, of taking all of Indochina. Chou En-lai and Molotov preferred a peace of partial triumph in the interest of a global *détente*. Bidault, presiding over a lost cause, hoped to save what he could. Eden sought compromise. Dulles, in a mid-April trip to London and Paris and in subsequent efforts, strove in vain for a "united front" for defense of Southeast Asia. He studiously ignored Chou En-lai. President Eisenhower overruled initial French pleas and later advice from the U.S. Joint Chiefs of Staff for American military intervention. The final result was distasteful to all, but was accepted as preferable to continued hostilities with no prospect of early victory and with grave peril, in the event of open Chinese and American involvement, of World War III.

Hopes in Berlin that the Geneva Conference might achieve the unification of Korea were disappointed. Seoul resisted proposals for all-Korean elections. Pyongyang demanded unity on terms threatening the Communization of both Koreas. The USA insisted on UN supervision of elections. No formula for compromise was discovered. On June 15 the Korean discussions were terminated on American initiative, despite British objections. Churchill and Eden came to Washington ten days later in an effort to resolve Anglo-American differences. Western spokesmen at Geneva asserted that no accord was possible as long as the Communists rejected free elections and de-

nied the authority of the UN. Communist spokesmen declared that the Western Powers were resolved to perpetuate partition in preparation for further "aggression."

Meanwhile Eden, Bidault, Chou, and Molotov bargained for a cease-fire in Vietnam. Dulles, leaving Walter Bedell Smith in his place, returned to Washington on May 4 to face severe criticism for diplomatic ineptitude. A deadlock was reached by mid-June over the status of Laos and Cambodia and over the composition and authority of an international supervisory commission. Smith returned to Washington on June 21. Two days later Chou and Mendès-France reached agreement in Bern. The new French Premier and Foreign Minister, who declared he would get an armistice by July 20 or resign, arrived in Geneva on July 10. Following urgent French appeals, Dulles flew to Paris on July 13 to confer with Mendès-France and Eden. But he refused to return to Geneva, sending Smith back in his place. In the final bargaining Chou asked U.S. participation in guaranteeing an Indochinese settlement. Washington limited its obligations to "respect" for such a settlement and adopted an attitude of "innocence by dissociation." The Geneva Conference closed on July 21, 1954, after 75 days of arduous labor.

Vietnam, now partitioned at the 17th parallel, was at peace. In Indochina, as in Korea and Germany, the global giants, having marched to the brink of global war and then drawn back, accepted a stalemate offering a prospect of global peace. But Soviet efforts to achieve such a peace, both before and after the cease-fire in Southeast Asia, met with little success during the second year of Malenkov's Premiership.

On March 31, 1954, the USSR proposed that the "Cold War" be ended by a new European security organization and by Soviet membership in NATO. The United States rejected this proposal on May 7, asking for "concrete evidence of good intentions." Soviet diplomats and propagandists wooed Tito; courted Japan; warned Pakistan, Turkey, Egypt, and Iran against American alliances; evolved a "Point Four" program of their own in Afghanistan, India, and Burma; welcomed Attlee and Bevan, other British missions, and a few American students and Congressmen; sent cultural missions abroad on an increasing scale; and dispatched numerous notes to the Western Powers. Following French rejection of EDC, Molotov reiterated his warnings against "German militarism" and renewed his bid for a new conference on European security. By October he was

asserting that German rearmament would mean the indefinite partition of the Reich, and appealing anew for a meeting to reunify and neutralize Germany.

Another Soviet note of October 23 proposed a November conference on Germany and European security. A note of November 13, addressed to 23 European governments and the USA, urged such a conference in Moscow or Paris on November 29. When all these overtures were rejected, Moscow convened a conference of Premiers and Foreign Ministers of the Soviet bloc in late November to consider countermeasures against the Paris Pacts. At year's end the USSR was warning London and Paris that it would terminate the alliance treaties of 1942 and 1944 if the pacts were ratified.

The tempo of Muscovite diplomacy was accelerated in 1955. On May 7 the Presidium of the Supreme Soviet abrogated the alliance treaties of 1942 with Britain and of 1944 with France, holding that London and Paris had violated their obligations by ratifying the accords of 1954 for German rearmament. On May 14 Bulganin and Molotov, meeting in Warsaw with envoys of Poland, Czechoslovakia, Hungary, Rumania, Bulgaria, Albania, and East Germany, signed an 8-Power, 11-article, 20-year Treaty of Friendship, Cooperation, and Mutual Aid, setting up a Communist counterpart of NATO with Marshal Ivan S. Konev as Chief of the unified command.

But these militant gestures of defiance were overbalanced by active pursuit of the goal of an East-West *modus vivendi*. In reconsidering the problem of Austria, Soviet policy-makers abruptly reversed their previous posture of obstructionism, with heartening results. The new dispensation first became manifest when Molotov, in talks with Ambassador Norbert Bischoff on February 25 and March 2, 1955, proposed fresh negotiations. He indicated that the USSR, as he had told the Supreme Soviet on February 8, would no longer demand the retention of foreign troops in Austria until the signature of a German peace treaty, providing Vienna would give pledges against any new *Anschluss* and agree not to join any military coalition. Following a favorable reply, Molotov on March 24 invited Chancellor Julius Raab to Moscow. On April 5 Washington, London, and Paris cautioned against bilateral commitments. Molotov expressed confidence that the Austrian mission would lead to the signature of the treaty acceptable to all.

On April 11 Raab reached the Soviet capital in a snowstorm, via a Soviet plane, accompanied by Vice-Chancellor Adolf Schaerf, For-

eign Minister Leopold Figl, and Deputy Foreign Minister Bruno Kreisky. Amid much cordiality, shared by Ambassador Charles Bohlen and other Western diplomats, the talks with Molotov and Deputy Premier Mikoyan ended on April 15 with agreement, registered in an Austrian-Soviet communiqué: Austria agreed "not to join any military alliances or permit military bases on her territory" and to "pursue a policy of independence"; the USSR agreed to accept payment of the $150,000,000 provided by Article 35 of the draft treaty in the form of Austrian goods, to transfer to Austria the properties of the Danube Shipping Co. and the Zistersdorf oil fields and refineries in exchange for deliveries of crude oil, to normalize trade relations, and to accede to President Koerner's plea for the release of all Austrians still held in Russia; both governments urged a 4-power conference to conclude the treaty.

On April 19 Moscow proposed to the West a conference of Foreign Ministers in the Austrian capital. The Western Powers, still cautious, countered on April 22 with a proposal for a conference of Ambassadors. Moscow promptly concurred, meanwhile beginning the release of prisoners and easing controls in the Soviet zone. On May 2 Ambassadors Llewellyn E. Thompson, Ivan I. Ilyichev, and Sir Geoffrey Wallinger, and Minister R. Lalouette met with Figl and Kreisky in the Allied Council building. Ilyichev initially objected, but soon yielded, to Western and Austrian insistence on modifying Articles 16 and 17 of the draft, respectively pledging Austria to repatriate displaced persons and limiting the army to 53,000 men. He later opposed any change in Article 35, arguing that Soviet economic concessions to Austria should be embodied in a bilateral treaty, but again yielded.

By May 13 the conference ended with approval of a text. On May 15, amid much wining and dining, John Foster Dulles, Harold Macmillan, Antoine Pinay, Vyacheslav Molotov, and Leopold Figl, having swiftly foregathered on the Danube, signed the document in Belvidere Palace after deleting a clause in the preamble implying Austrian war guilt. The treaty thus signed was promptly ratified by the appropriate authorities in Austria (June 8), the USSR (June 11), the USA (June 17 by a Senate vote of 63 to 3 with Senators McCarthy, Jenner, and Malone opposed), the U.K. (June 29), and France (July 12). With the deposit of ratification in Moscow, it became legally effective on July 27, 1955, to the tune of celebrations throughout Austria on the end of the occupation.

By the terms of the 38 articles of the compact, the four "Allied and Associated Powers" recognized the restoration of Austria as a "sovereign, independent, and democratic State" and declared their will to "respect the independence and territorial integrity of Austria" within the frontiers of January 1, 1938. *Anschluss* with Germany was forbidden. Vienna agreed to keep in force anti-Nazi legislation and to maintain the exile of the Hapsburgs under the law of April 3, 1919. Austrian armed forces were limited not in size but in weapons and in recruitment of ex-Nazis. Occupation troops would be withdrawn within 90 days. In supplementary accords, Austria agreed to deliver one million tons of oil annually for 10 years to the USSR, plus industrial and consumers' goods in discharge of the debt of $150,000,000. On September 28, in the wake of an Austrian economic mission to Moscow, an Austrian-Soviet trade agreement was signed, providing for a $50,000,000 exchange of goods over a 5-year period.

French troops withdrew in June and Soviet forces in September. The occupation ended with the withdrawal of the last British and American units on October 13 and 14. Austria's status as a "neutral" was not formally incorporated in the treaty or encompassed in any formula of international neutralization, but left as a principle of national policy. Chancellor Raab's oft-expressed hope was realized: when the rebuilt Vienna State Opera reopened on November 5 with Beethoven's *Fidelio*, Austria was free, sovereign, and independent.

What followed was even more dramatic, although less productive of tangible agreements. For the first time in ten years the heads of State of the major Powers met together in 1955 in an effort to alleviate international tensions and to promote the settlement of problems of power by bargaining rather than by violence. The former purpose was well served. The latter remained in suspense, thanks to the reluctance of policy-makers in Moscow, Washington, London, and Paris to redefine their goals in terms conducive to mutually acceptable formulas for German unification, disarmament, and enlarged contacts between East and West.

The two conferences at Geneva, despite their paucity of concrete results, registered the will of all the participants to renounce war as obsolete in the thermonuclear age, to mitigate the "Cold War" in its more incendiary aspects, and to strive, however hesitantly, for some minimum common ground as a context for a "coexistence" which might be at least non-violent even if "competitive"

and not altogether "peaceful." The discussions led to no specific accords, but created a "new atmosphere" in East-West relations.

A "summit" conference to negotiate a settlement had long been urged by Winston Churchill as the only alternative to coannihilation. No such conference had been held since the meeting at Potsdam, July 17–August 2, 1945. Early in 1955 the inexorable fact of stalemate, coupled with a dawning realization of the intolerable costs and fantastic risks of a continued contest for global hegemony, sufficiently impressed decision-makers in Moscow and Washington to admit of a new departure. Churchill revealed in the House of Commons on March 14 that he had vainly sought in the summer of 1954 to arrange an Anglo-Soviet parley, that Moscow had argued for a quadripartite conference, and that President Eisenhower had declined. Each side was resolved to "mend its fences" before embarking on bargaining.

This condition was met with Western ratification of the Paris accords of October 23, 1954, and the Warsaw Conference of May 1955, which fabricated a Communist counterpart of the Western coalition. Meanwhile, a "Big Four" parley was urged by Senator Walter F. George (March 20), ambiguously endorsed by the Eisenhower Administration, favored with "a positive attitude" by Premier Bulganin (March 26), championed anew by Churchill (March 29), made the subject of Anglo-French-American discussions, and furthered by exchanges of greetings between Eisenhower and Marshal Georgi K. Zhukov.

On May 8 the Foreign Ministers of France, Britain, and the USA, met in the name of NATO with Chancellor Adenauer participating, considered prospects in Paris. On May 10 the USSR publicized an elaborate plan for disarmament (envisaging partial military evacuation of Germany and limitation of American, Soviet, and Chinese armies to 1,500,000 troops each and of British and French armies to 650,000 each), while Bulganin in the Polish capital, in a mild and conciliatory statement, foreshadowed the shape of the Warsaw Pact.

Also on May 10 Washington, London, and Paris formally invited the USSR "to join with us in an effort to remove sources of conflict," to begin with "a meeting of the heads of governments, accompanied by their foreign ministers, for an exchange of views," and to be followed by further conferences on concrete issues. "We

stand ready," declared President Eisenhower to the Republican Women's National Conference, "to do anything, to meet with anyone, anywhere, so long as we may do so with self-respect . . . and there is any slightest chance of furthering this great cause of peace."

A Soviet note of May 26 accepted the Western invitation, though rejecting Dulles's suggestions for discussion of the "liberation" of the Soviet satellites. Agreement in Vienna on May 15 smoothed the way for later talks. As for place, Eisenhower and Dulles suggested Lausanne or possibly Stockholm, while Bulganin and Molotov favored Vienna. Geneva was agreed upon as a compromise. As for time, the Western Powers proposed July 18, with Moscow concurring, though objecting to a four-day limit.

A Western note of June 6 proposed a meeting in Geneva, July 18–21. A Soviet note of June 13 assented. At San Francisco, in connection with the 10th anniversary of the United Nations, Dulles, Molotov, Macmillan, and Pinay dined at the Pacific Union Club on Nob Hill on June 21 and ironed out remaining details. On June 22 the U.S. Senate, 77 to 4, voted down a proposal by Senator McCarthy, supported by Senators Jenner, Malone, and Langer, seeking to make Eisenhower's participation contingent upon discussion of the end of Communist rule in Europe and Asia.

Long before Geneva, policy-makers on both sides had publicly committed themselves to positions on Germany and on disarmament which were irreconcilable. These positions remained unchanged during 1955. They precluded any serious diplomatic bargaining and therefore doomed both conferences to discord on basic issues.

Both sides were agreed "in principle" on the need of German unification. But the West insisted on unity through free elections (spelling the end of the "German Democratic Republic"), with the reunited Reich deemed incapable of "neutrality" on the Austrian model and free to choose its alignments, and with projected guarantees of Soviet security to be conditional upon German membership in NATO. Moscow insisted on unification through parleys between the "German Federal Republic" and the "German Democratic Republic" (which Bonn and the Western Powers refused to recognize), with the unified Reich, *à la* Austria, pledged to no alliances and no foreign troops or bases on its territory.

Both sides were equally agreed "in principle" on the need of disarmament. But the West insisted on "fool-proof" arrangements of inspection and control as a prerequisite. The USSR argued for the

priority of commitments to reduce arms and to ban atomic weapons as a condition for any accord.

On both issues neither side had any means of coercing or inducing the other to accept its own position, nor did either display sufficient flexibility or ingenuity to evolve any formula acceptable to both. The result was continued deadlock—significantly alleviated, however, by a fresh climate of cordiality (the "Spirit of Geneva") productive of fruitful results in other areas of contacts, although viewed with understandable suspicion by the more ardent Western foes of Communism, the more so as the new "Spirit" was at once transposed into a *leitmotif* of Communist propaganda.

On July 15 Bulganin, in a press conference in Moscow, asserted that "even a bad peace is better than a good quarrel" and opined that "it would be naïve to think that we shall be able to solve all international problems." Yet he contended that "we can and must discuss these questions patiently and in good faith and find peaceful solutions for them." On the same evening Eisenhower, in a radio and television address, welcomed the Soviet Premier's remarks and bespoke hope for things to come: "The free people of the world hate war and want peace." He flew to Geneva on the 16th and lunched with Faure and Eden the next day while Bulganin, Khrushchev, and Zhukov toured the city of Calvin and Rousseau.

The conference opened on July 18 in the Palace of Nations, former headquarters of the League of Nations and now a UN building. Dag Hammarskjold briefly welcomed guests, who proceeded at once to set the "tone" of the meeting by delivering long daily speeches restating the positions each of their governments had already taken. Diplomacy can be conducted only in private. Since the proceedings at Geneva were conducted in public, no diplomatic negotiations took place, nor were any possible under such conditions.

Eisenhower proposed an "alarm system" of arms-inspection to prevent "frightful surprises" or "sudden attack." Eden proposed a mutual-defense treaty among the four Powers plus a unified Germany and a demilitarized security zone in East-Central Europe. Bulganin, after pledging his government to participate in the projected "atoms-for-peace" pool, proposed an exchange of guarantees between the signatories of NATO and of the Warsaw Pact. Faure proposed budgetary limitations on armaments, with the funds thus saved to be devoted to aid to underdeveloped countries. On July 21 Eisenhower made headlines by suggesting that the USA and USSR

exchange blueprints of military installations and agree to reciprocal aerial inspection of each other's territories.

This arresting proposal was widely hailed throughout the Western world as a constructive contribution to peace, as indeed it might have been and, conceivably, may yet become. At the time it was made, however, official Soviet anxieties over "enemy espionage" were such as to dictate absurd "security" regulations (not modified until the summer of 1956) that forbade the publication in any of the cities of the USSR of street plans, guidebooks, or even phone directories. Under these circumstances, the men of Moscow were compelled by their fears to view Eisenhower's proposal with the utmost suspicion and obliged by their hopes to equivocate, delay, and postpone lest, by flat rejection, they appear "uncooperative."

The Geneva Conference closed July 23, 1955, amid general expressions of cordiality, with a directive to the Foreign Ministers to meet in Geneva in October to discuss "European security" and "reunification of Germany," "to develop an acceptable system for disarmament," and to "bring about a progressive elimination of barriers which interfere with free communications and peaceful trade between peoples."

The absence of tangible accords, disguised by agreement on abstractions, did not minimize the value of a week of wining and dining among heads of States. Faure and Pinay were cold and cautious. Eden and Macmillan were correct and cordial. Eisenhower, Bulganin, Khrushchev, and Zhukov were "old friends" and "comrades-in-arms," as shown by Eisenhower's prompt dispatch of a fountain pen and portable radio to Zhukov's daughter when he was informed by Khrushchev of her impending marriage to Klimenti Efremovich Voroshilov, a nephew of the President of the USSR, and Zhukov's subsequent gift of a family portrait to the American President. The post-Geneva public utterances of all the participants bespoke "friendship," "understanding," and "success" in the quest for peace.

Early in August Eisenhower expressed willingness to accept Soviet proposals for inspection teams at key strategic points if the USSR would accept his plan for aerial inspection. Bulganin, in paying tribute to Eisenhower's "sincerity," cast doubt on the practicality of this proposal. But on August 5 the Soviet Premier, again addressing the Supreme Soviet, denied press reports that his comment constituted a "rejection" of Eisenhower's plan and declared it worthy of serious study.

In exchanges of messages during September, Bulganin voiced willingness to accept the Eisenhower proposals on condition that they should include U.S. overseas bases and be part of a comprehensive disarmament program including prohibition of the use of nuclear weapons. U.S. expressions of official disappointment at this reply were followed on September 24 by President Eisenhower's heart attack in Denver and by his consequent inability to assume active direction of policy-formulation, although he agreed, in a reply of October 12 to Bulganin, to accept Soviet proposals for checkpoint control.

The British, French, and U.S. Foreign Ministers met in New York, September 27–8, conferred with Molotov and the West German Foreign Minister, and resolved that priority in the coming discussions should be given to German unification. They publicly reiterated their view that the *status quo* in Berlin should remain unchanged, that the East German regime was unworthy of recognition, and that "the final determination of the frontiers of Germany must await a peace settlement for the whole of Germany." Diplomatic exchanges led to minor modifications in, and disputes about, various formulas for German unity, European security, and global disarmament, without producing any alteration of basic positions.

On October 27, 1955, the four Foreign Ministers with their staffs reassembled in Geneva's Palace of Nations, in a dampened atmosphere, and again resorted to public speeches elaborately restating their previous opinions, which, as expressed, admitted of no compromise on crucial questions. Complex proposals by both sides effected no change of policies. When discussion of Germany got nowhere, the Foreign Ministers turned on November 9 to discussion of disarmament, which also got nowhere.

Informal consideration, outside the agenda, of the mounting tension in the Middle East precipitated by Communist offers of arms and economic aid to Egypt and other Arab States was likewise without result. Molotov rejected Western proposals for a general accord on cultural interchange, obviously preferring to pursue this goal through bilateral agreements and unilateral modifications of the Soviet "Iron Curtain." On November 16, 1955, the conference adjourned amid mild recriminations.

The final communiqué recommended that "the future course of discussions should be settled through diplomatic channels." The participants were unanimous on the need of reducing tensions and pro-

moting disarmament, but noted that "it was not yet possible to reach agreement on effective methods and safeguards for achieving" these objectives. "They believe that their exchange of views has been useful in clarifying their respective positions." They "further reaffirm the obligation of their governments to refrain from the use of force in any manner inconsistent with the Charter of the UN." A simultaneous communiqué of the three Western Powers blamed the USSR for refusing to accept Western terms for German unity "since that would lead to the liquidation of the East German regime. . . . It is for this reason that the negotiations have failed. . . . The three Western Powers themselves will not cease their efforts to end the injustice and wrong now being done by dividing the German people and will continue to stand ready to contribute to the security which can be enjoyed by all only when Germany is reunified."

Following the Big Four Conference in Geneva, Khrushchev and Bulganin visited East Germany (July 24–6). West Germany's Chancellor Adenauer and Foreign Minister von Brentano and their aides accepted a Soviet invitation to visit Moscow (September 9–13) and there agreed to diplomatic relations and repatriation of remaining prisoners and displaced persons. Immediately thereafter East Germany's Minister President Otto Grotewohl and his aides went to Moscow (September 16–20) and signed a new treaty affirming complete equality of rights, mutual respect of sovereignty, and noninterference in domestic affairs, cooperation for peace, mutual aid, German unity, and temporary retention of Soviet troops in East Germany. In the face of the new deadlock among the Foreign Ministers at Geneva, Soviet policy-makers were prepared to perpetuate the partition of the Reich, to build an East German army, and to seek in due course a bilateral bargain with Bonn.

The visit of Premier Nehru of India (June 7–23) led to a joint declaration espousing peaceful coexistence, a ban on nuclear weapons, disarmament, extension of cultural and economic relations, and Red China's claims to Formosa and to a seat in the UN. In July 1955 Soviet leaders received Ho Chi Minh and a 12-member farm delegation from the United States. September found Bulganin and Khrushchev greeting Senators Kefauver, Frear, Malone, Dworshak, and Young (all of whom visited the Soviet atomic-energy plant) and welcoming the Finnish President, Premier, and Defense Minister, who agreed (September 19) to a 20-year renewal of the mutual-defense pact of 1948 and the return to Finland of the Porkkala naval base.

During October, Canadian Foreign Secretary Lester Pearson and Burmese Premier U Nu visited Moscow. The Norwegian Premier followed and reiterated (November 15) that Norway would not grant bases to her NATO allies unless attacked or threatened.

Khrushchev, Bulganin, Mikoyan, Gromyko, and Shepilov, visiting Jugoslavia May 26 to June 2, expressed regret to Marshal Tito for the "break" of 1948, and signed a joint declaration bespeaking normalization of relations, mutual respect and non-interference, condemnation of all aggression, peaceful coexistence regardless of ideological differences, and recognition that the policy of military blocs increases international tension. Moscow and Belgrade agreed that atomic weapons should be banned, that Germany should be unified on a "democratic" basis, and that Red China was entitled to admission to the UN and to satisfaction of her "legitimate rights with regard to Formosa." On June 1, in London, Ambassador Jacob A. Malik opened negotiations with Shunichi Matsumoto for a Soviet-Japanese peace treaty. Moscow indicated willingness to restore the Habomai and Shikotan islands to Japan, but rejected Tokyo's claims for the return of Southern Sakhalin and the Kuriles.

To the alarm of Israel and the consternation of the Western Powers, the Soviet bloc leapfrogged over the "northern tier" of "containment" in the Middle East by sending arms and economic and technical aid to Egypt and other Arab States opposed to the Baghdad Pact. Moscow warned Teheran on October 12 that Iranian adherence to the Pact "contradicts good neighborly relations" and accused Iran on November 26 of violating the Soviet-Iranian treaty of October 1, 1927.

Between November 17 and December 22, 1955, Khrushchev, Bulganin, and their aides made a triumphal tour of India, Burma, and Afghanistan, criticizing Western policies, supporting Indian claims to Goa and Kashmir, and reaffirming cordiality, self-determination, and coexistence. Soviet purchases of Indian raw materials and manufactures and Soviet sale, over three years, of a million tons of steel to India were agreed upon, as was Soviet purchase of one-half of Burma's rice exports for three years. Soviet technical aid was pledged to Burma. A bargain was concluded in Kabul (December 18) whereby the Soviet-Afghan treaty of neutrality and non-aggression of 1931 would be extended for ten years and the USSR would lend $100,000,000 to Afghanistan for economic development.

At year's end the USSR had cause for satisfaction, and the

Western Powers occasion for concern, over the international events of 1955. France was embroiled in colonial rebellions and deeply split in domestic politics. Britain, clinging to Cyprus, was at odds with Greece, which in turn was at swords' points with Turkey and veering toward neutralism. Soviet diplomacy had buttressed the Communist bloc, gained credit for bringing 16 new members into the UN, won Jugoslavia to the neutralist camp, strengthened ties with the major neutralist nations of southern Asia, gained new influence in the Arab world, and frustrated Anglo-American efforts to build effective coalitions in Southeast Asia and the Near East. With the "Cold War" mitigated by the Spirit of Geneva and moving from the military plane to the arena of economic and ideological competition for influence among the world's poor, the USSR posed a new challenge to America.

These remarkable achievements of Soviet diplomacy, to which Western responses were hesitant, confused, and unimaginative, were to be jeopardized, as we shall see, by the Muscovite fumblings and blunderings of 1956—matched, however, by comparable blunderings and fumblings within the Western coalition. The ancient and honorable, even if now obsolete and deadly dangerous, game of *Machtpolitik* moved in 1956 into a new phase and a pattern of drastic transformation.

6. THE CRISES OF THE COALITIONS

DURING the thirty-ninth year of the reign of the Marxists over Muscovy, domestic developments in the economy, society, and polity of Sovietland were overshadowed by the sensational international events of the autumn. The whole structure of the "Warsaw Pact" alliance and the previously solid edifice of the "Western bloc" were both shaken to their foundations by recourse to violence on the part of men and statesmen reduced to desperation. The violence, to be sure, was limited, localized, and temporary. But its impact was shattering for those in East and West alike who had staked their hopes on an assumption of the enduring unity of the new empires of Marxland and Freeland—both elaborately built out of mutual fear during the decade of "Cold War." The disintegration of the two systems was in neither case irreparable. Yet the old molds were broken.

The wonder-working magic of earlier years had lost its power. Whether new patterns in each half of a divided world could be so devised as to prove viable no one could say with assurance in the fortieth year after 1917.

The breakdowns of the *status quo* on each side of the line of demarcation, albeit unique in each instance in causes and consequences, had common denominators. Policy-makers in Washington had long eagerly anticipated, and indeed sought to foster, the dissolution of the Soviet coalition with no suspicion that their own policies might lead to comparable schisms in the Atlantic alliance. Policy-makers in Moscow had long entertained expectations of the disintegration of the Western bloc with few fears that their own policies might jeopardize their control of Eastern Europe. Had the opportunity of 1953–5 been used to negotiate a comprehensive and global bargain between East and West, the tragedies of 1956 would never have taken place. When Great Powers are agreed on a common program, lesser States must acquiesce. The opportunity was wasted. With each camp striving futilely to gain advantages over the other, both were obliged to pay the painful penalties of a failure of statesmanship.

The exciting, inspiring, and irrational imperatives of nationalism, as a secular religion far more appealing to most of contemporary mankind than the creeds of Marxism or democracy, were of the essence of the miseries of 1956. The imposition of Soviet (i.e., Russian) rule on the minority peoples of the USSR, widely denounced in the West as Communist "colonialism," was endurable to the non-Russian communities of Transcaucasia and Central Asia (most of whom had had no recent experience with independent political life) insofar as it meant the advent of schools, factories, hospitals, and improved living standards. The same rule in Eastern Europe, where it signified a loss of freedom and a decline of living standards, proved unacceptable, despite a decade of indoctrination, to large masses of people cherishing memories and dreams of national independence. Conversely, Western colonialism in Asia and Africa, beneficent in avowed purpose but exploitive in sober fact, begot fierce nationalist resistance, exploding in anti-Western violence throughout many of the colonial or formerly colonial communities. The men of Moscow strove to exploit, for their own purposes, these ferments of resentment throughout Africa and Asia. The men of Washington sought to exploit, for their own purposes, popular opposition to Communist

rule in Eastern Europe. In this competition the Kremlin was relatively more successful than the Pentagon and the State Department. But the rivalry itself was to prove highly hazardous for both contestants, with each "hoist by his own petard."

Before considering the double tragedies of late 1956, it will be well to note the broad pattern of Soviet politics at home and abroad prior to the autumnal convulsions. The February resolves and concluding verbal bombshell of Party Congress XX have been discussed above (see pp. 428 and 191). In the sequel the tasks of "de-Stalinization" were vigorously pursued on several fronts. More past purgers were purged. In late May, M. A. Bagirov, T. M. Borshchev, K. I. Grigoryan, and R. A. Markaryan were executed as "Beria's accomplices in crime." Stalin's staunch "dictator of literature," novelist Alexander A. Fadeyev, aged 55 and reputedly a chronic alcoholic, killed himself on May 13. Stalin's "dictator of biology," Trofim D. Lysenko, was replaced (April 9) by Pavel P. Lobanov as Director of the All-Union Academy of Agricultural Sciences. Plans were announced to republish John Reed's *Ten Days That Shook the World*, suppressed by Stalin because it made no mention of his role. On September 7 the Supreme Soviet changed the name of the "Stalin Peace Prizes" to "International Lenin Prizes for Strengthening Peace Among Peoples."

De-Stalinization was further fostered in the somewhat macabre form of posthumous "rehabilitations" of Stalin's victims. *Voprosy Istorii* (April 13) exonerated nine purged Army leaders of the 1930's: Alexander I. Yegorov, Vasili K. Bluecher, Jan B. Garmarnik, Andrei S. Bubnov (the only survivor), V. A. Antonov-Ovseyenko, Sergei S. Kamenev, M. S. Kedrov, Moissei L. Rukhimovich, and I. S. Unschlicht. Soviet Premier (1924–30) Alexei I. Rykov, who had been shot in 1938 and ever since treated in the press as an unperson, was mentioned without condemnation by *Pravda* on April 22. The Academy of Sciences in September 1956 rehabilitated three jurists liquidated by Stalin in the 1930's: N. V. Krylenko, O. B. Pashukanis, and N. E. Cheliapov. Among the Jewish victims of the purgers, Isaac Babel and Vsevolod E. Meyerhold, director of the Revolutionary Theater, along with sundry Yiddish writers, including Parets Markish and Itsik Feffer, who were done to death during Stalin's last years, were restored to respectability in various Soviet journals. A Hebrew Prayer Book was published in midsummer, for the first time since the Revolution, although other steps toward reviving Jewish life and Yiddish culture were halting. Some signs of persisting anti-

Semitism appeared in the fall. In January 1957, however, a rabbinical seminary was opened in Moscow.

At a New Year's Eve party, December 31, 1956, Khrushchev, either elated by beverages or worried over new storms among the comrades abroad, was quoted by diplomats as saying that Stalin, after all, had been "a great Marxist" and "a great fighter against imperialism" and that, as against imperialism, "we are all Stalinists." Yet the quest went on for the rule of law, for local autonomy, and for a softening and decentralization of power. The obscure Sergei N. Kruglov, Beria's successor as Minister of the Interior, was replaced on February 1, 1956, by the even more obscure N. P. Dudorov. As work continued on the preparation of new civil and criminal codes, the Presidium of the Supreme Soviet on April 23, 1956, created a special division in the Chief Prosecutor's Office to supervise all security agency—above all, the MVD—in order to prevent abuses. Who was to supervise the supervisors, and how new abuses in place of old were to be avoided in what was still an arbitrary police state, no one knew. Nor did any public figure in the USSR dare to voice the demand of the Hungarian rebels for the abolition of the political police.

Lesser steps were nevertheless taken. On April 25 the Presidium repeated legislation forbidding workers to leave their jobs and punishing absenteeism. Not yet was any "right to strike" acknowledged. But on May 13, 1956, the MVD announced that all forced-labor camps would be closed within 18 months and their inmates freed. A popular new pension law—sketched in February, announced in May, enacted by the Supreme Soviet in July, and put into effect in October 1956—provided full salary for workers earning 350 rubles monthly and half-salary for those earning 1,000 or more rubles a month after retirement because of age or disability.

In the face of difficulties and confusions, further attempts were made by the oligarchs to restore meaning to federalism, to downgrade and decentralize the bloated central bureaucracy, and to encourage local initiative in decision-making. That this campaign left much to be desired and that it represented, as yet, no true comprehension of functioning federalism as practiced in the West was shown by the circumstances of the abolition of the Karelo-Finnish Republic and its annexation to the RSFSR in July 1956. The decision was jointly decreed, as is customary with major matters in Soviet political practice, by the Party Central Committee and the Council

of Ministers. Participation by the federal Supreme Soviet or the Karelo-Finnish Supreme Soviet or by the people directly involved or affected was non-existent or *pro forma*. A vast decentralization of the swollen administrative machinery of business management was nevertheless begun in 1956, at least on paper. The extent to which this process could or would eventuate in anything resembling a restoration of local Soviet "democracy" at the grass roots remained to be seen forty years after the October Revolution.[1] (See p. 508 below.)

The Soviet economy meanwhile continued to flourish despite lags and lapses in the intricate tasks of organizing all saving and investment, spending and construction, production and distribution in a totally socialized and totally planned system of business. In agriculture, marketable output depended upon 9,000 machine and tractor stations, 5,000 state farms, and 87,500 huge consolidated collective farms, representing a reduction of the *kolkhozi* from 121,400 in 1950 and 235,700 in 1940. Increased production was largely dependent upon the new state farms, manned by youthful pioneers, in the freshly opened lands of Siberia and Central Asia, and upon the success or failure of the nation-wide campaign to grow maize for fodder. In one sense the result was unimpressive: in 1957 the total output of foodstuffs of Soviet farms, worked by 50,000,000 farmers, was roughly equal in volume to the total output of American farms, worked by 6,000,000 farmers. The discrepancy was only partly due

---

[1] The legislative and administrative details of this undertaking are too complex for brief review. Two examples must suffice. On May 31, 1956, the Party Central Committee and the Council of Ministers, with the Presidium of the Supreme Soviet approving, jointly decreed the transfer from the USSR to the Republics of all establishments under the Ministries of Foodstuffs, Meat, and Dairy Products, Fishing, Procurement, Light Industry, Textiles, Building Materials, Paper and Wood, Auto Transport and Highways, Inland Waterways, and Public Health, along with retail stores; the merging of the federal Ministries of Light Industry and Textiles into one Ministry of Light Industry; the transformation of the federal Ministry of Procurement into a joint Union-Republican Ministry of Grain Products; the abolition of the federal Ministries of Auto Transport and Highways, of Inland Waterways, and of Justice, with their functions transferred to the Republics. Appeals for further decentralization were publicized during the autumn and given concrete form in the spring of 1957.

Meanwhile, the survivors of the brutal deportation in 1943–4 of the Karachai, Kalmyk, Chechen-Ingush, and Kabardino-Balkar peoples of the North Caucasus were permitted in 1956 to resume "cultural autonomy" and, early in 1957, were promised a return to their homelands, which were to be restored to their pre-war political and legal status. No mention was made in official statements of the Crimean Tartars and the Volga Germans, who had suffered a like fate.

to the less favorable climate of the Eurasian steppes. In another sense the result was success: Soviet agriculture in 1956 produced the largest grain crop in Russian history, exceeding the previous all-time record of 103,000,000 metric tons in 1955. The number of cattle rose from 64.9 millions in 1954 to 67 millions in 1955, including an increase of cows from 27.5 to 29 millions; of hogs, from 51.1 to 52.1 millions; and of sheep from 117.5 to 124.9 millions. It is probable, four decades after October, that Soviet consumers, urban and rural alike, were eating more and better food than most of them had ever had before.

Soviet factories, mills, and mines, as in earlier years, were more effective in meeting the grandiose targets of rapid industrialization than in satisfying mass demand for housing and consumers' goods. Gigantic apartment projects in most cities, to be sure, were supplying millions of new residential units, some of them hopefully equipped with garages. Clothing, furniture, bicycles, motorcycles, radio and television sets, household utensils and appliances, and even, on a small scale, motor cars, were pouring off assembly lines. Yet the new apartments were scarce and crowded, and many store inventories were inadequate to the desires and buying capacities of their customers, even at prices that still were high despite another price cut on August 1, 1956. Steps were under way to reduce the gap between low and high incomes. On January 1, 1957, the first (and quite modest) Soviet minimum-wage law went into effect, stipulating that no workers was to be paid less than 350 rubles monthly. Plans were made to put all workers on a seven-hour day by 1960. Scales of wages, salaries, and bonuses were simplified and rationalized. The "common man," although better off than previously, was still poor by American or Western European standards. A full abundance of goods and services for the "proletariat" was still "pie in the sky by and by."

But in bone and muscle, if not in fat, the Soviet economy continued its extraordinary growth. Suslov reported in November 1956 that Soviet steel production had increased tenfold since 1929, oil sixfold, and electric power 31 fold. Soviet heavy industry, while still far from the goal of overtaking America's, was moving in swift strides from an over-all level of output approximating one-third of its American counterpart to a level nearer to one-half, thus exceeding the combined totals of all of Western Europe and, indeed, of all of the world's economies outside the USA. The changes of person-

nel in the Gosplan in late 1956 reflected no crisis in Soviet industry
but rather a decision of the Party leadership to "upgrade" the planning function in the interests of greater efficiency and productivity.[2]

How did the power-holders in this prospering community, towering giant-like over Eurasia, cope with new problems posed in relations with the outer world? The "Marxist dialectic," by which Soviet
policy-makers swore as a guide to action, offered no assurance of infallibility and many possibilities of error, some of which were realized. Muscovy's *Realpolitik* objective was, as always, to maximize
Soviet power and to divide and disintegrate the Atlantic alliance by
exploiting its weaknesses and inner contradictions. The far-off divine
event of the Marxist cosmology—i.e., the universalization of Communism through world revolution—could well be deferred to the Greek
Kalends if considerations of expediency, flowing from appreciation
of reality, so dictated.

Moscow's ends, as in previous years, were to win sympathy
abroad in the interest of the security and prestige of the USSR; to
consolidate the Chinese alliance and the Warsaw Pact; to buttress
foreign Communist parties, the better to fulfill their long-standing
function as adjuncts to Soviet diplomacy and propaganda; and to

[2] Following a five-day meeting of the Party Central Committee devoted
to economic problems, the Council of Ministers on December 25, 1956, dismissed Maxim Z. Saburov as Chairman of the State Commission for Current
Planning and replaced him by Mikhail G. Pervukhin, to be aided by Alexei N.
Kosygin and Vyacheslav A. Malyshev as First Deputy Chairmen and by
Mikhail V. Khrunichev, Vladimir A. Kucherenko, Vladimir V. Matskevich, and
Ivan A. Benediktov as Deputy Chairmen. Benediktov had long served as Minis-
ter of State Farms. Matskevich, Minister of Agriculture, who led the Soviet farm
delegation to the USA in 1955, had succeeded Pavel P. Lobanov as a Deputy
Premier in April 1956. Malyshev died early in 1957.

For further light on recent internal developments in the USSR, see Paul
Babitsky and John Rimberg: *The Soviet Film Industry* (Praeger, 1955);
Frederick C. Barghoorn: *Soviet Russian Nationalism* (Oxford University Press,
1956); R. A. Bauer, A. Inkeles, and C. Kluckhohn: *How the Soviet System
Works* (Harvard University Press, 1956); Harold J. Berman and Miroslav
Kerner (eds.): *Documents on Soviet Military Law and Administration* (Har-
vard University Press, 1955); M. Gardner Clark: *The Economics of Soviet Steel*
(Harvard University Press, 1956); David J. Dallin: *The Changing World of
Soviet Russia* (Yale University Press, 1956); Nicholas DeWitt: *Soviet Profes-
sional Manpower: Its Education, Training, and Supply* (National Science Foun-
dation, 1955); Otto Heilbrunn: *The Soviet Secret Services* (Praeger, 1956);
Gerhart Niemeyer and John S. Reshetar, Jr.: *An Inquiry into Soviet Mentality*
(Praeger, 1956); Nicholas Vakar: *Belorussia* (Harvard University Press, 1956);
Alexander Vucinich: *The Soviet Academy of Sciences* (Stanford University Press,
1956); and Bertram D. Wolfe: *Six Keys to the Soviet System* (Beacon Press,
1956).

split and discredit the Western coalition. The means to the ends consisted partly of efforts to negotiate diplomatic settlements in the "Spirit of Geneva" and, in larger part, of attempts to capitalize upon world-wide hopes for "peace" and "disarmament" and to portray the USSR as the champion of Asian-African nationalism against "Western imperialism." The unexpected impact of de-Stalinization upon the Cominform and the satellites engendered the October crises in Warsaw and Budapest, which in turn further demoralized many Communists *in partibus infidelium*. The interrelations and interactions among tangled skeins of events, each woven of a warp of astute high policy and a woof of ghastly blundering, can best be suggested by tracing first the course of Soviet contacts with "bourgeois" States and then considering intramural conflicts among the faithful.[3]

In marked contrast to the achievements of 1955, Soviet diplomacy in 1956 could register to its credit only one enduring accomplishment: an accord with Japan. The initial negotiations in London were broken off in March because of Soviet refusal to consider Tokyo's hopes for recovering Southern Sakhalin and the Kuriles or at least Kunashiri and Etorofu at the southern extremity of the island

[3] On Communist politics and propaganda and on Soviet foreign policy in general in the mid-1950's, see Chester Bowles: *Africa's Challenge to America* (University of California Press, 1956); J. C. Hurewitz: *Diplomacy in the Near and Middle East* (2 vols., Van Nostrand, 1956); John H. Kautsky: *Moscow and the Communist Party of India* (Wiley, 1956); George N. Kahin: *The Asian-African Conference* (Cornell University Press, 1956); Evron M. Kirkpatrick: *Target: The World* (Macmillan, 1956); Klaus Knorr: *The War Potential of Nations* (Princeton University Press, 1956) and *Ruble Diplomacy* (Princeton University Center of International Studies, 1956); Walter Z. Laqueur: *Communism and Nationalism in the Middle East* (Praeger, 1956); George Padmore: *Pan-Africanism or Communism?* (Roy, 1956); Henry L. Roberts: *Russia and America: Dangers and Prospects* (Harper, 1956); Robert Strausz-Hupé *et al.*: *American-Asian Tensions* (Praeger, 1956); Harold M. Vinacke: *Far Eastern Politics in the Post-War Period* (Appleton-Century-Crofts, 1956); and Henry Wei: *China and Soviet Russia* (Van Nostrand, 1956). On Eastern Europe on the eve of the abortive anti-Communist revolutions, see Stefan Brant: *The East German Rising* (Thames and Hudson, 1955); Glorney Bolton: *Czech Tragedy* (Watts, 1955); Alexander Cretzianu (ed.): *Captive Rumania* (Praeger, 1956); Stephen B. Kertesz (ed.): *The Fate of East Central Europe* (University of Notre Dame Press, 1956); Siegfried Kracauer and Paul L. Berkman: *Satellite Mentality* (Praeger, 1956); Anatole G. Mazour: *Finland Between East and West* (Van Nostrand, 1956); Elizabeth Wiskemann: *Germany's Eastern Neighbors* (Oxford University Press, 1956); and Robert L. Wolff: *The Balkans in Our Time* (Harvard University Press, 1956). Cf. also the Russian Institute: *The Anti-Stalin Campaign and International Communism* (Columbia University Press, 1957).

chain. In early August, Foreign Minister Mamoru Shigemitsu was told in Moscow by Bulganin, Khrushchev, and Shepilov that no territorial concessions were possible but that political and economic accords could be negotiated. Tokyo hesitated. Bulganin exchanged letters with Premier Ichiro Hatoyama. On September 25 Sunichi Matsumoto came to the Soviet capital as Special Ambassador. Three days later agreement was reached.

Hatoyama, flying from Copenhagen in a Soviet plane, was met on October 12 by Bulganin, Pervukhin, and Gromyko. On October 19 signatures were attached to a "Peace Declaration" ending the state of war, resuming diplomatic and consular relations, reaffirming the obligations of the Charter, pledging Soviet support for Japanese membership in the UN, providing for the repatriation of Japanese nationals, and renouncing all claims for reparations or war damages. The tiny islands of Habomoi and Shikotan would be transferred to Japan "after the conclusion of a peace treaty." A "Trade Protocol" established reciprocal most-favored-nation treatment. Ratification by the Presidium of the Supreme Soviet was reported by Tass on December 9, 1956.

In dealing with the West, Moscow continued to strive for agreement on reduction of armaments and made further concessions to Western views, only to discover, as before, that Washington, reluctantly followed by Paris and London, had no interest in disarmament beyond lip service and fatuous formulas for "foolproof" inspection schemes. On August 13, 1955, the Council of Ministers nevertheless announced the release from service of 640,000 Soviet troops; plans were revealed on May 4, 1956, to reduce the armed forces by May 1, 1957, by another 1,200,000 men, to disband 63 divisions and brigades, to close several military schools, to put into reserve 375 war vessels, and to cut the military budget by an undisclosed amount. Further reductions were offered if other Powers would reciprocate. Washington was skeptical and unresponsive.

On May 24 Moscow invited Washington to send top Air Force officers to Soviet Aviation Day exercises on June 24. President Eisenhower authorized Air Force Chief of Staff Gen. Nathan F. Twining to attend, but rejected as "impracticable" a Soviet invitation to all the U.S. Joint Chiefs of Staff. Twining and six aides were warmly welcomed on June 23, 1956. They observed four new types of Soviet planes in the air show (which emphasized defensive, rather than offensive, capabilities), toured Stalingrad, visited an atomic plant, and

RUSSIA AND THE FAR EAST

SCALE OF MILES
0   50 100 150 200

U. S. S. R.

SIBERIA

Sea of Okhotsk

PETROPAVLOVSK

KAMCHATKA

PARAMUSHIRU

Okha

Nikolayevsk

Komsomolsk

SAKHALIN

URUPPU

Smirnykh

50

Ilynski

Kholmsk

Yuzhno-Sakhalinsk

ETOROFU

Blagoveschensk

Amur

Khabarovsk

Gornozavodsk

Korsakov

KUNASHIRI

SHIKOTAN

Nunkiang

HABOMAI

Asahigawa

Kushiro

MANCHURIA

Sapporo

HOKKAIDO

Tsitsihar

Otaru

Hakodate

KURILE ISLANDS

Harbin

Mutankiang

Voroshilov

Aomori

Hachinohe

Changchun

Kirin

Vladivostok

Najin

J E H O L

Chungjin

Nigata

Mukden

Sea of Japan

Chinchow

Antung

Wonsan

Pyongyang

38

KOREA

Yokohama

TOKYO

PEKING

Port Arthur

Dairen

Inchon

Seoul

Nagoya

Kyoto

Tientsin

Osaka

Chefoo

Taegu

Pusan

Hiroshima

Wakayama

Masan

Shimonoseki

SHIKOKU

Tsingtao

Mokpo

Sasebo

KYUSHU

Licheng

Nagasaki

Miyasaki

Yellow Sea

Kagoshima

Pacific Ocean

Tungshan

Yangtze R.

Nanking

Shanghai

MONGOLIA

C H I N A

JAPAN

returned on July 4, with Twining darkly warning, as he had done before this journey, that the USSR was rapidly overcoming America's lead in air power.

Eisenhower meanwhile continued his private correspondence with Zhukov and his public correspondence with Bulganin. Zhukov, while touring India early in 1957, hinted that his exchanges with "Ike" were ending. The regular publication of the Eisenhower-Bulganin letters suggested, as always in Great Power relationships, that neither side was trying to negotiate an accord, a feat quite impossible without privacy and secrecy. Both were seeking to influence public attitudes. On January 23, 1956, Bulganin proposed a 20-year American-Soviet pact of friendship, non-aggression, non-intervention, and cooperation. Eisenhower on January 28 amiably rejected the draft treaty and appealed for Soviet acceptance of Western terms for disarmament, "open skies," and German unity. Subsequent exchanges revealed Muscovite ingenuity in impressing uncommitted peoples with the "reasonable" and "constructive" character of Soviet proposals, matched by American ingenuity in evasiveness and irrelevance. Bulganin's suggestions during the U.S. election campaign for a ban on H-Bomb tests, echoing Adlai Stevenson, were rejected as intolerable "interference" in American politics. The exchanges came back to their starting-point at year's end. Bulganin on November 17 proposed limited aerial inspection in a thousand-mile zone in Central Europe and a Five-Power conference, including India, to promote disarmament. Eisenhower on January 3, 1957, expressed "basic disagreement," once more denounced Soviet action in Hungary, and urged further negotiations on disarmament through the UN—where all previous "negotiations" had gotten nowhere. In a year of lost opportunities, another opportunity was here lost.

Soviet cultivation of British "friendship" in the spring was transmuted into Anglo-Soviet enmity in the fall. Again a chance was lost for an accord, thanks to a long heritage of mutual suspicion. In mid-year of 1956 London, Paris, Tel Aviv, and Moscow could conceivably have negotiated an agreement on their respective interests and aspirations in the Middle East. Such an accord would have been acquiesced in, however reluctantly, by the Arab States and by Washington, since no alternative would have been available. Such a bargain could have averted the Suez débâcle and even promoted a sane solution of the Hungarian crisis by demonstrating that the "Great Powers" had a common policy. Conversely, an American-Soviet

agreement on problems of power in the Middle East and Eastern Europe, however distasteful to Britain, France, and Israel and to those who were to attempt revolution in Hungary, would have served the interests of all concerned far better than the anarchy and bloodshed that were to come because of the lack of any Concert of Powers.

The politicians of Moscow, still bewitched by their dogma of anti-capitalism, were incapable of coming to terms with Washington against London and Paris, or with London and Paris against Washington. They preferred to cultivate Arab nationalism against "Western imperialism." The men of Washington, hypnotized by anti-Communism, could not conceive of any bargain with Moscow to liquidate the remnants of Anglo-French "colonialism" in the Middle East, even though this was a shared American-Soviet objective—motivated in Moscow by ideological and strategic considerations and in Washington by solicitude for the interests of American oil corporations, whose billions of investments in the Arab States it sought to make secure by "appeasement" of Arab nationalist fanaticism. Policy-makers in London and Paris, desperate in their resentment at U.S. policy or lack of policy, were yet incapable of striking a bargain with Moscow, thanks to their anti-Communism and their conviction that their security depended upon U.S. support, even when they feebly defied Washington. Such "support," as defined by Dulles and Eisenhower, was mathematically calculated to reduce Britain and France to impotence in the Middle East and to destroy forever their status as "Great Powers."

Amid these confusions, the pattern of irresponsibility in East and West alike in 1956 was comparable to its counterpart in 1936. The results, happily, were less grim. While Col. Nasser, the "Hitler of the Nile," obviously had the will to attempt world conquest, he did not have at his disposal such means as were available to *Führer*, *Duce*, and the Japanese warlords of the 1930's. Stalin, reposing beside Lenin in the marble tomb on Red Square, must have rejoiced in the correctness of his absurd prognosis of 1952 that war among the "bourgeois" States was far more likely than any "capitalistic" war against the USSR.

In this context of impending disorder, unanticipated by all, Bulganin and Khrushchev visited Britain in the spring of 1956. The futility of their endeavors was symbolized by the preliminary arrival in London on March 22 of Gen. Ivan A. Serov to discuss se-

curity arrangements with Scotland Yard. He arrived in a TU-104, a fabulous new jet transport capable of flying 500 miles per hour, inspiring British awe and envy rather than admiration. He was head of the State Security Committee and had had a long career in the MVD. The British press denounced him as "odious," a "Himmler," a "jackal," and a "thug." This inauspicious beginning was followed by Malenkov's three-week tour, ending April 7, which evoked friendly interest and respect, thanks to the ex-Premier's subtlety and suavity. Bulganin and Khrushchev arrived on April 18, occupied the royal suite at Claridge's, and departed on the 27th after much wining, dining, speechmaking, touring, and conferring—all, as matters turned out, to little purpose. The visitors, hailed in India and Burma in 1955 as heroes, were received by the British public without enthusiasm and occasionally with hostility, to which they injudiciously responded with resentment. Farewell addresses and communiqués were filled with platitudes, recording the lack of any concrete agreements apart from plans to increase trade.

Other festive comings and goings turned out, for the most part, to be equally pointless. Mikoyan visited India in March. Mollet and Pineau went to Moscow, May 15–19, 1956, and were content, as were their hosts, with the "vodka circuit" and with vague expressions of "friendship" instead of carefully negotiated and precisely defined accords regarding the matters with respect to which French and Soviet interests were in harmony or in discord. Shepilov went to Cairo on June 16, to Athens on June 28, and home on July 1. He affirmed Soviet-Egyptian amity, but denied reports of Soviet plans to build the Aswan Dam. The Shah of Iran arrived in Moscow, June 25. Ekaterina Furtseva was in London in July and in Italy in November. In mid-September, Mikoyan attended the 8th Congress of the Chinese Communist Party in Peiping. President Kuwatly of Syria visited Moscow on November 4. Few tangible results came from these travels save a $100,000,000 Soviet loan to Indonesia in the wake of President Sukarno's fortnight in Sovietland in September.

The qualities of statesmanship required to avert threatening calamities were conspicuous by their absence in all capitals, including Moscow, in the summer of 1956. The "Cold War" was ended. But the chance thus offered to negotiate a general East-West settlement, as Churchill had long urged, was sacrificed on the altars of suspicion, prejudice, and grievous miscalculation. Therefore the "Cold War," was soon to be resumed. Even prior to its resumption,

the course of East-West relations was characterized by the customary incidents, recriminations, and absurdities typical of previous years.[4]

[4] The most recent "cloak-and-dagger" episodes, still being multiplied as these pages went to press, are too numerous to recount. But, for the record, the major incidents of 1956 were as follows: Moscow in March, departing from precedent, paid Washington $724,947.68 as half the cost of the shooting-down of a Navy Neptune bomber over the Bering Sea on June 22, 1955. Meanwhile, on February 5 and thereafter the USSR accused Turkey and the USA of sending radio-equipped photographic balloons across Soviet frontiers in an attempt at "aerial inspection" without permission. Following initial denials, Washington on February 8 agreed to halt the launching of weather balloons from West Germany and Turkey. In a public display of captured equipment, Moscow insisted that their purpose was espionage, not meteorological research, and further protested, as a violation of sovereignty and a peril to air navigation, the launching of "Crusade for Freedom" propaganda balloons from West Germany. On May 14 and July 10 Ambassador Georgi N. Zaroubin protested alleged incursions by U.S. aircraft over Soviet territory. Washington rejected the charges as fabrications.

Incidents involving persons aroused wider public attention. On February 11, 1956, Donald Maclean and Guy Burgess, senior officials of the British Foreign Office who vanished in May 1951, reappeared in a Moscow hotel to meet the press. They conceded that they had been Communists in Cambridge, denied they had ever been Soviet agents, and explained their defection in terms of a desire to promote East-West understanding, an objective which they held had not been "seriously pursued" by Anglo-American policy-makers.

On April 7, five of nine Soviet seamen from the tanker Tuapse, seized off Formosa by Chinese Nationalists in June 1954 and subsequently granted "asylum" in the USA, departed for home, thus marking another apparent victory for the Soviet campaign to reconvert defectors. On April 25 the State Department expelled Alexander K. Guryanov and Nicholai Turkin, members of the Soviet delegation to the UN, on the ground that their activities in connection with the seamen had been "improper." The five sailors in Moscow charged that American authorities had sought to bar their departure. The remaining four sailors in the USA charged that their colleagues had not returned "voluntarily." Amid these exchanges, Soviet officials in Berlin on April 23 showed newsmen a tunnel they had discovered from the American to the Soviet sector, allegedly built to enable U.S. intelligence agents to tap East Berlin telephone cables.

During the Bulganin-Khrushchev visit to Britain, Commander Lionel Crabb, a British frogman, lost his life while engaged in underwater operations in Portsmouth Harbor near the Soviet cruiser *Ordjonikidze*. A Soviet protest of May 4 evoked British official denial of the fact, then denial of responsibility, and finally an apology and expression of "regret," coupled with the comment that Crabb's action was unauthorized and unknown to the Cabinet.

Life was made livelier by the arrest in London on August 29, 1956, of Nina Ponomareva, 27-year old, 210-pound discus-throwing champion with the Soviet Olympic track team. She was accused of stealing five hats, worth $4.68, in a chain store on Oxford Street. In the sequel, athletic meets were canceled, the Bolshoi Ballet threatened not to come to London, notes were exchanged, diplomats conferred, and indignation meetings were held. The lady, long in

In what followed, Washington and Moscow became competitors in errors of judgment. In his courtship of Arab favor, Secretary
of State John Foster Dulles denied arms to Israel, acquiesced in the
Egyptian blockade and murder raids against the Israelis, and pressed
Britain to abandon its bases and garrisons in the Suez Canal Zone—
with an accord to this effect concluded in 1954 and the last British
troops departing in mid-June 1956. In his "pactomania" or single-
minded conviction that the challenge of Communism could best be
met by military alliances, he concocted devices to "save the Middle
East" following his journey to the area in the spring of 1953. Turkey
and Pakistan, and then Turkey and Iraq (February 24, 1955), were
persuaded to sign military accords. Britain, Iran, and Iraq subsequently joined the cause, finally embodied in the Baghdad Pact of
November 22, 1955. Four Moslem Premiers, plus Harold Macmillan,
then British Foreign Secretary, solemnly declared their intention "to
work in full partnership and with united purpose for peace and security in the Middle East, to defend their territories against aggression or subversion, and to promote the welfare and prosperity of the
peoples of that region." The USA refused to become a signatory, lest
Arab critics be offended.

This feckless formula, designed to unite all the Middle Eastern
States in an alliance against the USSR—which was in no way threatening the area and had little interest in, or influence among, its
peoples or governments—had paradoxical consequences. Since all
the Arab States, save Iraq, were committed to "neutralism" in the
East-West struggle, all took counter-measures against the Baghdad
Pact. Egypt and Syria cultivated Moscow and bought arms from the
Soviet bloc. Russian policy-makers, seldom slow to take advantage of
the blunders of their rivals, championed Arab "independence,"
adopted an anti-Israeli orientation by way of cultivating Arab

---

hiding, appeared before a London court, pleaded "not guilty," was found
guilty of shoplifting, was freed on payment of three guineas, and sailed at
once for home. Meanwhile, 2½-year-old Tanya Chwastov, claimed as a citizen
by both the USSR and the USA, aroused an international furor of only slightly
smaller proportions. The father, Alexei, having resolved to return to the USSR,
successfully hid the child on the *Queen Mary* in New York harbor despite efforts
by the U.S. Immigration Service to locate and detain her. The mother, now
Mrs. George Dieczok, received official support from Washington in her attempts
to recover Tanya. Father and daughter reached London October 9. On October
12, 1956, she was taken off the Soviet ship *Molotov* on the basis of a British
court order and sent back to the USA, amid American satisfaction and Soviet
indignation.

amity, and vastly enhanced Communist prestige throughout the Levant. Dulles offered, and then withdrew, U.S. aid for construction of the Aswan Dam. When Nasser in retaliation "nationalized" the Suez Canal on July 26, 1956, Downing Street and the Quai d'Orsey moved to protect their vital interest in international control of, and unimpeded traffic through, the waterway that was the channel for most imports and exports between Europe, Asia, and Africa and for indispensable shipments of oil to Western Europe.

When Nasser proved recalcitrant, Dulles dedicated himself to restraining London and Paris from any remedial action. By October, French Socialists (because of their hopeless war against the Algerian rebels, supported and armed from Egypt), British Tories (because of their conviction that all British power in the Middle East would be ended by acquiescence in Nasser's outrages), and Israeli Zionists (because of their knowledge that Nasser was resolved to destroy Israel once he had accumulated sufficient arms) were all of one mind: Nasser must be "cut down to size" by a "preventive war" in defiance of the USA, the USSR, and the UN.

Moscow's role in the tedious and futile negotiations of the summer was conciliatory. Soviet intelligence services were evidently more competent than those of the USA. Official Washington professed astonishment and resentment at knowing nothing in advance of the Anglo-French-Israeli plans. As early as September 15 Moscow publicly accused Paris and London of plotting to seize the Canal in "an act of aggression" against Egypt in violation of the UN Charter, with prospective "irreparable damage" to the waterway and to the cause of peace, while Tass (September 21) asserted that Israel was seeking "maximum profit" from the conflict and might serve as the springboard for an invasion of Egypt. But if Washington had neither any policy, nor any knowledge of the extremities to which its conduct had pushed its allies, Moscow, with knowledge, also had no policy beyond capitalizing upon the mistakes of the Western Powers. The men of Moscow, moreover, were meanwhile entangled in the unforeseen consequences of "de-Stalinization," which exploded in their faces simultaneously with the outbreak of violence in the Middle East.

Menace from without begets unity within. The waning of the "Cold War" and the relaxation of Stalinist techniques of terror fed a rising yeast of discontent in all the satellites, as already shown by

the East German riots of June 17, 1953. Even in the USSR the processes of de-Stalinization begot violence in Tiflis on March 9, 1956,
with a loss of life of uncertain proportions. In late June and early
July, Polish workers, long weary of alien domination and exploitation and now hopeful of achieving a new dispensation, fought Communist police and troops in Poznan and other Polish cities and
yielded only to *force majeure* after many casualties. In what followed, Rumanians, Bulgarians, and Albanians remained quiescent
while, in a current Warsaw witticism, "Hungarians acted like Poles,
Poles acted like Czechs, and Czechs acted like pigs." The surging
tide of revolution in Poland, restrained from futile mass violence by
the wisdom of the Polish Communist leaders and by Stefan Cardinal
Wyszynski's pleas for order and moderation, led the Party Central
Committee on October 20 to restore to membership Wladyslaw Gomulka, ousted in 1947 and jailed as a "Titoist" in 1951.

On the same day Khrushchev, Zhukov, Molotov, Mikoyan, and
Kaganovich arrived in Warsaw as Soviet troops maneuvered in an
apparent effort to forestall any triumph of "National Communism."
Precisely what was said and done is still unknown. Jozef Cyrankiewicz remained Premier. But Gomulka's admission to, and Rokossovsky's exclusion from, the new Politburo was a portent, emphasized
by Gomulka's restoration to the decisive post of First Secretary of
the Party. The Muscovites, whatever threats they may have made,
finally accepted a new order in Poland. Rokossovsky, symbol of Soviet domination, returned to Russia on October 28 and was replaced
as Polish Minister of Defense on November 13 by Gomulka's colleague in earlier disgrace, Gen. Marian Spychalski. In later negotiations Moscow came to terms with the new "Titoist" Polish regime,
still Communist-ruled but liberalized and no longer controlled from
the USSR. Debts were remitted. Credits and grants of grain were
extended. Soviet troops in Poland were restricted. In short, a new
and viable pattern of Soviet-satellite relationships seemed in process
of emerging from the Polish crisis.

The shape of things to come was quite otherwise in Hungary,
where local patriots—some of them deluded over the years by promises or implications of "liberation" broadcast by the Voice of America and Radio Free Europe, operated from Munich by the "Crusade
for Freedom"—vainly essayed a total revolution by violence against
Communist rule. What transpired in the land of the Magyars is inseparable from earlier Muscovite efforts to achieve a *modus vivendi*

with Tito, symbol of "National Communism" independent of Moscow.

On April 17, 1956, the Central Committees of the Communist Parties of the USSR, Poland, Czechoslovakia, Hungary, Rumania, Bulgaria, Italy, and France jointly decreed the dissolution of the Cominform as having "exhausted its uses" under changed conditions. This regional Comintern, which had "expelled" Tito as a schismatic in 1948 under Stalin's delusion that Tito could readily be disposed of, thus readmitted him to the fold and dissolved itself in proof of repentance and in hope of reconciliation. Tito had meanwhile obtained almost a billion dollars from America, while Moscow had extended long-term credits to other Communist countries, chiefly for industrialization, to the amount of 21 billion rubles. The policy-makers of both the Super-Powers, all "materialists" in their divergent ways, were evidently persuaded that every man has his price. Many do. But fanatics never do. Such devoted souls always put "principle" above advantage and sometimes above life itself. Eastern Europe and the Middle East were both seething in 1956 with the fanaticism of nationalism.

Tito arrived in Moscow on June 1, enjoyed a gala performance in his honor at the Bolshoi, and departed on June 20, 1956, after a trip to Stalingrad. His joy in the journey was enhanced by Molotov's resignation as Foreign Minister on the day of Tito's arrival in favor of 51-year-old Dmitri Trofimovich Shepilov. The new incumbent, son of a Don metal worker and a 1926 graduate of Moscow State University, was tall, burly, handsome, and charming. After serving as a local prosecutor and agricultural student, editor, teacher, and Major General (Deputy Chief of Agitation and Propaganda for the Armed Forces in World War II), he became chief editor of *Pravda* in 1952. This representative of the "new man" among the Soviet elite was without previous diplomatic experience, aside from having joined Bulganin and Khrushchev on various missions abroad in 1954–5 while the veteran Molotov was ignored. (Molotov was named Minister of State Control, November 22, 1956; the import of the appointment was uncertain because of the ambiguities of its duties.) Shepilov's promotion in the context of Tito's advent suggested that he was believed by the top Party leaders to possess some special talent for coming to terms with schismatics, heretics, and dissidents within the Red Empire. No such talent was displayed in his activities, as publicly recorded, during 1956.

At the close of the Tito-Kardelj visit a joint communiqué of June 20 bespoke friendship, "common aims" and "mutual understanding," and espoused peace, disarmament, coexistence, Red China's entry into the UN, and German unity only through negotiations between the two German States. Economic and cultural contacts would be enlarged. Cooperation between the Soviet and Jugoslav parties would henceforth be based on "complete freedom of will and equality, on friendly criticism, and on the comradely character" of controversies, all on the premise that "the roads and conditions of socialist development are different in different countries."

In a further effort to reorder relations among the faithful and resolve confusions among the comrades abroad, the Central Committee of the CPSU drafted in late June, and released on July 2, a lengthy "Marxist-Leninist" exposition of the new orientation. Khrushchev's indictment of Stalin was reiterated. The abuses of the "cult of personality" were attributed to "conditions of enemy encirclement and a constant threat of attack from without." This menace, coupled with "the successes of socialist construction," had made any action against Stalin impossible, since it "would not have been understood by the people." Yet the view that Stalin's crimes were attributable to the Soviet social order or to its "degeneration," as alleged by Togliatti, was "absolutely wrong." "The 20th Congress indicated that the most important feature of our era is the conversion of socialism into a world system. The most difficult period is behind us." The resolution ended with a new attack upon American "cold warriors" and "imperialists" and an expression of confidence in Communist solidarity and the inevitable global triumph of Marxism-Leninism.

The most difficult period lay ahead. Such verbalizations, while not unimpressive to "hard-shelled" Communist converts imbued with a will to believe, had little effect upon doubters within the ranks and none upon the non-Communists and anti-Communists whose hopes of freedom, particularly in Hungary, rose week by week with each new piece of evidence that their Marxist masters were quarreling among themselves. Khrushchev appeared mysteriously in Jugoslavia, "on vacation," on September 18. Ten days later Tito conferred at Yalta with Khrushchev, Bulganin, and Erno Gero from Budapest. At month's end Belgrade revealed that the Central Committee of the CPSU had again warned other Eastern parties against "Titoism" and

that the recent parleys concerned "ideological differences" not unrelated, we may assume, to growing tensions in Hungary.

The sequel was interpreted by most Americans and many West Europeans as a heroic struggle against "tyranny" and for "democracy" by the Hungarian people. All Communists still faithful to Moscow interpreted it as an abortive effort by "Fascists" and "subversive" agents of "Western imperialism" to destroy the Danubian "People's Democracy" by force. The truth lay somewhere between— if truth can ever be arrived at in efforts to comprehend the irrationalities and brutalities of men. Magyar patriotic traditions included fanatical revolt against alien rule, best exemplified by Louis Kossuth's ill-fated revolutionary "Republic" of 1849, also suppressed by Russian troops. They included no legacy of democracy. The thousand-year-old feudal kingdom of Hungary, united with Austria in the Dual Monarchy of 1867–1918, suffered the Communist dictatorship of Bela Kun in 1919 and then passively acquiesced for decades in the Fascist dictatorship of Regent Nicholas Horthy (in 1956 an 88-year-old exile in Portugal), who came to power amid the "White Terror" of 1920 and delivered Hungary to Hitler during World War II. During the past several centuries Hungary had enjoyed democratic government not longer than a total of five years and this only during spasmodic and ephemeral interludes between various types of despotism. In the middle decades of the 20th Century Hungary, no less than Poland and the Balkan States, was condemned by the balance of forces within, and by implacable pressures from without, to choose between Fascism and Communism as alternative forms of dictatorship. Western and Soviet preferences between these options could scarcely be expected to coincide.

The immediate background of the disaster to come is worth noting, if only as illustrative of the dilemmas confronting Communist power-holders in the era of de-Stalinization and "peaceful coexistence." Premier Imry Nagy's "new course" had been denounced as "Titoism" and "Right Deviationism" by veteran Party boss, Matyas Rakosi. Nagy had been ousted from the Premiership in favor of Andres Hegedus on April 18, 1955, and later expelled from the Party. Stalinist Rakosi nonetheless felt obliged in March 1956 to "rehabilitate" Lazlo Rajk, Andras Szalai, Tibor Szoenyi, and Gyorgy Pallfy (all hanged for "treason" and "Titoism" on October 15, 1949, on Rakosi's orders), along with Bela Kun, purged in Russia in the

1930's. Early in October 200,000 people marched by the coffins in Budapest's central cemetery in a ritual designed to demonstrate the Cabinet's concern for "justice" but having the effect of discrediting the regime. Meanwhile, Rakosi made sundry "concessions," all too little and too late, and, under popular pressure, finally resigned as First Secretary of the Party on July 18, 1956, in favor of Erno Gero, who bespoke reconciliation with Tito and "no Poznans here."

On the advice of Mikoyan, on his way to Jugoslavia, the Polit-buro presently released from jail and readmitted to its ranks several former "Titoists," including Janos Kadar. Other concessions and re-shuffles proved vain. Between October 15 and 23 Gero, Hegedus, Kadar, and other leaders were in Belgrade, where they espoused "cooperation" and "friendly relations" with Tito's regime. During their absence Hungarian students organized mass demonstrations to demand freedom of the press, abolition of capital punishment, and, finally, the restoration of Imry Nagy as Premier, the punishment of Rakosi, the freeing of Cardinal Mindszenty, and the withdrawal of Soviet troops. The young intellectuals, whom the Communists had flattered, pampered, and regimented, and the workers, in whose name the Communists purported to rule, were in the forefront of rebellion, thereby demonstrating anew that the "dictatorship of the proletariat" as a façade for the rule of an intellectual elite was often deemed abominable by intellectuals and proletarians alike.

On October 23 mobs in Budapest demolished Stalin's statue, tore down the red star atop the parliament building, and in the eve-ning sought to storm the radio station from which Gero had just spoken. First blood was shed when the Security Police (AVO) opened fire. There ensued a popular uprising, apparently without central leadership, direction, or purpose, marked by book-burning, the murder of many of the hated Security Policemen, the defection to the rebels of many units of the Hungarian Army, and the indis-criminate killing of Jews and Communists by hooligans and mob-sters. In the early morning hours of October 24 the panic-stricken "rulers" of Hungary promised concessions and named Imry Nagy as Premier. He and Gero summoned Soviet troops to crush the rebels. On October 25 Suslov and Mikoyan arrived from Moscow as Russian forces mowed down demonstrators and bombarded factories and apartment buildings. Gero, later reported killed, gave way to Kadar as First Secretary of the Party. Kadar promised to negotiate for the withdrawal of Soviet forces as soon as order should be restored.

The men of Moscow, faced with anarchy on the Danube, were evidently prepared (unless their gestures be interpreted as hypocrisy) to swallow, as the lesser evil, a drastic alteration of their relations with Hungary, including acceptance of a non-Communist coalition and perhaps of an anti-Communist regime. On October 29–30 they announced their willingness to withdraw Soviet troops from Hungary and the other Warsaw Pact States. What course of belated concessions they were ready to pursue may never be known, thanks to new events in Budapest and in Egypt which led them, in new fear, to a wholly different decision.

The events in Budapest were these: while Bishop Groesz appealed for peace, Cardinal Mindszenty, freed by rebels on October 31, lauded the insurgents, appealed for Western aid, and hinted at his availability as head of an anti-Communist regime. The frantic Nagy, in hope of causing the rebels to lay down their arms, told the Soviet Ambassador on November 1 that the new Hungary was denouncing the Warsaw Pact, asking Western help, soliciting intervention by the UN, and demanding the immediate evacuation of all Soviet troops. As for Egypt, the Israeli Army on October 29 launched a massive invasion of the Sinai Peninsula in obvious connivance (despite denials) with Anglo-French policy-makers, who, following rejection of an ultimatum, began bombarding Egyptian airports on November 1 and prepared to seize the Suez Canal. Faced with the prospect of an anti-Soviet regime in Hungary and of open warfare in the Middle East, the policy-makers of Moscow decided to crush the Hungarian revolution by force.

Few decisions in Soviet history could have been more painful than the one here taken. The members of the Party Presidium well knew that what they were about to do would alienate many Western Communists, already confused by the weird politics of de-Stalinization, and would "throw onto the garbage heap of history" (to use a favorite Communist phrase) all of the Western and much of the "neutralist" good will they had so painfully cultivated since 1953. But, as so often, Soviet strategic interests were deemed paramount over all considerations of international Communist solidarity or Western "friendship."

What ensued in Egypt must be left to others to recount elsewhere. Let it only be noted that the Israeli invasion was brilliantly executed and that the soldiery of the new Zion, if left to their own devices, could doubtless have occupied the Canal before Nasser

wrecked it, taken Cairo, and ousted the "Hitler of the Nile"; that
Anglo-French policy, aimed at keeping the Canal open, ousting
Nasser, and reducing Soviet influence in the Middle East, led to the
closing of the Canal, the apotheosis of Nasser into a martyr and
hero, and a vast enhancement of Soviet influence; that Anglo-French
diplomacy and strategy, measured by the disastrous consequences of
total mismanagement, constituted a final demonstration that France
and Britain were no longer "Great Powers"; that Eisenhower and
Dulles, motivated by hopes of appeasing Arab nationalism and by
devotion to "legalistic-moralistic abstractions," consigned America's
major allies to helplessness through threats and pressures and
through complete solidarity in the UN Assembly with the Soviet
and Arab-Asian blocs in condemning Israeli-Anglo-French "aggression"; that London and Paris, thus menaced from Washington, ignominiously abandoned (November 6), on the eve of partial success, a
mistaken enterprise whose abandonment made it no longer a mistake but an irreparable calamity; that the Muscovite threat to send
"volunteers" to Egypt was an idle bluff, since no such forces could
have arrived at their destination without traversing waterways controlled by hostile Powers or violating the territory or air space of
intervening States and thereby inviting a world war—the last thing
the Soviet leaders were prepared to risk; and that the net result of
the ubiquitous political follies of 1956, embellished by a raucous
counterpoint in which all pots called all kettles black, was the disruption of the Atlantic alliance (despite verbiage to the contrary),
unaccompanied by any comparable collapse of the Soviet bloc, despite inner tensions, the demonstrated unreliability of satellite armies, and the discrediting and partial disintegration of Communist
Parties in Western Europe. In 1956, as in 1849, the USA could do
no more to "liberate" Hungary than pass resolutions and welcome
fugitives. Washington was wholly incapable of compelling Moscow
to abide by the rules of "morality" which it sought to impose upon
Tel Aviv, Paris, and London.[5]

　　Confronted with the spectacle of violence in the Levant, the
rulers of Muscovy emitted cries of outrage, blustered and postured
as heroic defenders of an innocent Egypt against the wicked Anglo-

[5] See Hans J. Morgenthau: "The Decline and Fall of American Foreign
Policy" in the *New Republic*, December 7 and 13, 1956; Louis Halle: "A
Touch of Nausea" in the same journal, January 21, 1957; and this writer's
letter in *The Nation*, December 22, 1956.

French "imperialists," and issued orders to do what they deemed necessary on the Danube. At dawn of Sunday morning, November 4, 1956, thousands of Soviet tanks moved into Budapest and other Magyar cities. All opposition was pitilessly smashed. Pathetic rebel appeals for Western aid elicited no response save sympathy and shouts of "Murder!" The Nagy Cabinet was suppressed. The luckless Premier, long a fugitive in the Jugoslav Legation, was ultimately deported to Rumania despite protests from Belgrade at violation of a promise of "safe-conduct" to his home. The Cardinal sought safety in the U.S. Legation. A new "Revolutionary Workers' and Peasants' Government" headed by Kadar acquiesced in the flight of 175,000 refugees to Austria and thence to other lands (with a conscience-stricken America generously supporting the escapees) and strove to restore order by a combination of concessions and repressions, while rejecting all proposals for UN "observers."

How many perished is uncertain. Budapest acknowledged 2,000 dead. Nehru, relying on reports by Ambassador K. P. S. Menon, who shuttled between Moscow and Budapest during the rebellion, calculated that 25,000 Magyars and 7,000 Russians had been slain. This estimate was undoubtedly exaggerated, perhaps by a factor of ten. The abortive attack upon Egypt probably sacrificed more lives than were lost in Hungary. And the French war in Algeria was far more costly in blood. The French Army boasted of killing 18,000 rebels in 1956 alone. The Hungarian martyrs aroused fierce anti-Soviet indignation throughout the Western world and evoked few echoes elsewhere. The Algerian victims of French arms elicited only mild regret in the West, but stirred millions to indignation throughout the Arab-Asian lands. Here, as always, moral indignation at man's inhumanity to man is a matter of whose ox is gored.

In the dismal dawn of 1957 the oligarchs of Sovietland were troubled and puzzled men. The Communist coalition, thanks to the Muscovite mailed fist, was still intact on paper. Yet all now knew that the satellite armies were not assets but liabilities for the USSR; that without radical reforms and a reordering of relationships within and among the States of the marchlands and between each and all and the Soviet Union, the carapace wrought by Stalin would inexorably disintegrate; and that the tasks of building a viable new order between the Baltic and the Adriatic, like those of liberalizing the Soviet State at home, were barely begun. Chou En-lai's January journey of good will, reconciliation, and new unity, taking him from

Rangoon, New Delhi, and Karachi to Moscow, Warsaw, and Budapest, offered a possible promise of progress.

Some comfort, albeit cold, could be derived by the masters of
Muscovy from the spectacle of even greater disorder and confusion
in the Atlantic alliance. France remained paralyzed by the never-
ending fighting in Algeria. Both France and Britain, where an ailing
and discredited Eden stepped down as Prime Minister in favor of
Harold Macmillan on January 10, 1957, were more than ever dependent upon an America whose President continued to rely upon
an ailing and discredited Dulles—wholly distrusted and cordially
hated by Downing Street and the Quai d'Orsay. Helpless in Hungary
and having no policy designed to halt continuing violence in Cyprus
and Algeria or to forestall a recurrence of violence in Egypt and Israel, Washington policy-makers retreated to the musty formulas of
the "Cold War," based on the demonstrably false premise that the
Communist challenge could best be met by more military alliances
—after existing ones had proven illusory and self-defeating. In asking Congress to embrace the "Eisenhower Doctrine," the President
of the United States was proposing irrelevant means to meet a non-
existent danger in a patent evasion of the real problems of the Middle East.[6]

[6] On January 5, 1957, in a warmed-up version of the Truman Doctrine
of March 12, 1947, and the Formosa Resolution of January 24, 1955, the President asked Congress for authorization to "undertake, in the general area of the
Middle East, military assistance programs with any nation or group of nations
of that area desiring such assistance. Furthermore, he is authorized to employ
the armed forces of the United States as he deems necessary to secure and
protect the territorial integrity and political independence of any such nation
or group of nations requesting such aid against overt armed aggression from any
nation controlled by international Communism. . . ." Expenditures of $200,-
000,000 a year for military and economic aid to such Middle East nations were
contemplated. The problems and conflicts of the area, notably the status of the
Canal and the reiterated resolve of the Arab States to destroy Israel, had no
relationship to any threat of Communist aggression. Nothing was less likely
than any Soviet military attack unless it might be American military intervention against renewed aggression by the Arab States or by Israel or by France
and Britain, none of which could be regarded by the remotest stretching of
the imagination as "controlled by international Communism." The new "doctrine" was thus meaningless and was perfectly calculated not to reduce but to
increase Soviet influence throughout the region, as the disastrous Baghdad
Pact had already done.

Dean Acheson aptly described the purpose of the doctrine: "To fight an
enemy that is not going to attack with forces that do not exist to carry out a
policy you have not yet decided upon." Moscow's response to this new challenge
in the renewed "Cold War" was adroit. On February 11, 1957, Shepilov deliv-

Under these circumstances the men of Moscow could confidently look forward to new rifts in the Western coalition, flowing from new miscalculations, and to fresh opportunities to influence people and win friends in the Middle East and to embarrass and befuddle the Western Powers. But the advantages to be derived by the USSR from the failures of Western statesmanship were negative, ephemeral, and hazardous. They could contribute nothing toward a restoration of unity within the Communist bloc unless a new image could be persuasively projected throughout Eurasia of a unified coalition of "Western imperialists" poised to assault the East. What was imperatively demanded by the facts of the present and the opportunities of the future was the over-all East-West bargain or settlement in Central Europe and the Middle East alike which Churchill had been vainly calling for since 1946. The new possibilities that opened in 1953 for negotiating such a settlement had been dissipated in empty verbiage. Early in 1957 no influential voices were raised in the West in favor of serious negotiations. Without such a settlement, further confusion and chaos were inevitable.

The men of Moscow, wiser in such matters from painful experience than the men of Washington, perceived the need of returning to diplomacy in order to recapture, if possible, the wasted opportunities of 1953–5. On February 15, 1957, following a two-day meeting of the Party Central Committee, Shepilov was replaced by Andrei A.

---

ered notes (at once made public) to the U.S., British, and French Ambassadors, proposing a "six-point program" for peace in the Levant. The four Great Powers should pledge themselves to a settlement by way of (1) "exclusively peaceful means on the basis of the method of negotiation"; (2) "non-interference in internal affairs" and "respect for the sovereignty and independence" of all Near and Middle Eastern countries; (3) "refusal to undertake any attempts to draw these countries into military alignments with the participation of the Great Powers"; (4) "the liquidation of foreign bases and the withdrawal of foreign troops"; (5) "joint refusal to supply arms to countries of the Near and Middle East"; and (6) "assistance in economic development . . . without putting forward any political, military, or other conditions incompatible with the dignity or sovereignty of these countries." Three days later Moscow asked the UN Assembly to consider U.S. "aggressive acts constituting a threat to security and peace"—e.g., the Eisenhower Doctrine, new atomic bases abroad, enlarged appropriations for arms, the "militarization" of West Germany, etc.

The appeal to the UN, as expected, was rejected. The "six-point program" was at once dismissed by Washington officialdom as "propaganda." So it was. Yet it was shrewdly calculated to make a powerful appeal, as in fact it did, to all Arab-Asian "neutralist" leaders, and to embarrass an America which, early in 1957, had no policy for dealing with the issues of the hour except more military alliances against a non-existent threat of Communist aggression.

Gromyko as Soviet Foreign Minister. Shepilov, whose skills were those of a publicist and propagandist, resumed work in the Party Secretariat. Gromyko, a career diplomat who shared honors with Molotov for negotiating the limited East-West settlements of the early "thaw," despite his record as Stalin's "Nyet"-man in previous years, was obviously expected to find ways and means of renewing negotiations. At the same time F. R. Kozlov, Leningrad Party leader, was named an alternate member of the Party Presidium while Nikolai S. Patolichev became a First Deputy Foreign Minister under Gromyko. The shift did not signify, as some Western commentators currently assumed, a "return to Stalinism." It symbolized a determination by the power-holders in Moscow to attempt a resumption of bargaining, from a position of strength, with the aid of a professional bargainer in the hope of giving to "coexistence" a meaning more concrete than the confusions and tensions of 1956. What was likely to come of this endeavor depended less on Moscow than on Washington—where, in February 1957, old formulas were still preferred to new departures.

In the fortieth year of the Soviet regime the Marxist oligarchs faced the future with many uncertainties and numerous unsolved problems. Their new European "empire" was in jeopardy, not from outer assault but from inner decay and from lack of the vision and foresight needed to give it new form and new prospects of enduring. The many dilemmas posed at home by strivings toward "socialist legality," the "rule of law," and meaningful federalism and democracy were baffling. On the other hand, the global deadlock or stalemate of the coalitions on which peace precariously depended had not been disrupted and seemed likely to persist into the far future. And the fact of the industrialization, urbanization, and education of Russia, as the most mighty and magnificent accomplishment of four decades dedicated to "building socialism," was irrevocable and irreversible.

Russia would long remain the second-greatest industrial Power of the world. Despite all difficulties and dilemmas, its leaders and people, given a modicum of wisdom and patience, could therefore face the future without panic and could entertain reasonable hopes, after infinite deprivations, disasters, follies, and crimes, for a freer and richer life in days to come.

EPILOGUE

A Time for Peace

1. IN SEARCH OF THE GOOD SOCIETY

W HAT SHALL we do to be saved? This timeless question admits of answers on various levels of experience and varying degrees of awareness of the paradox of the human condition. The simple answers of satisfied pigs differ from the complex answers of dissatisfied philosophers. No man's answer is ever wholly persuasive to another. All answers taken together have little in common save that each faces the universal afflictions of suffering and sin and recognizes that the earthly abode of humankind is as often a vale of tears as a garden of joy.

For many "salvation" means an eternity of bliss in a life after death for an immortal soul rescued from damnation by a loving God who gives man moral freedom of choice even as He rewards virtue and punishes vice. For others salvation is defined in secular terms of enriching man's mundane transit here below from cradle to grave, from sperm to worm, from womb to tomb. To these come visions of a polity founded upon love, brotherhood, justice, freedom, and equality (all abstractions admitting of a bewildering variety of meanings) and a society and economy offering to all members a maximum of self-fulfillment in security, peace, and plenty and a minimum of "social injustice," exploitation, oppression, and other variants of the cruelties that humans habitually inflict upon each other.

During the long past of primate experimentation with community life—embracing the life spans of the literate cultures or "civilization" of mankind during the past 7,000 years; the previous 40,000

years, more or less, of non-literate and pre-civilized *Homo Sapiens;* and the much longer life on the planet of *Homo Neanderthalensis* and his precursors—most men and women have found their satisfactions and sense of salvation in unquestioning acceptance of the order of things inherited from their ancestors. Within the walls of such defenses, people can enjoy such pleasures as daily life affords and endure the inevitable pains and griefs of the mortal adventure. In this way lived, during endless millennia, all the peoples of all the "folk cultures" of mankind. So also, as best we can judge from the record, lived most of humanity through many centuries since the advent of "civilization," with each accepting and making the best of his lot as slave, serf, or peon, landlord, soldier, or bureaucrat, merchant, lawyer, or manager. So also lives much of humankind today, though few are wholly untouched by the winds of change and the manifold schemes of a better life spun by reformers and rebels out of star dust and the stuff of dreams.

It is of the essence of Marxism as a "Jewish-Christian heresy," to use Toynbee's perceptive term, that its disciples repudiate the passivity and placidity of times gone by. They assert, as revolutionists, the possibility of a rationally conceived and consciously planned reordering of human relations for the purpose of arriving at self-mastery and self-realization. They profess to seek a more adequate fulfillment in the daily lives of men of the ideals of the good life derived from the Jewish-Greek-Christian tradition. It is the tragedy of Marxism, as of many other systems of belief, that the means deemed necessary and proper to arrive at the goal have, more often than not, been self-defeating and destructive of the ends pursued. This tragedy is age-old. It was known to Ikhnaton and the Hebrew Prophets. It concerned Plato—first among Western thinkers to envisage the possibility of a reasonably contrived "Republic" to be ruled for the good of all by an elite of enlightened guardians and philosopher-kings. It troubled Confucius, Buddha, and Jesus of Nazareth. It worried Alexander of Macedonia, the Cæsars of Rome, and the founders of the Christian church. When blueprints of social salvation become sacrosanct and the means thereto are clothed in the stiff dignity of dogma, the result is less likely to be a creative reformation than a hideous orgy of persecution of infidels and heretics whose resistance to new "truth" is intolerable.

The preceding pages, it is hoped, shed some light on how this came to pass among the Marxists, and particularly among their Rus-

sian converts, whose views of life and society and politics and the world at large were necessarily colored by memories of the Romanov Tsardom, the Grand Duchy of Muscovy, and the Khanate of the Golden Horde. As atheists and agnostics, they repudiated Church and State, God and Tsar. As men in need of faith, as all men are, they dedicated themselves to the worship of Man and to the deliberate fashioning of a new social order. How the enterprise might have proceeded and eventuated had the West left them in peace to pursue their fantasies we can never know. Since they had "declared war" against the West, the West waged war upon them from the outset and intermittently thereafter. The wars of East and West, thus far, have never been wholly won or wholly lost by either contestant. But violence insured that the "building of socialism" in the USSR would be a task of toil and terror, of inspiration and persecution, of devotion and hatred in a struggle for "freedom" from ancient evils waged by methods begetting a new tyranny productive of new abuses.

Whatever other "lessons of history" may be drawn from this undertaking, at once sublime and absurd, one at least is clear: "socialism," contrary to the messianic expectations of its early disciples and of most of its contemporary apostles, is no magic spell for the attainment of social justice, political freedom, equality, brotherhood, and love among men. Quite the contrary would seem to be the case on the basis of Soviet experience. Communal ownership and operation of the "means of production" and centralized political planning of the economy put an end, to be sure, to the exploitation of the "proletariat" by the "bourgeoisie" and to business cycles of "boom" and "bust." But they bring into being new patterns of exploitation and deprivation and new forms of oppression and dehumanization deemed far worse than the old by all who are unconvinced that the end justifies the means, who are skeptical of any ultimate arrival at the Utopian goal of "communism," and who doubt, should the goal ever be reached, that it would make men free.

Four decades after the October Revolution these issues are already stale and have little relevance to human destinies today and tomorrow. The 19th-Century "capitalism" which 19th-Century "socialists" rebelled against no longer exists. Industrialization is now the god of all mankind. Its initial costs are always high in the impoverishment, forced labor, and misery of the masses who must be compelled to produce more than they consume if capital is to be accu-

mulated for investment. The Marx who was outraged by the processes of capital accumulation in the Western Europe of the 1830's and 1840's, under the private auspices of capitalist entrepreneurs dedicated to *laissez faire*, might have been equally outraged a century later by the processes of capital accumulation in the Soviet Union of the 1930's and 1940's, under the public auspices of Communist Commissars dedicated to Marxism. All of this is long since gone in the West, is passing in the USSR, and still lies ahead in China, India, and the other slumlands of the earth where men are determined to achieve industrialization, whatever the cost, as the only means of moving from poverty toward plenty.

Contemporary industrial societies, whether "capitalist" or "socialist," pose comparable problems of management, of recruitment of leadership, of social mobility and conformity, and of production, consumption, saving, and investment. Alexis de Tocqueville in 1839 opined that Russia and America, "starting from different points, tend toward the same end." A century later his prophecy has a new meaning. A lately industrialized, urbanized, and educated Russia confronts an America long since educated, urbanized, and industrialized. These common conditions of community life, despite all ideological and institutional differences, have already produced a degree of "cultural convergence," to resort to the vocabulary of the anthropologists, which is only dimly appreciated in either the USSR or the USA. In the name of Marxism, Soviet power-holders, bent upon achieving a prosperous industrial economy, have long ago adopted the "capitalistic" devices of piece work, sharp differentials of income, Taylorism (Stakhanovism), payment of interest on bonds and bank accounts, rewards for profit-making, and innumerable other incentives for enhanced productivity and increased savings. In the name of "People's Capitalism," the rulers of America, bent upon maintaining a prosperous industrial economy and aided in their endeavors by the imperatives of war and of the "Welfare State," have long ago adopted the "socialist" devices of social security, drastic taxation, huge public spending, governmental control of prices and wages, and public planning of the economy.[1]

[1] From the data available from the U.S. Department of Commerce and the *Federal Reserve Bulletin*, the new dynamics of the American economy are plain for all with eyes to see. In a gross national product in 1929 of $104 billions, personal consumption accounted for $78 billions, private investment for 16, and government purchases of goods and services for 8. By 1933, at the nadir of the Depression, these items *seriatim* stood at 46, 1, and 8 in a gross

Remaining distinctions between the two systems, to be sure, should not be ignored or minimized. Prosperity in America is dependent upon a slow but steady inflation of prices. Prosperity in Russia is dependent upon a slow but steady deflation of prices. No one in the USSR can live a life of leisure by virtue of ownership of rent-producing property, or of corporate stocks and bonds, even though some members of the economic elite derive substantial income from royalties, bank accounts, and State Bonds. Few among the poor in America can become millionaires through hard work and demonstrated productive or managerial competence, though some can achieve the coveted status through shrewd investment or speculation. But similarities outweigh differences. Beginning with a centralized managerial bureaucracy, insistent upon conformity and uncritical obedience from lesser executives and workers at the bench, the economic planners of the USSR are now striving to encourage individual initiative, local autonomy, and decentralization of managerial functions. Beginning with decentralization, local autonomy, and individual initiative, American corporate business now strives for obedience and conformity and a centralized managerial bureaucracy.[2]

Only a rash prophet would venture to forecast that the two systems of business will be indistinguishable by 1984 or some earlier date. Yet the trends of change in each are making them more and more alike, institutionally and behavioristically, despite persisting

---

national product of $55 billions. After two decades of pre-war, war-time, and post-war boom, the same items in 1955 constituted 255, 59, and 75 billions in a gross national product of $387 billions. The "government sector" of the economy thus represented less than 8% of all transactions in 1929 and 20% in 1955. Advance estimates for 1957 postulated a gross national product of $425 billions, of which purchases of goods and services for private investment would represent 15% of the total and government purchases over 20%. In President Eisenhower's projected federal budget of almost $72 billions for 1957–8, 75% of the items, directly or indirectly, represented costs of past, present, and future wars. For a perceptive running analysis of the American transition to "socialism" via military spending and creeping inflation, see Lawrence Dennis's bimonthly bulletin, *The Appeal to Reason* (Becket, Mass.).

[2] On various aspects of these American transformations, whose counterparts in the USSR have been discussed in the preceding pages, see C. Wright Mills: *The Power Elite* (Oxford University Press, 1956); William H. Whyte, Jr.: *The Organization Man* (Simon & Schuster, 1956); and various studies in *Fortune* magazine. The fall 1956 issue of *Dissent* contains illuminating articles on some of these changes by Harold Rosenberg, John Strachey, Michael Reagan, Paul Mattick, and others. See also the *Monthly Review*, edited by Leo Huberman and Paul M. Sweezy, and Russell Lynes: *A Surfeit of Honey* (Harper, 1956).

divergencies in creeds and public professions of purpose. In both communities time-honored semantic devices of indoctrination are tangential to the facts of power and the new realities of economic management, social stratification, and the daily experiences of many-millioned multitudes in coping with problems of earning bread-and-butter and "keeping up with the Joneses" or the Ivanoviches.

Given these circumstances, each may learn from the other to the advantage of both. Quite apart from science and technology, where the gains to be derived from a sharing of knowledge are obvious, each might learn much of value from the efforts of the other to cope with the problems of a dehumanized and impersonal mass industrial society: *anomie* or loss of faith; the transition, in David Riesman's language, from "tradition-directed" to "inner-directed" to "other-directed" patterns of motivation; the stultifying tyranny of "conformism"; the disturbing manifestations of rebellion—e.g., juvenile delinquency, adult crime, racketeering, graft, alcoholism, family disorganization, and an apparently growing incidence of hypertension, psychosomatic diseases, neuroses, and psychoses. These "social problems" are common to America and Russia in the 1950's. Also common are the managerial problems implicit in Big Government, whether democratic or oligarchic, and in Big Business, whether privately owned or socialized.

Russians could profit greatly by availing themselves of accumulated American wisdom in the politics and economics of federalism and in the science of public administration, particularly as exemplified in federal grants-in-aid, the city-manager movement, the "civil-service" tradition, and new departures in state and local government. America and Western Europe could profit from a reconsideration of crazy-quilt patterns of taxation, involving confiscatory levies on high incomes, in the light of the relatively simple and painless Soviet device of raising revenues through the turnover tax. Other instances will come readily to mind among those familiar with Soviet and American fiscal and administrative practices and with the similar problems of human engineering confronting both communities.

These convergences, with their possibilities of a fruitful interchange of experience, should not obscure a basic distinction between contemporary "socialism," Soviet-style, and contemporary "capitalism," American-style. Even if all similarities be granted, the fact remains that the Soviet system of capital accumulation has, thus far, made possible an annual rate of economic expansion

roughly double that registered in the USA. This extraordinary tempo of growth will not persist in the USSR. The American rate of growth may increase. The implications of current trends are nevertheless momentous for the long future and should cause Americans to take thought anew regarding their economic arrangements.

In terms of social function and mass appeal, the "meaning of Marxism" in our time is not to be found, as Marx assumed and as many Marxists still believe, in a remedy for the evils of "capitalism." It is rather to be found in the fact that the Marxists of Muscovy have devised a method, "out-capitalizing" the "capitalists," whereby the accumulation and investment of capital, in an initial context of mass poverty, proceeds at a more rapid rate than "capitalism" in its heyday ever achieved or is now achieving in its semi-socialist maturity. The method, on the basis of Russian experience and prospectively of Chinese experience, constitutes a way whereby desperately poor societies can lift themselves by their bootstraps to a prospect of plenty. The record of Soviet accomplishment is here incontrovertible and conclusive. And since most of mankind is still desperately poor and clamoring for freedom from poverty, at whatever the cost in other freedoms, the contemporary challenge of Communism to America and the "Free World" lies precisely here in its largest dimension rather than in threats of conspiracy, subversion, sedition, or military aggression. To misconceive the nature of the challenge, as many in the West were doing in the 1950's, is to invite frustration and defeat in the contest. To fail to find effective means of countering the challenge is to court disaster.

Politicians and propagandists in the Atlantic communities deceive themselves and evade the issue when they seek comfort in the conviction that Soviet Communism, whatever its material achievements, spells "tyranny" and a denial of civil rights and human dignity—as, unquestionably, thus far it does—and that mankind in general prefers political liberty and democracy to totalitarian methods of economic and social advance. This dichotomy is meaningless to the masses of Asia, Africa, and even much of Latin America, where "liberty" and "democracy" have for generations been empty words and where poverty, ignorance, illiteracy, and disease have for centuries been the lot of most men and women. The deception of the West is twice compounded by the nascent prospect that the USSR, having brought into being an economy of relative abundance, may presently find ways and means of discarding the odious attributes of

the totalitarian police state and arriving at a relatively free and democratic system of public policy-making.

Whether "democracy" in any meaningful sense can or will replace despotism and oligarchy in the Soviet structure of power was an issue still beclouded on the 40th anniversary of the October Revolution. But this much was clear: the USSR as a highly industrialized, wholly literate, and largely urbanized community could not continue indefinitely to be governed by the Byzantine and barbaric devices of Stalinism, as Stalin's successors well understood. Their groping efforts to invent an alternative had not eventuated in any radical transformation of the Soviet State by 1957. Yet the efforts were continuing, not from choice but from necessity. They could conceivably fail altogether, leaving no options save a reversion to Stalinism or an extension to the USSR of the revolutionary ferment in the satellites in 1956. Indeed, any return to Stalinism might well spell ultimate revolution. The eternal Russia that finally revolted against a Tsardom seeking to perpetuate Autocracy long after such a mode of governance had become obsolete will find means of rebellion against Marxist oligarchs who strive to repeat the errors and resume the terrors of the past.

But these speculations, comforting as they may be to Westerners, have little relevance to the realities of Soviet politics on the eve of the fifth decade of the Red regime. Stalin's heirs have abundantly demonstrated their deep concern with reform as the price of survival. Despite their blunders and crimes, they were earnestly striving, forty years after October, for a new dispensation. In the light of their past accomplishments, the West could have no certitude of their failure in the new enterprise.

The pattern of an emergent Soviet democracy, it must be conceded, was foggy and confused in 1957, despite opportunities for a transition to a truly federal and genuinely parliamentary Union of Republics with no changes in the Constitution. A copying of Western recipes for freedom was precluded by Marxist dogma and by the traditions of the Russian community. Not soon or easily, if at all, will the USSR reproduce in its own political arrangements the designs of the West for "government by the consent of the governed," free elections of candidates among a multiplicity of parties, executive responsibility to the legislature, and liberty for all to criticize, propagandize, and organize to elect law-makers of their choice, with defeated minorities cheerfully acquiescing in the decisions of victori-

ous, albeit tolerant, majorities. Such attitudes and practices have few parallels in the history of Muscovy and little meaning to the peoples of Russia.

Some alternative form of "freedom" must doubtless be devised in Sovietland if it is to be acceptable, viable, and effective. As yet its contours cannot be discerned. They may be long in taking shape. What is certain from the record—unless the entire enterprise, most improbably, should fail utterly—is that the legal rights of Soviet citizens will be more and more adequately protected against arbitrary action; that decision-making in Party organs and governmental bodies will increasingly be based upon free discussion, debate, and voting (as in the first years of the Soviet regime) rather than upon dictation from above; and that popular "elections" will cease to be formal exercises in the rituals of unanimity and will offer voters some choice among candidates.

The latter prospect does not postulate the likelihood in any visible future of a two-party or multi-party political scheme on the Western model. This is far off and may never come to pass. It assumes no more than the possibility of multiple candidacies, perhaps on the model of the Polish election of January 20, 1957. It is probable that the Soviet transition to "democracy" will be influenced less by Western practices than by the attempts of the rulers of China and of the European "satellites" to improvise patterns of popular participation in policy-making. Great empires have not infrequently been liberalized by the experience of allies, subject peoples, and marchmen. The final result, whatever its image, is likely to negate a widespread Western conviction that the Soviet State is irrevocably and forever an unrestrained despotism whose rulers govern by terror. Such a transition will render it all the more imperative that Western peoples reconsider the problem of how best to meet the Communist challenge.

2. THE FAMILY OF MAN

IT is widely believed among men and women of good sense that another war of East and West waged with atomic weapons would eventuate not in one Rome but in two Carthages. Malenkov, Bulganin, Khrushchev, and their colleagues have all in their several

ways concurred with Eisenhower's comment of 1954 that "in the thermo-nuclear age there is no alternative to peace" and acknowledged that an atomic Armageddon would spell the doom not of "capitalism" but of civilization itself in East and West alike. No such proposition can be conclusively validated save through the experimental method. Some experiments, however, can be performed only once.

The considerations which may be adduced in support of the view that no such experiment is ever likely to be undertaken have been discussed in previous pages. The conclusion toward which they point is nevertheless a negative one, leaving unanswered many questions regarding the most probable, to say nothing of the most desirable, future pattern of East-West relations and of the global State System *in toto*.

If in such matters "freedom consists in the recognition of necessity," as Engels once wrote, then the scope of what is desirable, while it may be limitless in fancy-free fantasy or day-dreaming, is narrowly circumscribed for the practitioners of "practical" politics by the limits of what is possible in relationship to what is necessary. All men, with at least part of their personalities, are in favor of virtue and against sin. The virtuous, we must nonetheless grant, often sin—and never more grievously than when they do so in the name of vindicating virtue, as in all "Crusades," "Holy Wars," and Inquisitions. And all sinners either repent and seek forgiveness, or make virtues of their sins, or persuade themselves that their crimes are indispensable means toward noble ends, or embrace hypocrisy as the tribute that vice pays to virtue. Moral choices are seldom simple.

All men of reason, moreover, want peace, order, and security under law and abhor war, violence, anarchy, and lawlessness. For the attainment of the former goods and the avoidance of the latter evils, men have concocted and relied upon those formalized relations of command and obedience known as "government"—having, thus far here below, found no means of inventing any alternative procedures more adequate to the tasks in hand. The device is faulty, since men are fallible and ambivalent. All governments rob, enslave, and kill, always in the name of peace and security, with these operations usually dignified as taxation, punishment of crime, and national defense. Most citizens concede that such activities, if so named, are desirable or at least necessary to forestall greater ills. Political decisions are seldom simple or unmixed as to motives. Some

tolerable modicum of order and justice is nonetheless commonly achieved through these arrangements.

But what is possible within national communities is not possible in the international community in its present form for the obvious reason that all national communities have governments and the international community has none. If war be deemed the product of international anarchy, the assumption of violence, and the game of power politics (no other kind of politics being possible whenever men try to live without government), then it follows that the abolition of war can be achieved only through replacing anarchy by government in the community of nations. Something of the sort has been repeatedly attained during centuries long gone whenever men have enjoyed the blessings of "Universal States" or "World Empires." Such structures of authority have invariably been reared through the military subjugation of all members of the State System by one. But in our own constellation of sovereignties such efforts have always been thwarted through those combinations of the weak against the strong known as the "balance of power." And there are no sound grounds for supposing that either the USSR or the USA can establish a World State by conquest during any future now to be foreseen.

The only alternative means of replacing anarchy by government in the community of nations is the method of voluntary agreement among sovereignties to establish supra-national institutions vested with adequate powers, above and beyond those of national governments, to tax, to legislate, to enforce law, to administer common functions—in short, to govern the world. Many among the wise have long contended that such an innovation is needed if we are to be assured against the nuclear coannihilation of mankind. What can be persuasively demonstrated to be necessary can also persuasively be demonstrated to be possible. And, in truth, World Government is quite possible—save for the fact that most people and politicians deem it neither necessary nor desirable and prefer to cling to the ancient ways of national sovereignty and international anarchy, all the while hoping that eloquent advocacy of the "world rule of law" and eager recourse to UN resolutions will abolish violence and insure order in a global community without government.

These hopes are, of course, vain. The ancient ways are obsolete. Yet here Russians and Americans are wholly of one mind except for a semantic difference: in the USA apostles of world government are commonly denounced as "Communists," while in the USSR they are

invariably labeled agents of "capitalism" and "imperialism." It is arguable, as Clarence K. Streit and others have argued, that should either of the Super-Powers act to promote international federation within the areas under its influence as a regional step toward a Parliament of Man and a Federation of the World, it would thereby gain decisive advantages over the other in stirring the imaginations and winning the minds of men. But the proposition is not demonstrable, since nothing is less likely, now or in the near future, in either Moscow or Washington.[3]

It must therefore be taken as certain, for the years and decades immediately before us, that the world community will continue to lack world government and that problems of power will continue to be dealt with through the competitive strivings of rival national sovereignties. In the future, as in the past, no union of wills can emerge from these complex interactions of thrust and parry, threat and response, menace and defense, with their current formulas of "containment," "liberation," "peace pacts," "disarmament" programs, "massive retaliation," "brink of war," and the like. Nor can any citizen or statesman foresee, save through a glass darkly, what the operational consequences of any particular decision in so anarchic and disorderly a game are likely to be—as was dramatically demonstrated anew by the events of 1956.

Given this prospect, policy-makers, tax-payers, and even writers of books on world affairs may understandably despair of any possibility of anticipating things to come. *Weltpolitik* may readily, if not reassuringly, be envisaged as a jumble of hazardous guesses, dubious inferences, and trial-and-error fumblings and bumblings, all rather more likely to lead to calamity than to any contributions to the security of survival of *Homo Sapiens*. But so dismal a view may be slightly brightened by the reflection that amid the disorder a few

---

[3] The widespread public interest in America during 1944–7 in programs and prospects for world government had waned to a bare minimum of attention by 1952, when my previous book, *The Commonwealth of Man*, dealing in detail with these matters, was published by Knopf. Such interest has since approached the vanishing-point. Communist stereotypes in this area of inquiry are well exemplified by E. Mamedov in *Pravda*, October 30, 1953, who in a six-column "review" of *The Commonwealth of Man* demonstrated to his own satisfaction—and to the satisfaction of the editors, of the Party leaders, and perhaps of his readers—that the author was "a frank apologist for power politics and war," "a master of misinformation and slander," an "insolent propagandist" of American "world domination," an "active ideologist of American imperialism," a defender of U.S. "aggression," etc.

relatively "fixed points" and "enduring realities" can yet be espied through the murk and that some at least among these continuities offer promise of salvation from irreparable disaster.

World War III, it has here been contended (see pp. 400 f.), is wholly improbable because of the equipoise of forces achieved by the Soviet bloc and the Atlantic coalition in their struggle for hegemony. The global deadlock is quite unlikely to be disrupted or even significantly altered by anything done, or left undone, by policy-planners on either side so long as each is sufficiently wary of the other to keep its own fences mended. As of 1957, new dangers of a "breakthrough" in the stalemate were looming in Eastern Europe and in Western Asia and Africa. Unless decision-makers in both camps could summon up a greater measure of the ingredients of all successful statesmanship—vision, foresight, courage, magnanimity, and imagination—further violence in these troubled regions of past mistakes was all but inevitable, with results unpredictable but ill calculated to maintain in any orderly and stable pattern the local and global balance of influence upon which peace precariously depended.

The quest for more secure bases of coexistence appeared to require in 1957 and for long thereafter a return on both sides to the efforts of 1953–5 to negotiate settlements through bargaining and bartering. Problems of power in a world without government can be resolved only by war, whereby the contestants seek to impose their will upon one another by force, or by diplomacy, whereby they seek *quid pro quo* to compromise their divergent interests in a *modus vivendi* necessarily unsatisfactory to either side but at least tolerable to both. War is now impossible unless, as is quite unlikely, policy-makers on one side or the other or both should become so demented as to suppose that "victory" could be won or that the atomic incineration of civilization could somehow be averted in a future global trial by battle. Only diplomacy is left as a procedure of accommodation.

In the use of diplomacy in all such contests, three levels of adjustment are distinguishable: (1) a "stand-off" without agreement, wherein each side tacitly refrains from overt challenge to the other—e.g., the USA and Red China vis-à-vis Formosa since 1950 and East and West in Germany since 1949; (2) a negotiated truce or armistice, following stalemated hostilities, involving *de facto* partition of disputed areas—e.g., Korea in 1953 and Indochina in 1954; and (3) the negotiation of treaty terms *de jure*, as exemplified in the pacts

of 1947 and the Austrian treaty of 1955. That the third method is much to be preferred is self-evident from the record of recent years and from the whole history of the diplomatic art.

Since "Grand Alliances" facing "Great Coalitions" necessarily strive, as do individual sovereignties, to negotiate in a context of apparent unity and strength, rather than disintegration and weakness, preparations for bargaining usually involve efforts to heal rifts among allies and to present an appearance of solidarity. Such was the purpose of Chou En-lai's journeys in December 1956 and January 1957, whereby the Sino-Soviet alliance was consolidated and new unity was furthered within the Communist bloc, even though many problems of Soviet-satellite relations in the Warsaw Pact coalition were still unresolved.[4]

Such also was the purpose of Anglo-French-American efforts

[4] The long communiqué issued in Moscow on January 19, 1957, by Premiers Bulganin and Chou En-lai opined that the earlier hopes of "*a détente* in the international situation" and of "peaceful coexistence between States with different social systems" had "run up against obstacles" attributed to the "armed attack of the imperialist aggressive forces against Egypt and their subversive activities in Hungary." Both communities, however, were said to have "achieved victory in their heroic and resolute struggle" and to have inflicted "utter defeat" on the "imperialists." "Contradictions and disagreements in the camp of imperialism arising from the struggle for raw material resources, markets, and spheres of influence are growing more deep and acute every day. With the exception of the aggressive forces in a few imperialist States, the peoples of all the world yearn for peace. . . . If all the peaceable forces in the international arena unite, join efforts in a resolute struggle, any intrigues of the aggressive imperialist quarters will definitely be frustrated."

Amid further conventional Communist jargon, including condemnation of the "Eisenhower Doctrine," the Premiers vaguely pledged "support of the peoples of the Near and Middle East so as to prevent aggression and interference in the affairs of the countries of this area." They asked reparations for Egypt, expressed opposition to any "imperialist machinations aimed at placing the Suez Canal under 'international control' and are for the settlement of the question of free passage of shipping through the Suez Canal by way of negotiations between the States concerned on the basis of complete respect for Egyptian sovereignty." After rejoicing in the defeat of "imperialist counter-revolution" in Hungary, they reaffirmed Sino-Soviet solidarity and espoused anew "peaceful coexistence with the USA" and the replacement of NATO, SEATO, the Baghdad Pact, and the Warsaw Pact by multilateral accords in Europe and Asia for "collective security." China and the USSR were said to be united in pursuit of "victory in the common cause of struggle against imperialism; of victory in the cause of building socialism in different countries, of victory for the triumph of Communism. . . . There are no essential contradictions and conflicting interests in the relations between the Socialist States, even if in the past there were some mistakes and shortcomings. . . . The friendship and unity of the Soviet Union and China constitute a most important factor in the great unity of Socialist States."

during the same span of time to restore some semblance of unity in the disrupted Atlantic coalition. But the building of alliances is futile when they involve more costs, risks, and losses than benefits—as was plainly the case with SEATO, with the disastrous Baghdad' Pact, and with the amorphous "Eisenhower Doctrine." And the consolidation of viable alliances under such circumstances as we are here considering is pointless save as a step toward serious negotiations between antagonists. This elementary fact appeared, early in 1957, to be better appreciated in Moscow and Peiping than in Paris, London, or Washington.

To speculate upon the possible shape of such negotiated bargains between East and West as must be arrived at in the years to come would be a thankless and futile task. Yet it may be surmised that no stable structure of peace and security in Central Europe can be attained unless some form of the various patterns of "neutrality" now enjoyed by Jugoslavia, Austria, Switzerland, Sweden, and (with qualifications) Finland is extended to a reunified Germany, thence to all the Soviet satellites, and prospectively to all of *Mitteleuropa,* including Scandinavia, the Central and Eastern Mediterranean lands, and all of Danubia and Balkania.

By the same token, it may be surmised that the security of Israel, the welfare and stability of the Arab States, the safety of waterways and foreign investments throughout the Middle East, and the reduction to some tolerable dimensions of local and international tensions in the area will require a comprehensive East-West settlement. If any such settlement is to be possible, the Western Powers will be obliged to concede that the USSR has "rights" in a vast region on its very doorstep at least as legitimate as those of France, Britain, and America, including access to at least some of the vast oil reserves of the area (e.g., northern Iran); Moscow, confronted with dangers of anarchy in the Levant, will be obliged to modify its "anti-colonial" line of policy and propaganda and concede the legitimacy of Western rights and interests; and both will agree to act together, instead of against each other, to promote the diversion of Arab nationalism into constructive channels and the economic development of the whole huge region in a context of order assured by an accord of the Powers.

One might further surmise that a stable settlement in the Far East will require Communist acceptance of "two Chinas"—i.e., the indefinite postponement of hopes of reuniting Formosa with the

mainland—and American abandonment of the feckless doctrines of non-recognition of Red China and the denial to Peiping of China's seat in the UN. Only through full diplomatic and consular relations, an end of embargoes and boycotts, and the furtherance by all the governments of the area, including Japan, of a maximum measure of trade among all the peoples of the Orient can there emerge any prospect of order and plenty for the vast and restless masses in Eastern Asia. Other surmises are best deferred.

Whether those who wield power in East and West possess, or are likely to acquire, the needed skills of flexibility, adaptability, and compromise to effect such settlements is a question currently unanswerable. If not, the years ahead will be years of more disorder and recurrent threats of disaster. If so, the years ahead will be years of creative competition between the two halves of a divided world, each striving to outdo the other not in rivalry for power or for superiority in the weapons of destruction but in contributions to a better life for all and to the progressive amelioration of the miserable lot of that majority of humankind still living in illiteracy, poverty, and disease.

The dogmas of Marxism-Leninism, still coupled with vestiges of Stalinism, constitute an obstacle to the success of the enterprise. The American dogma of "anti-Communism" constitutes a comparable obstacle. In their more extreme versions both dogmas are fallacious, irrelevant, and hazardous. All Americans will be obliged to live in the same world with Communism for the rest of their lives and their children's lives. No "liberation" of Russia or of China, no establishment of Western-style "capitalism" or "democracy" in the Eurasian Heartland is conceivable through any imaginable magic of words or weapons. Conversely, the Communists' immortal hope of an overthrow of the Western "bourgeoisie" by the "proletariat" is pure fantasy, wholly remote from all present or future political or economic realities.

Whichever side can first abandon illusions and face facts will win major advantages over the other in the unending contest for the sympathy of that immense majority of humanity which lies outside the Soviet bloc and the Atlantic coalition. The record of recent years suggests that Russians, in some respects, are more capable of confronting realities than are Americans. But no American and no Russian need doubt America's ultimate capacity to accept the facts of

life in the world of the late 20th Century and to so act as to promote the survival of America and the welfare of the world.

Russia's century-long "mission" of saving the world from sin can never be achieved by any imposition of Russian doctrines or practices on the rest of mankind. It can be realized only by the demonstrated ability of the new Russia to attain within its frontiers a richer, fuller, and freer life for its people, unmarred by terrorism, injustice, and ruthless regimentation at the hands of an arbitrary oligarchy, and offering opportunities for popular participation in the planning of community life. America's more recent "mission" of saving the world from sin can never be fulfilled by attempts to "Americanize" other peoples. Its promise lies in the ability of Americans to renounce militarism as a way of life; to achieve racial equality and dignity; to bring Big Business, Big Labor, and Big Government alike under effective popular control; and to contribute constructively to the abolition of poverty both at home and abroad. If "victory" is conceived in terms of achieving the ruination of the "enemy," neither Super-Power can "win" the long and interminable struggle to gain friends and influence people among the many millions of men and women who are neither Russian nor American. Each of the combatants will gain honor and prestige to the degree to which it displays talent in sensing the aspirations of dark and fumbling multitudes, now aflame with hopes of a better life, and in contributing practically to the progressive fulfillment of their dreams.

Competition in the enterprise is inevitable. Cooperation in some of its aspects will serve the best purposes of both better than they could be served by a rivalry pursued in mutual ignorance and enmity. Given the productive resources at the disposal of each of the Super-Powers, both patterns of relationship can contribute to the amelioration of the condition of much of mankind. A mutually acceptable maximum of cooperation, moreover, may restore the initial premise of the United Nations—a concert of Great Powers devoted to pursuit of common purposes. Such a restoration would make the UN, even though lacking any attributes of a "world government," a highly useful and effective agency, as its founders hoped it would be, for the promotion of order, security, and a better life throughout the world community. Such a transformation might conceivably even reopen the possibility of the ultimate conversion of the UN into the embryo of a federation of the world.

All Russians, all Americans, and all other peoples everywhere have nothing to lose, save their stale superstitions and obsolete prejudices, and everything to gain from the fulfillment, in whole or in part, of the prospects here suggested. Whether they are able and willing so to act as to promote such realization was still uncertain in the fortieth year of the Soviet regime. But there was hope, in the words of Jeremiah, of "health and cure" and a "cleansing of iniquity. . . . Again there shall be heard in this place, which ye say shall be desolate without man and without beast . . . the voice of joy, and the voice of gladness, the voice of the bridegroom, and the voice of the bride, the voice of them that shall say, Praise the Lord of Hosts: for the Lord is good; for His mercy endureth forever. . . ."

APPENDIX

Constitution

(FUNDAMENTAL LAW)

OF THE

Union of Soviet Socialist Republics

AS AMENDED AND ADDED TO

AT THE FIRST, SECOND AND FOURTH SESSIONS

OF THE SUPREME SOVIET OF THE U.S.S.R.,

FOURTH CONVOCATION

CHAPTER I: THE SOCIAL STRUCTURE

ARTICLE 1. The Union of Soviet Socialist Republics is a socialist state of workers and peasants.

ARTICLE 2. The political foundation of the U.S.S.R. is the Soviets of Working People's Deputies, which grew and became strong as a result of the overthrow of the power of the landlords and capitalists and the conquest of the dictatorship of the proletariat.

ARTICLE 3. All power in the U.S.S.R. belongs to the working people of town and country as represented by the Soviets of Working People's Deputies.

ARTICLE 4. The economic foundation of the U.S.S.R. is the socialist system of economy and the socialist ownership of the instruments and means of production, firmly established as a result of the liquidation of the capitalist system of economy, the abolition of private ownership of the instruments and means of production, and the elimination of the exploitation of man by man.

ARTICLE 5. Socialist property in the U.S.S.R. exists either in the form of state property (belonging to the whole people) or in the form of co-operative and collective-farm property (property of collective farms, property of co-operative societies).

ARTICLE 6. The land, its mineral wealth, waters, forests, mills, factories, mines, rail, water and air transport, banks, communications, large state-organized agricultural enterprises (state farms, machine and tractor stations and the like), as well as municipal enterprises and the bulk of the dwelling-houses in the cities and industrial localities, are state property, that is, belong to the whole people.

ARTICLE 7. The common enterprises of collective farms and co-operative organizations, with their live-stock and implements, the products of the collective farms and co-operative organizations, as well as their common buildings, constitute the common, socialist property of the collective farms and co-operative organizations.

Every household in a collective farm, in addition to its basic income from the common collective-farm enterprise, has for its personal use a small plot of household land and, as its personal property, a subsidiary husbandry on the plot, a dwelling-house, live-stock, poultry and minor agricultural implements—in accordance with the rules of the agricultural artel.

ARTICLE 8. The land occupied by collective farms is secured to them for their use free of charge and for an unlimited time, that is, in perpetuity.

ARTICLE 9. Alongside the socialist system of economy, which is the predominant form of economy in the U.S.S.R., the law permits the small private economy of individual peasants and handicraftsmen based on their own labour and precluding the exploitation of the labour of others.

ARTICLE 10. The personal property right of citizens in their incomes and savings from work, in their dwelling-houses and subsidiary husbandries, in articles of domestic economy and use and articles of personal use and convenience, as well as the right of citizens to inherit personal property, is protected by law.

ARTICLE 11. The economic life of the U.S.S.R. is determined and directed by the state national-economic plan, with the aim of increasing the public wealth, of steadily raising the material and cultural standards of the working people, of consolidating the independence of the U.S.S.R. and strengthening its defensive capacity.

ARTICLE 12. Work in the U.S.S.R. is a duty and a matter of honour for every able-bodied citizen, in accordance with the principle: "He who does not work, neither shall he eat."

The principle applied in the U.S.S.R. is that of socialism: "From each according to his ability, to each according to his work."

CHAPTER II: THE STATE STRUCTURE

ARTICLE 13. The Union of Soviet Socialist Republics is a federal state, formed on the basis of a voluntary union of equal Soviet Socialist Republics, namely:

The Russian Soviet Federative Socialist Republic
The Ukrainian Soviet Socialist Republic
The Byelorussian Soviet Socialist Republic
The Uzbek Soviet Socialist Republic
The Kazakh Soviet Socialist Republic

The Georgian Soviet Socialist Republic
The Azerbaijan Soviet Socialist Republic
The Lithuanian Soviet Socialist Republic
The Moldavian Soviet Socialist Republic
The Latvian Soviet Socialist Republic
The Kirghiz Soviet Socialist Republic
The Tajik Soviet Socialist Republic
The Armenian Soviet Socialist Republic
The Turkmen Soviet Socialist Republic
The Estonian Soviet Socialist Republic
The Karelo-Finnish Soviet Socialist Republic. (abolished July, 1956)

ARTICLE 14. The jurisdiction of the Union of Soviet Socialist Republics, as represented by its higher organs of state power and organs of state administration, embraces:

a) Representation of the U.S.S.R. in international relations, conclusion, ratification and denunciation of treaties of the U.S.S.R. with other states, establishment of general procedure governing the relations of Union Republics with foreign states;

b) Questions of war and peace;

c) Admission of new republics into the U.S.S.R.;

d) Control over the observance of the Constitution of the U.S.S.R., and ensuring conformity of the Constitutions of the Union Republics with the Constitution of the U.S.S.R.;

e) Confirmation of alterations of boundaries between Union Republics;

f) Confirmation of the formation of new Territories and Regions and also of new Autonomous Republics and Autonomous Regions within Union Republics;

g) Organization of the defence of the U.S.S.R., direction of all the Armed Forces of the U.S.S.R., determination of directing principles governing the organization of the military formations of the Union Republics;

h) Foreign trade on the basis of state monopoly;

i) Safeguarding the security of the state;

j) Determination of the national-economic plans of the U.S.S.R.;

k) Approval of the consolidated state budget of the U.S.S.R. and of the report on its fulfilment; determination of the taxes and revenues which go to the Union, the Republican, and the local budgets;

l) Administration of the banks, industrial and agricultural institutions and enterprises and trading enterprises of all-Union importance;

m) Administration of transport and communications;

n) Direction of the monetary and credit system;

o) Organization of state insurance;

p) Contracting and granting of loans;

q) Determination of the basic principles of land tenure and of the use of mineral wealth, forests and waters;

r) Determination of the basic principles in the spheres of education and public health;

s) Organization of a uniform system of national-economic statistics;

t) Determination of the principles of labour legislation;

u) Legislation concerning the judicial system and the judicial procedure; criminal and civil codes;

v) Legislation concerning Union citizenship; legislation concerning rights of foreigners;

w) Determination of the principles of legislation concerning marriage and the family;

x) Issuing of all-Union acts of amnesty.

ARTICLE 15. The sovereignty of the Union Republics is limited only in the spheres defined in Article 14 of the Constitution of the U.S.S.R. Outside of these spheres each Union Republic exercises state authority independently. The U.S.S.R. protects the sovereign rights of the Union Republics.

ARTICLE 16. Each Union Republic has its own Constitution, which takes account of the specific features of the Republic and is drawn up in full conformity with the Constitution of the U.S.S.R.

ARTICLE 17. The right freely to secede from the U.S.S.R. is reserved to every Union Republic.

ARTICLE 18. The territory of a Union Republic may not be altered without its consent.

ARTICLE 18-A. Each Union Republic has the right to enter into direct relations with foreign states and to conclude agreements and exchange diplomatic and consular representatives with them.

ARTICLE 18-B. Each Union Republic has its own Republican military formations.

ARTICLE 19. The laws of the U.S.S.R. have the same force within the territory of every Union Republic.

ARTICLE 20. In the event of divergence between a law of a Union Republic and a law of the Union, the Union law prevails.

ARTICLE 21. Uniform Union citizenship is established for citizens of the U.S.S.R.

Every citizen of a Union Republic is a citizen of the U.S.S.R.

ARTICLE 22. The Russian Soviet Federative Socialist Republic consists of the Altai, Krasnodar, Krasnoyarsk, Primorye, Stavropol and Khabarovsk Territories; the Amur, Arzamas, Arkhangelsk, Astrakhan, Balashov, Belgorod, Bryansk, Velikiye-Luki, Vladimir, Vologda, Voronezh, Gorky, Grozny, Ivanovo, Irkutsk, Kaliningrad, Kalinin, Kaluga, Kamensk, Kemerovo, Kirov, Kostroma, Kuibyshev, Kurgan, Kursk, Leningrad, Lipetsk, Magadan, Molotov, Moscow, Murmansk, Novgorod, Novosibirsk, Omsk, Orel, Penza, Pskov, Rostov, Ryazan, Saratov, Sakhalin, Sverdlovsk, Smolensk, Stalingrad, Tambov, Tomsk, Tula, Tyumen, Ulyanovsk, Chelyabinsk, Chita, Chkalov and Yaroslavl Regions; the Tatar, Bashkirian, Daghestan, Buryat-Mongolian, Kabarda, Komi, Mari, Mordovian, North Ossetian, Udmurt, Chuvash and Yakut Autonomous Soviet Socialist Republics; and the Adygei, Gorny Altai, Jewish, Tuva, Khaskass and Cherkess Autonomous Regions.

ARTICLE 23. The Ukrainian Soviet Socialist Republic consists of the Vinnitsa, Volhynia, Voroshilovgrad, Dniepropetrovsk, Drogobych, Zhitomir, Trans-Carpathian, Zaporozhye, Kiev, Kirovograd, Crimean, Lvov, Nikolayev, Odessa, Poltava, Rovno, Stalino, Stanislav, Sumy, Ternopol, Kharkov, Kherson, Khmelnitsky, Cherkassy, Chernigov and Chernovitsi Regions.

ARTICLE 24. The Azerbeijan Soviet Socialist Republic includes the Nakhichevan Autonomous Soviet Socialist Republic and the Nagorny Karabakh Autonomous Region.

ARTICLE 25. The Georgian Soviet Socialist Republic includes the Abkhazian Autonomous Soviet Socialist Republic, the Ajarian Autonomous Soviet Socialist Republic and the South Ossetian Autonomous Region.

ARTICLE 26. The Uzbek Soviet Socialist Republic consists of the Andizhan, Bukhara, Kashka-Darya, Namangan, Samarkand, Surkhan-Darya, Tashkent, Ferghana and Khoresm Regions and the Kara-Kalpak Autonomous Soviet Socialist Republic.

ARTICLE 27. The Tajik Soviet Socialist Republic includes the Leninabad Region and the Gorny Badakhshan Autonomous Region.

ARTICLE 28. The Kazakh Soviet Socialist Republic consists of the Akmolinsk, Aktyubinsk, Alma-Ata, East Kazakhstan, Guriev, Jambul, West Kazakhstan, Karaganda, Kzil-Orda, Kokchetav, Kustanai, Pavlodar, North Kazakhstan, Semipalatinsk, Taldi-Kurgan and South Kazakhstan Regions.

ARTICLE 29. The Byelorussian Soviet Socialist Republic consists of the Brest, Vitebsk, Gomel, Grodno, Minsk, Moghilev and Molodechno Regions.

ARTICLE 29-A. The Turkmen Soviet Socialist Republic consists of the Ashkhabad, Mary, Tashauz and Charjou Regions.

ARTICLE 29-B. The Kirghiz Soviet Socialist Republic consists of the Jalal-Abad, Issyk-Kul Osh, Talas, Tien Shan and Frunze Regions.

CHAPTER III: THE HIGHER ORGANS OF STATE POWER
IN THE UNION OF SOVIET SOCIALIST REPUBLICS

ARTICLE 30. The highest organ of state power in the U.S.S.R. is the Supreme Soviet of the U.S.S.R.

ARTICLE 31. The Supreme Soviet of the U.S.S.R. exercises all rights vested in the Union of Soviet Socialist Republics in accordance with Article 14 of the Constitution, in so far as they do not, by virtue of the Constitution, come within the jurisdiction of organs of the U.S.S.R. that are accountable to the Supreme Soviet of the U.S.S.R., that is, the Presidium of the Supreme Soviet of the U.S.S.R., the Council of Ministers of the U.S.S.R., and the Ministries of the U.S.S.R.

ARTICLE 32. The legislative power of the U.S.S.R. is exercised exclusively by the Supreme Soviet of the U.S.S.R.

ARTICLE 33. The Supreme Soviet of the U.S.S.R. consists of two Chambers: the Soviet of the Union and the Soviet of Nationalities.

ARTICLE 34. The Soviet of the Union is elected by the citizens of the U.S.S.R. voting by election districts on the basis of one deputy for every 300,000 of the population.

ARTICLE 35. The Soviet of Nationalities is elected by the citizens of the U.S.S.R. voting by Union Republics, Autonomous Republics, Autonomous Regions, and National Areas on the basis of 25 deputies from each Union Republic, 11 deputies from each Autonomous Republic, 5 deputies from each Autonomous Region and one deputy from each National Area.

ARTICLE 36. The Supreme Soviet of the U.S.S.R. is elected for a term of four years.

ARTICLE 37. The two Chambers of the Supreme Soviet of the U.S.S.R., the Soviet of the Union and the Soviet of Nationalities, have equal rights.

ARTICLE 38. The Soviet of the Union and the Soviet of Nationalities have equal powers to initiate legislation.

ARTICLE 39. A law is considered adopted if passed by both Chambers of the Supreme Soviet of the U.S.S.R. by a simple majority vote in each.

ARTICLE 40. Laws passed by the Supreme Soviet of the U.S.S.R. are published in the languages of the Union Republics over the signatures of the President and Secretary of the Presidium of the Supreme Soviet of the U.S.S.R.

ARTICLE 41. Sessions of the Soviet of the Union and of the Soviet of Nationalities begin and terminate simultaneously.

ARTICLE 42. The Soviet of the Union elects a Chairman of the Soviet of the Union and four Vice-Chairmen.

ARTICLE 43. The Soviet of Nationalities elects a Chairman of the Soviet of Nationalities and four Vice-Chairmen.

ARTICLE 44. The Chairmen of the Soviet of the Union and the Soviet of Nationalities preside at the sittings of the respective Chambers and have charge of the conduct of their business and proceedings.

ARTICLE 45. Joint sittings of the two Chambers of the Supreme Soviet of the U.S.S.R. are presided over alternately by the Chairman of the Soviet of the Union and the Chairman of the Soviet of Nationalities.

ARTICLE 46. Sessions of the Supreme Soviet of the U.S.S.R. are convened by the Presidium of the Supreme Soviet of the U.S.S.R. twice a year.

Extraordinary sessions are convened by the Presidium of the Supreme Soviet of the U.S.S.R. at its discretion or on the demand of one of the Union Republics.

ARTICLE 47. In the event of disagreement between the Soviet of the Union and the Soviet of Nationalities, the question is referred for settlement to a conciliation commission formed by the Chambers on a parity basis. If the conciliation commission fails to arrive at an agreement or if its decision fails to satisfy one of the Chambers, the question is considered for a second time by the Chambers. Failing agreement between the two Chambers, the Presidium of the Supreme Soviet of the U.S.S.R. dissolves the Supreme Soviet of the U.S.S.R. and orders new elections.

ARTICLE 48. The Supreme Soviet of the U.S.S.R. at a joint sitting of the two Chambers elects the Presidium of the Supreme Soviet of the U.S.S.R., consisting of a President of the Presidium of the Supreme Soviet of the U.S.S.R., sixteen Vice-Presidents, a Secretary of the Presidium and fifteen members of the Presidium of the Supreme Soviet of the U.S.S.R.

The Presidium of the Supreme Soviet of the U.S.S.R. is accountable to the Supreme Soviet of the U.S.S.R. for all its activities.

ARTICLE 49. The Presidium of the Supreme Soviet of the U.S.S.R.:

a) Convenes the sessions of the Supreme Soviet of the U.S.S.R.;

b) Issues decrees;

c) Gives interpretations of the laws of the U.S.S.R. in operation;

d) Dissolves the Supreme Soviet of the U.S.S.R. in conformity with Article 47 of the Constitution of the U.S.S.R. and orders new elections;

e) Conducts nation-wide polls (referendums) on its own initiative or on the demand of one of the Union Republics;

f) Annuls decisions and orders of the Council of Ministers of the U.S.S.R. and of the Councils of Ministers of the Union Republics if they do not conform to law;

g) In the intervals between sessions of the Supreme Soviet of the U.S.S.R., releases and appoints Ministers of the U.S.S.R. on the recommendation of the Chairman of the Council of Ministers of the U.S.S.R., subject to subsequent confirmation by the Supreme Soviet of the U.S.S.R.;

h) Institutes decorations (Orders and Medals) and titles of honour of the U.S.S.R.;

i) Awards Orders and Medals and confers titles of honour of the U.S.S.R.;

j) Exercises the right of pardon;

k) Institutes military titles, diplomatic ranks and other special titles;

l) Appoints and removes the high command of the Armed Forces of the U.S.S.R.;

m) In the intervals between sessions of the Supreme Soviet of the U.S.S.R., proclaims a state of war in the event of military attack on the U.S.S.R., or when necessary to fulfil international treaty obligations concerning mutual defence against aggression;

n) Orders general or partial mobilization;

o) Ratifies and denounces international treaties of the U.S.S.R.;

p) Appoints and recalls plenipotentiary representatives of the U.S.S.R. to foreign states;

q) Receives the letters of credence and recall of diplomatic representatives accredited to it by foreign states;

r) Proclaims martial law in separate localities or throughout the U.S.S.R. in the interests of the defence of the U.S.S.R. or of the maintenance of public order and the security of the state.

ARTICLE 50. The Soviet of the Union and the Soviet of Nationalities elect Credentials Committees to verify the credentials of the members of the respective Chambers.

On the report of the Credentials Committees, the Chambers decide whether to recognize the credentials of deputies or to annul their election.

ARTICLE 51. The Supreme Soviet of the U.S.S.R., when it deems necessary, appoints commissions of investigation and audit on any matter.

It is the duty of all institutions and officials to comply with the demands of such commissions and to submit to them all necessary materials and documents.

ARTICLE 52. A member of the Supreme Soviet of the U.S.S.R. may not be prosecuted or arrested without the consent of the Supreme Soviet or the U.S.S.R., or, when the Supreme Soviet of the U.S.S.R. is not in session, without the consent of the Presidium of the Supreme Soviet of the U.S.S.R.

ARTICLE 53. On the expiration of the term of office of the Supreme Soviet of the U.S.S.R., or on its dissolution prior to the expiration of its term of office, the Presidium of the Supreme Soviet of the U.S.S.R. retains its powers until the newly-elected Supreme Soviet of the U.S.S.R. shall have formed a new Presidium of the Supreme Soviet of the U.S.S.R.

ARTICLE 54. On the expiration of the term of office of the Supreme Soviet of the U.S.S.R., or in the event of its dissolution prior to the expiration of its term of office, the Presidium of the Supreme Soviet of the U.S.S.R. orders new elections to be held within a period not exceeding two months from the date of expiration of the term of office or dissolution of the Supreme Soviet of the U.S.S.R.

ARTICLE 55. The newly-elected Supreme Soviet of the U.S.S.R. is convened by the outgoing Presidium of the Supreme Soviet of the U.S.S.R. not later than three months after the elections.

ARTICLE 56. The Supreme Soviet of the U.S.S.R., at a joint sitting of the two Chambers, appoints the Government of the U.S.S.R., namely, the Council of Ministers of the U.S.S.R.

CHAPTER IV: THE HIGHER ORGANS OF STATE POWER IN THE UNION REPUBLICS

ARTICLE 57. The highest organ of state power in a Union Republic is the Supreme Soviet of the Union Republic.

ARTICLE 58. The Supreme Soviet of a Union Republic is elected by the citizens of the Republic for a term of four years.

The basis of representation is established by the Constitution of the Union Republic.

ARTICLE 59. The Supreme Soviet of a Union Republic is the sole legislative organ of the Republic.

ARTICLE 60. The Supreme Soviet of a Union Republic:

a) Adopts the Constitution of the Republic and amends it in conformity with Article 16 of the Constitution of the U.S.S.R.;

b) Confirms the Constitutions of the Autonomous Republics forming part of it and defines the boundaries of their territories;

c) Approves the national-economic plan and the budget of the Republic;

d) Exercises the right of amnesty and pardon of citizens sentenced by the judicial organs of the Union Republic;

e) Decides questions of representation of the Union Republic in its international relations;

f) Determines the manner of organizing the Republic's military formations.

ARTICLE 61. The Supreme Soviet of a Union Republic elects the Presidium of the Supreme Soviet of the Union Republic, consisting of a President of the Presidium of the Supreme Soviet of the Union Republic, Vice-Presidents, a Secretary of the Presidium and members of the Presidium of the Supreme Soviet of the Union Republic.

The powers of the Presidium of the Supreme Soviet of a Union Republic are defined by the Constitution of the Union Republic.

ARTICLE 62. The Supreme Soviet of a Union Republic elects a Chairman and Vice-Chairmen to conduct its sittings.

ARTICLE 63. The Supreme Soviet of a Union Republic appoints the Government of the Union Republic, namely, the Council of Ministers of the Union Republic.

Chapter V: THE ORGANS OF STATE ADMINISTRATION OF THE UNION OF SOVIET SOCIALIST REPUBLICS

ARTICLE 64. The highest executive and administrative organ of the state power of the Union of Soviet Socialist Republics is the Council of Ministers of the U.S.S.R.

ARTICLE 65. The Council of Ministers of the U.S.S.R. is responsible and accountable to the Supreme Soviet of the U.S.S.R., or, in the intervals between sessions of the Supreme Soviet, to the Presidium of the Supreme Soviet of the U.S.S.R.

ARTICLE 66. The Council of Ministers of the U.S.S.R. issue decisions and orders on the basis and in pursuance of the laws in operation, and verifies their execution.

ARTICLE 67. Decisions and orders of the Council of Ministers of the U.S.S.R. are binding throughout the territory of the U.S.S.R.

ARTICLE 68. The Council of Ministers of the U.S.S.R.:

a) Co-ordinates and directs the work of the all-Union and Union-Republican Ministries of the U.S.S.R. and of other institutions under its jurisdiction;

b) Adopts measures to carry out the national-economic plan and the state budget, and to strengthen the credit and monetary system;

c) Adopts measures for the maintenance of public order, for the protection of the interests of the state, and for the safeguarding of the rights of citizens;

d) Exercises general guidance in the sphere of relations with foreign states;

e) Fixes the annual contingent of citizens to be called up for military service and directs the general organization of the Armed Forces of the country;

f) Sets up, whenever necessary, special Committees and Central Administrations under the Council of Ministers of the U.S.S.R. for economic and cultural affairs and defence.

ARTICLE 69. The Council of Ministers of the U.S.S.R. has the right, in respect of those branches of administration and economy which come within the jurisdiction of the U.S.S.R., to suspend decisions and orders of the Councils of Ministers of the Union Republics and to annul orders and instructions of Ministers of the U.S.S.R.

ARTICLE 70. The Council of Ministers of the U.S.S.R. is appointed by the Supreme Soviet of the U.S.S.R. and consists of:

The Chairman of the Council of Ministers of the U.S.S.R.;

The First Vice-Chairmen of the Council of Ministers of the U.S.S.R.;

The Vice-Chairmen of the Council of Ministers of the U.S.S.R.;

The Ministers of the U.S.S.R.;

The Chairman of the State Commission of the Council of Ministers of the U.S.S.R. for Long-Term Planning of the National Economy;

The Chairman of the State Economic Commission of the Council of Ministers of the U.S.S.R. for Current Planning of the National Economy;

The Chairman of the State Labour and Wages Committee of the Council of Ministers of the U.S.S.R.;

The Chairman of the State Committee of the Council of Ministers of the U.S.S.R. on New Techniques;

The Chairman of the State Committee of the Council of Ministers of the U.S.S.R. on Construction;

The Chairman of the State Security Committee under the Council of Ministers of the U.S.S.R.;

The Chairman of the Administrative Board of the State Bank of the U.S.S.R.

ARTICLE 71. The Government of the U.S.S.R. or a Minister of the U.S.S.R. to whom a question of a member of the Supreme Soviet of the U.S.S.R. is addressed must give a verbal or written reply in the respective Chamber within a period not exceeding three days.

ARTICLE 72. The Ministers of the U.S.S.R. direct the branches of state administration which come within the jurisdiction of the U.S.S.R.

ARTICLE 73. The Ministers of the U.S.S.R., within the limits of the jurisdiction of their respective Ministries, issue orders and instructions on the basis and in pursuance of the laws in operation, and also of decisions and orders of the Council of Ministers of the U.S.S.R., and verify their execution.

ARTICLE 74. The Ministries of the U.S.S.R. are either all-Union or Union-Republican Ministries.

ARTICLE 75. Each all-Union Ministry directs the branch of state administration entrusted to it throughout the territory of the U.S.S.R. either directly or through bodies appointed by it.

ARTICLE 76. The Union-Republican Ministries, as a rule, direct the branches of state administration entrusted to them through corresponding Ministries of the Union Republics; they administer directly only a definite and limited number of enterprises according to a list confirmed by the Presidium of the Supreme Soviet of the U.S.S.R.

ARTICLE 77. The following Ministries are all-Union Ministries:

The Ministry of the Aircraft Industry;

The Ministry of the Automobile Industry;

The Ministry of Foreign Trade;

The Ministry of Geological Survey and Conservation of Mineral Resources;

The Ministry of Agricultural Stocks;

The Ministry of the Machine- and Instrument-Making Industry;

The Ministry of Merchant Marine;

The Ministry of the Defence Industry;

The Ministry of the General Machine-Building Industry;

The Ministry of Railways;

The Ministry of the Radio-Engineering Industry;

The Ministry of Inland Water Transport;

The Ministry of the Medium Machine-Building Industry;

The Ministry of the Machine-Tool and Tool Industry;

The Ministry of the Building and Road-Building Machinery Industry;

The Ministry of Construction of Metallurgical and Chemical Works;

The Ministry of Oil Industry Construction;

The Ministry of Coal Industry Construction:

The Ministry of Electric Power Station Construction;

The Ministry of Shipbuilding;

The Ministry of the Tractor and Agricultural Machine-Building Industry;

The Ministry of the Transport Machine-Building Industry;
The Ministry of Transport Construction;
The Ministry of the Heavy Machine-Building Industry;
The Ministry of the Chemical Industry;
The Ministry of Electric Power Stations;
The Ministry of the Electrical Engineering Industry.

ARTICLE 78. The following Ministries are Union-Republican Ministries:
The Ministry of Motor Transport and Highways;
The Ministry of the Paper and Wood-Processing Industry;
The Ministry of Internal Affairs;
The Ministry of Higher Education;
The Ministry of Town and Village Construction;
The Ministry of State Control;
The Ministry of Public Health;
The Ministry of Foreign Affairs;
The Ministry of Culture;
The Ministry of Light Industry;
The Ministry of the Timber Industry;
The Ministry of the Oil Industry;
The Ministry of Defence;
The Ministry of the Meat and Dairy Products Industry;
The Ministry of the Foodstuff Industry;
The Ministry of the Building Materials Industry;
The Ministry of Fish Industry;
The Ministry of Communications;
The Ministry of Agriculture;
The Ministry of State Farms;
The Ministry of Construction;
The Ministry of the Textile Industry;
The Ministry of Trade;
The Ministry of the Coal Industry;
The Ministry of Finance;
The Ministry of the Nonferrous Metal Industry;
The Ministry of the Iron and Steel Industry;
The Ministry of Justice.

CHAPTER VI: THE ORGANS OF STATE ADMINISTRATION
OF THE UNION REPUBLICS

ARTICLE 79. The highest executive and administrative organ of the state power of a Union Republic is the Council of Ministers of the Union Republic.

ARTICLE 80. The Council of Ministers of a Union Republic is responsible and accountable to the Supreme Soviet of the Union Republic, or, in the intervals between sessions of the Supreme Soviet of the Union Republic, to the Presidium of the Supreme Soviet of the Union Republic.

ARTICLE 81. The Council of Ministers of a Union Republic issues decisions

and orders on the basis and in pursuance of the laws in operation of the U.S.S.R. and of the Union Republic, and of the decisions and orders of the Council of Ministers of the U.S.S.R., and verifies their execution.

ARTICLE 82. The Council of Ministers of a Union Republic has the right to suspend decisions and orders of the Councils of Ministers of its Autonomous Republics, and to annul decisions and orders of the Executive Committees of the Soviets of Working People's Deputies of its Territories, Regions and Autonomous Regions.

ARTICLE 83. The Council of Ministers of a Union Republic is appointed by the Supreme Soviet of the Union Republic and consists of:

The Chairman of the Council of Ministers of the Union Republic;

The Vice-Chairmen of the Council of Ministers;

The Ministers;

The Chairman of the State Planning Commission;

The Chairman of the State Committee of the Council of Ministers of the Union Republic on Construction and Architecture;

The Chairman of the State Security Committee under the Council of Ministers of the Union Republic.

ARTICLE 84. The Ministers of a Union Republic direct the branches of state administration which come within the jurisdiction of the Union Republic.

ARTICLE 85. The Ministers of a Union Republic, within the limits of the jurisdiction of their respective Ministries, issue orders and instructions on the basis and in pursuance of the laws of the U.S.S.R. and of the Union Republic, of the decisions and orders of the Council of Ministers of the U.S.S.R. and the Council of Ministers of the Union Republic, and of the orders and instructions of the Union-Republican Ministries of the U.S.S.R.

ARTICLE 86. The Ministries of a Union Republic are either Union-Republican or Republican Ministries.

ARTICLE 87. Each Union-Republican Ministry directs the branch of state administration entrusted to it, and is subordinate both to the Council of Ministers of the Union Republic and to the corresponding Union-Republican Ministry of the U.S.S.R.

ARTICLE 88. Each Republican Ministry directs the branch of state administration entrusted to it and is directly subordinate to the Council of Ministers of the Union Republic.

CHAPTER VII: THE HIGHER ORGANS OF STATE POWER IN THE AUTONOMOUS SOVIET SOCIALIST REPUBLICS

ARTICLE 89. The highest organ of the state power in an Autonomous Republic is the Supreme Soviet of the Autonomous Republic.

ARTICLE 90. The Supreme Soviet of an Automous Republic is elected by the citizens of the Republic for a term of four years on a basis of representation established by the Constitution of the Autonomous Republic.

ARTICLE 91. The Supreme Soviet of an Autonomous Republic is the sole legislative organ of the Autonomous Republic.

ARTICLE 92. Each Autonomous Republic has its own Constitution, which

takes account of the specific features of the Autonomous Republic and is drawn up in full conformity with the Constitution of the Union Republic.

ARTICLE 93. The Supreme Soviet of an Autonomous Republic elects the Presidium of the Supreme Soviet of the Autonomous Republic and appoints the Council of Ministers of the Autonomous Republic, in accordance with its Constitution.

CHAPTER VIII: THE LOCAL ORGANS OF STATE POWER

ARTICLE 94. The organs of state power in Territories, Regions, Autonomous Regions, Areas, Districts, cities and rural localities (stanitsas, villages, hamlets, kishlaks, auls) are the Soviets of Working People's Deputies.

ARTICLE 95. The Soviets of Working People's Deputies of Territories, Regions, Autonomous Regions, Areas, Districts, cities and rural localities (stanitsas, villages, hamlets, kishlaks, auls) are elected by the working people of the respective Territories, Regions, Autonomous Regions, Areas, Districts, cities or rural localities for a term of two years.

ARTICLE 96. The basis of representation for Soviets of Working People's Deputies is determined by the Constitutions of the Union Republics.

ARTICLE 97. The Soviets of Working People's Deputies direct the work of the organs of administration subordinate to them, ensure the maintenance of public order, the observance of the laws and the protection of the rights of citizens, direct local economic and cultural affairs and draw up the local budgets.

ARTICLE 98. The Soviets of Working People's Deputies adopt decisions and issue orders within the limits of the powers vested in them by the laws of the U.S.S.R. and of the Union Republic.

ARTICLE 99. The executive and administrative organ of the Soviet of Working People's Deputies of a Territory, Region, Autonomous Region, Area, District, city or rural locality is the Executive Committee elected by it, consisting of a Chairman, Vice-Chairmen, a Secretary and members.

ARTICLE 100. The executive and administrative organ of the Soviet of Working People's Deputies in a small locality, in accordance with the Constitution of the Union Republic, is the Chairman, the Vice-Chairman and the Secretary elected by the Soviet of Working People's Deputies.

ARTICLE 101. The executive organs of the Soviets of Working People's Deputies are directly accountable both to the Soviets of Working People's Deputies which elected them and to the executive organ of the superior Soviet of Working People's Deputies.

CHAPTER IX: THE COURTS AND THE PROCURATOR'S OFFICE

ARTICLE 102. In the U.S.S.R. justice is administered by the Supreme Court of the U.S.S.R., the Supreme Courts of the Union Republics, the Courts of the Territories, Regions, Autonomous Republics, Autonomous Regions and Areas, the Special Courts of the U.S.S.R. established by decision of the Supreme Soviet of the U.S.S.R., and the People's Courts.

ARTICLE 103. In all Courts cases are tried with the participation of people's assessors, except in cases specially provided for by law.

ARTICLE 104. The Supreme Court of the U.S.S.R. is the highest judicial organ. The Supreme Court of the U.S.S.R. is charged with the supervision of the judicial activities of all the judicial organs of the U.S.S.R. and of the Union Republics.

ARTICLE 105. The Supreme Court of the U.S.S.R. and the Special Courts of the U.S.S.R. are elected by the Supreme Soviet of the U.S.S.R. for a term of five years.

ARTICLE 106. The Supreme Courts of the Union Republics are elected by the Supreme Soviets of the Union Republics for a term of five years.

ARTICLE 107. The Supreme Courts of the Autonomous Republics are elected by the Supreme Soviets of the Autonomous Republics for a term of five years.

ARTICLE 108. The Courts of Territories, Regions, Autonomous Regions and Areas are elected by the Soviets of Working People's Deputies of the respective Territories, Regions, Autonomous Regions or Areas for a term of five years.

ARTICLE 109. People's Courts are elected by the citizens of the districts on the basis of universal, direct and equal suffrage by secret ballot for a term of three years.

ARTICLE 110. Judicial proceedings are conducted in the language of the Union Republic, Autonomous Republic or Autonomous Region, persons not knowing this language being guaranteed the opportunity of fully acquainting themselves with the material of the case through an interpreter and likewise the right to use their own language in court.

ARTICLE 111. In all Courts of the U.S.S.R. cases are heard in public, unless otherwise provided for by law, and the accused is guaranteed the right to defence.

ARTICLE 112. Judges are independent and subject only to the law.

ARTICLE 113. Supreme supervisory power to ensure the strict observance of the law by all Ministries and institutions subordinated to them, as well as by officials and citizens of the U.S.S.R. generally, is vested in the Procurator-General of the U.S.S.R.

ARTICLE 114. The Procurator-General of the U.S.S.R. is appointed by the Supreme Soviet of the U.S.S.R. for a term of seven years.

ARTICLE 115. Procurators of Republics, Territories, Regions, Autonomous Republics and Autonomous Regions are appointed by the Procurator-General of the U.S.S.R. for a term of five years.

ARTICLE 116. Area, district and city procurators are appointed by the Procurators of the Union Republics, subject to the approval of the Procurator-General of the U.S.S.R., for a term of five years.

ARTICLE 117. The organs of the Procurator's Office perform their functions independently of any local organs whatsoever, being subordinate solely to the Procurator-General of the U.S.S.R.

CHAPTER X: FUNDAMENTAL RIGHTS AND DUTIES OF CITIZENS

ARTICLE 118. Citizens of the U.S.S.R. have the right to work, that is, the right to guaranteed employment and payment for their work in accordance with its quantity and quality.

The right to work is ensured by the socialist organization of the national economy, the steady growth of the productive forces of Soviet society, the elimination of the possibility of economic crises, and the abolition of unemployment.

ARTICLE 119. Citizens of the U.S.S.R. have the right to rest and leisure.

The right to rest and leisure is ensured by the establishment of an eight-hour day for industrial, office, and professional workers, the reduction of the working day to seven or six hours for arduous trades and to four hours in shops where conditions of work are particularly arduous; by the institution of annual vacations with full pay for industrial, office, and professional workers, and by the provision of a wide network of sanatoria, holiday homes and clubs for the accommodation of the working people.

ARTICLE 120. Citizens of the U.S.S.R. have the right to maintenance in old age and also in case of sickness or disability.

This right is ensured by the extensive development of social insurance of industrial, office, and professional workers at state expense, free medical service for the working people, and the provision of a wide network of health resorts for the use of the working people.

ARTICLE 121. Citizens of the U.S.S.R. have the right to education.

This right is ensured by universal and compulsory elementary education; by free education up to and including the seventh grade; by a system of state stipends for students of higher educational establishments who excel in their studies; by instruction in schools being conducted in the native language, and by the organization in the factories, state farms, machine and tractor stations, and collective farms of free vocational, technical and agronomic training for the working people.

ARTICLE 122. Women in the U.S.S.R. are accorded equal rights with men in all spheres of economic, government, cultural, political and other public activity.

The possibility of exercising these rights is ensured by women being accorded an equal right with men to work, payment for work, rest and leisure, social insurance and education, and by state protection of the interests of mother and child, state aid to mothers of large families and unmarried mothers, maternity leave with full pay, and the provision of a wide network of maternity homes, nurseries and kindergartens.

ARTICLE 123. Equality of rights of citizens of the U.S.S.R., irrespective of their nationality or race, in all spheres of economic, government, cultural, political and other public activity, is an indefeasible law.

Any direct or indirect restriction of the rights of, or, conversely, the establishment of any direct or indirect privileges for, citizens on account of their race or nationality, as well as any advocacy of racial or national exclusiveness or hatred and contempt, are punishable by law.

ARTICLE 124. In order to ensure to citizens freedom of conscience, the church in the U.S.S.R. is separated from the state, and the school from the church. Freedom of religious worship and freedom of anti-religious propaganda is recognized for all citizens.

ARTICLE 125. In conformity with the interests of the working people, and in order to strengthen the socialist system, the citizens of the U.S.S.R. are guaranteed by law:

a) freedom of speech;

b) freedom of the press;

c) freedom of assembly, including the holding of mass meetings;

d) freedom of street processions and demonstrations.

These civil rights are ensured by placing at the disposal of the working people and their organizations printing presses, stocks of paper, public buildings, the streets, communications facilities and other material requisites for the exercise of these rights.

ARTICLE 126. In conformity with the interests of the working people, and in order to develop the organizational initiative and political activity of the masses of the people, citizens of the U.S.S.R. are guaranteed the right to unite in public organizations: trade unions, co-operative societies, youth organizations, sport and defence organizations, cultural, technical and scientific societies; and the most active and politically-conscious citizens in the ranks of the working class, working peasants and working intelligentsia voluntarily unite in the Communist Party of the Soviet Union, which is the vanguard of the working people in their struggle to build communist society and is the leading core of all organizations of the working people, both public and state.

ARTICLE 127. Citizens of the U.S.S.R. are guaranteed inviolability of the person. No person may be placed under arrest except by decision of a court or with the sanction of a procurator.

ARTICLE 128. The inviolability of the homes of citizens and privacy of correspondence are protected by law.

ARTICLE 129. The U.S.S.R. affords the right of asylum to foreign citizens persecuted for defending the interests of the working people, or for scientific activities, or for struggling for national liberation.

ARTICLE 130. It is the duty of every citizen of the U.S.S.R. to abide by the Constitution of the Union of Soviet Socialist Republics, to observe the laws, to maintain labour discipline, honestly to perform public duties, and to respect the rules of socialist intercourse.

ARTICLE 131. It is the duty of every citizen of the U.S.S.R. to safeguard and fortify public, socialist property as the sacred and inviolable foundation of the Soviet system, as the source of the wealth and might of the country, as the source of the prosperity and culture of all the working people.

Persons committing offences against public, socialist property are enemies of the people.

ARTICLE 132. Universal military service is law.

Military service in the Armed Forces of the U.S.S.R. is an honourable duty of the citizens of the U.S.S.R.

ARTICLE 133. To defend the country is the sacred duty of every citizen of the U.S.S.R. Treason to the Motherland—violation of the oath of allegiance, de-

sertion to the enemy, impairing the military power of the state, espionage—is punishable with all the severity of the law as the most heinous of crimes.

CHAPTER XI: THE ELECTORAL SYSTEM

ARTICLE 134. Members of all Soviets of Working People's Deputies—of the Supreme Soviet of the U.S.S.R., the Supreme Soviets of the Union Republics, the Soviets of Working People's Deputies of the Territories and Regions, the Supreme Soviets of the Autonomous Republics, the Soviets of Working People's Deputies of the Autonomous Regions, and the Area, District, City and rural (stanitsa, village, hamlet, kishlak, aul) Soviets of Working People's Deputies—are chosen by the electors on the basis of universal, equal and direct suffrage by secret ballot.

ARTICLE 135. Elections of deputies are universal: all citizens of the U.S.S.R. who have reached the age of eighteen, irrespective of race or nationality, sex, religion, education, domicile, social origin, property status or past activities, have the right to vote in the election of deputies, with the exception of insane persons and persons who have been convicted by a court of law and whose sentences include deprivation of electoral rights.

Every citizen of the U.S.S.R. who has reached the age of twenty-three is eligible for election to the Supreme Soviet of the U.S.S.R., irrespective of race or nationality, sex, religion, education, domicile, social origin, property status or past activities.

ARTICLE 136. Elections of deputies are equal: each citizen has one vote; all citizens participate in elections on an equal footing.

ARTICLE 137. Women have the right to elect and be elected on equal terms with men.

ARTICLE 138. Citizens serving in the Armed Forces of the U.S.S.R. have the right to elect and be elected on equal terms with all other citizens.

ARTICLE 139. Elections of deputies are direct: all Soviets of Working People's Deputies, from rural and city Soviets of Working People's Deputies to the Supreme Soviet of the U.S.S.R., are elected by the citizens by direct vote.

ARTICLE 140. Voting at elections of deputies is secret.

ARTICLE 141. Candidates are nominated by election districts.

The right to nominate candidates is secured to public organizations and societies of the working people: Communist Party organizations, trade unions, co-operatives, youth organizations and cultural societies.

ARTICLE 142. It is the duty of every deputy to report to his electors on his work and on the work of his Soviet of Working People's Deputies, and he may be recalled at any time upon decision of a majority of the electors in the manner established by law.

CHAPTER XII: ARMS, FLAG, CAPITAL

ARTICLE 143. The arms of the Union of Soviet Socialist Republics are a sickle and hammer against a globe depicted in the rays of the sun and surrounded by ears of grain, with the inscription "Workers of All Countries, Unite!"

in the languages of the Union Republics. At the top of the arms is a five-pointed star.

ARTICLE 144. The state flag of the Union of Soviet Socialist Republics is of red cloth with the sickle and hammer depicted in gold in the upper corner near the staff and above them a five-pointed red star bordered in gold. The ratio of the width to the length is 1:2.

ARTICLE 145. The Capital of the Union of Soviet Socialist Republics is the City of Moscow.

CHAPTER XIII: PROCEDURE FOR AMENDING THE CONSTITUTION

ARTICLE 146. The Constitution of the U.S.S.R. may be amended only by decision of the Supreme Soviet of the U.S.S.R. adopted by a majority of not less than two-thirds of the votes in each of its Chambers.

[POSTSCRIPT: *The measures of decentralization mentioned on p. 450 above had not yet, at the time of writing, been translated into amendments of Arts. 77–8 of the Constitution. On March 30, 1957, Khrushchev outlined further measures, contemplating the transfer to new regional bodies of the planning and managerial functions, respectively, of the State Commission for Current Planning (cf. p. 422 n. above) and of the All-Union and Union-Republican industrial Ministries, most or all of which were apparently to be sooner or later abolished, at least in their previous form. Final decisions on these matters had not been reached as these pages went to press. When reached, they would involve amendment of the relevant articles of the Constitution, as would the abolition of tuition fees in educational institutions and plans for universal education through the tenth grade. For details, see the* Current Digest of the Soviet Press *for 1957 and beyond.—F.L.S.*]

An Index of Authors

N.B. *Most books and articles herein cited are set down in footnotes on the pages listed. A few are mentioned in the text of the work. Items from the Soviet and Western press are not indexed as to source. The abbreviation NYT in the text means* The New York Times. *Quotations, with citations as to source, are included in the General Index below.*

An Index of Persons, Places, Peoples, Postulates and Problems,

INCLUDING A GLOSSARY OF RUSSIAN TERMS, ABBREVIATIONS, AND INSTITUTIONS

N.B. *Communism, Socialism, and USSR are not indexed. See* passim *and entries under persons and problems. Fictional characters are not indexed. See names of authors. Entries under names of countries are limited to major wars, treaties, international conferences, and relations with the USSR. The symbols employed below have the following meanings: B. = battle; C. = conference, international: Q. or q. = quoted; R. = river; W. = war; f. = and pages following; n. = footnote.*

A NOTE ABOUT THE AUTHOR

FREDERICK L. SCHUMAN was born in Chicago in 1904. He was educated in the public schools there, and later attended the University of Chicago. After a decade of teaching in Chicago, he went to Williams College as Visiting Lecturer in International Relations, joining the Williams faculty as Woodrow Wilson Professor of Government in 1938. In addition to his teaching, Professor Schuman has had a distinguished career as lecturer and writer, gaining wide renown for his prophetic analyses of contemporary world politics and his vigorous defenses of civil liberties. An energetic traveler, he has visited and studied in almost every European country as well as in the Soviet Union. Dr. Schuman's *Soviet Politics*, published in 1946, was immediately hailed as an outstanding interpretation of Soviet domestic and foreign affairs. His other published works include the highly regarded *International Politics* (Fifth Edition, 1953); *The Commonwealth of Man* (1952); *Design for Power* (with Major George D. Brodsky, 1942); and *Night Over Europe* (1941).

A NOTE ON THE TYPE AND PRODUCTION

The text of this book is set in Caledonia, a Linotype face designed by W. A. Dwiggins (1880–1956), who was responsible for so much that is good in contemporary book design. Though much of his early work was in advertising and he was the author of the standard volume Layout in Advertising, Mr. Dwiggins later devoted his prolific talents to book typography and type design, and worked with great distinction in both fields. In addition to his designs for Caledonia, he created the Metro, Electra, and Eldorado series of type faces, as well as a number of experimental cuttings that have never been issued commercially.

Caledonia belongs to the family of printing types called "modern face" by printers—a term used to mark the change in style of type-letters that occurred at the end of the eighteenth century. It is best evidenced in the letter shapes designed by Baskerville, Martin, Bodoni, and the Didots.

This book was composed by The Plimpton Press, Norwood, Mass. and printed and bound by The Haddon Craftsmen, Inc., Scranton, Pa.